THRACE

Samothrace

Lemnos

★ Aegospotami

★ Granicus

Troy

MYSIA

Pergamum

A E O L I S

Lesbos

Phocaea

G E A N

Chios

Clazomenae

O

Claros

N

Ephesus

Sardes

LYDIA

E A

Andros

Samos

Priene

Tralles

Delos

Miletus

CARIA

DIDYMA

Paros

Naxos

S

P

O

D

Halicarnassus

Cos

R

Cnidos

A

D

E

S

Rhodes

A DICTIONARY OF ANCIENT GREEK CIVILISATION

A DICTIONARY OF ANCIENT GREEK CIVILISATION

METHUEN & CO LTD. LONDON

FOREWORD

Most of this dictionary has been written by three Hellenists: a philosopher, Pierre-Maxime Schuhl, a literary historian, Robert Flacelière, and an archaeologist, Pierre Devambez. In about four hundred articles, each of which, however short, had to be self-contained, they tried to describe Greek civilisation which took shape during the 2nd millennium B.C. and was still a living force when Christianity was triumphant. There is no need to emphasise the wealth and complexity of that civilisation which, although we are indebted to it for a considerable part of our own, was nonetheless founded on conceptions that make it more remote than we are often led to believe.

When we examine the religious beliefs, way of life, economy, social and political structure of ancient Greece in the light of historical events and the geographical setting of a naturally divided country, we are struck by everything that separates us from the men whose art, literature and philosophical ideas are nevertheless at the root of our own culture. This is why the dictionary has not been limited to the great names, however illustrious and numerous, nor have the writers tried to reduce Greek civilisation to its finest achievements; Athenians did not live on the Acropolis, where they only climbed for the celebration of festivals, any more than Londoners spend their time in the British Museum or visiting old churches; they passed their lives from day to day in the same humble occupations and small worries that fill the existence of men everywhere.

It was indispensable that this background should be given its due place so that the eminent figures and splendid creations could be seen in proper perspective. Consequently, the writers have made every effort, whenever it was possible, to give a decidedly familiar slant to the innumerable aspects of Hellenism. With the same end in view, the illustrations have been carefully chosen to throw light on the real, tangible things of the Hellenic world.

The dictionary is intended for cultivated readers, particularly students, not specialists, and it should be pointed out that it does not pretend to be more than an introductory source of information on Hellenic civilisation.

ACKNOWLEDGMENTS

Mr Leonard von Matt for permission to use some of the photographs illustrating his books, *Magna Graecia* and *Ancient Sicily* published by Universe Books, New York.

Hirmer Verlag, Munich, for permission to reproduce the plan of the Temple of Hephaestus, Athens, from *Greek Temples, Theatres and Shrines*.

Penguin Books for permission to quote from Philip Vellacott's translation of *The Eumenides*.

CONTRIBUTORS

PIERRE DEVAMBEZ

Head of the Greek and Roman Antiquities in the Louvre
Director of studies at the École Pratique des Hautes Études

and

ROBERT FLACELIÈRE

Professor of Greek Rhetoric at the Sorbonne
Director of the École Normale Supérieure

PIERRE-MAXIME SCHUHL

Professor in the History of Ancient Philosophy at the Sorbonne

ROLAND MARTIN

Professor of Classical Grammar and Philology at the University of Dijon.

The publishers would like to thank the following for their help in compiling this dictionary

JEAN BEAUJEU, PATRICE BOUSSEL, MARIE-CLAIRE GALPÉRINE,
PIERRE HADOT, JACQUES PIQUEMAL, BERNARD NOËL,
JEAN TROUILLARD, MARIE-ANTOINETTE VINCENT-VIGUIER.

Illustrations and captions are by René Ben Sussan.

ACADEMY. This was the open-air gymnasium situated on the outskirts of Athens like the Cynosarges and the Lyceum. The Academy owed its name to a local hero, Academus or Hecademus, who once had a rustic sanctuary on the same site. Access to this sacred wood, which was surrounded by a wall in the 6th century B.C. by Hipparchus, son of the tyrant Pisistratus, was by a tree-lined avenue some two thirds of a mile in length, which ran from the Dipylon gate in the Ceramicus district of Athens and which was the route followed by the Bacchic procession of the Greater Dionysia. The Academy was dedicated to Athena and was the place of the twelve sacred olive trees, which provided oil for the victors of the Panathenaea. In the 5th century, Cimon laid out wide, tree-lined alleys in the Academy which became a favourite resort for the city dwellers especially in the summer, because of its shade and coolness.

In about 387 B.C., when he was some forty years old, Plato consecrated the area to the Muses, and it was there that he founded his philosophical school. The Academy thus became the world's first university. Plato taught there until his death in 347 and was buried on the site. His first successors at the head of the school were Speusippus (347-339) and Xenocrates (339-314). In the Hellenistic period, there was a considerable divergence from Plato's views when the Platonic philosophers of the " New Academy ", like Arcesilas and Carneades, upheld the theory of probabilism, maintaining that objective, absolute, truth is unknowable. In 86, the Academy was destroyed by Sulla. Today, the site is being excavated by Greek archaeologists.

R.F.

ACARNANIA. A province facing Leucas and Ithaca. Although remote and rather poverty stricken, it played an important part in the political history of Greece on several occasions. In 454 B.C., Pericles made a vain attempt to capture the town of Oeniadae. From 391 to 387, during the war between Athens and Sparta, Acarnania was again an important centre of operations. In 341, during the struggle against Philip, Athens sought the support of the cities in this region. Finally, Acarnania was a region which particularly attracted the Romans when they began to take an interest in Greece.

P.D.

ACHAEANS. The name that Homer gave to the Greeks in his epic poems. This term is both more precise and convenient than the more restricted appellation of Mycenaeans, which is usually employed by archaeologists to denote the peoples who settled in Greece in the second millennium B.C. The Achaeans formed part of the first wave of invaders who came from the north in about the 20th century B.C. and who occupied the southernmost extremity of the Greek peninsula. The route taken by the invaders is still a subject for controversy. At the time of their first appearance in Greece, the Achaeans were still barbarians. Their arrival met with fierce resistance, nevertheless, some of their beliefs and customs took root in Greek soil, and they were influenced by Cretan civilisation once they had established maritime links with Crete. This was the origin of Mycenaean power and culture (*See* Mycenaean Civilisation). A small province of the Peloponnesus is still called Achaea.

P.D.

ACHERON. The Acheron is a real river that flows into the Ionian Sea after running through the wild regions of Epirus. At one point it disappears from sight to run underground. This may explain why the same name was given to the mythical river that the dead had to cross before penetrating into the infernal regions. All those who had not been buried or cremated according to the approved rites were unable to cross it, remaining tormented souls, forever condemned to wander miserably along its banks clutching the reeds that grew on its shores. The more fortunate souls embarked on the boat rowed by the sinister boatman, Charon, and they alone were able to enter into a kingdom which was certainly joyless but where, at least, they felt they had a place.

P.D.

ACHILLES. Achilles was the son of a goddess, Thetis, and a mortal, Peleus. According to the legend, when he was born, his mother plunged him into the Styx so that the waters of the infernal river would make his body invulnerable; and it was only in the heel by which she was holding him that he could be wounded. The youth's education was placed in the hands of Chiron, the wisest of the Centaurs, who taught him the arts of war and hunting and the principles of morality and gave him a taste for beautiful things. When the Trojan War broke out and Thetis and Peleus learned from an oracle that their son would perish in the conflict, they gave him into the care of Lycomedes, king of Scyros, who hid him among his daughters so that the Greeks could not mobilise him to make him one of their leaders. Ulysses learned of this subterfuge and visited Lycomedes, disguised as a merchant of fine cloths and ornaments. The king's daughters, with Achilles in their midst, were admiring the wares when Ulysses suddenly displayed naked swords to the sound of warlike trumpet calls. While the terrified girls fled, Achilles enthusiastically rushed towards the weapons, thus making himself known.

He covered himself with glory before the walls of Troy, leading the Myrmidons who were ruled by his father. But he felt slighted by Agamemnon who deprived him of Briseis, one of the slaves he had received in his share of the booty, and withdrew from the fight. It was only at the last moment, when the Greeks were in an almost desperate situation, that he agreed to lend his armour to Patroclus, the friend he loved above all others. When they saw Patroclus coming, the Trojans mistook him for Achilles and fled in terror but Hector faced him and slew him. After holding a sumptuous funeral feast in honour of Patroclus, Achilles revenged his death by challenging and killing Hector, dragging his corpse behind his chariot around the walls of Troy and only returning it to the aged Priam after an enormous ransom had been paid. The *Iliad* has made this the best known episode of the life of Achilles. A short time after this exploit the hero died from the wound of an arrow shot by Paris, the least courageous of the Trojans, and Ajax and Ulysses then quarrelled over his weapons. His son Neoptolemus, crueller and less valiant than his father, took part in the final battle and showed no mercy in his fury to Hector's son Astyanax and to Priam.

Although the Greeks' admiration for the heroism of Achilles was unbounded, and they celebrated his exploits in art and literature on countless occasions, they do not seem to have regarded him as being typical of their race. To this eminently moderate and reasonable people, Achilles' exclusively warlike spirit, his violent reactions, and his unbridled wrath marked him as an exceptional being of a temper alien to their own.   P.D.

ACHILLES TATIUS.   Greek novelist, author of the *Adventures of Leucippe and Clitophon (See* Romances).

ACROPOLIS. The common noun "acropolis" means high city. No Greek city was without its acropolis. Because it was easy to defend, it was generally the original core of a town, where the gods and notables would dwell from

Achilles. Detail of an Attic amphora by the Achilles Painter. About 450 B.C. Rome, Museo Etrusco Gregoriano. *Photo Anderson-Viollet.*

The Acropolis at Athens: view from the south-east. *Photo H.W. Silvester*

the moment of foundation, just as in many country towns of today the centre is built on the highest part and the houses of the oldest families are to be found clustering around the cathedral.

Today, the best known acropolis of all is that of Athens. It is a steep sided plateau, which rises abruptly to a height of two to three hundred feet above the surrounding plain and valleys. When it was first inhabited at the beginning of the second millennium B.C. the 900 foot long summit running from east to west did not have its present table-like appearance, with its gentle inclination towards the west, and the almost geometrically precise contours surrounding it. The crest was then narrower, being furrowed by fissures and probably studded with outcrops, which were gradually, until the 5th century B.C., filled in or flattened so that new buildings could be set on a more or less level foundation. It was also in the 5th century that the buttressing walls were built which gave the plateau its definitive width, 480 feet, and transformed the natural escarpments so that the Acropolis became accessible from one side only. Short sections still exist of the

original Mycenaean ramparts that followed the contours of the original summit. They formed an enormous wall, built in cyclopean style, probably about thirty-eight feet high and nineteen to twenty-three feet thick. Access to the plateau was by the gentlest slope on the western side, but a sally-port with a stairway was also built on the northern flank. Apart from private dwellings, the surrounding wall also enclosed the king's palace, which stood on almost the same site now occupied by the more recent Erechtheum. Even at this remote period the citadel was dedicated to a female divinity, Athena, who, the legend says, fought for it with the sea-god Poseidon who left traces of his trident in the rocks near the spot where the olive tree given by Athena grew. We do not known what happened to the Acropolis between the end of the Mycenaean age and the middle of the 6th century B.C. When Pisistratus seized power in 561, sacred and profane buildings stood side by side on the Acropolis and it was not until 480 that the site was completely cleared of all profane dwellings and reserved exclusively for the immortals. Remains of pediments show

11

The Acropolis at Athens. Model by the archaeologist, G.P. Stevens, of its appearance in the 1st century A.D. 1: Propylaea. 2: Temple of Athena Nike. 3: Sanctuary of Artemis Brauronia. 4: The Chalcotheke. 5: Parthenon. 6: Temple of Rome and Augustus. 7: Precinct of Zeus Polieus. 8: Erechtheum. 9: House of the Arrephoroi. 10: Colossal statue of Athena Promachos by Phidias. 11. Pinacotheke. *Photo American School, Athens.*

the existence of small buildings for worship in the second quarter of the 6th century, but their exact site and purpose are not known. Only one has been identified: the old temple of Athena, called the Hecatompedon because it was one hundred Attic feet long, which Pisistratus's sons embellished with a new marble façade in about 520. It was also Pisistratus who gave the Acropolis its first monumental entry. Ambitious schemes were already under way when the Persians sacked the Acropolis in 480 and again in 479. It was not until 447 that the reconstruction of the sanctuary was seriously undertaken, on the initiative of Pericles who wanted to heighten Athens' prestige and also provide his compatriots with work. The leader of the enterprise was Phidias, who was assisted by numerous assistants, architects, sculptors and ordinary workmen. Less than forty years saw the building of the Parthenon (447-432) on the south side of the plateau, the Propylaea (437-432) which replaced Pisistratus's former entrance way, the Erechtheum (430-410) which alone sheltered nine different cults, and lastly, outside the walls, the little temple of Athena Nike (about 428) which stood in an adjoining sanctuary and was surrounded by a sculptured balustrade in about 410. Although Athena was the real mistress of the Acropolis, other divinities, Artemis and Zeus, also had their own enclosures within the sanctuary. Besides the buildings that had already been built, countless sacred buildings ranging from modest stelae to the colossal bronze statue of Athena Promachos, standing nearly fifty feet high, were crowded within the sacred precincts. The aspect of the Acropolis remained practically unchanged until the Christian era; the number of ex-votoes increased; a pedestal was built before the Propylaea near the ramp leading to the sanctuary, in the late 2nd century, which supported a statue of Agrippa from 15 B.C. onwards; a little round temple was set up to the glory of Augustus and Rome in 27 A.D. to the east of the Parthenon; and, lastly, the zigzagging path which had led up to the Propylaea was replaced by a monumental stairway begun in the reign of Caligula or Claudius and only completed a century later. It was not until Christianity had become established that the Acropolis and its monuments underwent any great changes in their appearance. P.D.

ADONIS. The legend of Adonis is very probably of Syrian origin, but it soon spread throughout Greece to such an extent that festivals in honour of the god became very popular during the classical period. Adonis was the son of Myrrha, who had been turned into a tree after committing incest with her father. Nine months after this metamorphosis, Adonis was born out of the bark of this tree and picked up by Aphrodite who gave him into the care of Persephone. Adonis spent alternate times of the year with Persephone and with Aphrodite, who had fallen in love with him and was loved in return. This touching idyll was brutally ended when Adonis was killed by a boar which Artemis had set against him. The goddess was inconsolable after her lover's death and afterwards mortal women used to weep, too, for the beautiful youth during annual ceremonies. Hellenistic art and literature often used this legend because of its sentimental appeal. Several variants and added embellishments are known.

P.D.

ADRASTUS. Legendary king of Argos. To obey the oracle who had told him that his offspring would be a lion and a boar, Adrastus gave two of his daughters in marriage to Tydeus and Polynices whose shields bore images of these animals. Polynices was the son of Oedipus. Tydeus's father was Oeneus, the king of Calydon. To restore Polynices, when he had been expelled from his kingdom, Adrastus led a vast expedition against Thebes, which was known as the war of the Seven against Thebes because six heroes led the army at his side. Only Adrastus survived this disastrous campaign and he then made the sons of his six companions in arms swear to avenge their fathers. The result was the war of the Epigoni (the descendants). Adrastus's own son lost his life in this war and he himself died of sorrow.

The soothsayer, Amphiaraus, took part in the first of these wars, although he left unwillingly for he already knew what fate awaited him. He had hidden himself rather than answer Adrastus's appeal, but his wife, Eriphyle, delivered him up after being tempted with the promise of a magnificent necklace as a reward for her betrayal.

P.D.

AEACUS. It was not until Plato's time that Aeacus was considered as one of the judges of the underworld. He had long been known as the legendary king of Aegina, the little island that Zeus had peopled at his request by transforming ants into men who became known as Myrmidons, a Greek word whose root means ant". Aeacus exiled one of his sons, Peleus, the future father of Achilles, for having killed his brother. Phocus, with the aid of a third brother, Telamon. Aeacus was held by the Greeks to be a model of piety.

P.D.

AEGEUS. Aegeus was a legendary king, who was believed to have been the father of Theseus. When he caught sight of the black sail on the boat that was bringing his son back from Crete, he mistakenly thought that Theseus was dead and threw himself into the sea which was henceforth to bear his name. The Aegean Sea extends from the coasts of Macedonia and Thracia in the north, between mainland Greece and the western shores of Asia Minor, as far as the Mediterranean, properly so called; that is, as far as the latitude of Cape Malea and Rhodes. Many islands lie scattered throughout the Aegean, the main groups being the Sporades in the north, the Cyclades in the south-west, and the Sporades, or Dodecanese, in the south-east. The name Aegean is sometimes given to the civilisation that arose in this region during the 2nd millennium B.C.

P.D.

AEGINA. The history of the little island of Aegina (only 33 sq. m. in area) was largely determined by the poverty of its soil and its geographical situation. It is situated in the centre of the Saronic Gulf, between Attica and Argos, overlooking the Isthmus of Corinth in the distance. We know little about the population of which traces have been found, dating from the Mycenaean period, but we do know that, from the 8th century B.C. onwards, the Aeginetans were forced to seek a living in far-off countries. Unable to cultivate the barren soil, they became seafarers and roamed all over the Mediterranean. After their ruler, Pheidon, the king of Argos, had introduced the circulation of the coinage he had invented in the island, coins from Aegina became current in every port and their wide diffusion is a proof of the successful commerce of the island. The Aeginetans sold products manufactured on the island—mostly bronzes—and they also transported merchandise for other peoples with less developed fleets. In the 7th century B.C., they shook off the yoke of Argos and remained independent

until 455 B.C., when they fell under the sway of Athens, but the loss of their autonomy did not affect their prosperity, although they were never to be as rich again as they had been during the archaic period. Their prosperity had shown itself in the early years of the 5th century by the construction of a temple to the goddess Aphaea, the marble pediments of which were found in 1811, revealing the charm of pre-classical Greek art to the world. Remains of the pediments are now in Munich and represent fights between Greeks and Trojans in the presence of Athena. P.D.

AEGOSPOTAMI. The River of the Goat, Aegospotami, owes its fame to the battle fought by it in 405 B.C., when the Athenians were defeated by the Spartans after the Spartan general had managed to take their fleet by surprise and destroy most of it. The defeat led to the capitulation of Athens in 404. P.D.

AENEAS. Aeneas was the most valiant of all the defenders of Troy, except Hector. He did not belong to the reigning family, but was the son of Anchises and the goddess Aphrodite who constantly protected him and even placed herself between him and Diomedes, consequently receiving the blow that the Greek hero had intended for her son. As Aphrodite was injured, Apollo

took over the role of Aeneas' protector. Aeneas took part in many battles, opposed Achilles and was saved from his adversary's arrow by Poseidon. He was not only protected by the gods because of his divine descent, but also because a prophecy had stated that he was to be the sole heir of the Trojan race, which was to be perpetuated by his descendants. When Troy fell and was sacked, he fled carrying his father Anchises on his back, dragging his son Ascanius behind him and carefully holding the Trojan sacred idol, the Palladium. He withdrew to Mount Ida where he gathered the surviving Trojans around him. Then, according to the legend that Virgil has immortalised, he landed on the shores of Latium after a long and arduous voyage. The famous episode with Dido was not altogether unknown to the Greeks and may be of Phoenician origin, but it only became popular with the Romans. P.D.

AEOLIS. According to tradition, one of Orestes' sons left Aulis together with many companions in order to settle in Asia. He himself never reached his goal but after a complicated voyage his descendants arrived in the region extending between the Troad and the gulf of Smyrna. Most of these colonists seem to have been of Boeotian or Thessalian origin and certain affinities in their dialects confirm this hypothesis. These Aeolians,

14

as they were called, did not confine themselves to the coast of Asia Minor but also seized Lesbos and Tenedos. They founded a fair number of towns, none of which ever became very important for, as the country's main resources were agricultural, they always kept a rural character.   P.D.

AEOLUS. According to a tradition which was already known to Homer, Aeolus was the guardian of the Winds, which he kept shut up in a goatskin or in a cavern and let loose or called back according to the will of Zeus.

AESCHINES. Athenian orator, born in 390 B.C. He had a poverty stricken childhood, for his father was an ill paid schoolmaster. Aeschines was a scribe and then an actor before becoming secretary to the Council and making his first speech to the Assembly at about the age of forty. In his first speech, in 348, he denounced the threatening behaviour of Philip of Macedonia, but he soon changed sides and joined the party of Eubulus who wanted nothing more than to keep the peace by coming to a friendly agreement with the king. Aeschines was to spend the rest of his career as the main adversary of Demosthenes, the spokesman of the patriotic party which advocated resistance.

Aeschines' three surviving speeches all relate to his merciless fight against Demosthenes. In *Against Timarchus* (345) he attacked the ally of Demosthenes who had accused him of breach of duty when the embassies had been sent from Athens to Philip to conclude the peace treaty of Philocrates in 346; in *On the Embassy* (343) he replied to Demosthenes' speech on the same subject; lastly, in *Against Ctesiphon* (330) he spoke on the affair of the crown which Ctesiphon had suggested giving to Demosthenes as a reward after the battle of Chaeronea (338). Aeschines won the first two cases, for Timarchus was condemned for unworthy moral behaviour and vanished from political life, and when the affair of the embassies was thoroughly argued, Aeschines was acquitted. But he lost the last bout in 330; Demosthenes' speech *On the Crown* won over the judges and Aeschines did not even receive one fifth of the votes which meant that as he was the accuser he had to pay a fine of a thousand drachmas. Unable to pay, he had to go into exile and went to employ his talents as a rhetor in Asia, at Ephesus, and perhaps also at Rhodes. Neither the place nor the time of his death is known to us.

Aeschines' speeches sometimes sound rather hollow, as do those of the sophists, but in style they are pure, brilliant and beautiful. He showed himself a consummate artist in his use of vehemence and irony, indignation and sarcasm. He knew both how to excite and to relax his audience. He was more graceful and witty than Demosthenes, although he had much less power and presence. He twice defeated his terrible adversary and was certainly a great lawyer. There is no evidence that he was a traitor in the pay of Philip of Macedonia as Demosthenes had so often al-

Wounded warrior. Detail from the pediment of the temple of Aphaea at Aegina. Early 5th century. Munich, Glyptothek.
Photo L. von Matt

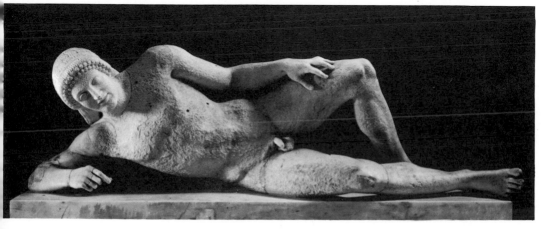

leged. It may well be that the skilful king knew how to delude Aeschines without actually bribing him. Aeschines was sincere in his belief that Athens needed peace and a naïve pride made him all too open to the king's flattery.   R.F.

AESCHYLUS. Athenian tragic dramatist (525-455 B.C.). Aeschylus was born at Eleusis and took part in the battles of Marathon (490) and Salamis (480). He made his début in the theatre at the age of twenty-five in 500, but he did not win the first prize in the tragedy competition until 484, after a laboured and difficult early career. In 472 he won a great triumph with his play the *Persians* and was invited by Hieron, the tyrant of Syracuse, to his court to perform the play. On his return to Athens, Aeschylus presented his Theban trilogy of which only one tragedy, the *Seven against Thebes,* has survived.

In 458 he triumphed again with the *Oresteia* which is his only trilogy to have survived in its entirety. He then returned to Sicily and died at Gela.

Although Aeschylus wrote 90 tragedies or satiric dramas, only seven of his tragedies are still known to us. Modern scholars believe the *Suppliants* to be one of Aeschylus's last works although in its structure it is certainly one of the most archaic. It is predominantly lyrical in spirit and the real protagonist of the drama is the chorus of the Danaidae, pursued by their cousins who wish to marry them in spite of their reluctance. The *Persians* was written eight years after the battle of Salamis and in it Aeschylus represented the consequences of the Greek victory at the royal palace of Susa, the capital of the Persian empire; one of the play's greatest moments is when the old king Darius makes his appearance after being conjured up out of his tomb by the incantations of the chorus of the faithful. The whole play was an exaltation of the Greek national spirit and it was Pericles himself who served as Aeschylus's choragus. In the *Seven against Thebes* Eteocles, defending his country against the coalition of the seven chieftains formed by Polynices, is perhaps the most impressive male figure in the whole of Greek drama. *Prometheus Bound* is a " metaphysical " tragedy in which both the actors and the chorus (the Oceanidae) are all divinities. Lastly, there are the three plays with consecutive plots of the *Oresteia* trilogy: *Agamemnon*, in which the chief of the Achaeans, the conqueror of Troy, returns home to his palace at Mycenae and is murdered by his wife Clytemnestra, the *Chœphoroe*, in which Clytemnestra is killed in her turn by her son Orestes to avenge his father Agamemnon; the *Eumenides*, in which Orestes goes to Delphi to purify himself of the matricide he has committed on the orders of Apollo, but is pursued by the Erinyes until he is finally acquitted at Athens by the tribunal of the Areopagus, instituted by Athena; on this occasion, the vengeful furies transform themselves into the Eumenides, meaning " benign divinities ".

Aeschylus introduced several technical innovations (*See* Tragedy). Like his contemporary, Pindar, he was a believer and a metaphysician who was always inclined to reflect on the gods. Aristophanes has represented him in his play the *Frogs* as a man of passionate and haughty character. Aeschylus's tragedy is a highly spectacular representation which is designed to arouse feelings of disquiet, fear, anguish, horror and terror in the audience. In the choral parts his lyricism is distinguished by its power and brilliance; instead of winning the admiration of the spectator it overwhelms and dazzles him. His style is characterised by the use of a vocabulary full of neologisms and composite words which are often very long, an abundance of strong and expressive images, and a tone which is nearly always noble and high-flown although it does not exclude extremely realistic expressions and action.

At the centre of Aeschylus's metaphysical thought lies the idea of Nemesis or divine justice. Both Xerxes and Agamemnon are shown as victims of their own pride, for they forget the limits imposed on the human condition by destiny. Are the gods themselves just? Aeschylus puts the question in his *Prometheus Bound;* this and the other plays of the trilogy to which it belonged end with the conclusion that even if the supreme god, Zeus, had not always been just in the past, he had become so. For Aeschylus, divine will always had a meaning even if an obscure one; it was the pious man's first duty to know it and then to conform to it in his deeds. Although he had killed his own mother, Orestes was finally absolved because he had obeyed the gods.

As Aristophanes said, Aeschylus " taught the people " and, although his drama presents a terrifying picture of man's destiny, it is optimistic in the final analysis. But it was only after a long and bitter debate with his conscience that Aeschylus arrived at this lucid optimism, strengthened by a faith which, instead of being blind, tirelessly sought for its rational justification through ancient myths. The nobility of his inspiration, the power of his creative imagination and his unfailing sense of theatre make Aeschylus incontestably one of the greatest of the Greek tragic poets. R.F.

AESOP. From earliest times the Greeks liked to express their experience of life in fables in which animals spoke with the tongues of men, as in Hesiod's fable of the *Nightingale and the Sparrow-hawk* and in Archilochus's *Eagle and the Fox*. While these fables were in verse, those that have come down to us in the collection attributed to Aesop are in prose. Aesop seems to have lived in the 6th century B.C. and to have been a slave of Phrygian or Lydian, in any case Asiatic, origin. He became a legendary figure. If we are to believe Herodotus, Aesop had the same master as the famous courtesane Rhodopis: the Samian Iadmon. He won a great reputation with the fables he invented and recited during his journeys, but he also made enemies. The Delphians were offended by his irony and after falsely accusing him of sacrilege, put him to death.

The collection of Aesop's fables that we now know contains more than 350, but it is no longer certain which were really by his own hand. He enjoyed great celebrity at Athens where a statue was raised to him. In his comedies, Aristophanes makes several allusions to Aesop's fables and, according to Plato's *Phaedo,* Socrates put several of his fables into verse before dying. P.D.

Aesop talking to a fox. Inside of a cup by the Bologna Painter. About 470 B.C. Vatican Museum. *Photo Alinari-Viollet.*

AETOLIA. Aetolia was a vast mountain province lying to the north of the Gulf of Corinth and west of Locris and Phocis. For a long time the Greeks regarded its inhabitants as barbarians. They lived dispersed in villages and their only important town was Thermum, which was very modest compared with those in the rest of Greece. From at least the beginning of the 1st millennium B.C., it had been the site of the successive temples of Apollo that had been raised one after another on the same foundations. The temples are a precious source of archaeological information; they have enabled scholars to follow the various transformations of the original design and several decorative fragments of the 7th century building have been found (painted metopes and terra-cotta antefixes). It was not until Hellenistic times that Aetolia became important in Greek politics. Its people were brave warriors and at the end of the 4th century B.C. they grouped themselves in a league that united almost the whole country. Formerly despised by the other Greeks, the peasants of Aetolia became a force to be reckoned with. During almost the whole of the 3rd century, the Aetolian League exercised its authority over the sanctuary of Delphi through its delegates and it introduced a new festival, that of the Soteria, in the universally revered sanctuary. The league increased its territories and its influence and it was largely because of its collaboration that Rome was able to triumph over Macedonia and Greece. P.D.

AGAMEMNON. The son of Atreus, Agamemnon was the most famous victim of the curse that weighed upon all the descendants of Pelops. He was ruler of Argos and as such seems to have exercised a kind of moral authority, at least, over the princes of the Peloponnesus. He was therefore entitled to lead the expedition against Troy, launched to bring back the unfaithful Helen who had abandoned her husband, Menelaus, king of Sparta, to follow her lover, Paris. Fate turned against the unfortunate Agamemnon from the very beginning of the venture; the fleet which was to take the warriors to Troy was unable to leave the little port of Aulis because of contrary winds. When an oracle was consulted it declared that the winds would only turn if Agamemnon's own daughter were sacrificed to Artemis. With a heavy heart, Agamemnon ordered his wife, Clytemnestra, who had remained at Argos, to bring him their child, Iphigenia, on the pretext that he wanted to marry her to Achilles. On her arrival, heedless of his wife's curses, Agamemnon handed his daughter over to the soothsayer, Calchas, who slit her throat upon the altar to Artemis (some versions of the legend claim that at the last moment the goddess substituted a doe for the young girl whom she brought up as her priestess in far-off Tauris).

The expedition set off and Agamemnon fought against the Trojans for ten years, not without having many difficulties with his fellow-countrymen. His quarrel with Achilles, whom he had deprived of Briseis, inspired the many episodes in the *Iliad*. When the city was taken, Agamemnon returned home, bringing with him a Trojan princess, Cassandra.

During her husband's absence, Clytemnestra had taken her cousin, Aegisthus, for a lover. The adulterous couple savagely assassinated Agamemnon and Cassandra on the day of their return. But the king left two children: the unhappy Electra, whom Clytemnestra married to a poor peasant to prevent her from claiming the throne, and Orestes, who grew to manhood in the crime-haunted palace, then went into exile and eventually killed Aegisthus and Clytemnestra to avenge his father's murder. Because of his tragic fate, in the many dramas that this story inspired in ancient Greek literature, Agamemnon appears in a rather sympathetic light despite his many faults, perhaps also because he was regarded as a personification of legitimate power. P.D.

AGATHARCHUS. A painter from Samos, he worked in Athens at the same time as Zeuxis in the last third of the 5th century B.C. He was famous because of his dealings with Alcibiades, who shut him up in his house until he had finished painting the decorations. According to Vitruvius, Agatharchus invented perspective while painting a tragic scene. He afterwards commented on the painting in a written work and this commentary provided the original basis for the theories of the philosophers, Anaxagoras and Democritus, on geometrical perspective. R.M.

AGATHON. Athenian tragic poet of the second half of the 5th century B.C. None of his work has survived but he enjoyed great fame. In his *Poetics* Aristotle mentions him more often

than Aeschylus. Aristophanes made him one of the characters in his comedy the *Thesmophoriazusae*. He also appears as one of the speakers in Plato's *Symposium* in the framework of which it seems that it was Agathon himself who had invited Socrates, Aristophanes and several other guests, including Alcibiades who arrived late, in order to celebrate one of his victories in a competition of tragic drama. Agathon influenced the evolution of tragedy by replacing the songs of the chorus with simple musical interludes without any relation to the theme of the play. R.F.

AGELADAS. Ageladas was the most famous representative of the school of sculpture of Argos where, in the early 5th century B.C. the heavy, powerful style of archaic Dorian art became modified by influences from the east which were transmitted through Corinth and Sicyon. It is said that Ageladas' fame was so great that he attracted Polygnotus and Phidias as his pupils. He carved many figures of athletes that were mentioned by Pausanias when he visited Olympia, but he also sculptured images of the gods including that of Zeus Ithomatas, which was particularly famous. He was also an animal sculptor. At Delphi he had carried out an offering made by the Tarentines: a file of bronze horses accompanied by Messapian captives. He made the famous racing quadriga which Cleosthenes of Epidamnus offered to Olympia. The various genres in which Ageladas worked show him to have been the master of the great sculptors of the 5th century. R.M.

AGESILAUS. After defeating Athens in 404 B.C. and thus bringing the Peloponnesian War to an end, Sparta began a series of campaigns against the Persian territories in Asia Minor. The most brilliant of these offensives was led by Agesilaus, who had become king in 397. His fellow-citizens mocked him because he was short and lame, but he was courageous and a good general. He advanced deep into Phrygia and even occupied Sardes, the capital of Lydia. He avoided pitched battles and his campaigns were mostly plundering enterprises without any political significance. They allowed those of the Greeks who had not accepted Lacedaemonian supremacy full freedom to prepare their revenge. His successes were short-lived and the destruction at Cnidos of the Spartan fleet by Conon, an Athenian in the service of the Persians, prevented the Spar-

Agora at Athens.
Processional way of
the Panathenaea.
Modern reconstruction
of the Stoa of Attalus
in the background.
Photo Hassia.

tans from striking any more blows against the Persian king on his own territory.　　　　P.D.

AGORA. The agora has no equivalent in our modern civilisation. The very word itself, still used today by Greeks when speaking of a market place and employed by translators of ancient Greek texts to denote a centre of public affairs, no longer evokes what was, for the ancient Greeks, the essential and meaningful aspect of the Agora. It was the open place we usually imagine it, but it was only at a late date in ancient Greek history and at certain sites that it assumed the majesty we usually associate with the word. It was in the agora that meetings were held and that merchants had their booths, but—and it is this that is so difficult to comprehend in its entirety—it was first and foremost the sacred centre of the civic body, the heart and brain of the institution that has now disappeared for ever and that remains alien to us—the *polis*, which we now give the inexact term of city. It was a sacred place in the full meaning of the words. In 4th century Athens, according to what must have been a very ancient custom, vases were placed at the points where roads led into the agora, containing water with which the passer-by ritually purified himself, as he entered the agora as though into a shrine.

Access to the agora was forbidden to men of dissolute lives and, after the time of Draco, to anyone accused of murder. Like a sanctuary, the perimeter of the agora was indicated by boundary stones. It was in the agora that the body of the city's founder was buried whenever it had been preserved. Other equally venerable tombs were placed there and altars and temples were consecrated to the gods who protected the state. Ceremonies were held in honour of these gods and heroes so that the agora was not only a place of worship but also of festivals. It was sometimes specially designed for this purpose, as at Corinth, where traces have been found of the starting-line for torch races. If so many political assemblies were held, so many tribunals situated in the agora, and if official buildings, such as meeting halls and archives, were built along its limits, it was precisely because the tutelary gods and heroes, who could inspire the deliberations of the citizens, were to be found there.

It can be seen from this that the agora was far more than just a public place, but it only assumed its full importance once the royal power had disappeared. The kings had their residences on the Acropolis, where they rendered justice, summoned their councillors and sometimes even their subjects to inform them of the decisions they

Harvesters. Detail of a vase in steatite from Haghia Triada. 18th century B.C. Heraklion Museum. *Photo Hassia.*

had taken. When the monarchy fell, although the Acropolis still dominated the town below because of its historic prestige, the seat of the collective government was removed, to be situated among the dwellings of the citizens. This is how the agora of Athens was founded in about the 8th century B.C., at the foot of the ancient rock in an available space that had formerly been used as a necropolis. In Athens, as in all other cities founded in ancient times, many centuries elapsed before the agora took on an imposing aspect in about the 2nd century B.C. A series of successive enlargements gradually transformed the character of the agora. It had been very small at first, was later embellished by Cimon immediately after the departure of the Persians, and was then filled with new buildings until finally the enlarged esplanade was adorned with sumptuous porticoes by the kings of Pergamum.

In more recent cities, first in Ionia, then at Miletus and Piraeus, which were examples of rectilinear city planning, a central space was left in the grid pattern to be occupied by the agora. Consequently, from the very beginning architects were able to give the agora an imposing character by surrounding it with porticoes on three of its four sides. Naturally, people did not gather in this vast square at the very heart of the city for political and religious reasons alone, and the agora inevitably became a business centre as well. This last function may seem the most important one to us today; it was not the first and many high-minded citizens lamented the fact that at the very centre of that organism which was the city, among the altars and at the foot of the statues that had been set up to honour the liberators of the homeland, merchants now spread their wares, and commercial interests tainted a place where the only interests should have been those of the state. Nevertheless, commerce took hold in the agora so strongly that the officials responsible for the administration of the markets came to be called *agoranomoi*. At the most, the Athenians made efforts on several occasions to forbid mercantile activities in certain areas reserved exclusively for worship and public affairs. A more radical solution was adopted in Piraeus and other towns, where a second open square was built especially for commerce, and therefore situated alongside the port. Later, even when Greece lost her independence, it was the agora, like the Acropolis, with all its historic associations, that remained the symbol of that community spirit which had once informed the city.

P.D.

AGORACRITUS. A native of Paros, Agoracritus was Phidias's favourite, if not his best, pupil. It was said that Phidias loved him so much that he let him put his name to his own works. We only know Agoracritus by his reputation. One of his main works was a colossal cult figure in marble (*See* Statues) for the sanctuary of Nemesis at Rhamnus in Attica; the only fragments that we know come from the sculptured base and are carved in a very classical style, but it is not certain whether this relief, representing Helen and Leda, was by the same hand as that which carved the statue in the round of Nemesis.

P.D.

AGRICULTURE. According to legend, it was Demeter (the Ceres of the Romans), the corn-goddess, who gave the first ear of corn to the Attic hero, Triptolemus, but it may well be that Demeter was a substitute for Isis, since the Greeks believed that their agriculture came from Egypt. The Mycenaean tablets, which Michael Ventris deciphered in 1953, throw some light on the agricultural economy of the Achaeans in about the 13th century B.C. They stress the importance of agriculture and livestock breeding, and mention corn, barley, figs, honey, sheep, goats, pigs, horses and donkeys. Homer, especially, described the vast royal domains, as in Book XVIII of the *Iliad* for example, with its description of the tilling of the soil, the harvest, the grape-harvest, and stock-breeding: " Next he depicted a large field of soft, rich fallow, which was being ploughed for the third time. A number of ploughmen were driving their teams across it to and fro... He also showed a king's estate, where hired reapers were at work with sharp sickles in their hands. Armfuls of corn fell down in rows along the furrow, while others were tied up with straw by the sheaf-binders. Three of these were standing by, and the boys who were gleaning behind came running up to them with bundles in their arms and kept them constantly supplied. And there among them was the King himself, staff in hand, standing by the swathe in quiet satisfaction. Under an oak in the background his attendants were preparing a feast. They were cooking a great ox that they had slaughtered, and the women were sprinkling the meat for the labourers' supper with handfuls of white barley. The next scene was a vineyard laden with grapes. It was beautifully wrought in gold, but the bunches themselves were black and the supporting poles showed up throughout in silver... He also showed a herd of straighthorned cattle, making the cows of gold and tin. They were mooing as they hurried from the byre to feed where the rushes swayed beside a murmuring stream. Four golden herdsmen accompanied the cattle, and there were nine dogs trotting along with them... To this picture the illustrious lame god added a big grazing ground for white-fleeced sheep, in a beautiful valley, complete with its farm buildings, pens and well-roofed huts. " (*Translated by* E.V. Rieu.) In the part of the *Odyssey* which takes place at Ithaca, Homer describes Eumaeus's herd of swine, other herds of sheep and goats, and the little plot of land with its beautiful orchard outside the town, which was tended by the aged Laertes.

Sowing and ploughing. Detail of a black-figure cup. Third quarter of the 6th century B.C. British Museum.

While Homer showed us a great estate, Hesiod, writing in the late 8th century B.C., left us the description of a humble peasant holding. This was his own property at Ascra in Boeotia, an " accursed estate, unpleasant in winter, hard in summer, and never agreeable ". His didactic poem *Works and Days* is the first known textbook on agriculture. First, Hesiod tells us how to make a plough : " First, take home a bough of ilex for it is the strongest for ploughing with oxen once Athena's servant has fitted it into the sharebeam, and nailed and fitted it to the pole. Make yourself two ploughs in your own home, one of one piece, the other of several pieces all fitted together... For the plough, laurel and elm are the woods least likely to be eaten by worms; for the frame, oak is the most suitable, for the handle, ilex. " Hesiod then recommends the different and most suitable times for various agricultural tasks: " When the Pleiades, daughters of Atlas, rise in the heavens, begin your harvest, but when they set, begin to plough... When the violence of the keen sun abates its sweat-making heat and all powerful Zeus sends down the autumn rains... wood is least liable to be attacked by worms if felled with the axe; it is then that you must cut your wood if you can still recollect the work to be done in each season... Take heed, as soon as you hear the yearly cry of the crane high out of the clouds, for it brings the signal for sowing-time and heralds the rainy winter. Its cry gnaws at the heart of the man who has no oxen... "

In the 4th century, Xenophon wrote his *Oeconomicus* on the theme of domestic " economics ", the management of family inheritances. As this inheritance happened to be in the country, the work ended with a treatise on agronomics. In it, Xenophon advises the reader how to distinguish between different kinds of land, how to prepare fallow land, how to sow, hoe, harvest, thresh and winnow grain and how to tend fruit trees, especially olive and fig trees, and vines. Unlike Hesiod's modest field, the land in question was a great estate where the owner did not work with his own hands but supervised a large team of agricultural workers so that, consequently, the art of commanding men was one of the many things that the would-be farmer had to learn. Xenophon enthusiastically sings the praises of agriculture, declaring that " this activity is not only a source of pleasure, but also a means of increasing one's estate and of training the body to do all that is fitting for a free man to be able to do ".

After holding forth at length on these three points, Xenophon finally concludes, " Agriculture is the mother and nursemaid of all the other arts ".

In classical Greece, the system of land tenure varied greatly from one region to another. In Sparta, each citizen possessed, in principle at least, an inalienable holding *(kleros)* of medium extent which was cultivated by helots with an average yearly yield of eighty *medimnoi* of corn (about forty hectolitres) as well as olives and grapes, but in practice some families enriched themselves at the expense of others, and a small number of citizens ended by possessing vast *latifundia* while others had just enough land for their subsistence. In Thessaly, large estates were always the rule. In Attica, the great estates of the Eupatridae had long been parcelled up. At the time of Solon, the foremost class of citizens who alone could accede to the archonship, included those Athenians whose annual revenue equalled or exceeded five hundred *medimnoi* of corn (about two hundred and fifty hectolitres). They were known as the *pentakosiomedimnoi*. Next came the knights and the *zeugitai*, with a respective annual revenue of at least three hundred and two hundred *medimnoi*. The largest class of citizens was that of the *thetes*, the poor, who could only rely on a wage for their subsistence; they were often in debt and no longer owned their properties which had passed into other hands. Solon re-established a fairer system in 594 B.C. by means of the *seisachtheia*, and celebrated his act in verse: " She may bear witness at the court of Time, the venerable Mother of the Olympians, the black Earth out of which I tore the boundary stones that were set in it everywhere: once it was a slave, now it is free. "

In the 5th century, three kinds of land-owners could be distinguished at Athens: the small landowner *(autourgos)* who worked his land either with his own hands, as Hesiod had done in the past, or with the help of a few slaves; the landowner who contented hinself with supervising the slaves and agricultural workers who laboured on his estates, like Xenophon at Scillus, or Ischomachus, the main character of the *Oeconomicus;* lastly, the absentee landlord, who lived in the town, and appointed a steward to look after his lands and send him either produce from his estate or its equivalent in money, as Pericles did when he was detained at Athens by his activities as a statesman.

From the time of Solon's reforms to the Peloponnesian War, the condition of the Attic peasantry seems to have been pleasant enough. In Aristophanes' play the *Clouds,* Strepsiades harks back to the time he spent in the country before the war made him flee to Athens: " What a pleasant humdrum life one leads there, lazing in the shade of cedar trees, surrounded by bees, lambs and olive oil. " Indeed, " the plains of Mesogaea, Cephissus and Eleusis produced fine crops of cereals and vegetables, Diacria was covered with lovely vineyards; pastures and brushwood were plentiful along the Parnes Mountains; on the heights, like those of Mount Hymettus, the hives were filled with bees and everywhere olive trees produce an oil worth its weight in gold " (G. Glotz). During the Peloponnesian War, the enemy invaded Attica with the coming of every spring and ravaged it, cutting down the vines and olive trees before settling down at permanent quarters at Decelea. The war also brought about a general rise in prices, which caused the small land-owner to fall into debt as he was no longer able to make a living out of his tiny parcel of land. This is why the peasants in Menander's plays are no longer like those of Aristophanes, but ceaselessly lament their unhappy fate and the ingratitude of a soil covered everywhere with sterile pebbles.

Agricultural techniques were always at a very rudimentary stage. The land was usually ploughed three times in the year: in the springtime, in the summer, and in the autumn, but rotation of crops was unknown and farmers contented themselves with leaving their land to lie fallow every second year. Chemical fertilisers were also unheard of and there was a lack of dung in regions unsuited to stockbreeding. Nevertheless, from the 4th century B.C. onwards, agronomists began to study questions of land improvement, and researches were made into arboriculture where several improvements were achieved. The plough, which had not been improved since the time of Hesiod, was still pulled by an ox or mule, making such a shallow furrow in the soil that the work had to be completed with a pick axe or hoe. Corn was threshed as it still is today in certain remote parts of Greece; the sheaves were laid out on a tiled threshing-floor in a place exposed to the wind and were then trodden upon by a team of horses or mules, walking in a circle around a central post to which they were tied by a long cord. The grain was then ground by female slaves in mortars with the aid of wood or stone pestles. Attica produced insufficient corn and barley for its own needs and the Athenians were obliged to import large quantities of cereals at great expense from Egypt, Sicily or the Pontus on the north shore of the Black Sea, the Crimea of today. Olives were pressed in a mortar with a spout or an outlet at the bottom for the marc, which was used as a fertiliser. Use was also made of what was really a kind of oil-mill, consisting of two stones, one fixed and the other mobile, which was rotated by slaves. Work at this mill was reputed to be almost as hard as that at the mines at Laurium.

Vegetables were rare and expensive, for they mostly came from the neighbouring countries of Megara or Boeotia, but in the 4th century B.C. the Attic peasants were able to produce cabbages, lentils, peas, onions and garlic, and even managed to adapt Egyptian gourds to the Greek climate. In Attica there were no good grazing grounds for horses, while Boeotia and especially Thessaly had fertile plains which allowed intensive stockbreeding. As late as 490, at the battle of Marathon, the Athenians had no cavalry. They constituted a cavalry corps at a later date, but its strength never went beyond a thousand horses. On the other hand, there were numerous pigs, sheep and goats in Attica, where goats and sheep were led to pasture in the mountains at the confines *(eschatiai)* of the country. In Aristophanes's *Clouds,* Strepsiades tells his son: " When you are grown up you will bring your goats back down from Mount Phelleus, wearing a goatskin like your father. " This costume was none other than the *diphthera,* the typical attire of the Greek peasant. R.F.

AGRIGENTUM. Of all the ancient sites in Sicily, Agrigentum is now one of the most magnificent with its line of buildings on the crest of the hill, overlooking the sea separating the island from the African coast to the south: the temples of Hephaestus and the Dioscuri, the Olympieion with its giant figures which once stood between the columns and held up the jutting architrave with their bent arms, and the temples of " Heracles " and " Juno Lacinia ". They still stand there in a line, at irregular intervals, all well enough preserved to produce a monumental effect, all in a sufficient state of ruin to give the landscape that picturesque quality so esteemed by 18th century connoisseurs.

All this splendour dates only from the 5th cen-

Agrigentum.
Temple D,
called the Temple
of Juno Lacinia. The
altar seen from the
pronaos.
About 440-425 B.C.
Photo Hirmer.

tury B.C., when Agrigentum had only a brief history behind it. It was founded in 580 by settlers from Gela. From 565 to 549 it had suffered the tyrannical rule of Phalaris whose cruelty became legendary. It then went to war against its neighbours and finally became strong enough during Theron's period or rule (488-472) to crush the Carthaginian army at Himera in 480, with the aid of the Syracusans. This victory and the booty that went with it made for the sudden prosperity of the city, filling it with thousands of slaves and ensuring its domination over all the surrounding territory. It was then that those edifices were built which made it, in Pindar's words, " the most beautiful city of mortals ". So much care was lavished on the city's embellishment that the vital needs of the state were neglected and during the republic that followed a period of tyranny the inhabitants neglected their training so that in 406 the Carthaginians were able to take the city and set fire to it. It was resettled during the 4th century but neither then nor during the successive domination by the Romans, the Carthaginians, and then again the Romans did it ever recapture its past splendour and glory.   P.D.

AJAX. Two Greek heroes who took part in the Trojan War were both called Ajax. The first was a Locrian and the son of Oïleus. Although a courageous warrior, he was unpleasant by nature

and never slow to mock the gods. When Troy was being sacked, he dragged the prophetess, Cassandra, down from the altar of Athena where she had taken refuge. Later, on his voyage back home, he was caught in a tempest called up by Athena and only escaped with his life owing to the intervention of Poseidon. He then took shelter on a rock where he boasted of being more powerful than the goddess. No longer able to bear his repeated blasphemies, she then commanded the same Poseidon who had saved him from the sea to break the reef on which he was standing with his trident. The second Ajax was the son of Telamon, king of Salamis, and he was as pious as his namesake was disrespectful. He was equally courageous and was the foremost warrior of the Greek army after Achilles' death. But being disappointed at not receiving the Palladium, the divine statue that had protected Troy, in his booty, he ran himself through the heart with his own sword.   P.D.

ALCAEUS. He was a lyric poet of the isle of Lesbos, probably born about 630 B.C. and a contemporary of the famous poetess, Sappho. He was in love with Sappho, who refused him, the encounter being immortalised on a beautiful painted vase, now in the Museum Antiker Kleinkunst, Munich. Only a few fragments survive of Alcaeus's works. We know that he led a very stormy life in which politics, war, adventure and amorous activities all had a place. He played an active part in the civil wars in Lesbos during the troubled period preceding the rule of the wise Pittacus and then refused the amnesty offered him by the generous tyrant and remained his irreconcilable enemy, only returning to Lesbos after Pittacus's abdication. He also fought in the war against Athens, which was disputing the possession of Sigeum in the Troad with the Lesbians. Like Archilochus, Alcaeus threw his shield away in battle and later good-humouredly recounted his misadventure in a poem. Several of the surviving fragments express the violence of the partisan, but they mostly sing of the joy of life and the pleasures of drinking and love. Alcaeus's style is always very personal and his poetry easily becomes sensual, as when he sings of the boy Lycus, with his black hair and eyes, or of the gracefulness of some girl or other. R.F.

ALCAMENES. Alcamenes was one of the followers of Phidias and one of the most successful in keeping his own originality while still remaining faithful to his great master's precepts. It may well have been Alcamenes who succeeded Phidias as supervisor of public works in Athens after the master had left the city, but he did not have the same universality, for although he was a good sculptor he was never anything more than a sculptor. Some of the works of Alcamenes that were most admired by his contemporaries have survived in the form of replicas, and include a Hermes, which stood in the Propylaea of the Acropolis and which was distinguished by a serene sweetness that was rather revolutionary in about 430 B.C. Apart from a somewhat sentimental sculpture of Procne and Itys, he carved an Ares, which may have been a copy of the famous Borghese Mars, and was commissioned by the Athenians to chisel the gold and ivory cult image for the new temple of Dionysus. P.D.

ALCESTIS. Alcestis was the daughter of Pelias, the old king who was boiled in a cauldron by his daughters who hoped to rejuvenate him by following Medea's wicked advice. She was the only one to refuse to take part in the magic rite, which was of course intended to result in the frightful death of the sovereign. Her hand had been sought in marriage by Admetus, a Thessalian prince, who was only successful after he had managed to drive a chariot drawn by a lion and a wild boar. The couple were devoted to one another and when Admetus was at the point of death the gods agreed to let him go on living if someone else would consent to take his place. He vainly begged his aged parents to sacrifice themselves for him, nor was he any more successful with his debtors. Only Alcestis readily volunteered and he accepted her offer. She was already buried when Heracles visited Admetus, finding him in

Suicide of Ajax. Detail of an amphora attributed to Execias. About 540 B.C. Museum of Boulogne-sur-Mer. *Photo D. Widmer.*

tears and unwilling at first to tell him the cause of his grief. But when he finally broke the news to the hero, Heracles himself descended into Hell and brought back the heroic wife who had so loved her husband that she had given her life for him. In the play that Euripides based on this legend, one of the most moving scenes is that in which Alcestis says good-bye to her young children. P.D.

ALCIBIADES. Just as Alcibiades is always popular with schoolboys when they have to read the dry account of the Peloponnesian War because of his devil-may-care cheek and his panache, so he was a favourite with the Athenians in the time of Pericles. He was a spoilt child throughout his life, whether he was holding up the traffic in the streets as a little boy so that he could play with his friends, or whether he was anticipating modern publicity techniques by such expedients as cutting the tail of his dog in order to be the centre of attention in discussions with his contemporaries. The Greeks of his day do not seem to have realised that Alcibiades, who was descended from a noble family which counted many turbulent politicians among its ancestors, was the personification of a spirit that could only be fatal to Greek democracy and even the fate of the country. He introduced a scorn for laws and an indifference to the public interest into the republic under the most attractive guises and, as a pupil of the sophists, he was able to convince both himself and others that such a peerless individual as himself was entitled to every right. He was by birth an aristocrat, became the ward of Pericles and a pupil of Socrates, and entered into politics in his youth, as a champion of the people. The prestige he had won by his extravagant career, his remarkable intelligence and distinguished military record (he had fought at Potidaea) helped to get him elected a strategus in 420 B.C. After discrediting Nicias, the leader of the conservative faction, he pursued a complicated policy towards Sparta, sometimes opposing it with a confederation of Peloponnesian cities and sometimes flattering it. The climax of his political career came when he encouraged the Athenians to attack Syracuse. It would seem that this obviously dangerous and badly handled expedition (Alcibiades was to have been one of the leaders but at the very moment of departure was implicated on a charge of sacrilege, he was accused, probably rightly so, of being one of a merry

band of iconoclasts who had mutilated the sacred hermae placed at every cross-roads in Athens) was only a stepping stone towards even greater popularity. For Sicily, whose wealth was proverbial, was a tempting prey for a democracy on the look-out for easy gains. After being accused of impiety, Alcibiades escaped sentence by fleeing to Sparta, where the advice he gave his hosts led to the failure of his countrymen's expedition, which he himself had advised. After quarrelling with the Spartans, he fled to Asia Minor where he continued to intrigue at a distance. Then he returned just in time to help the Athenians free themselves from the Four Hundred Tyrants who had been ruling over the city for some time. He obtained his pardon (411). He led the fleet that had been entrusted to his command and won two victories over the Spartans and a fair amount of glory during the campaigns to the east between 410 and 408. In 407 he was given a true victor's welcome in Athens, but his popularity rapidly waned in later years and he died wretchedly in 403. P.D.

ALCIPHRON. Rhetorician and sophist of the 2nd century A.D., almost contemporary with Lucian. He has left a collection of a hundred and eighteen fictional letters divided into four books: letters of courtesans, fishers, peasants and parasites. They are, in the opinion of M. Croiset '' one of the most agreeable productions of second century sophism ''. Like Lucian, Alciphron borrowed ideas wherever he could find them in earlier books; he was considerably influenced by the new style of comedy, notably Menander's, and also by novels such as Longus's pastoral *Daphnis and Chloe*. He gives an invaluable and charming picture of social manners in his description of the facile, glittering life of the courtesans, but he did not forget the misery of the poor common people or the hard life of the peasants on their lands. R.F.

ALCMAEON of CROTON. One of the first great doctors of ancient Greece. A medical school had been founded at Croton by Democedes, the son of a priest of Asclepius at Cnidos, who had been doctor at the courts of Polycrates of Samos and King Darius before returning to his homeland, where he married the daughter of the athlete, Milo, who attended the meetings of the Pythagoreans. Alcmaeon was one of Pythagoras's pupils and first disciples. He compared the human organism to the state saying that the preponderance of any one element would cause an illness in the body and could thus be compared to the monarchy. He compared the life of the human race and the movement of the stars, which were immortal because at the end of their orbits they came back to the beginning again, achieving a renewal that was beyond the capacity of an individual life. He practised dissection and understood the part played by the brain in the physiology of sensations and especially that of sight, and was able to comprehend the function of the optic nerves. Animals, he remarked, can only feel, but man can understand; but whereas the gods have a full knowledge of the invisible world, men can only speculate about it. We may recognise in his ideas the probabilism of a scientist who was the first to link medicine with philosophy.   P.-M.S.

ALCMAN. Lyric poet of the second half of the 7th century B.C. He was born at Sardes in Lydia, but mostly lived in Sparta. His poems are all written in the Lacedaemonian dialect and were choral lyrics or *parthenia,* hymns designed to be sung by choirs of young girls. The few fragments that are extant suggest a gracious and homely poetry, somewhat banal and far removed from the fiery genius of Sappho and the excesses of Alcaeus. The only time when Alcman's poetry attains a certain grandeur is in some of his descriptions of nature which are reminiscent of Hesiod's style.   R.F.

ALEXANDER. There are few great figures in the history of ancient Greece whose career is as well known to us as is that of Alexander, owing to the number of reliable records, just as there are few whose life and actions have been the object of greater controversy. Whatever other words we may be tempted to use in describing such an overwhelming personality, we cannot call him enigmatic. Alexander seems to defy understanding by being outside the normal human scale and by possessing so many seemingly contradictory qualities, all intensified to an unprecedented degree and exceeding by far those that are usually only granted singly and sparingly to ordinary mortals.

Alexander came from a country which was considered barbaric even though it had been touched by Greek influence. Although the family of Alexander claimed descent from Heracles,

thereby being entitled to participate in the Olympic games, both Alexander and his father Philip were lacking in such typically Hellenic traits of character as poise, moderation and that profound conviction that man neither can nor should attempt to equal the gods. When, after many victories, Alexander insisted on honours normally only accorded to the immortals in Greece, he was probably only conforming to the customs of the peoples he had conquered. He was never reluctant to enhance his authority with such superhuman prestige but, even before winning his great victories, he was already treating the Olympians as his equals, pretending that his true father was a god (331 B.C.), extorting a reply from the Pythian oracle at a time of year when it was usually silent (336), and forcing fate by severing the Gordian knot after being told that he must first untie it if he was to be certain of conquering Asia (334).

Alexander possessed something that was rarely found among the Greeks and that was the quality of imagination. Although he had been tutored in his youth by Aristotle, the teachings of that most critical of philosophers had been unable to curb the exuberant flow of ideas and projects that was to lead Alexander into undertakings of such daring that their failure would have provided to minds nourished on Aeschylus and Pindar a perfect example of how the gods punished foolhardy mortals. But Alexander succeeded in everything he attempted, for he had had the good fortune to be born at a time when the world was ageing and when the structures of its societies were crumbling, and because the passion and almost pathological violence of his character were combined with a keen sense of realities and an extraordinarily clear understanding of the methods to be used in accomplishing his projects.

He was born in July 356 B.C. in the palace of Pella, the capital city of Macedonia. His father was Philip II (q.v.) and his mother, Olympias, a princess from the barbaric tribe of the Molossi in Epirus. Alexander was brought up to love poetry so that, when he was razing the city of Thebes to the ground, the only house he ordered his troops to spare was that where Pindar had lived. The *Iliad* was his constant bedside companion and he recognised the talent of such artists as Apelles and Lysippus by granting to them alone the right to make his portrait. Although he had taken lessons from Aristotle, little trace of the philosopher's teachings was to be found in his later career. He also conformed to native tradi-

Alexander at the battle of Issus. Detail of a mosaic from Herculaneum copied from an original painting of the 4th century B.C. Naples, Museo Nazionale. *Photo Anderson-Viollet.*

tions by hardening his body with warlike exercises and by displaying his courage in such legendary feats as the taming of his wild horse Bucephalus. There can be little doubt that he observed another native Macedonian custom by indulging in wild drinking bouts, which were later to lead him to commit such irreparable acts as the slaying of his most faithful friend, Clitus, in 328, when he was in a state of blind drunkenness.

He was only sixteen years old when he was appointed regent by his father, who had gone to war against Byzantium, and it was then that he led his first campaign and founded the first of the cities that were to bear his name, Alexandropolis in Thracia. In 338, he led his cavalry in a charge against the Sacred Band of the Thebans, and shortly afterwards he headed the delegation which came to Athens bringing the ashes of the warriors who had died in this battle.

In 336, his father was murdered by Pausanias and he succeeded to the throne after first eliminating his rivals in a blood-bath, with the aid of his mother. Greece was preparing to shake off the yoke of Macedonian domination, but a military excursion was enough to confirm Alexander in his father's rights. He then spent the next few months subduing the various Balkan tribes that were menacing his kingdom, such as the Thracians, the Triballi and the Illyrians, and in a lightning offensive against the Greeks who had been encouraged to revolt by false rumours. The capture and total destruction of Thebes, however,

proved sufficient to reassert his royal authority, and by autumn 336 Alexander, who had shown mercy to the Athenians, no longer had anything to fear from this quarter.

The year before, he had followed his father by receiving the title of commander-in-chief against the Persians from the Greeks. He spent little time in lengthy preparations for he was determined to make this title into a reality. He started his campaign almost without money and with a much weaker fleet than that of his adversary. He relied upon his army which was few in numbers (less than 40,000 men) but hardened to war and well organised and headed by his élite corps, his 1500 Macedonian horsemen, called *hetairoi*. He also relied on the phalanx formations of his infantry and their long spears *(sarissa)*, his corps of engineers and their siege machines, his general staff of generals and administrators some of whom had proved their worth in the reign of his father (Craterus, Parmenion, Clitus the Black, Antigonus, Nearchus, Eumenes of Cardia, Lysimachus, Ptolemy, Hephaestion) and also on the fundamental feebleness of the Persian empire, under its weak emperor, Darius III Codomanus, for he was always very well informed about the real state of his enemies. Finally, and perhaps above all else, he relied on his own genius and on the help of the gods whom he considered as his equals. Like a new Achilles, he was always confident of victory and, when his troops were disembarking on the shores of Asia, he took possession of the country

28

by hurling his javelin into the beach and by being the first to leap ashore. Almost immediately afterwards, he was faced by the Persian army which had been drawn up to meet him along the banks of the little river Granicus. He routed the army and the audacious victory gave him and his men a confidence that was to be fortified by future events. He marched through defenceless Phrygia, Lydia, Ionia where he liberated the Greek cities, and collected overdue tribute wherever he went. He stayed for a while at Ephesus and Miletus, then made a rapid raid into Lycia and Pamphylia. By the spring of 333, less than a year after beginning his campaign, he was the master of a large part of Asia Minor. He then crossed the mountains of Cilicia and in the following November met Darius himself, who was waiting to repulse him with an enormous army, on a carefully prepared battlefield. The result was the battle of Issus, of all Alexander's battles the most glorious and the best conducted, which ended with the panic-stricken flight of the Great King.

A famous mosaic from Herculaneum, which is a faithful reproduction of a painting of Alexander's time, depicts this battle and shows Alexander attacking Darius at the height of the battle. Alexander's features are easily recognisable, because we know them well from coins and good replicas of the portraits sculptured by Lysippus. He had a long face with a regular and energetic profile, a determined chin, a resolute expression which could be either cold or impassionned, and disordered hair falling in long locks down each side of his forehead.

After the battle of Issus, Alexander was free to choose from among the various possibilities that destiny offered him, being all the freer as he had nothing to fear from the Greece he had left behind or the provinces he had conquered. Not only was there little likelihood of any serious revolt (attempts at revolt in Aegae a year later were easily put down), but he had set up an administrative and financial system in the lands he had subdued, which was in the hands of experienced and faithful subordinates. The alternatives before him were to bring his conquests to an end and accept Darius's offer of a pact of friendship; strike towards the capital of the Persian king and the heart of his empire, or take the more methodical course of subduing Phoenicia and Egypt and thereby destroying the naval power of an enemy which was threatening his lines of communication with his homeland. He decided on the

third course and, strengthened by the booty his victories had brought him, followed the Mediterranean coast-line, accepting the submission of Sidon but only taking Tyre in 332 after a seven months siege during which every resource of siege craft had been employed. He advanced as far as Damascus where he allowed the Persian governor to retain his post, after naming one of his Macedonian officers as adjutant. After taking Gaza, not without difficulty, he then advanced into Egypt without striking a blow. The conquest of this country, which had been restive under the Persian yoke and which made no attempt to defend itself, was not one of Alexander's most glorious exploits, but it marked a decisive step in his career, not because the treasures it yielded him enabled him to continue the war, but because it was here that he first applied the policy that he was henceforth always to adopt in conquered countries. Instead of coming as a victorious warrior, he assumed the role of a legitimate sovereign who was the heir of the pharaohs. He sacrificed to the local gods, appeared before the people wearing the traditional head-dress of the pharaohs, the *pskhent*, symbol of royal power, restored the sanctuaries and founded the city of Alexandria. He intended it to unite Egyptian with Greek civilisation; later, it in fact became the chief port of the Mediterranean and the capital of art and letters during the whole Hellenistic period. Even more important, it was at this time that he formed a more precise idea of his destiny. He made a journey across the desert to visit the shrine of Zeus Ammon, the Egyptian divinity which was also honoured by the Greeks, and, after closeting himself with the god, went away convinced that he was indeed the son of Zeus (" When will Alexander stop making trouble between me and Hera ? " Olympias was supposed to have said at the time) and fortified by the promise that his empire would be universal.

In the spring of 331 he left Egypt at the head of his army, determined to fulfil the prophecy of Ammon. Darius had assembled all his troops behind the Tigris but, when Alexander met him between Gaugamela and Arbela, the result was a new victory for the Greeks. The Great King managed to escape, but at the cost of losing all his treasure, his family, and his army (October 331). Alexander made a triumphant entry into Babylon, Susa and Ecbatana, but it was not until July 330, after a hot pursuit that he finally caught up with Darius by the shores of the Caspian Sea, finding the wretched king betrayed and dying by the hand of one of his own subjects. Alexander then installed himself on the throne, proclaiming himself the successor of the Achaemenids and began to practise on a grand scale the policies he had first tried out in Egypt, now applying them to a vast empire. He adopted the customs of the sovereigns he had displaced, ruled supreme over an empire in which Greece and Macedonia were now mere provinces, treated his new subjects and his old companions on an equal footing, and attempted a fusion of all races so that the ancient quarrels between Medes and Hellenes would be forgotten. In the years that remained to him he applied these principles with the utmost tenacity and never hesitated to put even the most faithful of his captains to death when they rebelled against a policy which abolished all differences between conqueror and conquered. He appointed Darius's former servants to high posts and, not content with practising the Great King's polygamy by marrying Roxana and then other Persian princesses, held a gigantic wedding ceremony in which he married off more than ten thousand of his officers and soldiers to local women in a single day (in 324), bestowing a gift and a dowry on each couple. He also participated in the various religious rites of the different regions through which he passed. The extent of his domains was constantly increasing and, far from resting on his laurels after acceding to the throne, Alexander undertook new campaigns to subdue the oriental satrapies. From 330 to 327 he led his army through mountain regions populated by warlike, hostile tribes, fighting hard all the way and slowly advancing towards Parthia and then on to the high valley of the Cabul river, to Samarkand and then to Bactria where he called a halt. He subdued Sogdiana and appointed Persian governors in the newly conquered territories. Then, in 327, when he decided that these savage regions had been sufficiently pacified, he began his fabulous expedition which was to take him into India, well beyond the river Indus. He defeated King Porus and was hoping to reach the Ganges when his army refused to follow him any further, worn out and terrified of being so far from its base. The return journey began in 326 and was accomplished partly on land, partly by sea in a fleet commanded by Nearchus. After many trials, Alexander led his army back to Babylon after prolonged stays at Susa and other cities. He immediately began to re-establish order throughout his empire and to punish those of his governors and stewards who

had taken advantage of his absence to commit acts of insubordination or to embezzle funds. Alexander was only thirty-three years old, but it was not enough for him to have won the greatest empire ever possessed by any ruler and to have founded countless cities, which bore his name or commemorated his victories. There is no knowing what his plans may have been in June 323 when a short illness, malaria perhaps, brought his career to an end. The projects he was supposed to be harbouring were the most ambitious yet and so fraught with risks that we might almost be tempted to consider his premature death as a final sign of that affection the gods had always shown him. Who knows whether Napoleon did not one day regret that he had not died beneath the walls of Moscow? P.D.

ALEXANDRIA. Of all the cities named after Alexander of Macedon, Alexandria in Egypt was by far the most famous and most important. Alexander had founded it in 331 B.C. In order to spite Tyre, which he had just subdued, he wished to create a great new port on the Egyptian coast-line, which would centralise all the trade of the eastern Mediterranean. According to Plutarch, the site of the future city was shown to him by Homer in a dream: " Rising immediately, he made towards Pharos which was then an isle a little above the canopic mouth of the Nile, now attached to the mainland by a causeway. When he saw the advantages of this site, he declared that Homer, who was so accomplished in all things, was also the cleverest of architects, and ordered the plan of the city to be drawn up, in conformity with the nature of the site." Responsibility for supervising the work went to Dinocrates of Rhodes, who chose the sites for the main buildings, traced the avenues and streets and made them intersect at right angles according to the newly established laws of town-planning. The main highway, which was laid out more or less in the centre of the city, ran from east to west and measured almost a hundred feet in width, according to the writers of the period. Although archaeologists have not yet found remains of any such vast highway, it may well have been along such an imposing avenue that the lavish processions described by Theocritus in his XVth idyll made their way. From the time of its foundation, and even more from the time that it became the chosen capital of Ptolemy I, Alexandria was the greatest city in the whole Hellenistic world. In size alone it was the greatest since it extended over the then unprecedented area of almost ten square miles, in which blocks of dwellings, sometimes reaching a height of sixty feet, were interspersed with parks and public monuments in specially reserved areas. Alexandria was the first great precursor of the modern city, but it was also one of the cultural capitals of the Hellenic world. It was there that shortly before his death in 285, Ptolemy I Soter established the famous Library, which was to be the model for similar foundations at Pergamum and elsewhere. It was more than a repository for an ever growing collection of manuscripts; works of art were also exhibited in the building, which had been dedicated to the Muses —hence the word " museum "—and thus the library became a real shrine of the arts, where sages and poets of the past were revered. The result in the cultural life of the city was the so-called Alexandrian school, which was characterised not only by a somewhat precious refinement and a tendency to archaise, but also by a very lively sense of family life and picturesque detail. The basis for this great cultural upsurge was the material richness of Alexandria due to its commercial importance; it was to its wonderfully constructed port, dominated by the colossal three-storey Pharos, over three hundred and sixty feet high and one of the Seven Wonders of the World, that ships from every country came to fetch the agricultural produce brought from far inland by the barges of the Nile. P.D.

ALEXANDRIANISM. After Alexander's death in 323 B.C., Alexandria became the capital of the kingdom of the Ptolemys. Under the rule of these Greek sovereigns, in the 3rd and 2nd centuries B.C., the city became the main centre of Greek culture, chiefly because of such special institutions as the Royal Library and the Museum (a foundation for the maintenance of scholars and scientists), although it never rivalled Athens for supremacy in the domain of philosophy. This is why Hellenistic civilisation is called Alexandrian despite the competition of Pergamum and then Rhodes. Alexandrianism was characterised in the first place by a rapid development of the physical, astronomical and biological sciences, as well as those of philology and literary history. In poetry, it was the age of Callimachus, Theocritus, Apollonius of Rhodes and Lycophron. Some of these poets' works were rather overburdened with erudition or else tended towards affectation, but others are full of vigour, picturesqueness and beauty. For a long time Alexandrianism was unjustly considered to be a period of decadence in comparison with the Attic culture of the so-called classic period. R.F.

ALEXIS. Dramatist of the Middle Comedy. (*See* Comedy).

ALPHEUS. The Alpheus is a little river in the Peloponnesus which crosses Elis to flow into the Ionian Sea. It waters Olympia where it is joined by its tributary, the Cladeus.

ALTAR. An altar is a site where worshippers prepare and leave food and drink required for the sustenance of a divinity. Like the human beings in whose shape they are conceived, the gods can go without sleep at night but not without food and drink. The altar, therefore, is more important than the temple and many sanctuaries in ancient Greece contained altars well before temples were built within them. It was at the altar, not the temple, to which access was often forbidden, that human and immortal met; it was in front of the altar that prayers were accompanied by sacrifices or libations; and it was against the altar that suppliants would kneel when demanding a favour or divine protection, since the god would surely come there. In earliest times, when the priest was also the king, the divinity used to live in the same palace and consequently the altar, as the common hearth of the state, the priest-king and the divinity, was situated in the most important room in the palace. Certain primitive temples still conform to this pattern as the altar is within their walls. Once the monarchy had been abolished and the god was no longer the personal guest of the ruler, but rather that of the people as a whole, it was necessary to build a new dwelling place for him, near the first altar and facing it so that his eyes might behold the offering and his nostrils might smell the smoke of the meat that was being cooked for him.

The original altars were built simply by the accumulation of the ashes of the victims, and a row of stones would limit the hearth. As it grew in height, the altar had to be enlarged in its entirety, as happened at Samos when the surface area of the altar grew sevenfold between the 10th and the 8th centuries B.C. Soon, the altar became a rectangular or circular mass of masonry, its summit circled by a ridge to hold the wood or coals, and crowned with acroteria. A step was often set beside the altar on one side where the sacrificer could stand while stoking the fire and cooking the meat of his victim. There were altars, too, at ground level, really ditches in which the blood of the sacrificial beasts was offered to the deity of the place. This type of altar was consecrated to gods of the dead, who did not reign in the upper air, or dead heroes, who also lived in the depths of the earth.   P.D.

AMASIS. With Execias, the Amasis painter dominated Greek black-figure vase painting between 550 and 525 B.C. Although he relied heavily on legend and mythology for his themes, his paintings show that he had a greater gift for rendering movement, the picturesque and even caricature. He was often particularly attracted by scenes of family life, women conversing by fountains or at work in their apartments, and homely every day incidents. He specialised in the decoration of vases with very lively and well characterised miniature figures. His use of palmette friezes,

lotus flowers and delicate running spirals as borders to set off the main scene in his painting, instead of rather abruptly breaking it off like a metope, as Execias did, was in character with his liking for minute detail, which he indicated by a profusion of incisions. It was this gift for engraved detail in his decoration that made him the great master of miniature painting in the second half of the 6th century.   R.M.

AMAZONS. These were a legendary tribe of warlike women believed to inhabit a barbaric country to the east or north of Greece. The legend was already known to the Greeks in the time of Homer, but as their geographical knowledge grew, the supposed site of the Amazons' home became increasingly distant. According to the legend, the Amazons had fought with the Greeks on several occasions, either because the Greeks had attacked them and the heroes had made incursions into their territory (as when Heracles and Theseus attempted to carry off the Amazon queen, Antiope, or Hippolyta as she was sometimes called) or because they themselves had waged war in the west, advancing as far as the gates of Athens. Achilles was supposed to have fought against them and killed one of their number, Penthesilea. However, no historical confirmation of the legend has been found, despite the investigations of modern scholars. Nevertheless, the Amazons were a living reality to the ancient Greeks as indicated by the considerable number of works of art in which they feature. In a comparatively short time, the struggles between Greeks and Amazons assumed a symbolical significance and were considered as an episode in the victory of civilisation over barbarism, which largely explains the popularity of the myth during the classical period. As Greek art often tended to transpose reality into myth, the Amazons came to personify the Persians whom the Greeks had vanquished in the Persian Wars.

The Greeks did not always depict the Amazons in the aspect that is best known to us in classical art, as vigorous women, only clothed in a short tunic tied at the waist, with one breast left bare, nor were they always shown mounted. On 6th century B.C. painted vases, where their exploits constituted a favourite theme, we may see them on foot, equipped like hoplites, with crested hel-

Maenads. Detail of an amphora by the Amasis Painter. About 530 B.C. Paris, Cabinet des Médailles. *Photo Hirmer.*

Fight between Greeks and Amazons. East frieze of the Mausoleum at Halicarnassus by Scopas (?).
About 355-330 B.C. British Museum. *Photo Hirmer.*

mets, a cuirass and leg-guards, and armed with a bow or a spear. In the early 5th century, they were represented as Persian or Scythian warriors, with their bodies covered by a kind of tights, and wearing a Phrygian cap or foxskin toque; for weapons they usually had a single or double bladed axe, and they dexterously wielded a little round shield with a notch cut in it, called a *pelte*. It was then that they began to be shown as the horsewomen we have always imagined them to be, riding astride like men. They figured in great art when painters and sculptors, such as Micon and Phidias, depicted them on the Parthenon of the Throne of Zeus and established the patterns for future representations, and the priests of Ephesus held a competition between the greatest sculptors of the time to carve a figure in the round of a wounded Amazon. The types created during these competitions, by Polycletus and Phidias, popularised the image of the young woman with a short tunic and one breast laid bare. The figure of an Amazon with a breast cut off was still unknown. From the 4th century B.C. onwards, combats between Greeks and Amazons are often to be found carved on funerary monuments, but so far no very clear explanation has been found for the connexion between the barbaric female warriors and the idea of death.

AMBASSADORS. Book IX of the *Iliad* tells how Agamemnon acted on Nestor's advice by sending an embassy to Achilles comprising Ulysses, Ajax, and, somewhat lesser in rank, Achilles' old tutor, Phoenix. During the classic period, ambassadors were joined by heralds who were held to be inviolable. The ambassadors never resided in foreign countries, for the role of permanent representatives abroad was held by the *proxenoi* (q.v.). The *presbeis* were always entrusted with specified and temporary missions such as the settlement of a dispute, the conclusion of a peace treaty or an alliance, etc. At Athens, embassies consisted of three, five or ten citizens who were chosen by the people instead of by lot. Their instructions were determined by decree of the people who had chosen them and they were rarely granted full powers. The daily pay of an ambassador seems to have been two or three drachmas at the time of Aristophanes, a drachma and a half at the time of Demosthenes. The records providing most information on Greek embassies are the decrees honouring foreign ambassadors (at Athens they were often invited to a banquet at the Prytaneum) and especially the speeches of Demosthenes and Aeschines on the Athenian embassies sent to Philip in 346 B.C.

From these sources we have learnt that Attic

33

law provided severe penalties for ambassadors who might be guilty of any breach of duty during the period of their functions *(parapresbeias graphe)*. R.F.

AMBRACIA. The city of Ambracia once stood on the site of present Arta, and has given its name to the gulf opening into the Ionian Sea, almost directly facing the gulf of Leucas where the famous battle of Actium took place. Ambracia itself did not have a particularly distinguished history, although during the Peloponnesian War it became allied with Sparta against Athens. P.D.

AMPHIARAUS. A hero of Argos, Amphiaraus was a valiant warrior chieftain and an infallible soothsayer. He was obliged by a promise which he had made, to follow his cousin Adrastus, king of Argos, on the expedition of the Seven against Thebes although he knew that it was foredoomed and that the warriors were already marked by death. He had made a vain attempt to escape, but his wife delivered him up to Adrastus, receiving a necklace as a reward for her treachery. Once before the walls of Thebes, Amphiaraus fought bravely but during the final rout he took flight like the others and would have been killed as well had not Zeus opened up the earth in front of his chariot, hidden him in the depths of the earth and given him immortality. At the very spot where Amphiaraus had vanished at Oropus in Attica, a sanctuary was built to which pilgrims came in search of a cure or an oracle. Amphiaraus would reveal himself to them in a dream and advise them what they had to do. P.D.

AMPHICTIONIES. "The same spirit that had inspired the foundation of cities had also inspired different cities to make sacrifices together, brought together by proximity and mutual necessity, they celebrated festivals and sang panegyrics together and thus a bond of friendship was formed between them as they held their sacred feasts in common and united in offering libations." The associations thus described by Strabo were called amphictionies and were frequent in ancient Greece. The most famous were those of the Ionians (in Asia Minor) at the Panionia in the sanctuary of Poseidon, that of the Dorians at Cape Triopium in the Peloponnesus in honour of Poseidon and Apollo, that at Mount Lycaeus in adoration of Zeus, and lastly, and most important of all, that at Delphi. That such associations had been founded in very remote times is proved by the esteem accorded to certain of the participating cities which had lost their one-time grandeur by the classical period. Each of the states taking part had an equal vote and was represented by delegates who, at Delphi, were named *pylagorai* and *hieromnemones*. It was the duty of these associations to assume responsibility for all questions of administration, religious ceremonies and the communal festivals held at the sanctuaries. Because of the political jealousies between the cities, these festivals remained strictly religious in scope and never played the unifying role they might have assumed. They were sometimes used for political ends, but always in a limited way and for the benefit of some member state that wished to increase its power, as in the amphictiony of Delphi when the Thessalians launched the Sacred War at the beginning of the 6th century B.C. in order to subdue the city of Crisa, which was hampering their communications with the sea. This almost systematic abstention from politics and this insistence on neutrality helped to give the amphictionies a moral prestige like that of Delphi, which was respected throughout the whole of Greece. P.D.

AMPHIPOLIS. In 436 B.C. the Athenians founded the city of Amphipolis, near the mouth of the river Strymon, in order to assure their supremacy over northern Greece and to safeguard their annexation of the gold-mines of Mount Pangaeus and the forests on which they depended for wood for their ships. It was a strategic position of the first importance, both for the economy of Attica and naval communications. But some years later, during the Peloponnesian War, the city fell to the Spartan, Brasidas. In 371, the so-called Peace of Callias restored the city and its surroundings. to Athens, but this restitution was brief since Philip captured the city in his turn in 357. Despite the promises he made to the Athenians, he never returned it to them and it remained a Macedonian possession until the heritage of Alexander fell into the hands of the Romans. P.D.

AMPHITRITE. Wife of Poseidon, daughter of Nereus, leader of the choir of the Nereids, Amphitrite was the queen of the seas. A famous red-figure Attic cup, dating from about 500 B.C.,

Amphitrite, in the presence of Athena, gives Theseus the golden crown. Cup by the Panaitios Painter. About 500 B.C. Paris, Louvre. *Photo Hirmer.*

shows Amphitrite giving Theseus the golden crown that proved his divine descent. In other representations, Amphitrite is shown surrounded by her band of sisters.   P.D.

AMPHITRYON. Amphitryon, king of Thebes, married Alcmene, who took the fancy of Zeus, but she proved so virtuous that the god was obliged to assume the appearance of her legitimate spouse before winning her. Alcmene later gave birth to two sons, one of whom, Iphimedes, had been fathered by Amphitryon while the other, Heracles, by far the strongest and bravest of the two, was the son of Zeus.   P.D.

AMYCLAE. The sanctuary of Amyclae, a few miles from Sparta, was consecrated to the hero Hyacinthus, who was said to have been loved by Apollo who had killed him by mistake. It was one of the most ancient of all the sacred sites in the Peloponnesus. In the 6th century B.C., an Ionian, Bathycles of Magnesia (q.v.), was entrusted with its restoration. What is now rather incorrectly called the Throne of Amyclae was once

a vast complex of buildings, dominated by a colossal statue of Apollo, decorated by a great number of reliefs with scenes from the myths and legends that were most in vogue at the time of its building.   P.D.

ANACREON. Lyric poet of the second half of the 6th century B.C. born at Teos in Ionia. He first lived in Samos at the court of the famous tyrant, Polycrates, and then at Athens in the service of Hipparchus, the son of Pisistratus, where he became friendly with Xanthippe, the father of Pericles. Anacreon was the typical court-poet, amiable, witty, frivolous, and remained joyous and good-natured even in old age (he was 85 years old when he died). His poetry is mostly in praise of Eros, the god of love, and the beauty of young girls in the full bloom of life, and he made scornful fun of those of his rivals who were fortunate. Of his authentic works only a few fragments now survive, but his renown was so great that he was often imitated in antiquity. A whole collection of " anacreontic " poems have come down to us; they are inspired by the style of

35

Anchises flees from Troy carried by Aeneas. Detail of an Attic oinoche. About 530 B.C. Paris, Louvre. *Photo Giraudon.*

the poet from Teos just as the "marotic" verses in France were inspired by the real work of Clement Marot. Such lively, witty and graceful odes as *Ode to his Lyre*, the *Silver Cup*, *Love and the Bee* were later imitated in their turn by the French poets of the Pléiade.   R.F.

ANATOLIA. Anatolia, or Asia Minor as it is usually called, is very close to Greece and practically linked to it by the islands scattered throughout the Aegean. As early as the 10th century B.C., its western shores were densely populated by Ionian settlers, and the cities that later sprang up near the coast were among the most important and prosperous in the whole Hellenic world. Nevertheless, the interior remained "barbarian" to the Greeks. The whole of the immense plateau in the interior, surrounded by mountains, was covered by little kingdoms, which had arisen out of the ruins of the Hittite empire and which were later transformed into satrapies after the Persian conquests from the 6th century onwards. The Anatolian plateau was quite different in climate, appearance and culture from the land the Greeks knew and loved so much. For the Greeks, such provinces as Phrygia, Caria, Lydia and Lycia may well have been different countries, but they resembled each other in that incomprehensible languages were spoken there, gods different from any on Mount Olympus were worshipped, and

ideas and customs held sway that Hellenic rationalism found astonishing if not shocking.

Even though there was not a single province which had not been at least sporadically penetrated by the Greeks from the very earliest times, even though contacts with the interior became increasingly frequent from the 4th century B.C. onwards and even more so in the Hellenistic period, and even when Greek sovereigns held their courts in capitals such as Pergamum and appointed Greek governors to the cities to which they had given Greek names, only a thin layer of the population could boast of its Hellenic origins while the great mass of the people continued to live as before, unaffected by the influence of Hellenic civilisation.
     P.D.

ANAXAGORAS. Anaxagoras was a philosopher from Clazomenae in Ionia, who lived some thirty years at Athens, between 460 and 430 B.C., and became both Pericles' master and friend. When the Athenians, who were discontented with Pericles' rule, brought lawsuits against the persons in his entourage at the beginning of the Peloponnesian War, Anaxagoras was accused of impiety, forced to leave the city and settled at Lampsacus where he died. Anaxagoras's contribution to philosophy was to have replaced Empedocles' (q.v.) concept of a duality of cosmic forces ruling the universe—love and hatred—with the idea of the single animating principle, which he called the *Nous* (Mind). The Nous orders the world and is " infinite and absolute master; alone it is in itself and for itself "; it is an ordering intelligence and a kind of soul of the world. Extremely subtle, but not immaterial, this spirit had a physical effect on the primordial mixture of the universe, composed, according to Anaxagoras, of qualitative particles possessing the property of infinite divisibility. To these elements Aristotle gave the name of " homoeomeries " which is still used today. Anaxagoras's theory was quite opposed to that of the atomists who did not admit the existence of any infinitely divisible element. The action of the Nous on this mixture caused it to revolve outwards and finally constitute the universe by a kind of centrifugal process.

It is hardly surprising that Anaxagoras was accused of impiety, for he had affirmed that the sun and the moon were not gods, as most ancient peoples believed, but simply material bodies.

Moreover he did not believe in divination, as Plutarch has related; when the soothsayer, Lampon, had wanted to extract a prophecy from a one-horned ram that had been found on a farm belonging to Pericles, Anaxagoras had offered an anatomical explanation for the phenomenon which tended to ruin the soothsayer's reputation. Anaxagoras may be regarded as one of the founders of Greek rationalism. He also said that man is the most intelligent of all the animals as he has hands.   P.-M.S.

ANCHISES. To have been a shepherd on the slopes of Mount Ida near Troy must have been an agreeable occupation, for even before the three goddesses had appeared there to Paris to ask him to judge which of them was the most beautiful, it was there that Aphrodite had visited Anchises as he was tending his cattle and mated with him. The fruit of their love was Aeneas to whom Anchises later owed his life, when the Trojans had to flee from their city after it had been captured by the Greeks.   P.D.

ANDOCIDES (1). Athenian orator, born about 440 B.C. He came from a noble family and belonged to that elegant and gilded youth which had Alcibiades as its idol. In 415 he was thrown into prison for alleged complicity in the

affair of the mutilated hermae and was only released after denouncing those who were supposed to be guilty. After being deprived of certain political rights, he went into exile and led an adventurous life abroad. He returned to Athens in 403 after a general amnesty and attempted to take part in politics, but was accused again in 399 of impiety, this time for having profaned the Eleusinian mysteries. He was acquitted after making his defence with the speech *De Mysteriis* which has still survived. In 392 he was sent to Sparta as ambassador and, when he returned, he made the speech *De Pace* which also survives, but the people's assembly disowned the negotiators and banished them, and Andocides went into exile once more. Although he was traditionally considered as one of the ten best Attic orators, Andocides' eloquence was of a rather dull and mediocre nature.   R.F.

ANDOCIDES (2). The Athenian vase painter of the potter, Andocides, was one of the first to adopt a transformation in the style of vase

painting at the end of the 6th century B.C., which was to give rise to the red-figure style. He evolved a new technique whereby the red of the clay was reserved for the figures, against a background which had first been glazed with black. Whereas earlier black-figure painters, who painted their figures in black against the natural clay ground, had no other means than engraving or touches of white and violet for rendering details of clothes or muscles, the red-figure painters were able to fill in all details by using a very thin brush dipped in the black glaze, a process of great delicacy and unlimited possibilities. Composition kept pace with technique; the red-figure artists attempted to escape from the limitations of the frontal style, which had restricted such black-figure masters as Execias and Amasis. They had been forced to show the parts of a figure all on the same plane, either full face or in profile, or, as was often the case, with the head and torso depicted frontally while the legs were drawn in profile. The red-figure painters introduced the three-quarter view which led to many other variants. From then onwards, there was a marked evolution in the composition of the scenes themselves. The artists went on to make continuous cyclical compositions instead of single, isolated scenes on the vases; a single scene was developed on various parts of the vase, back and front, whence the name, binary composition. The new style soon attracted other painters, such as Psiax, the famous painter of cups, who was another very sensitive draughtsman and extremely skilful in his delicate rendering of draperies.   R.M.

ANDROMACHE. She was a Trojan princess and wife of Hector. It was Andromache who waited on the ramparts of the beleaguered city while her husband covered himself with glory, and who furiously defended her son Astyanax with a pestle, all in vain, against the fury of the victorious Greeks after the fall of Troy. She was taken to Epirus as a captive by Neoptolemus, son of Achilles, married his brother-in-law, Helenus, and reigned with him over Epirus. She finished her days after an extraordinarily adventurous life, at Pergamum, the city founded by the son she had borne by Neoptolemus. The Andromache of

Bull. Ass laden with pitchers.
Late Minoan. Clay. Heraklion Museum. *Photos Hassia.*

Rhyton in the form of a dog's head. About 490 B.C.
Rome, Villa Giulia. *Photo Hirmer.*

Young men inciting a dog and cat to fight. Attic bas-relief. About 510 B.C. Athens, National Museum.

classical Greek tradition is quite different from the lamenting, obstinate widow whom Racine immortalised in his play.   P.D.

ANDROMEDA. Daughter of Cepheus, king of Ethiopia. Andromeda's father offered her up to the monster who was ravaging his kingdom in order to appease it. Andromeda was later delivered by Perseus who killed the monster, on his return from his expedition against the Gorgons, and married her.   P.D.

ANDROS. Despite its area—it measures more than twenty miles in length—and its comparative fertility, the isle of Andros, lying south-east of Euboea as the direct prolongation of the promontory, has never had any importance in Greek politics, economy, art or literature.   P.D.

ANIMALS. In Mycenaean and archaic times, lions, bears and other wild beasts roamed the forests of Greece. In later times, their memory was kept alive in legend and religion, as in the story of the Nemean lion, which Heracles killed, and the worship of Artemis Tauropolus, notably at Brauron in Attica. During the funeral of Patroclus in Book XXIII of the *Iliad,* Achilles cuts the throats of " two dogs, out of the nine that Patroclus kept by his table " and offers their bodies up as sacrifices on his friend's funeral pyre. Many vase paintings of the classic period show dogs at banquets, gnawing the bones and picking up

the fragments that the guests had thrown to them. Dogs were so indispensable for hunting that the Greek word for hunter, *kynegetes,* meant " leader of dogs ". In his *Cynegeticus,* Xenophon dwelt at length on the training and breeding of hunting dogs and coursers. Some breeds from Laconia were especially famous. There was no lack of game in the mountain regions, hares and foxes being especially plentiful, not to mention birds, countless species of which are mentioned by Aristophanes in his play the *Birds.*

An archaic bas-relief has been found showing two young men sitting in front of each other, one holding a dog on a leash, the other a cat, while the two animals engage in a strange kind of fight. Behind the youths stand two men who follow the course of the fight with impassioned interest, probably because they have wagered on the outcome. Nevertheless, cats were rarely mentioned in texts and figured infrequently in works

An owl. Proto-Corinthian perfume flask. Paris, Louvre. *Photo Giraudon.*

of art. The Greeks often employed tame weasels in their houses to catch mice. In the women's apartments, young children raised dogs and weasels as well as ducks, quails, mice and grass-hoppers. In the 4th century B.C., some young dandies would even go about carrying a quail under their cloak, as Plutarch has told us in his *Life of Alcibiades* (Chapter X). From the 5th century onwards, rich Athenians imported " birds from Phasia ", or pheasants, from far-off regions and also raised peacocks. The animals most frequently found in ancient Greece were goats, pigs, sheep and mules. Oxen and horses were most numerous in Boeotia and Thessaly, where the great fertile plains were suitable for large-scale stock-breeding. Shepherds would lead their herds of goats and sheep to pasture in the mountainous frontier regions *(eschatiai)*.

The Athenians were so fond of cock-fighting that the city magistrates organised special fights in the theatre every year. The fighting-cocks were fed on garlic and onions to make them more combative and metal spurs were fixed to their feet. Bets were placed on the results of the fights and a good fighting-cock fetched a high price.

Animals played a considerable part in religion, for as in Egypt, Greek religion had passed through an early phase of zoolatry. Thus, Apollo was believed to have been a wolf at first, Artemis a bear, and Athena an owl, before these animals were simply regarded as attributes of the divinity which had assumed human shape. The species, sex, and characteristics of the animals that were sacrificed to the different gods were determined by precise, detailed rules. Except in the case of a holocaust, all sacrifices normally ended with feasting, and many poor Greeks only ate meat during family ceremonies or public religious occasions. The sacrificing priest would also perform the duties of a cook as we may see in Menander's *Peevish Man*. Soothsayers would inspect the entrails of the sacrificed animals, especially the livers, in order to read the future. They would also observe the flight and cries of birds which, as they were inhabitants of the skies, were considered the most important of divine messengers *(See* Divination, Fishing, Food, Hunting, Oracles, Sacrifices). R.F.

Kore by Antenor. About 525-520 B.C.
Athens, Acropolis Museum.
Photo Deutsches Archäologisches Institut, Athens.

ANTENOR. The sculpture of the late archaic period was dominated by the Athenian 6th century sculptor Antenor. His most important work was the group sculpture of the *Tyrranicides*, the two brothers Harmodius and Aristogiton who had freed Athens from the tyranny of the Pisistratids. This famous work was cast in bronze and lost after being carried off by Xerxes during his sack of Athens in 480 B.C. All that remains of it are the copies of the work executed to replace it by Critius and Nesiotes. The authentic style of Antenor may be seen in a colossal *Kore* (now in the Acropolis Museum); larger than life, it marks a break with the older, excessively linear, decorative style and shows a new feeling for plasticity. The architecture of form and the structure of the body are both stressed and reinforced by the fullness of the flowing draperies and the fall of the folds which, in spite of a slight stiffness, underline the balance of the hips and the imperceptible movement of the legs, which derives more from the impression of inner vitality than any suggestion of actual physical movement. Unlike previous korai, the statue is not smiling and the face is also treated in the same forceful style, its strong structure giving it a determined and decisive expression. The stylistic affinities between the Kore of the Acropolis and the female figures from the east pediment of the temple of the Alcmaeonidae at Delphi would appear to justify the attribution of the latter group to Antenor. Despite the bad condition of the sculptures, they still reveal the same full, majestic composition which makes the Kore of the Acropolis such an original work. R.M.

ANTIGONE. The Greek tragedians, and especially Sophocles, have made Antigone into one of the noblest characters in the whole of Greek mythology. They have depicted her as the living symbol of filial devotion and moral courage, and the revolt against man-made laws that violate the rules of justice as laid down by human conscience and divine will. The whole of Antigone's life was a drama. She was born of an accursed family; unknown to her, her father Oedipus had married his own mother Jocasta. When the truth was known and his wife took her own life, he blinded himself before being banished by his subjects who were afraid that the whole community would be punished for the taint on the king.

Antigone faithfully followed her blind father into exile, through towns and provinces where no one would give them hospitality, until they finally came to Athens. But almost as soon as they had arrived, Oedipus recognised the spot where he was destined to die and, in obedience to the gods, sent Antigone away. After his death, near the small village of Colonus, she was unable to find his body.

Antigone then returned to Thebes, to her sister, the sweet and frail Ismene, who could only lament their fate, and her two brothers Eteocles and Polynices, whom their father had cursed for their lack of filial piety and who had gone to war against each other. They both perished in battle and her uncle, Creon, seized power. As Polynices had taken up arms against his country, he was refused burial by Creon. But despite her uncle's prohibition, Antigone accomplished the symbolic burial rites for her brother, well aware that she was risking death as a punishment for her disobedience. In a magnificent scene, Sophocles has shown her justifying her act and, instead of protesting her innocence, defending her obligation to obey those unwritten laws of conscience which are stronger and more compelling than any human laws. She accepted her punishment while remaining convinced that it had been her duty to pay her last respects to the dead whatever their faults might have been in life and went steadfastly to her execution, unable to foresee that her example would be followed by innumerable and often unknown heroes who were prepared to die for what they believed to be right. P.D.

ANTIGONUS MONOPHTHALMOS. The dynasty that came to power in Macedonia early in the 3rd century B.C., like those in Egypt and Syria, was founded by one of Alexander the Great's former officers, Antigonus, nicknamed Monophthalmos or the One-eyed. After Alexander's death he had been appointed governor over Pamphylia, Lycia and part of Phrygia. In a short time he subdued most of the provinces in Asia Minor and became one of the most important of the diadochi (the generals who disputed the succession to the empire after Alexander's death). After his son, Demetrius, called Poliorcetes, had defeated Ptolemy's fleet at Cyprus in 306, he proclaimed himself king, not of the region he officially governed, but of Macedonia itself, thereby showing that he considered himself as Alexander's rightful successor. The other diadochi refused to recognise him as such, assumed the same title themselves and mobilised against him. In 301 he was defeated and slain at the battle of Ipsus. His son, Poliorcetes, took refuge in Macedonia, named himself king in 297 and died in captivity at the court of Seleucus in 282 after having restored the oligarchy in Greece.

Once the empire had been dismembered, Poliorcetes' son, Antigonus Gonatas, inherited Macedonia and was officially proclaimed king in his turn. His reign, which lasted until 239, was mostly taken up by wars against the Greek provinces which were in a constant state of rebellion against his rule, against Ptolemy who was backing the rebels and wanted to assure himself of bases in the Aegean, and lastly against Pyrrhus who even replaced him for a time as king. It was during Antigonus' reign that two rival leagues were formed in Greece. One was the Achaean League, led by Aratus of Sicyon, and the other was formed around Aetolia, which was used by Antigonus in his attempt to keep the Peloponnesus under his domination. In spite of many difficulties, he almost succeeded in making Macedonia into a great nation, but the advantages he had won were thrown away during the ten years reign (239-229) of his successor Demetrius II. When Antigonus Doson came to the throne in 229, he found himself confronted by the Achaean and Aetolian leagues united against him. He managed to defeat them and, shortly before his death, succeeded in subduing Sparta, which had been a centre of opposition to his rule.

When Philip V succeeded in 220, the kingdom seemed solid and safe, but apart from having to contend with the rebellious Greeks, he also had to face the Romans in Illyria, where they had been making their first tentative encroachments since 228. Philip was thus obliged to divide his attention between the Romans in the west and his enemies in the east, notably the kingdom of Pergamum. In the end it was the Roman armies who struck him the worst blow by defeating him in 197 at the battle of Cynoscephalae. This was the first step towards complete collapse. His son, Perseus, who succeeded him in 179, was defeated at Pydna by Aemilius Paullus in 168, and Macedonia became a Roman province in 148, two years before the Romans became masters of the whole of Greece by capturing the key city of Corinth.   P.D.

ANTIOCH. Of all the different cities bearing the same name, Antioch on the Orontes was one of the most important. It had been founded after

the battle of Ipsus in 300 B.C. by Seleucus Nicator who had given it his father's name. The four quarters of the city were surrounded by a common line of fortifications and each had its own set of walls. Shortly after the city's foundation, the sculptor, Eutychides, cast a bronze statue of a female figure to personify the city; it was the first of a long series of similar allegorical figures. Antioch was the capital of the Seleucids and became an important commercial centre, retaining its prosperity long after its capture by the Romans in 64 B.C. Numerous mosaics have been found in the city, dating from the 4th and 5th centuries A.D., which indicate the wealth of the inhabitants.   P.D.

ANTIOCHUS III. *See* Seleucus I.

ANTIPATER. While Alexander the Great had been making war in Asia, he left Antipater behind in Greece to look after his kingdom. After the conqueror's death, Antipater continued to fulfil his official functions and it was in his capacity as viceroy that he crushed the revolt of the Greeks who had hoped to win back their independence. During a short war, known as the Lamian War, he seized Athens, killed Hyperides, made Demosthenes commit suicide and installed a garrison at Munychia. In 321 B.C., a coalition of the diadochi allowed him to replace Perdiccas as regent and to become virtual ruler of Macedonia, but he soon died and left his succession to his son, Cassandra.   P.D.

ANTIPHANES. Dramatist of the Middle Comedy. *(See* Comedy).

ANTIPHON. Orator and Athenian politician, born about 480 B.C. He was a member of the aristocratic party and, after Thucydides, was the main inspirer and organiser of the oligarchic revolution of 411 which only had a very brief success. In the course of the purge which followed it, Antiphon was condemned to death and executed.

Two different styles may sometimes be distinguished in the work that has come down to us under Antiphon's name. In it, Antiphon appears both as an orator and as a sophist, but it is probable that both styles are by the same hand. As a teacher of rhetoric, Antiphon has left us his *Tetralogies*, groups of four fictitious speeches made comprising an accusation, a defence and the replies of both prosecution and defence. As an orator, we know Antiphon by his three speeches during trials for murder, but his most remarkable speech, according to Thucydides, was made during his own defence in 411. It has unfortunately been lost. R.F.

ANTISTHENES. Philosopher and founder of the Cynic school. *(See* Cynicism).

AOIDOI. Epic poets who declaimed their own works as they accompanied themselves on the cithara. *(See* Epic; Homer).

APELLES. Although nothing is now known of Apelles or his contemporaries, we do know that he was considered by the ancient Greeks to have been the finest painter of the 4th century B.C. In any case, it was Apelles alone who had the privilege of portraying Alexander the Great (in sculpture, the same privilege had been given to Lysippus). Apelles was born in Colophon, near Smyrna, and had made many portraits of Alexander, his father Philip, and several lesser personages. He had also done paintings of Aphrodite— then the most popular goddess with artists and their public—and Lucian has left us an account of his allegorical painting *Calumny,* the description of which was to inspire Botticelli in the Italian Renaissance. P.D.

APHRODITE. Aphrodite was the goddess of beauty and love. According to tradition she was born out of the spray of the sea at Cyprus. The legend may represent the survival of the memory of the oriental goddess, statues of whom have been found in Syria, dating from remotest times showing her with her hands holding her breasts as though to inundate the whole world with her milk. The Greeks were not slow to transform this patron goddess of fertility into a somewhat more subtly characterised personage. They believed that Aphrodite was the daughter of Zeus and Dione and credited her with romantic adventures in which romantic feeling was almost as important as elementary sexual instinct. She was married to the deformed, ill shaped god Hephaestus, and consoled herself with Ares, but the two lovers were caught by the deceived hus-

Aphrodite, called the Venus de Milo. About 100 B.C. Paris, Louvre. *Photo Tel.*

band and their misadventure vastly entertained the whole of Olympus.

Aphrodite betrayed her oriental origins in showing a marked predilection for the enemies of the Greeks, for she supported the Trojans in the war and was even said to have bestowed her favours on Anchises. It was also in the orient that she later picked what may have been her most tenderly cherished lover, Adonis, whose death she was to lament together with her worshippers after the handsome young shepherd had been mortally struck by a boar. Aphrodite is often shown with her son Eros, Love, and it was she who guided the arrows that the young archer would let fly at the hearts of those whom the goddess wished to touch with love.   P.D.

APOLLO. Apollo made his appearance in the world of the Greek divinities at a comparatively late date, and the island of Delos, where he was supposed to have been born, had no tradition of a male god before the end of the second millennium B.C. at the very earliest. According to tradition, Apollo was the son of Zeus and of the Asiatic Leto, and his sister was supposed to have been Artemis. It is difficult to account for his exact origins, as they differed according to the regions in which he was worshipped. According to the myth of Delphi, which was one of his main sanctuaries, he had killed and replaced the serpent, Python, who had reigned before him and given

Statuette of Apollo dedicated by Manticles. About 700-680 B.C. Boston, Museum of Fine Arts.

Apollo Pythios seated on the omphalos. Silver stater. About 355 B.C. Basel, Antiken Museum.

44

Apollo. Detail of the central figure from the west pediment of the Temple of Zeus at Olympia. 465-455 B.C. Olympia Museum. *Photo Émile.*

APOLLODORUS. "The painter of shadows" who was active in the last quarter of the 5th century B.C., was according to Plutarch the first artist to use mixed colours and to use different tones in painting shadows. He had a far reaching influence on the progress of painting at the end of the 5th and at the beginning of the 4th centuries.

We may now study the technique evolved by Apollodorus on two white lekythoi, where the folds of the draperies are accentuated by shadows, and in the Roman imitations of classical paintings, such as the painting on marble of the *Knucklebone Players* in which the clothing of the players is shaded in grey and brown. R.M.

APOLLONIUS of RHODES. He was a poet, born at Alexandria in about 300 B.C. His master, Callimachus, obtained the post of director of the Library at Alexandria for him in about 270 *(See* Alexandrianism) and had him chosen as tutor for the future king Ptolemy III Euergetes. At the Library, Apollonius devoted himself to study for a while, then began his great poem, the *Argonautica,* but this project was not approved by Callimachus who favoured short works. In about 250, Apollonius read part of his poem in public, but the recital was a failure and he was obliged to relinquish his post at the Library, where he was replaced by Eratosthenes, and sought refuge at Rhodes. There he completed his poem and was granted the rights of the city. It was there, too, that he became famous, founded a school and died, apparently without ever returning to Alexandria. The four books of the *Argonautica* constitute an epic in the Homeric style and are written in hexameters. The work describes the voyage of the heroes led by Jason, who sailed on the ship Argo to Colchis, where Jason won the Golden Fleece with the aid of Medea, the daughter of the king of that remote country, who had fallen in love with him. Apollonius's poetry is often erudite and cold, but not without brilliance and vigour, especially in Book III in which, in a style partly derived from Euripides and partly original, Apollonius describes the emotional anguish of Medea, inflamed with love for Jason. R.F.

oracles. In his turn, Apollo began to foresee the future and it was to him, despite all Heracles' attempts to seize the symbolic tripod, that thousands of Greeks made their way throughout antiquity to ask what the future held in store for them. Apollo also fulfilled the functions of oracle in other sanctuaries, like Clarus in Asia Minor. He was eternally youthful and distinguished himself, not only by his countless amorous adventures but also, rather like Achilles, by his quick temper, his pride, his violence and the frequent harshness of his reactions. He implacably shot down with his arrows all who offended him, massacred the sons of Niobe to avenge his mother and spread plague among the peoples who had not shown respect to his priests. He was the perfect image of athletic beauty and it was only in the time of Praxiteles that his vigorous body began to show signs of effeminacy. His cult was widespread, but certainly would not have been so popular if it had not been for the fact that he had been first and foremost an oracle. P.D.

APOLLONIUS of TYANA. Philosopher and Pythagorean miracle-worker of the 1st century A.D. His most important writings comprise a *Life of Pythagoras,* an astrological treatise, a book on sacrifices, and his letters. All that remains of his work are a few fragments. Like Pythagoras, Apollonius became a legendary figure and it is to the legend rather than to authentic history that Philostratas owed most of the details for his *Life of Apollonius,* written in the 3rd century A.D.   R.F.

ARATUS of SOLI. Poet, philosopher, and mathematician of the Hellenistic period, and author of the *Phaenomena. (See* Astronomy).

ARCADIA. Arcadia was not the idyllic country that the 17th century believed it to be. Although it was one of the greenest parts of Greece, it was surrounded by high mountains, isolated in the very heart of the Peloponnesus, and inhabited by peasants and primitive shepherds who were very different from the poetic shepherds depicted by Poussin. They were descendants of the Achaeans who had fled before the Dorian invaders and found refuge in this inaccessible region. The Arcadians pretended to be natives of the region and their language, bristling with archaisms, proved both their ancient origins and their isolation. As a defensive bastion against all foreign invasions and a point of departure for attacks in remote areas, Arcadia constantly aroused the covetous instincts of its neighbours, such as Argolis, Messenia and Laconia, and was all the more tempting a prey as it hardly ever succeeded in achieving political unity. Its towns were few and unimportant: Tegea, which had kept the Spartan army at bay for a time during the early 6th century B.C., owed its most durable glory to the temple that Scopas had built and decorated in honour of its patron goddess, Athena Alea; Mantinea, site of a battle where the Spartans, led by Agis, had crushed the army of the Athenians and the Argives in 418, and where the Thebans would have beaten the Spartans in 362 if their chief, Epaminondas, had not been mortally wounded in the melée; Orchomenus, which must not be confused with the city of the same name in Boeotia; and lastly, Megalopolis, founded by Epaminondas in 371, which was inhabited by settlers transferred from neighbouring villages and was for a short time the capital of an ephemeral Arcadian confederacy.   P.D.

ARCESILAUS. Arcesilaus was born at Pitane in Aeolia in about 316 B.C. He succeeded Crates as head of the Academy from 268 to 241. He brought about a renewal in the spirit of the Academy by returning to the principles of Socrates, whose dialogistic method he used to espress a sceptical position. Under his direction the school became known as the New Academy, it was there that Arcesilaus vigorously criticised the dogmatism of the Stoics and evolved the theory of probabilism, taking reasonableness as a criterion.   P.-M.S.

ARCHERMUS. Sculptor, born at Chios, probably in the 7th century B.C. His signature has been found at Delos and the works of his two sons, Athenis and Bupalus, won considerable success later at Rome.   R.M.

ARCHILOCHUS. Lyric poet of the 7th century B.C., born on the isle of Paros. He was the illegitimate son of Telesicles, who had led the colony from Paros that had been sent to the isle of Thasos. Archilochus's life was that of a poor and needy adventurer and he became a soldier of fortune, fighting notably at Thasos. Once, he threw away his shield in order to make his escape from the battlefield more quickly and, far from concealing this inglorious episode in his career, he related it with good humour in his verses. He finally died in battle in about 640. All that now remains of his work are some fragments. His poetry, especially his iambic verses, was highly personal and original in style. It was often written in a mocking, scornful and satirical tone that was later to be adopted by Aristophanes in his Attic comedies and represented an innovation in Greek literature. The poet was particularly fond of satirising his superiors, especially those who had wronged him in some way like the rich Lycambes, a nobleman of Paros, who had refused to let him marry his daughter, Neobule, with whom Archilochus had fallen in love. Archilochus's surviving verse is full of mordant flashes of wit, spontaneity and freedom of expression, and bears out the judgment of his time which considered him to be almost as talented as Homer.   R.F.

ARCHIMEDES. Mathematician, physicist and one of the greatest scientists of antiquity. He was born in Syracuse about 287 B.C., lived for many years in Alexandria and then returned to

Palace at Cnossos.
*Photo Bernard
Aury-Arthaud.*

his home town. When the city was besieged by
the Roman general, Marcellus, from 214 to 212,
Archimedes became an engineer and invented
numerous machines to break up and set fire to
the Roman ships. When Marcellus finally captured the city, Archimedes was killed. He had been
so absorbed by a geometrical problem that he
ignored the questions of a Roman soldier who
slew him in a fit of rage.

Archimedes was interested in all branches of
science, especially astronomy, and built a planetarium which became famous. In geometry, he
worked out the ratio between the surface and
volume of a sphere and its circumscribing cylinder, which is why he requested that the only
engraving on his tomb should be that of a sphere
inscribed in a cylinder. After the whereabouts
of his tomb had been forgotten by the Syracusans,
it was later discovered by Cicero. Archimedes
invented the pulley, the winch, the endless screw.
The story of how he discovered the basic principle
of hydrostatics in his bath tub is well known
(" Eureka! "). Several of his written treatises
have survived, among the most important are the
two books on *Floating Bodies*. He was also
the originator of the notion of specific gravity.

Hieron II, the king of Syracuse, asked him to
inspect a gold crown in which he suspected the
goldsmith had mixed a certain amount of silver.
By means of a bucket full of water and by measuring the overflow when an object was put in it,
Archimedes was able to establish: 1) the volume
of gold equal in weight to that of the crown,
2) the volume of silver equal in weight to that of
the crown and 3) the volume of the crown. As
the last turned out to be somewhere between the
first two, it was an easy matter to calculate the
proportion of silver to gold.   R.F.

ARCHITECTURE. Architecture is perhaps
the most glorious and the least known achievement of Greek art. It flourished at every period
in Greek history but, with rare exceptions, all
that now survives of it are the foundations and
scattered stones on which archaeologists now
depend in their endeavour to reconstruct the
great buildings and monuments of antiquity
with results that are only too often mere speculation. It is important to make a distinction between the Greek architecture of the 2nd and that
of the 1st millennium B.C., for there were marked
differences in style, function, and techniques,

47

Temple of Hera, called the Temple of Poseidon, at Paestum. About 460 B.C. *Photo L. von Matt.*

owing perhaps to the differences between the societies that created them.

In the civilisations of Crete and Mycenae, the most important buildings were palaces, for the cities were ruled by sovereigns who were all-powerful and were the intermediaries between the people they ruled and their gods. As a result, the greatest architectural achievements of the time were to be found in the royal residences. In such peaceful states as that of Crete, palaces were designed with a view to the maximum pleasure and comfort of their inhabitants. They were planned after oriental models, generally centring on a vast inner courtyard, which both separated and united all the different quarters of the building. These palaces were at one and the same time the residence of the king and his family, the administrative centre, the main depository for archives, the cultural centre and the centre for all the industries and manufactures necessary to the maintenance of the royal family and its retainers. At Mycenae, as at Troy in the very earliest times, the ruler was a warrior and consequently, the palaces were built more for security than for personal comfort and were fortresses rather than residences. As the powerful enceinte that

surrounded them could not be too long for strategic reasons, more careful attention was paid to the planning of the interior. In Mycenae, more than in Crete, the siting of the different buildings within the walls was determined by considerations of terrain, since the site chosen was usually on a steep sloped height, which could be more easily defended. Other differences between Cretan and Mycenaean palaces could be accounted for by differences in climate.

Both on the mainland and the isle of Minos, stone was used for building. Although the masons were sometimes skilled enough to be able to cut the stone with sharp edges, they usually cut irregular, polygonal blocks, in what was to be called the " cyclopean " style, and filled up the interstices between them with earth and pebbles. This was not because they were unable to build with regular blocks, but because the polygonal masonry was better suited for defence, being both stronger and more imposing. In Crete and on the Greek mainland, shrines were built inside the buildings and were usually so small that they have often been compared with the Roman sanctuaries for the *lares* or household gods, or the chapels of medieval castles.

Although domestic architecture naturally preceded palace building, it cannot be considered here. The dwellings of primitive Greece are of more interest to the ethnographer than the art historian and later houses were built in light, perishable materials. Only in Crete do private houses deserve our attention, for this was the only country rich enough to permit a well-off middle class to build themselves sumptuous dwellings, some of which were so luxurious that they could be compared with royal residences, and where even the most modest houses were still far more than mere shelters against the elements.

Apart from palace architecture, the Mycenaeans, in contrast to the Cretans, attached great importance to funerary architecture, a difference which might be explained by dissimilar attitudes towards death. At Mycenae, the tomb became a chamber in which the body was laid to rest and it was there that the " cupola tomb " was developed. In shape it was like a beehive, and the finest surviving example is that of the famous Treasury of Atreus.

The Dorian invasions marked a turning-point in the history of Greek architecture, especially as during the last centuries of the 2nd millennium B.C., economic and political conditions were highly unsuitable for any kind of building. The new, and henceforth Hellenic society no longer had any place for a king who ruled over his people and represented them before the gods. No matter what form was assumed by the supreme power in the state, the city regime was collective. Palaces no longer had a purpose and, indeed, no more were built until the restoration of the monarchy in the 4th century B.C., but a new home was needed for the gods, who had hitherto lived in the royal palaces, and so the first temples were built. In the beginning, the temple was built on the same plan as a human habitation, which in the 8th and 7th centuries B.C. was a very modest dwelling indeed, but it was not long before the temple began to distinguish itself from the houses of ordinary mortals. For centuries afterwards, Greek architects worked exclusively for the gods, after undergoing their period of apprenticeship by building sanctuaries. During the long intervening period of the Dorian invasions the country had become so poor and conditions so barbaric that architects no longer built in stone. The first temples were made of brick, standing on stone foundations, and the roofing was originally made of thatch, the beams and pillars of wood. From about 600 B.C. onwards, architects began to build walls in stone, and baked earth and wood gradually gave way to more durable materials. In a very short time the masons gave proof of a remarkable technical skill. Not until the Roman period did they make use of mortar. They carefully cut the stone into jointed blocks and, after partially polishing them, bound them together with clamps and dowels, sometimes of wood, more often of bronze. While the bronze was still molten, it was poured along channels grooved in the thickness of the stone into specially prepared cavities. According to different periods or the type of building, the blocks were either left irregular or else were chiselled to have regular angles. The bare walls were either rough-coated and then smoothed, or left rustic, according to the preference of the clients who were either representatives of the gods or the people, and always magistrates. From surviving inscriptions of the time, we have now learnt that specifications were very precise, estimates were demanded and accounts were regularly kept of all building operations. We also have a considerable amount of interesting and curious information on the life of the builders and know that many building methods used today already existed in ancient Greece.

Like the temples, theatres also were the result of community enterprises, but it was not until the late 4th century at the very earliest that they were built in stone. As might be expected, it was the city that commissioned the building and paid the costs of such edifices as the prytaneum (q.v.), the senate (bouleuterion) and archive depository. It is worth noting that buildings, where only a few people assembled together, were at first as modest as private dwellings, and that those designed for large meetings were only built at a comparatively late date, for in the Greek democracies, assemblies were often held in the open.

The most suitable site for these vast meetings was the agora (q.v.), or market-place. It was only very late in Greek history that the agora took on its imposing aspect, and until the 4th century B.C. it merely consisted of an open space among the surrounding houses. It was sometimes lined by porticoes, but in the beginning these were only covered arcades without any great architectural distinction. The agora could only be a work of architecture in its own right once it had been planned as an integral part of a larger architectural complex. The origins of town-planning

The theatre at Segesta. *Photo Hirmer.*

(q.v.) as such are still a subject for controversy. They may lie in the 5th century B.C., if the famous Hippodamus of Miletus (q.v.) really was more than just a skilful surveyor. What we do know is that town-planning made its greatest progress during the Hellenistic period. This is not really surprising since it was then that the city magistrates lost any important political power they may once have had and were able to devote themselves entirely to the embellishment of their cities. The inhabitants, many of whom had grown rich through commerce and industry, demanded large, convenient streets and vast open spaces, as at Alexandria, where lavish ceremonies could be held. In some cities, the rulers or governors built themselves palaces which became centres for the whole city. While the Greeks of archaic and classical times had merely regarded their houses as a shelter for their wives, children and slaves, and as a place to spend the night, the private citizens and their wives, too, who now played an important part in Hellenistic society, made their dwellings into pleasant residences where they no longer need feel ashamed to receive their friends.

It was also in this period that the palaestrae, where athletes trained, became buildings of architectural worth, for formerly they had only consisted of a few rooms grouped around a courtyard. The Greeks had always paid particular attention to their fountains and as early as the 6th century B.C. covered them with colonnades. Later and probably due to Roman inspiration, vast baths and thermae with a great variety of installations were built beside them.

Such then were the main types of buildings in ancient Greece. Despite differences of design, they all showed affinities of style and decoration, deriving from the common spirit that informed them. In particular, the importance of the column and the different orders (*See* Orders) in Greek architecture cannot be overestimated, for few Greek buildings were without porticoes and pillars. Although the tendency to give buildings an increasingly richer and more majestic appearance began in archaic times and continued to the period of Roman domination, the essential principles and the spirit of Hellenic architecture remained remarkably consistent from the very earliest times.   P.D.

ARCHON. The Greek word *archon* meant someone who commanded and this somewhat vague term was also used to denote the supreme magistrature of certain cities as well as the leader of confederations of states. Best known to modern historians is the archonship of Athens, whose development is closely linked with the political evolution of the city. In the beginning, the archons were two officials chosen by the nobles to govern together with a king whose sole, absolute sovereignty they were no longer willing to recognise. We do not know either when these two posts were first created or whether one preceded the other. The appointments represented an empirical solution to the political problems of the time and must date from the reigns of the weak kings, probably towards the end of the 9th century B.C., which archaeological evidence has shown to have been a period of extreme prosperity for the aristocracy. The king was not deposed but was deprived of all political powers and left with only his religious attributes which, however, remained very important and which he retained for life, for a time at least. Of the two archons, one was the real leader of the government and the other, known as the polemarch, commanded the army. Aristotle stated that these two magistrates exercised their functions for a ten year period, but this statement has given rise to considerable controversy. We also do not know when the king or, as he was henceforth called, the *archon basileus*, was made to submit to the same rules as his colleagues. What is certain is that in 686, while still keeping their respective attributes (worship, administration, war), the three personages combined to form a college of archons which was open to all the nobles and which was renewed annually. The most important of the three was the archon who presided over the political life of the state; the fundamental idea of the office was vested in him and his name figured in all official decrees. His mention in these texts as the *archon eponymos*, as he was later called, has given historians a sound basis on which to establish Greek chronology as he was appointed once a year. But the social upheavals of this period, the weakening of the aristocratic families, the development of an economy that was no longer exclusively dependent on agriculture, and the need to protect a whole class of the population from famine and poverty all created so many problems that by the middle of the 7th century B.C. the number of archons was raised to nine by the appointment of six *thesmothetai*. These *thesmothetai* were responsible for the introduction and application of new legislation that answered the needs of the times and by their appointment the judiciary powers, which had formerly been in the hands of the heads of families, were transferred to the state. It was as a thesmothetes that Draco drew up his famous code of laws in 621. Upon relinquishing their appointments, after holding office for a year as explained above, the nine archons automatically became members of the council of the Areopagus, which held its sessions upon the Areopagus hill. The archonship continued unchanged during the 6th century and membership was reserved for the wealthiest class of citizens who were knowns as *pentakosiomedimnoi*. Solon retained the aristocratic character of the archonship and when Cleisthenes added a tenth archon as secretary, it was only to make the number of the archons correspond to that of the tribes. They were appointed by the drawing of lots and until 487 B.C. forty proposed names would be put in an urn, ten by each of the four tribes, but after Cleisthenes' reform the number of candidates was raised to five hundred, all being nominated by the demes, both to make the proceedings more democratic and to reduce the risk of fraud. At the same time, membership was opened to the second class of citizens, the knights *(hippeis)*, and from 457 onwards it was opened to virtually all citizens, but by then the office had lost almost all its former importance. From the early 5th century the government was in the hands of the strategi and, although the archons were covered with honours, they only dealt with matters of no great political importance. Similarly, although they were still automatic members of the Areopagus tribunal, they only dealt with crimes in which state interests were not directly involved.   P.D.

AREOPAGUS. " Citizens of Athens! As you
                    [now try this first case
Of bloodshed, hear the constitution of your court.
From this day forward this judicial council shall
For Aegeus' race hear every trial of homicide.
Here shall be their perpetual seat, on Ares' Hill.
Here, when the Amazon army came to take
                    [revenge
On Theseus, they set up their camp, and fortified
This place with walls and towers as a new
                    [fortress-town
To attack the old, and sacrificed to Ares, whence

This rock is named Areopagus. Here, day and
[night,
Shall Awe, and Fear, Awe's brother, check my
[citizens
From all misdoing, while they keep my laws
[unchanged.
If you befoul a shining spring with an impure
And muddy dribble, you will come in vain to drink.
So, do not taint pure laws with new expediency.
Guard well and reverence that form of government
Which will eschew alike licence and slavery;
And from your polity do not wholly banish fear.
For what man living, freed from fear, will still be
[just?
Hold fast such upright fear of the law's sanctity,
And you will have a bulwark of your city's strength,
A rampart round your soil, such as no other race
Possesses between Scythia and the Peloponnese.
I here establish you a court inviolable,
Holy, and quick to anger, keeping faithful watch
That men may sleep in peace." *(Translated by
Philip Vellacott).*

Such were the famous lines spoken by Athena in Aeschylus's play the *Eumenides,* written
in 458, to tell the Athenians how one of the
city's most ancient assemblies, the council
of the Areopagus, had been originally created in
order to judge Orestes for the murder of his mother.
Although its power had been reduced by Aeschylus's time, the council must certainly have been
the same as that summoned by the kings of Athens
to discuss affairs of state in the Homeric age. In
that remote period it was certainly composed of
the heads of the leading families and it had
survived the fall of the monarchy. It included all
the archons who had completed their terms of
office and therefore only represented the Eupatridae, who constituted the richest and noblest
class of citizens. Its powers must have been
as vague as they were far reaching since in every
primitive state there is no clear-cut separation of
powers. According to Aristotle, its function was
that of a watchdog for the laws: " It was responsible for the greater and more important part of
the administration and it meted out punishment
from which there was no appeal, either by fines
or corporal chastisement, to all who disturbed
the peace. " In a short time the council was
specifically charged with the judging of crimes
and this judicial function was soon to be the
only one to survive. Democratic reformers were
hostile to it; again according to Aristotle, in 462
" Ephialtes deprived it of all the attributions which

had made it a guardian of the constitution and
distributed them among other political and judicial
assemblies " At about the same time, the fact
that the lower classes could become members
of the archonship inevitably modified the character of the old council. It gradually continued
to lose its prerogatives, for the tribunal of the
Heliaea held most of the more important trials,
and by the 4th century B.C. the Areopagus only
judged cases of premeditated murder, poisoning,
arson, and, in certain cases, accusations of
impiety. Nonetheless, its glorious past preserved
its prestige and it was able to intervene in times of
great emergency. Its attitude in the tragic period
following the defeat of Athens in the Peloponnesian War showed that it was still just as capable
as in the past of maintaining respect for the laws.
P.D.

ARES. Ares was one of Zeus' few children by
Hera but his regular and legitimate birth was not
enough to give him an important place among the
gods. He was the lord of war and violent combat.
He was represented wearing a helmet, armed with
a cuirass and a spear and the Greeks believed they
could sometimes see him in the midst of battles,
uttering war-cries with his deep voice. When
he was not fighting, he was not a particularly
impressive god, for Athena could always defeat
him whenever intelligence was needed in a fight
as well as mere brute force. Even in hand-to-
hand fighting he was not always the winner and
Homer has told how he was wounded by the
Greek hero, Diomedes. His misfortunes were not
confined to war alone, for his love affair with
Aphrodite ended very badly when the goddess's
husband caught them both in a magic net and
summoned all the gods of Olympus to witness
how he had been betrayed. The story of Ares'
life is not very rich in events and his popularity
was always slight; for even if they did make war
almost constantly, the Greeks, like other peoples,
preferred to live in peace. P.D.

ARGOLIS. Even in the periods when its
power and political importance were in decline,
Argos still enjoyed an extraordinary prestige in
the eyes of the Greeks. It was reputed to be the
oldest of all Greek cities and its name was linked
with certain legends which the Greeks considered
to be part of their most ancient history. It was
near Argos that Heracles had accomplished his
first exploits, killing the lion at Nemea, and slaying

the Hydra in the marshes of Lerna.

Although the primitive Greek cultures made greater progress in Thessaly and the Cyclades during the 3rd millennium B.C., Argolis became the most brilliant centre of political and intellectual life in the time of the Achaeans. There is reason for thinking that Argolis was the first part of the mainland to have relations with Minoan Crete; for, although further from the island than the southernmost points of the Peloponnesus, it was a more tempting region for navigators. It is a peninsula stretching southwards and it offered the Cretan ships a largely open roadstead, which was very well sheltered from the northern winds by mountains. At the foot of these stretched great plains, which offered their inhabitants an abundant variety of such agricultural resources as cereals, vines, vegetables and fruits. Consequently, although small in area, the province became covered by towns, all near to one another and of considerable importance, judging by the richness of the tombs discovered by modern archaeologists. Besides Argos, Mycenae and Tiryns were the chief towns, but mention should also be made of Midea and Asine among others. It is hard to say whether Argos or Mycenae was the leading town and even the Greek tragedians often confused one with the other. According to the Homeric poems, it would seem that, although they were not quite the heads of empires, the rulers of Argolis—Agamemnon being the most famous held sway over fiefs which were frequently fairly remote from their capital.

Argos rapidly regained a considerable importance after the Dorian invasion. After Mycenae and the other towns were subdued by it, one of its kings, Pheidon, attacked Sparta, the most redoubtable city of the Peloponnesus, and after his victory made himself the president of the Olympic games in which representatives from the whole of Greece were already taking part (about 670 B.C.). Besides its military success, Argos was the first state in Greece to introduce the circulation of coinage, which it may also have been the first to invent. The new coins spread throughout Greece from Aegina which was subject to Argos. The ancient sanctuary of Hera, only a few miles from the city, drew pilgrims from all parts of the Peloponnesus. This brilliant period was brief; for the different states into which Argolis was divided refused to unite against the common enemy and were constantly menaced throughout the 6th century by Sparta, which had become their neighbour after conquering the province of Tegea. Nevertheless, Argos continued to prosper and produce brilliant artists. The two early 6th century statues of Cleobis and Biton that were consecrated at Delphi indicate that Argos was a great centre of sculpture and its bronze workshops produced mirrors with anthropomorphic handles of admirable elegance and solidity. At the very end of the archaic period it was from an Argive sculptor, Ageladas, that young Greek sculptors took lessons, one of them, it is said, being Phidias. A few years later it was the turn of Polycletus to bring glory to the city, a glory far greater than any in war or politics. Argos easily vanquished its neighbours, Tiryns and Mycenae, which it destroyed in 468 B.C. It underwent a period of civil strife between aristocrats and democrats in the course of which the latter took power in about 460, and attempted to cause the utmost damage to Sparta by its system of alliances. But the city was living mainly on its past memories and was never to recapture its former power which, from the time of Agamemnon to that of Pheidon, had made it one of the first cities in the Hellenic world.   P.D.

ARGONAUTS. The main protagonists of the rather patch-work legend of the Argonauts were Jason and Medea. Jason was born in Iolcus in Thessaly. His uncle Pelias had usurped the throne and ordered him to go to Colchis on the far shores of the Black Sea, in order to fetch the Golden Fleece. This was the hide of the marvellous ram which had carried Phrixus and his sister Helle to that far-off region, when they had been threatened with death by their father, and had then been consecrated to Ares by Aetes, the king of Colchis. At the head of some fifty fellow-adventurers, including Orpheus, and for a time, Heracles, Jason embarked on a boat that had been built with the aid of Athena by a certain Argos, whence the name of Argonauts for the members of the expedition. After a voyage punctuated by various adventures, all related to local legends, the expedition arrived in Colchis. There, helped by the sorcery of the witch, Medea, daughter of Aetes, Jason successfully passed the tests, which had been set him by the king before he would give him the Fleece. Once victor, Jason would still have been killed on the spot if he had not fled with the precious booty and Medea, whom he had promised to marry. We need not follow the complicated course of the homeward

expedition from Colchis back to Thessaly. Suffice it to say that the itinerary varies according to different traditions. It was supposed by various story-tellers to have gone along the Danube and the Po, the coasts of Italy, Sicily, Africa, Crete and the islands of the Cyclades, full of fabulous adventure such as mariners have always told in the heroic early days of sea travel. Many too were the various sites that the inhabitants of the ancient world proudly pointed out to strangers as the scene of the exploits of Jason and his crew. P.D.

ARGUS. Great grandson of a personage of the same name, who was the son of Zeus and Niobe. After many exploits, Argus was entrusted by Hera with the care of Io who had been metamorphosed into a cow; for, as he was supposed by some people to have two pairs of eyes, one in front and one behind, or by others, to have eyes all over his body, nothing could escape his notice. But Zeus was in love with Io and had her delivered by his messenger Hermes who killed Argus.
P.D.

ARIADNE. Daughter of Minos and Pasiphaë. Ariadne fell in love with Theseus, when he came to Crete to kill the Minotaur, and helped him to find his way through the labyrinth by giving him a spool of thread, which he unwound behind him as he went. She then followed him when he left Crete, but he abandoned her on the isle of Naxos, where she was discovered by the god, Dionysus, and became his mistress. Ariadne has often been represented together with Dionysus and it is highly probable that originally she had been a goddess. P.D.

ARION. Lyric poet of the 6th century B.C., born at Methymna on the island of Lesbos. Arion was a citharist who mostly composed dionysiac dithyrambs and may have been a pupil of Alcman. He travelled a great deal and like Alcman stayed at Sparta, but spent most of his time at Corinth at the court of the tyrant, Periander. From there he went to Italy, where he made a great deal of money, and then embarked on a Corinthian boat to return to Greece. It was then that the marvellous adventure related by Herodotus befell him: the sailors had wanted to kill him and take his riches, but Arion persuaded them to let him sing one last song, dressed in his magnificent costume of a *kitharaoidos*. When he had finished singing he leaped in to the sea where a dolphin, charmed by his music, took him on its back and carried him to Cape Taenarus. R.F.

ARISTARCHUS. Philologist of the Alexandrian period, born in Samothrace about 215 B.C., died at Alexandria about 143. He was both the disciple and the successor of Aristophanes of Byzantium (q.v.) at the head of the royal library of the Ptolemys. Aristarchus is especially famous for his edition of Homer which was so authoritative that his name became the synonym for rigorous and impeccable criticism.

R.F.

ARISTARCHUS of SAMOS. Astronomer of the Hellenistic period. *(See* Astronomy).

ARISTIDES. Son of a good family, treasurer of Athena, archon and strategus, Aristides was born in 540 B.C. and died in about 468. He was of legendary honesty and high moral character and has figured in anthologies for high-minded schools, but it must be admitted that his personality pales beside those of such figures as Miltiades or Themistocles, who, if less honest, were among the great architects of Athens' glory in the crucial years following the defeat of the Persians. Aristides was put forward by the party of the moderates to oppose the democrats and paid for the enthusiasm of his supporters with a brief period of exile in 483. There is a well known, edifying story of how he wrote his own name on the voting form for ostracism that had been given to an illiterate voter. Recalled to Athens together with other exiles when the city was directly menaced by the Persians under Xerxes, he showed great courage in the Persian Wars but no particularly important operation which saved the capital is to his credit. He did, however, render his country the invaluable service of lending his name to give an aura of integrity to the most questionable enterprises. Themistocles made use of him when he swindled the Spartans during the rebuilding of the walls of Athens in 478. His personality also must have contributed to the rapid success of the Delian League, the members of which had been so firmly convinced that they would all be equal that it was not for fifteen years that they found out that they had been duped and were really nothing more than subjects of the Athenians.

P.D.

ARISTIPPUS of CYRENE. Born about 390 B.C., Aristippus was a follower of Socrates. Like the Cynics, he had a low opinion of speculative knowledge which he regarded as being inferior to manual activity. He appears to have been influenced by the relativistic theories of Protagoras, and to have only attributed value to the inner sentiment of pleasure at the moment it was felt, for he considered pleasure to be an ephemeral sensation. According to him, the wise man enjoys the present and dominates circumstances. He was uninterested in civic life and went to the court of the tyrant, Dionysius of Syracuse, where he met Plato. When he returned to the town of his birth, he founded the Hedonist or Cyrenaican school as it was called, and was succeeded at the head of it by his daughter, Arete, and then his grandson Aristippus the Metrodidact who had been his mother's pupil. Of the Cyrenaicans, Hegesias Peisithanatos, who, as his name indicates, advocated suicide, evolved a philosophy of radical pessimism which was challenged by Epicurus. It was in order to escape from this pessimism that Anniceris gave social ties their former importance. After him, his follower, Theodorus the Atheist, who lived with Ptolemy I Soter, Lysimachus, king of Thracia, and Demetrius of Phalerum, recommended cosmopolitanism and indifference to all things except prudence and justice. We may find strong traces of the Cynics' influence in his theories and, to a lesser extent, those of his pupil, Bion the Borysthenite. Certain Cyrenaican elements of thought can also be detected in the thought of Anaxarchus of Abdera, the master of Pyrrhon, who flattered Alexander but bravely defied Nicocreon, the tyrant of Cyprus. He recommended both indifference and the sense of opportunity. But it was above all to Epicureanism that the Cyrenaic school opened the way.

P.-M.S.

ARISTONOUS of CORINTH. Lyric poet of the 4th century B.C. A hymn to Hestia and a paean to Pythian Apollo by him have been found engraved on a stone discovered at Delphi.

ARISTOPHANES. The greatest dramatist of the Old Comedy *(See* Comedy). He was an Athenian (although his enemies pretended he had usurped the title of citizen), was born about 445 B.C. and may have died in about 380. The story of his life is the story of his plays. Of the forty-four comedies he wrote, only eleven have come down to us : *The Acharnians* (425), a courageous plea for peace, when Greece was torn by six years of the Peloponnesian War; *The Knights* (424), a satire on the demagogue, Cleon, and on the Athenian people, personified by the senile old man, Demos, who had allowed themselves to be gulled by him; *The Clouds* (423), a criticism of the sophists and especially of Socrates who had become associated with them; *The Wasps* (422), a satire on the common Athenian mania for trials; *Peace* (421), in which a peasant, Trygaeus, rises into the sky on the back of a snail in order to beseech Zeus to stop war and deliver Peace who has been imprisoned in a cavern; *The Birds* (414), one of Aristophanes' most poetic and imaginative plays, in which two Athenians, tired of paying taxes, found the new city of CloudCuckooville in the sky; *Lysistrata* (411), which shows us the women of Athens finding an unusual way of forcing their husbands to make peace with Sparta; *The Thesmophoriazusae* (411), in which Euripides is shown fearing the fate women have in store for him after he has said so many hard things about them; *The Frogs* (405), a literary satire in which Dionysus, the god of the theatre, goes down to hell to bring back a good dramatist after the death of the last of the three great Athenian tragedians (will he come back with Aeschylus or Euripides?); *The Ecclesiazusae* (392), in which Aristophanes alludes to certain feminist-communist ideas that were then current in Athens by representing the Athenian women seizing power and deciding that henceforth all goods and all women would be shared in common; lastly, *Plutus* (388) in which he dealt with the social problem of the distribution of riches, and in which Plutus, the blind god of Fortune, is cured of his blindness at the sanctuary of Asclepius at Epidaurus.

Aristophanes' imagination and gift for comedy knew practically no limits. He was unable to renounce the coarse humour and obscenity that were traditionally a part of the Old Comedy, but we have reasons for thinking that he made less use of them than most of his rivals in the theatre. What Aristophanes was trying to do, above all, was to make people laugh so that he could win the competition among playwrights, and, secondly, to criticise the social, political and literary customs of his time in order to better them. He was far from being a mere jester and proudly proclaimed that " comedy also knows what is right ". He made fun specially of demagogues and sophists, and seems to have had rather con-servative opinions, but he was not a party man and every now and again he made fun of the traditional-minded Athenians, the " Marathonomachi ", whom he so admired. His plays show a surprisingly irreverent attitude towards the gods —even the god of the theatre—but this also was part of a literary tradition and there is no reason to conclude that Aristophanes was a free-thinker or an atheist. He showed himself to be a great lyric poet in the choruses and sometimes even in the dialogue of his comedies, but it was as a comic genius that he was unequalled, both in Greece and in other countries.   R.F.

ARISTOPHANES of BYZANTIUM.
He was a great philologist of the Alexandrian period (about 250-175 B.C.), a grammarian, lexicographer, bibliographer and editor of texts. He created the theory of analogy in grammar and, as head of the Royal Library of Alexandria, completed Callimachus's catalogue. Above all, he obtained famous editions of Homer, Hesiod, the main Greek lyric poets, and tragic and comic dramatists. Aristarchus (q.v.) was one of his pupils.   R.F.

ARISTOTLE. Aristotle was born in 384 B.C. at Stagira (Greek colony in Chalcidice near Macedonia to the north of Athos) and was the son of Nicomachus, personal physician and friend of Amyntas II, king of Macedonia. In 367, aged seventeen, he came to Athens and joined the Academy of Plato where he remained twenty years until the death of the master in 347. Plato soon noticed the exceptional gifts of this pupil, whom he called " the mind " or " the reader ", for indeed Aristotle had read everything and was a kind of walking encyclopaedia. In 347 Aristotle and his friend, Xenocrates, went to Atarneus, a city on the coast of Asia Minor, facing Lesbos, where the dynastic ruler, Hermias, had been converted to philosophy by some old pupils of the Academy who had settled in the neighbourhood. The first group of disciples began to form around Aristotle at Assos in the Troad and then at Mytilene in Lesbos. In 342, Philip II, King of Macedonia, entrusted Aristotle with the education of his son, Alexander, then aged fourteen. From then, until 335, Aristotle lived in Macedonia, usually in the royal palace of Mieza, near Pella, with his royal pupil. It would seem that Aristotle's intellectual and moral influence on Alexander was far-reaching. Once he was in Asia,

Alexander constantly sent his former master specimens of plants and all kinds of rare animals. In 341 Aristotle married a sister of Hermeias, Pythias, who died shortly after giving him a daughter. He later married a woman from Stagira, Herpyllis, who gave him the son, Nicomachus, to whom he dedicated his famous *Ethics*. In 335, when Alexander had left to conquer Asia, Aristotle left Macedonia and settled down in Athens where he founded his school in the gymnasium of the Lyceum (q.v.), and taught there for thirteen years. In 323, news of Alexander's death provoked a rising in Greece against Macedonia and it became dangerous for Aristotle to remain in the city as he was such a great friend of the Macedonians. A charge of impiety was brought against him in the courts and he withdrew to Chalcis in Euboea, the capital of Stagira where a stomach illness from which he had long been suffering caused his death in 322.

Aristotle's work is immense; it may be divided into two parts, that of his youth and that of his mature period. Like that of Plato, Aristotle's youthful work was destined for a non-initiated public whom he wished to lead progressively towards philosophy and science. It included dialogues like the *Eudemus*, which dealt with the survival of the soul, or works such as the *Protrepticus* and the treatise *On Philosophy*. The ancient Greeks greatly admired these works, even from a literary viewpoint, but all that now remains of them are a few fragments which modern scholars are now carefully studying in order to determine the exact evolution of Aristotle's thought and to see the way in which it gradually diverged from that of Plato. Aristotelian philosophy is, in fact, a kind of reformed Platonism which combines the taste for general knowledge which he owed to his master with a very lively sense of empiricism and the concrete. This was the great quality that characterised Aristotle's mature works, which were written for his disciples and not a wide public. This part of his work was a virtual scientific and philosophical encyclopaedia, and included more than four hundred works of which only forty-seven have come down to us in a more or less complete state. In this vast body of work Aristotle was able to co-ordinate one of the greatest collections of knowledge that any man has ever been able to constitute. To do this he made use of a certain number of notions and oppositions many of which have now become a part of current language, which, in fact, was where Aristotle often found them in the first place.

The then current interpretation of the theory of Ideas *(See* Plato), which made them into transcendent entities, was unacceptable to Aristotle. To him, the Idea (or Form) is immanent in the individual: it is its specific structure which makes a being what it is, but this Form can only be achieved in and by a matter in which it is immersed and which individualises it. The essence (later called quiddity) of a being is defined by form inasmuch as it is form that determines matter.

Aristotle also had recourse to several couples of opposed notions: substance (subject of the verb) and its attributes; accidents (whose presence is fortuitous) and special properties (linked to the essence and whose presence determines the species); power (or virtuality) and action (or realisation); the final cause (answer to the question: why?) and the efficient cause (answer to the question: how?) It should be added that the different types of attributes are grouped in a certain number of different classes called " categories ". These different notions are studied more thoroughly not only in the *Metaphysics* (the work which owes its name to the place that was given to it in Aristotle's series of works, after *Physics*) but also in a particular aspect in the works on logic. These last are grouped together under the name of *Organon* or instruments of knowledge. Together with the *Sophistici Elenchi* and the *Topics* or commonplaces, they include the *Categories* which study terms, the *De Interpretatione* which studies propositions, and the *Analytics* which deal with the syllogism, Aristotle's great discovery: the basic reasoning by which if two propositions are put forward, a third proposition, the conclusion, must necessarily result. By these different treatises Aristotle gave a definitive form to the formal logic he had constituted.

The *Physics* is essentially a treatise on the theory of movement and change in the domain of nature, in opposition to that of art, and the skies, to which he devoted a special treatise *(De Caelo)*. Natural movement is spontaneous, artificial movement is provoked, the movement of the planets is circular, as is (in an inverse sense) the eternal movement of the sphere of Fixed Stars which limits the universe. The *Physics* then, led to a theology which centred on a unique divinity, a pure act, a thought which thought itself into being and which moved the sphere of the Fixed Stars by its power of attraction; an imperturbable order

reigns in the celestial domain while a large place is left to hazard and liberty in the sublunary domain. Among Aristotle's other treatises, mention should also be made of the *Meteorologica* and the *De Generatione et Corruptione*.

We now come to the biological writings which play a central part in Aristotle's work. Most important are the voluminous *Historia Animalium* (or rather *Enquiry on Animals*), the treatises *De Partibus Animalium* and *De Generatione*. The crowning treatise is the *De Anima* in which the soul is defined as the form of the organised body with the capacity for life. In it, various theories are elaborated at length: first, that of perception, then that of intellectual activity which proposes a passive and active intellect—a theory which was to give rise to many debates in the Middle Ages. Some commentators on Aristotle's works identify the active intellect with Aristotle's God or Prime Motive Force. The *Poetics* contains Aristotle's famous theory of the purging of the passions, or catharsis, which played such a great part in French 17th century drama, not to speak of modern psychoanalysis.

In order to write his *Politics*, Aristotle, with his pupils, devoted precise, preliminary studies to 158 constitutions of which only one was rediscovered in the 19th century—that of Athens, the *Athenaion Politeia*. Like Plato, but using different means, Aristotle wished to reform the ancient city and free it from its troubles. He also dealt with economic problems, criticising the economy founded on profit, condemning usury, and recommending a return to the small family economy. The treatise on *Politics* is crowned by moral works, the most important being the *Nicomachean Ethics*, in ten books, written for the instruction of Nicomachus. In it, Aristotle affirmed the superiority of contemplative values; he made a very subtle study of voluntary action and the theory of the virtues which are able to find a just mean between opposing extremes. He made a very important study of friendship and left the description of human characters to his pupil, Theophrastus (q.v.). Finally a treatise on *Rhetoric* has come down to us.

Aristotle taught in a gymnasium called the Lyceum (q.v.) and the school was soon called Peripatos or the Peripatetic School because it was the custom to discuss problems while walking

Hoplite. Funerary stele of Aristion, the work of Aristocles. 510 B.C. Athens, National Museum. *Photo Hirmer.*

around it. Aristotle's first successors made remarkable additions to his work but the school was soon eclipsed by the success of the great Hellenistic schools of Epicureanism and Stoicism. Aristotle's "esoteric" writings disappeared for a time but were found again and re-edited in the time of Sulla (86 B.C.). They gave rise, especially from the 3rd century A.D. onwards, to the exegesis of such penetrating commentators as Alexander of Aphrodisias (3rd century), Themistius (4th century), Philopon (6th century) and Simplicius, the pupil of Damascius (q.v.). Mention must also be made of the *Introduction to the Categories* or the *Isagogus* by Porphyry (q.v.), which was translated into Latin together with the first two treatises of the *Organon* by Boethius in the 5th-6th centuries. These two short translations were all that was known of Aristotle's work in the early Middle Ages. Aristotle's works were translated into Arabic in the 9th century by order of the Caliphs of Baghdad, and the great Arab and Jewish philosophers of Asia, North Africa and Spain built up their systems while trying to reconcile their beliefs with the Aristotelian ideas. Latin translations were made in Spain in the 12th century and soon reached France, where they provoked great controversy and a law was passed forbidding the teaching of the doctrines (1210 - 1277). Notwithstanding this interdict, they were studied by such scholars as Siger of Brabant and St Thomas Aquinas who created a synthesis which scholasticism soon made well known. Galilean science and the classic philosophies of Descartes and Malebranche were opposed to Aristotle's theories, but Locke retained and developed their empirical elements, and Leibnitz was inspired by them to a certain extent. Today, modern scholarship is taking a fresh interest in the interpretation of Aristotle's ideas by stressing the importance given by him to the study of the difficulties, or *aporia*, resulting from the confrontation of contrary opinions on a given problem which all appear to be equally valid.

P.-M.S.

A R M Y . Between the mass of warriors that a coalition of kings flung against the walls of Troy and the organised, well equipped divisions of the Hellenistic period, the difference is as great and as similar as that between the hosts of medieval lords and modern military divisions. Very little is known about the Cretan armies, but the inventory of the arsenal at Cnossos suggests that chariots played an important part in battles of the time. Homer gives more explicit information about the troops under Agamemnon's command and it is likely that the text of the *Iliad* combines memories of the Mycenaean period with the realities of the 8th century B.C. Each king had his own soldiers under his absolute authority, having recruited them from among his vassals by demanding the heads of the various families to furnish him with the required number of soldiers. He would draw them up " phratry by phratry, tribe by tribe ", in Nestor's own words, and each of these groups would fight for itself in the hand-to-hand mêlées which were the battles of the time. But the most important part was played by the chieftains, who would ride onto the battlefield in their chariots and then fight in single combat on foot before their assembled soldiers. Their equipment consisted of a great crested helmet (like the one that so frightened Astyanax in the *Iliad*), a short cuirass, a large shield with a notch in the middle, which covered the whole body, a spear and a sword.

It seems that Sparta made the first progress in military art. Its citizens were soldiers all their lives, and nothing but soldiers, for even in times of peace they were constantly in arms. Their chieftains were more than isolated members of a warrior-élite whose single-handed prowess could decide the issue of a battle for it was their responsibility to coordinate the action of the whole army; the soldiers were no longer grouped according to families but according to age in sections, companies and battalions (the *lochoi*), the last unit comprising 640 combatants. Frequent exercises made the soldiers accustomed to combined movements carried out to the accompaniment of trumpets, which have been compared to the movements of a ballet. Besides the citizens, who made up the heavy infantry and who were grouped by their leaders into phalanxes, were the engineers, recruited from among the *perioikoi*, the commissariat, and sometimes light troops who were recruited, when necessary, from outside the citizen body, but commanded by Spartan officers. They were all heavily armed and their leaders counted on mass attacks to win the day. The whole army was at first placed under the command of two kings, and then one only, from the late 6th century onwards. They were supreme commanders, directed the campaigns and had power of life and death over their men. It was due to this powerful organisation that Sparta was

Warriors. Detail of the Warrior Vase. Mycenae.
13th century B.C. Athens, National Museum.
Photo H. Müller-Brunker.

until the age of sixty. In case of war, as many as were needed could be called upon to serve. Each soldier joined his unit with the equipment he had received as an ephebe and, as long as he was under arms, he received pay and a maintenance allowance. His posting depended on his private means; the rich usually served in the cavalry; others were hoplites, and the light infantry of archers, sling-throwers, peltasts (who fought with the javelin) were usually recruited from among the poorest and the metics. Officers were appointed by election and command of the operations was placed in the hands of one or several of the ten strategi who were annually chosen by popular vote. Discipline was freely consented to and was less strict than in Sparta; although the strategus could put a bad soldier into irons, dismiss him from the ranks, or court-martial him, he preferred to reason with him. '' To be obeyed by one's soldiers '', said Xenophon, who was very Athenian in his outlook despite his Spartan sympathies, '' one should show them the advantages resulting from obedience, and prove by practice how discipline benefits those who observe it, and causes harm to those who violate it. ''

The impoverishment of Greece, the waning of the civic sense, then the disappearance of the city

the most formidable military power in the whole of Greece during the archaic period. From the 5th century onwards, the diminution of the number of citizens reduced the strength of the army, for, in addition to the true Spartans, ever increasing numbers of soldiers who had no right to citizenship were recruited, such as perioikoi, even helots, and mercenaries whenever necessary.

Although different Hellenic cities were soon obliged to adopt the tactics which had proved so successful for the Spartans, the composition of their armies reflected quite a different spirit. Everywhere, and at all times, it was the citizens who formed the nucleus of the fighting forces, and each of them had to be ready to sacrifice his life for the sake of the homeland. But even if, as was usual, mobilisation was frequent (it was almost always partial), it was always something of an exception in their lives, for the soldiers were first and foremost civilians. In Athens, for example, citizens were obliged to serve from the age of eighteen to twenty, and they constituted the units of ephebi (q.v.) who were responsible for the defence of the national territory. After their period of service they went back to civilian life, although they could always be called up again

Corinthian helmet. Mid-7th century B.C.
Olympia Museum. *Photo Deutsches
Archäologisches Institut, Athens*

Hoplites. Detail from an Attic bas-relief. Beginning of the 5th century B.C. Athens, National Museum. *Ph. R. Zuber*

state and the creation of the great Hellenistic kingdoms profoundly modified the organisation and the spirit of the Greek army. As in Sparta, in former times, these new kingdoms mainly depended on their military might and everything was done to give their troops a crushing superior-

Bronze helmet and gold funerary mask. Macedonia. 6th century B.C. Athens, National Museum. *Photo S. Meletzis.*

ity, but the sovereigns could count neither on the patriotism of their subjects nor on their combative instincts; so the national army was replaced by the professional army composed of trained mercenaries ready to serve whoever paid them. At the same time, although the final issue of a war still depended largely on the courage of the soldiers, new techniques and strategies made their appearance. Siege warfare was developed, which required special experts and engineers. Supply problems, which were easy to resolve when wars were fought on the national territory or in neighbouring regions, became more difficult when expeditions were launched in far-off regions. Such problems must have been closely studied by Alexander during his Indian campaign. Past methods no longer sufficed and the army became an organised body existing outside civic life, which could impose its will and could play an important part in the politics of the state. P.D.

ARRIAN. Historian and essayist, born at Nicomedia in Bithynia (about 95-175 A.D.). In his youth Arrian had been an enthusiastic disciple of the Stoic philosopher, Epictetus (q.v.), and showed his influence in two works: the *Discourses* and the *Manual*. Through the favour of the emperor, Hadrian, who held him in high esteem, he became a high official in the Roman empire. He was an admirer and imitator of Herodotus and Xenophon. He wrote a *Treatise on Tactics*, a *Treatise on Hunting* and historical works of which the most important were the *Anabasis*, the recital of Alexander's conquests, and the *Indike*, probably rewritten, but full of interesting information, particularly in the section devoted to the voyage of Nearchus. R.F.

ART. Greek art has shown such a consistent unity of style throughout all its different periods that ideally it should be studied in all its simultaneous manifestations, in architecture, sculpture, painting and all the minor arts such as ceramics, terra-cotta figurines, coins and jewellery. Unfortunately this cannot be done in a dictionary like the present one but, nevertheless, a few remarks of a general nature must be made.

In the first place, we must remember that except in its very latest periods, Greek art was closely linked with religion. Even in the Minoan civilisation, when artistic creation seems to have been so spontaneous that it is difficult to explain it by anything other than the sheer joy of representing life, the only themes we find are divinities, scenes of worship and festivals held in their honour. Even the famous *Parisienne* was not the isolated figure we now know, but one of several female figures shown participating in some religious ceremony. Only decoration was profane, with its flower motifs, leaf patterns and sea creatures. In Greek art properly speaking, it should be noted that the civic buildings which were erected later than the sacred buildings were also invested with a sacred character by their builders; no man, for instance, might set foot in the agora unless he was first in a state of spiritual purity. Of profane sculpture and painting there was none until the 5th century B.C. at the very earliest. The making of statues and pictures to decorate shrines was an act of piety and its purpose was to provide the people with images of the divinity and to commemorate the exploits of past heroes. Even the minor arts were governed by this general rule and although many vases were painted with profane scenes, they were often made to be placed in tombs or else offered as ex-votos, and they were then painted with ritual scenes (such as funeral lamentations) or some other subject dear to the immortal who was to be placated. Not even the terra-cotta figurines were designed as mere ornamental knick-knacks until very late in Greek art.

It is for this reason, among others, that the artists lavished such loving care on their works. The same word was used for both art and technique and when we read the texts of the time we are often given the impression that the ancient Greeks believed that the first essential for an artist was to be a master of his craft. The Seven Wonders of the World were admired less for their intrinsic beauty than for the skill that had been required to make them, but this does not mean the Greeks were indifferent to beauty. They were often so demanding that artists strove hard to excel each other.

If we follow the course of Greek art from beginning to end, we shall find that it was singularly unrevolutionary. The contrast offered by Greek art of the 2nd and that of the 1st millennium B.C. is accounted for by the two or three centuries of the intervening period that separates them. But even in this obscure intermediary period, the few surviving works all bear witness to the slow transformation of an ideal that was never rejected. Once Hellenic art had taken root, in the early 8th century B.C., it evolved regularly, never meeting any obstacles, with each successive generation of artists trying to perfect what it had learnt from its ancestors. This fidelity to past tradition was so great that scarcely had the archaic period come to an end than some artists were looking back on it with nostalgia and trying to prolong it; the first archaising schools of art date from the 5th century B.C.

These considerations do not only apply to technique; the continuity of artistic inspiration is even more striking. Greek art always concentrated on the representation of the human figure; the Greeks believed that, as Sophocles said, " if marvels are many in this world, the greatest marvel of all is man himself ". The glory of Greek art never depended on originality. It was during the geometric period, after a long interval in which sculpture had ceased to exist and in which painting was non-figurative, that the human figure made its entry into Greek art and took that pre-eminent place it was always to keep, as a result of Egyptian and oriental influences. But in neither type nor theme was there ever to be any great variety. The statues of Polycletus were inspired by the ancient kouroi, the exploits of heroes like Heracles and Theseus were repeated indefinitely and the plan and aspect of temples were fixed once and for all in the 6th century B.C. Although a growing prosperity

Artemis and Actaeon. Detail of an Attic krater by the Pan Painter. Second quarter of the 5th century B.C. Boston, Museum of Fine Arts.

and the birth of a kind of romanticism and climate of spiritual unease, and contacts with Asia in the 4th century may be said to have brought new elements into Greek art, this unprecedented quality of spirituality was given to figures that had remained essentially unchanged. In their proportions, their attitudes and their external appearance they hardly differed from those that had been made as soon as artists had succeeded in overcoming the technical difficulties which alone had prevented them before from giving expression to an ideal that remained astonishingly consistent throughout the whole Hellenic period. This conception of art, in which beauty was equated with technique, was justified; for it was by technique that the ancient Greeks were able to give their works of art that perfection which, to our eyes, sets them outside space and time, in a world more beautiful than any we now know.   P.D.

ARTEMIS. The cult of the goddess, Artemis, was one of the most widespread in the whole of ancient Greece. Alone or else accompanied by her brother, Apollo, she presided over countless sanctuaries, among which the most important were those at Ephesus, Delos and Brauron in Attica. In the classical period she was usually represented as a virgin goddess, who reigned over the animal kingdom and hunted wild animals with a bow and arrows. It would appear that she was originally a substitute for the Asiatic Great Mother who ruled over all living beings and that she had assumed the same role and even the same personality. In early representations Artemis retained the oriental appearance of her forbear, for she was shown dressed in a long robe, wearing a cylindrical tiara, with two wings with the tips swept back in a scallop-shape, and flanked by two lions whom she held either by the necks or the feet. Later, she became a young woman of rather boyish aspect, wearing a short tunic, as in the 4th century statue of Artemis and the hind —almost certainly by the hand of Leochares—and the well known Diana of Gabii perhaps by Praxiteles.

Artemis retained several of her original features. She was always the fierce goddess who dealt death with her arrows and showed special severity towards mortals who had been guilty of impiety, like the children of Niobe whom she helped Apollo to massacre; Actaeon, who, according to some authorities, had been guilty of daring to compete with her in archery, and according to others (this being the most widely accepted version in Hellenistic times) had con-

Votive relief
dedicated to
Asclepius.
About 380-350 B.C.
Athens, National
Museum. *Photo
Spyros Meletzis.*

templated her naked as she was bathing; and
many others.

The nature of her cult varied according to the
region. In Sparta she was known as Orthia and
presided over the sanguinary rites of young people who fought one another before her altar. In
Attica she was served by young girls called little
bears. In Ephesus, she was worshipped according to rites of a more oriental nature.   P.D.

ASCLEPIUS. Asclepius was the son of
Apollo and a mortal woman, Coronis. His mother
had been killed by her divine lover for deceiv-
ing him; he had torn the child out of her womb
and had him raised by the Centaur, Chiron.
Asclepius learnt the art of medicine from his
master and became so expert that he was able to
bring the dead back to life again, but Zeus could
not tolerate this defiance of the established order
of the world and struck Asclepius down with a
thunderbolt. The famous tholos at Epidaurus
may, in fact, be nothing else than Asclepius's
funerary monument, for it was at Epidaurus that
Asclepius had his greatest sanctuary after he had
been deified. He became a new god and took
the place of his father, for although Apollo was an
implacable slayer of his enemies, even he had
need of the healer's art. Asclepius was the

patron of medicine and won a considerable vogue
from the late 5th century B.C. onwards. Countless pilgrims came to Epidaurus to seek cures at
his shrine and he would appear to them in dreams
to tell them what treatment was needed. It was
under his patronage that what were virtually
schools of medicine sprang into existence, notably on the island of Cos.

Asclepius belonged to that category of gods
who were comparative latecomers and who only
existed by virtue of their functions, for their
rather uneventful and shadowy lives gave
rise to no substantial body of legend.

Asclepius was represented by artists as a
benign, bearded, thoughtful man and is generally accompanied by a serpent. Certain of
his images resemble the portraits of philosophers that were widely diffused from the 4th
century onwards.   P.D.

ASIA. Although the Greeks had penetrated
in the time of Alexander into the western provinces of India and had even inspired a Graeco-
Buddhist style of Indian art and although they
even had some rather tenuous links with the Far
East through intermediate peoples, Asia for them
signified Anatolia (q.v.), Persia, Syria and Mesopotamia. For the Greeks, Asia was more than a

geographical entity; it was the perfect example of a foreign land, a world entirely different from theirs by its customs, its languages, its religions and its system of ethics. The two sisters of royal blood, who personify Asia and Hellas and who appear to Atossa in a dream in Aeschylus's play *The Persians*, are as different as can be: one is ready to accept a life of slavery whereas the other is willing to die rather than lose her liberty. Although Asia became identified with the Persian king after the Persian conquests, it was first identified with less powerful sovereigns who reigned over nearer regions like that of Lydia especially, with its famous prince Croesus, who was on friendly terms with the Greeks and whose wealth had dazzled the entire world. During the archaic period Lycia, Phrygia, Mysia in Asia Minor, and more distant Phoenicia were also well known to Greek traders and sailors.

Whether it was united under the rule of the Persian king or divided into a number of smaller kingdoms, Asia never ceased to fascinate the Greeks although they were rather loth to admit it and even then felt rather guilty at having fallen victim to its fascination. The attraction of Asia for the Greeks was compounded of curiosity, because of its different civilisation and envy of its somewhat grander and often sumptuous way of life. It was from Asia that the Cretans derived certain traits which were to make the richness of Minoan civilisation, it was into Asia that the Mycenaean kingdom expanded, and it was to Asia that the Greeks went from the 8th century B.C. onwards to seek new inspiration for their art. After the Greeks had repulsed Xerxes' armies in 480 B.C. and no longer feared the threat of an invasion and after they had signed a new treaty with the Persians in 448, the orient became fashionable again; Asiatic beliefs made their way into Greece, a taste for the sumptuous Asian way of life replaced former austerity and, when Pericles and Phidias rebuilt the Acropolis, they may even have secretly wished to rival the colossal monuments of Persepolis. After the misfortunes of the late 5th century, the richness and power of Persia attracted the envious looks and solicitations of nearly all the Greek cities until, finally, Alexander stepped into the glorious place that had been occupied by the Great King and advanced as far as India to accomplish the fusion of the two civilisations by reducing Hellas, once so restive under the yoke of a king, to obedience under his rule together with her sister Asia.

ASSEMBLIES. The ancient Greeks never practised an oriental despotism and, even at times when the state was ruled by a single leader, he would never ignore the opinions of his fellow-citizens. Homer's poems, which are probably a fairly accurate picture of Mycenaean civilisation, describe how kings would assemble restricted councils of noblemen to discuss affairs together and how they would summon the people to acquaint them with the decisions they envisaged. This system of a double assembly survived almost everywhere in the Greek world until the end of antiquity. It persisted more or less in its primitive state in Sparta where the *Gerousia* or group of twenty-eight elders, chosen in theory for their virtues, would assemble in the presence of the two kings, while all the people had to do was to approve by popular acclamation the proposals put before them. In more democratic states the system evolved until the two assemblies finally became the sovereign rulers of the state. This is what happened at Athens where the council of the Areopagus had inherited the functions of the private council of the kings and had very wide but ill defined powers at first until, in the time of Solon, its competence was confined to the judiciary. The political authority was then assumed by a new assembly known as the *Boule* or Senate, composed of four hundred members, *Bouleutai*, of which a hundred were chosen from each of the four tribes. But the part played by the Boule was so insignificant under the Tyranny that its existence has sometimes been doubted. We do know that the whole of the people was sometimes consulted as indicated by the voting which designated the members of Pisistratus's bodyguard.

The system changed entirely in the late 6th century B.C. when Cleisthenes introduced the double assembly regime into Attica. From then onwards, the Boule was formed by a council of five hundred members who were chosen by lot, fifty being taken from each of the ten newly constituted tribes. The only conditions for membership of the Boule were to be a free citizen, to be over thirty years of age, and to have passed the *dokimasia*, which was a purely formal examination of morality that every magistrate had to undergo. The Five Hundred were nominated for a year and were not allowed to hold office more than twice in a lifetime which allowed at least half the elder Athenians to be senators at some time in their lives. In the 4th century B.C. they were paid an indemnity of five obols for every sitting they attended. Sessions were held every day except during festivals, and for periods of 35 to 39 days a section of 50 members, representing one of the tribes, would take turns in officiating and ensure a permanent assembly by day and night. These fifty members were called the *prytaneis* and their president *(epistates)* was chosen by lot every day and also acted as chairman for the assemblies that were held during the duration of the *prytaneia,* as the period was called. He was helped in his duties by a secretary who was recruited from among the council and who had to write the minutes of the sessions and inscribe and display the texts of the measures which had been decided. The Boule played a double role; it had to prepare the measures that were to be put before the public assembly and it had to ensure the execution of the measures that had been decreed by the public assembly. The Boule had therefore to deal with a great variety of affairs and as a pamphlet, which has been falsely attributed to Xenophon, stated, " it deliberated on such matters as wars, finances, the passing of new laws, the everyday details of administration, allies, tributes, arsenals, temples ". In principle —a principle that was faithfully respected up to the beginning of the 4th century—no proposal was ever submitted to the public assembly that the latter had not originally proposed. The Boule would put forward names for ambassadors, present envoys from other states to the people, supervise the activities of the different magistrates, discuss finances and reserve the right to judge certain cases. In short, its scope was universal and the multiplicity of its functions justified the frequency of its sittings. The last word of course rested with the public assembly, but the Bouleutai were certainly not ignorant of the fact that there is an art in swaying crowds. The public assembly called the *Ecclesia,* or more simply, the People *(Demos)* was composed of the whole of the civic body. The result was that while the Boule sat indoors in the *Bouleuterion,* the public assembly was held in the open. In the time of Cleisthenes it met in the agora, then on a hill (the Pnyx) to the west of the Acropolis until the middle of the 4th century, and finally in the theatre of Dionysus.

At no time were all the Athenians present at the sessions and even the institution of the system whereby attendance vouchers were distributed, which could be exchaged after the meeting for three obols, did not do away with abstentions. This is hardly surprising since the assembly regularly met four times in each prytaneia, not to mention special meeting in times of great emergency, and many citizens lived in the country where they were detained by agricultural work. The attendance was still heavy and certain decisions, particularly those with regard to ostracism, could not be taken if less than six thousand were present. The result was that the public assembly was more like a political meeting than a parliament in the modern sense. The meetings were well behaved and not disturbed by latecomers since, once the meeting had begun, the Scythian policemen would set up a rope barrier to prevent access to the assembly. The assembly assumed a religious significance and began with sacrifices, prayers and solemn curses against any who should deceive the people. There was no competition for the office of president which went by right to the epistates of the prytaneis until 378, after which it went to one of the nine *proedroi,* who were chosen by lot from among the bouleutai of the nine tribes who were not in charge during that prytaneia. No proposal was discussed that had not already been examined by the Boule but this did not prevent anyone from putting forward counter-proposals or amendments, nor from exercising the right to ask the Boule to consider a new proposal which would then come back to the public assembly. The president gave permission to speak to anyone who requested it and the speaker would then mount the rostrum, wearing the myrtle crown which placed him under divine protection and assured his inviolability. He would expose his views, which others might criticise later, to a public that might react vigorously but, according to Aristophanes, usually listened to him with rapt attention. When the discussion was closed, the vote would be taken by a show of hands in nearly all cases (although a secret ballot was sometimes taken, as in debates on ostracism) and the public assembly was not bound in any way to follow the recommendations of the Boule. Once the result of the vote had been declared, each citizen had the right of insisting that the matter should be reconsidered at a further session and, should the adopted proposal be found to be illegal, its author was liable to heavy penalties.

It would be hard to imagine a more liberal and prudent system; everything was specially designed to allow each citizen the greatest possible

Orators' tribune on the Pnyx, a hill west of the Acropolis where the assembly of the Ecclesia was held until the mid-4th century B.C. *Photo Hassia.*

initiative while at the same time eliminating the risk of ill considered decisions. But this rather cumbersome system proved unsatisfactory to the Athenians by the 4th century B C and they began to make a habit of discussing proposals in the public assembly that had not been previously examined by the Boule. After all, both assemblies dealt with the same matters, drew up the same decrees and laws and decided on relations with other cities, financial policies and the designation and supervision of magistrates.

Such then were the two main assemblies which presided over the political life of the Athenians. In the strict sense of the word, there were other assemblies too: the colleges of magistrates, restricted as they were, the tribunals, the Aeropagus (q.v.) and especially the Heliaea (q.v.) whose six thousand members sat in groups of several hundreds. Evidently, although it was the rule at Athens to respect the initiative and freedom of every individual, it was considered advisable to introduce a system of checks by submitting this initiative and freedom to the judgment of a group.
P.D.

ASTRONOMY. The impressive achievements of Greek astronomical science, based on geometry, owed little or nothing to the Babylonian astronomers. All that the Greek scientists owed to the Chaldaeans were a few elementary, practical notions such as the Zodiac and its twelve signs, the divisions of the circle and of time (still in use today), useful records of observations, particularly of eclipses, that had been made over a period of centuries and, finally, the main principles and methods of astrology. From the Homeric poems and Hesiod's *Works and Days* we may see that in its beginnings Greek astronomy was limited to a few rudimentary and practical observations. We know that Ulysses took his reckoning by the Great Bear, which never sets, in order to keep a straight course at night, and that sailors and farmers kept watch for the heliacal rising and setting of various constellations—notably the Pleiades, the Hyades and Arcturus—as heralds of changes in the weather, and that their first appearance of the year in the evening sky or their last appearance at dawn was noted down in agricultural calendars. During the whole of antiquity, in Greece and in Rome, these Prognostics were gathered in collections which were precursors of the more modern almanac. But cosmology as such was limited to myth and fable and there was no coherent theory of the universe until the philosophers, who lived in the Greek colonies in Asia Minor and south Italy between the early 6th century and the middle of the 5th century B.C., made astronomy into an empirical science by freeing the study of nature and physics from the domain of myth and magic. For the physicists of Ionia, the essential aim of philosophical reflection was to discover first the constitution and transformation of matter and, secondly, the structure and laws of the universe. The result of their studies was a series of global, cosmological theories in which astronomy played a part; for example, the theories of Thales of Miletus (about 625-585 B.C.), who represented the world as a bubble of air in the midst of an aqueous mass. Thales seems to have been the first astronomer to affirm that the light of the moon was derived from that of the sun and, by making use of Babylonian astronomical tables, was able to predict an eclipse of the sun (that of the 28th May, 585 ?). Anaximander of Miletus (about 570 B.C.) has been credited with several important discoveries: the curvature of the earth's surface, (he drew the first map for use by navigators), the suspension of the world in space, the infinitude of space and the plurality of worlds. Another less fortunate and stranger theory of his was that the two luminous discs of the sun and moon and the shining dots we call 'stars' correspond to holes pierced in immense hollow rings, made of opaque air and filled with fire, the higher wheel being that of the sun, the lower that of the Milky Way. He also discovered the obliquity of the ecliptic. The adventurous speculations of later astronomers—Anaximenes, Xenophanes, Heraclitus, Empedocles and Anaxagoras—marked a regression rather than a step forward in cosmography.

At the same period, the principles of geometric astronomy were being elaborated by another school of philosophers, for it was in the south of Italy from the late 6th century B.C. that the Pythagoreans (the dates and even the very existence of Pythagoras of Samos, the legendary personage who was supposed to have fled from the Persian menace in about 520, are most uncertain) brought about a kind of revolution in physics by considering that numbers were the archetypes of all things, at once the constituent elements of matter and diagrams for all structures. It was they who introduced the idea that the cosmos incarnated a rational order and a divine harmony, a conception that was to endure for centuries to come. From the very start, they had stated the sphericity of the

earth as a dogma that Parmenides (about 500-450) accepted and Plato respected. They also made a firm distinction in the world between the sublunary region where generation, corruption and disorder held sway, and the space above the moon which was a domain of eternal order and purity. One strange astronomical theory that has come down to us has been attributed to Philolaos, a Pythagorean of 450-400 B.C.; according to his theories, there was a central Hearth (Hestia) in the middle of the world, around which revolved ten celestial bodies which were, working outwards, the Anti-Earth (like the central Hearth, invisible from our hemisphere), the Earth, the Moon, Mercury, Venus, the Sun, Mars, Jupiter, Saturn and the sphere of the Fixed Stars; the number and distances of these spherical bodies corresponded to arithmetical properties and composed a musical harmony which could be detected by sufficiently instructed spirits. The theory of the Central Hearth and the Anti-Earth met with little success, but the doctrine of the central position of the spherical earth, at rest in the centre of the celestial sphere, as formulated by the great Parmenides of Elea, became one of the fundamental and least questioned dogmas of scientific astronomy until the time of Copernicus. The other main dogma that Plato, heir to the Pythagorean tradition (428-348), bequeathed to succeeding astronomers was that of circular and uniform movement, which was the only perfectly beautiful and rational movement, in conformity with the divine nature of the sideral world; the planets were situated in succession between the earth and the sphere of the Fixed Stars and all the stars revolved around the earth.

Starting from these principles, Greek astronomers went on to evolve two great rival systems. The first had been sketched out by Plato, completed by Eudoxus (about 368 B.C.), retouched by Callippus (about 335 B.C.) and then complicated by Aristotle (384-322 B.C.). In it, the stars were attached to a series of concentric transparent spheres, each one fixed within the other, and all with the centre of the earth as their common centre. The outermost sphere of the Fixed Stars turned on its axis from east to west in a simple " retrograde " movement, one complete revolution being accomplished every twenty-four hours. The problem was much more difficult with regard to the seven so-called " wandering " stars or " planets ", that is, the sun and the moon, whose course shows certain irregularities, and especially the five " little " planets of Mercury, Venus, Mars,

Jupiter and Saturn. To the terrestrial observer, the apparent displacement of these last planets is the projection onto the sphere of the Fixed Stars of their revolution around the sun, combined with the earth's annual rotation around the sun. As Eudoxus and his successors supposed that the earth was immovable in the centre of the whole universe and that the five " little " planets gravitated around the earth and not the sun, they were obliged to have recourse to a system in which each planet was accompanied by a succession of homocentric spheres in order to account for their displacements by uniform circular movements. According to Eudoxus, there were three spheres for the sun and the moon and four for each of the " little " planets, making a total of twenty-seven in all, including the sphere of the Fixed Stars. In each cluster, the two or three inner spheres each revolved independently around its own axis, which was different from the axis of the sphere in which it was set. As the movement of the main sphere affected that of each inner sphere, the movement of the innermost sphere to which the planet was fixed was the result of the movement of the three or four spheres of the cluster. By suitably adjusting the speed of the spheres and inclination of their axes, it was possible to " save appearances ", at least approximately, to use the expression of the astronomers of antiquity. The main sphere, in which each cluster was set, transmitted the diurnal movement governing all stars, the second the individual movement of the planet in the zodiac in a straight line, the third and the fourth spheres, its anomalies such as delays, accelerations, stations and retrogressions.

There was a serious defect in this system: as all the spheres were concentric to the earth, each planet would always remain at the same distance from the earth, which was manifestly not the case. Consequently, the system was perfected by the addition of the theory of eccentric circles around the earth and " epicycles": by giving the circular orbit of the planet a centre that was different from that of the earth it was possible to account for the varying distances of the planet from the earth and the varying times taken by the planet to describe an equal arc and it was also possible to explain the " zodiacal anomaly " in the movement of the sun and the moon which was the only one to have been observed during centuries. The explanation given of the " heliacal anomaly " of the " little " planets such as stations and retrogressions, was either that the centre of the eccen-

tric circle described by the planet around the earth itself described a small circle; or, which was simpler, that the planet described a smaller circle known as an " epicycle " around an ideal point, which itself described an eccentric circle around the earth. This theory, already familiar to Apollonius of Perga (about 200 B.C.), was applied to observed phenomena by the two greatest astronomers of antiquity: Hipparchus of Nicaea (active 161-127 B.C.), in his studies of the sun and the moon, and Claudius Ptolemy (active 127-151 A.D.) in his studies of the planetary system as a whole. The theory found supporters throughout the Middle Ages, as did also the theory of the spheres whose scientific inferiority found compensation in the authority of Aristotle.

A few bold spirits rejected the dogma of the central position of the earth and its immobility in the universe and it seems that Heraclides Ponticus explained diurnal movement by the earth's rotation on its axis and maintained that Mercury and Venus turned around the sun whereas the sun and the moon and the other three planets turned around the earth. Aristarchus of Samos (about 280 B.C.) evolved the heliocentric theory by which the sun was at rest in the centre of the universe while the planets revolved around it, including the earth which also accomplished a complete rotation on its axis every twenty-four hours. But with the exception of a certain Seleucus of Seleuceia (2nd century B.C.), all the scientists and philosophers of the time indignantly contested Aristarchus's hypothesis, which was in opposition to the dogmas that associated perfect movement with the divine purity of the empyrean and the central position and immobility of the earth with its weight.

Hipparchus also discovered the procession of the equinoxes, the annual displacement of the points of intersection of the ecliptic and the equator, but calculated it at only 36 " instead of 50 ". He also compiled a *Catalogue of stars* (more than eight hundred, defined by their ecliptic co-ordinates) to which Ptolemy added another three hundred unities. The best approximate calculations of the distance of the sun from the earth and the sun's diameter were made by Posidonius of Apamaea, a Stoic philosopher and physicist (135-51 B.C.). He estimated the distance of the sun to be 62 million miles (in reality the mean value is 93 million) and its diameter to be 39 times 114 times the diameter of the earth (in reality 109.5 times). He also explained so-called

" horizontal " eclipses of the moon by atmospheric refraction, and the phenomenon of the tides by the double attraction of the moon and sun.

On the fringes of Hellenic astronomy properly speaking, with its geometrical basis, lay a Babylonian astronomical tradition based on simple arithmetical methods. It flourished during the Hellenistic and Roman periods in the form of popular astronomical texts and above all in astrology. As the art of determining the influence of the seven planets on the whole or part of the earth and on mankind, and more particularly on each individual according to his position in the zodiac at some crucial point in time such as his birth or conception, astrology was born in the late 5th century B.C. in Mesopotamia (the earliest known horoscope has been found on a clay tablet of 410 B.C.). Astrology did not really become popular until the 3rd century and doctrinal works of astrology (of which the best was Ptolemy's *Tetrabiblos*) were all the products of Hellenistic thought.

The extraordinary vogue enjoyed by astrology in the Graeco-Roman world was not only a result of the growing influence of oriental beliefs, but also of the idea which was widespread among philosophers and public alike that, as the sky and the stars were of divine nature, they could act on the course of earthly matters. This belief seemed to receive confirmation from the observed mechanism of the seasons, the tides, and the connexions between the rising and setting of the sun and certain regularly occurring meteorological phenomena.   J.B.

ASTYANAX. The son of Hector. In the *Iliad* Homer has described how the sensitive child was frightened by the waving plumes on his father's helmet as he said good-bye to him before the battle. According to the most widely accepted tradition, Astyanax did not survive long after his father, for although his mother Andromache vainly tried to protect him from the fury of the Greeks, he was pitilessly slain and his brains dashed out against the ground. Some versions maintain that he escaped and was taken by his mother to the court of Neoptolemus in Epirus.   P.D.

ATALANTA. The Arcadian Atalanta was almost certainly a goddess before she became a king's daughter in popular tradition. Like Artemis, by whom she was soon eclipsed, Atalanta was the protectress of wild nature, sometimes taming and sometimes hunting and slaying wild beasts. According to the legend, it was she who triumphed over the boar that had ravaged Calydon, a theme that proved immensely popular with writers as well as artists. Like Artemis, she wished to remain a virgin; it was said that the only reason she had consented to marry Melanion was because he was the only man who had ever succeeded in outrunning her, by ruse rather than his own fleetness of foot.   P.D.

ATHENA. Like Hera and Artemis and all the other female divinities of ancient Greece, Athena must have been a descendant of the goddess whom the Cretans and Mycenaeans worshipped in the 2nd millennium B.C., but it was Athena more than any other goddess who personified the Hellenic ideal. She was the daughter of Zeus from whose head she sprang fully armed. She was the symbol of wisdom and intelligence

Astyanax, on Priam's knees, fatally wounded by Neoptolemus. Detail of a hydria by the Cleophrades Painter. About 480 B.C. Naples, Museo Nazionale.

Atalanta, Melanion, Peleus and Meleager chasing the Calydonian Boar. Detail of the François Vase. About 570 B.C. Florence, Museo Archeologico. *Photo Hirmer.*

as well as being a warrior. She protected all heroes who fought for the good of mankind, such as Heracles and Theseus, and aided all who represented the ideals of Hellenism such as Ulysses, the whole race of the Achaeans during the Trojan War, and most of all, the people of Athens whose special patron she was. Like Artemis, but with less prudish sensitivity, Athena preserved her virginity. At a very early date, Greek artists endowed her with attributes which made her easily recognisable at first sight: a helmet, lance, and especially her shield, a goat-skin on which the petrifying head of the Gorgon was attached. Her favourite bird was the owl. Despite her warlike panoply, which was defensive rather than offensive, Athena presided over many peaceful activities; she was invoked by women spinning and weaving, by workers and by craftsmen. She was represented on the base of Phidias's great gold and ivory statue in the Parthenon helping Hephaestus bring the clay figure of Pandora to life.

ATHENAEUS. Athenaeus was a sophist and grammarian of the 3rd century A.D., born at Naucratis in Egypt. His *Deipnosophists,* which he seems to have published in about 230, is an immense, erudite compilation which was later abridged by revisers. The setting of the work is a banquet, following the tradition established by Plato in his *Symposium,* Xenophon, and Plutarch in his *Quaestiones Convivales.* A rich Roman pontiff, Larentius, invites numerous friends, who are all specialists in different branches of knowledge, to a dinner. This rather indigestible work

contains many curious and instructive passages and innumerable quotations from authors whose works no longer survive, and is consequently a precious source of knowledge for almost every aspect of ancient life and customs. R.F.

ATHENS. The city of Athens already existed during the Mycenaean period but it was only a small town and far inferior in importance to Argos or Mycenae although the remains of an impressive palace and fortifications of the time have been discovered. According to ancient tradition, one of the kings of Athens, Theseus, extended his rule over all the different villages surrounding Athens, which had been hitherto independent, in order to form a single kingdom (the process was known as synoecism) and defended his state against various enemies, the most notable being the Amazons. The names of all his successors were preserved, including the last, Cecrops, who had sacrificed his life for the common good. Athens does not seem to have suffered overmuch from the Dorian invasions, for Attica was protected in the north-west by the barrier of the Cithaeron and the city was not rich enough to excite the cupidity of the invaders. It seems that the ancient Greeks were right in supposing that Athens was the point of departure for numerous emigrants who settled on the islands or Asia Minor; it would explain the close contacts that the city was able to maintain with the Ionian civilisation. In any event, it is quite certain that during this kind of medieval period in Greece at the beginning of the Iron Age, Athens had already become a leading centre of civilisation through its industry and commerce. Athenian ceramics were of a high quality and were exported not only to neighbouring regions but as far as Delphi, Ithaca, Thessaly and the coast of Asia Minor. At this time it was governed by a small number of aristocrats, the Eupatridae, who were both land-owners and ship-owners, whose vessels were able to ensure the city's hegemony and to carry its products to distant lands. Tombs of the Eupatridae have been found in the cemetery of the Dipylon. They were surmounted by enormous vases bearing scenes of their exploits and their retinues of serv-

ants who took part in the funeral ceremonies. Almost all these aristocrats must have lived on the Acropolis like the kings whose powers they shared, but nothing now remains of the architecture of this period.

Like all the other Greek states, Athens was torn by civil strife provoked by the greed of the aristocrats in the 8th and 7th centuries B.C. As everywhere else the people endeavoured to obtain control of the executive power, the law, and the economy, despite the opposition of their rulers. Even before the 7th century had drawn to a close, a certain Cylon had tried to seize power, but he failed in his endeavour (628). A few years later Draco codified the laws that were later to be considered archaically ferocious, but nonetheless they represented a considerable progress since they were written down on tablets that could be consulted by anyone, which put an end to the arbitrary power of the judges. But civil harmony was far from having been achieved and the condition of the common people remained as precarious as ever. The early years of the 6th century were marked by the powerful personality of Solon, who had become famous after leading his fellow-citizens in the conquest of Salamis. He made an attempt to reform the economic and social structure of the state and established just and human agreements between debtors and creditors by measures whose details are no longer known to us. He also wrote poems which include allusions, now unfortunately obscure, to the very real benefits of his administration. He was also responsible for political progress and it was during his administration that the first timid steps were taken towards a form of democracy. The Athenians had to wait for the intervention of a tyrant before many of their problems could be resolved; it was during the reign of Pisistratus (561-528 B.C.), twice interrupted by revolutions, that the city reached an unprecedented degree of splendour and prosperity. Although we do not know how, we do know that when his sons and successors, Hipparchus and Hippias, were respectively assassinated and overthrown (514 and 510) the social problem had been resolved.

We also know that the appearance of the city had completely changed during the fifty years' du-

Athena Promachos. Bronze statuette found on the Acropolis at Athens. 6th century B.C. Athens, National Museum. *Photo Spyros Meletris.*

ration of the tyranny that he had established. Temples had either been built or embellished on the Acropolis and in the lower city; the Hecatompedon was one of the most important. Fountains had been built, the most notable being that of Callirhoë.

Deprived of political power by Pisistratus, the aristocracy still played an important social role but the ranks of the wealthy were swelled by many newcomers of common descent, and merchants and manufacturers were henceforth able to make lavish offerings to the gods. A great quantity of korai and kouroi, reliefs, panel paintings and vase paintings date from this time and their remains have been found on the sacred hill of the Acropolis. Much of this new wealth was due to the export of manufactured products and especially the pottery that Athenian ships sold in the ports of Etruria and elsewhere. It was at this time, in the course of the 6th century, that Athens began to take on the aspect of a great city. The centre was still on the steep—sided hill of the Acropolis that dominated the surrounding plain, but the main part of the city was built on the northern part of the plain next to the ruins of an old cemetery, which had been disused for more than a century, and consisted of humble dwellings which huddled closely together, separated by narrow winding streets, mostly inhabited by the craftsmen and the potters who gave the name of Ceramicus to a whole district. The market place, or agora, had not yet taken on its monumental aspect. The rock of the Areopagus, which faced the Acropolis to the north-east, was where the tribunals held their sessions. The southern part of the city was still largely uninhabited and it was there that Pisistratus laid the foundations of a gigantic temple whose construction was almost immediately interrupted.

Once the Athenians had resolved their most pressing financial problems, they followed the general trend in the whole of Greece by aspiring after political liberty and freed themselves from the tyranny in 510. Under the guidance of Cleisthenes, a regime was established which might already be considered as democratic, but it did not really come into its own until from about 450 onwards in the century of Pericles. From about the last years of the 6th century, the executive power lay in the hands of all the citizens who met in a deliberative assembly, justice was administered by popular tribunals, and except during a brief interval, property qualifications were no longer demanded from candidates for administrative posts. This regime was in the process of establishing itself, not without some difficulties when the whole of Greece was faced by one of the greatest threats in its history; in 490 the Persian army, led by Darius, made a deep incursion into Greek territory until it was turned back by Miltiades and the Athenian army at Marathon. Ten years later it was the Athenians again who led the resistance against a new Persian offensive and who won the victories of Salamis and Plataea under the leadership of Themistocles. These brilliant successes did more than all the splendour of Pisistratus's reign to make Athens one of the foremost cities in Greece, the equal and the rival of Sparta, which was then considered the greatest state in the whole of the Hellenic world.

In a few years, Athens rose again from her ruins and created a real empire by her skilful policies while she fought against both the Persians on one hand and her Greek enemies on the other. The master of this empire, between 448 and 429, was Pericles, a wise statesman who respected the laws and the forms of the democracy he himself had done so much to promote, while at the same time persuading his fellow citizens to keep him in power and follow the policies he had originated. This was the most brilliant period in the city's life. With the aid of Phidias, Pericles raised the buildings on the Acropolis which alone would have sufficed to ensure his glory for posterity, while tragedy and comedy flourished in the Greek theatre. The citizens lived in ease on the prosperous commerce of their city and the enforced tributes brought each year by the other Greek cities who had joined Athens to fight against the Persians and had been reduced practically to the rank of subjects of their all-powerful ally.

The Peloponnesian War, which divided the whole of Greece into two armed camps, ranged around Sparta and Athens respectively, brought this golden age to an end. In 404 B.C. Lysander captured the city and imposed an oligarchic regime on its citizens, exacted an enormous financial tribute and destroyed its fleet. Even after expelling the government of the Thirty Tyrants set up by the enemy, and after forming a new confederation in 377, similar to that which she had organised a century earlier against the Persians, Athens never regained the prestige and prosperity she had enjoyed in the time of Pericles. She still took part in the struggles for supremacy between the Greek states which lasted until the Macedonian con-

Jumping, wrestling and javelin-throwing. Attic bas-relief. About 510 B.C. Athens, National Museum.

quest, but proved incapable, despite Demosthenes' *Philippics*, of resisting Philip of Macedon's offensives and her political role came to an end when Alexander captured the city. From then onwards, Athens was a city like any other with its municipal crises and longings for independence, but in reality ready for total domination which became its fate when it was conquered by the Romans in 146 B.C.

Athens might be a subject city but it was still important. The crises of the 4th century did not diminish the city's artistic activity; it remained the home of such great artists as Praxiteles, and was embellished with beautiful buildings, in particular its marble theatre and agora, which was gradually surrounded by porticoes. Imperceptibly it became the city-museum whose splendour so excited the enthusiasm of the rich Atticus, who has left us a striking picture of the city's splendour in the letters he sent to his friend, Cicero. No man's education was accounted complete if he had not visited the city, listened to the speeches of its philosophers and orators, and imbibed the spirit of its glorious past. As a result, the generosity of foreigners, governors and emperors further enriched the city with new monuments. The Acropolis and its surroundings became crowded with buildings which were not always of the highest quality, such as the Roman Odeum built at his own expense by Herodes Atticus in 161 A.D. beside the theatre of Dionysus, and the library founded by Hadrian that prolonged an already enlarged agora towards the north. The gigantic temple of the Olympieum, whose foundations had been laid by Pisistratus was finally built. But when

the schism occurred between the Roman empire of the west and that of the east in the 4th century A.D., Athens no longer had any chance of becoming the chief city of the eastern Mediterranean again, for it was Constantinople that was henceforth to represent the new Hellenism, a Hellenism that had been transformed by the new Christian religion. Athens had been too profoundly penetrated by its past beliefs to be able to survive the new faith.   P.D.

ATHLETES. The important part played by gymnastic exercises in education (q.v.) in Athens and other towns and especially in Sparta, served to prepare young Greeks to become champions and athletes like those who competed against each other in the panhellenic games, whose victors were immortalised by Pindar's odes. Thucydides wrote: " The Lacedaemonians were the first to show themselves completely naked in public and would rub themselves with oil before taking part in sporting contests. In olden times, athletes would wear a garment like trunks even when taking part in Olympic contests. " The vital equipment for an athlete consisted of a sponge for ablutions, a small bottle of oil *(alabastron)* and a bronze scraper or comb (strigil) which was a sort of spatula with a groove and one, curved end, which was necessary for scraping the skin clean of its layer of oil and dust mingled with sweat.

The five tests of the *pentathlon* were: running, jumping, wrestling, discus and javelin throwing. The pentathlon, boxing and the pancratium were the classic forms of Greek athleticism which does not seem to have included swimming even though

Running race. Detail
of a black-figure
Panathenaic amphora.
About 530 B.C.
New York,
Metropolitan
Museum of Art.

children were taught to swim at an early age. In jumping, the Greeks only seem to have practised the running long jump. The athletes would jump holding a stone or lead dumb-bell in each hand in order to reinforce the swinging of the arms. The famous athlete, Phayllus of Croton, was supposed to have made a jump of 55 feet in this way. Wrestlers would fight with head lowered, arms outstretched and try to seize each other by the wrists, the neck or the waist in order to throw their adversary while remaining themselves upright. Each match consisted of three bouts.

During the contests, pairs of wrestlers were drawn by lot with beans of which two were marked with an alpha, two with a beta, etc. If there was an uneven number of contestants, five for example, one bean marked with a gamma was put in the urn and whoever drew it was kept in reserve to fight the winner of one of the first fights, between whom lots were drawn a second time and so on. The discus was made of bronze and might weigh as much as eight pounds. The throwing-point was only marked out in front and on the sides. The discus was rubbed with sand

Boxing. Detail of a
black-figure
Panathenaic
amphora. 6th century
B.C. Paris, Louvre.

Discus thrower. Detail of a krater by the Cleophrades Painter. About 500 B.C. Tarquinia Museum. *Ph. Hirmer.*

time-limit to boxing matches and no rounds. The same applied to the pancratium which was a more brutal sport because almost every kind of blow was allowed including kicks and punches, as well as a wrestling-hold and twisting of limbs, etc. All that was forbidden was to poke one's fingers in the eyes of one's opponent. The fight ended when one of the combattants was worn out and raised an arm to show that he gave in. Spattered with blood and rolling in the mud, these pancratiats must have presented a very different spectacle from that imagined by the neoclassical poets when they wrote of " naked athletes under the blue skies of Hellas ". The winning athletes were the gods of the stadium and the great honour of having gained a victory in the panhellenic games reflected on the family and the city of the victor. The Athenian Olympic athletes were fed at the expense of the state in the Prytaneum. It was said that one city even tore down part of its walls so that the winning athlete might enter by a gateway that none had been through before him. *(See* Games; Stadium). R.F.

ATLANTIS. Atlantis was a fabled continent which was supposed to have been situated in the south Atlantic and overwhelmed by the rising of the waters. In the *Timaeus* and the surviving fragment of the *Critias* Plato has given a

to prevent it from slipping in the fingers. The spot where it fell was marked with a peg so that the throws of the various contestants could be measured. Myron's statue, the *Discobolus,* faithfully reproduces the second phase of the discus thrower's movement, after he has first pivoted on his own axis. The javelin was frequently used in hunting and warfare. That used by athletes was without a point in order to avoid accidents but one end was weighted; at its centre of gravity it was given a lace sling to make it rotate in flight and thereby increase its range. It was used for target practice and also for long-distance throwing competitions. For boxing, athletes wore leather straps wound round their hands. There was no

Athletes jumping with the help of jumping-weights. Cup attributed to the Euergides Painter. Last quarter of the 6th century B.C. Paris, Louvre.

Bronze discus. About 500 B.C. It weighs about 8 lbs., double the weight of the modern discus. Vienna, Kunsthistorisches Museum.

wondering and detailed description of this immense island which was as large as Asia and Africa united, a kind of Eldorado where justice reigned during the golden age of the reign of the god, Poseidon. The Atlanteans had tried to conquer the world and had gone to war with Athens but had been defeated by the city some 9000 years before the time of Plato, who lived in the 4th century B.C. In modern times, certain geographers and geologists have tended to favour the theory of the existence of such a continent, stretching from the shores of Africa to those of America and embracing the isles of Cap Verde, the Canaries and Madeira. Observations of flora and fauna have seemed to indicate a kind of relationship between the coastlines of Africa and South America, whose outlines seem vaguely to fit, thus favouring the hypothesis of " the drift of the continents ". Plato's Atlantis probably has no more historical reality than Bacon's *New Atlantis* or Pierre Benoit's famous novel *L'Atlantide*.   R.F.

ATLAS. Like his brothers who had been defeated by Zeus, Atlas also had to suffer punishment for his rebellion and it was he who had to bear the weight of the celestial vault on his shoulders. He helped Heracles to steal the Golden Apples from the garden of the Hesperides for Eurystheus, either by showing him the way to this place of marvels or, according to the most popular and most frequently illustrated version of the legend, by shifting the sky onto Heracles in order to fetch the precious fruits himself and bring them faithfully back to the son of Zeus and Alcmene. According to other sources, he tried to rid himself for ever of the burden that he had trans-

ferred onto Heracles' shoulders, but when the hero threatened to let it fall he took it back again.   P.D.

ATRIDAE. In art and literature no family is better known for its tragic destiny than that of the Atridae. The founder of the family, Atreus, was the son of Pelops and Hippodamia who may still be seen sculptured on the pediment of the temple of Zeus at Olympia at the moment when the chariot race was about to start that was eventually to dispossess and cause the death of Oenomaus, the former master of the Peloponnesus. Atreus's younger brother was Thyestes and when they were cursed by their father they took refuge in Mycenae at the court of Eurystheus. Upon Eurystheus' death, Atreus was called upon to succeed to the throne. Political jealousy and rivalry in love caused an unrelenting hatred to flare up between the two brothers. Atreus secretly killed Thyestes' three sons, cut them to pieces and served them up to their father in the course of a banquet and, after revealing to Thyestes the secret of what he had eaten, he drove him from the kingdom. Another son of Thyestes then avenged his father by killing Atreus. The king had left two sons: Agamemnon who was king of Mycenae and Menelaus who reigned over Sparta. The curse which hung over the family struck them both, but with unequal severity. By marrying Helen, Menelaus condemned himself to the fate that has made him famous, whereas Agamemnon was recognised as chief by all the Greeks of the time and married Helen's sister, Clytemnestra, by whom he had several children. When he was chosen to lead the panhellenic expedition against Troy, he was obliged to begin by sacrificing his own daughter, Iphigenia, whose death was demanded by Artemis before she would grant the Greeks a wind to take their vessels across the sea to Troy. During the ten years that the Greek army was encamped below the walls of Troy, Clytemnestra took Aegisthus for a lover, perhaps to avenge herself for the death of her daughter and it was in a doom-laden atmosphere that the young Orestes, Agamemnon's son, grew to manhood. After Troy had fallen and Agamemnon returned to his palace, accompanied by his captive, Cassandra, he was murdered by Aegisthus whose arm was guided by Clytemnestra. Orestes killed the two lovers to avenge his father and was then pursued as a parricide by divine vengeance. He was tracked down by the pack of the Erinyes, or Furies, and only found peace when Apollo himself purified him on the omphalos at Delphi. According to the Athenians, Orestes had only been purified after a tribunal composed of their ancestors and presided over by Athena had met on the rock of the Areopagus (q.v.) in their city and decided on the acquittal of the accursed hero. Orestes then became king of Mycenae in his turn and the story was told how, after his acquittal, he had first gone to Tauris in southern Russia on Apollo's orders, where he had found his sister Iphigenia who had been miraculously saved by Artemis at the very moment when she was about to be offered up as a sacrificial victim by her father, and brought her back together with a statue of the goddess whose priestess Iphigenia had become.

Several very different elements may be detected in this complicated story. Some belong to universal mythology and others may perhaps belong to a historic reality that became distorted with time like the epic of Charlemagne. Certainly, the relationship between Agamemnon and his Greek vassals as described by the *Iliad* seems to correspond with reality and the fact of Argolis's political supremacy cannot be contested. What made the celebrity of this unhappy, fate-haunted, and partially legendary family in Greek literature and thought was the fact that it provided a striking example of the force of destiny; for since the very beginning, when Pelops had gained power in the Peloponnesus at the price of Oenomaus' death, and since he had cursed both his sons, the curse had fallen on all the descendants and had made its blinded victims commit a number of crimes for which the direct responsability—as the judges of the Areopagus were the first to realise—was to be imputed to the fates alone.   P.D.

ATTALUS I. Attalus I was the first sovereign to reign officially over the kingdom of Pergamum, but he was not the founder of his country's glory and prosperity. The beginnings of Pergamum had been modest enough; Lysimachus had appointed one of his officers, Philetaerus, to keep guard over Alexander's treasure in this eagle's nest. Philetaerus had betrayed his commander and appropriated the money which had allowed him to aid Seleucus at the time of the battle of Corupedium (281 B.C.) and thus gain the friendship of the Syrian dynasty. The treasure was still an important factor when his nephew, Eumenes, known as Eumenes I, succeeded him as the governor of the province and obtained recognition of its independence in 261. When Attalus, Eumenes' nephew, succeeded him, he was able to profit from the weakness of the Seleucids by proclaiming himself king, a title that he transferred to Eumenes II in 197.

This was a magnificent period for the small state, wisely governed by intelligent princes who unscrupulously extended its frontiers. With the aid of the Egyptians, its rulers followed a consistently hostile policy against the Seleucids from whom they acquired new provinces, the most notable being the whole of the Aegean littoral, from the Dardanelles to the gulf of Smyrna. The arts also flourished. When Attalus I defeated the Galatians, he commemorated his victory by an offering of four marble groups of sculpture on the Acropolis of Athens and it was also to glorify his victory that Eumenes II built the great altar to Zeus at Pergamum, which was to have such a great influence on Hellenistic art. Eumenes II was not content with merely embellishing his capital and founded numerous towns and developed the country's economy. His armies defeated the Galatians, Pharnaces king of Pontus, and Prusias of Bithynia. He was succeeded by his brother, Attalus II, in 159 and the new king won the friendship of the Romans to whom Attalus III, the last ruler of Pergamum, left his treasures and territories at his death in 133.   P.D.

ATTICA. We cannot fully understand the history of Athens if we consider it in isolation from the province whose capital it became, probably about the 12th century B.C., after the political unification of the area that was credited to Theseus and known by the name of synoecism. The area of Attica only covered some 1100 square miles. It was composed of a triangular peninsula whose base, in the north-west, was formed by the rocky barrier of Cithaeron and the Cerata mountains, while the other two sides were bounded by the sea, the extreme south-east point formed by Cape Sunium. The coast-line, known as Paralia, measured some 120 miles and was very indented. The mountain region alone, Diacria, covered some 600 square miles, the main peaks being those of Parnes (5453 feet), Pentelicus (3638 feet), and Hymettus (3368 feet). The plains, or Pedion, lay in the mountain valleys except for those of

Eleusis, Mesogaea and Marathon which covered a wider area. There was little water and the Illissus and the Cephisus, which run through Athens, were among the few rivers that watered the country when it had rained sufficiently.

The mountains provided stone and marble (Pentelic), the little Laurium mass in the south held silver bearing lead deposits from which the Athenians made a considerable profit and the sea was rich in fish along the coast-line; agriculture was confined to the plains and was not enough to feed the whole population. Even during the time of Athens' greatest glory, the inhabitants were mainly a country people and the citizens nearly all owned land, whether it was a small plot or a vast plantation, somewhere outside the city walls and it was from their fields quite as much as from their professions that they made their living. The peasants were reluctant to come to Athens and it was a real disaster for them when war forced them to take refuge in the city.

The economic and sentimental ties that bound the country people and the townsmen together were reinforced by the administrative system. It was in order to break the social classes of the past that Cleisthenes grouped all the citizens of Attica together in ten tribes in 508 B.C. Each tribe was formed one third of city-dwellers, one third of coast-dwellers, and the remaining third with inhabitants of the hinterland. As the tribes represented the political unity of the new democratic state, a fusion was accomplished between town and country. But this did not prevent territorial districts from being constituted throughout the whole of Attica, Athens included, which were known as demes and were vital to the organisation of the state.   P.D.

AULIS. The town of Aulis was named after a bay in the passage separating Euboea from the mainland, on the eastern coast of Attica some miles from Euripus. It was an insignificant town and its fame is only due to the fact that it was there that the Greek fleet assembled before sailing to Troy, and Agamemnon had to sacrifice his daughter Iphigenia before the goddess Artemis would send the expedition a wind for sailing.   P.D.

BACCHYLIDES. Lyric poet, born at Iulis in the isle of Ceos, and a near contemporary of Pindar (520-440 B.C.). Bacchylides was the maternal nephew of the great poet, Simonides,

who may have given him his first lessons in poetry and music. After a democratic revolution, he was banished from Ceos and settled in the Peloponnesus. Before his exile he had sent a triumphal ode to Hieron, the tyrant of Syracuse. As Hieron liked to gather poets and artists around him, he invited Bacchylides to his court where Simonides and Pindar were also residing. All that was known of Bacchylides' work was a few short fragments until 1897 when an Egyptian papyrus was discovered containing some twenty of his poems, most of which were mutilated, though some were almost intact. They included *epinikia* (odes composed in honour of victors in athletic games), heroic hymns, paeans and dithyrambs. In his treatise *On the Sublime*, Longinus said that Bacchylides was " an impeccable poet whose style was brilliant and perfect " and indeed it was clear, flowing, and decorative. Although his songs are lit by a consistent gentle inspiration, they have none of the lightning strokes of genius that distinguish many of Pindar's works.   R.F.

BAND (SACRED). The Sacred Band was composed of élite Theban troops at the beginning of the short period during which the city practically dominated the whole of Greece, and was founded by Epaminondas and Pelopidas (qq.v.). The Band was formed by three hundred young men of noble family who fought in pairs united by lifelong friendship, and it particularly distinguished itself at the battle of Leuctra in 371 B.C.   P.D.

BANQUET. The Spartans used to eat regularly in common and their meals were known as *syssitia*. The Greeks of other cities were also greatly given to banquets and almost any pretext served as an excuse for a *symposion*, such as a family festival, a city festival, success in a sporting, musical or theatrical competition, the arrival or departure of a friend. The exact meaning of the word *symposion* was " a meeting of drinkers ". All dinners to which guests were invited or banquets of a religious confraternity *(thiasos)* were divided into two halves: first, the meal properly speaking, to satisfy the hunger of the guests, and then a gathering in which wine was drunk, conversation was made, word-games were played, music and dancing and other amusements entertained the guests. It must not be thought that there was no drinking in the first part and no eating in the second. Eating and drinking continued throughout the whole of the banquet, and the guests would nibble at fresh or dried fruits, cakes, and grilled beans and chick-peas in order to stimulate their thirst throughout the evening. Freewomen were rigorously excluded from banquets and only serving maids, female musicians, dancers and courtesans were allowed to appear.

A banquet was called an *eranos* when members of a club *(hetairoi)* met in turn at each other's homes and each brought his share of food and drink. More often, the banquet would be given by a host who was rich enough to pay all the expenses. Invitations were sometimes spontaneous when a friend might be encountered in the street or some public place and be invited to dinner on the spot. Greek comedies satirise parasites who would haunt public places in the hope of being wined and dined at no expense to themselves. When they arrived at their host's house, the guests took off their shoes to have their feet washed by slaves before entering the banqueting room, crowned with garlands of leaves or flowers. They ate in a reclining position, usually with their legs stretched out on a couch, the upper part of their body propped up by cushions and bolsters, but women and children would eat in their quarters seated on chairs. Each banqueting couch was usually large enough to hold two or three guests. The tables were small, easily portable and usually round and there might be one for each guest or couch. Slaves would serve prepared portions of each dish in bowls and plates. As soon as the guests had taken their places, servants would bring them ewers and basins so that they could wash their hands, a particularly useful custom since fingers were used for eating (knives and spoons were also used but forks were unknown). The meal began with a kind of aperitif, the *propoma,* a cup of aromatic wine which was passed round the table. No napkins were used and guests wiped their hands with pieces of bread which they then threw, with bones and other leavings, to the dogs of the household who wandered between the tables and couches. The symposion properly speaking began with customary libations in honour of the gods and especially Dionysus, the god of wine. The libation rite consisted in drinking a small quantity of undiluted wine and then scattering a few drops while invoking the name of the god before singing a hymn to Dionysus. Next, the " king of the banquet " *(symposiarchos)* was chosen, usually by lot. His main duty was to decide the proportion of wine to water in the krater and how many cups each guest was to quaff. Anyone who disobeyed the symposiarchos was punished by a kind of forfeit, such as having to dance naked or run round the room three times carrying a female flute-player in his arms. Banquets frequently ended in general drunkenness.

The frequency of banquets in the lives of the

Banqueting scene. Heracles at the house of Eurytus. Detail of a Corinthian krater. About 590 B.C. Paris, Louvre. *Photo Giraudon.*

Bassae. Temple of
Apollo Epicurius.
End of the
5th century B.C.
Photo Hirmer.

Greeks gave rise to a literary genre, for example Plato's *Symposium,* Xenophon's work of the same title, Plutarch's *Symposiaca* and Athenaeus's *Deipnosophists.*

Of all these works, Xenophon's *Symposium* appears to give the most faithful description of a Greek banquet. A foolish parasite, Philip, asks for a dinner to be given for him and his slave and in exchange he undertakes, without any great success, to make the other guests laugh. " As soon as the tables had been taken away, libations made and the paean sung ", that is as soon as the symposion proper, after the meal, had begun, a Syracusan impresario appeared with a troupe of three young performers to offer an entertainment consisting, as we should say, of several music hall and cabaret turns. The impresario had certainly been hired in advance by the master of the house, Callias, to amuse his guests. After a concert given by the flute and cithara players, Callias suggests that perfumes be brought as usual, but Socrates objects. A young dancing girl of the troupe then juggles to the rhythm of the flute with twelve hoops and executes a series of daring somersaults over a circle of swords. A boy then dances and sings to his own accompaniment on the cithara. Meanwhile the guests continue to converse. Following a suggestion by Socrates, they all state which virtue or art they prefer and try to prove its merit. Later, they amuse themselves

with a " portraits' game " and Socrates sings them a song himself. Finally, the Syracusan has his troupe perform a kind of mime in which the male and female dancers play the parts of Ariadne and Dionysus at Naxos to the accompaniment of the flute. This graceful spectacle soon became very realistic and suggestive so that " seeing the young people in close embrace as though they were about to go to bed together, the bachelor guests swore that they would soon marry and those who were already married mounted their horses and galloped off to their wives ". A game of skill that was often played at banquets was *kottabos (See* Toys and Amusements). R.F.

BARBARIAN. Our xenophobia has inevitably given the word " barbarian " a pejorative sense that it did not originally have for the Greeks, for they simply used the word to denote all non-Greek peoples (another word, translatable as " foreigner ", designated all Hellenes from another town). The Barbarians might either be almost completely savage tribes or else such civilised peoples as the Persians and Egyptians whose wisdom was admired by the whole of Greece, and who contributed much to Greek civilisation. To the Greeks the main characteristics of all these " barbarians " or " non-Greeks " were that they all spoke incomprehensible tongues which sounded " like the twittering of birds "; they blindly

81

Young girl having a bath. Cup by Onesimos. About 480 B.C. Brussels, Musée du Cinquantenaire. *Photo Hirmer.*

accepted the authority of sovereigns who were above all laws and considered themselves essentially superior to other mortals; they worshipped gods who were not in the image of man; and, in general, lacked confidence in the human condition and the fundamental qualities of humanity, in the humanity that the Greek gods themselves, despite their superiority, never failed to respect.
P.D.

BASSAE. The temple of Bassae, standing amidst mountains in the very heart of Arcadia, is one of the best preserved in the whole of Greece. It was built by the inhabitants of the neighbouring town of Phigaleia as a sign of gratitude to Apollo who had saved their region from the plague. The architect was Ictinus (q.v.) who also built the Parthenon. Like the Parthenon, the temple was built in the Doric order but in a somewhat different style; the inner colomns are attached to the wall of the *naos* by spur walls; there is a side as well as a main entrance; and the back of the naos is isolated by a Corinthian column, the oldest known to us. The frieze is now in the British Museum and represents a combat between Greeks and Centaurs.
P.D.

BATHING. Greek children learnt to bathe and swim in rivers and in the sea at an early age and in Sparta they bathed daily in the river Eurotas all through the year, even in winter. A proverb said that " he is a fool who can neither swim nor read ". In the 6th century B.C., Pisistratus and his sons provided Athens with monumental fountains where the women would come to fill their water-jugs, but the spouts were placed sufficiently high for one to be able to take a shower bath beneath them. Such bathing scenes have been found in several Greek black-figure vase paintings. Palaestrae and gymnasia (qq.v.) contained bath tubs and round swimming-pools. In the classical period, the Greeks not only took baths to clean themselves, they also used the bath as a place to relax as Homer's heroes did long before. The bath tubs were either built in moulded terracotta, stone, or small bricks dipped into a mortar and covered with glaze. The baths at Olynthus are more or less rectangular in shape and one end is raised to provide a seat as in modern sitting-baths. They were without a drainhole. They were not deep enough for the body to be completely immersed and the bather either had to sprinkle himself or be sprinkled by a servant with a vase

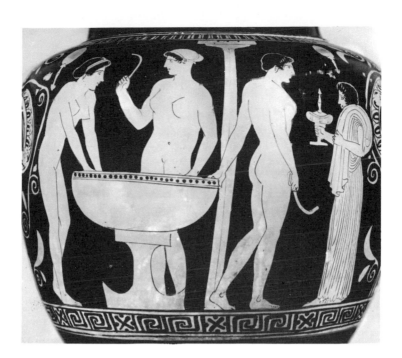

Young women holding strigils at their toilet. Detail of an Attic stamnos. 5th century B.C. Boston, Museum of Fine Arts.

or a sponge. Shallow metal bowls on a tripod with the legs shaped like lions' claws were used for foot-baths. The most usual washing tub in the classical period seems to have consisted of a large, deep, circular tub supported by a high pedestal which widened towards the base and was surmounted by a capital which was usually Ionic. This was the type of bath most frequently depicted inside houses and palaestrae in scenes from red-figure vases. The tubs were made of stone or terra-cotta and were both filled and emptied by hand, heated water being used in winter. From the 5th century onwards, and particularly in the 4th century, the city of Athens possessed several public bathing establishments which included swimming-pools and shallow bath tubs like those found at Olynthus. The tubs were set around a circular hall, and several of these rotundas were transformed into sweating-rooms. The " master of the baths " (balaneus) took the minimum entrance fees (two chalkoi, the equivalent of about 2/3 of a halfpenny) and supervised the work of the slaves or " bath boys " who looked after the heating, sprinkled the bathers, and then rubbed them with oils. The public baths were also used as a place for meeting friends and for conversation

and, in winter, poor people would stay as long as possible to take advantage of the cheap heating. There was no soap and an impure sodium carbonate, a solution of potassium extracted from wood cinders (also used for washing clothes) or a special clay from the Cycladic island of Cimolus was used. In the 3rd century, the Syracusans in the reign of Theocritus used to wash their hands with a kind of thin, creamy paste.

It was customary to take a bath before the evening meal so that the expression " to take a bath " was practically synonymous with " dining ". In Plato's *Symposium,* when Socrates was invited by the poet, Agathon, he is described as arriving " well washed and wearing sandals, which was unusual for him ". R.F.

BATHYCLES of MAGNESIA. Architect and sculptor, born in Ionia. In about 530 B.C, Bathycles was called to Sparta where he built a curious monument known as the *Throne of Amyclae* which brought the Ionian spirit of exuberance and profusion into the rather dry severity of Spartan art. By its complexity of style, the *Throne of Amyclae* seems to have disconcerted even the prolix Pausanias. By his description, and the remaining vestiges, it would appear to have been a monumental complex which comprised porticoes with galleries and sacred chambers surrounding an altar, possibly in the Ionian style, which constituted the base for an archaic statue, a *xoanon* of Apollo. R.M.

BELLEROPHON. A Corinthian hero. It was said that his real father was not Glaucus, son of Sisyphus, who had married his mother, but Poseidon. Because of a murder, Bellerophon was obliged to exile himself to Tiryns where he was purified by the king, Proetus, but the king later suspected him of making love to his wife and sent him to the court of Iobates, king of Lycia, who had been asked to put him to death. Iobates ordered Bellerophon to kill the Chimaera, which was a monster with the body of a lion, a flame-breathing goat's head sprouting out of his back, and a serpent for a tail. Mounted on the winged horse Pegasus, Bellerophon flew through the sky and effortlessly slew the Chimaera to the great surprise of Iobates, who thought he would never return. He was then sent on several other perilous expeditions but as he always returned triumphant, Iobates finally recognised his divine origin and left him his kingdom of Lycia. The hero then returned again to Corinth to punish Proetus's wife who had falsely accused him before her husband. She tried to flee on Pegasus but the horse threw her and she fell to her death. P.D.

BOEOTIA. The Athenians had maliciously spread the widely held belief in ancient times that Boeotia was a province exclusively peopled by boors. This supposed dull-wittedness of the Boeotians was readily attributed to geographical reasons, for the province was surrounded by mountains with only a few passes, such as the Cithaeron chain, and only had indirect access to the sea, into the Euboic Gulf. The climate was stifling, but the land was particularly fertile so that the main occupation of the inhabitants was with their fields and their cattle. But it should not be forgotten that both Hesiod and Pindar came from Boeotia, and that a considerable number of works of art were found in the archaic sanctuaries of Orchomenus and Ptoios, which may not have been as beautiful as those of Athens but which still merited great admiration and esteem. Also in Boeotia was Tanagra, world famous for its delicate pottery figures. Even before archaeological excavations had revealed the remains of Boeotian grandeur in Mycenaean times, it was obvious that the historical importance of Boeotia in the 2nd millennium B.C. was scarcely inferior to that of Argolis; for this was the region that had given birth

Bellerophon. Melian terra-cotta. About 475-450 B.C. British Museum.

84

to the legends of such heroes as Heracles, born in the palace of Amphitryon, Oedipus, and the Seven Chiefs whose exploits were immortalised in poetry and drama.

There were two distinct regions of Boeotia, one in a plain, with its capital at Thebes, the other on the slopes of the mountains, the site of the city of Orchomenus and of sanctuaries of famous heroes, such as that of Ptoios in the north-east and Tropho-nius in the west. The powerfully fortified island of Gla was surrounded by the lake of Copaïs which has now dried up. In the south, the names of Mount Helicon and the Vale of the Muses conjure up many famous poetical memories. Once it had lost its former splendour in the Mycenaean age—a splendour that can only be dimly glimpsed now—Boeotia only rarely played an important part in Greek history. It was an agricultural pro-vince covered with vast plantations and was al-most continuously governed by an oligarchy of great landed proprietors; there was never a suffi-ciently developed artisan class for a democratic constitution to evolve. But Boeotia did provide the rare and almost unique example of a confede-ration of cities that were obliged for mainly econo-mic reasons to group together while still preserv-ing their autonomy. From the middle of the 5th century B.C., not content with meeting in a reli-gious ceremony at the sanctuary of Athena Itonia, where decrees decided in common were written down on stone, they formed a common army commanded by ten Boeotarchs, and a common federal currency with coins bearing the symbols of the various cities on one side and the round, twin-notched Boeotian shield on the reverse. It was this Boeotian Confederacy that was later to be taken as a model for the Arcadian League. The ancient Greeks and especially the Athenians bitterly reproached the Boeotians with having betrayed the Hellenic cause during the Persian Wars, for Boeotian contingents had fought in Xerxes' army. The most brilliant period in Boeo-tian history was in the mid-4th century when Epa-minondas and Pelopidas (qq.v.) had shaken off Spartan domination to give Thebes and the Boeo-tian Confederacy a hegemony over the rest of Greece, but their success was short-lived for it did not survive Epaminondas and Thebes was later defeated and completely destroyed by Alexander in 336. Even the ruin of this city did not discourage the Boeotians, for in the late 4th century the enormous marsh of the Copaïs was drained for the first time. This gigantic enterprise later came to nothing from lack of maintenance, but it justified the following judgment that was then made on Heraclean Thebes: " an astonish-ing people for the faith they have in life ".   P.D.

BOOKS. Children learning to write at the school of the *grammatistes* used wooden tablets coated with wax on which they formed their characters with a stylet. The same kind of tablet was used by adults for making rough notes, but books were written with ink on rolls *(volumina)* of papyrus and also, later on, of parchment. The pith in the stems of the papyrus, a plant that grew principally in Egypt, was treated with a special process so that it could be written on and would retain the writing (q.v.). This process consisted in moistening the pith and pressing it flat into strips, which were stuck together lengthways to form a roll. A literary work of any length, the *Iliad* or *Odyssey* for example, could not have been contained on a single roll, which would have been too large and difficult to handle, and several were used for it. One consequence of this form of book was that early authors could not put a note at the side or foot of the text; the remarks, sometimes long ones, which a writer today would relegate to a footnote or an appendix at the end of his book, had to be integrated into the text and appear like digressions to us. The reader held the roll in his right hand and unrolled it as he read with his left, which at the same time rolled up the part he had finished.

Parchment *(Pergamene)*, made from sheepskin, got its name from the town of Pergamum, where it was said to have first been made. Parchment, because it was thicker than papyrus, would take writing on both sides, which is why under the Roman Empire the idea developed of arranging the leaves of parchment like a modern book and sewing them together in the margin to form the codex. R.F.

Young woman reading a scroll. Detail of a red-figure lekythos. About 440 B.C. Paris, Louvre.

BRASIDAS. Brasidas was one of the most distinguished figures in the Peloponnesian War. He was a skilful diplomat and brave general and during the first part of the war proved a formidable adversary to the Athenians. He was ordered by Sparta to lead an offensive in northern Greece, which was of vital importance to the Athenians, and in the space of a few months captured Acanthus, Stagira and Amphipolis. Brasidas was killed in 422 B.C. while defending Amphipolis against a counter-attack led by the strategus, Cleon. P.D.

BRAURON. Recent discoveries have focussed the attention of archaeologists on the sanctuary of Brauron near the east coast of Attica. It was already known that Artemis had been venerated there from earliest times. According to the legend, after the inhabitants had killed a she-bear, an animal sacred to the goddess, she demanded that she should be worshipped on the site of the killing, and that young girls between the ages of seven and eleven should be consecrated to her and serve her while living in her temple. Brauron was also supposed to be the burial place of Iphigenia after she had been sacrificed by her father in nearby Aulis. Excavations led on the site by J. Papademetriou have confirmed the tradition. In an architectural setting which included a temple, a portico and propylaea, all of the classical period, inscriptions, a great quantity of statuettes of young girls, and vases have been found, proving that the site had been consecrated to the worship of Artemis. P.D.

BREAD. This was a basic element in the Greek diet, particularly of the Athenians, who imported large quantities of cereals because their country could not produce sufficient for their needs *(See* Agriculture). Homer already called men "flour eaters". Round cakes of barley meal *(maza)* were eaten every day even by poor people and slaves. Bread made from wheat *(artos)* could only be eaten on feast days, according to one of Solon's laws, and was roughly shaped into a round ball. In early times, barley or wheat bread was baked in the house, but in Pericles' day, bakeries existed and by the 4th century B.C. the mistress of the house made the bread in the poorest homes only. Alexander's messengers, Plutarch tells us, were very surprised to find Phocion's wife busy kneading flour before she baked the household bread herself.   R.F.

BRIDGES.   In a country where most of the rivers are dry, except for a brief period when they are transformed into raging torrents, and where goods, if they were not sea-borne, were carried by donkey or mule, bridges had little importance. The river beds were crossed on foot and, if the current was too strong, time was not so precious that the travellers could not wait until it abated. Consequently, while the Romans were great bridge-builders, the Greeks hardly built any; they may have used wooden foot-bridges where necessary, which were repaired after the winter. However, we do know of the existence of several bridges. Some in Argolis seem to have been extremely old; they were of cyclopean construction, little more than thick walls with a narrow passage left in the middle for the water. Others were built with a much more skilled technique borrowed from the Romans in the age of imperial Rome; the bridge thrown over the Cephissus at Eleusis is an example. But the skilled design of a recently discovered bridge at Brauron in Attica, belonging to the 5th century B.C., shows that the Greek architects were expert in this branch of their work, too, when the need arose.
P.D.

BRISEIS.   Briseis was taken captive at Troy by Achilles and was tenderly loved by him, but was then delivered up to Agamemnon as a slave when he was obliged to return Chryseis to her father in order to appease the wrath of Apollo. Once deprived of his mistress, Achilles refused to take any more part in the war against Troy, but when he was reconciled with Agamemnon after Patroclus's death, Briseis was returned to him.
P.D.

BRONZE.   From the late 2nd millennium B.C., a bronze of copper and tin was already being made in the Aegean basin. Copper was not a rare metal in the Mediterranean countries, but tin had to be brought from afar, from northern Europe and also Britain. The peoples of ancient times used bronze for many purposes such as weapons, tools of all kinds, utensils, sculpture and coins.

Bronze is not a metal that withstands the ravages of time as well as is often believed but it is relatively precious, and in times of poverty, statues and other important bronze works were often melted down with the result that very little has survived of the immense bronze production of ancient times.

It was either hammered into shape or cast. It was usually beaten for thin objects such as a vase or cuirass, and in the archaic period, sculptors used to hammer it in thin sheets over a wooden core. Casting was reserved for heavier and more delicate works. Full casting, which consisted of pouring molten bronze into a hollow mould, was especially practised in primitive art and for small statues. Larger statues or welded attachments, such as the handles for a vase, were cast by the *cire perdue* process; the molten metal was poured into a narrow space between an inner core, or armature, and a matrix that was then broken open when the metal had cooled and hardened. If the statue was a large one, it was made with several pieces that had been cast separately and were

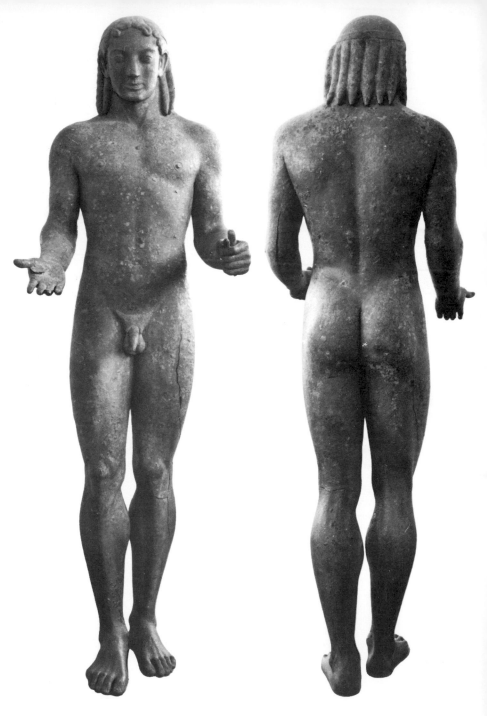

Kouros from Piraeus. Bronze statue. About 520 B.C. Athens, National Museum. *Photos Boudot-Lamotte*.

Horseman. Bronze statuette. About 550 B.C.
Athens, National Museum. *Photo Spyros Meletzis.*

The ephebe of Anticythera. End of the 4th century B.C.
Athens, National Museum. *Photo Hirmer.*

then soldered together. The whole object was worked over with a burin, a file and a polishing-tool; faults in the casting were covered over with incrusted pieces and an artificial patina was given to the work. Most great sculptors were bronze-workers and many marble statues in museums today are ancient replicas of works originally cast in bronze. P.D.

BRYGOS. Brygos was in the first rank of the magnificent, red-figure vase painters who

flourished around the year 500 B.C. We do not know whether it was he himself or an artist work-ing under his orders who painted the decoration on the vases he signed. He was, anyway, one of the purest representatives of Attic art and the vase in the Louvre painted with the scene of the taking of Troy is rightly considered to be a master-piece. P.D.

BURIAL. During some periods, the Greeks practised both burial and cremation; in other

Fall of Troy. Cup by Brygos. About 490 B.C. Paris, Louvre.

periods, one custom ór the other was followed. The tombs varied in aspect according to the procedure employed. Among the Cretans, as in Mycenaean civilisation, burial was the rule. Burials were often communal for, when nothing remained of the body but the skeleton, it was pushed aside if room was needed for a fresh corpse. Objects recovered from these tombs seem to show that it was believed necessary to place food and drink with the dead person, as well as his weapons and apparel, but their very nature makes the existence of any real funerary cult improbable. Some tombs, known as " chamber tombs " were tiny rooms cut into the rock. Access was by a long, narrow corridor called the *dromos* which would be blocked up and then opened again for each new burial. From the 15th century B.C. onwards, actual buildings shaped like bee-hives were built. They have been called cupola tombs or *tholoi* (sing. *tholos*). Larger thaǹ the chamber tombs, the *tholoi* were reserved for the princely families and also used to contain several bodies. The Dorian invasion brought the practice of cremation into Greece. Tombs then became nothing more than narrow graves dug in the ground and covered with a slab. The same type survived on a larger scale when the habit of burial was taken up again, without, however, completely abandoning the practice of cremation. The offerings that were placed in the coffin or near it were still very modest and were of a utilitarian nature which would lead us to suppose

that the Greeks had a belief in the at least temporary survival after death of the deceased.

Even in the earliest periods, the site of a tomb was marked by a mound or a vertical slab or stele. This custom survived throughout the whole of antiquity. Another custom, which only lasted a short time, was current in the first centuries of the 1st millennium B.C. A vase, often of colossal size, was placed on the tomb, with a perforated base through which libations might be poured at various times, which proves that a funerary cult existed at this time. From then onwards, the principle of burial never changed. Certain eastern regions in the Greek world followed Asiatic practices by often burying the dead in a chamber over which an artificial hillock or tumulus was raised. As a result, it was necessary to place the body not only in the modest wooden coffin used in ordinary tombs, but in a sarcophagus made of terra-cotta or carved in marble.   P.D.

BYZANTIUM. There was nothing in the early history of Byzantium to suggest that Constantine was to make it the glorious capital of a great empire in 330 A.D. It was then renamed Constantinople, the modern name being Istanbul. First founded by the Megarians before the mid-7th century B.C., it resembled many other cities throughout antiquity, but grew prosperous because of its key position on the Bosphorus. It had suffered the same fate as Ionia both before and during the Persian Wars and was as ready to revolt against Darius as to shrink from the consequent repression. It was freed by the Spartan king, Pausanias, after the battle of Plataea and entered the Delian League but vainly tried to leave it in 440 B.C. and hesitated between the two sides during the Peloponnesian War. Its policies were equally undecided during the first half of the 4th century; it concluded an alliance with Athens in 390, denounced it in 362, and in 340 called on Athens for help out of fear of Philip of Macedon. It only escaped Galatian occupation in 279 by paying a heavy tribute, and later allied itself with the Romans.   P.D.

CADMUS. Cadmus was a Phoenician and the brother of Europa. When she had been carried off by Zeus, Cadmus was ordered by his father to pursue her and sailed to the north of Greece. After many wanderings he consulted Apollo who told him to found a town at the spot where a magic cow would stop which Cadmus would be able to distinguish from its herd by the signs on its flanks. The place where the exhausted cow fell to earth was the site of Thebes, but before founding the new town Cadmus had to kill a dragon whose teeth, scattered on the earth, were immediately transformed into the Spartoi, savage warriors, who attacked Cadmus as soon as they were engendered, but then let him alone to massacre each other. Cadmus then founded Thebes, married Harmonia, and then left the throne to his grandson Pentheus and went to reign in Illyria.   P.D.

CALAMIS. Calamis was one of the most important of the sculptors working in the second quarter of the 5th century B.C., immediately before the great classical period. He was an Athenian and, apart from the mysterious Sosandra, which Lucian described as an incomparable masterpiece, he sculpted an Apollo of which the Choiseul-Gouffier Apollo in the British Museum is believed to be a replica. It has also been thought, without any proof, that the bronze Zeus or Poseidon that was found in the sea by northern Euboea was also by his hand (Athens, National Museum). According to tradition, Calamis was the sculptor of figures

of gods that were greatly admired for their severe nobility.   P.D.

CALAURIA. Calauria was a very small island in the Gulf of Argos, and only famous because it was there that Demosthenes took refuge in the temple of Poseidon and put an end to his own life.

CALCHAS. Calchas was a soothsayer who accompanied the expedition against Troy. He had announced that the presence of Achilles was vital to the success of the expedition and that the offensive would last ten years. He is notorious for having obliged Agamemnon to sacrifice his daughter so that the Greek ships would be given a wind to take them across to Troy.   P.D.

CALENDAR. *See* Chronology.

CALLIMACHUS (1). Scholar and poet of the 3rd century B.C. and one of the most typical representatives of Alexandrian culture or Alexandrianism (q.v.). He was a nobleman, the son of

Cadmus killing the dragon at the fountain of Ares.
Detail of a krater from the workshop of Polygnotus.
440-430 B.C. New York, Metropolitan Museum of Art.

Caryatid head with a kalathos. About 540 B.C. Delphi Museum. *Photo G. de Miré.*

lyric, and a short epic, the *Hecale,* which relates a little known episode in the legend of Theseus. In the second part of his life, Callimachus was an official court poet and leader of the school of Alexandrian poetry. This aristocratic poet claimed that he only wrote for an élite of "connoisseurs" and despised the vulgar public whom he considered to be mainly ignorant and incapable of appreciating his refined and delicate art. He was the theorist of the *oligostichia,* that is a short but extremely polished and formally perfect work in a fresh but erudite idiom.   R.F.

CALLIMACHUS (2). Callimachus was a sculptor of the second half of the 5th century B.C. and, with Alcamenes, he was Phidias's most important follower. He was more a metal-worker than a sculptor and the gold lamp that burned night and day in the Erechtheum was his work. It was surmounted by a bronze palm leaf which served as an outlet for the flame and smoke. The ancient Greeks also considered him to have been the inventor of the Corinthian capital. It is not certain that he collaborated in the decoration of the parapet that ran round the terrace of the temple of Athena Nike, but the grace of the winged figures corresponds with what we know of his style. Some experts have been tempted to credit him with the original work that has been reproduced by the charming Fréjus Aphrodite; with its finely modelled drapery clinging to the body as though it were wet, revealing every detail of the goddess's beauty, it has a refined sensuality that was later to characterise the work of Praxiteles.
                    P.D.

CALYPSO. The nymph Calypso lived on a remote island that has still to be located by classical scholars and that Homer seems to have situated in the western Mediterranean. When Ulysses set foot on her domain in the course of his long voyage back to Ithaca, Calypso fell in love with him and only let him leave her years later when formally ordered to do so by Zeus's emissary, Hermes. She gave Ulysses instructions for returning to his homeland and taught him how he might consult Tiresias by conjuring up his ghost and summoning him from the kingdom of the dead for a few moments.   P.D.

Battus, and was born in about 315 at Cyrene in Africa. He went to Athens to study philosophy and then settled in Alexandria where he earned a modest living at first as a school-teacher. He had probably already written many poems by this time, even during his early years at Cyrene. He was honoured by the king, Ptolemy Philadelphus, who gave him a post in the Library, where he wrote his famous *Pinakes* or *Bibliographical Tablets.* His poetical work notably included the *Aetia,* which was a kind of erudite chronicle in verse that related the founding of various cities and the legends connected with them. Some fragments have survived, the finest being the beautiful love story of *Acontios and Cydippe.* Like many other Alexandrian poets, Callimachus had a penchant for stories of love and passion. He wrote a number of hymns which have survived *(To Zeus, To Apollo, To Artemis, To Delos, For Pallas's Bath, To Demeter)* and several were directly commissioned by the king of Egypt or the priests of a sanctuary for religious ceremonies. They are full of mythological erudition, geographical and theological detail, but have many lively, brilliant passages. His surviving work also includes epigrams, fragments of elegies, iambic poems, every kind of

Caryatids of the Erechtheum porch on the Acropolis at Athens. About 420 B.C. *Ph Hassia.*

CANACHUS. Canachus was a sculptor and one of the great masters of the workshops of Sicyon in the 6th century B.C. He was invited to Miletus to cast a bronze statue of *Apollo Philesius* for the archaic temple of Didyma. He specialised in bronze casting and the *Apollo of Piombino,* which is now in the Louvre, has been attributed to him, but this attribution has often been contested as its rather flaccid form and weak lines do not seem to correspond with the ampler, more solidly constructed design of certain cast and chased, male and female bronze statuettes that almost certainly come from the workshops at Sicyon.

R.M.

CANON. From the time of the Dorian invasions at least, the Greeks had a taste for mathematics which may be seen not only in the science of geometry, which they created, but also in the forms of their thought and their art. Although they always closely observed nature, sculptors and painters endeavoured to endow it with an order that would correspond with their rationalism. They attached a great importance to the mathematics of proportions which is particularly evident if we compare their art with that of the Cretans.

This preoccupation with mathematics was not confined to the major arts alone, for it can also be detected in ceramics. Like statues, Greek vases are conceived in obedience to a law of numbers of which the secret has yet to be discovered. It is hardly necessary to add that architecture also obeyed the same imperatives.

There is no one Greek canon, for taste changed at different periods and the Greeks of one generation would prefer slenderness of outline, while those of the next would favour a somewhat heavier solidity of form. Polycletus's canon was far more thick-set than that of Lysippus, just as 7th century art, many years previously, had refined the silhouette of geometric vases. The practice of Polycletus, whose *Doryphorus* seemed to the ancients its most characteristic example, shows that the calculation of proportions was very advanced and that treatises were written on the numerical relationships between the different parts of the human body. These treatises were partly inspired by Pythagoras's teachings and have unfortunately been lost. They would have been highly instructive to modern scholars and might have helped us to understand how the Greek artists were able to create so many works which

Cassandra, attacked by Ajax, takes refuge by the Palladium. Detail of a hydria by the Cleophrades Painter. About 480 B.C. Naples, Museo Nazionale. *Ph. Hirmer.*

give a perfect illusion of life with such subtelty, on the basis of abstract mathematical theories.

P.D.

CARIA. The vast region of Caria extended between the area of Smyrna and Lycia. The Greeks of the classical period considered the Carians of past times as their predecessors in the possession and civilisation of the Aegean basin, but nothing has been adduced to support this contention and, on the whole, Caria seems to have remained largely isolated from the Hellenic world until the 4th century B.C. at least. Caria had become somewhat Hellenised during the rule of Mausolus, one of the satraps who had succeeded in obtaining some independence from the Persian king. The funerary monument that Mausolus and his wife had built for themselves in about 350, at Halicarnassus, shows a disconcerting mixture of Greek and barbarian stylistic elements throughout *(See* Mausolus*)*. Like other provinces in Asia Minor, Caria kept its own language, customs and religious practices even when the élite of its population had learned to speak Greek and were raising temples to the gods of Hellas.

P.D.

CARYATID. The etymology of the word '' caryatid '' has been a subject of much controversy, but it is usually used to denote any standing female figure serving as an architectural support (in the far rarer case of male figures, the term is '' Atlantes ''). Caryatids frequently appear in the minor arts of the archaic period, when numerous tripods and basins were made with supports in the shape of graceful female figures bearing the basin on their heads or their outstretched arms. Caryatids are much rarer in architecture; those on the façade of the Treasury of Cnidos, and of Siphnus at Delphi belong to the third quarter of the 6th century B.C.) Best known are the caryatids of the Erechtheum on the Acropolis at Athens. They were six in number, four for the façade, one on each side, against a wall which concealed the hidden staircase leading down to the sacred platform inside the temple. The fact that they took the place of the customary columns certainly cannot be due to chance. Once a year the secret staircase served as a passage for two young priestesses, the Arrephoroi, who carried mysterious ritual objects in a basket on their heads from the Erechtheum to the sanctuary of Aphrodite on the northern slope of the hill. The capitals between the heads of the caryatids and the architrave they support are splayed out in a basket shape and may well be a discreet allusion to the ceremony. The name of the sculptor responsible is unknown, but the similarity between the figures and the *ergastinai* on the east frieze of the Parthenon has often been commented upon. Although their architectural function has given the caryatids a rather stiff attitude, they are full of robust grace, and the skilful modelling of the austere draperies suggests the youthful charm of the bodies underneath. P.D.

CASSANDRA. Daughter of Priam, king of Troy. Cassandra had the gift of prophecy, she foretold that Paris would bring about the downfall of the city and knew that the wooden horse the Greeks had left outside the city represented a danger for the Trojans, but none of her predictions, which should have put them on guard against these very real dangers, were ever taken seriously. When Troy was captured, she took refuge on the altar of Athena, embracing the statue of the goddess, but Ajax the Locrian tore her away from her asylum. She was given as a captive to Agamemnon and followed him to Argos. In the play *Agamemnon*, Aeschylus has shown her terror-struck at the idea of entering the doom-laden palace in which Clytemnestra and her lover were to massacre her and Agamemnon. P.D.

CASTALIA. Castalia is a sacred spring near Delphi. According to legend, it was there that a young girl of the same name drowned herself to escape from Apollo's advances.

CECROPS. According to legend, Cecrops was the first king of Athens. He had been born out of the soil of Attica and he had kept traces of his earthly origins since, although his torso was that of a human, the lower part of his body was a serpent, essentially a creature of the earth. He married Aglauros and had a son named Erysychthon. It was said that he was chosen as arbiter in the quarrel between Athena and Poseidon for the possession of Athens, and that he had taught men the rudiments of civilisation, the building of cities, and the burial of the dead. P.D.

CENTAUR. With the Amazons, the Centaurs were among the most popular figures of Greek mythology. We do not know the origins of this ancient myth of creatures with the body of a horse and the torso and head of a human being. They were symbols of wild savagery and barbarism, and first appear in the 8th century B.C. on painted vases and in bronzes. They lived in the woods and lived by hunting and their intempe-

rance made them so violent and aggressive that it was not thought advisable to invite them to banquets. When invited to the wedding festivities of Deidamia, daughter of the king of the Lapiths, because they had been on good terms with this peaceful and rustic people, they attacked their hosts during the banquet. They attempted to carry away the women and children and the intervention of Apollo and the aid of Theseus were needed before they would let go their prey, an episode that was often represented in Greek art, most notably on one of the pediments of the temple of Zeus at Olympia. Heracles also fought against the Centaurs and triumphed over them at Mount Pholoë. Many vase paintings represent the hero fighting against the Centaurs who are armed with stones and branches. When they were not being swayed by the basest passions, the Centaurs were a likeable enough tribe; one of their number, Chiron, even acquired a reputation for wisdom and goodness, and it was to him that Thetis and Peleus entrusted the education of Achilles.

The subject of the Centauromachy lasted until the end of the classical world. It inspired some of the greatest artists and was used as a symbol for the victories won by the Greeks over the barbarians. One of the most famous works on this theme is Phidias's series of metopes on the south side of the Parthenon, but it was also frequently taken up again by many other sculptors and painters. Like the battles of the Amazons,

Centaur fighting a Lapith. Metope from the Parthenon. About 447-443 B.C. British Museum.

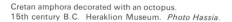

the theme of fights with Centaurs later assumed a funerary significance whose origins are now hard to explain.   P.D.

CERAMICS. The importance of ceramics in Greek art has no equivalent anywhere else. The fact is that apart from its own intrinsic qualities, it is our only means of knowing Greek painting. Modern museums are rich in Greek vases, and surviving works and fragments run into several hundreds of thousands. There is nothing surprising about such an abundance, for in a country where wood was scarce, where glass was infrequently used although known, and metal was dear, it was only natural that clay or terracotta should be used for the majority of utensils which are now made of different materials. Apart from every kind of recipient for liquids, potters in ancient Greece also made coffers, boxes, and even sarcophagi, as in the region of Smyrna.

Pottery techniques did not vary greatly from the early Bronze Age to the end of antiquity and astonishingly perfect results were obtained by almost rudimentary processes. The kilns resembled those now used in many country regions for the making of charcoal and the temperatures obtained were far lower than those now required, the maximum being some 700 or 800 degrees centigrade. The various stages of manufacture were determined by the materials used: earth was carefully chosen and cleaned before being kneaded and left in water to rid it of all pebbles and impurities; the various parts of a vase were turned on a wheel and then fastened together with a kind of glue with a resinous base called barbotine before being hardened by a slight firing; before being finally returned to the kiln a layer of colour would be added, to be followed by the application of figurative or non-figurative decoration. The most notable progress in techniques, after the very ancient invention of the wheel, was in the more delicate treatment of earthenware, and the invention of a kind of varnish (glaze) with an iron-oxide basis which could be given an incomparable lustre according to the way in

Krater of the geometric period from the Dipylon Cemetery 8th century B.C. Athens, National Museum.

KRATER
A vase for mixing wine with water.
New York, Metropolitan Museum of Art.

which the temperature in the furnace was regulated.

This lustrous coating already existed on pottery from the region of Troy before the end of the 3rd millennium B.C.; excavations have revealed ceramics which were often complicated in design, shaped into anthropomorphic urns to contain the ashes of the dead; the vase was roughly moulded as a body (canopic vases) with handles in the shape of arms, pellets added for breasts, and lids formed into heads. Minoan pottery was more sober in style although it was only rarely characterised by a logical and geometric decoration. Drinking bowls, vases for liquids, jugs for pouring were all given fanciful shapes which corresponded with the imaginativeness of their decoration. The impression is often given that the potter was more interested in the beauty of the form than in the functional necessities of the product. Unlike the pottery of the Greek period, it is difficult to give precise names to the different pottery wares which did not obey any fixed rules in design. Such apparently precise terms as amphora, krater and cups have been used for vases which often differ greatly from one another, and such vague terms as urn, for example, have often been employed to denote forms that seem to obey no particular canon. There was nothing clumsy about Cretan pottery; the fantasy of shapes and the refusal to conform to any fixed standards of design was due to a spirit of individuality. Potters showed great skill in the way they gave balance and symmetry to their slender vases whose thin bases often

AMPHORA
A vase for carrying liquids.
Brescia Museum. *Photo Hirmer.*

HYDRIA
A pitcher for fetching water from a fountain.
Paris, Louvre. *Photo Hirmer.*

seemed too delicate to support the wide bowls.

The Mycenaeans were the first to bring logic and discipline into the construction of pottery shapes and they were also the first to make clearly defined distinctions between the different parts of a vase, but organic structure in ceramics only made its definite appearance with the coming of the Dorians, and it was only then that a strict repertory of forms can be said to have been evolved. The amphora served either as a bottle or a carboy according to its size and was generally oval in shape and covered by a lid which could be fastened with string to the two lateral handles. The hydria was used for carrying water from a foun-

tain and to the two side handles, which were used for lifting it, a third was added so that it might be lifted sideways for pouring. Another pouring vessel was the oinochoe, meaning literally a wine-jug, which was smaller in size with a trilobate or trefoil mouth to facilitate pouring. The oinochoe was filled with a ladle from a wide-mouthed krater in which wines of different strength were mixed. Apart from the oinochoe, which was passed from hand to hand, these vessels were generally fairly large and their average height was usually about 18 inches. They were rarely very large although in the early archaic period and in the late classical period, in the 8th century, and

KYATHOS   SKYPHOS   KANTHAROS
Drinking cups. Paris, Louvre. *Photos Tel et Hirmer.*

98

STAMNOS
A vase for holding liquids.
Brussels, Musée du Cinquantenaire. *Photo Hirmer.*

OINOCHOAI
Jugs for pouring.
Paris, Louvre. *Photos Tel et Dräyer.*

in Italy in the 4th century, some amphorae and kraters were made measuring more than five feet in height, and were used either for decorative or ritual purposes. Drinking bowls and perfume flasks were naturally much smaller and were either bowls and goblets (kotylai and skyphoi), or cups which changed in shape according to different periods and workshops, or narrow tapering vases to contain oil for medicaments, such as alabaster or aryballoi. Derived from these vessels were the lekythoi, which were nearly cylindrical vases with a circular base, a flattened shoulder and a thin neck. Mention must also be made of the pyxides which were used as boxes for containing jewels.

Despite all these minor variations, each category possessed sufficient individuality for each type to be easily recognisable and for a precise name to be given to each type of vase. This was one of the features which especially distinguished Greek ceramics from Minoan productions.

Another very Hellenic trait was the style of decoration. Some Greek vases were left undecorated, either because they were very common pieces or else because their form was esteemed so beautiful in itself that no need was felt for decoration, and indeed some vases which were only decorated with glaze were judged so beautiful that they bear the potter's signature. Generally,

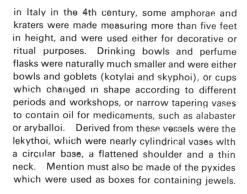

KYLIX
A drinking cup. Tarquinia Museum. *Photo Hirmer.*

RHYTON
A drinking cup. Paris, Louvre. *Photo Tel.*

LEKYTHOS
Vase mainly for funerary use.
New York, Metropolitan Museum of Art.

SQUAT LEKYTHOS
Vases for oil and perfume.
Paris, Louvre. *Photos Giraudon et Dräyer.*

ARYBALLOS

even the cheapest vases were usually painted. Sometimes they were painted with simple decorative patterns, but more frequently with a figurative motif which might be either an isolated figure or a detailed scene. At first, the scenes were painted in black silhouette against the clear ground of the clay as in the so-called geometric style which reigned from the time of the Dorian settlements in the 10th century until well into the

PYXIS
Jewel box.
New York, Metropolitan Museum of Art.

8th century B.C. The technique survived until the end of the archaic period, but during the so-called orientalising period of the 7th century vase painters often practised line drawing, only outlining the figures and adding a few touches in red or white for detail. This was the black-figure style in which the figures stood out against the background of natural, red-coloured clay. Then, in about 530, the Athenians discovered a more visually effective process known as the red-figure style. The figures were surrounded by a thin black outline and kept the red of their clay ground but were set against the background of black varnish. They were no longer indistinct silhouettes and details of muscles or facial expressions were added with a fine brush ending in a single pig's bristle *(See* Painting for the history of Greek vase painting styles). The vase painters often transcribed the style and sometimes even the subjects of large painted compositions and this is why Greek vases are so vital for a knowledge of Greek painting.

Much of the ceramic production of the 5th century B.C. possesses this documentary value, and the diffusion of a new technique which consisted in adding a white coating to the clay which could hold a more varied range of colours, brought vase painting even closer to classical fresco or easel painting. Towards the end of the 5th century the ceramic industry was faced by a double peril; on the one hand, the technical developments and progress of fresco painting deprived the humbler vase painters of their last hopes of ever being able to compete with the masters they continued to copy, and on the other hand, bronze crafts-

The Ceramicus Cemetery at Athens. *Photo Hassia.*

manship had reached such great heights that many clients preferred the lustre and solidity of metal to the fragility of ceramics. Now, it is a fact that the very perfection of Greek ceramics often leads us to forget that vases were industrial products which were made, not to be sold as luxury objects, but as basic necessities. Even when they were of the highest quality, their price remained modest (often the equivalent of the cost of a few working days) and potters were, first and foremost, merchants. They sought custom everywhere and always; they exported their wares. Many of the Corinthian and Attic vases now in museums come from Etruria, and their makers signed them as much for reasons of publicity as from an artist's pride. In the 4th century, in order to win back a hesitant clientele, potters began to make vases to which they endeavoured to give a bronze-like appearance and from which painted decoration was necessarily excluded, and thus put low-priced imitations of metal objects on the market. This attempt was soon to prove futile and the ceramics lost their artistic importance.

While some potters started to compete with the bronze artists, other, more traditionally minded potters refused to lose hope and painted ceramics reached new heights during the whole of the 4th century, mostly in Athens and southern Italy. While the Attic potters remained faithful to the principles of moderation and discretion that had brought such glory to their art, the vases placed in the tombs of rich people in Italy were often oversized and cumbersome in form, with excessive and over-elaborate decoration. The death of the art of painted ceramics might be said to date from the middle of the 3rd century B.C. were it not that the potters of the Nile Delta and certain centres in Sicily had endeavoured, with only slight success, to produce wares that were rather like the finer, white-ground vases of the Athenians. Their ceramics were covered with a fairly clear coating on which real polychrome paintings with a wide range of tones were made, but the excessive fragility of the decoration doomed the attempt to failure. A more successful technique which bore greater results and even lasted into Roman art and its derivatives, was that of relief decoration, known by the long series of incorrectly called " Megarian " bowls. Stamped motifs were also attached with barbotine to the bowls of vases. This was an imitation of a current practice among

metal-workers who would solder or rivet decorations onto the bronze vessel which could not be painted because of the material used.

It was thus that bronze finally triumphed over clay after a long fight, during which ceramicists lived in a constant fear of being replaced in the public taste by the metal workers, even at a time when they had reached the greatest heights in their art. As a matter of fact, the fight between the more costly but more solid bronze vases and the more fragile but cheaper ceramics was always unequal. Had the ceramics not been painted with decorations that were so often of the highest quality and always interesting, inspired by the finest fresco painting, Greek amphorae, hydriai, calices and other earthen vessels would soon have been replaced by their bronze equivalents.

CERAMICUS (Necropolis of). From at least the 3rd millennium B.C. it was the general rule in ancient Greek civilisation to bury the dead only outside the city precincts, and necropolises were usually sited on each side of the roads leading out of the main gateways. Athens was a notable example of this; there the oldest and most important cemetery faced the Dipylon, the double gateway on the road to Eleusis. The cemetery was gradually enlarged and the most ancient part was incorporated within

Heracles drags
Cerberus in chains
into the presence of
Eurystheus who hides
in terror in a pithos.
Detail of a hydria from
Caere. About 525 B.C.
Paris, Louvre.

the city walls. It was generally known as the Ceramicus because of the potters who had established themselves nearby. The most ancient tombs dated from the Mycenaean period and the necropolis was in constant use until the beginning of the Christian era. Archaeologists have thus been able to follow changes in burial customs; at the end of the Bronze Age tombs tended to contain the ashes rather than the bodies of the deceased but later on cremation was less frequent than burial. As was usually the case, the cemetery was not arranged according to any particular plan and it was enlarged wherever space was found for it. The necropolis has yielded many important objects illustrating the history, civilisation and art of Athens; most are now exhibited in museums, one of the most famous being the Hegeso stele. P.D.

CERBERUS. This monstrous dog kept guard in front of the palace of Hades and Persephone in Hell. It was usually represented in Greek art with two or three heads although according to certain traditions it had as many as fifty or a hundred. Its back was covered with serpents' heads and it also had a serpent for a tail. It was considered to be the brother of the Hydra of Lerna and the Nemean Lion. One of Heracles' most famous exploits had been to tackle it unarmed and bring it in chains to Eurystheus' dwelling.
P.D.

CHAERONEA. This Boeotian town was famous because of the two battles fought near it.

It was there that Philip of Macedonia defeated an army composed of Thebans and Athenians and contingents from other parts of Greece (Megara, Corinth, Achaea, Locris, Phocis) in 338 B.C. and that Alexander distinguished himself by annihilating the famous Sacred Battalion (q.v.). The victory assured Philip's triumph over the Greeks. The second battle was fought in 86 B.C. between one of Mithridates' generals, Archelaus, and Sulla during the Roman invasion of Greece. P.D.

CHALCIDICE. Chalcidice was a wide mountainous outcrop which bordered the gulf of Salonica to the east and extended into three thin peninsulas to the south, the easternmost being that of Mount Athos. The region owed its name to the thirty or so colonies that had been founded there by the Chalcidians of Euboea, but one of its most important cities, Polidaea, had been founded by the Corinthians. Another famous city was Olynthus. During the rivalry between Athens and Sparta and the campaigns of Philip of Macedon, Chalcidice was one of the most contested regions. P.D.

CHALCIS. Chalcis is situated in Euboea at the point where the island is nearest the mainland from which it is separated by the Euripus, a tumultuous channel some 200 feet wide. With its rival Eretria, Chalcis was the most important town on the long island, and owed much of its prosperity to the rich pastures where the nobles raised their horses, as well as its vineyards, olive groves and forests. There were many bitter conflicts between the two towns and the war lasted nearly a hundred years until, in the 7th century B.C., Chalcis was finally victorious. As its name indicates, Chalcis was a centre for the bronze industry; its citizens were a bold seafaring people and it was one of the most important colonising cities in Greece. From the 8th century onwards, its pioneers moved mainly towards Thracia and Macedonia. They settled in the region named Chalcidice after their town, but also sailed to the west, founding Naxos, and Zancle in Sicily. At the end of the 6th century B.C. the town lost almost all its former importance.   P.D.

C H A N C E. " In order to declare that a man is dear to the gods, and that he is happy, we have recourse to chance. Chance picks out the man who must command; chance rejects the man who must obey. Nothing could be more just, for chance is a god. " With these words Plato was expressing an idea that was deep-rooted in the minds of the Greeks for, from the time of Homer to the latest written texts, it is clear that they were persuaded that both the blind hand that took a counter from out of an urn and the dice that rolled on the ground were guided by a supreme will. Cleromancy, or divination by lots, was practised in many sanctuaries and, even if it was more the concern of Hermes and the three nymphs known as Thriae, it was not despised by Apollo himself, and it was by shaking knuckle-bones in a tripod bowl that the Delphic Pythia answered questions. Chance served especially to point out those for whom some honour or benefit was reserved, or else the unfortunate individual who was to carry out a difficult and dangerous mission. It was said that Zeus, Hades and Poseidon had recourse to chance to decide which part of the world would fall to each of them, and the same procedure was followed in sharing out the booty among victorious soldiers, or land among settlers in a new colony. It was more than a convenient means of avoiding disputes, for it was an authentic judgment of god—and far superior to any human decision. Consequently, the Greeks had recourse to chance in every circumstance, in weighty or frivolous matters, in political or private life. Chance was called upon to decide how the paternal legacy should be shared by the heirs if no will had specified their respective portion; the place and order of candidates in competitions was settled by chance; chance decided who was to preside over banquets, and chance again decid-

ed most appointments to the magistrature. Such a procedure was long established and was probably the legacy from a very remote past. Political magistrates, judges in tribunals, priests and members of assemblies nearly all owed their posts to the white bean that was picked out of the urn when their name was called.

That there were dangers in such a system is evident enough and Socrates himself was not unaware of them: " It is folly that a bean should decide the choice of the leaders of the republic whereas neither pilots, architects, flute-players nor other artists, whose mistakes are much less dangerous than those of magistrates, are drawn by lots. " But long before Socrates, statesmen had already taken the necessary measures to guide the choice of the gods, for when lots were to be drawn, only hand-picked men were candidates. They were selected, according to the times, from those classes which alone had the right to power, but even among those who might legitimately aspire to high office there were many who voluntarily withdrew their candidature either because they feared the responsibility, or, more often, because they found it impossible to combine an unpaid or badly paid state appointment with the profession that earned them their living. At Athens, where names were put forward by the tribes, it is noticeable that the same persons, or at least the same families, always used to appear most frequently when appointments were decided. Moreover, certain particularly responsible posts, like that of strategus, were decided by election, which avoided the constant danger of a whim of chance, even when it was guided.   P.D.

C H A R E S. Chares of Lindus was the pupil of Lysippus in the second half of the 4th century B.C. and the founder of the Rhodian school of sculpture which had a considerable influence on Hellenistic and Roman art. From its very beginnings, the school of Rhodes, and Chares in particular, showed a stylistic tendency towards the colossal and the emphatic. The sculptor, Lysippus, had already executed a statue of Helios, the sun god, standing in his quadriga, and Chares returned to the theme by making a monumental statue of Helios to stand by the entrance of the port. This was the famous *Colossus of Rhodes,* 105 feet high, and one of the Seven Wonders of the World. It is now very difficult to reconstitute the exact attitude of the statue and, even more its style, although certain indications have been given by the sculptures found at Pergamum, in particular, where the groups from the frieze show the Sun's position. An idea of the style of the face can be gained from a colossal head found at Rhodes which may also be compared with certain 3rd century B.C. coin effigies. R.M.

CHARITES. The Charites, or, to give them their English name, the Graces, were originally nature divinities and it was only at a comparatively late date that they were attributed with the functions that 17th century poets praised. In the beginning, they reigned over the countryside and plants and were local divinities whose number, finally fixed at three, might change according to place. They were represented austerely veiled in an attitude suitable for inspiring feelings of awe and veneration in spectators but later, in Hellenistic times, they tended to be shown unclothed and in a more seductive posture. P.D.

CHARITON. Greek fiction writer, author of the *Adventures of Chaereas and Callirhoe (See* Romances).

CHARON. Roughly swaddled in his sombre cloak, wearing a wide traveller's hat over his untidy hair, his beard untrimmed, and with a general air of abstraction, Charon was the sinister boatman who used to ferry the dead

across the river Acheron once they had received the ritual funeral honours. He mercilessly rejected all other poor suffering souls and prevented any living being from entering into Hell. Two mortals did however succeed: Heracles whose might made Charon allow him to pass, and Orpheus in his search for Eurydice, through the charm of his songs. P.D.

CHARYBDIS and SCYLLA. Charybdis and Scylla were two monsters who guarded the Straits of Messina. Charybdis would swallow up a great deal of the sea, together with the vessels that might be sailing on it, three times a day, and then spit it out again, while opposite her Scylla set a pack of six ferocious dogs, which she always kept by her, on the hapless sailors. It was only with the greatest difficulty that Ulysses succeeded in making his way through the straits past these fearsome monsters. P.D.

CHERSONESUS. The name Chersonesus means a peninsula and was often coupled with an adjective to denote a precise geographical locality. For example, Tauric Chersonesus was the ancient name for the Crimea, Thracian Chersonesus for the Gallipoli peninsula on the north coast of the Dardanelles. The first was peopled by settlers who mostly came from Miletus, and served as an intermediary between the

The sea-monster, Scylla, and her ferocious dogs. Silver tetradrachm, Agrigentum. About 415 B.C. *Photo L. von Matt.*

104

Greeks and the peoples of southern Russia; the second, the key to the straits, was fought over by the Athenians and Philip of Macedonia. One of Demosthenes' most famous speeches was entitled *Speech on the Chersonesus*. P.D.

C H I L D R E N . Even in Athens in the classical period, the father of a family had the right to decide whether to keep a new-born child or to expose it, which meant that he could abandon it wherever he pleased without worrying whether anyone would pick it up, or whether it would simply perish. In Sparta it was the community of the *homoioi* (citizens with equal rights to hold offices of state) who could alone decide, without asking the father's advice, whether the infant seemed robust enough to be worthy to be allowed to grow up a Spartan, or if it should be exposed.

In Laconia, in Athens or elsewhere, the infant's early years were spent with the mother and if the father ever paid any attention to his babies he certainly did not boast about it. Homer has told us that Hector was content to frighten Astyanax with his warlike mien and we may well believe that, as in our own day, even if a father liked to play with his toddler sometimes, he was all too likely to be a figure of ridicule if he played the nurse like Strepsiades in Aristophanes' comedy. Many Greek vase paintings show little children held in their mothers' arms, crawling on the ground, or else well settled in a kind of armchair which held them fast by the thighs and buttocks so that their parents might have some much longed-for quiet.

The child began to come out of the family circle at the age of seven. In Sparta a boy was brutally separated from his mother and enrolled in brigades that were already of a practically paramilitary nature, under the direction of a magistrate, the *paidonomos*. From then on he belonged to the state which never returned him to his family. He moved from one class to another as he grew up and, with each automatic promotion, he was enclosed in a still stricter discipline and a still harsher life.

By contrast, in other cities and in Athens particularly, the child remained dependent on the family, under its protection, even while attending school. It was his father who decided what his education (q.v.) was to be (at Athens every citizen was obliged to assure his son a minimum education), who chose the school and who had his son accompanied to the teacher by the pedagogue-

slave. We may well conclude from this that the life of an Athenian child was not so very different from that of a modern child, for their games and toys (qq.v.), mechanical toys excluded were more or less the same. Like today, some children were spoilt, and Strepsiades, whom we have mentioned already, was to repent bitterly of having given way to all the caprices of his child, Phidippides, when all he received in return was ingratitude. P.D.

C H I M A E R A . The Chimaera was a monstrous animal born of Typhon and Echidna. It was a kind of fire-breathing lion with a serpent for a tail and a goat's head on its back. It was originally an oriental creation but it was adopted by the archaic Greeks. It frequently appeared in Greek art of the 7th and 6th centuries B.C. and was killed by Bellerophon on the orders of Iobates, king of Lycia, according to the Greek legend.
P.D.

C H I O S . Like its neighbours, Lesbos and Samos, the island of Chios seems to have once been part of the nearby Anatolian mainland, with which it always remained in close contact during the course of its history. Like the two other islands, its fertile plains sheltered by mountain chains gave it a prosperity that was greatly envied by the arid and less fortunate Cycladic islands. It was settled early in the 1st millennium B.C. by colonists from Euboea and, like Greece, it underwent a political evolution that began with a monarchy, continued with the aristocratic government of Basilides, and culminated with a regime of public assemblies which may have served as a model later for that of Athens. But its political role in Greek history was slight. In the 6th century B.C. it was a member state of the Panionion which was a fairly loose amphictionic league of a dozen Ionian cities. After being conquered by the Persians in 498 B.C. it revolted against them and in 477 put its fleet at the disposition of the Athenians; as a member of the Delian League, it was one of Athens' most faithful allies until the final defeat of the Peloponnesian War, then it wavered between Athens and Sparta until 355 when it won its independence. It was incorporated into Alexander's empire and was involved in all the vicissitudes of Hellenistic history until it fell under the domination of the Romans who allowed it a semblance of autonomy from 86 B.C. onwards.

Chios's finest period was in the 7th and 6th

centuries when it was the home of a school of sculpture led by Archermus (q.v.), Bupalus and Athenis, none of whose works have survived, and a bronze industry (it seems that it was at Chios that iron soldering was first practised in the 7th century by Glaucus). A considerable ceramic industry also flourished on the island and foreign trade was developed, notably with Egypt. Although the merchants and sailors of Chios always held an acknowledged position in the Hellenic world, its artistic importance was short-lived for, like many other islands, Chios was completely eclipsed by Athens' prestige in the 5th century B.C. and counted for no more than a provincial outpost.   P.D.

CHORAGUS. Citizen designated by the archon to train and instruct a lyric or dramatic chorus at his own expense. *(See* Theatre).

CHOREUTUS. Member of a lyric or dramatic chorus. *(See* Theatre).

CHRONOLOGY. The ancient Greeks had no precise method for counting the divisions of the day or hours. Various times of the day were roughly designated by the dawn, the time when the " market was fullest " (about mid-morning), mid-day, afternoon and evening. But from the 5th century B.C. onwards two time-measuring devices were used: the sun-dial or gnomon, which came from the orient, and the clepsydra or " water clock " in which water ran out of a vase at a constant rate.

The Greek month was a lunar month and in theory it corresponded to the interval between one new moon and the next but in practice the twelve months of the year were alternately given 29 and 30 days. A month was divided into three decades; the first day of the first decade being the day of the " new moon ", the second day the " second of the new month " and so on until the tenth day; the eleventh day was known as the first day " of the middle of the month ", but after the twentieth day the count was kept in reverse so that the 21st would be " the tenth (or the ninth, if the month only had 29 days) before the end of the month ". The names of the months were usually those of religious festivals but they varied from one city to another. At Athens, the civic year began, in principle, with the summer solstice and the twelve months were named: Hecatombaeon (about July), Metageitnion (August),

Boedromion (September), Pyanopsion (October), Maemacterion (November), Poseideon (December), Gamelion (January), Anthesterion (February), Elaphebolion (March), Munichion (April), Thargelion (May) and Scirophorion (June).

Six months of 29 days and six of 30 only make a total of 354 days whereas of course the solar year lasts 364¼ days. In order to make up the difference the Athenians customarily intercalated a month of 30 days every 3rd, 5th and 8th year of every eight year cycle. The intercalary month was added after Poseideon and was known as " the second Poseideon ". In 432 B.C. the Athenian astronomer, Meton, invented a 19 year cycle with seven intercalary months, a system to which Aristophanes made witty allusion in his plays, the *Clouds* and the *Birds*. To indicate years the Greeks of the classical period used the names of the *archon eponymos* which naturally differed from one city to another. In Athens the name of the principal archon was used, in Sparta it was that of the chief ephor. Then, in the 3rd century B.C. the scientists of the Alexandrian period worked out a chronology applicable to all the Greek states on the basis of the Olympiads. The first Olympic games for which the names of the victors had been recorded was held in 776 B.C. As the games were held every four years, an Olympiad was a four year cycle. The Greek date, Olympiad 75, 1, denoted the first year of a four year cycle after 74 previous Olympiads had elapsed. To work out the date in our chronology we simply have to multiply these 74 cycles by 4, making 296, and substract this number from 776 which gives us 480 (the year of the battle of Salamis).   R.F.

CHRYSEIS. Chryseis was taken captive by Agamemnon during the Trojan War and was the cause of the wrath of Achilles. As Agamemnon had refused to return the young girl to her father, Chryses, the indignant parent besought the aid of Apollo whose priest he was. The Greeks were immediately struck by a plague and were told by an oracle that it would only come to an end if Agamemnon returned the girl. He accordingly did so, but then demanded Briseis, who was loved by Achilles, in return.   P.D.

CIMMERIANS. What the Huns were to the Europeans of the Dark Ages, the Cimmerians were to the ancient Greeks. They were a nomadic people of Thracian origin who had almost certainly assembled together in the steppes of southern Russia in about the 10th century B.C. After the Scythian invasions, they split into two main branches, one settling in the Crimea and near the mouth of the Danube, the other pushing towards the mountains of the Caucasus and the north-east of Asia Minor. In the first quarter of the 7th century B.C. the Cimmerians made a combined attack against the Assyrian provinces but were repulsed by Esarhaddon; they then turned against Phrygia and defeated the king, Midas, who committed suicide in about 676. In about 663 they attacked Lydia and the Greek cities of Ionia, captured Sardes, pushed on to Ephesus where they set fire to the temple and to Magnesia in Meander which they sacked. They were severely defeated in Cilicia in about 637 but their armed bands constituted a serious menace until about 575, when they were finally expelled from Anatolia. P.D.

CIMON. Cimon was a citizen of Athens and the son of Miltiades, the victor of Marathon, and a Thracian princess. He had a brilliant military career but he was less fortunate in politics. In 476 B.C. he conquered the Persian stronghold of Eion in Thracia, thus opening the way towards the riches of Mount Pangaeus for his fellow-countrymen, and in the following year he captured the isle of Scyrus where Theseus, the founder and patron hero of Athens was buried, and brought back his remains to the city. He destroyed Xerxes' fleet in a battle at the mouth of the Eurymedon on the south coast of Asia Minor in 468, won new victories in Thracia and subdued the city of Thasos which had rebelled against the Delian League. But in his own country he was the embodiment of the conservative spirit in politics and when Pericles became head of the democratic party in 463, he accused Cimon of having allowed himself to be corrupted by the king of Macedonia. The accusation misfired, but when the king of Sparta dismissed the expeditionary force the Athenians had sent him in response to his plea for help against the rebellious helots in 461, Cimon was held responsible for what the Athenians considered an insult, for he had commanded the expedition and was responsible for the decision. He was ostracised but returned to Athens ten years later to continue the fight against the Persians. After decisively defeating the Persians at Cyprus he died on the island in 451. P.D.

CIRCE. In the *Odyssey* Homer tells how Ulysses escaped the enchantments of the sorceress, Circe. She prepared a special brew for his shipmates which transformed them into swine, but armed with the moly, a miraculous plant that Hermes had given him, Ulysses avoided this disagreeable metamorphosis and forced Circe at the point of his sword to give back their human aspect to his companions who had been herded into her pig-sty. P.D.

CITY. The Greek word *polis* which we usually translate as " city " meant far more than a mere agglomeration of houses and dwellings. Whereas the word city is now used to denote any important urban complex, the Greek polis embraced a community of citizens who were united by common origins and interests and who often lived outside the city proper, in the neighbouring countryside or in small villages and farms. Greek cities even survived the destruction of the town proper in times of war, for they were as much an institution and a concept as a precisely located geographical phenomenon. The city was a purely Greek institution which owed nothing to Egypt or the peoples of Asia; it was an institution peculiar to Greece and without it, it is hard to imagine a Greek civilisation; at the same time, it was a product of and moulding influence on, Hellenism.

Although its origins are obscure, the Greek city did not suddenly spring into being like Athena out of Zeus's forehead, fully developed without any preparatory period. The polis of the Homeric epics was quite different from that of the 5th century B.C. for it was only the fortified dwelling place of a chieftain, which later became known as the acropolis to distinguish it from the surrounding habitations; as many as a hundred could be counted in Crete alone, which explains why Agamemnon and Menelaus were able to make gifts of one or several of them to their friends. The lands surrounding the polis were an integral part of the possession and their produce went towards the maintenance of the lord and his family. The peasants who worked the land and who followed their master to the wars, the Homeric *laos,* only gathered together to hear the decisions that their lord had taken, although they did participate in the religious ceremonies held by the lord in honour of the divinity who protected the community. The social groups that were formed around the common altars on each of these parcels of land were the embryo of the future cities. The only effect the downfall of the monarchy had on these groupings was to increase their vitality, for once he no longer owed allegiance to a sovereign, the country squire in his polis was obliged to shoulder the responsibility for the defence of his domain against the encroachments of his neighbours and for its administration without the possibility of having recourse to royal arbitration and intervention. It was this, as much as the geographical nature of Greece, that explained the political fragmentation of the peninsula.

The Greek city did not really take shape until the period of economic and social upheaval in the 8th and 7th centuries B.C. The power of the local nobility was gradually eroded during these troubled times but the communities around them survived. Life did not come to a halt, the divinities still protected the communities and the political groupings that had formed around the chieftain's dwelling in the course of centuries still remained. All that changed was the source of authority, for the members of families that had enriched themselves by annexing surrounding lands were not strong enough to dominate the others and were obliged to share the administration of the community, with the consequence that a system of electoral colleges and assemblies came into being. Even when only a few privileged citizens, chosen from among the highest social categories, had the right to sit in the colleges and assemblies—and the oligarchy which was the rule everywhere at this time was to maintain itself vigorously in a number of cities—and even when tyrants appointed their minions to all the key posts, the system of government had become irrevocably rooted in the community. Even though they did not all have a voice in the councils, all the free men descended from the original members of the social group of the polis were citizens; they were all under the direct protection of the patron divinity of the city, and it was in the interest of all to encourage the development of a civic body in which they hoped either to keep or to win an important place.

As the city was both an urban grouping and a sovereign state, the problems facing the citizens were far more vast and complex than any that modern city dwellers have had to contend with. The inhabitants of the modern city delegate their responsibilities to their representatives and are often ignorant of the precise issues at hand in city administration, but in the Greek polis the citizen not only had a direct say in the appointment of his

administrators, whose every action he closely scrutinised, but he was also expected to give his opinion on a wide variety of subjects such as local interests, roads, taxation and budgets, relations with foreign states, the choice of ambassadors, declarations of war, treaties, and even the administration of justice. Every issue was so immediate, the results of every decision taken were so important to the citizens of these small states, that it was only natural that the sense of political and civic responsibility, as well as patriotism, should be developed to the highest degree. The exercise of his duties and the knowledge of his rights gave even the humblest citizen a feeling of superiority over the less privileged part of the population living around him, such as the slaves, and especially the metics *(metoikoi)*, who were free and often rich foreigners living in the city without really forming part of the civic community.

The community was essentially moral in character. It has already been pointed out that the citizens of a city did not necessarily live inside the same town. They might live side by side with the metics and although it might be necessary for the polis to have a centre (the word " capital " would be out of place here), this centre was not distinguished by any particular architectural feature (such as the belfry in the medieval communes which had a certain resemblance with the Greek polis), nor was it necessary for the city to be surrounded by walls; Athens remained an unfortified city for many centuries. Nevertheless, certain buildings were considered to be indispensable to the life of the polis such as the *prytaneion* (or prytaneum), the hearth of the entire community and the shrine for the sacred flame that once burned in the house of the lord, the *bouleuterion* where the Senate met, temples and buildings for civic worship, the gymnasium where the young could train for athletic events, a theatre and above all, the agora, or public meeting-place, where the people could assemble to debate public issues or transact business. The golden age of the city in Greece lasted from the end of the 6th century B.C. until Alexander's conquests and it was during this period that the democratic regimes that sprang out of the city state and that favoured its growth spread throughout Greece. Once the conqueror had imposed his own law on the country the city tended to be reduced to the status of a mere municipality and, even when it still maintained diplomatic relations with other states, its sovereignty had become greatly diminished. But never had the citizens been more avid for public honours, and never had so many decrees been passed to proclaim the merits of some benefactor whose generosity had made it possible to set up a statue or repair a building. General poverty brought financial problems to the foreground and it became a fairly common custom to sell civic rights to all who could pay, whereas in the past they were only accorded to those whose families were natives of the state.   P.D.

CIVILISATION. We have often been told that our modern western civilisation is the daughter and the heir of the civilisation of ancient Greece. We have been told this so often that it is not surprising if we sometimes forget the difference between being a daughter and an heir. We are confirmed in our illusions by transpositions rather than translations of words, which confuse two different notions in our minds. Although it is true that the Greeks were rationalists like us, to an even greater extent perhaps, their rationalism was based on notions quite different from ours and foreign to our way of thinking. Greek religion was an anthropomorphic polytheism; for them, divinity was not something to be revealed through human beings and phenomena, for they believed that each phenomenon could be considered as a divinity in its own right. For the Greeks, abstract ideas became alive and, to take an example, an oath or a curse had an existence of its own and a body as tangible as our own. Zeus protected Justice and condemned Injustice, but both these notions were living beings to the Greeks; Justice appealed to Zeus for aid but was to a certain extent independent of him. The Greek world was peopled by so many divinities that, although the religious sense was strongly developed, it often became confused with superstition.

It is said that Greece had similar political institutions to ours but this is to forget that for the Greeks the homeland was never larger than a county, that the state was never anything else than the administration of a city and its surroundings. Rather than the Greeks, it was the barbarians who possessed the notion of empire that is now so familiar to us. What exactly was the city in ancient Greece? It was the agglomeration of a restricted and privileged class of citizens, who were unable to live without the help of metics who were denied any say in public affairs, and slaves who did not even own their own bodies. Even in the most democratic of the Greek states, the majority of the inha-

bitants were without the most basic civic rights.

It should be added that even in these states the slaves and metics were not on the same level, as they were classed in strictly hierarchical social categories by the laws of the city. Although the barriers between the classes later tended to break down, the principle underlying this division was never questioned. What should we think of certain customs that are as strange to us as they were natural to the Greeks, particularly the way in which the magistrates of most cities were chosen by lot? The Greeks thought that such a system was the surest way of obeying the divine will since the final decision was left to the immortals. Even so, this primitive sovereign rule underwent certain modifications and the choice of the gods was guided by only the worthiest candidates being put forward, but the actual method itself was never abolished. Many other such examples could be given to illustrate the fundamental differences between the ideas of the Greeks and our own and we might well be tempted to ask ourselves if it is not in its most material aspects that Greek civilisation is closest to our own. Methods of cultivation, hunting and fishing, eating and drinking customs, and amusements may have changed somewhat in form, but they respond to the same needs and are inspired by the same feelings; there was a similarity in technology until not so very long ago, when new methods were invented and new ways found of harnessing the powers of nature, and there is not much difference between the bricklaying and carpentry techniques of the 20th century and those of 5th century Athens. What does separate us from Greek civilisation by a great gulf are the main ideas and beliefs underlying our society and that of the ancient Greeks.   P.D.

CLAROS. The sanctuary of Claros was situated to the south of Smyrna at a short distance from the sea and was one of the most ancient to have been consecrated to Apollo. Homer himself mentioned the god as being the protector and patron of this site. The god delivered oracles in the sanctuary which drew pilgrims from Ionia and the neighbouring islands. We know practically nothing about the early history of the sanctuary, but recent excavations have uncovered the enormous buildings that were erected in honour of the god in Roman times, and a considerable mass of inscriptions has confirmed the popularity of Apollo at the period. A chamber, the adyton, had been built under the temple and must certainly have been used for prophetic consultations.

P.D.

CLASSES (SOCIAL). Every society in ancient Greece was more or less hierarchical; but we should also take account of the Hellenic character and the respect for the human person that reigned in Greek civilisation; there was neither arrogance, nor servile humility. Although many Greek families proclaimed their heroic descent at the beginning, it was richness rather than blue blood that separated the upper classes from the common ranks of society. It should also be stressed that in many Greek states democracy became the rule fairly soon and that a levelling process was taking place at the bottom of the social pyramid in most cities before the end of the 5th century B.C. Two great exceptions were Sparta where the *homoioi* (citizens with equal rights to hold offices of state), a diminishing class, continued to dominate the subject peoples, and Thessaly, where the system of great landed properties favoured an aristocratic regime.

The Homeric poems, Hesiod's writings and the little we know of the history of this remote period have all confirmed that in the first centuries of the 1st millennium B.C. social divisions were fairly clear-cut; there was no middle class that might have served as an intermediary between a miserable peasant class, bound to the soil by the debts it had made, and an aristocracy wholly given up to war, which derived its income from lands that it never cultivated itself. The development of commerce and craftsmanship and the export of manufactured products to foreign countries and colonies created a class that did not live by agriculture, that gathered together in cities and modified the social structure of ancient Greece. At the same time, a massive emigration to far-off regions, the promulgation of laws like those of Solon, about which we still know little, concerning mortgages and debts, remedied the situation.

It is Athens that furnishes us with the clearest picture of social conditions prevailing at the beginning of the period when the first democratic aspirations were making themselves felt and when tyrants had to win the support of the lower classes in order to seize power. The great families, who were the descendants of the Eupatridae, were still flourishing at the beginning of the 6th century B.C. They had been a sufficiently powerful class to overthrow the ancient monarchs and force them to share their powers, at some time towards the end of the 9th century perhaps; the exact date is difficult to establish. They were a turbulent class of nobles who were always given to conspiracy (Cylon is an instance in about 630 B.C.) but above all they were a landed aristocracy whose power was based on wealth. They were called the *pentakosiomedimnoi* (those whose lands produce an enormous quantity of grain); the name was coined when agriculture was mainly devoted to cereals, but the name remained even when their plantations consisted of vineyards and olive groves. The class immediately below was that of the *hippeis* who were also landed proprietors but who lived closer to their farmers and had lesser resources. At some time in the 7th century, a law was passed which reserved public offices for these two classes, but the hippeis were only allowed to hold the secondary posts. During this period the two lower classes played no part in political life; they were the *zeugitai* who only possessed small plots of land, and the *thetes* who were the poorest freemen of all.

It was not until the reforms of Cleisthenes, and even more, those of Ephialtes (462 B.C.), that the political barriers between the classes were removed. The Peloponnesian War, economic developments, commercial links with foreign countries, the growing importance of slaves and freemen in business, all naturally encouraged a radical transformation of the situation of the different classes of the population. Although attempts were made after Athens' defeat in 404 B.C. to re-establish a copy-holding system, all citizens were equal before the law, no matter what their income might be. Although most of the wealth might be in the hands of bankers and ship-owners they themselves were often of lowly birth, and sometimes even ex-slaves, who had been freed by their masters in gratitude for their services and who had managed to make their fortune by their talents.

P.D.

CLEISTHENES. Two outstanding Greek statesmen bore the name of Cleisthenes. The first was a tyrant at Sicyon during the first twenty years of the 6th century B.C., while the second, an Athenian, was his maternal grandson. The latter was related through his father to the family of the Alcmaeonidae who had already played an important part in Athenian political life. Despite his aristocratic birth, Cleisthenes became a democratic reformer. He came to power in 508, two

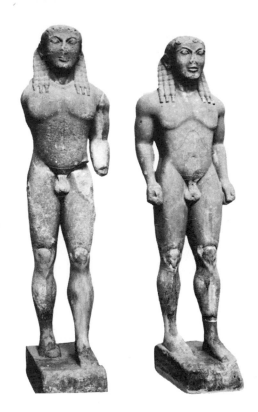

Cleobis and Biton. Votive statues. About 600 B.C. Delphi Museum. *Photo Spyros Meletzis.*

years after the fall of the Pisistratids, opposed the supporters of tyranny and the nobility who wished to bring back an oligarchic regime in Attica, and led a popular movement that was strong enough to succeed in defeating a contingent from Sparta that had been called in to aid the enemies of democracy. Cleisthenes preserved certain ancient institutions, but he created others which were more vigorous and effective and it was during his period of government that the old *naukrariai* (administrative districts) lost much of their power and that the Areopagus lost some of its prerogatives. In order to destroy the old territorial divisions, Cleisthenes created the demes *(demoi)* which he grouped together into ten tribes, each of which was composed of one third city-dwellers, one third inhabitants of the coastal regions, and one third peasants living in the interior. The result was that nothing was left of the former administrative divisions and the spirit of the reform may be compared somewhat to that which inspired the division of France into departments after the Revolution. Henceforth, the tribes were the basis of all political organisation; each tribe sent fifty representatives, chosen by lot, to the Senate (the Boule) and they were renewed each year. For one tenth of the total session *(prytaneia)* the representatives of one tribe were responsible for the government. The assembly of the people (Ecclesia) held sessions next to the Boule at least once during each prytaneia and had the final say in discussions of each measure that was proposed to them. These reforms, which transformed the whole character of the Athenian state, were pushed through in a few months, for in 506 Cleisthenes vanished completely from the scene. But before this disappearance, for reasons unknown to us, he had established a very special institution in order to protect his achievements in the field of political reform; this was none other than the system of ostracism (q.v.) by which any citizen whose activities might seem dangerous to the state could be banished for ten years.   P.D.

CLEOBIS and BITON. In the first years of the 6th century B.C. the Argives consecrated the statues of Cleobis and Biton at Delphi. They were, Herodotus tells us, the sons of a priestess of Hera. According to legend their mother was waiting in her chariot for a team of horses to take her to the sanctuary to make a sacrifice and, as they never arrived, her own sons pulled the chariot in which their mother rode all the way from Argos to Hera's sanctuary, nearly five miles away, in time for the ceremony, and then dropped down dead from exhaustion.   P.D.

CLEOMENES. This was the name of several kings of Sparta. We need only mention Cleomenes I who reigned from about 510 until 490 B.C. and who intervened on several occasions in Athenian politics, in an attempt to delay the democratic evolution that was taking place in the city after the downfall of the tyranny; and Cleomenes III who attempted to modify his country's constitution and give it a regime more in keeping with the new ideals of the time, between 237 and 219. He abolished the ephor system, redistributed lands, and tried to integrate his fellow countrymen into a social world from which Sparta had voluntarily isolated herself for centuries, but his efforts came to nothing when he was defeated by Antigonus Doson at the battle of Sellasia and died in exile at Alexandria.   P.D.

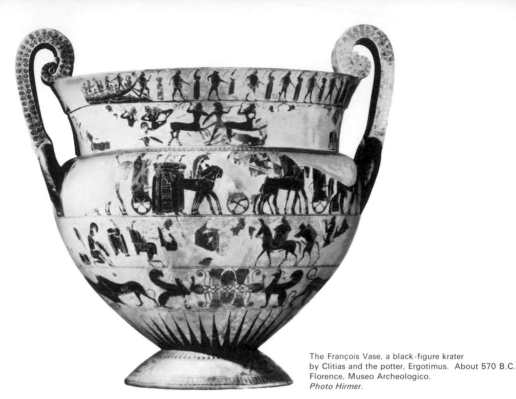

The François Vase, a black-figure krater
by Clitias and the potter, Ergotimus. About 570 B.C.
Florence, Museo Archeologico.
Photo Hirmer.

CLEON. Cleon was a Greek statesman who had the misfortune to have his life chronicled only by his worst enemies. Both Aristophanes and Thucydides painted the blackest of portraits of Cleon, representing him as cowardly, venal, crafty, avid for popularity and only concerned with his own interests. According to them, this rich tanner, who had entered into politics, did not scruple to use the lowest methods in order to accomplish his ends. It was certainly true that Cleon was a demagogue and the violence of his language combined with the coarseness of his attitudes probably impressed the mob more than the cold refinement of Pericles' oratory. Nowadays we might regard him as a determined war leader, for when Athens was fighting for its life in the Peloponnesus he advocated every measure in order to achieve victory; when the Mytileneans revolted in 428 B.C., Cleon demanded the death penalty for them all, and when there was a financial crisis he suggested a special tax on incomes. It was not therefore so very surprising that he was a resounding success in the assembly. He also took part himself in several campaigns and in 425 captured some 400 Spartans that the strategus,

Demosthenes, had been unable to drive out of Sphacteria. He died in 421, fighting before Amphipolis. According to Aristotle, no other man " had countributed more to the corruption of the people by letting it follow its instincts ", but might it not be more exact to say that he was only the spokesman of a people who were tired of the aristocratic distinction and moderation of Pericles ? P.D.

CLEPSYDRA. Water clock which was used rather like an hour-glass in order to limit the time in which an orator was allowed to hold the tribunal *(See* Chronology *and* Justice).

CLERUCHY. Although Athens had not founded a single city during the great period of Hellenic colonisation, it inaugurated a policy of territorial expansion towards the end of the 6th century B.C. The Athenian settlements, or cleruchies, were quite different from colonies *(See* Colonisation). Whereas in former times colonists had fled from the poverty of their native land to seek their fortune in barbarian countries, the cleruchs, or holders of lots, were almost always

Cretan dress. The "Snake Goddess" Minoan art. About 1500 B.C. Heraklion Museum. *Photo Hassia.*

sent to Greek regions that were often close to Athens like, for example, Euboea. Although, like the colonists, the emigration of the cleruchs was directed and led by a chief, they still kept their Athenian citizenship and all the rights and duties that went with it. It was Athens that assigned them their place of residence and their parcel of land *(kleros)* which was taken from the local population. A cleruchy then, was a settlement of Athenians in a precisely defined locality; unlike the colonial cities of former times, the settlement remained dependent on Athens and also kept guard over the state that had been obliged by Athens to offer them its hospitality.

Naturally enough, cleruchies were usually established in allied states whose loyalty was uncertain or in important strategic areas. The result was that the indigenous population found themselves living under a virtual occupation, and their lands taken from them by the victors, or " protectors ", who enjoyed all the privileges of Athenian citizenship, who paid less in taxes and military exactions, and who behaved as though they were in a conquered country. The system had been started by Cleisthenes, spread widely during the 5th century B.C. and was largely responsible for Athens' unpopularity when the Peloponnesian War broke out.   P.D.

CLITIAS. Clitias was a Greek vase painter, associated with the potter, Ergotinos, and considered one of the most brilliant representatives of the early Attic black-figure style in the second quarter of the 6th century B.C. His masterpiece is the François Vase, now in the Museo Archeologico, Florence (about 570-560). The survival of oriental decorative traditions may be seen in the way the vase is painted in successive bands, and by the fact that the sixth band depicts a procession of animals whereas the other five feature human figures. In this " kind of illustrated Greek Bible " (E. Pottier) we may see numerous heroes of the *Iliad*, or of Attic legends, combined with themes that had already been treated by sculptors in the past. More than two hundred and fifty figures and animals engaged in various activities have been counted on the vase. The spaciousness of the composition and the liberty with which movements and attitudes are treated are in striking contrast to the orientalising style and prefigure

the great achievements of later Greek vase painting. The careful rendering of detail, the liveliness of the compositions and the mastery of miniature painting, shown in this work, prove that the black-figure painters were already in full command of their medium, although certain archaic traits still persist, notably in the rendering of heads and limbs in profile, in contrast to the frontal aspect of the trunk, and the hieratic postures of the divine personages.   R.M.

CLOTHING. Nothing illustrates more clearly the difference between the Minoan civilisation and the civilisation of Greece itself than the differences in clothing. A fair number of Cretan images in paintings, engraved stones and figurines have survived, showing men wearing nothing but a rather short loin-cloth fastened at the waist by a broad belt under which they sometimes slipped a

113

which came down over the thighs. Women's clothes were more directly influenced by Cretan models but the long cloak was more common.

The Dorians brought entirely different fashions with them. After their arrival, both men and women's clothing was draped instead of close-cut, and waists were much less emphasised. The cloths they wrapped round their bodies were only rarely held by seams or buttons; they mostly used fibulae which were a kind of safety-pin. As a result, they had a much greater freedom of choice in the way they tightened their costumes, or in the height at which they fastened them so that the plastic effects they obtained in the way they dressed were far more striking than if they had worn close-fitting garments. There was little practical difference between the main parts of men's and women's clothing. It consisted in the first place of a more or less long tunic, which was a rectangular piece of cloth, hanging from the shoulders and leaving the arms free. The chiton, as it was called, remained fairly short for men and rarely fell below the knees. So that they might move more easily, they often only attached the ends of the tunic over one shoulder; the belt they wore around the waist, which made the garment pouch slightly, was only intended to prevent the tunic from flapping as they walked. Female tunics were similar, but they were longer and generally covered the whole of the legs. Except in Sparta, on one side of the body the two edges of the cloth were always brought together and sewn or attached by a number of hooks. There were two varieties of this tunic: the peplos, which was mostly worn by the Dorians, and the Ionian chiton. The peplos was made of a heavier material, such as wool, and because of its weight, it fell in long vertical folds that artists often treated like the fluting in a column. As it was very long, the upper part had to be folded back over the body so that it lay double over the chest. It could also be worn with a belt from which it flared out loosely Although the general build of the body, the squareness of shoulders, and the shape of the breasts could be seen under the costume, the details did not appear; the curve of the thighs and the narrowing of the waist were hidden by it. The Ionian chiton was made of linen and moulded the contours of the body far more closely, which permitted the wearer to indulge in a variety of seduc-

dagger. Women's clothing was more complicated but it also emphasised the waist and was in two parts: one a widely flaring skirt, which was often bell-shaped, the other a small, short-sleeved jacket, which tightly moulded the upper part of the body and was low-cut in front, finishing with a collar which rose behind the neck. A kind of chemisette was often worn under the jacket, and skirts usually had panels. A kind of hooded cape was always worn by men and probably also by women, when it was cold. Although their manner of living was so strongly influenced by the Cretans, the Mycenaeans dressed somewhat differently because of the difference in customs and the greater severity of the climate in mainland Greece. However, their clothing was also close-fitting and drawn in at the waist. The men wore drawers instead of loin-cloths and they covered the upper part of the body with belted tunics

Young women wearing a peplos and a chiton. Acroteria from the Temple of Aphaea at Aegina. About 500-480 B.C. Munich, Antikensammlung. *Photo Leonard von Matt.*

Horseman dressed for winter wearing a chlamys. Inside of a cup by the Pistoxenos Painter. About 480-470 B.C. Paris, Louvre. *Photo Tel.*

115

tive effects, first because it was finely and sharply pleated, which must have been very elegant, secondly because, although it was not transparent, it still hinted at physical details that the more austere peplos modestly concealed. The belt was only a thin cord worn rather high. The costume was generally sleeveless but, if the material was wide enough, the hems were fastened to the wrists and the elbows, giving a graceful wing-like effect.

Both chiton and peplos were worn alone. For walking, women put on a large piece of cloth, the himation, which ressembled a shawl rather than a coat. It was worn even more freely than the chiton: it could be hung from either one or both shoulders, slung transversely across the chest, or worn at equal length on each side of the body; one fold could be slung behind the back, or else hang down one hip and thigh, and some women even folded it over their heads as a hood. The material was usually rather heavy but sometimes, especially from the 4th century B.C., it was made of fine cloth and, when it was worn over the chiton, it clung fairly closely to the body.

Such garments were rarely white and were often lively and varied in colour. On the polychrome lekythoi of the late 5th century B.C., they are black, blue, yellow and various shades from red to violet. They were not always of one colour and the borders were often edged with wide strips of a different colour. They were also embroidered; the patterns were sometimes simple (there are plenty of examples in statuary and vase painting) or quite complicated. Exceptional garments, like the peplos that the Athenians offered their goddess every four years *(See* Panathenaea), would be embroidered. Theatrical costumes differed from everyday clothing by their richness as so often in later ages.

The way they wore these loose-fitting clothes distinguished the Greeks from the barbarians. When Greek artists depicted Scythian warriors or Persians, they gave them the long, close-fitting trousers, called *anaxyrides,* and the sleeved tunics they actually wore, which enabled a Greek to recognise at a glance that they were foreigners.
P.D.

CLYTEMNESTRA. Of all the crimes committed by the tragic family of the Atridae (q.v.) it was those of Clytemnestra that most fired the imagination of the Greek poets. Clytemnestra was the daughter of Leda, and therefore sister of Helen and the Dioscuri; she married Agamemnon and gave birth to Orestes, Iphigenia and Electra. She became filled by a bitter hatred for Agamem-

Amazon wearing a tunic and anaxyrides, or trousers. Detail of a pelike from the workshop of Polygnotus. About 440-430 B.C. Syracuse Museum. *Photo Hirmer.*

Palace at Cnossos.
Throne room.
Photo Hassia.

non after he had forced her to yield up Iphigenia to him for sacrifice and, during his ten years' absence during the Trojan War, she became the mistress of Aegisthus. When Agamemnon returned home, Clytemnestra incited Aegisthus to murder him and share the throne with her to rule over Argolis. Electra was then married to a poor labourer but Orestes fled for his life and later returned to kill his mother and the usurping lover.

Clytemnestra is one of the most tragic figures in Greek literature. Whether she was represented endeavouring to save Iphigenia, or else hypocritically welcoming Agamemnon after his triumphant Trojan campaign, or else as the mistress of Aegisthus and the perverse mother of Electra and Orestes, she was to remain a never failing source of inspiration for the greatest of the Greek playwrights.   P.D.

CNIDOS. Cnidos was one of the Dorian cities that were founded in the early Iron Age along the southern coast-line of Anatolia. Situated at the end of a peninsula separated by a narrow channel from the mainland, Cnidos owed its importance to its shipping activities and had few relations with the mainland. It is now mostly known because it was the centre of a cult of Aphrodite and the site of a temple which contained Praxiteles' famous statue of the goddess.   P.D.

CNOSSOS. Cnossos was one of the most important cities of ancient Crete and its site is only a few miles from the island's present capital. It was there that the Cretan princes, who became so powerful as early at least as the 18th century B.C., first built their palace in the 2nd millennium B.C. The site was particularly suitable for a capital city as it was near the sea, surrounded by a fertile plain, and the starting-point of the road which ran through the rich region of Mesara, linking the northern and southern shores of the island.

We know very little about the early city of Cnossos, for only a few buildings have been excavated; some are modest dwellings, others are more palatial residences. The palace itself has been totally excavated through the work of Sir Arthur Evans and his followers, and is famous as the finest known example of a royal residence of the Minoan age. Traces have also been found of successive alterations; the first ground plan, which dates from about 2000 B.C., underwent several changes until the completion of the palace in the 16th century and its destruction in about 1400 B.C. In its final form, the palace was a vast building which covered a rectangular area around a central courtyard. Extremely refined building techniques had been used in its construction and while stone was used for the base of the walls, the upper parts were built in brick and wood. The irregularities of the façades of the buildings seem to have been typically Cretan; a portico was set on the west side while access to the building was from the north and south. The exact purpose of the different quarters around the courtyard is not clear, although two types of " storeroom ", or cellars and warehouses, have been recognised, one situated at the end of a long corridor to the west, the other to the north-west. The Throne Room and its adjacent chambers were situated to the north-west of the courtyard, and included a chamber which was used as a votive store. The great Room of the

Double Axes owes its name to the signs that have been found incised in its walls, and is near the Queen's Apartments. Remains of staircases, of which the one to the east of the courtyard seems to have been particularly impressive, prove the existence of a second storey which has been rather audaciously reconstructed by the excavators. The presence of baths and latrines proves that the original inhabitants had a highly developed sense of comfort. The most important rooms were decorated with frescoes of which fragments have survived, the best known being the *Parisienne* and the famous *Prince with lilies* of which only a few pieces are authentic. The palace was destroyed at the end of the 15th century B.C. and the ruins themselves remained unoccupied. The site, however, was not deserted. Although the fine houses, whose rich decorations rivalled those of the palace, were also abandoned, a large number of people continued to live in more modest dwellings, built little by little on the remains of the ancient town, and until the Roman era Cnossos struggled to maintain its existence especially in

Palace at Cnossos.
Private apartments
on the first floor.
Photo Hassia.

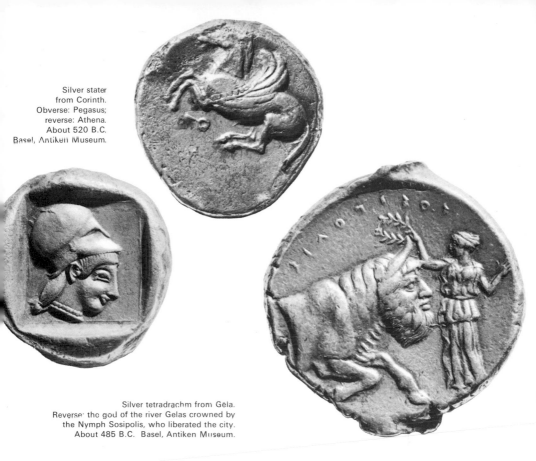

Silver stater from Corinth. Obverse: Pegasus; reverse: Athena. About 520 B.C. Basel, Antiken Museum.

Silver tetradrachm from Gela. Reverse: the god of the river Gelas crowned by the Nymph Sosipolis, who liberated the city. About 485 B.C. Basel, Antiken Museum.

the face of competition from the rival town of Gortyn. P.D.

COCYTUS. Tributary of the Acheron, the river of Hades.

COINAGE. Although Hellenic civilisation was far from being the earliest of those that developed in antiquity, and although a considerable volume of trade was done in Egypt, eastern countries and Crete, it was in Greece and then not until the 7th century B.C. that coinage was invented. Before that barter was practised, the unit of exchange being either a head of cattle or metal, which was either weighed at each deal or wrought in the form of axes, tripods and cauldrons. As early as the 8th century B.C., Greeks used iron spits, called obols, six of which made a drachma. We are not sure who first had the idea of a small easily handled ingot with a fixed value guaranteed by the official stamp of a public authority entitled to

certify its weight and alloy, in other words, a real coinage. Ancient traditions offer no reliable information. Among the innumerable names they mention, modern scholars have credited Pheidon, king of Argos, with introducing the new system into his own city and Aegina, about 650 B.C. There are some, however, who think that the honour of inventing it should go to the Greek cities of Asia Minor. Whatever the truth, the use of coinage spread as rapidly among the Greeks as among the barbarians because of its obvious practical advantages.

As coinage was at first a unit of weight, each state took one piece in its own system of weights as the standard and made the others its multiples and submultiples. At Aegina and in the Peloponnesus, the standard weight in trade was the mina, weighing 628 grammes, and the drachma, weighing one hundredth of this, 6.28 grammes, was chosen as the monetary unit. The didrachm, or stater, was about double this, 12.57 grammes,

Decadrachm from Syracuse. Head of the nymph Arethusa
surrounded by dolphins. About 495 B.C.
Sicily, Private collection. *Photo L. von Matt.*

Silver drachma from Selinus.
The trefoil of Selinus. Syracuse,
Museo Archeologico. *Photo L. von Matt.*

Silver coin from Metapontum.
A wheat-ear. *Photo L. von Matt.*

and its subdivision, the obol, weighing 1.04
grammes, counted as one sixth of a drachma.
In Euboea and Attica, where the mina weighed
436 grammes, the drachma was 4.36 and its multiples, the didrachm and tetradrachma, weighed
respectively twice and four times this, 8.73 and
17.46 grammes. The obol, a sixth of the monetary
unit, weighed 0.73 grammes.

For a long time, mainland Greece and the
Cyclades only struck silver coins, but Asia Minor,
on the other hand, practised bimetallism and even
trimetallism, from the very beginning, with gold,
silver and electron, a natural alloy of gold and
silver.

The business of finding equivalents between
these different systems made the fortune of the
money-changers *(trapezitai),* who pursued their
calling in the open air at ports and places where
trade was carried on. We know that, in early
times at least when polymetallism existed, gold
was worth thirteen and a third times of an equal

weight of silver. Equivalents were also worked
out between the different local systems. Although
attempts were made to reduce the variety of standard weights and although some of these standards, the Euboeic for example, were adopted
throughout the area where Athenian trade developed, the idea of international monetary conformity remained alien to the Greek mind, minting
its own coinage was a tangible proof for each
state of its autonomy.

The variety of coins in ancient Greece was very
great and they had nothing in common, if allowance is made for differences of period, except the
general appearance deriving from the minting
process.

The molten metal was first divided into ingots
that were weighed to ensure the legal weight.
They looked like a rounded or ovoid drop with
irregular edges. When the ingot had cooled, it
was placed on an anvil and struck with a bronze
or steel die bearing the hollowed image that

Decadrachm from Naples signed by Cimon. 5th century B.C. Naples, Museo Nazionale. *Photo L. von Matt.*

would be reproduced in relief on the coin. During the archaic era, only the obverse bore an image and the reverse was impressed by one or more rectangular shapes. At the beginning of the 5th century B.C., the reverse, too, was stamped with a design. The image selected had an official character and was in some way associated with the idea of the city that had struck it; it might be the head of a tutelary divinity (Athena at Athens), a local nymph (Arethusa at Syracuse), the image of a regional product (an ear of barley in the rich agricultural district of Metapontum) or even a sort of pun on the name of the town, like Zancle (a sickle), built on a sickle-shaped bay, whose coinage was stamped with dolphin in a sickle-shaped harbour.

Large quantities of Greek coins have been preserved and they are still being found accidentally or in systematic excavations on all ancient sites. They are extremely interesting for us. When there is no doubt about their origin, they provide evidence for the commercial exchanges between different cities and are consequently a major factor in reconstructing the history of trade. The changes in weight and the use, varying from period to period, of monometallism and bimetallism indicate the fluctuating prosperity of the issuing states. Although bronze coins were minted with less care than the gold and silver ones, they are often very beautiful. The Greek cities generally commissioned engravers of outstanding skill, who sometimes, like Evainetos and Cimon, signed their works, and some coins, especially at the end of the 6th century and during the 5th century B.C., are unquestionable masterpieces, like the Damareteion struck by Syracuse in 480 B.C. When the images have no particular aesthetic appeal, they are valuable as dated archaeological records; the style of paintings and sculptures can be compared with theirs and dated accordingly.

During the Hellenistic period, the device on the coin, as often before in the provinces of the Per-

Tetradrachm from Syracuse
struck at by the order of Agathocles
to commemorate his victory
over Carthage. About 310 B.C.
Agrigento Museum.
Photo L. von Matt

Athenian coin. Reverse: an
owl and three olive leaves.
Paris, Cabinet des Médailles.

sian empire, was the portrait of the sovereign who
had minted it. After Alexander, whose energetic
features were reproduced even after his death,
several kings stamped their heads on coins; this
is an invaluable contribution to our knowledge of
ancient iconography. The name was generally
engraved around the edge. Some kind of inscription was traditional, from the beginning, cities had
often inscribed an abbreviated form of their name
beside the device to indicate the origin of the coin,
like the three letters (TH is represented by a single
character in Greek) for ATHE on the Athenian
drachmas.   P.D.

COLONISATION. The original Greek
word for emigration is usually translated as
" colonisation " with the result that we are all too

likely to forget that there is a fundamental difference between the two concepts. In modern
times, the word colonisation is used when the
inhabitants of a more powerful state take possession of some more or less remote territory, whose
inhabitants are considered to belong to an inferior
civilisation and who are reduced to an inferior
status, while the colonising settlers retain the
citizenship of their mother country and all the
privileges that go with it, irrespective of whether
their stay in the colony is transitory or permanent.
This fairly recent historical phenomenon, which
first appeared in the 17th century, has been regarded as the sign of a nation's power. But it was
in the time of their greatest weakness and political
turmoil, in the period between the 8th and the
6th centuries B.C., that the Greek cities became

colonisers. They were almost all undergoing a period of growing pains which affected political and social as much as economic conditions. In almost every city the monarchy had given way to an aristocracy who ceaselessly enlarged their estates at the expense of the small landowners, who were forced by their debts to relinquish their small holdings with the result that there was an ever-growing disinherited class who were unable to make their living by trade or craftsmanship, then scarcely developed, and whose numbers were swelled by the people defeated in the many civil wars then raging throughout the states. The only course left to these wretched inhabitants of a country lacking in natural resources was to emigrate and this was the essential cause of Greek colonising activities. Rather than going abroad to seek their fortunes separately, those who decided to emigrate would ask their city to provide them with a leader and a fixed destination. This process of expatriation was more than an emigration or a colonisation in the accepted sense; it was more like the swarming of bees. Nothing was left to chance. Navigation was flourishing, the outer world was becoming better known and the oracle of Delphi was regularly consulted and would indicate the direction to be taken by the emigrants. An official ceremony would then be held before the departure of the expedition and its leader, who was to be the head of the colony once it had been founded.

Once they had arrived at their destination, the colonists not only founded a city but built temples to the divinities whom they continued to worship as before. The new city organised a life of its own and was independent of the homeland with whom it only maintained diplomatic relations; for it was a new state in its own right with its own administration, coinage, and diplomacy. It concluded its own treaties with neighbouring states and made its own declarations of war, sometimes even against the mother country. Relations with the local inhabitants might be good or bad, but whether the colonists traded with them or reduced them to servitude, they did so of their own accord without referring to the homeland. They relinquished their former nationality.

This movement of populations may be regarded as a kind of prolongation, after a long interval, of the migrations which had led the Balkan tribes into continental Greece in the late Bronze Age and sent the earlier Ionian inhabitants towards the islands and the coasts of Asia Minor. The new emigrants were impelled by poverty rather than invasions but the result was the same, with the essential difference that this time, the settlers had already formed their roots, organised cities and developed their own civilisation. The emigrants who began to swarm from the 8th century B.C. onwards, along the shores of the Mediterranean and the Black Sea, did not have to undergo the same period of apprenticeship as the less civilised tribes who had invaded mainland Greece and the islands from the regions of the Danube. Although the movement of colonisation spread in every direction, it was at its most marked in the more fertile regions and it avoided territories that already lay under powerful civilised rule. From about 775 B.C. onwards, expeditions from Euboea settled in Italy, along the gulf of Naples, and shortly afterwards in Sicily, and the occupation of southern Italy became so extensive that the whole of the southern peninsula became known as Magna Graecia. Other colonists sailed further westward and settled at Marseilles and even Spain, while countless others moved northwards and eastwards, to Macedonia and Thracia, the shores of the Sea of Marmara and the Black Sea. A Greek city was founded on the shores of Syria at Al Mina and in the 6th century B.C. the Egyptian pharaohs granted the concession of the site of Naucratis to a consortium of Greek cities.

Not all the states of ancient Greece were colonisers and neither Sparta nor Athens ever sent part of their population overseas. But Chalcis and Eretria in Euboea, Corinth and Megara, certain islands like Paros and Thera, and especially the city of Miletus in Ionia were among the most prolific colonising states. This colonising process, which must not be confused with the institution of the cleruchy (q.v.) in the 5th century B.C., had a great effect on the history of the Hellenic world. It spread Hellenic culture abroad and went a long way towards resolving the economic and social problems of the old cities. Not only were the Greek cities relieved of the burden of their surplus population, which they could no longer feed, but the commercial exchanges between the mother countries and the colonies, whereby the latter exported such raw materials as wood and grain to the parent metropolis, encouraged the growth of industries, whose products were in turn exported to the new settlements. Furthermore, as the new colonies did not have to bear such a heavy burden of local traditions, they were able to innovate in many fields and their

Restored column of the palace at Cnossos. Doric and Ionic columns of the Propylaea at Athens. *Photos Hassia.*

contribution towards the development of city planning has often been stressed as an example of their freedom to experiment.   P.D.

COLUMN. The column was a very important element in Greek architecture. It was not only used in the interior of large rooms as an additional support for the beams that had to bear the weight of the roof but was employed even more frequently on the exterior as a support for open galleries and porticoes which would provide indispensable shade from the burning Mediterranean sun. It was therefore in constant use. At the beginning, and for a long time afterwards, at least until the end of the 7th century B.C., columns were made of wood. As late as the 2nd century A.D., Pausanias noticed a single, remaining wooden column still supporting the structure of the temple of Hera at Olympia, which had been gradually rebuilt in stone. Cretan and Mycenaean

columns were made of a single tree-trunk cut into a tapering shaft; the thin end was placed downwards and inserted in a ring-shaped base while a square block was inserted between the top of the shaft and the beams it had to support. In Greek architecture, by contrast, the shaft tapered upwards and in the classical period the shaft was made to swell slightly in the middle to avoid the optical illusion whereby a perfectly straight shaft appears to be narrower in the centre.

The Greek column was one of the essential elements in the orders of architecture and whether it stood on a base or not (Ionic or Doric column) it was nearly always fluted; there were twenty grooves in the Doric order and twenty-four in the Ionian. The purpose of fluting was to avoid an impression of monotony, to give a vertical, linear rhythm to the colonnading and to catch the light. The system whereby only one side of a column would be fluted with the rest faceted only dates from the Hellenistic period. The capital *(See Orders)* may be considered as an integral part of the column in Greek architecture.　　　P.D.

COMEDY. In its early literary origins, the Greek comedy was derived from the *Margites* (a satirical and burlesque poem attributed in ancient times to Homer of which only a few scraps have now survived) and the iambic poetry of Archilochus (q.v.). But the real source of comedy in the theatre, as well as of tragedies and satiric drama, was the cult of Dionysus. The word *komos* (q.v.), whence *komodia*, was used to designate the burlesque and unruly processions of the worshippers of Dionysus under the sign of the *phallos*. These drunken roisterers later became the comic chorus, but the comedy properly speaking did not begin to exist until it had evolved dramatic action and a plot and until the associates who gave the cues to the chorus had become actors.

Unlike tragedy (q.v.), Greek comedy was not purely Attic in its origins. Such Dorian states as Sicyon, Megara and Sicily seem to have played an important part in the evolution of the comedy and Greece's first comic poet was a Sicilian named Epicharmus. He seems to have been born in about the middle of the 6th century B.C. and stayed at the courts of the tyrants of Sicily, Gelon and Hieron, where he may have met Simonides,

Bacchylides, Pindar and Aeschylus. The titles of the plays of Epicharmus that we now know were derived either from mythology *(Alcyone, The Wedding of Hebe, The Cyclops, Philoctetes, Chiron, Busiris)* or everyday life *(The Peasants, The Plunderers, Riches, The Refined Man, The Cooking-Pots, Hope, The Megarian Woman)*. The few surviving fragments of Epicharmus's plays are full of wit, verve, and lively dialogue. Epicharmus was particularly interested in depicting character and ways of life which brings him closer in spirit to Menander than Aristophanes. He was also greatly interested in the theories of philosophers. Despite Epicharmus's importance, it was at Athens that comedy developed most fully. Although competitions of tragedies had started under Pisistratus in 534 B.C., comedy did not appear in the programme of the Great Dionysia until 486, although a certain kind of comic representation known as *komoi* had been performed as early as 501.

In the 5th century B.C. the ancient comedy was rather rigid in structure and was formed of three parts: 1) the play opened with a kind of dialogue-prologue which often resembled the burlesque turn given outside the booth of a travelling show; the choir then entered on the scene and engaged in a lively struggle with the protagonist; this skirmish often ended in a debate *(agon)* and the victory of either the actor or the chorus brought

Scene from a comedy. Zeus, carrying a ladder and Hermes a torch, engaged in an amorous adventure. Detail of a Paestan krater. Late 4th century B.C. Vatican, Museo Gregoriano Etrusco. *Ph. Alinari-Giraudon.*

this first part to a conclusion; 2) the *parabasis:* a kind of entr'acte without actors in which all dramatic action was suspended and the chorus revealed the author's reflections, complaints or hopes to the public; 3) a loosely linked series of scenes in which the consequences of the situation that had been created at the end of the first part were amusingly developed. The scenes were punctuated by the satiric songs of the chorus who left the " orchestra " in a noisy finale thus bringing the performance to an end. The themes were very varied but always drawn from political, social or literary topics. The poet's main aim was to excite mirth at the expense of powerful or fashionable personalities, often by the crudest means and coarsest jokes. Not even the gods, with Dionysus, the god of the theatre, at their head, were spared by this biting satire. Aristophanes (q.v.) is the only poet of the Old Comedy whose plays are still known to us, for we only have fragments of the works of his predecessors and contemporaries such as Magnes, Cratinus (whose *Bottle* was crowned at the expense of Aristophanes' *Clouds),* Crates, Pherecrates, and Eupolis. Aristophanes' two last surviving plays illustrate the transition from Old to Middle Comedy in the first half of the 4th century B.C.; the role of the chorus was reduced and the parabasis tended to disappear. The leading comic poets of this period are Antiphanes and Alexis, but only fragments of their work survive.

The period from about 350 to the 3rd century B.C. was that of the so-called New Comedy and its main exponents were Menander (q.v.) and Philemon. The chorus practically disappeared, or rather, its only function was to provide dance and music interludes without any connexion with the play, in between each act or scene. The greatest difference between the Old and the New Comedy was in the nature of the subjects treated and in the general tone of the works. Political satire gave way to a comedy of intrigue and character which centred entirely on the private lives and manners of society, and the former vein of crudeness or obscenity gave way to the tone of " good society ". Although he was not an Athenian, Philemon won his greatest fame and glory at Athens. He was born in 361 and only just missed becoming a centenarian for he died in 262. He was often Menander's successful rival and more than sixty titles of his comedies are known to us although only scattered fragments have survived.   R.F.

COMMERCE. Although Greek roads were merely rough tracks which crossed rivers at fords, they were used by travelling merchants who made long journeys with their bundles and beasts of burden, such as donkeys or mules, laden or dragging their two or four-wheeled carts, in order to sell the produce of such regions as Boeotia or Megara in the agora of Athens. Such overland commerce was relatively unimportant; the way merchants *(emporoi)* made their fortunes was by maritime trade. The merchants were obliged to invest large capital sums in their enterprises and were sometimes helped by bankers who lent them money at usurers' rates. By farming out the taxes to a company, the state levied customs of a hundredth, and then a fiftieth, of the value of all merchandise that came in through the harbour of Piraeus. Apart from this tax, all products except cereals were allowed free passage. The college of *sitophylakes* supervised the importation of corn that the Athenians bought at a high price in Egypt, Sicily, and across the Pontus Euxinus, as well as the sale of flour and bread. Its political hegemony enabled Athens to enjoy several monopolies such as that of vermilion, which came from the island of Ceos. The author of the *Polity of the Athenians,* a work which has come down to us under Xenophon's name, gives the following picture of Athenian commerce: " In the whole of Greece and among the Barbarians, is there any other people as capable of enriching themselves as the Athenians ? Indeed, even though building timber may abound in such and such a town, or copper or linen in another, how can this merchandise be marketed if the city that is mistress of the seas is not given its share of these interests ? Consequently, one of our ships will provide us with wood, another with iron, one with copper, another with linen, and another with wax... Without getting anything out of the earth I obtain everything by sea. " In exchange for varied and massive imports, Attica exported nothing except its oil, its wine and its pottery. But in the Hellenistic period the commercial centre of the Aegean moved successively towards Delos, Alexandria and Rhodes *(See* Shipping).   R.F.

COMPETITION. The Greeks were among those fortunate peoples whose citizens did not spend their best years studying to pass tests in order to obtain administrative posts, all too often of a mediocre nature, since administrative, religious and political appointments were decided by elections or, more often, by lot. Moreover such professions as that of medicine were open to all. But they did not ignore the fact that the spirit of emulation is inherent in human nature and they enjoyed holding competitions for their own sake in which honour and glory were the sole prizes to be won. Games were held in which the champions of different cities competed against each other, playwrights, actors and musicians were classed according to their merits by specially qualified judges, and the famous judgment of Paris on the three goddesses was only the most celebrated of the many beauty contests that were very popular in archaic times, notably in the eastern regions of the Hellenic world. P.D.

CONCUBINAGE. Although the Greeks were always a monogamous people and unfaithful wives were severely punished, great indulgence was shown in the classical period to unfaithful husbands who might even install another woman, often a slave, in the conjugal household as a concubine. But the children of concubines did not have the right of citizenship unlike those of the legitimate wife. When fathers sometimes legitimised their bastards, the inheritance was often disputed in the courts. In a plea which has been attributed to Demosthenes, but which seems to have been written by another hand in the same period *(Against Neaera)*, the speaker declares, as if it was the most natural thing in the world: " We have courtesans for pleasure, concubines to minister to our daily needs, and wives to give us legitimate children and to be the faithful guardians of our households. " In the Hellenistic period the principle of moral equality between the sexes, which several philosophers had proclaimed after Socrates, tended to pass from theory into practice, as may be seen in the marriage contract dating from 311 B.C. quoted in the entry on Contracts (q.v.). R.F.

CONON. In the last years of the Peloponnesian War, the Athenian, Conon, played a fairly important part as a strategus. In 413 B.C. he was sent to Naupactus to intercept the enemy convoys on their way to Sicily, in 406 he was given the task of reorganising the Athenian fleet and tried to establish smaller but more effective naval units. Unfortunately he allowed Lysander to capture thirty of his ships at Mytilene and his negligence was largely responsible for the disaster of Aegospotami (q.v.). Not daring to return to Athens

after this defeat, he fled to Cyprus and entered the service of the Persian king. In 394 he led the Persian fleet and defeated the Lacedaemonian navy at Cnidos, which frustated Agesilaus's efforts in Asia Minor. His success compensated for his past mistakes and he returned to Athens in triumph. P.D.

CONSTITUTION. We should not be misled by the word constitution, which has been used in the translation of certain treatises and pamphlets which were very popular at the end of the 5th century B.C., especially among the Peripatetics, such as the *Constitution of the Lacedaemonians*, falsely attributed, it seems, to Xenophon, Aristotle's *Athenaion Politeia*, etc. All these treatises describe an already existing political state with a greater or lesser degree of objectivity, but there was never any mention of a constitution in the modern sense. The concept of a written charter and a fundamental law, which laid down the rules of government and defined the respective rights and duties of government and citizens, was unknown to the ancient Greeks. The Greek city state developed gradually and its form of government was decided by civil or religious traditions which themselves could be modified if necessary. P.D.

CONTRACTS. The earliest Greek contracts *(synthekai, symbolaia)* were probably those which bound a debtor to his creditor. The pledge of one's own person was not abolished in Athens until 594 B.C. by Solon, and meant that an insolvent debtor could be sold as a slave together with the whole of his family by the creditor. Commerce and especially maritime trade gave rise to many contracts between bankers and shipowners, shipowners and captains, but they were generally verbal agreements made in the presence of witnesses as may be seen from the speech *Against Zenothemis* which Demosthenes wrote as a logographer. Another kind of contract was the fictitious sale of a slave to a divinity as an act of enfranchisement; the practice became increasingly frequent in the 2nd and 1st centuries B.C. The acts were inscribed on stone in sanctuaries such as that of Delphi and often included certain special clauses such as that of *paramone* which obliged the enfranchised slave to remain in the service of his master until the latter's death. With regard to marriage, it would appear that payment of the dowry was guaranteed verbally before witnesses,

Pediment from the Temple of Artemis at Corcyra. About 600 B.C. Corfu Museum.
Photo Deutsches Archäologisches Institut, Athens.

during the ceremony of *engyesis (See* Marriage).
A number of marriage contracts written on Egyptian papyrus and dating from the Hellenistic period
have been found. The following dates from 311
and was signed on the isle of Cos:

" 7th year of the reign of Alexander, son of
Alexander, 14th year of the satrap, Ptolemy,
month of Dios.

" Contract of marriage between Heraclides and
Demetria.

" Heraclides takes Demetria of Cos for his legitimate wife and receives her from her father, Leptines of Cos, and her mother, Philotis. He is free
and she is free. She brings clothing and jewels to
the value of a thousand drachmas. Heraclides
undertakes to provide Demetria with everything
necessary for a free woman. They will live in a
place to be chosen by Leptines and Heraclides
jointly.

" Should Demetria be found committing any
act likely to harm her husband and bring shame on
him, let all the possessions she has brought with
her be confiscated, and let Heraclides declare why
he has reproached Demetria before three arbiters
whom they will choose jointly. Let it not be per-

mitted to Heraclides to take another wife, which
would be to do wrong to Demetria, nor to have
children by another woman, nor to harm Demetria
on any pretext whatsoever. If Heraclides be
found committing any similar wrongs, he will be
accused by Demetria before three arbiters whom
they will have chosen jointly. Let Heraclides
then return the dowry of a thousand drachmas that
Demetria brought him and also pay a fine of a
thousand silver drachmas of Alexander.

" There shall be distraint on Heraclides and all his
goods, both on sea and on land, to the benefit of
Demetria and her authorised agents after executory
judgment. The contract is executory in any place
pleasing to the parties' Witnesses. " This contract
shows a noticeable evolution in family law in classical Greece, in favour of the woman. R.F.

CORAX. Sicilian rhetorician and master of
Tisias. *(See* Rhetoric).

CORCYRA. The island of Corcyra, or Corfu
as it is now called, facing Epirus, is the largest of
all the islands lying off the Adriatic coastline of
Greece. It is usually identified with the island of

Scheria where the Phaeacians lived according to Homer's *Odyssey*. The capital, named like the island, was founded in remote times by colonists from Euboea, who were later expelled in the 8th century B.C. by the Corinthians. The early 6th century temple of Artemis at Corcyra is one of our main sources of knowledge of archaic architecture and sculpture. The pediment was decorated with an enormous figure of the Gorgon, showing Chrysaor and Pegasus being born out of its blood. It was flanked on either side by animals resembling panthers, while the angles were somewhat clumsily filled with representations of the giants fighting the gods. Once the great wave of colonisation towards the west of Greece had subsided, Corcyra only had a minor importance in Greek history. The island quarrelled with the mainland and also with the city of Epidamnus, which it had founded, and it was one of these disputes that led to the first clash between Athens and Sparta on the eve of the Peloponnesian War. It was also at Corcyra that the Romans made their first contact with the Greeks on Hellenic territory (228 B.C.). P.D.

CORINTH. Corinth was one of the most important cities of ancient Greece. It was not one of the oldest cities and does not seem to have played the slightest part in the Mycenaean period.

It first appeared in history in the early 1st millennium B.C. and was flourishing for the whole of the archaic period. Its situation in the centre of Greece at the end of the narrow isthmus which linked the Peloponnesus to the mainland, its direct access through its gulf to the Adriatic and the proximity of the Aegean sea on the other side, and the surrounding fertile plains where wine and olives could be cultivated made it a commercial centre of the first order. Its industries were developed by a dynasty of tyrants, the Cypselidae, and during the whole of the 7th, and a part of the 6th century B.C., Corinthian potters exported countless thousands of vases throughout the Hellenic world, usually small in size but often of the highest quality. Bronze was another industry that developed at the same time. After the downfall of the tyranny, Corinth held a minor position in Greek politics; its population of rich merchants was afraid of being engaged in foreign adventures and the city only reluctantly took part in the Persian Wars. Although it later joined the intrigues and struggles that ravaged the Greek world, it did so without any great show of enthusiasm and, so it was said, most unwillingly. The city's real ambition was to become rich and the riches found by the Romans when Mummius captured and sacked the city in 146 B.C. proved that it was successful in this aim.

Temple of Apollo at Corinth. About 540 B.C. *Ph. Hirmer.*

The Diolkos, a causeway made for hauling boats across the Isthmus of Corinth. *Photo Georges Roux.*

Although this vast undertaking was never accomplished in antiquity, a passage, the *Diolkos,* was built acccross the isthmus, on which fully laden boats were slid or pushed from one gulf to the other. It was only natural that such an important site should be consecrated to a god and recently the famous sanctuary of Poseidon, which was described in the texts of the time, was uncovered by archaeologists. The sanctuary was one of the sites of the great international games that were held every two years in ancient Greece and some of Pindar's most famous odes, the *Isthmian,* were specially commissioned to commemorate the athletes who had triumphed in the games.   P.D.

COS. A small island in the Dodecanese and a neighbour of the island of Rhodes. Cos was only saved from total obscurity because of its sanctuary of Asclepius, built near a sulphurous spring. The sanctuary's most important period dates from the middle of the 4th century B.C. when its temples and porticoes were built and enlarged as the fame of the god spread. It was a dependency of Epidaurus at first, and soon became one of the most important sanctuaries in the whole of Greece. Famous doctors came to the island to practise their profession and they founded a school of medicine which seems to have been outstanding in its time.   P.D.

COSMETICS. Women often singed or shaved their superfluous hair (the razor belonged to the woman's, not the man's, toilet equipment) and also used beauty creams, perfumes (q.v.) and rouge. In his *Economy,* Xenophon Ischomachus says that one day he found his young wife " all made up with ceruse to give her a clearer complexion than usual, all painted with alkanet so that she would look more rosy than she really was ". Courtesans (q.v.) not only used the white of ceruse and the pink of alkanet, but also heightened their eyes and eye-brows with black and brown lines.   R.F.

COURTESAN. The custom of sacred prostitution existed in ancient Greece as in many other ancient countries and its most important centre was at Corinth in the sanctuary of Aphrodite (Venus), the goddess of love. The rather

The loss of their independence did not particularly effect the Corinthians, for the numerous remains of buildings dating from the period of Roman domination show that the city soon regained its former prosperity.   P.D.

CORINTH (Isthmus of). The Peloponnesus, which was one of the most important regions of ancient Greece and the cradle of Hellenic civilisation, and such important northern provinces as Boeotia, Attica, Phocis and Delphi were linked by only a narrow strip of land scarcely four miles in width, the Isthmus of Corinth. It was a natural defensive position, for the presence of an army across its width was enough to hold back invaders from the north, but it was also an obstacle to maritime traffic since it blocked the route between the gulf of Aegina and the Aegean sea in the east and the Gulf of Corinth and the Adriatic in the west. In 480 B.C. a wall was built from east to west across the isthmus as a defence against the Persian invaders under Xerxes; it was later rebuilt and repaired on various occasions. The idea of cutting a channel through the isthmus to facilitate sea communication was a very old one and the first known project dates from the time of Periander in the 7th century B.C., but all the many successive projects came to nothing until the canal was finally cut in the 19th century A.D.

special priestesses who served the goddess were called *hierodouloi* (sacred slaves). A Corinthian athlete, whom Pindar has celebrated in his odes, once made a vow to offer fifty *hierodouloi* to the Aphrodite of his native town if he won in the Olympic games, and when he did so, kept his promise. "Secular" courtesans, as they might be called, were known as *hetairai* (companions or friends). Some became famous like Rhodopis, the 6th century B.C. courtesan, whose life has been related by Herodotus. She was so rich that she was reputed to have paid for the building of one of the great pyramids of Egypt. When Solon was archon of Athens in 594 B.C., he opened the first public brothels in order to avoid the family disturbances that were being caused by over-amorous young people. The Attic temple of Aphrodite Pandemos (the Popular) was built with the yield of taxes that the inmates of the brothels were obliged to pay to the public treasury. Xenophon's *Memorabilia* (III, 11) contains an amusing description of Socrates' chaste visit to the courtesan, Theodota. After Rhodopis, the most famous courtesans were Lais, and then the Thespian, Phryne (q.v.), the model and mistress of the sculptor, Praxiteles. Phryne appeared in a court case in which she was defended by the orator, Hyperides, who influenced her judges by suddenly ripping open her dress and showing her bare bosom at the most moving moment of his peroration. The court was suddenly seized by religious scruples and did not dare to condemn "the priestess and servant of Aphrodite", but the Athenians took precautions against the repetition of such incidents by passing a decree which forbade the accused to remain before the judges when they came to the vote. The authenticity of this story, which inspired many sculptors and painters, has often been contested, but is not so unlikely when we consider the enormous respect that the art-loving ancient Greeks had for physical beauty.

Many courtesans were also talented musicians (particularly as flute-players) and dancers who would perform at banquets. In 4th century B.C. Athens, they were so sought after that a law was passed fixing their maximum fee for one evening at two drachmas, and it was decided that lots should be drawn when they were demanded by several clients at the same time.

Several hetairai, such as Neaera, succeeded in finding husbands and becoming respectable family women in the end. The greatest period of the

Courtesan dancing in front of a guest at a banquet. Detail of a cup by Brygos. About 490 B.C. British Museum.

statues of Zeus and Athena, who became a virtual " minister of Fine Arts " through his friendship with Pericles. Greek artists did not become rich and Plato has told us that a fashionable sophist like Protagoras would earn ten times as much as Phidias. As private houses were always very modest residences until the Hellenistic period, artists rarely worked for private citizens but were commissioned by the state, especially to build and decorate temples. In the 5th century B.C. artists were mainly employed on the great project of the Acropolis in Athens. In the 4th century, art became decentralised: Scopas, Bryaxis, Leochares and Timotheus went to work in Asia on the Mausoleum of Halicarnassus. Lysippus was Alexander's accredited sculptor and from the Hellenistic period onwards, as artists came to depend almost exclusively on kings and princes for their commissions, they were obliged to become courtiers as well.

R.F.

CRATES. Comic dramatist, slightly earlier in date than Aristophanes. *(See* Comedy).

CRATINUS. Great comic dramatist and Aristophanes' rival *(See* Comedy).

CREON. Two legendary kings were both called Creon. The first ruled over Corinth and gave his daughter, Creusa, in marriage to Jason, but the unfortunate girl fell victim to the jealousy of the sorceress, Medea. The other Creon was the brother of Jocasta and ruled Thebes after the old king, Laius, had been killed by an unknown assassin. Then Oedipus came to the town, saved it from the Sphinx, married Jocasta without knowing that he was his own mother, and ascended the throne. It was Creon's destiny to take the place of dead kings; after he had succeeded Laius, he came to the throne again after his nephews, Eteocles and Polynices, had killed each other. Literature has represented him as a cruel tyrant in the present sense of the word, because he would not allow Polynices to be buried for having taken up arms against his own country, and condemned his niece Antigone to death when she disobeyed his ruling. Before this, he also pursued Oedipus, who had taken refuge in the village of Colonus near Athens, not out of pity for the blind man, but because an oracle had told him that, even though

hetairai was the Hellenistic age, when prevailing customs made it easy for them to climb the social ladder, and some " could trample on kings' diadems " in Plutarch's words; courtesans like Lamia, the mistress of Demetrius Poliorcetes, Belestike, Ptolemy II's mistress, and Agathocleia, Ptolemy IV's mistress, were almost queens. R.F.

CRAFTSMEN and ARTISTS. All talented Greeks had a great sense of beauty and this was why ancient Greece produced so many great artists. There was no really radical distinction between artists and craftsmen. Potters signed their graceful wares, as did the artists who painted them. A craftsman like Aison, who left his signature on a bowl depicting the exploits of Theseus, was just as much an artist as Phidias, the decorator of the Parthenon and the creator of admirable

Vase decorated with a sacred knot in relief, found in the Little Palace at Cnossos. 16th century B.C. Heraklion Museum. *Photo Hassia.*

he had exiled Oedipus, the hero's presence was necessary for the prosperity of Thebes.   P.D.

CRESILAS. This sculptor came from Crete. He left the island, probably in his youth, to go to Athens where he arrived just as Phidias was to begin the great works on the Acropolis and fell under the master's influence, although he does not appear to have been either his pupil or collabora- tor.   What was probably one of his earliest works is the famous *Wounded Warrior,* shown on the point of death.   He was also the artist of the famous portrait of *Pericles* of which two good replicas have survived until the present day. It was almost certainly an idealised portrait, for the intelligent, refined and noble face of the great strategus has been deliberately represented without any of the traits that might indicate old age or fatigue.   Cresilas took part in a sculpture contest for a *Wounded Amazon* for the sanctuary of Artemis at Ephesus, together with Phidias and Polycletus, but his work was not chosen (the prize went to Polycletus); it has survived in replicas, which indicate a talent depending largely on technical skill.   P.D.

CRETE.   In size, Crete is the largest of the Greek islands, in influence it was once the most important.   With a length of 160 miles from east to west and with a maximum width of 35 miles, it forms a kind of barrier enclosing the Aegean Sea to the south.   A high chain of mountains runs along its length like a spine, each side being somewhat different in aspect.   Because of its position, the island flourished during the troubled period around the year 2000 B.C. and developed the so called Minoan civilisation, which already foreshadowed the glory of Greece and was a kind of forerunner of Hellenism.   Crete was far enough from the continent not to have to fear the invasions that were then ravaging the Greek peninsula, rich enough in such agricultural resources as vines and olive trees and in sheltered harbours like the

Faience plaques showing houses, found in the Palace at Cnossos. 18th century B.C. Heraklion Museum. *Photo Hassia.*

present port of Candia, as important now as was ancient Cnossos, to be able to lead an independent existence and maintain or sever relations as it liked with the Cycladic islands and the Peloponnesus, as well as the old civilisations of Egypt and Asia. The island's greatest period was between the 18th and 15th centuries B.C. Earlier, either in the Neolithic period or else in the Early Minoan period, whose origins are obscure but which came to an end in about 2200, the island was already peopled by a race who showed signs of great industry but no particular talent for creating a civilisation. In about 2000 the first palaces were built, towns were founded and life seems to have been both peaceful and prosperous, with princes trading the products of their not very extensive domains. There were frequent exchanges with foreign countries and many Cretan techniques were derived from the Egyptians such as pottery making; stone and terra-cotta vases seem to have been inspired by Egyptian models. Private citizens of the time built themselves roomy houses of several storeys, and curious tablets have been found which depict these dwellings vividly.

In the 18th century B.C., Crete was struck by disaster. We do not know what it was, but it was more probably an earthquake than an invasion. New, larger, and more beautiful palaces were built on the ruins, specially designed for the comfort of their inhabitants, with vast central courtyards, and various quarters for the royal family, the courtiers and the servants. The ruins of Cnossos, Mallia and Phaestus and those of the villa of Haghia Triada point to the extraordinary prosperity of the period. Surprisingly enough, little place seems to have been reserved for worship in these buildings. The Cretans seem to have considered small chapels and household shrines as being sufficient for their religious needs. The reason was that the celestial beings were mostly worshipped in the open; the chief divinity was female and represented the principle of fertility. She resided on the peaks of mountains, near springs or in the shade of a great tree. The festivals held in her honour were in the open, often in the courtyard of the palace before the eyes of assembled spectators who either stood or sat on steps. Wild bulls were brought in, and both male and female athletes would accomplish the most dangerous and spectacular feats such as turning somersaults over the animals' backs. The apartments of the palace consisted of small rooms opening on to narrow corridors; the fragments of paintings which have

Tauromachy.
Impression
of an agate seal
from Praisos.
16th-15th century B.C.
Heraklion Museum.
Photo Hassia.

Suppliant goddess. Terra-cotta from the Palace at Cnossos. 13th century B.C. Heraklion Museum
Photo Hassia.

been found on the walls show an astonishingly high level of technique and inspiration. The feebleness of the fortifications is proof that the inhabitants of these vast buildings had an almost complete sense of security. It was not war that brought wealth to the Cretan princes and their subjects but agriculture, commerce and industry. It seems that the harmony was only rarely disturbed among the " hundred cities ", which existed in Crete according to classical sources; if their number was exaggerated, excavations have proved that they were in fact extraordinarily numerous. This peace was probably the source of Crete's legendary reputation among the Greeks in the classical period; they spoke admiringly of the sovereign, Minos, who was traditionally supposed to have ruled over the island. The names of other kings were mentioned, such as Rhadamanthys, whose sense of justice was such that he continued to judge the dead in the underworld. Although they no longer knew the vast palace of Cnossos, the Greeks created the legend of the labyrinth. Probably the Minotaur, devouring the young captives whom defeated peoples were forced to sacrifice to him, represented the power rather than the cruelty of the Cretans. In the 16th century B.C., when mainland Greece had finally emerged from the troubled period marking the beginning of the millennium, firm links were established between Crete and the Peloponnesus, as is attested by the discovery of Minoan works that had been imported into Greece or else copied by local artists. It was largely owing to Cretan influence that Mycenaean civilisation came into being. We do not know the exact date when the relations between the two countries changed in character, but towards the end of the 15th century Crete entered into a decline and it would seem that the Mycenaeans triumphed by force over the kings of Crete; Argolis then became the new centre of civilisation. Like other regions around the Aegean, Cretan civilisation fell into a kind of slumber after the collapse of the Mycenaean world, only to be awoken by the shock of the Dorian invasions. But it would seem that Crete remained somewhat isolated from events

Steatite vase from Haghia Triada. About 1500 B.C. Heraklion Museum. *Photo Hassia.*

Head of the Kritian boy. About 490-480 B.C. Athens, Acropolis Museum. *Photo Giraudon*.

because it no longer lay on the main shipping routes. From the 6th century B.C. onwards the isolation that had once been a source of strength to the island became the cause of its inferiority. Although it remained rich and materially prosperous it no longer had any great part to play in the Hellenic world. Crete distinguished itself neither in politics nor in intellectual life and the most talented of its natives, like the sculptor Cresilas (q.v.) in the 5th century, went elsewhere to find a field for their activity. P.D.

CRITIAS. Critias (450-403 B.C.) was an Athenian politician and writer, the pupil of Socrates and a relative of Plato who named one of his dialogues after him (the one in which Atlantis is mentioned). He was exiled from Athens during the Peloponnesian War because he led the aristocratic party which was favourable to Sparta, but he returned when the city had been captured by Lysander in 404 B.C. and proved himself to be one of the cruellest of the Thirty Tyrants who were supported by the armed might of the Lacedaemonian garrison. When Thrasybulus brought back the exiled democrats, Critias was killed during the fighting at Piraeus. He was both a poet and prose writer, and wrote tragedies, elegies and historical works of which only short fragments have survived. R.F.

CRITIUS. The Athenian, Critius, is one of the very few archaic sculptors who are more than just names to us. His famous sculpture of the Tyrannicides, Harmodius and Aristogiton (qq.v.), seems to be fairly faithfully reproduced by the Roman copy in the Museo Nazionale, Naples. In order to cast it in bronze, he was helped by the founder, Nesiotes. It is also thought that he was the sculptor of a marble Kouros now in the museum of the Acropolis, a work of high quality which shows the beginnings of the classical spirit while yet retaining a certain fidelity to tradition. P.D.

CROESUS. King of Lydia, who reigned from 561 to 546 B.C. He amassed a great fortune from the resources of his kingdom, was on excellent terms with the Greeks and lavishly subsidised the embellishment of the sanctuary of Delphi in particular. Herodotus has told of Croesus'

on the mainland, as in the early 2nd millennium B.C. In pottery, wares show the influence of the geometric style, but both shapes and decoration differ from continental models and the survival of a native tradition is fairly strongly perceptible, the Cretan style showing greater freedom of imagination than in the rest of Hellas. Again, as in the early 2nd millennium, Crete was in fairly close contact with Asia and Egypt, and it was on the island that some of the most characteristic traits of the coming Greek culture were first to be found. During the whole of the 7th century, cultural activity seems to have been intense; it was from Crete that the inhabitants of the continent brought their legislators at this period, as well as most of the techniques that were to be developed in the Peloponnesus, Attica or the Cyclades after having been tested and perhaps invented on the island. Cretan derivation is particularly marked in bronze work and terra-cotta, but it was probably also in Crete that the first stone sculptures were made. Cretan architecture does not seem to have had a great influence on that of the continent, although there was no lack of buildings on the island, like the little temple of Prinias with its curious sculptured decoration, in the central plain of Messara.

After being the crucible of Greek inventions, Crete fell into a complete decadence, perhaps

King Croesus on the pyre. Detail of an amphora attributed to the painter Myson. About 490 B.C. Paris, Louvre. *Photo Hirmer.*

interview with the wise Solon and how he tried to make Solon tell him that he was the most happy of mortals to which the sage replied that no man could be considered happy until his life had come to an end. Still according to Herodotus, Croesus found that this judgment was only too true, for his capital, Sardes, was later taken by Cyrus and he was condemned to be burnt alive on a pyre. His life was only spared at the last moment when he repeated the wise sayings of Solon to his conqueror.   P.D.

CRONUS. Cronus was the son of the Sky and the Earth. In order to reign over the world he castrated his father and mated with his sister, Rhea. He had numerous children but, afraid that they might dethrone him later, he ate them alive. When she had given birth to Zeus, Rhea substituted a stone for the child, as she was tired of seeing her progeny disappear in this way, and Cronus unwittingly swallowed it. Zeus was brought up by the Corybantes and on the appointed day he triumphed over Cronus and restored all the children that had been devoured to life again by

means of a magic brew; and so began the reign of the Olympians.   P.D.

CROTON. Croton was one of the colonies of Magna Graecia, founded by Achaeans from the Peloponnesus. It was the homeland of the famous athlete, Milon, and Pythagoras.

CUMAE. Although of all the Greek colonies founded in Italy and Sicily, Cumae was the farthest removed from its metropolises, Eretrea and Chalcis, it was also the most ancient. It had been founded in about the middle of the 8th century B.C. by pioneers from Euboea, who had settled on the plateau dominating the Campanian plain, not far from the present Pozzuoli. For twenty years they had installed themselves on the island facing the site, that of Pithecusae, but before they could settle permanently, they first had to expel the Opici who occupied the site of the future city. Cumae became prosperous in a very short time and in its turn founded Dicaearchea and Neapolis and had a far reaching influence. In 474 B.C. the Cumaeans, united with Hieron of Syracuse,

Head of a large Cycladic statue from Amorgos.
3rd millennium B.C. Athens, National Museum.
Photo Spyros Meletzis.

defeated the Etruscans in a naval battle, but in 421
they were conquered by the Samnites. The city
was finally conquered again by the Romans in
334 and was left with nothing but memories of
its former Hellenic greatness. P.D.

CUSTOMS. The establishment of the system of customs duties seems to be a very old one
for, as early as the Homeric period, kings were
demanding gifts from merchants before they
would allow their goods to circulate. The system
soon spread widely throughout Greece and taxes
were paid on all goods coming into a state. Most
commerce was by sea, consequently duties were
levied in ports, where inspection was easy. In
most cities, duties were low enough not to discourage exporters. It was two per cent in Athens, a tax
that should not be considered as a device to protect local manufactures but as a source of revenue
for the city. The customs control of the different
states was not exercised only on their own territory, for when their hegemony extended over other
cities they took care to supervise their commerce
and to levy taxes on it. It was in this way that
Thasos controlled the shipping entering the ports
of the Thracian-Macedonian coast and made them
pay duties, before it was conquered by Athens in
462 B.C. Similar to these customs duties was
the toll exacted by the inhabitants of Crisa, for
example, from pilgrims who went through their
territory on the way to Delphi, or the tithe established in Byzantium in 411 and 390 by Athens,
on boats crossing the Bosphorus. It was so
fruitful a source of revenue that once Byzantium
won its independence it re-established the tax for
its own profit. P.D.

CYCLADES. The Cyclades are a group of
islands scattered in a circle, whence their name,
between the Greek coast and Asia Minor. They
vary in size; the largest are Naxos and Paros but
the island that had the most important position in
the Greek world was the tiny isle of Delos, in the
centre of the circle. It was on the Cyclades that
the earliest and most curious signs of the Greek

Seated musician playing the harp. Cycladic statue from
Keros. 3rd millennium B.C. Athens, National Museum.
Photo Spyros Meletzis.

genius appeared in the 3rd millennium B.C. These were the anthropomorphic but highly stylised, sculptured idols, made of a marble found in abundance throughout the islands and particularly on Paros and Naxos. They were placed in tombs and probably represented a protective female deity. This early period was a brilliant time for the islands, for navigation had already begun to flourish and obsidian was being used at Melos for razors, knives and cutting instruments. The diffusion of bronze and the establishment of Cretan naval power brought this source of wealth to an end and reduced the Cyclades to the status of Cretan satellites. Although we do not know exactly what happened to the islands during the Mycenaean period, we do know that Delos had become the centre of an important cult whose popularity has been proved by the remains of rich offerings that have been found. Some of these offerings have an oriental character revealing Asian influence in the islands and, indeed, relations seem to have been particularly close between the Cyclades and Anatolia during the whole of the archaic period. From the 7th to the 6th century Delos became the religious capital of the Ionian world, and pilgrims came from all the other islands and the Asian coast to worship at the shrine of Apollo. Although each city of the Cyclades kept its autonomy, as in the rest of Greece, some tried to dominate others either by their commercial or their political activity. Paros was the main centre for pottery but Naxos, whose craftsmen also appear to have exported their products, seems to have dominated its neighbours for a time. From the end of the 6th century B.C., the Cyclades were no more than pawns in international politics, directed by more important states. They were reduced to a passive role and neither in the Persian Wars, nor during the period of Athenian domination, nor during the Peloponnesian War, nor later when they were theoretically autonomous again, do they ever seem to have played any active part in the great movements that were transforming Greece. Their inhabitants lived on the meagre resources provided by fishing and the cultivation of the arid soil. Only Delos played a part of any note until the beginnings of the Christian era, on account of its reputation as a religious sanctuary and its international port. *(See Delos, Melos, Naxos, Paros).* P.D.

CYCLOPES. The word Cyclops naturally suggests the cannibal monster Polyphemus, who devoured Ulysses' companions before being blinded by the hero, and who, long after Homer, was described by Theocritus as being a passionate lover at the feet of Galatea. For the people of antiquity a whole category of Cyclopes were wild, gigantic monsters who lived far from civilisation, looking after their herds and jealously defending their country against all foreign intrusions, but also, because of their great strength, the Cyclopes were also renowned as builders of cities. It was believed that the first walls of Athens had been built by them under the guidance of Athena. This episode has been illustrated by a 5th century B.C. vase painting and gave rise to the term "cyclopean" to describe a certain kind of masonry in which walls were made of enormous, irregular blocks of stone piled on top of one another. It was also believed that the Cyclops worked as blacksmiths under the orders of Hephaestus and that the first generation was even earlier than that of the Olympians. It was owing to the arms provided by three of the Cyclopes, thunder and lightning, thunderbolts, a helmet which conferred invisibility on its wearer, and a trident, that Zeus, Hades and Poseidon were able to seize power. In art the Cyclopes were represented with features stressing their brutality or their rusticity and the tradition by which they only had one eye in the centre of their forehead is far from being a general one. P.D.

CYNICISM. This philosophical school was founded by the Athenian, Antisthenes, a pupil of Socrates, in the gymnasium of the Cynosarges (the agile dog), whence the name of Dogs or Cynics for the followers of the school. It not only perpetuated its origins, but symbolised "their snarling, ceaseless barking and moral vigilance, and, to a certain degree, their mode of life" (L. Robin). It was above all the appeal to virtue and the austerity of Socrates' teaching that the Cynics retained. They opposed nature to culture and despised all social conventions. Man, they believed, should only seek for the good of his soul and consider all the rest, honours, wealth and reputation, as vain trifles. Sincere Cynics would therefore give up all the goods of this world, beg what was necessary for them to live, and become wandering preachers who, by their violent diatribes, confounded ignorant souls who had been unable to find the true road to happiness, and attempted to convert them to their doctrine. Zeller has called the Cynics the "Capuchin friars of

Horseman. Terra-cotta from Cyprus. Beginning of the 1st millennium B.C. Paris, Louvre. *Photo Tel.*

Another Cynic of the same time, Crates of Thebes, married the sister of his friend Metrocles, the beautiful and rich Hipparchia, who renounced all her worldly goods despite her parents' protests, in order to follow him and share his life as a vagabond. It was thus that Hipparchia won the right, rare for a woman, to be mentioned in Diogenes Laertius' *Lives of the Philosophers*. Crates was the first master of Zeno, the founder of Stoicism. In the 3rd century B.C. the best known Cynics were Bion the Borysthenite, whose *Sermons* served Horace as the model for his *Satires*, Menippus of Gadara to whom Lucian often proclaimed his debt, and Teles. During the Roman empire, Cynism had a great influence, for the diatribes of Cynic preachers won a large public and the Stoicism of Seneca comes close to the purified Cynicism of Demetrius whom he praised highly.

antiquity ". The Cynics' chosen patron was Heracles, whose labours symbolised the permanent effort of the worthy man to gain virtue.

The founder, Antisthenes, was a prolific writer. His works included speeches in the manner of the sophists on themes borrowed from the poets, and Socratic dialogues, all of which were greatly admired in antiquity but which have only survived in small fragments. Antisthenes is one of the speakers in Xenophon's *Symposium,* where he criticises Plato's theory of Ideas and says: " I can certainly see horses but I don't see Horseness ", that is, the idea of the horse.

Antisthenes' successor, Diogenes of Sinope, was famous for his witticisms. He lived in a " tub " or a huge jar and his sole utensil was a ladle, which he finally threw away as superfluous after seeing a boy drink water out of his cupped hand. He armed himself with a lantern and went out into the world in search of one true man without ever finding him. When Alexander the Great asked him whether he requested any favour, Diogenes' only reply was to ask him to move out of his light.

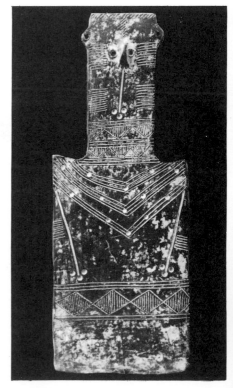

Female idol. Terra-cotta from Cyprus. 3rd millennium B.C. Paris, Louvre. *Photo Tel.*

Demetrius was the friend of the Stoic, Thrasea Paetus, who dared to defy Nero. The moral preachings of the Stoic, Musonius Rufus (Mousenilos), who was exiled by Nero, are also very close in spirit to this new Cynicism.   P.-M.S.

CYPRUS. Cyprus has a place apart in Greek history. Situated as it is in the north-east corner of the Mediterranean, less than 60 miles from the coasts of Asia Minor and Phoenicia, it was a compulsory port of call during the whole of antiquity for Greek and Asian navigators and it was in frequent contact with Egypt which had economic and military interests in neighbouring regions.   Cyprus lay at the cross-roads of different empires and civilisations and it could not fail to be affected by their material splendour and cultures, so that throughout the course of the island's history its people were influenced by the various countries with which they were in close contact. But they remained faithful to their own local traditions which were of such marked individuality that their language, customs and art were quite different from all others during the whole of the classical period and gave the civilisation of Cyprus a distinct character of its own. Everything they adopted from abroad, probably unconsciously, was assimilated and adapted to their character and rather rustic way of life.   That this process of absorption never gave rise to any great works of art is almost certainly due to the fact that the Cypriots were lacking in those natural gifts that enabled the Athenians or Corinthians, for example, to create glorious masterpieces on the basis of cultural elements that were not always indigenous.

The complicated and often obscure history of the island can only be resumed briefly here.   The few Neolithic sites that have been found on the island seem to have been already abandoned by the beginning of the Bronze Age in about 3000 B.C., when a pastoral people, probably from Anatolia, settled on the island.   These settlers were almost certainly politically dependent on the countries from which they came and they gradually developed relations with Asia Minor and Africa.   The production of pottery in a style to which the Cypriots remained amazingly faithful for so long, dates from the coming of these settlers and consisted of bottles, gourds and vessels with rounded bases which were frequently clay facsimiles of metal, wicker-work and leather receptacles. A turning point in the history of the island was the massive arrival of the Achaeans in the 15th and 14th centuries B.C.   They came from Greece and brought with them their culture, their institutions, including doubtless their special brand of non-absolute monarchy, which was to persist throughout antiquity, their language, which never changed, since the Cypriot dialects always kept their archaic character, and finally their art and their new techniques.   The Mycenaean period lasted longer at Cyprus than anywhere else, well into the troubled period of the early 1st millennium B.C. Cyprus then fell under the sway of the Phoenicians and it was almost certainly at this time that the inhabitants began to use a writing system that was to be adopted and slightly modified by the Greeks.   Cyprus was divided into small kingdoms, the number of which varied between seven and ten, with some, like Idalium or Salamis, becoming rather strongly Hellenised while others, such as Amathus, remaining more faithful to local traditions and Phoenician influences.   The island had been a Hittite possession at one time and after an obscure period fell under the domination of Sargon II in about 715 B.C.   In 626 Cyprus became an Egyptian possession after the collapse of Syrian power and in 526 it became part of the Persian empire at the same time as Egypt, with the kings continuing to rule their cities while being dominated by a foreign sovereign.   Various attempts at a revolt during the Persian Wars all ended in failure, but the most brilliant period in

King Arcesilas
supervising the
weighing and storage
of silphium. Laconian-
cup. About 560 B.C.
Paris, Bibliothèque
Nationale.

the island's history was during the reign of Evagoras I (410-374 B.C.) who extended his authority over the whole of Cyprus and was recognised by the Persian king. After the battle of Issus in 333 B.C., Cyprus enthusiastically welcomed Alexander's domination and foreign elements became absorbed by Hellenism. Cyprus was then conquered with some difficulty by the Egyptian sovereigns and did not finally become a Roman province until 22 B.C.

Although it might appear to have remained rather isolated, Cyprus played a role of considerable importance in the history of the Hellenic world, for it was from there that many oriental elements were transmitted into Greek civilisation, all the more easily because they had lost their more obviously exotic characteristics. Some types of Cretan and Corinthian vases of the late 8th century B.C. seem to have been directly copied from Cypriot models, as to a somewhat lesser extent do some of their decorative patterns. But religious beliefs and legends owed even more to Cyprus; according to certain traditions, Aphrodite herself was a native of the island, having been born at Paphos. P.D.

CYRENE. Few colonies were founded as reluctantly as Cyrene, on the coast of north Africa. In about 644 B.C. the inhabitants of Thera had been ordered by Apollo to send an expedition to Libya, but they turned a deaf ear to the command. As a punishment, the god afflicted their island with a drought. They then decided to send off a few pioneers, who never set foot on the continent but contented themselves with camping opposite the shores on the little isle of Plataea, before returning home to give an account of their mission. Led by the archegetus, Battus, two ships then left Thera, bearing a few dozen men who settled on Plataea where they led a painful existence until they returned home less than two years later, deeply discouraged; but the Therans would not let them land and again Apollo sent the colonists to Libya, telling them to settle on the continent proper this time. Battus and his companions finally took their task seriously and in about 630, after first having lived on a less favoured site, they founded the city of Cyrene at some distance from the coast near a spring and on a site that was easy to defend.

The colony gradually prospered so that in 575,

during the reign of Battus II, it was necessary to send reinforcements from the Peloponnesus, Crete and Rhodes, for the exploitation of the site. Dispossessed of their lands by these new arrivals, the older settlers revolted but, despite the aid of the Egyptians, they were defeated. Later, other campaigns were less successful and troubles broke out which resulted in important changes being made in the regime. But during the reign of Arcesilaus II in particular, Cyrene continued to prosper, from the richness of the soil and the cultivation of a plant called siphium and large-scale horse-breeding. For several centuries the colony was content to exploit its natural riches and never attempted to play any part in international politics, but its wealth made it a tempting prey for its neighbours and, not surprisingly, the Ptolemys added it to their empire.   P.D.

CYTHERA. The associations of this small desolate island to the south of the Peloponnesus are modern inventions; its only renown in ancient times was due to its sanctuary of Aphrodite. It was not one of the goddess's most favoured abodes, and it was far from being the enchanted island that was so popular with 18th century artists and poets.   P.D.

DAEDALUS. Daedalus was a legendary personage to whom the naturally industrious Greeks attributed many inventions of all kinds. He was believed to be a Cretan, probably because the Greeks remembered how much their civilisation originally owed to the Minoans. He was especially famous for having found a way of flying by means of wings made of birds' feathers. He attached these to his shoulders and his son, Icarus, met his death by falling into the sea, after the wax holding his wings had melted because he had flown too near the sun. Daedalus was also given the honour of making the first statues. Archaeologists do not accept this completely unsupported tradition, but they have given the name Daedalic to the sculptural style of the 7th century B.C. These statues were characterised by their rather dry and summary execution and the rather excessive emphasis on facial structure and on expression, by use of abnormally wide eyes and mouth. Although his personality is vaguer, Daedalus may be compared with Ulysses as one of the most typical representatives of the Greek spirit, with its practical intelligence and skill in execution.   P.D.

DAMASCIUS. Last scholar of the school of Athens. He was deprived of his post by Justinian's decree of 529 A.D. which ordered the closure of the Academy. Followed by some of his disciples, including Simplicius, he took refuge at the court of King Chosroes in Persia, where he remained for two years. We no longer know what happened to him on his return to Greece nor the dates of his birth and death. All we do have are a few fragments of his master, Isidore of Alexandria, one of Proclus's successors. These precious texts constitute the history of the last period of the school of Athens. In them, we find the atmosphere of an intense intellectual life which reigned in the 6th century A.D. in the last pagan circles of Alexandrian and Athenian society. A commentary on the *Philebus*, hitherto falsely attributed to Olympiodorus, was recently published by Westerinck (Amsterdam, 1959). But Damascius's essential work is still that published by Ruelle in 1889. *Problems and solutions on the First Principles*. It is the last monument of Greek thought and comprises two distinct works: a *Treatise on Principles* and a commentary on the *Parmenides* of Plato, the great dialogue whose exegesis, together with that of the *Timaeus*, was used as the basis for the teachings of the Neoplatonists. Damascius's Commentary was intended to be an answer to Proclus's interpretation of the *Parmenides*. For Proclus as for Plotinus, the supreme Principle was the One. But it is even higher, beyond the One itself, to the Ineffable absolute that Damascius's theories lead us to, to the point where our thought has no other knowledge than that of its own impotence, nor any other experience than that of inner nothingness. The question was, is it nothingness that it then encounters, and is one to conclude that nothing exists beyond the One? At this point language becomes misleading. Since we can no longer make any statements, we give the name of " Nothingness " to that abyss out of which all things come, and to that other abyss in which all things vanish.

Damascius's thought is the profoundest reflection of antiquity on the relativity and limits of human knowledge.

Knowledge is by its essence a relation and there can be no thought of the Absolute or of the absolute Principle. The notion of principle also implies a relation, for every principle is a principle " of " something. This philosophy of knowledge is also a philosophy of language. No more precise, penetrating, " modern " critique of abstract and general thought is to be found anywhere else in Greek philosophy, and Damascius often reminds us of Bergson. Damascius did not inspire mystic theology, as Proclus did through the work of the Pseudo-Dionysius. Denser, more obscure, and more difficult, its very profundity isolated it. What now astonishes us is its admirable critical lucidity and its intense awareness of the difficulties in Neoplatonism.   G.

DAMOPHON. Damophon was a Greek sculptor, famous for the cult statues that he made for the temple of Demeter and Despoina at Lycosura in Arcadia. Damophon of Messene worked in the early 2nd century B.C. and represented a classical tendency which was distinct from the tormented and sometimes rococo plasticity of the island schools, in particular, that of Rhodes. He was requested to repair Phidias's statue of Zeus at Olympia, after it had been damaged by an earthquake in 183, and studied the technique and style of the great Athenian artist whom he afterwards tried to imitate in the works he later made on commission in Messene, Megalopolis and other towns of the Peloponnesus.

The group of statues for the temple of Lycosura is known to us by Pausanias's description and various important fragments, in particular the heads of the Titan, Anytus, and Despoina. The same group also inspired designs for coins, in which the two goddesses, Demeter and Despoina, were represented seated and flanked by the standing figures of Artemis and Anytus. The group was presented in frontal view without any attempt at giving an effect of perspective, a method which was far removed from the spirit of the sculpture of Pergamum or Rhodes at the same period, but which recaptured the calm and the serenity of classical sculpture.   R.M.

DANAË. An oracle predicted that the son of Danaë would kill his grandfather, Acrisius, the king of Argos. When the young girl reached a marriageable age, Acrisius shut her in a dungeon to escape his destiny, but Zeus fell in love with her and managed to come to her in the shape of golden rain. As a result of the union, Danaë gave birth to the hero, Perseus. Acrisius then shut both mother and child in a coffer which he threw into the sea, but Zeus saved their lives and they

Danaë. Detail of a Boeotian krater. End of the 5th century B.C. Paris, Louvre.

Dancers and a woman musician. Terra-cotta from Palaikastro, late Minoan. Heraklion Museum. *Ph. Hassia.*

landed on the isle of Seriphus where they were welcomed by the king Polydectes, and his brother Dictys.   P.D.

D A N A I. Like that of " Achaeans ", Danai was the name given by Homer and other poets to the Greeks who assembled to fight against Troy. It seems to have been a generic term with no relation to any particular region, and was meant to perpetuate the memory of a common ancestor, the mythical Danaus.   P.D.

D A N A I D A E. King Danaus was born in Egypt and fled from the country with his fifty daughters, the Danaidae, to escape the enmity of his fifty nephews, and settled in Argos. The nephews followed them to Greece and demanded the hands in marriage of their cousins. During the wedding night, all the wives except one cut the throats of their husbands and then cut off their heads in obedience to their father's orders. The Danaidae were punished for their crime in Hell by being made ceaselessly to fill pitchers with holes in their bottoms.   P.D.

D A N C E. Dancing was far more important in ancient Greece than in modern society. It was not a gratuitous amusement but rather the expression of such deep feelings as joy and sadness. It was therefore linked with the cult of certain divinities such as Artemis, who were particularly pleased by the sight of their worshippers dancing in their honour. Minoan and Mycenaean works of art of the 2nd millennium B.C. include representations of young women taking part in violent dances which may have been ecstatic in character. When Theseus and his companions returned in triumph from Crete they landed at Delos and performed a dance in honour of Apollo, which seems to have been an imitation of the flight of cranes, probably a kind of farandole like those which may still be seen in the south of France and other Mediterranean regions. Apart from solemn dances, some, like the cordax, performed by the worshippers of Dionysus, were violent and lascivious in character. Many early 6th century vases bear representations of cordax dancers, who imitated the amorous frolics of sileni and satyrs and attached a false tail to their buttocks to make their movements even more obscene. Sparta was one of the Greek cities where dancing was most popular but there were few regions where choruses were not formed under the guidance of experts. There is no need to point out the importance of these choruses in the theatre, where their songs were accompanied by rhythmical movements.

Dancing was not reserved for the young alone and Socrates himself, in his old age, spoke of his wish to learn the art which he had always neglected. We shall not list all the different kinds of dance; suffice it to say that they were as numerous as they were varied. At all periods, certain performers had become virtuosi of their art, and professional dancers became more and more numerous as time went on. Naturally enough, the more dancing became a simple exercise intended to charm onlookers, the more its religious character tended to diminish, but nonetheless, its religious origins and significance were never forgotten by the Greeks.   P.D.

DAPHNE. Daphne was one of the countless nymphs beloved of Apollo. When she was pursued by the god, she besought her father, who, according to various legends was the river Ladon

Dionysiac dance. Detail of a krater by the Karneia Painter. About 410 B.C. Taranto Museum. *Ph. Hirmer.*

or Peneus, to help her in her difficult situation. He replied by metamorphosing her into a laurel tree, which became Apollo's favourite tree.
                                                                                P.D.

DECELEA. Situated some fifteen miles to the north of Athens, the deme (q.v.) of Decelea was one of the key-points of Attica, for it was traversed by the great road that led to Euboea and Boeotia. It was at Decelea that the ephebi spent their year of military service. The occupation of the site by the Lacedaemonians during the Peloponnesian War proved fatal to Athens. It was not surprising, therefore, that a fortress was later built by the entrance to the defile which led northwards at Decelea.   P.D.

DEFILEMENT. The idea that anyone who had committed a crime suffered in consequence from a material, physical and even contagious defilement lies at the root of many beliefs and customs that now astonish us. Whoever had shed blood, except in a regular combat, became and remained impure until a ritual ceremony rid him of what the Greeks called the " miasma ". When Oedipus was found guilty of having killed his father, his subjects expelled him from Thebes, not for any moral reason, but because his presence alone had been enough to bring an epidemic of plague which could only cease after his departure. Despite the fact that the ancient Greeks held the virtue of hospitality in such high esteem, he was badly received everywhere he went in his pitiful wanderings because his presence would irremediably defile the homes and families that had given him lodging. Even a god had to wash away his crime if he had spilt blood in certain circumstances; Apollo went into exile among the Hyperboreans after killing the serpent, Python. Even when murder was involuntary, the killer was still defiled. Consequently, a complete purification ritual was provided for the many in need of it.   P.D.

DEIANIRA. Deianira was the daughter of Oeneus, king of Calydon, and became the wife of Heracles after repulsing the amorous advances of the river deity, Achelous. She gave birth to a son named Hylas. The episode of her abduction by Nessus is well known and has been frequently

Delos.
Avenue of Lions.
7th century B.C.
Photo Chéruzel.

illustrated in Greek art. Nessus was a Centaur who practised the profession of ferryman and carried on his back travellers who did not want to swim across the river. After he had taken Deianira to the other bank, he tried to rape her but was killed by Heracles. Before dying, Nessus gave the young woman some of the blood running from his wounds and told her that if her husband should ever prove unfaithful, she could bring him back to her again by making him wear a shirt dipped in this blood. This is what Deianira did when Heracles fell in love with the young Iole. But the advice she had been given turned out to be Nessus's posthumous vengeance, for the blood was a poison which burned Heracles when he wore the shirt. Unable to relieve his horrible sufferings by taking off the shirt, he was said to have built a pyre on which he burnt himself in order to find a quicker death.   P.D.

DELOS. For the small, rocky and almost ceaselessly windswept isle of Delos to have become one of the great centres of the Hellenic world, nothing less than the presence of a god was needed. When Leto was pursued by the jealousy of Hera and sought for an asylum where she could give birth to the son she had conceived by Zeus, only the island of Delos, which was so poor it had nothing to lose, accepted her request. The island made Leto promise that Apollo, her son, would never despise it but honour it above all other parts of the earth and have a magnificent temple built on it. It was there therefore that Leto gave birth to Apollo, leaning against a palm tree which became sacred as a consequence, by the foot of the rocky height of Cynthus whose majestic appearance is only due to its isolation.

We do not know when this legend originated, but excavations have proved that, before Delos became the island of Apollo, it had a goddess as its patron divinity. There is no lack of Mycenaean remains on the island, which was at first inhabited by a few fisher folk before becoming an important harbour when navigation had increased in extent. The Mycenaean goddess, who reigned at this time and seems to have been a precursor of Artemis, received many offerings, a pile of which has been discovered ritually embedded in the structure of a temple. The goddess may also have been accompanied by a masculine deity whose modest role gave no signs of his later brilliant destiny, for, it seems, this companion was none other than Apollo in his first image. When the cleavage occurred in the Aegean world at the end of the 2nd millennium B.C., the goddess was eclipsed by her *paredros* (fellow-deity) who was then held to be her brother. At the same time, these two divine figures were given a mother. This was the Asiatic goddess, Leto, who was believed by legend to have been the mistress of

147

Delos.
Statues of Cleopatra
and Dioscorides
2nd century B.C.
Photo Georges Roux.

Zeus. In less than two centuries, the new cult spread to such an extent that Delos had become, and was to remain, the queen of the Cyclades, gathered, in the words of a poet, around her like a chorus. A belief took firm hold that it was impossible to dominate the Aegean without the consent of the Delian Apollo. Consequently, offerings began to pour in which brought an unhoped for prosperity to the barren island. Periodic festivals were held and a 7th century hymn has survived in which the sumptuous spectacle of all the Ionians assembled in their finest raiment is described in glowing terms. Buildings rose on the island, but at first these were modest temples or rather barbarian sculptures, like the row of lions along the Sacred Way leading to the sanctuary of Leto. At first, Apollo only had a humble shrine which was far inferior to that of Artemis beside it. Then, in his turn, a statue was built in his honour in the 6th century B.C., and statues were dedicated to him, including one which reached the colossal height of fifty feet. The temple and the offerings were consecrated by the inhabitants of Naxos, a nearby island that was then attempting to dominate the whole of the archipelago. In the course of the 6th century the Athenians in their turn sought the aid of the god in order to ensure their supremacy, and told how their national hero, Theseus, had established the sacred rites, still celebrated on the island, on his

return from Crete where he had vanquished the Minotaur. They looked after Apollo's interests and to ensure that the shrine should remain unsullied, followed the advice of an oracle by removing the tombs, which previous generations had set in the immediate vicinity of the divine dwellings, to a site where they could no longer be seen by the god. In this way they became the protectors of the cult and defenders of Apollo to whom they dedicated a great number of korai and kouroi.

It was not until the 5th century B.C. that the Athenians exercised their strongest and almost official sway over Delos. In 477 they made the sanctuary the headquarters of an alliance against the Persians, and until 454 they placed the wealth of the league on the island under the protection of the god; as a result they acquired and retained control of the administration of the sacred domain. In 425, when the difficulties encountered in the Peloponnesian War made the support of Apollo all the more necessary for them, they reorganised the great festivals or Delia, made a new purification of the island and henceforth forbade anyone to be born or to die on it; pregnant women and the dying were taken to the nearby island of Rheneia. They then began to build a new temple which was to replace the old shrine of the 6th century, which they considered to be too small and old fashioned. Except for a brief interval, they continued to dominate the island from 402 to 393, but as the Cyclades no longer played a very important role in political life or economy, the Athenians were less interested than in the previous century in embellishing the domain of the god.

When Alexander's successors gave a new importance to mastery of the seas in 315, Delos was freed from the authority of Athens and became a great Hellenic centre again as in the archaic period. Commerce was in full expansion and the island provided a safe and convenient harbour where freight from all parts could be transferred from one ship to another. After the middle of the 2nd century B.C., when Delos had been declared a free port and had inherited the commerce of Rhodes (166) and Corinth (146), it became the great centre of the slave and grain trades. Drawn by the lure of ready wealth, foreigners came to the island from all countries and mingled with the Delians; Asians, Egyptians, and even Romans came to open up agencies near the port. They also brought new beliefs with them and were authorised by Apollo and the Delians to build temples to their barbarian deities outside the limits of the sanctuary. The town grew and fairly well preserved ruins of residential quarters have enabled us to form a picture of the swarming life that once existed in the narrow streets winding between the houses *(See* Town-planning). With its quays, warehouses, mooring points, and rules of navigation, the port received vast quantities of merchandise which increased every year and enriched the population. The sanctuary also benefited from this prosperity, for the Macedonian kings, Antigonus and Philip, embellished it with beautiful porticoes, sovereigns consecrated their portraits to the god, and nobles set up statues and exedrae. Semi-religious, as well as semi-commercial establishments were installed near the sacred domain, and the wealthy inhabitants commissioned artists, sculptors, painters and mosaicists to make images to be consecrated to the divinities honoured on the island or else to adorn the finest rooms of the houses. The quality of these works was not always of the highest for, although the artists were skilful they were working for a nouveau riche clientele, many of whom were mere businessmen whose interest in art was superficial and whose taste was ostentatious. Notwithstanding, its wealth made Delos into an important artistic centre from the end of the 3rd to the beginning of the 1st century B.C.

Commercial prosperity did not save Delos from political misfortunes. In 166, when the Romans had conquered Greece, they made a gift of the sacred isle to the Athenians as a reward for their fidelity and once again, as in the 5th and 6th centuries, Athenian tyranny reigned ruthlessly over

Delos. Residential quarter. Hellenistic period. *Photo Jacqueline Staméroff.*

what was considered to be no more than a colony. Even greater misfortunes were in store; in 88 and then 66 B.C. the armies of Mithridates and bands of pillagers captured the isle without difficulty, for its only protection was its holiness, and they only left it after having despoiled it of all the riches they could carry, leaving nothing behind them but ruins and mourning. Delos never recovered from this double blow. Pilgrims gradually ceased to honour a god who lived in solitude on an island without resources, and before the end of the classical period, Delos had become what it was to remain until the end of the 19th century: a heap of ruins whose marble was used in limekilns.

P.D.

DELPHI. The site of Delphi in Phocis, almost in the centre of mainland Greece, by Mount Parnassus above the gulf of Corinth, is one of the most wild and majestic in Greece. It must have fired the imagination of the Greeks at an early date, for they believed that Zeus had sent two of his eagles to the ends of the earth (which was held to be a flat disc) in order to determine its centre : the divine birds had met at Delphi over the *omphalos* or navel, a sacred stone of a vaguely conical shape, a sort of dwelling place of the god. The name of Delphi is similar to the word *delphys* or " womb " and the place was considered to be

Delphi. Omphalos, the sacred stone that was considered the centre of the world. *Photo Spyros Meletzis.*

the " navel of the earth " and the centre of the universe. In any case, it was the most influential and the most important religious centre in the whole of Greece. It was inhabited and had temples well before the arrival of the Olympians, Apollo and Athena, the son and daughter of Zeus. Excavations carried out by the French School of Athens have uncovered the ruins of houses and sanctuaries of the Mycenaean period. The ancient Great Mother of the Minoan religion also left her traces on the site. She was identified with the Earth and was, according to Aeschylus, " the first prophetess ", whose oracle was guarded by the dragon, Python, which explains why Homer called Delphi " Pytho " or " the rocky ". In order to install himself as the master of Delphi, Apollo killed the dragon and thus became the Pythian god. His oracles were transmitted by a woman of Delphi named Pythia, and every four years, in the course of an Olympiad, the great Pythian games, which were both athletic and musical in nature, were held at Delphi with the participation of Greeks from every part of Greece. The games, and even more the oracle, made the Apollo of Delphi quite as panhellenic as the Olympian Zeus.

The traveller coming to Delphi from Athens by the overland route (it could also be reached by the port of Itea, the former Cirrha, on the gulf of Corinth) first came to the sanctuary of Athena Pronaia (" before the main temple ") or Pronoia (foresight) as it was sometimes called in a pun. It was in this sanctuary that the splendid and

Delphi. Treasury of the Athenians, dedicated between 490 and 485 B.C. *Photo Hassia.*

enigmatic round monument, the *tholos,* was to be found. From there the way led to the gymnasium where athletes used to practise before the Pythian Games. Next came the fountain of Castalia, whose water spurted out of the deep gorge between the two high, dazzling cliffs of the Phaedriades, and then, at last, the main sanctuary of Apollo. Because of the steepness of the sloping ground the Sacred Way ran in a great V between the offerings of every kind, which in the classical period made the sanctuary a kind of crowded open-air museum. These offerings included isolated statues, which sometimes stood on high columns or else in rows on plinths, and Treasuries, which were a kind of shrine where the cities would heap up both private and public ex-votos. In modern times the Treasury of Athens has been reconstructed by archaeologists. From there, one went on to the great altar outside the entrance to the temple of Apollo. The temple was destroyed in the 6th century, then again in the 4th century B.C., and was rebuilt each time in the most lavish manner from the generous contributions of the whole Greek world. The Pythian sanctuary was both protected and administered by a league of neighbouring cities, the Amphictiony (literally " neighbours "). This league was first formed around the sanctuary of Demeter at Anthela near Thermopylae and had two centres, Delphi and Thermopylae, which was why it was called the Delphic Pylaean Amphictiony. Each of the twelve member states sent two main representatives to the sessions or Pylaiai of the League. They were known as the *hieromnemones,* and the *Pylagorai* whose duty it was to assist the hieromnemones in this kind of international assembly.

After Apollo, the most important deity at Delphi was Dionysus, the god of wine, drunkenness and frenzy. Although he was in principle immortal like all the Olympians, Dionysus had his misfortunes like the Egyptian Osiris; it was said that he had died and then been resurrected and that his tomb was precisely in the " holy of holies " of the temple of Apollo, in the subterranean chamber, the *manteion* or *adyton* where the Pythia would be seated on a high tripod and render the " true "

Delphi. Column from the Athenian Stoa and the polygonal wall. *Photo Georges de Miré.*

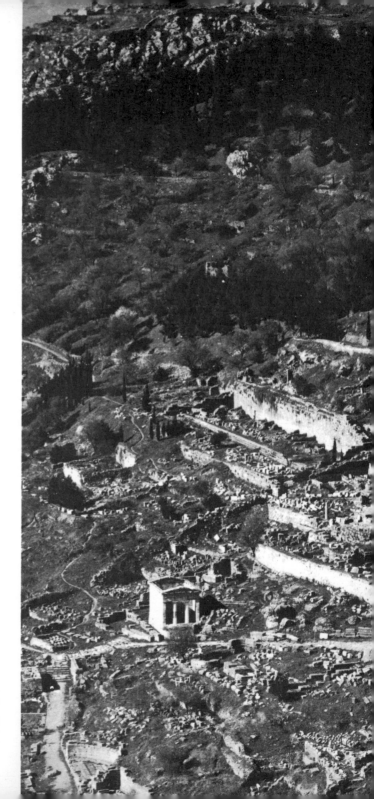

Sanctuary at Delphi. The Sacred
Way enters on the lower left
from the main entrance. The
rectangular foundation of the
Treasury of Siphnus lies on the
left before it makes a sharp turn
to the right. A little further on,
it passes the Treasury of the
Athenians on the left, then the
three columns of the Athenian
Stoa, standing in front of the
polygonal wall, before ending at
the Temple of Apollo. Beyond
it, lies the theatre and, right at
the top, the stadium.
Photo Spyros Meletzis.

Delphi. Temple of
Apollo at the foot of
the Phaedriades.
4th century B.C.
Photo Aury-Arthaud.

and "infallible" oracles by which Apollo kindly
revealed the will of his father, Zeus, to mortals.
It might have been the influence of the orgiastic
cult of Dionysus that made the Pythia a kind of
ecstatic or "possessed" Maenad when she
prophesied. Despite a recent theory according
to which the Pythia was always calm and serene,
all the writers of antiquity from Plato to Cicero
and Plutarch, represented her as being seized by a
kind of *mania* or delirium, called *furor* by Cicero,
induced by the god who inspired her. Apart from
the consultation in the adyton at Delphi, other
prophecies were given by divination, notably by
cleromancy or fortune-telling by drawing lots
(See Oracles).

Both private citizens and the delegates of cities
came crowding to Delphi to question the Pythia
who would only answer on certain days and in
certain conditions. As long as their religious
faith endured and remained profound, the peoples
of antiquity would never dare to undertake any
important enterprise without first having sought
the advice and the revelations of the god. The
Delphic oracles played a role that was important
although difficult to explain, in the great move-

ment of Greek colonisation, which established
Greek settlements along the shores of the Mediterranean from Spain to the far shores of the
Pontus Euxinus (Black Sea), especially from the
8th to the 6th century B.C. The Pythia would
provide the founders of new cities with ritual
prescriptions for the forms of worship and the
religious institutions to be established abroad,
and also, it seems, with geographical information
on the remote regions to which they were sailing.
It was natural enough that Delphi should become
an admirable information centre because of the
great number of pilgrims who came from every
region to consult the oracle, all the year round and
in even greater numbers during the Pythian
Games.

The golden age of the sanctuary and the
oracle of Apollo was the 6th century B.C. Until
the Persian Wars, the authority of the Delphic
revelations was practically uncontested. But
when Xerxes invaded Greece in 480, the attitude
of the Pythia was not of a nature to encourage
the defenders of Greek independence. It appears
that the envoys of the Persian king were well
received at Delphi. The peoples of the Amphic-

Delphi. The theatre. 4th century B.C. Below it, the Temple of Apollo and the Treasury of the Athenians.

tionic League who nearly all lived to the north of Thermopylae, and even the Boeotians, were reluctantly compelled to support the invader even though they themselves were the most directly menaced. The Pythia prophesied nothing but misfortunes for the Greeks but, when the victories of Salamis and Plataea had saved the situation, the explanation was given that the oracles of Apollo had foreseen and prepared them, and the offerings of the triumphant Greeks came flooding into the sanctuary again. But the hitherto almost blind faith of the Greeks in the veracity of the god of Delphi had received a severe blow. With the Persian Wars, the political independence of the sanctuary came to an end. Henceforth, the oracle was to be under the patronage of the dominant state which exercised a hegemony: Athens in the 5th century, then Sparta, Thebes and Macedonia in the 4th, the Aetolians in the 3rd, and finally the Romans. Nevertheless, the sanctuary remained very influential, at least until the time of Alexander who came to Delphi before setting off on his great expedition in order to have himself proclaimed " invincible " by the Pythia. In the 2nd century A.D. Delphi underwent a virtual renaissance, even though it was of a somewhat " archaeological " character, thanks to the philhellenism of several emperors, notably Hadrian. Associated with this ephemeral renaissance is the name of Plutarch, the author of the *Lives,* who was a priest of Delphi and became the fervent apologist of the Delphic religion in his *Pythian Dialogues;* for, although there was not a Delphic " doctrine " properly speaking, there was a " spirit " which had a great influence on the religious and moral beliefs of ancient Greece. Far from being the cruel and inhuman archer and spreader of plague as he is represented in the *Iliad,* Apollo became the most " philanthropic " of the gods with the progress of theology, not only by his oracles, by which he illumined and guided men, but also by the " cathartic " rites he presided in his role as Purificator of all moral stains and faults. Aeschylus, Pindar and Herodotus are among those who owed much to the Delphic spirit, and they also gave back much.

The intellectual and literary influence of Delphi was considerable. The temple of the Pythian

Delphi. Sacred way and Altar of Chios. *Photo Spyros Meletzis.*

Apollo contained the portraits of Homer and Hesiod and Pindar's iron seat. In Pindar's own lifetime, the oracle ordered the Delphians to give him a part of the tithes that had been offered to the god. Apollo, leader of the chorus of the Muses as Musagetes, was the natural patron of poetry and poets and the fact was not overlooked by the Pythia. He was also the protector of the sciences and it was said that when he was on the sacred isle of Delos, where he had been born, he had ordered them to double the cubic volume of an altar, thereby making them undertake the study of geometry; for, like the squaring of a circle, the doubling of a cube is an insoluble problem. Various maxims by sages who had been more or less inspired by Apollo, such as " Nothing excessive ", " Learn to know yourself ", " If you participate, misfortune will attend you ", as well as the mystic epsilon to which Plutarch devoted the whole of the dialogue *De E apud Delphos* were inscribed on the entrance to the temple. The oracles of the Pythia considered that the immortality of the soul, which Socrates had tried to prove in Plato's *Phaedo,* was implicitly admitted. Socrates advised his disciples to consult the Pythia, and when his friend asked at Delphi whether the world contained any man wiser than Socrates, the oracle replied that it did

not. Plato, in the ideal and Utopian city he constructed through reasoning gave a preponderant role to the god of Delphi in all matters concerning religion and morality. He also wrote in the Republic: " It is Apollo who should dictate the most important, the most beautiful and the first of all laws... We shall follow no other guide, for this god who is the traditional interpreter of religion, has settled at the centre and the navel of the earth to guide mankind. " R.F.

D E M E . In order to break the power of the aristocratic classes of the Athenian state, the reformer, Cleisthenes (q.v.), divided the territory of the city and the surrounding Attic countryside into some hundred territorial divisions known as *demoi.* Many small and unimportant localities were grouped together to form a single deme in the system, whereas thickly populated areas were broken down into several such divisions. The deme was the basic unit of the state; in the year following his birth, every freeborn Athenian was inscribed on the register of the deme to which his father belonged, and his name was always followed by the demotic, that is, the name of the deme. By being inscribed on the register of his deme, he automatically enjoyed all civil rights and the rights of the city. But the deme was more than an

Demeter and Persephone giving an ear of wheat to the young Triptolemus. Votive relief found at Eleusis. About 450-440 B.C. Athens, National Museum.

administrative convenience; it constituted a community, led by a *demarchos* who was elected, somewhat like a mayor, and who administered local affairs with the help of the popular assembly. He also acted as an intermediary between the central power and administration, and the inhabitants of his deme. Each deme had its divine protectors, its sanctuaries and its festivals, as well as its own finances which were increased by sacred property and residence taxes paid by foreigners.　　　　　　　　　　　　　　P.D.

DEMETER. The goddess, Demeter, played a very important part on Olympus because of her well specified attributes: she gave the earth its fertility and it was she, above all, who made the corn grow; while this ensured the spread of her cult, it gave a very special character to the ceremonies held in her honour. In the sanctuaries where she was worshipped, especially at Eleusis in Attica, secret rites or mysteries (q.v.) were performed before an assembly of initiates. We have no details of these mysteries but it would seem that their profoundest significance was derived from the idea that life is eternal and always repeating itself. An illustration of this idea may be seen in the legend of Demeter. The goddess had a daughter, Persephone, by Zeus, and cherished her tenderly. One day, while Persephone was playing in the fields with her friends, she was carried off by Hades who took her down to the underworld and made her his wife. Demeter did not know what had happened to her daughter and searched for her all over the face of the earth, imploring human aid in many places that were later to be pointed out by the ancient Greeks as they recounted her pathetic wanderings. Weary and despairing, the goddess refused to ensure the fertility of the earth and famine threatened the world, whereupon Zeus ordered Hades to return Persephone to her mother. But as Persephone had eaten some seeds of a pomegranate (held by the Greeks to be a fruit of the dead) she was enthralled by their magic power and obliged to spend half of every year with Hades. As a result, vegetation only appears on the earth for six months in every year. When Demeter had recovered her daughter, she wished to show her gratitude to all who had helped her in her distress,

and gave Triptolemus (q.v.), son of the king of Eleusis, an ear of corn which he was to cultivate and whose virtues he was to reveal to mortals. Triptolemus then travelled around the world, on a winged chariot according to the legend, teaching agriculture and the art of taming nature wherever he went.

Demeter and Persephone, also called simply Kore, the girl, are inseparably linked in tradition and were represented together by artists, often shown embracing one another tenderly as on the east pediment of the Parthenon. It was also said that Demeter had a son, Plutus, who symbolised wealth.

Demeter was one of those divinities in the Greek world who were not only the object of a formal worship, but who aroused a genuine mystic sentiment among their faithful. Those who had been initiated into their mysteries could rely on Demeter and Persephone to ensure the survival of the soul in the sad domain of the dead.

Artists have represented both mother and daughter under rather similar aspects: grave and severely dressed in long flowing robes. As was only natural, Demeter was given a more matronly appearance, but they both had the same benign expression. They may be seen together on a famous relief from Eleusis, flanking the young Triptolemus to whom they give the ear of corn. Demeter was usually shown holding a sceptre, while Persephone's most frequent attribute is a torch, a funerary symbol.   P.D.

DEMETRIUS of PHALERUM. In the fighting which broke out after the death of Alexander, one of the claimants to the throne of Macedonia, Cassander, managed to capture Athens which had supported his rival Polyperchon. He then placed the city under the authority of one of his friends, Demetrius of Phalerum, who ruled from 317 to 307 B.C. He was a disciple of Aristotle and his first measure was to establish an oligarchic regime based on the census. He was famous for his lavish living, but passed a law forbidding luxury for tombs—an important law with regard to the history of art since it put an end to the making of carved funerary stelae in Attica. He governed as a tyrant, without cruelty, but also without the slightest regard for the prestige of Athens which, as a modern historian has remarked, he reduced to the rank of a small country town. In 307 Demetrius Poliorcetes seized Athens and, to the great joy of the population, expelled the tyrant who took refuge at the court of Ptolemy.   P.D.

DEMETRIUS POLIORCETES. Demetrius Poliorcetes succeeded his father Antigonus I the One-eyed who had proclaimed himself king in 306 B.C. and governed most of the provinces of Asia Minor. After being expelled by the Diadochi after his defeat at Ipsus in 301, Poliorcetes fled to Macedonia where he proclaimed himself king in 297. After a two year siege, he seized Athens and then re-established oligarchic regimes in the Greek cities. He was chased from his kingdom by a coalition in which Pyrrhus, the king of Epirus, played a leading part, and then went to Asia Minor. There, he captured the city of Sardes before being taken prisoner by Seleucus and dying in captivity in 283. He gave his name to a new science, poliorcetics, the science of siege warfare, but his character was not equal to his intelligence and he made himself hated for his luxurious way of living and his arrogance. Plutarch called him a shadow king.   P.D.

DEMOCRITUS. Democritus of Abdera was a disciple of Leucippus, himself the disciple of Parmenides, and was a contemporary of Socrates. He was born in about 460 B.C. and lived to a very old age. He was a great traveller, a great observer and a great writer, producing more than fifty treatises which composed an encyclopaedic work of which only fragments have survived. In them, we find a morality of happiness and serenity and the first discussion of an atomistic philosophy. Parmenides affirmed the existence of an immutable Being and denied Nothingness or Non-Being. But, as Leucippus and Democritus then remarked, the Non-Being exists, for it is the emptiness without which there can be no movement. Being itself was not a solid block of matter which would rule out the existence of generation and corruption: rather, it was composed of solid and indivisible particles, or atoms, invisible to our sight because of their smallness. These particles only differed from one another by their position (like Z and N), their order (like AB and BA) and their form or figure (like A and B), whence the name of « ideas » which was given to them by Democritus. These atoms moved in emptiness and encountered one another, producing a whirlwind which led to a mechanical selection by a centrifugal process; this allowed Democritus to explain the whole system of the world. Sensations can be explained by the passing of light atoms, either effluvia or simulacra, through the pores of organs, but the actual knowledge that results from this is obscure, unauthentic and purely conventional. The only legitimate knowledge comes from reason which postulates the atoms and space. The soul is composed of subtle and mobile atoms which are renewed by respiration. Plato and Aristotle subordinated the mechanical explanations of the atomists to the finalistic considerations which were to dominate classical thought. Only Epicurus adopted the system of atomist physics, although not without some modifications and additions. The poem *De rerum natura* by his disciple, Lucretius, gives us an overall picture of ancient atomist thinking. Democritus now appears as a precursor of modern physicists, whose corpuscular and mechanistic ideas he heralds.   P. M.S.

DEMOSTHENES (1). The greatest of all the Athenian orators (384-322 B.C.). His father was a rich arms manufacturer who died when Demosthenes was only seven; he had chosen three tutors for his son but they squandered the inheritance. When he was eighteen years old, Demosthenes decided to make them disgorge their ill-gotten wealth and learned the secrets of legal oratory from the orator Isaeus. When he was twenty-one he pleaded in person against his tutors and won the case but he was only able to recuperate a small part of his inheritance. He was therefore obliged to earn his living as a logographer by composing speeches for litigants less skilful than him with words. He then took the rostrum of the assembly where, at the age of thirty, he made his first political speech, which has still survived, *On the Symmories*.

At that time, the king of Macedonia, Philip II, was attempting to add Greece to his empire. Many Athenians gave way, faced by the dangers of war, and preferred to make concessions to keep the peace. Demosthenes joined the ranks of the patriotic orators who were determined to defend the liberty of the Greek cities at all costs. In 351 he delivered the 1st *Philippic,* and for the next ten years he made one fiery, violent speech after another until the 4th *Philippic* in 341. He finally succeeded in shaking the Athenians out of their lethargy and, after winning the confidence of the people, he took charge of their affairs from 340 to 338. One of his most notable achievements was the alliance with Thebes which could have saved the independence of Hellas, but in 338 both Athenians and Thebans were crushed by the Macedonian phalanx at Chaeronea. The affair of the crown, which followed after Chaeronea but was not taken to the courts until 330, gave Demosthenes the opportunity to offer an apologetic for his political career which had been under heavy fire from Aeschines, who only received less than a fifth of the votes and had to go into exile after paying a heavy fine. In 324, occurred the case of Harpalus in which Hyperides, Demosthenes' former ally in the patriotic party, became his accuser. Demosthenes was suspected of venality, was sentenced and had to go into exile, but he was soon recalled to Athens when the news of Alexander's death provoked a rising against Macedonia. But the Lamian War ended in defeat for the Greek cities and Demosthenes was once again exiled and pursued. He took refuge in the sanctuary of Poseidon on the island of Calauria and when his pursuers were about to seize him, he committed suicide by poison.

Some sixty speeches have come down to us under the name of Demosthenes but some, espe-cially civil pleas, are suspect or else completely spurious. Nearly all his published speeches have survived. The most regrettable loss is his speech in his own defence in the Harpalus affair. He was, first of all a great man of action and an energetic teacher. His ideas were inspired by an ardent patriotism, a great love of liberty, and the high notion he had of the role of a " counsellor ", that is, a political orator, in a democracy. He had read and re-read Thucydides' works from which he derived both political wisdom and elegance of style. His adversary, Aeschines, said of him that when he mounted the rostrum he bounded and postured " like a tiger ". The written phrases of his speeches still suggest the violence of his oratorical approach, for, as Montaigne said, " Demosthenes on paper is Demosthenes speak-ing ". The summit of his art was in the way in which he succeeded in making his audience for-get him as a man, and he scorned the precepts of rhetoric. He was an inimitable speaker of great persuasion, with a nervous, incisive and striking style. R.F.

DEMOSTHENES (2). He was an Athe-nian general who played a role of some impor-tance together with Nicias in the Peloponnesian War. He was one of the leaders whom his com-patriots chose for the expedition to Sicily.

DEUCALION. Deucalion and Pyrrha were the only mortals that Zeus spared when he decided to drown the whole of mankind in a great flood. They had both built an ark on which they floated until the day the waters receded. They interpret-ed Zeus's orders which had been transmitted to them by the intermediary, Hermes, and threw the bones of their mother over their shoulders, that is, the stones that are the skeleton of the earth. From these stones there then sprang human beings who henceforth peopled the world. In this legend, which was one of the lesser known in Greek mythology, a transposition of oriental flood myths is easily apparent. P.D.

DIADOCHI. When Alexander the Great died without leaving any other legitimate heirs than his imbecile half-brother and a hoped-for but still unborn child, his generals never imagined for a moment that the empire in whose creation they had so proudly participated was to be dismembered. A king had to reign in Macedonia and accord-ingly, the throne was given to a feeble-witted man who was shortly afterwards joined by the son to whom Roxana gave birth. To protect these weak sovereigns and to exercise the power in their name, two of Alexander's best lieutenants were chosen: Perdiccas and Craterus, both of whom had distinguished themselves in the Asian expedition and notably in the Indian campaign. Next, governors were appointed for the various provinces of the empire. Antipater kept his post of strategus responsible for affairs in Greece which he had held for so long, and it was he who put down the Greek revolt that was provoked by news of Alexander's death, condemning Hyperides to death and making Demosthenes commit suicide. Ptolemy, the victor of Halicarnassus, was given the satrapy of Egypt, Antigonus I, known as the One-eyed *(Monophthalmos)* received that of Pamphylia, Lycia and Phrygia, and Eumenes was given the unenviable post of governor for the as yet unsubdued provinces of Cappadocia and Paphlagonia, while Thracia went to Lysimachus. The eastern territories were divided among less important personages who played a more modest role.

In a very short time, each of the successors *(diadochi)* of Alexander became convinced that he was the best qualified to rule over the empire. The result was that for more than forty years they all fought mercilessly and intrigued endlessly against one another until 277 B.C., when the last of the heroic old guard had died and what was left of the empire was split up into independent kingdoms.

Perdiccas was the first to aspire to the control of Greece and the royal throne. His ambition resulted in a coalition being formed against him of all the diadochi and a war in which both he and Craterus were killed. Their death made a new partition necessary in 321, in which the regency was given to Antipater, Antigonus's position in Asia Minor was consolidated, and another of Alexander's officers, Seleucus, was appointed in Babylonia. But shortly after Antipater's death, his successor, Polyperchon, whom he had himself nominated, found himself faced by a new coalition: Cassander, Antipater's son, led an offensive in Greece, set up Demetrius of Phalerum as tyrant in Athens, and seized power in Macedonia after having killed Alexander's widow and son in 316. But in the years that followed he was eclipsed by the personality of Antigonus I, who was opposed by a new coalition of Ptolemy, Cassander, Lysimachus and Seleucus once he had

revealed his ambitions to rule the empire. War broke out, interrupted by a short truce in 311, and Antigonus placed his troops under the command of his son, Demetrius, who later won the title of Poliorcetes, the besieger of towns, and defeated Demetrius of Phalerum in 307, driving him out of Athens where he had reigned for ten years as tyrant. Then in 306, at Salamis in Cyprus, he defeated Ptolemy's fleet which had been threatening the Aegean isles in the preceding months. As a result of his victory, Antigonus declared himself king, and not to be outdone, Ptolemy, Seleucus, Cassander and Lysimachus all followed suit.

The clash of so many rival ambitions soon led to a new war. In 301, the armies of all the kings met at Ipsus where Antigonus died in the battle and Poliorcetes was driven from the field. A third and last partition was then made, in which Macedonia and Greece were officially given to Cassander, Ptolemy was confirmed in his dominion over Egypt, and Seleucus over Syria, while Lysimachus received Antigonus's former territories in Asia Minor in addition to Thracia, which he already possessed. But Demetrius Poliorcetes refused to acknowledge defeat and, while a new conflict over Syria opposed Seleucus and Ptolemy, he returned to Greece. There, taking advantage of Cassander's death in 297, he proclaimed himself king of Macedonia, set up an oligarchy in the Hellenic cities and made himself hated by all. He was attacked on one side by his Thracian neighbour, Lysimachus, on the other by Pyrrhus, the king of Epirus, and lost Macedonia in 287. He was unable to prevent Ptolemy's fleet from taking control of the Cyclades, and died in 282 after being taken prisoner by Seleucus. The other diadochi soon met similar fates; for Seleucus was killed in the battle of Corupedium (281) in which he was opposed by Lysimachus who himself died a year later.

Weary of fighting and despairing of ever preserving the unity of the empire after so many disputes, the later generations of the diadochi resigned themselves to dividing Alexander's heritage into a number of large, independent kingdoms. The family of the Lagides, to whom Ptolemy belonged, kept Egypt, while Poliorcetes' son, Antigonus II, established his dynasty in Greece and Macedonia, and the Seleucids reigned over Syria.   P.D.

DIALECTS. In classical times, although the Greeks were so often divided by cities and

Temple of Apollo
at Didyma.
Photo Hirmer.

civil wars, they shared a common sentiment of ethnic unity because of their language which distinguished them, in their eyes, from all the " barbarians " who neither spoke nor understood Greek. But there were numerous dialectic differences which distinguished, for example, the Greek spoken at Athens from that spoken in Sparta, Thebes or Cyprus. Nowadays, we can no longer study the Greek dialects without taking into account the " Mycenaean " and pre-Homeric language of the inscribed tablets found at Mycenae, Pylos and Cnossos *(See* Linear B). In 1953, by a brilliant discovery, Michael Ventris was able to decipher the writing which was syllabic and not alphabetic, and showed that it was a kind of archaic Greek which had preceded the dialects of the classical period.

It is now customary to distinguish between four groups of dialects, which we give chronologically, in the probable order of their appearance:

1) the Arcado-Cyprian group, comprising Arcadian (spoken in the centre of the Peloponnesus), Cypriot and Pamphylian;

2) the Attic-Ionic group: Ionian of Asia Minor and the islands, Ionian of Euboea, Ionian of Attica;

3) the Aeolic group: Aeolic of Asia Minor or Lesbian, Thessalian, Boeotian;

4) western Greek: Phocidian, Locrian, Aetolian, Elean; and Dorian proper: Laconian, Argolian,

Corinthian, Syracusan, Megarian, Cretan, Rhodian, dialects of Thera and Cyrene.

There are so many affinities between groups 1 and 2 on one hand, and groups 3 and 4 on the other, that some linguists now tend to reduce these different groups to two great categories of dialects: " southern dialects, with the archaic residue of Arcado-Cyprian and the vigorous new development of Attic-Ionic; and northern dialects with the marginal and complex remainders that had constituted the Aeolic dialects, and the youngest group of Dorian and north-western dialects which the Greeks themselves considered as being frankly opposed to Attic-Ionian " (P. Chantraine). According to these views, each group of dialects would have been due to one of the two great waves of invasions which swept over Greece in the early period. Thus, Homer's Achaeans would have been the originators of " Mycenaean ", Arcado-Cyprian and Attic-Ionic, while the Dorian invaders would have originated Aeolic and then Dorian.   R.F.

DIDYMA. Didyma was the great sanctuary of Miletus that was consecrated to Apollo. In the archaic period a triumphal way led from the city to the sacred site several miles distant, bordered by statues of high dignitaries of the cult, belonging to the family of the Branchidae. A colossal temple with an adyton was raised in the sanctuary in the Hellenistic period but it was never completed. P.D.

DIO CHRYSOSTOMUS. He was a sophist and philosopher of the 1st century A.D., born at Prusa in Bithynia, and nicknamed Chrysostomus or " golden mouth " because of his eloquence. Like the sophists of ancient times, Dio travelled from country to country, made brilliant speeches on the slightest pretext and won enthusiastic applause everywhere. He stayed at Rhodes, in Egypt and especially in Rome, from where he was exiled by the emperor Domitian in 82. The exile lasted fourteen years until the death of the emperor and changed not only Dio's life but also his character and ideas. He became converted to philosophy and travelled throughout Asia wearing the mantle and carrying the staff of the Cynics. His speeches were no longer trivial discourses on the merits of small boys or parrots, but grave, moral exhortations. In the reigns of Nerva and Trajan he was again well received at court, but he remained a philosopher and never ceased to preach in favour of conversion to the philosophical way of life so that his numerous voyages of the time tended to resemble missions. He died about 112. In his speeches as a philosopher Dio showed little originality. His morality was that of the Cynics and Stoics, his theology was that of Platonism, but his preachings were imbued with a talent, a wit and a grace which is well evident in such surviving works as *The hunter* and the *Euboicus*. R.F.

DIODORUS SICULUS. Diodorus was a historian of the 1st century B.C. and author of a monumental *Bibliotheka* (World History) which claimed to relate the history of all the peoples of antiquity. He was only a compiler though an accurate and conscientious one, and what now remains of his gigantic work is extremely valuable for our knowledge of the ancient world. R.F.

DIOGENES LAERTIUS. Historian of philosophy and probably a native of Laertia, a town in Cilicia, he lived in the 3rd century A.D. His *Lives and Doctrines of the Philosophers* is a mediocre compilation, devoid of all critical spirit, but indispensable for our knowledge of Greek philosophy, of which so many original works have vanished, because of its wealth of information, which is often picturesque. P.-M.S.

DIOGENES of SINOPE. *See* Cynicism.

DIOMEDES. Diomedes should not be confused with the Thracian king of the same name whose mares devoured strangers and who was slain by Heracles; he was one of Ulysses' most faithful companions in the Trojan War. He went with Ulysses to Scyrus to seek Achilles, encouraged Agamemnon to sacrifice his daughter, was one of the ambassadors sent by the Greek chieftains to Achilles to beseech the latter to return to the fight, and accompanied Ulysses in order to capture the Trojan spy, Dolon. He was a valiant warrior and in the course of a battle, wounded the goddess, Aphrodite, when she descended to earth in order to protect Aeneas.
P.D.

DIONYSIUS I and II. In the years which followed the ill-fated Athenian expedition (413 B.C.) Syracuse did not profit as much as might have been expected from her victory. She allowed the Carthaginians who had settled in the west of Sicily to seize Selinus, raze Himera to the ground, and annex Agrigentum. An obscure citizen named Dionysius, known as the Elder,

Diomedes carrying his share of the booty : the Palladium, a statue of Pallas Athena, protectress of Troy. Decoration inside a cup. About 400-380 B.C. Oxford, Ashmolean Museum.

aroused the anger of the Syracusans against the spiritless attitude of their leaders and succeeded in getting the assembly of the people to nominate him as strategus. He decided that it was too late to stop the Carthaginians from conquering Camarina and Gela and that it would be wiser to negociate with them to put an end to their progress. He then created a fleet of two hundred vessels, reorganised the army into which he brought mercenaries from Campania, fortified the city and even barred the entry to one of the ports by means of a dyke which allowed the defenders to keep a watch on all ships that entered. Without directly attacking Carthage, he attacked the villages where the enemy might have found allies, and then turned on the Greek cities, destroying Etna and Naxos and occupying Leontini and Catania. The capture of Sicily made the Carthaginians recommence hostilities and in 397 they even threatened Syracuse after having defeated Dionysius' fleet, but Dionysius ended by winning a victory and the struggle went on indecisively until his death. Far from devoting the whole of his energies to the defeat of the Carthaginians, Dionysius played a very important part in Magna Graecia between 390 and 373, the year of his death. He annexed many villages, military posts and even Hellenic cities like Croton. In fact, he carved himself a vast empire which extended from Ancona to the tip of Sicily. If we also take into account that he was greatly admired by the Spartans in spite of their hostility to tyranny, Dionysius I must be accounted one of the greatest figures of the early 4th century B.C., an age lacking in great men.

His son, Dionysius II, known as the Younger, was quite different. He was an indecisive personality, always in an open or secret state of hostility against his half-brother, Dion, the friend of Plato, and quite incapable of ensuring a normal existence for Syracuse so that at his death the once-brilliant city, deprived of its empire, was no more than a solitude, to use the words of a contemporary. P.D.

DIONYSIUS of HALICARNASSUS.

Dionysius was a grammarian and historian of the 1st century A.D. who mostly lived in Rome. He was the author of numerous treatises on style, notably *On the force of Demosthenes' style*, the second section of *On the ancient Orators*, for he was a passionate admirer of the great Athenian. He also wrote the *Antiquitates Romanae*, a weighty tome on the origins and first centuries of Rome, which is a compilation of no historical or literary merit. R.F.

DIONYSUS.

Dionysus seems at first to have been a somewhat minor figure in the Hellenic pantheon, but in the course of time his popularity increased to such an extent that by the Hellenistic age he was considered as one of the most important deities of Olympus. The reason was that he had gradually become the focus for mystic ideas which, as the spiritual needs of the Greeks became more pressingly felt, made him one of those rare immortals who might be approached for hope and consolation. He was the son of Zeus and a Theban princess called Semele. When she was already pregnant, Semele besought Zeus to reveal himself to her in all his glory, but when the god did appear, the sight of his splendour was too much for her and she died thunderstruck. Zeus then kept the embryo of the child in his thigh until it was time for it to be born. He then confided it into the care of the Boeotian king, Athamas, and his wife, Ino, but Hera was inflamed by jealousy and pursued the illegitimate child with her hatred. She afflicted the infant's adoptive parents with madness and Zeus then ordered Hermes to take the child to the care of the nymphs in a mysterious country called Nysa, an episode immortalised by Praxiteles in his great group sculpture. When he had grown to manhood, Dionysus discovered the vine and its uses, thus becoming the god of wine, and also that of ivy, that plant whose perennial hardiness may be taken as a symbol for the continuity of life. After many vicissitudes, owing to Hera's jealousy, Dionysus took the place that was rightly his on Olympus. He was said to have travelled as far as India, in the midst of a triumphal procession, dwelt in Thracia and after an adventurous sea voyage in which he was nearly captured by pirates, met Ariadne on the isle of Naxos, where she had been abandoned by Theseus, and made her his mistress.

God of intoxicating plants (like the vine, ivy can produce a certain state of euphoria if masticated), Dionysus was a god who loved joy and merry tumult, whence one of his nicknames, "the noisy one". He would go surrounded by his thiasos which he would lead to the rhythm of his thyrsus—a miraculous stick with ivy leaves entwined around it, made by the spirits of the woods —and satyrs and maenads who would dance to the sound of the flute and the tambourine. Inspired by the example of this divine procession, in the course of certain festivals, women imitated these Bacchantes by succumbing to delirious enthusiasm and would run wild through the forests, in Boeotia especially, in a state of hysteria which sometimes attained such a degree that they would tear apart any animals that might happen to cross their path. One such band of women was once seen to arrive in a state of exhaustion, after their ecstasies, in the town of Amphissa in the middle of the night. The town was being sacked by enemy warriors at the time but, completely unaware of anything happening around them, the women collapsed in the main square and fell soundly asleep. Such a frenzied cult could not fail to strike the Greeks who were by nature rationalist and little given to such excessive displays of emotion and both Euripides' play *The Bacchae* and a statue by Scopas which we now know by a copy, survive as witnesses to the profound impression that such sights made on the Greek mind. 6th and 5th century vases often bear paintings representing the thiasos. It should, however, be noted that in the middle of these wild processions, Dionysus is shown standing calm and majestic, holding a vine-stock and a cantharus, a kind of drinking cup reserved for his personal use; he wears a long and richly embroidered robe and his face is framed by a majestic beard. He is often shown accompanied by his favourite animal, a panther.

In the course of the 5th century B.C. at the latest, Dionysus became a god of the dead, whose survival he ensured, perhaps because he was already the deity of plants whose existence shows such tenacity. He became a kind of replacement for Hades and he was sometimes held to be the husband of Persephone. About the time of the Peloponnesian War, in the second half of the 5th century, a new image of Dionysus came into favour with both Athenians and the Greeks in general; his idyll with Ariadne was stressed and the two lovers were often represented in a tender embrace, with Dionysus often bearing

Dionysus, god of wine, in a ship canopied by a vine. The sea is symbolised by dolphins. Cup by Execias. About 540 B.C. Munich, Antikensammlung. *Photo Hirmer.*

Dionysus, holding a kantharos, watches a dionysiac dance. Detail of an Italiote krater by the Karneia Painter. About 410 B.C. Taranto Museum. *Ph. Hirmer.*

away the young woman in his arms. His godlike appearance became somewhat transformed and he was shown no longer with beard and flowing heavy costume, but as a beautiful, naked young man with long ringlets of hair falling on his shoulders. Such an image was far from being a simple depiction of an amorous scene and it has been rightly considered as a symbolic representation of the god leading a mortal soul to immortality. This was the conception that was henceforth to dominate the legend and that was to make Dionysus so beloved by mortal minds troubled by intimations of mortality. P.D.

DIOSCURI. The Greek word Dioscuri means sons of Zeus. They were Castor and Polydeuces (or Pollux in Latin) and their mother was Leda. Helen and Clytemnestra were their sisters and each of the sons was said to have been born in an egg which he shared with one of the sisters. The event occurred near Sparta, on the river Taygetus, and the Dioscuri were typically Laconian heroes. As warriors they took part in many expeditions, delivering the young Helen whom Theseus had abducted, embarking with

the Argonauts to seek the Golden Fleece and defeating Talus, a giant with a bronze body who massacred strangers in Crete. Finally, after stealing a herd or after having kidnapped the two daughters of King Leucippus, they were slain in a brawl with their cousins, Idas and Lynceus. Zeus granted them immortality which they shared on alternate days. They were not only patrons of Sparta, but became protectors of mariners and they were often invoked during dangerous voyages, which is why so many shrines consecrated to them have been found near seaports. P.D.

DITHYRAMB. Round chorus, in honour of Dionysus. *(See* Lyric Poetry).

DIVINATION. Following Plato, Cicero made the distinction between two kinds of divination: one due to art and consisting in the interpretation of signs provided by birds, the entrails of sacrificial victims, drawing of lots, etc.; and the other which is due to nature, that is, to the soul of the prophet or prophetess who is directly enlightened by the divinity. The first

One of the Dioscuri leaping from his horse carried by a triton. Acroterion from the Ionic temple at Locri. End of the 5th century B.C. Naples, Museo Nazionale. *Photo L. von Matt.*

a fatal link between the presage and its accomplishment.

Apart from such prodigies that diviners did not always have at their disposal, signs of divine will were also to be observed from the normal behaviour of animals, for animal instinct has an astonishing certitude and permanence and seems to be a manifestation of a supernatural power. Besides, the majority of animals were worshipped, not only in Egypt, but also in Greece where they were at first considered as gods before being associated with the Olympians as their attributes: Zeus's eagle, Apollo's wolf, Artemis's bear and Athena's owl were all reminders of the ancient period when these creatures themselves were the object of worship. Aquatic animals were rarely used by diviners, as fish are dumb; terrestrial animals such as snakes, lizards, rats, weasels and bats were used somewhat more, but the best messengers of the gods were held to be the birds who lived in the sky. Ornithomancy, as the science of divination by birds is called, was very widespread in the archaic period and was a highly complicated affair. The diviner had to interpret the species of the bird (some were held to bring good fortune, others not), the direction and destination of its flight (if to the right of the observer a good sign, if to the left, a " sinister " sign), its cry, and lastly, its degree of activity *(energeia)* and its *hedra* (seat).

In the classical period, ornithomancy gave way before other methods which came from Etruria: divination by the examination of the entrails of sacrificed animals. This science of hieroscopy was based on the postulate that Providence had disposed the answers she wished to give men in the viscera of animals. All the viscera could provide indications, but the liver was especially important, a fact which caused the progress of anatomical knowledge of this organ at an early date. The diviner would examine the appearance of the lobes, the biliary vesicle and the portal vein. An anomaly such as atrophy or the absence of a lobe enabled diviners to foretell the speedy deaths of Cimon, Agesilaus and Alexander the Great.

The priests might also burn parts of the victims on the altars, such as the legs, and the diviners would then observe the way in which the flesh burned and sizzled, the intensity of the flame and

method may be called artificial or inductive, the second, inspired or intuitive. In this article we shall deal with the first, the second being treated in the entry on Oracles.

The most ancient Greek diviners known to us are those of the *Iliad,* especially Calchas among the Achaeans and Helenus among the Trojans. They revealed the will of the gods or the future by interpreting signs furnished either by prodigies or by such natural phenomena as the flight of birds, and sometimes, although rarely, received an immediate revelation from the gods. While the leaders of the Greek army were making a sacrifice at Aulis before setting sail for Troy, a serpent suddenly darted out from underneath an altar and devoured nine sparrows perched nearby on a plane tree; immediately afterwards, the serpent changed to stone. Calchas concluded from this prodigy that the siege of Troy would last nine full years and that the town would fall in the course of the tenth. This was an example of a " determining, figurative omen ". According to the ancient belief, the extraordinary acts of animals determine what men will accomplish; they are not merely signs, but causes, and there is the aspect of the smoke. Another sort of pyromancy, or fire-divination, consisted in the interpretation of the smoke of incense, the smouldering of laurel and barley flour in the flames, as was practised at Delphi for example. There were also very many ways of divining by means of inanimate objects. Especially used were water (hydromancy), mirrors (catoptromancy) and trees like the oaks of Dodona. The oracle of Dodona in Epirus was already known to Homer and was reputed to be the most ancient in Greece. Among other methods also practised in this sanctuary, the Selli, priests of Zeus, and the Peleiades, priestesses of Dione (a divinity identified with the earth) interpreted the noise made by the wind as it rustled through the leaves of the oaks, which were trees consecrated to Zeus. At Dodona and also at Delphi, divination was practised by lots, or cleromancy. The peoples of antiquity ceaselessly had recourse to the drawing of lots which was held to show, not the laws of hazard, but the will of the gods, even when it was a matter of choosing the magistrates of cities. Cleromancy was practised by means of dice, knuckle-bones or beans.

Atmospheric phenomena, *meteora,* were also held to show signs of the will of Zeus, who was god of the sky and the atmosphere. Thunder and rain were omens. Then there were the stars above the clouds. Astrology was imported into Greece from the orient. At an early date the Greeks already had astral superstitions and the Pythagoreans were not alone in considering the stars as the most powerful of gods. After Alexander's conquests, the beliefs of the Chaldaeans penetrated deeply into Greece and astrology assumed the importance it was to retain under the Roman empire.

Divination by words was halfway between inductive divination and inspired divination. As man, a free and intelligent being, sometimes speaks or acts in an involuntary or unconscious manner, he might also be moved by divine will, like the birds. " Every word ", writes Bouché-Leclercq, " every phrase, isolated word or exclamation, heard by a man who is preoccupied by ideas foreign to the person speaking, may become a prophetic sign for the hearer, which the Greeks called *kledon*. It is an unforeseen conjunction, a fortuitous consonance, which might contain a providential warning. " Words in themselves have an intrinsic influence, some being fortunate, others " sinister ". Those pronounced

by human beings whose reason has not yet developed, in other words, children, have a special value in this kind of divination and we still say, " out of the mouths of babes truth is spoken ". Not only involuntary words, but even the movements and sudden twitches of the human body could serve as omens, such as the convulsions of epileptics, struck by the " sacred malady ", as well as such ordinary phenomena as sneezing or hearing a buzzing in one's ears. The distinction was made between the sneeze heard from the left and that heard from the right, the one being a favourable and the other a bad omen.

Besides Calchas, mention should be made of the great diviners of the Theban epic cycle: Amphiaraus, the prophet-king, and Tiresias, the old blind man who is linked with the Oedipus legend and who makes such remarkable appearances in Sophocles' *Oedipus Rex* and *Antigone.* In the first rank of those diviners who belong, not to legend, but to history is the soothsayer Megistias who accompanied Leonidas to Thermopylae and who refused to leave the king when the latter ordered him to go so that he should not perish with him, preferring to die at his post. His epitaph was written by the poet Simonides: " A prophet, he had clearly seen the approach of his destiny, but he did not want to abandon Sparta's chieftains ". The most famous diviner in 5th century Athens was Lampon, a friend of Pericles, who made him a kind of " minister of worship ". The most notable functions of this official personage were those of exegete, or interpreter of religious laws and customs, as well as oracles. He contributed to the foundation of Thurii, the new Sybaris. At the beginning of his *Life of Pericles,* Plutarch has described the diviner, Lampon, interpreting a prodigy. One day, the head of a ram with only one horn was brought to Pericles on his country estate. Lampon declared that the power of the two parties led by Thucydides and Pericles, which were then dividing the state, would become that of a single man, the man to whom this prodigy had been shown. True enough, a short time afterwards, Pericles succeeded in getting Thucydides ostracised. A less clever diviner was Nicias's soothsayer, for he delayed the retreat of the vanquished Athenians because of an eclipse of the moon, and was thus partially responsible for the final disaster of the Sicilian expedition. He should have known that for an army about to retreat, a moon that hides its light is a favourable omen. We should also distinguish between diviners properly speaking and collectors of oracles (which, though they would never admit it, they sometimes fabricated themselves) such as the Athenian, Onomacritus, who was caught *in flagrante delicto* by Pisistratus's son Hipparchus, as Herodotus has related.   R.F.

DIVORCE. In ancient Greece a husband always had the right to repudiate his wife, even without a motive being declared, but in such cases he had to return the dowry and the prospect of such a restitution must certainly have kept the number of divorces down. If the wife should commit adultery, then divorce was compulsory, and over-complaisant husbands could be punished by *atimia,* the deprivation of all civic rights. As the Athenians mainly married to have a son who would ensure the continuity of the family and the cult of the ancestors, to divorce a barren wife was obligatory. But even pregnant wives could be divorced. After Pericles had met Aspasia, he divorced his wife, who had given him two sons, and married her off to another Athenian. In Euripides' play, Medea says: " It is infamous for a wife to leave her husband and she is not permitted to divorce him ". The Athenian woman lived in a perpetual state of minority and was always rendered an inferior by the laws. She only had one recourse: to go to the archon, who was the legal protector of the defenceless, and give him a written explanation of her reasons for asking for a separation. The patent infidelity of the husband was an insufficient reason, for prevailing customs were tolerant of this, but serious misdemeanours might induce the archon to pronounce the divorce. When Alcibiades' wife wanted to divorce him, he refused to give her back the dowry, went to the archon after his wife, picked her up and brought her home again in his arms.   R.F.

DODONA. Even if it were not indicated by tradition, the antiquity of the sanctuary of Dodona could be deduced from its situation outside Greece proper, in Epirus near the modern Janina; by its association with the union of Zeus, the patron deity, and Dione who was an almost forgotten goddess in the classic period; and lastly, by the customs of the priests, the Selli, who slept next to the ground and walked barefoot in order to lose nothing of the emanations from the earth. Dodona was near the region where the people lived who gave their name to the Greeks, the

Graeans, and remained a much frequented site despite its remoteness, especially because of the oracles rendered by the god. He would reveal his will by the rustling of the wind in the leaves of the sacred oak trees, by the flight of doves, the fall of dice, or by the sound made by a sacred cauldron when struck by the thongs of a whip held by the statue of a child. Although it did not have as great a reputation as the oracle of Delphi, that of Dodona was still one of the most important in Greece, and among the pilgrims who came to it was Croesus. Alexander later offered an important sum of money to the sanctuary and the riches that had piled up in the temple were enough to make the writer, Polemon, describe them in his now lost work.

Excavations began on the site almost a century ago and have recently been resumed after a long interval, by the Greek Service of Antiquities. The most notable discovery has been a theatre, but the most important information has been provided by a mass of archaic, bronze, ex-voto figures, mostly consisting of animal figurines which were consecrated by local stock-breeders who hoped to see their herds increase.   P.D.

DOKIMASIA. Before taking up their duties, Athenian officials underwent an examination, the *dokimasia,* which was not concerned with their competence, but with their good citizenship and piety. It made sure that the candidate for office had conducted himself properly towards the state and the gods. The Boule *(See* Assemblies) asked him whether both his parents were Athenians, whether he had behaved filially towards them, whether there were family tombs, and whether he honoured his ancestors, and finally whether he joined in the worship of Apollo Patroos and Zeus Herkeios.   P.D.

DORIANS. Although the ancient Greeks made a very strict distinction between the Ionians and the Dorians, we should not necessarily conclude that they were two different peoples. They themselves considered themselves as being part of the same family and descendants of Hellen, the founder of the race. Some descended from Hellen by his son Dorus, the others by his grandson Ion, the nephew of Dorus. Despite differences of character, customs and language both Dorians and Ionians felt themselves related by close ties of consanguinity, and modern

168

historians have acknowledged that they were not mistaken in this. In the early 2nd millennium B.C., barbarian tribes from the north invaded what was later to be known as Greece. Although they found only a slightly developed civilisation, they were intelligent, energetic, and full of initiative and were able to adapt themselves to their new home and adopt everything they found worthy of admiration from their Cretan neighbours. This trait is already characteristically Greek and we now know that they were soon speaking Greek and worshipping the gods that were later to be in the Greek pantheon. It was they who transformed what had been almost barbarian regions into the cradle of Mycenaean civilisation and their exploits, glory and riches won them such a renown that their memory was preserved in epics and lasted during the whole period of antiquity. It is believed that these first Greeks, called Achaeans by Homer, were the ancestors of the Ionians.

They were submerged towards the end of the Bronze Age by waves of invaders who also came from the Balkans and who seized the territories that they had conquered seven or eight centuries earlier by a series of campaigns and peaceful infiltrations that lasted for at least two centuries. In these invasions, the peoples of antiquity saw the return of the descendants of Heracles, the Heraclidae, to take possession again of the country from which their forefathers had been expelled after the death of the hero, according to legend.

The main difference between the Achaeans and these newcomers, the Dorians, lay in the inequality of their cultural level; for the latter had not benefited from the centuries of apprenticeship during which the earlier invaders had built their civilisation. This civilisation was sufficiently in decline for it to be completely destroyed by the conquest; nonetheless, it had retained enough of its brilliance to dazzle the barbarians. Their education was a lengthy process, for the country they settled in was empty of inhabitants who had fled either into the more inaccessible mountain districts like Arcadia (it should be noted that even in classic times the Arcadians still spoke a dialect which had remained unchanged since the time of the invasions) or, in even greater number, across the sea to the coast of Asia Minor around the Gulf of Smyrna, a region known as Ionia, and to the large neighbouring islands of Chios and Samos, and the Cyclades. They still kept a bridgehead on mainland Greece in the extremity of Attica which was relatively protected by the barrier of the Cithaeron mountains. The populations who had been the first to stand in the way of the advancing Dorians were the first to cross the Aegean and settle in the north of Ionia and on the island of Lesbos, where they became known as the Aeolians. The Dorians laid waste the country around them and pushed on as far as the Peloponnesus where they were so numerous that the region became the centre of the Dorian civilisation. Some went even further to Crete and then Rhodes. As a result, the beginning of the 1st millennium B.C. saw the establishment of large geographical regions, each with its own distinct population.

When economic and social circumstances led to a vast movement of colonisation in the 8th and 7th centuries B.C., Dorian expansion was mostly directed towards Sicily and southern Italy while the Ionians settled in Macedonia, Thrace and the shores of the Black Sea, as well as the western Mediterranean basin, where the Samians explored as far as Gibraltar and the city of Marseilles was founded by the Phocians. After this period, territorial limits tended to become blurred between the different branches of the Hellenic race, and Ionians and Dorians often closely intermingled, without, however, forgetting their origins. Commercial interests and the pattern of international politics easily effaced the differences between them, which were too slight in any case to affect their unity in an ideal common to all Hellenism. Superficial evidence of these differences was found in dialects; there were more profound differences in the character of the peoples. The Dorians were characterised by their austerity, their moral rigour, and admiration for intellectual and physical strength, whereas the Ionians were of a more easy-going disposition and preferred the pleasure of a banquet and the joys of a conversation, which was often refined, to the turmoil of battle and athletic exercises. These different tendencies were reflected in literature and art; the sobriety of Doric architecture contrasts with the graceful elegance of Ionic buildings, and Ionian sculpture is without the solid structure and terse simplicity of Dorian works. Historians have also stressed certain differences in the constitution of Ionian and Dorian society and political regimes; the number of tribes differed, for example. But it is also evident that many of these original differences disappeared with time and that political evolution saw the replace-

Young women undressing.
Cup by Douris.
About 490-480 B.C.
New York, Metropolitan
Museum of Art.

ment of the original regimes by constitutions which corresponded to the changes taking place in a world where questions of race no longer had any great meaning. P.D.

DORIS. Doris is a small province to the north of Parnassus comprising a mountainous district between Phocis, Locris and Aetolia. The same name is used for the Dodecanese islands and the south-western Anatolian coast because they were colonised by the Dorians during the great migrations at the end of the 2nd millennium B.C. P.D.

DORYCLEIDAS. Sculptor of the Spartan school, trained by the Cretans, Dipoenus and Scyllis, who settled in Sparta. Little is known of his work, but from this school of the 7th and 6th centuries B.C., the bronze and ivory ex-voto figurines, offered to Artemis Orthia, are characteristic examples. This plastic art was to develop in bas-reliefs and statuary in the early 6th century and shows the links between Spartan art and that of the Cretan and oriental centres of Cyprus,

Ionia, and perhaps also Lydia and Syria. These workshops specialised in lead and ivory-work. They also developed the technique of chryselephantine sculpture in which the richer and more decorative materials of gold and ivory were sometimes combined with stone. R.M.

DOURIS. Douris was one of the most esteemed of Athenian vase painters, working around 500 B.C. His success is proved by the great number of vases which have been found bearing his decorations. They were very varied in theme, ranging from a charming representation of children at school to the tragic image of Eos holding the corpse of her son Memnon on her knees and frank scenes of banquets with courtesans in attendance. Douris' qualities are such that he may be cited as the most typical representative of vase painting at the time, but although he possessed an excellent knowledge of drawing and was a skilful composer of the varied scenes he delighted in painting, his eclectic inspiration does not always have that depth we find in the works of some of his followers. P.D.

170

DRACO. From the middle of the 7th century B.C. the Athenian college of archons included six *thesmothetai* who were specially responsible for the passing of laws. For a long time the activity of these magistrates remained largely ineffective but in 621 B.C., one of them, Draco, drew up a code which became famous for its severity and which imposed the authority of the state in legal matters for the first time in the history of Athens. It did not mean that the city intervened in purely family matters, and the father remained the sole authority over his wife, children and slaves; but a family that had been injured by another was no longer allowed to take justice into its own hands, and although peaceful agreements were welcomed, vendettas were no longer tolerated. This explains the severity of the new code; for having been deprived of their ancient privilege of punishing those who had offended them, the families would never have accepted the intervention of the state if it had not given them a satisfaction equal to that which they themselves would have demanded from the guilty parties. This measure was an enormous step forward in the acquisition of power by the community and represented a severe blow to the old aristocratic regime. Even the conception of the family was affected by the new laws, which determined the exact degrees of relationship allowed before joint transactions or civil actions could be undertaken. Draco also laid down a distinction between premeditated and involuntary crime, thus proving that he was less cruel than was said.

P.D.

DRAMA (SATYRIC). Each tragic dramatist of Athens who took part in the competitions of the Dionysiac festival *(See* Theatre) presented three tragedies and a satyric drama. This fourth play was quite unlike a comedy, although it contained such burlesque elements as a chorus of satyrs who were blustering, roguish, cowardly and lecherous companions of Dionysus. The only satyr play to have survived in its entirety is Euripides' *Cyclops*. Its hero is Ulysses, as in Book IX of the *Odyssey*, but Polyphemus's servants are the satyrs, Silenus and his son. Like tragedy, the satyric drama dealt with an episode in the legendary life of the hero, but in a witty and parodying manner.

R.F.

DREAMS. Dreams have always been believed to have a premonitory and prophetic value and even today the public still buys *Keys to Dreams*. Oneiromancy has existed at all times and in every country. Homer knew that

"The Horsemen". Scene from a satyr-play. Detail from a black-figure Attic amphora. End of the 6th century B.C. Berlin Museum.

of the observations mentioned tally with those of modern psychologists. At Epidaurus, in the sanctuary of the god of medicine, Asclepius, it was in their dreams that the patients were revealed the treatment that would cure them. *(See* Oracles).

R.F.

EDUCATION. The Athenian citizen began his existence by being tightly swaddled in a cocoon of bandages wound round him. Cradles were either wicker baskets or something like a wooden manger and infants were customarily rocked to sleep. Generally mothers nursed their children themselves but they might also call in wet-nurses who might be either freewomen or slaves, and the sturdy wet-nurses from Laconia were particularly sought after at Athens. Until about the age of seven, small boys were raised by their mothers in the gynaeceum (q.v.), where girls remained until their marriage when they went to reign over the gynaeceum of their husbands. Disobedient children were threatened by bogey-men with such names as Acco, Alphito, Gelo, Gorgon, Empusae, Lamiae or Mormo as well as the big, bad wolf. Good children were told amusing stories in which animals played the main parts as in the tales of Aesop (" Once upon a time there was a rat and a weasel... ") and were also given toys *(See* Toys and Amusements).

Athenian parents do not seem to have been obliged by law to send their children to school but they were practically compelled to do so by prevailing custom. The city magistrates, notably the strategi, had the right to supervise education. At Athens, unlike Sparta (to which we shall come later) education was left to the initiative of private persons who opened schools of letters, music or gymnastics—the trivium of Greek education—and who were paid by the parents. It was only for sons of citizens who had died for the homeland that the state paid the fees of private teachers.

The child would go either successively, or sometimes at the same time, to the school of the *grammatistes,* the *kitharistes* and the *paidotribes* (physical trainer). The grammatistes would teach him the letters of the alphabet and the rudiments of arithmetic. He taught him to read and write by first using the poets, and the first of these was Homer. " Homer is not a man but a

dreams were ambiguous and that it is difficult to distinguish between true dreams, those that come to us through the door of horn, and those lying dreams that come through the door of ivory. His epic poems are full of dreams sent by the gods either to guide the heroes or to lead them astray. In Attic tragedy, the most ancient example is the dream of Atossa, the mother of Xerxes, in Aeschylus's the *Persians.*

Dreams might include every kind of prodigy and presage that could be observed in a waking state. As a result, a good interpreter of dreams had to command the whole of the diviner's science and dream divination developed into a body of complex, detailed doctrines known to us by the five books compiled by Artemidorus of Ephesus and edited in the Roman period. The Pythagoreans, and later the Platonists, believed in dreams but thought that it was necessary to prepare for them by means of a real ascetic discipline in order to avoid nightmares and demoniacal dreams and only experience true dreams sent by the gods. Aristotle wrote a very curious treatise known as *De divinatione per Somnum* and many god " was what children copied in one of their very first writing lessons. A mother was proud when, on asking the tutor of her son how the child was doing, she was told, " He is already studying Book VI of the *Iliad*." (H-I. Marrou). In the schools, such as those we see in vase paintings, there were no desks; the children would sit on low stools facing the master's chair and write on their knees, which was easy enough, for they used hard wax tablets on which they either wrote directly or laid sheets of papyrus.

Greeks have always been fond of music and dancing and the best proof of this is the importance laid on singing and musical instruments in their education. The very word *mousike* is derived from 'Muses', who were the patrons of all intellectual activities. The cultured man was a *mousikos aner*. The existence of music, for the Greeks, was the first, indispensable condition of civilisation. Children not only learned to sing but also to play the cithara or the aulos. The cithara, or lyre, is a stringed instrument with a sounding box; there were usually seven cords which were plucked with the fingers or with a plectrum. One might sing like the Homeric bards while accompanying oneself on the cithara, but not on the aulos, which was a wind instrument

usually known as a flute, although it was more like a clarinet and usually had two diverging mouthpieces. It had nothing in common with Pan's famous pipes, the syrinx. Music was taught empirically and entirely by ear, without any written scores. Greek music was always monodic, for polyphony was unknown. Young people, who had thus been trained in singing, instrumental music and dancing, might take part in choruses, of various kinds. The most famous at Athens were the dithyrambs which led to competitions every year between children's and adults' choruses from different tribes. Greek tragedy was born out of the dithyramb and this is why the chorus played an essential role at first.

The love of the Greeks for bodily exercises is as old and as fervent as their love for music, and we may judge how strong it was from the description of the funeral games held by Achilles in Patroclus's honour in Book XXIII of the *Iliad*. The palaestra of the paidotribes, or master of gymnastics, was a private institution like the schools of the grammatistes and the kitharistes. Pupils were divided into two classes; the small from the age of 12 to about 15, and the older pupils, from the age of 15 to 18, which was the age when the youth, or ephebe, became liable for

Music lesson. Detail from a skyphos by the Pistoxenos Painter. About 480-470 B.C. Schwerin Museum. *Photo Hirmer.*

Music and reading lessons. Detail from a cup by Douris. Early 5th century. Berlin Museum.

military service. The five classic tests of the pentathlon date from the 6th century B.C. and were: wrestling, running, jumping, throwing the discus and throwing the javelin. The paido-tribes, wearing a purple mantle and holding a long forked stick, would direct the exercises and harshly punish the lazy and the disobedient. Limbering-up exercises, rather like those of so-called Swedish gymnastics, were performed to the rhythm of an aulos, which was as necessary to the palaestra as the oil the children rubbed themselves with and the scraper, or bronze comb, they then used to clean their skin of dust, oil and sweat. In the palaestra, the children were completely naked of course. The atmosphere of the palaestra favoured '' special friendships '' between younger and older boys, and between youths and adults, and it is known that paederasty played a role of some importance in Greek education in both Athens and Sparta (See Love). Other sports beside the pentathlon, included pugilism (a kind of boxing) and the pancratium, a combination of wrestling and boxing which was the most violent and brutal of all the sports.

It was only from the period of the sophists onwards, in the second half of the 5th century, that the adolescent Athenians received what we should now call a '' secondary '' or '' higher '' education, when they began to study rhetoric and philosophy.

In Sparta there was never any question of education at such a level because education was entirely organised and controlled by the state and was aimed at one thing only, the production of future warriors. As stress was also laid on eugenics, young girls, unlike their sisters in Athens who lived in seclusion, also took part in many public sports like the boys, and not only practised dancing (the choruses of young Spartan girls were famous throughout Greece) but also running, wrestling, discus and javelin-throwing. The young Lacedaemonians were only allowed to stay with their families until the age of seven. From earliest childhood, they were subjected to a training and special upbringing which was intended to accustom them to a frugal and hardy life. At the age of seven, they were enrolled in troops of children, and the state, represented by the *paidonomos*, made itself responsible for their education. Each band was commanded by an *eiren*, a youth between sixteen to twenty years old, they were divided into packs which were led by the most alert member, the *bouagos*. The study of letters was kept to the strict minimum. Education consisted of learning to obey, to win at wrestling, and to endure fatigue patiently. After twelve years of age, the conditions of life became increasingly harsh; boys no longer wore a tunic and were only given one cloak a year. They slept in dormitories on pallets of reeds and for even the slightest infraction of the rules they were cruelly whipped. They took their meals in common and were only given the coarsest nourishment on purpose, so that they would try to steal food and thus acquire cunning and endurance. At sixteen years of age the transition was made from childhood to adolescence. The eirenes had to undergo a series of successive tests which were both trials of endurance and ceremonies of a magical character, with masks and dances. The strangest of these tests was the *krypteia;* after a time of retreat in which the young man lived alone and hid in the countryside like a wolf, he would practise hunting helots, wandering by night, and would have to kill at least one. Apart from a summary instruction in letters and a serious grounding in music, the whole of the carefully organised Spartan educational system, supervised throughout by the state,

was based on physical training and was aimed at military efficiency.   R.F.

ELATEA. Small town in Boeotia dominating the road between southern and northern Greece. Its situation gave it a strategic importance which is borne out by a famous passage of Demosthenes, revealing how in 339 when Philip of Macedon took the town by surprise, the Athenians suddenly became conscious of the danger that was threatening and became panic-stricken at the thought that nothing stood between Attica and the invading enemy any longer.

P.D.

ELEATIC SCHOOL. Elea, the modern Velia, was a small town in Lucania, south of Naples, on the Tyrrhenian Sea, where one of the oldest and most important philosophical schools of Greece grew up. It was founded by Xenophon (q.v.), but the outstanding mind was Parmenides (end of the 6th—beginning of the 5th century B.C.), who wrote the poem, *On Nature*, fairly large fragments of which have come down to us. The

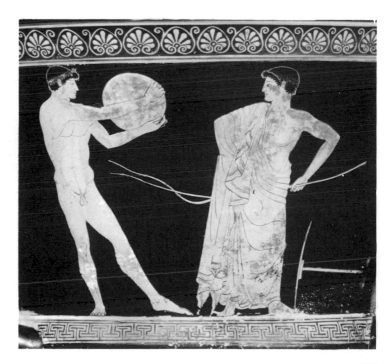

Exercise in throwing the discus supervised by the paidotribes. Detail from a krater by the Cleophrades Painter. About 500 B.C. Tarquinia Museum. *Ph. Hirmer.*

poem is written as a revelation; the truth revealed to the writer is that Being exists and Non-being does not. Thus the principle of contradiction is expressed in ontological form. " It is impossible either to say or think that Being does not exist. What necessity forced it into existence ? Why not earlier or later ? There is neither birth nor beginning in Being. It exists absolutely or it does not exist, and no force of argument will ever enable something to come out of it that is not a part of it. " The second part of the poem elaborates a natural philosophy of appearances. In denying (while at the same time offering its explanation) a multiple and changing reality in favour of immutable Being, Parmenides was setting a fundamental problem to which his successors, Empedocles, Anaxagoras, Democritus and Plato, offered various solutions.

Zeno of Elea, Parmenides' pupil, undertook the defence of his master's ideas by showing that notions of plurality and movement implied consequences which were absurd. He discussed them in a certain number of arguments traditionally called the Fallacies of Zeno. The two best known are that of the arrow; at any given moment, an arrow in flight is opposite a length of ground measuring its exact length and therefore, at any given moment, it is motionless; and that of Achilles and the tortoise : in order to cover a certain distance, a moving object must first cover half of it and, before that, half of this half, and so on; in other words, a spatial infinity and, as this infinity is endless, Achilles will never catch up with the tortoise he is pursuing. It is the *reductio ad absurdum* method of reasoning, used to reveal the unintelligibility of movement.

The last representative of the school of Elea was Melissus, admiral of Samos, who won a naval victory against Athens in 442 B.C. He wrote a book, *On Nature or Being,* in which he asserted the infinity, unity and immutability of Being. Plato severely criticised the positions of Parmenides, while paying him tribute. Eleatic doctrine had a particularly strong influence on the school of Megara (q.v.). P.-M.S.

ELECTRA. Although, in the beginning, Electra was such an obscure figure that even Homer did not seem to be aware of her name, the Greek poets of the 5th century B.C. made the young girl into an immortal figure, worthy of the tragic family of the Atridae to which she belonged. She was the daughter of Clytemnestra and Agamemnon, but she hardly knew her father for he had left for the Trojan Wars when she was still an infant, and as soon as he returned home ten years later, he fell under the sword of Aegisthus, the lover of Clytemnestra. Electra was raised by the adulterous couple, treated like a slave, and then was given in marriage to a poor peasant who never dared to consummate the marriage. She might have remained in this situation as a kind of minor Cinderella, but she refused to resign herself to her fate and became mistress of her own destiny. She lived in hatred of her persecutors and remained faithful to the memory of her father whose tomb she regularly visited. It was there that she eventually met her brother, Orestes, whom she believed to be dead since the time she had made him take flight to escape Aegisthus's cruelty. After a dramatic scene in which she recognised the vigorous young man as having once been the feeble infant she had protected, Euripides shows her urging the sole heir of the family to avenge his father. She helped him to slay the usurper and Clytemnestra and then, when Orestes was pursued by the Erinyes, she devoted herself to him, tending him like a loving sister and seeking to appease his painful madness.   P.D.

ELEGY. A genre of lyrical poetry characterised by alternating hexameters and pentameters. *(See* Lyric Poetry).

ELEUSIS. Eleusis, one of the most sacred sites in all Greece, is situated some twelve miles to the west of Athens, on the bay facing the isle of Salamis. It was there that the weeping Demeter had been hospitably received by King Celeus while she was wandering throughout the world in search of her daughter, Kore, and it was there also that she had given Celeus's son, Triptolemus, the ear of corn so that the young prince might teach mankind how to grow its own cereals, whence the cult and the mysteries (q.v.) whose reputation grew steadily from the beginning to the end of the pagan period and reached far beyond the frontiers of Attica. The fertility of the plain extending around Eleusis, known as the Thriasian plain, is itself by no means sufficient to explain the origin of the legend. What is certain, however, is that the site was one of the first to be inhabited in Attica and we know that as early as the first half of the 2nd millennium B.C. a settlement had been established on the heights of Eleusis, below which the sanctuary was to be placed. In the very heart of the sanctuary, below a later building, the Telesterion, ruins have been found of a Mycenaean megaron where a female goddess, who must certainly have been none other than the Cretan goddess, had been worshipped. She became Demeter shortly afterwards and was associated with the male god, Poseidon.

What made the glory of Eleusis were neither games such as those that were held at Olympus, nor the presence of an oracle, as at Delphi, but instead the initiation into mysteries whose character and significance are still an enigma to us. In the first place, we do not even know when they were first held. They were held under the supervision of the two families of the Eumolpidae and the Kerykes who prided themselves on being as old as the sanctuary itself, and who claimed that it was on Demeter's orders that Eumolpus had instituted the sacred ceremony.

In what did the mysteries consist? We know more or less for certain that the essential roles in the ceremonies were played by the *hierophantes,* the *dadouchos* and the *keryx* and from these names we may deduce that the function of the first named was to reveal sacred matters, that the second carried the torch and that the third had the role of sacred herald, and that all these dignitaries had, of necessity, to belong to the two families we have mentioned. The ceremonies were held twice a year, in the spring and in the autumn, but those in September were more important than those in March, for it was in September that candidates were initiated. Initiation was not reserved for a single class of the population but— quite exceptional in Greek religion—was open to all, Hellenes and barbarians, freemen and slaves, on condition that they had not been tainted by the sin of murder and that they knew enough Greek to be able to pronounce the sacred formulas. The ceremony lasted several days and more than a week elapsed between the first purification and the last two nights of the initiation ritual. This last consisted of two stages and was held in the Telesterion, a square hypostyle hall, where only the Mystai (candidates for initiation) were allowed to enter. What they saw and what they heard had to remain a secret, but it is probable that, among other things, they were shown symbols of fertility and fecundity.

Successive enlargements of the Telesterion in the time of Pisistratus and then of Pericles when the tiers built alongside the walls were no longer sufficient to accomodate all the faithful, were a witness to the growing popularity of these mysteries.

This popularity must be largely due in the first place to the fact that, as we have said, no man was excluded on grounds of class or race, and secondly, because the initiates believed that even in death they would continue to benefit from the protection of Demeter. It has often been discussed whether this religion was a purely formal one and the initiates were content only to learn formulas which in themselves had a saving virtue, or whether moral precepts and counsels of spiritual as well as physical purity were given to the initiates. Eleusinism evolved with the course of time and, although in the beginning it may have been no more than a quasi-magical religion, the distinction of its initiates, from the 5th century onwards at any rate (Pindar, Aeschylus, Polygnotus among many others) would seem to show that, in a fairly short time, it brought its followers a hope of survival after death that must certainly have been accompanied by moral obligations.

P.D.

ELIS. Elis was a province situated in the Peloponnesus between the central chain of mountains and the Ionian sea and would have played a very humble role in Greek history if it had not been the home of the panhellenic sanctuary of Olympia.

ELOQUENCE. *See* Rhetoric.

EMPEDOCLES. Empedocles was a philosopher of the 5th century B.C., born at Agrigentum in Sicily, and author of two poems written in epic hexameters, a treatise *On Nature* and a book on *The Purifications (Katharmoi)* of which fragments have survived. Empedocles certainly did not suffer from any false modesty for in his writings he presents himself not only as prophet, thaumaturge and magician but also as a god. Both scientific and mystical tendencies converge in his thought and his philosophical system combines the ceaseless flux of becoming of Heraclitus with the immovable Being of Parmenides (qq.v.). According to Empedocles, nothing is ever created or lost and the four elements (earth, air, water, fire) exist throughout all eternity. In the beginning they were all mingled in a spherical mass *(Sphairos)* which was maintained by love *(Philia)* before becoming progressively dissolved by strife *(Neikos)*. The evolution of the world is subject to the successive predominance and alternation of these two cosmic and opposing forces, which ceaselessly form and then destroy beings in order to compose others—always with the same four elements. Their combinations made it possible to construct a physical and a biological system containing evolutionist conceptions, which make Empedocles a kind of forerunner of transformism.

The poem of the *Purifications* is a religious work in which the influence of Pythagoras (q.v.) made its appearance. In it, Empedocles describes the downfall of a soul that has failed, its expiations and reincarnations in the form of various types of men, animals and even of plants. One consequence of Empedocles' conceptions was that he was led to recommend abstinence from meat. This astonishing personage soon became legendary. It was believed that he had not died but had mysteriously disappeared during a storm, or that he has thrown himself into the crater of Mount Etna and that the volcano had thrown up one of his sandals.

P.-M.S.

ENCOMIUM. Song of praise. *(See* Lyric Poetry).

EPAMINONDAS. The fact that Thebes could try to dominate the rest of Greece during the second quarter of the 4th century B.C. was mainly due to Epaminondas. He was of noble birth but so poor that he was said to have had to stay indoors while the one garment he possessed was being washed. He was both a friend of writers and a courageous soldier and his civic sense and feeling for discipline were so great that he even served as a simple hoplite after having been a general in command. In 379, he took part in the liberation of Thebes from the Spartan occupation, and then, in 374, he managed to unify Boeotia with the aid of his friend Pelopidas. In order to defend the Boeotian League which they had built against Sparta, Epaminondas and Pelopidas reorganised the army and it was then that the Sacred Battalion (q.v.) was formed. It consisted of three hundred young noblemen, who were maintained by the state and who had sworn never to separate, either in battle or in death. At the battle of Leuctra in 371, fought to defend Boeotian unity, this army used a new tactic which had been invented by Epaminondas and won a brilliant victory over the Spartans. This success enabled Thebes to bring Euboea and the peoples of central Greece within its sphere of influence, and some states left the Athenian alliance in order to group themselves around Boeotia. Epaminondas then intervened in the Peloponnesus (370-369) where he struck severe blows at the authority of Sparta by encouraging the constitution of an Arcadian League. Although he was in disgrace for a short time because of a setback before the city of Corinth, Epaminondas, helped as always by Pelopidas who took charge of negotiations, had the hegemony of his country recognised by the king of Persia in 367; it was at Thebes that, in the rescript of Susa. Artaxerxes granted the city the authority to take action against any other city that should violate the treaty of Antalcidas, signed between Persians and Hellenes in 386. In order to defend Boeotian prestige against the claims of other states. Epaminondas created a whole fleet whose arrival alone, in 364, was enough to detach Byzantium, Chios and Rhodes from the Athenian Confederation. After being called back in 362 by the Arcadians to the Peloponnesus, in which the Boeotians had somewhat lost interest, Epaminondas fell at Mantinea in the course of a battle, which his death alone prevented from being yet another triumph of his nation over the Spartans.   P.D.

EPHEBI. In the beginning, like all other primitive peoples, the Greeks classified society by age groups, by various, clearly defined categories, which distinguished between children, adolescents, mature men and old people, and the transition from one category to another took on the character of a religious initiation accompanied by ritual ceremonies—at least for the young. This ancient custom was perpetuated in certain Cretan cities and even more in Sparta; elsewhere the division of classes according to wealth soon replaced social divisions according to age. The only survival of the earlier system in the classical period was in the institution of *ephebeia,* which was common to most of the Greek states. Athens furnishes the best example of it for us. Although " ephebe " in its widest and vaguest meaning was applied to almost every adolescent, it particularly denoted young people who were doing their two year term of military service. When they reached the age of eighteen, they first had to appear before the deme to which they belonged and the Boule in order to undergo a double *dokimasia* (examination) concerning their age and their membership of a free Athenian family, before being registered as conscripts on a civil register. In the course of a religious ceremony, they then took an oath, the words of which have still survived; invoking the most ancient Attic divinities, they swore to defend the fatherland and never to forsake their companions in arms.

The chiefs who led or instructed them were elected by the people and were known as the *paidotribai,* the *sophronistai* and the *kosmoi.* After making a tour of the sanctuaries, led by these officers, the conscripts were garrisoned at Piraeus. At the end of a year, they paraded in the course of a public ceremony which was held in the theatre and received their arms, which consisted of a round shield and a lance. For the second year of their service, they were stationed in various strongholds in Attica, carried out military exercises and were responsible for the protection of the national territory. Once they were freed from such active service, they were incorporated into the mass of the citizens, with all the rights that

Éphebe. Detail of an amphora by the Andocides Painter. About 520 B.C. Berlin Museum. *Photo Hirmer.*

its glory to its military prowess, like Sparta, nor to
its wise political institutions but, as it was situated
at the end of the long road that ran through
Anatolia, it was the richest and busiest port in the
whole of Asia Minor and its inhabitants led a life
of such luxury that the Greeks were dazzled by it.
It was also the city that Artemis, a goddess of
markedly oriental characteristics, loved above all
others. Like most cities on the coast of Asia
Minor, Ephesus had been a Greek settlement in
the beginning of the 1st millennium B.C. According to tradition it was Androclus and a band of
colonists from Argos and Athens who had been
the first settlers on this site which had already
been inhabited by the Asians. Ephesus was also
like many other coastal towns in being under the
suzerainty of the kings of Lydia, and it never made
any very serious effort to free itself from their rule.
Its inhabitants were treated well by their rulers,
who showed both sympathy and admiration for
Greece, and it was with the financial aid of
Croesus that a magnificent temple to Artemis was
raised in the middle of the 6th century B.C. This
temple replaced more modest structures and,
although its architects, Chersiphron and Meta-
genes, were Cretans, it was built in a typically
Ionian style. Its dimensions were unusually
large, it was entirely in marble and the lower
drums of some of its columns were decorated
with bas-reliefs. When it was burned by a
madman, Eratostratus, in 356, it was replaced by
another temple built after the same design, on
the same site, which was considered to be one of
the Seven Wonders of the World.

There is no need to trace all the city's various
political vicissitudes throughout the centuries for
they were neither of great importance nor did
they greatly affect its prestige. Ephesus never
ceased growing in size and, after being under the
successive rule of the kings of Lydia, the Persian
king and the Hellenistic monarchs, it became one
of the greatest cities in the Roman Empire by the
2nd century A.D. Every kind of building, notably
a library, attests to the munificence of the city's
generous patrons. Glorious as the city's past
had been, it gained even greater fame in early
Christian times when it became linked with the
memory of St Paul and the legend of the Seven
Sleepers. P.D.

went with citizenship. During the period of
their service they benefited from certain privileges
but, although they received a maintenance allowance, they took no part in civic life and, with a
single exception, did not have the right to plead
in court.

Many documents dating from the last third of
the 4th century B.C. have enabled us to gain an
idea of the life of the ephebi, of their relations
with their officers on whom they often bestowed
honours, of the training they were made to undergo in the gymnasiums, and also of the care that
was taken to develop their literary culture.
Before this date, we can only rely on hypotheses.
But it seems probable that the institution is of
much earlier date; it certainly existed from the
most remote times and it can only be understood
if we remember that it was, as mentioned already,
a survival of earlier customs that became transformed as society evolved. P.D.

EPHESUS. Few cities in ancient Greece
could rival Ephesus for prestige. It did not owe

Library at Ephesus. Recesses in the far walls for book-cases. *Ph. Boudot-Lamotte.*

EPHORS. Ephors, or supervisors, was the name given in certain Dorian states to magistrates whose functions were of especial importance. From the middle of the 8th century B.C., at least, they were five in number and they may have been astrologers of some kind (which would explain the original meaning of their title) whose duty it was to say every nine years whether the signs in the skies were favourable or not to the continuing rule of the kings who depended on them. This function as interpreters of the divine will eventually gave the ephors such power that, from the 6th century onwards, they became the real source of power in the state. They were elected for one year by a system now no longer known to us, but which Aristotle called childish, and wielded a tyrannical power over the country. They supervised the rule of the kings who periodically had to take an oath before them to govern according to the laws; they examined both their public and their private conduct, even accompanying them to the wars; and sometimes took their place themselves, condemned, or fined them if they found anything reprehensible in their conduct. Their authority was no less great over the people, for they regarded it as their mission to see that they

remained true to Spartan traditions and social discipline. When they took office, their first act was to make a proclamation which ordered all citizens to " shave their moustache and obey the laws ", a typical example of the conservative spirit which accords equal importance to purely formal details and fundamental principles. They gave their own interpretations to the laws which at Sparta were more like unwritten customs. They acted in the interests of the state and attached particular importance to manners and education. They were only responsible to their successors to whom they felt bound by links of solidarity by virtue of their functions. Until the end of the 5th century B.C., at least, it would seem that most ephors remained faithful to their sense of duty and only acted out of patriotism, but their institution poses many questions. Modern historians have often regarded them as being the servants of the noble classes but, although this might have been true in the 4th century, it could not have been so before when there was no aristocratic class in Sparta. It should also be remembered that the ancient Greeks regarded Sparta as the most democratic city in the whole of Greece. The very regime of this state in which the citizens were by definition all equal, imposing their rule on the helots and the perioikoi (See Sparta), makes such a discussion futile. It has rightly been said of the ephors that they were " the all powerful delegates of a martial people, who were so imbued with a respect for tradition that they would impose it, if need be, by force, but who usually won the voluntary submission of their fellow-citizens who shared the same faith " (P. Roussel).

The great military triumphs that Sparta won over Athens had rather unfortunate effects on the ephorate, as on other institutions. Corruption began to permeate it and the ephors, who were often of humble and obscure origins, began to serve the interest of the new aristocracy of wealth that began to arise. In 227 B.C. the king, Cleomenes, avenged the long period of oppression that his predecessors had suffered under the ephors by putting an end to their power.
P.D.

EPHORUS. Historian of the 4th century B.C., born at Cyme.

EPIC. All we know of early Greek epic poetry is Homer's (q.v.) *Iliad* and *Odyssey* but it is certain that epic poems had already been written before this date, as certain passages in Homer himself indicate. In Book IX of the Iliad, that of the embassy, Agamemnon's envoys, Ulysses and Ajax, come upon Achilles engaged in whiling away his leisure time by playing the cithara while " singing of the exploits of the heroes ". In Book VIII of the *Odyssey*, " which constitutes the most important document we have with regard to the history of epic poetry in Greece " (M. Croiset), we are told how the bard, Demodocus, sang three rhapsodies *(See* Rhapsodes) in succession at the court of Alcinous, the king of the Phaeacians; they were the Quarrel between Ulysses and Achilles, the licentious episode of the loves of Ares and Aphrodite, and lastly, the taking of Ilium by means of the wooden horse (as we know, this last episode, like the two others, is not to be found in the *Iliad* which comes to an end with the account of the funeral of Hector). It is therefore clear that even before Homer there existed rhapsodies, either isolated or grouped together in poems, which related to the Trojan legend and also to that of Thebes, for several passages of the *Iliad* which allude to the expedi-

tion of the Seven Chieftains and that of their Epigoni against Thebes seem to refer to a *Thebaid* of still earlier date.

Like the Mesopotamian epic of Gilgamesh, the Greek epic related the adventures of the gods and the heroes but its originality resided in the fact that it concentrated on the deeds of men while the gods were relegated to the background. It has been claimed that the Greek epic originated with the priests and in shrines but such a theory has little to commend it, for both the *Iliad* and the *Odyssey* are incontestably secular in character and therefore the first witnesses to the Greek humanistic spirit. It is possible that the epic metre, the dactylic hexameter, might have been borrowed by the Greeks from some foreign literature, and the Homeric poems contain descriptions of both Cretan and Mycenaean civilisation which preceded the arrival of the Hellenes properly speaking. But the vision of mankind and the world that we find in these epics is specifically Greek in its nature.

After Homer, the brotherhood of the Homeridae not only added interpolations to the *Iliad* and the *Odyssey* but also elaborated on events that had taken place previous to the *Iliad* (Cyprian Songs), those which had occurred between the time of the *Iliad* and the *Odyssey (Aethiopis* and the *Destruction of Ilium* by Arctinus of Miletus) and lastly, events dating from after the time of the *Odyssey* (the *Telegonia* by Eugammon of Cyrene in which Telegonus was said to be the son of Ulysses and Circe, or Calypso, etc.). In the same manner, the epic poems came to form a complete cycle with regard to the Trojan War. With the *Oedipodea* and the *Epigoni* the same poetical treatment was applied to the Theban cycle. Finally, apart from the two great legendary cycles, Greek epic poetry also included a *Titanomachia,* an *Oechaliae Halosis,* a poem entitled *Danais,* a *Heracleis,* a *Theseis,* etc. With the exception of a few fragments, all these works are now lost for us; but Aristotle, who had read them, judged them as being of mediocre quality.

Epic poetry in imitation of the Homeric manner continued without interruption throughout the classical, Hellenistic and Roman periods in Greece. The *Argonautica,* a 3rd century B.C. epic poem on the legend of Jason and Medea by Apollonius Rhodius has survived, as well as the *Post-Homerica* by Quintus of Smyrna and Nonnus's *Dionysiaca,* both of the Roman period.
R.F.

EPICHARMUS. Comic playwright, born at Cos, who lived mainly in Sicily. *(See* Comedy).

EPICLES. The name of this master stone-cutter, which has been found associated with that of the architect, Cleomenes, in an inscription on the last step of the base of the temple of Apollo at Syracuse, deserves remembrance for the archaic text, dating from about 570-560 B.C. It is full of the pride of a craftsman who was one of the first to create a stone colonnade for a peristyle in western Greek architecture. It was a contribution to the diffusion of the architectural style that was so typical of the Greek temple. Epicles' columns are both heavy and massive since their height (26 feet) is little more than four times the diameter (6 feet 6 inches on the façade) and they mark the transition from the wooden archi tecture of the 8th-7th centuries to later stone structures. R.M.

EPICTETUS. In its last period, the Stoicism of the ancient world has left us the edifying picture of two men communing in the same doctrine, one an emperor, the other a slave, but also one a pupil and the other his master; the former was Marcus Aurelius who congra-tulated himself on " having been able to read the books that have preserved Epictetus's teachings for us ". Epictetus was born in about 50 A.D. at Hierapolis in Phrygia and lived in Rome as the slave of Epaphroditus, a freeman of the emperor, Nero, until his master's death. Once he had become a freeman himself, he devoted himself to the teaching of philosophy. When in 94 the last of the twelve Caesars, Domitian, had banished all philosophers from Rome by a *senatus consultum*, Epictetus retired to Nicopolis where he lived as a poor man and died in about 125. One of his disciples in Epirus was the general Flavius Arrian who wrote down the teachings of his master in dialogue form and collected them together under the title of *Discourses* (or *Diatribai*); he also wrote a kind of summary in fifty-three articles, the famous *Manual*.

Epictetus was far more a moralist, a spiritual director and a doctor than a philosopher in the classic sense of the word. What he wanted to do was to form the will of those who followed him and to teach them the meaning of liberty. " Philosoph-ical dogma ", he said, " raises the heads of those who have lowered them, and gives men courage to look straight in the eyes of the rich and power-

ful. " He did not seek for an audience and never took himself for a messenger of the gods. " The school of a philosopher is a doctor's consulting room... for you did not come there in good health ". Those who ignored their illnesses he left to themselves, and he cured others by showing them the path of liberty which had nothing whatever to do with legal enfranchisement: " When you make your slave turn round in front of the praetor, have you done anything ?—Yes, you have done some-thing.—What ?—You have made your slave turn round in front of the praetor.—Nothing more ?— Yes, you also have to pay the tax of one twentieth for him.—But then hasn't the man who was the object of this ceremony become free ?—Only in so far as he has acquired peace of mind. "

This peace of mind can only be acquired by knowing how to distinguish between those things that depend on us and those that do not. True liberty is obtained when we free ourselves from false opinions and it is also in " the use of ideas presented to our consciousness ", that is, images created by feelings. The tyrant may dispose of my body, my goods, my reputation and my friends but he cannot dispose of my opinions, for no one can force me to think what I do not think. " I must die. But need I die lamenting ? I must go to prison. But need I complain ? I must go into exile. But who can prevent me going with a smile, in high spirits and in peace ? " For man, good and evil reside in his judgment and in his will; if his judgment and will are sane and steadfast they will give him all the happiness he is capable of knowing. Even when subjected to the worst tortures, the Stoic will refuse to give way to unhappiness and will say: " Oh my representation, wait a little; let me see what you are and what your aim is, let me test you! " Once he is able to ratify or to invalidate representations, man—be he a slave or a king—commands all things and becomes the equal of the gods, or may be said to be no longer a work of God but a " fragment of God ". The result of this highly inspired morality is that in each of his deeds the Stoic engages the whole of humanity, and the final consequence is an apothe-osis of man. From the time that Arrian edited the *Manual,* there were many followers who attempt-ed to put these teachings into practice throughout the ages, and some succeeded. P.B.

EPICURUS. Epicurus was born in 341 B.C., six years after the death of Plato. His Athe-nian parents were cleruchs, or settlers, on the isle of Samos during the occupation of the island by the Athenians. His father, Neocles, was a schoolmaster. At Samos, Epicurus was the pupil of the Platonist, Pamphilus, and the result of this training was that he always felt a lively distaste for Plato's conception of education, founded as it was on geometry and dialectic with the theory of the Good as a final aim. At the age of eighteen he went to Athens to do his two years of military service *(ephebeia)*, during which Alexander the Great (323) and Aristotle (322) died. Epicurus went on with his studies, first, it is believed, with the Peripatetic philosopher, Praxiphanes, at Rhodes and then, as we know for certain, at Teos with Nausiphanes, a follower of Democritus and pupil of Pyrrho with whom he later quarrelled. Epicurus then spent several years with his family, who had been expelled from Samos together with the other colonists and settled at Colophon, where he elaborated his doctrine. In 311 he went to Mytilene and tried to expound his theories in public and converted the rhetor, Hermarchus, who was to become his successor. But his teachings aroused such hostility that he was forced to flee by sea in midwinter, taking refuge at Lampsacus where he was welcomed by Mithres, the finance minister of Lysimachus. Again, he converted many people, including Idomeneus who was to give him important financial aid, Leonteus and his wife Themista, the mathematician Polyaenus, Metrodorus and his wife Leontium, Colotes, Pythocles and many others. In 306 when Demetrius of Phalerum, the pupil of Aristotle and the governor of Athens, was expelled by Demetrius Poliorcetes, Epicurus went to live at Athens. There, he bought a cottage and a little garden, not far from the Academy, where he gave private lessons until his death in 270, whence the name of " Garden " that was given to his school. Epicurus suffered from a precarious health and patiently bore long sufferings (renal colic and gallstones); he was a bachelor and without children and looked after the children of his beloved disciple, Metrodorus, who died seven years before him. It seems that Epicurus was known for the exquisite delicacy of his thought and his feelings. He had been accompanied on his way to Athens by a whole group of his friends who helped him in his teachings. This group included several women who were the wives of his friends, cultured courtesans or slaves, some of whom wrote well known works, like Themista and Leontium.

Epicurus rejected both Plato's philosophy (" I spit on moral virtue, *to kalon* ") and Pyrrho's scepticism. He constructed a dogmatic system founded on the evidence of affective states and ideas presented to our consciousness which, according to him, do not deceive when they are not badly interpreted. Epicurus wished to find remedies for the anguish suffered by mankind. The mystery of the universe disturbs men who feel themselves subjected to the necessity of fate; they fear death and punishments in some life hereafter and the intervention of malignant gods; finally they are incapable of withstanding suffering and are never satisfied with material goods. He first of all explained the mystery of the universe by adopting the atomic theory of Democritus (q.v.), with a fundamental modification of his own; the atoms which fall vertically in the void may, at any moment, move sideways in an unexpected movement of " declination " and this movement corresponds to the unexpected manifestations of our personal independence. Moreover, as the soul, like the body, is made of atoms, although lighter in weight, neither death nor any punishments in a future life are to be feared, since death is only a dislocation of this unity of soul and body—a dislocation which brings an end to all sensibilities. As for the gods, Epicurus did not contest their existence since they are the object of a pre-notion, but he placed them in a kind of interworld, where he attributed them with a happy and serene existence in which they were quite indifferent to the fate of mankind to whom they should serve as examples. Finally, men ignore the fact that pleasure, which is the sovereign good for all living beings, immediately reaches its maximum as soon as suffering is avoided by the satisfaction of only the most natural and necessary needs. Rational calculation will make men prefer a sober life and teach them how to compensate for present sufferings by remembering past joys. Epicurus taught the value of virtues and gave the first place to the joys of friendship. For him, happiness essentially consisted in this absence of anxiety and passion, ataraxy, which make the wise man like a god. The authentic Epicurean philosophy can thus be seen to be ascetic in contrast to its vulgar form which is only a caricature, depending solely on a few of Epicurus's maxims taken out of their proper context, such as " the principle and the root of all good is the pleasure of the belly ".

Epicurus wrote many works of which only

fragments have survived but Diogenes Laertius has preserved for us three letters which Epicurus wrote to his friends Herodotus, Pythocles and Menoeceus, in which he resumed his physical, meteorological and moral systems. His thought is also known to us through collections of his " master thoughts ". Epicureanism enjoyed a widespread success, not only throughout Greece but also in Rome, where Lucretius enthusiastically expounded the doctrine in his poem *De rerum natura*. As late as the mid 3rd century A.D. a citizen of the little town of Oenoanda in Lycia had an outline of Epicurean philosophy engraved in letters on his porch for the edification of his fellow-citizens. The inscription was found in the late 19th century by some French archaeologists.

P.-M.S.

EPIDAURUS. Epidaurus owes its fame to the sanctuary of Asclepius which was established there in the 6th century B.C. at the latest. It was there that the tomb could be seen of the god, who had first been a hero, and was then struck by a thunderbolt sent by Zeus because he had been too skilful and conscientious a physician and had revived a dead man. The famous Tholos at Epidaurus was nothing other than the tomb of the god and it was there that patients came in search of a cure. The main buildings do not date from before the 4th century B.C., for it was then that Polyclitus the Younger transformed the humble circular labyrinth, where sacrifices were made to the hero, into the sumptuous Rotunda, or *Tholos*, of marble of which only the admirable ruins now remain. A short time before, a temple had been built there to Asclepius, and another to Artemis and the sculpted ornament of the two buildings, notably the figures of young women with their draperies clinging to their bodies in a gust of wind, heralds a new artistic style and may be the work of Timotheus. Finally the theatre was built, also in the mid-4th century, and by its size we may imagine the multitudes of pilgrims who came to the sacred site. In order to accomodate such a number a kind of caravanserai had been established. In order to allow the patients, who would sleep on the skins of the animals they had sacrificed, to see in a dream the treatment that the god advised for them, an incubation chamber or long dormitory, where every sort of patient passed the

night, had been installed. Many inscribed or carved ex-votos have been found, proving that the cures were often effective and that many worshippers returned home free from their ills. Once it had been well established, the fame of Epidaurus steadily grew throughout the centuries and although branches of the sacred sanctuary were also established in such other towns as Cos and Pergamum in particular, there was no decrease in the number of pilgrims to the sanctuary. It was only at the end of the pagan period that the site was abandoned and that the stone of the monuments was carried away by nearby masons or used to make lime.

P.D.

EPIGONUS. Greek sculptor and the son of Charias. Together with other sculptors whose names have been preserved by Pliny (Phyromachus, Stratonicus and Antigonus) he had the honour of working for the greater glory of the dynasty of Pergamum at the end of the 3rd century B.C. Epigonus was representative of the first school of Pergamum which aimed at realism rather than the expression of emotion. Typical of this are the portraits of Philetaerus, the founder

Epidaurus. Hieron of Asclepius. *Photo Boudot-Lamotte.*

of the dynasty, an unscrupulous conqueror whose hard, brutal features are also depicted on coins of the time. It is quite likely that we can credit Epigonus with some of the famous figures of the Gauls that recent studies have recomposed. In particular, mention should be made of the *Dying Gaul* in the Museo Capitolino, Rome; in this famous sculpture the dying man is shown staunching his flow of blood with his left hand while he supports himself with his right arm, his features tense with pain, his eyes already glazed by approaching death, his head falling loosely.

R.M.

EPIRUS. The mountainous region of Epirus is situated on the western coast of Greece, almost facing the island of Corfu. Because of its inhospitable shores and the high mountain chains enclosing it to the south and east, its contacts with the rest of Greece were restricted and as a consequence the ancient Greeks considered it as lying outside the Hellenic world. But nonetheless legend had it that one of its kings, named Neoptolemus or Pyrrhus, was the son of Achilles himself.

It was here that the famous and greatly venerated sanctuary of Dodona was established in remote times, and it was from Epirus that the small tribe of the Graeans, who were to give their name to the whole of Greece, first came. Some of the tribes who overran Thessaly and Boeotia towards the end of the 2nd millennium B.C. must also have passed through this wild region. Later, Epirus remained isolated behind its mountain barriers, always faithful to its monarchical system of government and, when the city of Corinth founded the colonies of Ambracia and Apollonia on its shores in the 7th century B.C., it was considered by the Greeks to be a barbarian country. Epirus remained unaffected by the great events that took place in its neighbouring Greek states in the 5th century B.C. and it only took part in Greek politics after it had fallen under Macedonian influence. The king of one of its tribes, the Molossians, gave his daughter in marriage to Philip II and Alexander the Great was born of this union. In 323, Epirus joined with Greece in her efforts to free herself from Macedonian domination, but it was during the reign of Pyrrhus I that

Epidaurus. Theatre.
4th century B.C.
Photo Hassia.

it played its greatest part in Greek history. It was involved in Greek and Italian politics and seemed likely to become a great power but its period of glory was short-lived. After Pyrrhus's death it became a republic and soon fell under Macedonian domination before finally becoming a Roman province. P.D.

ERATOSTHENES. Scholar and man of letters, born in 273 B.C. at Cyrene. After completing his studies at Athens, Eratosthenes, with the support of his fellow-countryman, Callimachus (q.v.), became head of the Royal Library of Alexandria in 235 and the tutor of the future Ptolemy Philopator. He died in about 192. He was a poet, a philologist, a geographer, historian, mathematician and natural philosopher. None of his literary works has survived but, notably through Strabo, we are still acquainted with his geographical and historical works which were of the first order. Eratosthenes was the founder of scientific geography and historical chronology. Among his most important achievements was his calculation of the circumference of the globe by a

new method which enabled him to come very close to the truth. His geographical map of the earth represented a considerable progress in relation to all preceding maps. He was the first to state clearly that the historical age began with the era of the Olympiads (776 B.C.) and that previous epochs were either completely unknown or else mythological. Nonetheless, his *Chronological Tables* begin with the Trojan War. They fully deserved to become and remain classics up to the present day. R.F.

ERECHTHEUM. The Erechtheum, on the Acropolis of Athens, was not only the temple of Erechtheus, for within its enclosure of 100 ft by 50 ft it contained no less than nine different shrines. It was built approximately between 430 and 408 B.C. by an architect whose name is no longer known to us, but who, judging by his ingenuity, might well have been Mnesicles (q.v.), the architect who had already built the Propylaea. It was composed of a central structure with two porticoes of unequal size projecting on the north and south sides. The interior of the central build-

Erechtheum: view from the west. Last decades of 5th century B.C. *Photo Hassia.*

ing contained two parts which remained quite separate without any communication between them: to the east, a sanctuary of Athena preceded by an Ionic colonnade; to the west, two adjacent shrines each one consecrated to a different cult, one being that of Erechtheus and Poseidon, the other, that of Hephaestus and the hero, Boutes. The two shrines were orientated from west to east and access to them was by a closed vestibule running from north to south, with each extremity opening onto one of the two porticoes already mentioned. This vestibule was built over the salt spring that Poseidon had struck from the rock with his trident during his quarrel with Athena. The porticoes themselves were the entrances to that part of the Erechtheum which did not belong to Athena. The main portico was monumental in appearance and was that of the north and the plinth of its six columns was built over the spot where traces could be seen of the lightning which had struck Erechtheus. The south portico was partly built over the tomb of Cecrops and concealed the secret staircase that was used once a

year by two priestesses for a sacred ceremony. The six caryatids with which the architect had replaced the customary columns may have been suggested by the maidens who carried on their heads the baskets containing the mysterious objects that were transferred in them from the Erechtheum to the neighbouring sanctuary of Aphrodite.

The whole building was given an apparent unity by the fact that it was covered by a single roof. It was girdled by two friezes, one of which ran around the main building, the other along the top of the north portico. As far as we can see from the few remaining fragments, they were mainly devoted to scenes of local legends, notably that of Erichthonius. The west façade consisted of a wall which supported, half way up its height, four columns flanked by two pilasters. To the west and adjacent to the building was a small open enclosure containing the olive tree which Athena had given to her people. Remains have been found under the building of a palace of the Mycenaean period and there can be no doubt that its historic associations and religious traditions

Erechtheum: the
Caryatid porch.
Photo Hassia.

made the Erechtheum the most venerated part of the Acropolis in the eyes of the Athenians.

P.D.

ERECHTHEUS. Grandson of Erichthonius (q.v.) who also seems to have been a ruler of Athens. He had numerous descendants. In a war against Eleusis, he killed the son of Poseidon, Eumolpus, provoking the wrath of the god who struck him with a thunderbolt on the spot where the Erechtheum was later to be built.

ERETRIA. Eretria was one of the two great towns of Euboea, the other being Chalcis. It was destroyed by the Persians in the early 5th century B.C. but it was soon rebuilt. Of the

remaining monuments, whose ruins may still be seen, mention need only be made here of the temple of Apollo Daphnephoria which once included a beautiful group sculpture in the round (Theseus carrying away Antiope?) dating from about 500 B.C., a temple of Dionysus and a theatre.

P.D.

ERICHTHONIUS. For the Athenians, the origins of their city were somewhat lost in the mists of time and certain parts of their history always remained vague. One consequence was that they sometimes confused Erichthonius with Erechtheus (q.v.). The first named was said to have been born as a result of Hephaestus's desire for the chaste goddess Athena, who hid the child in a basket which she gave to one of the daughters of King Cecrops, Aglauros, advising her not to lift the cover. Aglauros and her sisters were so curious that they disobeyed and when they saw a serpent, watching over the infant in the basket, they were so terrified that they killed themselves by throwing themselves off the top of the Acropolis. Erichthonius became king of Athens and was credited with many good deeds. It was believed that he was the first to harness four horses to a single chariot and that it was he who established the Panathenaea (q.v.) in honour of Athena.   P.D.

ERINYES. The Erinyes were very ancient and very powerful divinities who intervened among mankind in order to punish those who had committed crimes of a sacrilegious nature as, for example, in the case of Orestes. By killing his mother Clytemnestra, he had automatically exposed himself to the pursuit of these furies who followed him like bloodhounds, sending him mad and never giving him a moment's peace of mind. Although the concrete-minded Greeks probably did not conceive such a notion in any explicit manner, the Erinyes were the personification of the power of the conscience from the remotest times onwards.   P.D.

ERIS. The Greek tendency towards anthropomorphism naturally transformed all abstract conceptions into divinities and Eris, representing Disputes and Quarrels, was already personified as early as the time of Hesiod. She was a figure who held little inspiration for artists although she appeared as early as the 6th century B.C. on a vase, where she was expressly named by a inscription. But from the 5th century onwards, when allegory became fashionable, she won greater popularity with painters.   P.D.

EROS. The god of love. Eros had not always been the graceful little boy shooting arrows into the hearts of lovers as he appears in the poetry of Theocritus or Longus. According to the oldest legends, he was born at the same time as the Earth, and at Thespiae in Boeotia, he was worshipped in the form of a rough stone. Later, he lost this primitive aspect and from the archaic period onwards he was represented as the son of Hermes and Aphrodite, the latter having had another son by Ares, Anteros, representing mutual love.

In his new form Eros was involved in many adventures and he struck at mortals as much as at the gods. He was often shown accompanying Aphrodite; on the Parthenon frieze he is shown as a little child watching the procession of the Panathenaea together with his mother; but from as early as the late 6th century B.C. he was also shown as an adolescent, often with wings, who seemed to be floating in the air in search of victims. The bow and arrows by which he is so well known to us did not appear in the earliest representations of the god, and it was mostly from the 4th century onwards that he appears as the mischievous young deity shooting his shafts of love. He played a more important role in art and literature in the Hellenistic period, when the Greek public developed a taste for sentimentality, and it was then that the romantic and philosophical legend, associating the Soul and Love under the forms of Eros and Psyche, was born.
P.D.

ERYMANTHUS. It was on Mount Erymanthus in the heart of the Peloponnesus that Heracles accomplished one of his Twelve Labours on the orders of Eurystheus. He captured the boar that was ravaging the region and brought him back alive. Many vase paintings bear representations of the hero carrying the beast on his back before throwing it into the great jar in which the fearful tyrant had taken refuge.
P.D.

ETEOCLES. *(See* Seven against Thebes).

EUBOEA. Euboea is one of the longest of the Greek isles. It faces the shores of Boeotia and Attica and is barely separated from the mainland; its closest point is only some sixty yards away at the straits of Euripus, in front of the town of Chalcis. It is a fairly mountainous isle (its topmost peak is Mount Delphi, 5118 ft) and owed its richness to the timber of the forests that covered the slopes of the mountains, the fertile plains lying between the ranges which produced vines, olives and cereals, and lastly, its mineral resources. It was first peopled by Thessalian colonists, Thracians and Dryopians, and then by Greeks from the Peloponnesus and the islands. From the 8th to the 6th centuries B.C., its two main towns, Eretria and Chalcis, sent colonists to far-off regions to found cities in Sicily and the northern shores of the Aegean. Towards the end

Theseus abducting Antiope (?), Fragment from the pediment of the Temple of Apollo at Eretria, Euboea. Late 6th century B.C. Chalcis Museum. *Photo Hirmer.*

of the 6th century B.C. the island was so rich that the Eretrians built a temple to Apollo Daphnephoros from which the fine sculpture group of Theseus abducting Antiope has been preserved.

At the same time Athens made efforts to extend her sway over the island whose wealth she envied and which lay so close to her own frontiers. Cleruchs *(See* Cleruchies) were sent to the island and every effort of the Euboeans to free themselves was suppressed. Athens lost Euboea in 411 during the Peloponnesian War, although it succeeded in winning over most of the island's cities to the Confederation it organised in 378. After being under Theban domination from 371 to 358, Euboea became an Attic protectorate again until 350 when it fell under Macedonian domination. But despite the island's troubled history, its inhabitants were less interested in playing a political role in the world than in assuring their own prosperity by their agriculture and commerce.

P.D.

EUBULUS. Eubulus was one of the rare examples in Greek, and more particularly Athenian, history of a politician who was also a technician. From 354 B.C. and probably for eight consecutive years he administered the finances of Athens, his main aim being to create reserves and to ensure regular resources for the city. One of his special functions was to administer the funds of the *theorika* which was a special subsidy to enable poor citizens to pay for their seats at the theatre. He made use of his office in order to combat waste and to assure new resources. This enabled him to rebuild the Athenian fleet, which he increased to the number of three hundred and fifty triremes, to build an arsenal and to restore the port of Piraeus. As a good administrator, he disliked risky enterprises and opposed Demosthenes, who advocated war against Philip of Macedonia and attacked Eubulus in his famous speeches, accusing him of being an enemy to the public good and preferring to accumulate money for the pleasures of the citizens rather than taking arms against the menace to the homeland. Although Eubulus's conduct may not have been suited to the tragic situation of the city at that time, he conformed exactly to our own ideal of a finance minister.

P.D.

EUCLID. In the 3rd century B.C., the various sciences that had taken on an independent character and detached themselves from philosophy followed an autonomous existence, those of mathematics and astronomy notably being pursued by Euclid (330-270 B.C.), Archimedes (287- 212 B.C.) and Apollonius (260-200 B.C.). All we know of Euclid is that he taught mathematics at Alexandria in about 300, that he was of a kindly nature, and that he disdained the practical applications of what he taught. Once, when one of his pupils had asked him what he would gain by learning geometry, Euclid called a slave and said to him, " Give a drachma to this young man since he wishes to gain something from what he is learning. "

Quite apart from what had preceded it and what was to follow it, Euclid's *Elements* remains an outstanding geometrical text-book.

Although the book must certainly have been a compilation to a certain extent, because a fairly large number of theorems had been demonstrated before Euclid's time, no other mathematician had ever analysed problems with such precision, such attention to the logical sequence of ideas and such uncompromising refusal to make any affirmations that might be contested. Euclid preceded Book I of his *Elements* (it consisted of 13 books, numbers XIV and XV being additions of a later date) with a number of definitions, axioms and postulates. The definitions are made as clear as possible, are based on experienced facts and, in the words of the mathematician Paul Tannery, " seem to derive from the technique of the art of building ". According to the book, a point is something which is indivisible (Def. 1); similarly a length has no width (Def. 2) and a surface has only length and width (Def. 5). Consequently, points may be considered as the ends of lines (Def. 3) and lines as the extremities of surfaces (Def. 6). The axioms are a kind of mathematical syllogism: things equal to the same thing are equal to each other, thus if A equals B and B equals C, C will equal A—or else self-evident truths such as: the whole is greater than the part. Lastly, Euclid makes five demands or postulates which have to be satisfied before any further research can be undertaken. The fifth and most famous postulate is as follows: " If two straight lines are intersected by a third straight line, and the sum of the interior angles on the same side of the third straight line be less than two right angles, and if the two straight lines are produced to infinity they will meet on the side where the angles are smaller than two right angles ". In the 18th century, J. Playfair formulated another postulate: " Through one point only one straight line can be drawn parallel to another straight line ". It was the abandonment of these Euclidean postulates in the 19th century that was to lead to the non-Euclidean geometrical systems of Lobatchevsky, Bolyai and Riemann which were to prove more " convenient " (but not more true since one geometry cannot be any more true than another) for the interpretation of modern theories of generalised relativity.

The first four books of the Elements deal with plane geometry, Books 11, 12 and 13 with solid geometry. Books 7, 8 and 9 concern rational numbers (arithmetic). " With the fifth book, " wrote Leon Brunschvicg, " it seemed as if a new science had begun, having for its object the comparison of magnitudes in general. The basic unit then becomes the ratio of magnitudes, and the basic considerations of the science are those which establish the *similarity* (we should now say *equality*) of ratios (those that define proportions) ". In the 6th book the purely geometrical study of proportions is transformed into the application of a science of proportions in general. Finally, Book 10 deals with incommensurables, classifying irrationals provided by " geometric constructions... with their properties not only for quadratic equations and for the quartic equation with rational coefficients but partly even for the sextic equation " (Paul Tannery).

Euclid was also the author of an *Optic* in which he proceeds as in geometry and in which he postulates that rays of light move in a straight line, and of a treatise on *Porisms* which has not survived but whose meaning has been much discussed. P.B.

EUCLID the SOCRATIC. *See* Megarian School.

EUDOXUS of CNIDOS. Scholar and philosopher and friend of Plato, he was born in about 408 B.C. and died in 355. He was a geographer and made a long journey in the east, where he became acquainted with Persian dualism, and was also a great mathematician, a builder of astronomical instruments and the inventor of the system of homocentric spheres. His works in this last domain were the subject of a commentary by the astronomer, Hipparchus (about 161-126), and by the poet, Aratus, in his poem the *Phaenomena* (about 275). Although he led an austere life he considered that pleasure was the sovereign good, and he modified the theory of Ideas. He stayed at the Academy in 361 and directed it while Plato was away on his second Sicilian voyage. P.-M.S.

EUERGETES. What we now call a maecenas was known as an euergetes in ancient Greece, and euergetism became quite an institution, especially during the Hellenistic period. Generosity was one of the characteristics of the Greeks and there was also a certain glory to be won by rich Greeks who could perpetuate their name by some benefit they had conferred on the community. Even now, rich Greeks still donate hospitals and buildings to their country. From the 4th century B.C. onwards, the enrichment of some Greek citizens by commerce or manufacture was a phenomenon that accompanied the impoverishment of cities and, long before this date even, the city of Athens had created a form of compulsory euergetism by means of liturgies (q.v.). But donations for various foundations, which were later made in many other impecunious states, were spontaneous in nature and the benefactor would be rewarded for his generosity by an honorific decree and a crown. When the empire of Alexander was being divided, the princes taking part in the partition made conciliatory gestures towards some of the states involved by imitating the euergetes, and their wealth permitted them to build sumptuous monuments such as the stoas of Athens which have preserved the names of Attalus and Eumenes.   P.D.

EUHEMERUS. Very little is known to us of the personality of Euhemerus. We know that he lived at the end of the 4th century B.C. and in the early decades of the 3rd century, but whether he was born in Sicily, Messina or at Messenia in the Peloponnesus, whether he was really the friend of King Cassander of Macedonia who is supposed to have conferred high offices upon him, and whether he really did undertake great voyages is all far from certain and reliable evidence is lacking. On the other hand, much of his famous work, the *Sacred History*, written in the early 3rd century, is known to us. The most abundant and valuable extracts have come down to us from the historian, Diodorus Siculus, and from Lactantius who himself had been inspired by Ennius's translation of the work. The work was really a sort of novel and it is not surprising that it should have been so popular. In form, it was a kind of political Utopia, written to suit the taste of the day. It described a sea voyage around Arabia (a fabulous land for the Greeks) and the discovery of a group of blessed isles, the most beautiful being that of Panchaïa in the centre. Euhemerus described this island with such skill that it was long thought to have really existed. Minute descriptions were given of the customs, the caste system and the moderate form of collectivism that was practised on it. A second novel then begins, inserted in the first, and it soon becomes clear that it is the latter that forms the real theme of the entire work. Panchaïa had dedicated a temple to Zeus which contained a long recital engraved in hieroglyphics on a golden stele and Euhemerus pretended to give a transcription of this text which narrated the great deeds of Uranus, Cronus and Zeus when they were reigning on Earth. The narrator was Zeus himself although the second part of the stele concerned other gods, notably Apollo and Artemis.

The idea that the gods had first been men before being apotheosised, either during their lifetimes or after their deaths, was warmly welcomed by the public taste of the time. In the first place, the anthropomorphism of religious representations in Greece, the important place reserved for those heroes, who had been born as humans, and local traditions which assigned specific sites to the tombs of important divinities all contributed to the success of Euhemerus's work. Secondly, recent developments in Greece had made the public mind more receptive to his ideas; on the one hand, rationalist criticism of the heroic legends and philosophical criticism of religious traditions readily stressed their human (even all too human) elements. Also, the practice of apotheosis had made its appearance in Greece, for Alexander had made himself into a divinity. All that remained to be done was to popularise this thesis in a systematic form, and give it concrete and convincing illustration; this Euhemerus accomplished. His basic aim was to rethink the divine in rational and humanistic terms rather than deny it completely. It seems that he admitted the divinity of the stars, in any case he never denied it, and he mentions among the various important deeds of Uranus the fact that he had made them the object of a cult. His theories were only concerned with the more popular deities, not so much to devaluate them as to redefine their merits. The gods were certainly men, but by their qualities and the results of their deeds, these divine legislators, inventors, benefactors, or even conquerors were shown to be " beings apart ". It might be said that the gods embodied an element which was immanent in the whole of humanity, the counterpart of that contained by the stars in their transcendence.

Euhemerism very soon distorted the ideas of its founder on this subject. The tendency to give authenticity to all the local variants of divine figures and to seek for a prosaic transposition for each of their attributes often led the followers of Euhemerus (and there were many from the 3rd century B.C. onwards) to multiply the number of the gods and to diminish their lustre. Some followers transformed euhemerism into a bantering process of demystification with the exploits of great men giving place to banal or grotesque anecdotes. This degradation of Euhemerus's orig-

Heracles and Antaeus. Detail from a calyx krater by Euphronius. About 510-505 B.C. Paris, Louvre. *Photo Hirmer.*

inal inspiration is even more clearly apparent in the writings of early Christians. Euhemerism has often been cited with regard to these writers but the fact is that many did not know even the name of the author of the *Sacred History* and those who did mention him often lacked any precise idea of his work. Besides, it was difficult for the polemicists who tried to bring disrepute on paganism by associating it with the scandalous history of its gods to find suitable material in the works of Euhemerus. If we leave aside those texts in which the human nature of the gods is deduced from their vices, weaknesses or crimes, we shall see that the authentic euhemerism of the Church Fathers nearly always consisted of secondary arguments which were often obtained from second-hand sources. J.P.

EUMAEUS. Eumaeus was the son of a king who had fallen into slavery, and was the most faithful of all Ulysses' servants. Although he was only a humble swineherd he did his best to safeguard the possessions of his master, during Ulysses' twenty years' absence, and to protect Penelope against the importunate advances of her suitors. It was to Eumaeus that Ulysses first

made himself known when he returned to Ithaca incognito. P.D.

EUPHRONIUS. One of the finest ceramic artists in the last years of the 6th century B.C. He painted some of the vases he made himself, such as the Antaeus krater in the Louvre, and later seems to have opened a workshop in which he employed several vase painters as collaborators, the most famous being the Panaitios Painter. P.D.

EUPOLIS. Athenian comic dramatist of the 5th century B.C. *(See* Comedy).

EURIPIDES. Athenian tragic dramatist (480-406 B.C.). Euripides was born at Salamis in the same year as the famous naval battle. Aristophanes stated on several occasions that Euripides' mother used to sell chervil and other vegetables in the market, but if Euripides really had been born of a poor family, it would have been impossible for him to have afforded the expensive training of the sophists and then to have devoted himself entirely to a literary career. Euripides was both the disciple of Anaxagoras and Socrates. He was said to have been married twice, unhappily on each occasion, which would explain the misogyny that frequently appears in his plays, but it should be remembered that he was also the creator of such admirable heroines as Alcestis, Evadne (in the *Suppliant Women*) and Laodamia (in the lost tragedy of *Protesilaus*). Moreover, several passages in his *Medea* express " femininist " demands.

Euripides made his début in the theatre at the age of twenty-five in 455, the same year in which Aeschylus died. He wrote ninety-two plays but only won the first prize for drama five times. Aristophanes was merciless in parodying and mocking him and has left us a picture of Euripides as a vain and solitary man of letters who shut himself off from the rest of the world in his study in order to dream and meditate all day long with " his feet in the air ", in other words, stretched out on a couch. He never seems to have taken part in public affairs and with his gloomy and morose nature lived a very secluded life. Probably he was not so much of a misogynist as a misanthropist. Annoyed by his lack of success, he left the ungrateful city of Athens, as Aeschylus had once done, in order to live abroad. In 408 he went to Thessaly and then to Macedonia to the court of king Archelaus. He died in Pella in the same year as Sophocles, 406, leaving three sons of whom the youngest, who was also named Euripides, became a tragic dramatist in his turn.

Euripides was little appreciated in his lifetime but of the three great Athenian tragedians, his posthumous reputation was the most brilliant. His plays were frequently performed and this is almost certainly the reason why nineteen of his plays have survived, more than those of both Aeschylus and Sophocles combined. They are as follows: *Alcestis* (438), the wife of Admetus, king of Pheres, who is doomed to die unless he can find someone to suffer in his place; Alcestis agrees to die in his place and is shown dying on the stage, surrounded by her husband and children, but Heracles suddenly appears and after a struggle against the spirit of death, Thanatos, brings her back alive to her husband, who had offered the hero generous hospitality despite his grief;—*Medea* (431), Euripides' masterpiece, a brilliant representation of Medea's jealousy and indomitable character; abandoned by her husband Jason, who owed his life and the conquest of the Golden Fleece to her, she slays their children in order to wound him at his most vulnerable point;

—*Hippolytus* (428) in which the son of Theseus is falsely accused by his mother-in-law, Phaedra, who has fallen in love with him, and dies innocent, a tragedy that Racine was to imitate in his own *Phèdre;*—*Hecuba*, the wife of Priam, who sees her daughter, Polyxena, slain on the tomb of Achilles by the Achaeans after the capture of Troy and who then takes a cruel revenge on Polymestor, king of Thracia, who had killed her son Polydorus;—*Andromache* (420) in which the widow of Hector, now the concubine of Pyrrhus, the son of Achilles, has a son, Molossus, whom Hermione and her father, Menelaus, wish to kill; they are prevented from doing so by Peleus, Pyrrhus is then slain by Orestes; once again Racine was inspired by Euripides' play for his own *Andromaque;*—the *Children of Heracles* in which Eurystheus attempts to kill the sons of Heracles who are saved by the son of Theseus, Demophon, king of Athens;—the *Suppliant Women,* written in praise of Athens and of Theseus who forced the Thebans to return the bodies of the seven chiefs to whom they had refused burial rites;—the *Trojan Women* (415), a dramatisation of the horrible scenes that occurred when Troy was captured, including the distribution of the captured womenfolk among the victors, the sacrifice of Polyxena, murder of Astyanax and the burning of the city;—*Electra* (412) in which Euripides turned to the theme that had already been treated by Aeschylus in the *Choephoroi* and by Sophocles in his own *Electra;* in it Agamemnon's daughter is married to a peasant and lives in the countryside until the arrival of Orestes who makes himself known to her and kills Clytemnestra;—*Helen* (412), a play with a paradoxical theme; Paris flees to Troy with only the phantom of the real Helen, who has been carried off to Egypt, where she is found by Menelaus after the Trojan War;—the *Madness of Heracles* in which the hero first saves his children, whom the usurper Lycus wishes to kill, and then kills them himself after being bereft of his wits by a fit of madness provoked by Hera;—*Ion,* the son of Apollo and Creusa, is abandoned at birth and later becomes " sacristan " (*neokoros*) of the sanctuary at Delphi; as Creusa believes him to be the son of her husband, Xuthus, by a previous union, she tries to poison him, and Ion tries in turn to kill her until mother and son finally realise their true identities;—*Iphigenia in Tauris:* instead of having been sacrificed at Aulis, Agamemnon's daughter has been carried away by Artemis to Tauris in the Crimea,

Book IX of the *Odyssey;* Silenus and his sons, the satyrs, are all the slaves of the Cyclops and introduce a burlesque element into this heroic story; lastly, *Rhesus,* whose authenticity has been contested, probably wrongly, in which Rhesus, king of Thracia, is killed by Ulysses in the Dolonea episode in Book X of the *Iliad*. Important fragments of other plays by Euripides have also survived, notably of *Hypsipyle* and *Antiope*.

Aristotle said that Euripides was the " most tragic " of all the tragic dramatists. It is quite true that he had an even greater effect on his public than Aeschylus and Sophocles, and that he was able to arouse feelings of terror and pity by a great variety of means. For the statement of his themes he resorted to the convenient but artificial theatrical device of the prologue, a monologue in which the subject of the play was described by a character in it or by one of the gods. Euripides made even greater use than his predecessors of the *deus ex machina* for the ending of his plays. He was particularly brilliant in depicting the passions of love and jealousy, which he saw as irresponsible forces, destroying every vestige of decency and pity in the hearts they possessed. This feature of Euripides anticipated Hellenistic drama. His lyrical qualities were distinguished by elegance rather than by power, and sometimes tended to suffer from preciousness or banality. His drama was less exalted than that of Aeschylus, less noble than that of Sophocles, and reveals him to have had a less pure conception of his art. His skill as a dramatic writer tends to become too obvious and his philosophical and rhetorical passages often destroy the impression of realism in his plays, for he wrote innumerable speeches in which his characters served merely to express the personal ideas of the former pupil of the sophists. But the creator of Medea, Phaedra and Alcestis was nonetheless a great poet. R.F.

where she becomes priestess to the goddess and as such, is obliged to immolate all strangers who come into her domain; Orestes and Pylades are brought before her but she recognises them just in time and flees with them;—*Orestes* (408), the son of Agamemnon is condemned to death for the slaying of Clytemnestra but captures Menelaus's palace and is about to kill Hermione when Apollo, appearing as the *deus ex machina*, orders him to marry her;—the *Phoenician Women,* a kind of dramatic " abridgment " of the whole of the Theban cycle of legends;—*Iphigenia in Aulis:* Iphigenia is about to be sacrificed by the Achaeans in order to obtain a favourable wind for the departure of their fleet but she is saved by Artemis who has her replaced by a hind;—the *Bacchae,* a religious and mystical drama (or, on the contrary, one with rationalistic tendencies) describing the institution of the orgiastic cult of Dionysus in Boeotia; Pentheus, king of Thebes, opposes the new god but is slain by the Bacchae, one of whom is his mother, Agave;—the *Cyclops,* a satyr play about the stay of Ulysses and his companions in the cave of Polyphemus, as told in

EURIPUS. The part of the island of Euboea facing the city of Chalcis is separated from the mainland by a strait only sixty yards in width called the Euripus. Because of the double current in its waters it is extremely dangerous and subject to storms of great violence.

EUROPA. Europa was a young Phoenician princess, who was carried away by Zeus disguised as a miraculous bull, while she was playing with her friends on the beach at Tyre or Sidon. The strange couple crossed the seas and landed in Crete. Three sons were born of this union, Minos, Rhadamanthys and Sarpedon. Europa's brothers set off in pursuit of her and it was while seeking for her that Cadmus came to central Greece where he founded the city of Thebes.   P.D.

EUROTAS. The Eurotas was a river, flowing through the region of Laconia, which was famous for the coolness of its waters. It was said that young Spartans used to dive in it after violent exercise and emerge with enough appetite to take pleasure in eating the black, highly spiced broth, which they alone of all the Greeks could appreciate.   P.D.

EURYDICE. Eurydice was the wife of the mythical poet, Orpheus. She was bitten by a serpent one day and died. Orpheus was inconsolable and went to seek her in the underworld. The charm of his songs enabled him to penetrate the forbidden realm of the shades and won him permission to bring Eurydice back on earth, on condition that he did not turn back to look at her until he had left the underworld. According to the legend that only became popular at a fairly late date, Orpheus was unable to resist the temptation to gaze upon the features of his wife again and gave way to the pleading of Eurydice, hurt by his apparent indifference. He turned round too soon and Hermes, the leader of souls, promptly led Eurydice back again to the realm of the dead.   P.D.

EUXINE SEA. *See* Pontus Euxinus.

EXECIAS. One of the most brilliant of all the Attic vase painters, active in the second half of the 6th century B.C. between approximately 550 and 520. Execias was one of the last great artists to make use of the black-figure technique and also its finest exponent. One of his most famous works is that showing Ulysses and Ajax playing at dice (Museo Gregoriano Etrusco, Vatican). Another distinguished work is the magnificent cup in the Museum Antiker Kleinkunst, Munich, with its representation of Dionysus on a boat with the mast and main-yard loaded with grape-vines.   P.D.

FAMILY. Irregular relationships with a kept mistress were frequent and sometimes stable, but the family was normally founded on marriage

Achilles and Ajax playing dice. Detail of an amphora by Execias. About 530-525 B.C. Vatican Museum. *Photo Hirmer.*

ponsibility and were afterwards reluctant to surrender the relative independence that this period of emergency had afforded them. The Athenians then established a new magistrate, the *gynaikonomos,* who was entrusted on behalf of the city with watching over the behaviour of the women. Greek families were not prolific. The husband easily satisfied his sexual desires outside his home with courtesans (q.v.) and boys, or even inside it with servants, who could refuse nothing to the master and so became his mistresses. Then again, poverty or simply egoism made them afraid of having too many mouths to feed. The desire not to whittle away the family patrimony by sharing it among several children also contributed to the deliberate limitation of births. They were content when the birth of one or two boys into the family appeared to guarantee the continuity of its ancestor worship. When the head of the family died without a male descendant, his daughter, if he had one, was called *epikleros* and had to marry her youngest relative, who would inherit the patrimony and so avoid breaking off the worship paid to the family ancestors.

There was normally little intimacy or love between husband and wife, as the essential purpose of marriage was the upkeep of the house and the procreation of an heir. Divorce was very easy for the man, who had the right to repudiate his wife. Admittedly, if he did this, he had to return her dowry, which was often effective in preventing separation. Divorce (q.v.) for the woman, on the other hand, was extremely difficult, almost impossible in fact. At Athens, unhappy wives had only one course open to them: to go to the archon, who alone could decide how serious their sufferings had been. Recognised infidelity on the part of the husband was not sufficient ground, but blows and ill-treatment, if they could be established by enquiry, could lead the magistrate to grant a divorce.

Abortion was not forbidden provided that the father agreed to it; a free woman could not have an abortion without the consent of her husband, nor a slave without the permission of her master. In addition, the father of the family enjoyed an unquestioned right to abandon outside the newborn babies that he could not be bothered to bring up. The child was put in a receptacle or

(q.v.). The middle and upper class wife led a secluded life in the gynaeceum (q.v.), but morals were certainly more lax among the lower classes and cramped living conditions must have made a strict separation of the sexes inside the home impossible. The rights of the man were absolute; he was the master, the *kyrios.* He spent a great deal of his time outside the house; often he even had most of his meals with his friends or comrades (this was the institution of the *syssitia* in Sparta) and, when he invited other men to his home, his wife did not appear. However, a wife who enjoyed the confidence of her husband was on the whole mistress *(despoina)* in her own home. She kept the keys of the storeroom and supervised the young children and the domestic slaves, whose numbers varied according to the wealth of the family.

The Athenian family seems to have been well established until the time of the Peloponnesian War (431-404 B.C.), which brought great changes in its way of life. As the men were frequently away campaigning or occupied in guarding the ramparts, their wives had to assume more res-

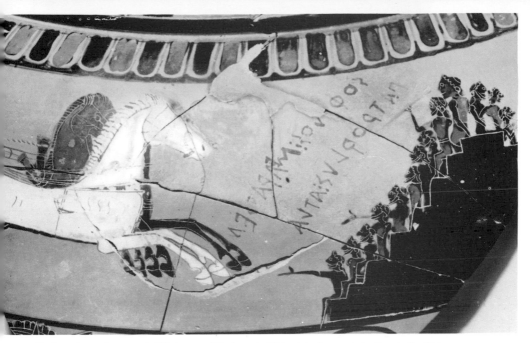

Chariot racing at the games held in honour of the funeral of Patroclus. Fragment of a dinos by Sophilus. About 480-470 B.C. Athens, National Museum. *Photo Hirmer.*

clay pot, which served for his " tomb ". Illegitimate children were exposed in greater number in this way than others, and girls more often than boys.

At Athens, when a child was acknowledged by his father, the family celebration of the *amphidromia* was held five or six days after his birth. The celebration included lustrations for the mother and everyone who had been in " contact " with the delivery, which would make them impure, then the child was carried running round the house whence the word *amphidromia*, meaning a " running round ", derives. After that, the newlyborn child was a part of the family and the father himself no longer had the right to get rid of him. On the tenth day after the birth, the members of the family gathered together again to offer a sacrifice, followed by a banquet. The child was then given a name. Generally the eldest boy was named after his paternal grandfather. Birthcontrol, abortion and the exposure of new-born babies contributed more even than epidemics and wars to *oliganthropia*, the depopulation from which Greece suffered during the Hellenic and Roman eras and which led to its decline. At the beginning of the 2nd century A.D., Plutarch stated that " the whole of Hellas can hardly muster three thousand hoplites, which was the number of the contingent sent to Plataea (479 B.C.) by the single city of Megara. " R.Γ.

FANS. As an accessory of feminine dress, the fan was very useful in such a hot and sunny country as Greece. The Greek fan was a simple screen with a handle, generally in the shape of an arum or palm leaf, whose stem served as a handle, or heart-shaped. Sometimes it was circular or like a palmette. Fans were usually green, blue or white in colour, sometimes gilded. They were rigid and often seem to have been made of a panel of thin wood with handles carved in the shape of elegant female figurines in the style of Tanagra. R.F.

FESTIVALS. " Life without festivals is a long road without inns, " said Democritus and Thucydides went further when he wrote, " The Athenians took care to provide plenty of relaxation for the spirit through games and periodical sacrifices. " Festivals, however, were not instituted to ensure leisure for working men at that remote period when social considerations played little part; in Greece, as elsewhere, they had a religious origin and there was not a single private or public festival from which the gods were absent. These, just like men, had their anniversaries, which it would have been sacrilegious to let go by without celebrating: birthdays, victories and their installation in their sanctuaries; and since no good fortune comes to human beings except through the will of the immortals, it would be unjust not to associate them with the rejoicings that are a manifestation of the happiness enjoyed by mortals through their gifts. One of the most ancient records in connexion with this subject, a vase with relief ornament from Haghia Triada, about 1500 B.C., shows us Cretan peasants, exuberant about the fine harvest, brandishing sheaves that they have just gathered and singing at the top of their voices, as they march along. There is no divinity in sight, but it is safe to assume from all we know from other sources that these good people have not forgotten to thank the Mother Goddess in their couplets.

About the same period, the games that Thucydides considered an essential element of every festival appear in the form of dances and acrobatics on the paintings of Cnossos. They take place in front of crowds of spectators massed on tiers or stairways like those that have been discovered at the palace of Phaestus and, when we see, as so often, a bull-fight depicted there, we can be sure that the death of the beast constitutes the sacrifice which, according to the same historian, was also an integral part of a festival.

Sacrifice and games alone constituted the festival (why not call them rejoicings?) that accompanied the funeral of Patroclus as it is described in the *Iliad*. Beasts—men too, but this was exceptional—were slaughtered on the pyre, then the participants competed in chariot races, running, boxing, wrestling, throwing the discus, shooting with the bow, and it was in an atmosphere of gaiety that these exercises and the distribution of prizes to the victors took place. The importance attached to sporting competitions in festivals may seem surprising. It is understandable if we remember that the Greek gods—and the deified dead, the heroes, even more so—had the appearance and temperaments of human beings and that the manly ideal was represented for Hellenism by the perfect athlete. So nothing could be more pleasing to the gods than to contemplate man made in their own image, in all his perfection. It should not be forgotten that at the end of these games there followed a music competition: *mens sana in corpore sano.*

Of course, the size and character of the Greek festivals depended on the setting and circumstances in which they took place. There were the family feasts on the occasion of a birth or a marriage and naturally these private celebrations did not include games; modest festivals that took place within the communities of the phratry, deme or one of the religious associations called a *thiasos;* city and national celebrations; and the panhellenic festivals. As soon as the participants were sufficiently numerous, instead of the straggling lines of private feasts pushing a piglet or sheep towards the altar for sacrifice, there was a solemn procession led by priests and official notabilities, the number of sacrificial victims increased and could be as many as a hundred, which made a hecatomb. The Panathenaea is the perfect example of the public festival where a whole city gathered together to celebrate the feast day of a patron deity.

The atmosphere of the festival varied according to its character. If it was celebrating Dionysus, the god of wine and fertility, instead of Athena, it was marked by jollity rather than the subdued and dignified joy of the faithful. A village celebration of the wine harvest was a country affair with uproarious laughter, bawdy jokes and copious bumpers of new wine. The atmosphere was hardly less free when an entire city held a thanksgiving to a rustic god whom it had once adopted; at the Anthesteria, a whole day was given over to drinking with trials of endurance, where the palm went to the toper who could drain the largest number of pitchers at one draught. At the end of March for a more important festival, the Great Dionysia, the god himself took his place in the procession, carried in a ship mounted on a waggon and accompanied by sileni, trumpeters and attendants holding phallic symbols. The competition, which followed the ceremony, was a poetry and music competition in which writers of tragedies, comedies and dithyrambs joined.

Everywhere—and this indicates both the ancient origins and rural character of Greek civilisation—most of the great festivals fell at the crucial points of the year: seed-time, harvest and grape-gathering. There were also the humbler festivals, those that were celebrated in the family circle. Their rites were no less strictly laid down than those of the public ceremonies and they varied naturally according to the nature of the event celebrated. The common elements in all these rejoicings were

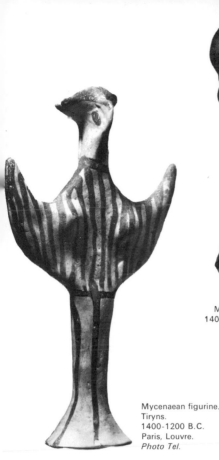

Minoan figurine. Haghia Triada.
1400-1200 B.C. Heraklion Museum.
Photo Hassia.

Mycenaean figurine.
Tiryns.
1400-1200 B.C.
Paris, Louvre.
Photo Tel.

Boeotian figurine.
Thebes.
Late 6th century B.C.
Paris, Louvre.
Photo Tel.

without any doubt the feeling of gratitude to the gods and, as with people the world over, the enjoyment of gathering together just like ours today.   P.D.

FIGURINES. Long before they carved sculpture, the peoples who had been living on the shores of the Aegean Sea since the 3rd millennium B.C., made figurines representing either beings in human shape or animals. The Roman Empire had already firmly established its sway over the Mediterranean world when on the same sites they often continued to produce small figures which, although the art was more refined, served the same purposes. All of them had a religious function. They were never intended as curios and were not exhibited in cabinets, like the Dresden china of collectors today; they were placed in tombs or consecrated in sanctuaries. The first kind represented goddesses entrusted with the protection of the dead person, or else they were intended as mementoes for him of his life on earth. The second kind were ex-votos offered by popular piety to a particular divinity as a thanksgiving for some favour. They could also be seen beside the household altar, protecting the family with their tutelary power. They only differed from statues in size and price and they were, like these, inspired by religious sentiment and not by aesthetic considerations.

The word " figurine " suggests to our minds the terra-cotta statues that the lay-man refers to by the generic term of " tanagra figures ", although Tanagra was only one centre of production among many; but, although for mainly economic reasons most of these " dolls ", as the Greeks called them, were made of terra-cotta, there were also figurines in bronze, wood and stone. As stone ones required individual work and could not be made in a

mould like terra-cotta or even bronze, they were naturally more expensive. They were widely distributed particularly after the beginning of the Hellenistic period, but the banality and weak execution of most of them show that they were produced by craftsmen whose standards remained low. On the other hand, there are real masterpieces to be found among the terra-cotta figurines whatever their period.

Their interest for us is not purely aesthetic; they provide important evidence for the history of religions and are often a source of information for large sculpture, which they sometimes faithfully reproduced. P.D.

FISHING. Fishing was common among the Greeks, who were fond of fish, but it was never for them the restful pastime that rouses the tired worker at dawn, reluctant to have anything to think about. In the first place, fresh water fish was rare in a country with so few rivers and, secondly, fishing was considered a mercenary occupation only fit for poor people. The techniques have hardly changed since antiquity. In a vase painting a young boy is depicted perched on

Figurine from Myrina.
Early 2nd century B.C.
Paris, Louvre.
Photo Tel.

Group from Myrina.
2nd century B.C.
British Museum.
Photo Hirmer.

202

Aphrodite. Terra-cotta figurine. Hellenistic period. Syracuse, Museo Archeologico. *Photo L. von Matt.*

a rock holding a line, but the more usual methods were with nets and pots, like our own, and fishing with a madrague with its complicated system of cords and winches was already practised, just as it has been recently described in a contemporary novel. Tunny fish were stunned with a gaff, a method that was sufficiently well known for Aeschylus to allude to it in the *Persians* when he was describing the slaughter of the conquered at the battle of Salamis. At night, since they had no acetylene lamps, the sailors brandished torches to attract their prey. P.D.

F O O D . The ancient Greeks were generally a very sober people, although the inhabitants of rich Boeotia were held by their neighbours to be great eaters and were mocked at for their gourmandise. By way of contrast the diet of the Spartans was even more frugal than that of the Athenians. Cereals, corn and barley especially, were the staple diet of the Greeks whom Homer had called "the flour eaters". Athens had to import large amounts of corn because the soil of Attica was sparse and poor. The main nourishment of poor people was *maza,* barley flour kneaded into cakes, some fish, olives and figs, although, by the time of Pericles, Athenian bakers were also making wheat bread which was somewhat more expensive.

Opson, that is everything in a meal that accompanied bread, was composed of vegetables, onions, olives, meat, fish, fruit and cakes. Vegetables were rare and costly in Attica, except for beans and lentils which were often eaten as purée. Athenians, and particularly their soldiers, ate a lot of garlic, onions and cheese, but to more refined stomachs such a diet appeared too monotonous and coarse. Olives were plentiful and they were used for making oil. Meat was expensive except for pork (a sucking pig cost three drachmas) and the poorer inhabitants of the city only ate it during festivals when sacrifices were followed by feasting. But well-off country folk were able to eat poultry, pork, goat meat, mutton and game caught during hunting expeditions *(See* Hunting). The majority of Athenian city-dwellers ate far more fish *(See* Fishing) than meat; as we may see in Aristophanes' plays, any rise in the price of

sardines and anchovies at Phalerum was a cause of great anxiety for the common people, and the fish-market was the most frequented and picturesque part of the agora. Such delicacies as eels from lake Copais, and tuna, were beyond the means of most customers, but shell fish, molluscs, cuttle-fish and squid were greatly appreciated. Merchants of salted provisions sold fish and meats which had either been smoked or pickled in brine. Meals often ended with a dessert which might consist of fresh or dried fruits, mainly figs, nuts and raisins, or honey-cakes. Honey made by the bees of Hymettus was famous but very expensive. Forks were unknown but spoons and knives were used at meals. At Sparta, one of the main dishes was the famous black broth, which was a very highly seasoned stew containing such ingredients as pork, blood, vinegar and salt.

Kykeon, the ritual beverage at the mysteries of Eleusis, was halfway between a solid food and a drink, and was very popular with peasants. It was a mixture of barley-gruel and water, spiced with aromatic herbs such as pennyroyal, mint or thyme.

The most common drink was certainly water, whose freshness and savour even gourmets

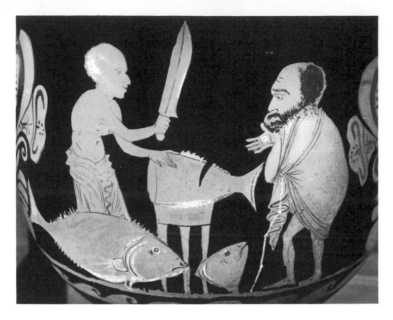

Tunny-seller. Detail of krater in the Italiote style. 4th century B.C. Cefalu, Mandralisca Museum. *Photo Leonard von Matt.*

learned to appreciate. Milk was drunk, especially that of goats, and also a kind of mead. The drink of kings and the " gift of Dionysus " came from the vine. Certain vineyards were famous, like those of Thasos. The ancient Greeks did not put resin in their wines but they did add aromatic herbs and spices, particularly thyme, mint, cinnamon or honey. Wine was rarely drunk on its own and was usually mixed with water before the meal in a large vase called a krater.   R.F.

FOOTWEAR. Socrates was not the only Greek to walk barefoot in the streets of Athens or its suburban roads, for figures on painted vases are rarely shown wearing footwear. Greek men and women were usually bare-footed, shoes and sandals only being worn when they went out on special occasions, and even then only by the richest classes of society. Sandals consisted of a simple cork, wood, or leather sole which was kept on the foot by laces tied around the ankle and the toes, and the top of the foot was left bare. The *embas* was a high shoe, laced up in front with the top turned down, so that it resembled a kind of half-length boot, which was often worn by travellers. The *endromis*, a similar type of boot, was without a turned down top. The *kothornos* (or *cothurnus*) Lydian in origin, was a

thick-soled shoe which was less tight-fitting than the others we have mentioned, since either shoe could be worn on either foot, whence the nickname of " kothornos " which was given to politicians who easily changed parties. It may have been Aeschylus who adapted the kothornos for the theatre where it gave greater height to actors on the stage.

Women's footwear was far more varied and elegant in design. The names of some varieties, such as *persikai* or *lakonikai* indicated their origins. In a mime by Herondas, a cobbler vaunts his wares to his customers in the following terms: " Just examine all these different samples: Sicyon, Ambracian, canary yellow, parrot green, canvas shoes, mules, slippers, Ionian shoes, high shoes, bed slippers, low cut shoes, lobster red shoes, sandals, Argive shoes, scarlet shoes for the younger man or for the market. " But the customers haggled hard as we may see in another scene, taking place in the shop of Kerdon, the cobbler:

" *A female customer:* What do you want for that pair you're holding there ? Only don't send us packing by charging the earth for it.

Kerdon: Value it yourself if you like and fix a price. But say a price that'll buy bread for the workers.

Female customer: What are you grumbling

about? Can't you be frank and say the price, whatever it is?

Kerdon: Madam, this pair is worth a *mina* [about a hundred drachmas, then a considerable sum]. Look at it all over if you like. Even if Athena herself wanted to buy it I couldn't knock the price down by a farthing.

Female customer: Now I see why so many beautiful and costly wares never leave your shop. Look after them well!".

Women who wanted to appear taller were unable to make use of high heels since it appears that cobblers never made shoes with heels, but they were able to solve the problem by inserting a kind of felt insole between their feet and the sole. Shoes were often made to measure; the cobbler cut the sole around the foot which the customer placed on a stool, as we may see from one vase painting.   R.F.

FORTIFICATIONS. The most ancient Greek fortifications that we know (those of the Neolithic Age are deliberately left out of this article) are those that the Achaeans built round

Woman tying her sandal. Detail of the neck of an amphora by Oltos. About 520-510 B.C. Paris, Louvre.

their towns. While in the apparently peaceful island of Crete, the town dwellers and the owners of palaces seem to have reduced their defence systems to a minimum, the remains of ramparts at Mycenae, Tiryns, Thebes, Athens and every agglomeration of any importance are astonishingly impressive. They are built according to a system called "cyclopean". The walls, with a double facing, filled inside with a packing of small stones and clay, consisted of piles of stone blocks, more or less roughly hewn and often enormous. The spaces between were filled with smaller stones wedged into them; there were no joints or sealings; the whole structure was held together by its own weight. A rudimentary technique, it may be said, but it was not the result of inexperience in masonry, because some parts of the wall at Mycenae are carefully bonded. Actually, building of this kind was economical because it dispensed with the slow labour of trimming stone and was quite adequate protection for a town from the arms of the period and against the attacks of an enemy who had no engines of war. To talk of inexperience is out of place when we examine the skilful planning of the casemates at Tiryns, the subterranean passages leading the besieged towards secret posterns, or the protective arrangement of the gates, which were approached by a passage open to the sky that forced the assailants to present to the defenders the right side of their bodies, which could not be protected by the shield.

It was some time after the Dorian invasions that fortifications reappeared round cities or simply round the citadels. These points were not left defenceless, but their occupants were content in the beginning with wooden palisades, like the Parian colonists when they arrived at Thasos. Ramparts of stone, or sometimes of brick on a stone foundation as at Gela towards the end of the 4th century B.C., were only gradually constructed.

As far as possible, the surrounding wall took advantage of the natural relief and followed its contours, sometimes breaking off where an insurmountable peak made its existence unnecessary. It was generally thick, consisting of two parallel walls with packing piled up between. Sometimes its material strength was reinforced by magical protection, just as at Thasos where two large apotropaic eyes were engraved in the walls to ward off all forms of evil. The rampart was often flanked by round or rectangular towers, which enabled the defenders to take the attacker on his flank if he tried to climb over or demolish the wall. An example of these are the towers, still in good condition, at Eleutherae, the fortress on the way to Boeotia that protected Attica. Particular care had been taken over the arrangement of the gates, which had to be placed where the lines of communication diverged. There were no drawbridges, because the towns were not surrounded by a moat as in the Middle Ages. There were portcullises, however, and the entrance was approached by a narrow, sometimes oblique, passage, which prevented the attacker from deploying his forces. Again at Thasos, there is an almost unique example in Greece of the city's two tutelary gods sculptured in the passage in the Hittite manner.

Such as they were, Greek ramparts were sufficient to protect the towns, at least up to the time in the Hellenistic period when siegecraft made immense progress. Until then, the enemy could only break down the resistance of a city by long sieges, famine and guile. P.D.

FOUNTAINS. Because of the dry climate, water supply was a constant and difficult problem for the Greeks particularly in built-up areas. The wells and cisterns were seldom adequate, which explains the importance of fountains in town-planning. The tyrants of the 5th and 6th centuries B.C. were popular with town dwellers because they brought water to the city centres, which they had been forced to fetch before from far away. The aqueduct, which Eupalinus constructed at Samos by order of Polycrates, was often referred to with admiration. It was a tunnel, pierced for nearly a mile through the heart of a hill, about 5½ft. in width and height and containing a channel of baked clay. It followed the different ground levels skilfully and at its outlet, a network of canals distributed the water through the town. Much later at Pergamum, the engineers of Eumenes II, working on the same principles, brought water from sources at a far greater distance in the mountains sixteen miles away, and by taking advantage of the pressure, they made the water flow to the top of the citadel.

Without resorting to so much technological knowledge, the Greeks had to devote a considerable effort to solving the problem of water supply and it is not surprising that special officials were designated to supervise the upkeep and cleanliness of the fountains and conduits. As this service required a certain competence and financial responsibilities were involved, these officials were appointed by election at Athens and not by drawing lots.

While water supplied to houses themselves was exceptional even at a late period, the remains of public fountains on the other hand can be seen in all the towns and sanctuaries. Sometimes the fountain took the form of a slightly built portico with pipes emerging from the lower part, generally through the muzzle of a lion or other decorative figures, and the jet of water fell into the receptacles placed on the ground. Sometimes it was a basin hollowed out in the pavement and people plunged their pitchers into it to fill them. Although this second type was rarely represented in the decorations of buildings, it seems to have been

Fountain. Detail of an Attic hydria. 510 B.C. British Museum.

Man and ephebe. Detail of an amphora by the Phrynos Painter. About 550 B.C. Würzburg, Martin von Wagner Museum. *Photo Hirmer.*

much more commonly used. Some of the fountains most famous for the purity of their water or the beauty of their construction were the fountain of Theognis at Megara, the Pirene Spring at Corinth, built by Periander, the Castalian Spring at Delphi, and at Athens, the Enneacrounos with its nine mouths, which was originally called the Callirhoë and whose water, Thucydides tells us, was used for marriage rites and other religious ceremonies.   P.D.

FRIENDSHIP. In ancient Greece, it was friendship *(philia)* that was honoured more than love *(eros)*. In fact, the word philia was used to denote a great variety of sentiments of attachment and affection between two persons, but the philosophers distinguished between four different types of philia: natural or parental philia *(physike)* uniting beings of the same blood; philia between a host and his guests *(xenike)*, a reminder of the importance of the virtue of hospitality (q.v.) in the ancient world; philia between friends *(hetairike)*, the only philia corresponding to what we now call friendship; and, lastly, amorous philia *(erotike)* between two persons of the same or different sex.

One consequence of this semantic peculiarity was that the famous adage of Pythagoras " between friends all is in common " normally applied to all four sorts of friendship. The friendship betwen Achilles and Patroclus, as described by Homer, is admirable for its strength and purity; it was to become proverbial and be regarded by the philosophers as representing the most typical and perfect example of this sentiment. Later, Aeschylus conformed to the tendency of his age by transforming the friendship of Achilles and Patroclus into a physical relationship, in his lost tragedy the *Myrmidons*. Friendship between men—and, more rarely, between women—often had an ambiguous aspect in ancient Greece.

" Philosophic " friendship was conducive to virtue. Socrates said that he " hunted for friends " and claimed that he plied the trade of go-between because he wanted to establish links of solidarity, mutual aid and affection between his disciples. Aristotle is the outstanding theorist of friendship and claimed that of all our affections it was the most valuable, because it was linked to

virtue, which is the essential element in morality. Love (q v.) was linked to beauty which, for Aristotle, was only a transitory quality based on pleasure which changed with the years. He admitted that love was certainly the stronger and more violent sentiment but maintained that friendship was more important since it was more long-lasting and constant. " Young people are given to love which is often only the result of desire and is aimed at pleasure. That is why they love and stop loving so quickly and change their tastes twenty times in a single day " *(Nicomachean Ethics, 8,3)*.

In Aristotelian morality, the greatest virtue was greatness of soul or magnanimity. Although the magnanimous man may be self-sufficient in a certain sense, he will still need friends because man is always a " social animal ". Indeed, Aristotle thought, friendship is necessary to us in order to practise virtue, and a virtuous friend is indispensable to a virtuous man; he will give him the opportunity to do good and nothing can be finer than to do good to a friend because of friendship or because one loves him. Friendship also teaches the magnanimous man to feel the joy of receiving and to give and sacrifice himself, which is the very acme of all moral grandeur and beauty.

In Epicureanism, friendship was also honoured. Epicurus and his friend, Metrodorus, were united by a fervent friendship which was celebrated by sculptors who represented them in twin busts. Friendship was to remain one of the essential principles of the Epicurean life, the element which was to bring ardour, cohesion and unity to the groups of the Garden. R.F.

FUNERALS. Although we know several tombs of the Minoan and Mycenaean periods, we do not known what happened between the death of a person and the moment when his body was buried. It is possible that the customs described in the *Iliad* which, it must be emphasised, only applied to the funerals of eminent persons, are still Achaean. The body was washed and perfumed immediately after death. Then it lay in state and was surrounded by mourning men and women, most of whom were hired for the ceremony and who lamented, sang the praises of the dead *(threnoi)* and tore their hair in the prescribed manner. After this, the corpse was placed on a pyre and burnt. If the preparations were likely to be long drawn out, the corpse was protected by anointing it with products that slowed down putrefaction, but not by embalming. Games were held in honour of the deceased and the victors were handsomely rewarded. The ceremony ended with a banquet.

During the Greek period proper, the funerals even of high ranking persons were more modest and from time to time decrees were issued forbidding anything in this kind of ceremony that would allow a family to make an ostentatious display of wealth. The body still lay in state and was mourned, but it was hurried to its final resting place, largely for hygienic reasons. Flasks or lekythoi, which had contained the perfumed oil used for anointing the corpse, were thrown into the tomb, and placed on it around the stele that marked the grave. The stele itself was considered not only as the indicator of the tomb, but also as a sacred stone marking the boundary

between life and death, and as such was a cult object. It was smeared with oil and paint, bound with bandlets and from time to time visits were made to the tomb and offerings placed on it. P.D.

FURNITURE. Vase paintings have given us an idea of the most frequent types of Greek furniture. The writings of ancient authors, especially Aristophanes, have given us additional information on the subject. Beds were simple wooden frames equipped with webbing on which a thin mat of rushes or reeds *(psiathos)* was placed as a mattress. Pillows and blankets were used but not sheets. Banquets (q.v.) appear frequently in vase paintings and from them we can see that the couches on which the guests reclined, propped up by cushions, were a kind of short but wide divan, as two and even three guests could lie on the same couch. The banqueting tables were small and easily portable, and there might be one for each guest or couch. Some were square or rectangular, others round and supported by tripods. The inventory of Alcibiades' possessions, which were sold in execution of the sentence after the case of the Hermae, do not suggest the luxury that might be expected in the household of such an illustrious personage; the richest item among his furniture was " a dining-room set " of four tables and twelve couches of " Milesian handiwork " to the total value of 120 drachmas. Chairs and stools often had very elegantly curved legs. Coffers and chests in which clothes, blankets and jewels were placed were usually made of wood, occasionally of bronze, and were sometimes richly decorated. Many of the painted vases, signed by famous artists, that are now admired in

Lying in state of a dead man. Terra-cotta funerary plaque. About 530 B.C. Paris, Louvre.

Young woman sitting on a chair. Detail of a lekythos by the Achilles Painter. About 440 B.C. Switzerland, Private collection. *Ph. Hirmer*.

Young women standing in front of a bed. Detail of a calyx krater. 4th century B.C. British Museum.

Chests. Terra-cotta plaques from Locri. About 470-450 B.C. Taranto Museum. *Photo L. von Matt.*

Incense-burner in terra-cotta. About 600 B.C. Naples, Museo Nazionale. *Photo L. von Matt.*

museums, were without any domestic purpose, for they were displayed as ornaments in the reception rooms just as fine dishes and vases are today.   R.F.

GALATIANS. At the beginning of the 3rd century B.C., Hellenism was threatened by one of the worst dangers it had known. A Celtic people from the north swept down towards the Aegean Sea and, in 280, their vanguard marched through the Pass of Thermopylae and penetrated as far as Greece. They reached Delphi, where the Aetolians succeeded in stopping them. A wave of terror ran through Greece before the irruption of these barbarians and, when the sanctuary of Apollo was saved, the victors instituted the annual feast of the Soteria in gratitude. Thrown back towards the north, the Galatians, as they were called, clashed with the army of Antiochus I and they then settled down in the Danubian region and Thrace, where they lived on trade and industry. However, a prince of Asia Minor, Nicomedes of Bithynia, invited them to help in the struggle against his brothers. They crossed the Hellespont in bands, pillaged the regions through which they passed, and attacked or threatened the towns on the Aegean coast from Cyzicus to Miletus. Antiochus I again stopped them in 270 in front of Sardes. This victory did not succeed in putting the dangerous invaders to flight and they settled down permanently in the valley of the Halys, which consequently came to be known as Galatia. They remained a constant menace to the neighbouring peoples ever afterwards, to Pergamum in particular whose rulers celebrated their victories over them with splendid ex-votos. P.D.

GALEN. Galen was born at Pergamum about 130 A.D. After studying languages, geometry, dialectic and the different systems of philosophy, he took up medicine at the age of seventeen. He associated with schools at Pergamum, Smyrna, Corinth and Alexandria before returning to his native town in 157, where he was put in charge of the medical care of the gladiators. He taught at Rome in 162 and, after scientific travels in the Middle East, he was appointed physician to Commodus, a post which he retained in 180 when Commodus became emperor. Thirteen years later, he went back to Pergamum and the end of his life is obscure. Galen wrote on a variety of subjects; he believed that "the good physician is a philosopher" and his thought is always clear. He is considered one of the greatest anatomists of ancient times; he discovered certain muscles, described the functions of arteries and veins, and analysed the nervous system. The discovery of recurrent nerves and the motor and sensory nerve roots would have alone ensured his fame. Galen was the founder of experimental physiology and showed that the brain was the centre of voluntary movement and sense-perception. Borrowings from his predecessors, violent criticisms and intransigent judgments are scattered through his works, the treatises on surgery, pharmacology, hygiene, dietetics and essays on medical philosophy, but he always succeeded in co-ordinating the disparate elements, synthetising them all into a vast system and building a significant structure. His writings and those of Hippocrates were the most important contributions to early medicine and formed an essential part of the training of western and arabic doctors for more than a thousand years, yet they are scarcely known today. P.B.

GAMES. The word Games, used again in the name of the Olympic Games, designated the periodical ceremonies, which accompanied cer-

Armed Pyrrhic dance. Athens, Acropolis Museum. *Photo Boudot-Lamotte.*

Boxer. Bronze by Apollonius. Mid-1st century B.C. Rome, Museo Nazionale. *Photo Hirmer.*

celebration, like those of the Ten Thousand (q.v.) at the end of their long tramp over the continent, the organisation of games nearly always assumed a religious character; they took place on fixed dates, at a sanctuary, and were bound up with a whole group of religious ceremonies. Legendary traditions connect the games with illustrious characters, like Heracles and Theseus, and with local heroes who instituted them or on whose tomb they were held for the first time.

Every Greek city had its own games organised on some festival, but there were also games shared by several states because they were neighbours or were drawn together by a common cult. Most important of all were the panhellenic games in which the whole Hellenic world joined through their official representatives. There were four of these panhellenic games, held at Olympia, Delphi (these were the Pythian games), Nemea and at the sanctuary of the Isthmus near Corinth. They were consecrated respectively to Zeus, Apollo, Zeus again, and Poseidon. Some were annual (the Great Dionysia at Athens, for example), some only came round every two years, others every three years, or even, like the Olympic and Pythian, every four years. In the games of an individual city or a group of states, the competitors had to belong in principle to the city or to one of the states associated with the religious ceremony. In the panhellenic games, all the Greeks were eligible; only Barbarians were excluded, and men who had incurred a penalty involving the loss of civil rights; Alexander the Great confounded those who denied that he was a Hellene by reminding them that he had competed at Olympia.

The games included all sorts of events and the most highly organised of them continued for several days. The events fell into three broad divisions: equestrian, athletic and musical competitions. These last acquired an increasing importance with time, although their beginnings stretched back to a very early period and at Delphi they may even have preceded the sporting competitions. They not only comprised musical recitals (the flute, lyre, cithara, songs and poetry accompanied by music), but also dancing, recitations of poetry, declamations and dramatic spectacles. Each event was judged and prizes solemnly distributed to the winners. The athletes were

tain religious festivals, during which athletes, musicians and declaimers competed with each other. The origin of these games is rather obscure. They do not seem to have had any direct connexion with the festivals of Minoan Crete in which, as far as we know, the salient features were tauromachies and acrobatic exercises. The first references appear in the Homeric poems; competitive sports in which the winners were awarded prizes added lustre to the funeral of Patroclus and entertained Ulysses during his stay with the Phaeacians. In neither instance did the games seem to be associated with a particular cult; they were not accompanied by any sacrifice and they were not celebrated in a sanctuary; nor, under the walls of Troy, is there even a suggestion that they were intended to appease the shades of the dead, so it is quite likely that they were held at a great gathering of people simply to satisfy the natural Greek taste for physical exercises. This was no longer true after the period, which was still Mycenaean, described by Homer. Although competitive sports may sometimes have been considered just as a spontaneous and joyful even more highly esteemed for their victories in various trials: running (speed and long-distance), chariot racing, wrestling, boxing, throwing the discus and javelin, the pancratium (a combination of boxing and wrestling), the pentathlon (five combined exercises: jumping, running, throwing the discus and javelin, wrestling), the lampadromia or torch race. These exercises were not all equally appreciated, but some of them, particularly the pentathlon, endowed their champions with a celebrity at least comparable to that enjoyed by our racing motorists and for at least the first fifty years of the 5th century, leading sculptors, like Myron, and the most famous poets, Bacchylides and Pindar for example, built their reputations on founding bronze statues of victorious athletes and composing odes in their honour.

Although the prizes awarded at the panhellenic games were often purely honorific—at Olympia it was an olive wreath—we can be certain that the participating cities who shared the glory of their representatives made sure that their champions enjoyed a material benefit from their efforts. Athletics was a career and Theogenes the Thasian, the winner of several hundreds of events in the panhellenic games, was not an isolated example of an athlete who ended his life admired by everyone and enjoying a fortune that neither trade nor agriculture could have given him. An athlete's training was not confined to the few weeks preceding the games on the grounds themselves, as at Olympia, but began in childhood. There is no doubt that the outstanding individuals were very soon picked out from among all the Greek boys who used to go to the palaestra and the city would take responsibility for them in the hopes that one day one of them would cover it with glory.

The competitions took place in the stadium before a vast and enthusiastic public. Even when the games were not part of a panhellenic festival, representatives of other states were invited to watch, but women were not admitted to most of them; at Olympia, the priestess of Demeter was the only one of her sex allowed to enter and, moreover, she was given the place of honour. There were, however, competitions for women and, as the owner of a chariot racing team was awarded the prize and not the driver, a woman was sometimes crowned victor. The judging

Young jockey, called the Jockey of Artemision. Hellenistic period. Athens, National Museum.

body was composed of officials, called *Hella-nodikai* at Olympia and, in other places, *agonothetai, athlothetai* or *epimeletai*. They were in charge of organising the games, sending out invitations, supervising the final training of the competitors and seeing that the regulations were properly observed. The festival began with a sacrifice to the patron deity of the sanctuary, then the president formally declared the games open. The musical competitions generally came first, followed by the sports and the equestrian events took place last. After this, the victors were announced and they marched in procession before going to the banquet held in their honour. The return to their native city, if they had won a stiff competition at a panhellenic meeting, was often like a triumph and countless honours were paid them by their fellow-citizens.

The games were not just an entertainment in the lives of the Greeks and it is impossible to exaggerate the part they played in the history of their civilisation. Around them crystallised national sentiment and a civic sense. They became for the inhabitants of the same city and the children of the same race, scattered all over the Mediterranean, the bond that reminded them of their common interests and their common origin. They had an influence on private as well as public life; they not only inculcated in everyone the idea that physical education should be encouraged by training young people in the palaestra, they also gave an opportunity to the scattered members of the same ethnic family to fulfill themselves in the pursuit of an ideal that distinguished them from the Barbarians. The celebration of this ideal put a temporary stop to the rivalries and hostilities between cities; the panhellenic games were accompanied by truces during which it would have been sacrilegious to begin or continue a war. The internal conflicts of cities died down too; public business lay idle, judicial actions, executions and even the seizure of securities were suspended. These truces took effect only locally for festivals of secondary importance, but they were general for the Olympics, which were the most important of this kind of celebration. An indication of their importance is that the Greeks made 776 B.C., the year of the first Olympic, the beginning of their chronology.

The glory surrounding the games was never completely dimmed until a decree of Theodosius in 392 A.D. abolished them and marked the end of the classical world. Their history had its vicissitudes. Their great period was in the 6th and first half of the 5th century, after which they were somewhat discredited by the contempt of the philosophers and kindred spirits who subordinated the life of the body to that of the soul. Sufficient respect for them survived, however, for their institution to spread in the Hellenistic period throughout the world conquered by Alexander. Games were founded in the capitals of the new kingdoms and in all the towns of any importance. They were often held, not only in honour of the gods, but also of joyful occasions for kings and generals, then the Roman emperors and the members of their family. P.D.

GANYMEDE. Ganymede was a very handsome young man of royal blood whom Zeus (some say the eagle of the god) abducted while he was guarding the flocks of his father near Troy. He remained with the gods, as their cup-bearer.
P.D.

GARDENS. The Greeks only succeeded after unremitting effort in growing the fruit and

Ganymede playing with a hoop. Detail of a krater by the Berlin Painter. About 480 B.C. Paris, Louvre.

Heracles and Cybele, in her chariot drawn by lions, fighting against the Giants. Detail of the north frieze of the Treasury of the Siphnians at Delphi. About 525 B.C. Delphi Museum. *Photo Hirmer.*

vegetables necessary for subsistence from their dry land, which meant that the art of gardening did not develop so long as the Hellenic world was bounded by the Aegean Sea. The descriptions of the grounds of Alcinous and Calypso in the *Odyssey* were purely imaginary. Gardens planted for religious reasons in some sanctuaries, the Academus at Athens or those of the Eleusinian goddesses for example, must have been very poor. The few trees growing round Xenophon's house at Scillus were probably only a faint reminder to their landlord of the parks, the "paradises", he had admired on his military expeditions in Asia Minor.

It was there, in fact, after Alexander's campaigns, that the victorious Greeks in imitation of the Persian nobles were able to practise horticulture and develop an art that they passed on to the Romans. We can imagine what those great gardens were like from the Pompeian paintings where buildings and statues are set in the midst of leafy groves. P.D.

GE (or GAEA). She was a very ancient goddess who, according to Hesiod, gave birth to all the divine races. She engendered the Heavens, Uranus, and from their union were born several children, one of whom, Cronus, dethroned his father and engendered Zeus. Complicated genealogies explain how all the evil and benign forces of nature descend either directly from Ge or indirectly through one or several intervening generations. Ge possessed sanctuaries in various places that go back to an era when the Olympians had not yet settled in Greece. She was gifted with oracular powers, which she gradually lost to the younger divinities; Apollo, for example, was no more than her successor at Delphi. P.D.

GIANTS. These should not be confused with the Titans. The Giants were the sons of Uranus, the Heavens, and Ge, the Earth. As soon as they were born, they attacked the Olympians whose power they wanted to usurp. The gods overcame them, but not without a struggle; the episode is one of the most important in mythology and numerous works of art have taken this Gigantomachy for a subject. The Giants piled two of the highest mountains in Thessaly, Ossa and Pelion, one on top of the other to attack Olympus. From there they mounted their assault by hurling stones. The gods could not on their own subdue the Giants, who were formidable, brutal looking creatures, some of whom, for example, are depicted on the frieze around the Pergamum altar as anguiform monsters. They could only be killed by the hand of a mortal, so Zeus called on Heracles, whose arrows finished off the wounded. All the gods joined in the battle, each with his special arms: Athena fought with a spear, Zeus hurled his thunderbolts, Poseidon struck with his trident, Dionysus with his magic thyrsus, Eros drew his bow, Cybele let loose her lions on them and Hephaestus burnt them with a mass of incandescent fire.   P.D.

GITIADAS. This Spartan was a characteristic figure of the archaic period (7th to the 6th century B.C.) when artists were passionately fond of sculpture and sometimes, like Gitiadas, of poetry as well. He is only known from literary tradition, so it is difficult to determine his style. In Greek tradition, the name of Gitiadas has remained associated with the engraved bronze facings that decorated the temple of Athena Chalkoikos on the acropolis of Sparta. These reliefs depicted scenes taken from the legend of Heracles, and the exploits of the Dioscuri and Perseus. Nothing of them has been preserved. Gitiadas also practised the art of founding; two bronze tripods were commissioned from him by the Lacedaemonians for the sanctuary of Amyclae, one supported by an Artemis, the other by an Aphrodite.   R.M.

GORDIAN (knot). In the town of Gordium in Phrygia, a chariot was preserved which, so it was claimed, had belonged to the founder of the city, Gordias. Its pole was tied with such a complicated knot that it seemed impossible to undo it. It was said that the man who untied it would become master of Asia. When he was passing through Gordium, Alexander the Great cut the knot with his sword.   P.D.

GORGIAS. Philosopher and rhetorician (485-380 B.C.). Gorgias was born at Leontini in Sicily and was the pupil of the rhetorician, Tisias. Like most of the sophists, Gorgias was also a philosopher. He professed a far-reaching scepticism in his book called *On Nature or Non-being* where he tried to prove: 1) that nothing exists; 2) that if something exists, it is incomprehensible by man; 3) that if a thing is comprehensible, that knowledge cannot be communicated to anyone. Gorgias's fame rested mainly on his reputation as a rhetorician. He wrote a manual of rhetoric *(Technikos)* and several set speeches *(Pythikos; Olympikos),* which he addressed to the Greeks assembled for the festivals at Delphi or Olympia, exhorting them to unity, concord and peace. He also composed a *Funeral Oration, In Praise of Helen* and an *Apologia for Palamedes.* Only fragments survive of these three works. His style can be assessed from these and also from Plato's amusing pastiche in his *Gorgias.* Considerable credit should also be given to this prince of sophists for his melodious and subtle " artistic prose ". His sentences, still short and much less elaborate than in Isocrates' period, leave an impression of harmony and brilliance from his use of studied antitheses, rhythmical parts of equal length *(parisa)* and internal rhythms and assonances *(homoioteleuta).* The styles of Isocrates, Thucydides and others owe much to Gorgias.   R.F.

GORGONS. These were three monsters, one of whom, Medusa, was a mortal. They had the body of a woman, a terrifying head, crowned with serpents for hair, a mouth from which protruded fangs like the tusks of a boar and huge eyes that petrified anyone who looked at them. They flew with wings that grew from their backs and ankles. They lived at the end of the world in the far west and there Perseus went to find them to

Perseus decapitating Medusa. Metope from Temple C at Selinus. About 530 B.C. Palermo Museum.
Photo Hirmer.

Gournia: the Minoan
village. About
2000 B.C.
Photo Hassia.

kill Medusa with the help of the gods. He stole
upon them in their sleep and when he cut off the
head of the monster, the winged horse Pegasus
and the horrible Chrysaor were born from its
blood, the progeny of Poseidon, the only immortal
who was not afraid of union with this dreadful
being. Athena placed Medusa's head in her
aegis which she carried as part of her armour.

P.D.

GOURNIA. On the northern coast of
Crete, beside the Gulf of Mirabello, the site of
Gournia was occupied as early as the Minoan
period by a town whose ruins can still be seen
today. It was situated on a hill and the houses
were built on the slopes in terraces. Two parallel
streets were paved; the agora has been identified
as has a palace, which was carefully built but
which was humble compared to the luxurious and
princely dwellings of Cnossos or even Mallia.
The individual houses were crowded between
the main streets and flights of steps led to the
terraces and narrow alleys. Most of these houses
comprised smaller rooms besides the principal
one, which was sometimes paved and stuccoed.
The remains of staircases indicate the existence of
an upper storey.

P.D.

GRACES. *See* Charites.

GRANICUS. It was on the banks of the
Granicus, a small river of Asia Minor, flowing into
the Sea of Marmara, that Alexander the Great
won his first victory over the Persian army in
334 B.C.

GREECE. From an obscure tribe, the
Graeans or Graii, who had almost died out by the
beginning of historical times, the Latins derived
the names of " Greek " and " Greece ". The
Greeks, at least from the 8th century B.C. onwards,
called themselves Hellenes and believed themselves to be descendants of Hellen, son of Deucalion, who would have reigned in legendary times

and whose son was Dorus, eponymous ancestor of the Dorians. Aeolus was the eponymous ancestor of the Aeolians and the sons of Xuthus, Ion and Achaeus, of the Ionians and Achaeans. Just as the Graeans had never occupied more than a narrow strip of Epirus, so Hellas properly so called was only a small district, which Aristotle situated near Dodona, and the *Iliad* in Thessaly. It must be remembered that Greece was never at any point in ancient times, as it is in our day, a state with a capital city, clearly defined frontiers, a central government and civil servants sent to different parts of the country; nor was it a federation of partially autonomous provinces that relied on an institution, representing all of them, to decide questions of general interest. The terms '' Greece '' and '' Hellas '' had no political significance; they designated for the ancients a community which was half-racial, half-cultural and whose essential characteristics constituted Hellenism. Colonisation from the 8th to the 6th centuries B.C. scattered the Greeks and spread Hellenism from the Straits of Gibraltar to the far shore of the Black Sea and the coasts of Lebanon. Without constituting a political federation, even when they were fighting each other, the Greeks considered themselves as belonging to the same ethnic group, quite distinct from the Barbarians, that is to say the non-Greeks; the Greeks of Marseilles and Naucratis on the Nile delta felt closer to each other than to the natives whose territory bordered on their own city.

However, although the words '' Greek '' and '' Hellene '' kept this meaning, '' Greece '' quite quickly acquired a geographical denotation that included the countries from which the colonists had swarmed; the southern extremity of the Balkan peninsula, south of a line running from near the Gulf of Volos to that of Ambracia with its ring of islands in the Adriatic (Corfu, Cephallenia, Ithaca, Zacynthus), in the sea to the south (Crete) and in the Aegean (Sporades, Cyclades, Rhodes). Although this area was comparatively small, it was from earliest times divided into a multitude of tiny states, each jealous of its complete independence, which it had to defend constantly against the ambitions of neighbouring cities. The geographical structure of the country has sometimes been held responsible for this extreme political fragmentation. Mountains cover about 80% of its surface; they are the extension to the south-west of the northern branch of the Balkan chain. Although no peak in Greece is

higher than the 9,570 ft of Olympus, the abode of the gods, a number of others approach it: Parnassus 8,062 ft, Taygetus 7,895 ft, Cyllene 7,792 ft. These are the greatest altitudes, but the chain rarely drops below 3,300 ft. The subsidence that accompanied the huge plications of the Tertiary Age only left a few plains between the mountains, which are all very narrow, except for the fairly broad Boeotian plain, but they were sometimes so deep that the sea swept in leaving islands, which are also mountainous. One of these subsidences cut the mainland of Greece in two parts, so that the peninsula of Peloponnesus is only joined to the continent by the Isthmus of Corinth, just 4 miles across. Thus, islands and narrow valleys form natural territorial unities, separated from each other by the sea or rocky barriers that are even more difficult to cross. The few rivers are short, generally torrential, with an irregular flow so that they are unsuitable for navigation and are not sufficient to water the stony soil. Only the lowest slopes and the plains reward the toil of their cultivators. Vines and olives are the only profitable types of cultivation; there is little cereal growing. Goats and sheep are the only livestock that can be bred on the thin soil.

It is not surprising that the Greeks were naturally attracted to more lucrative activities in commerce and that they emigrated, sometimes in large numbers, spreading their language, religion and customs to distant lands *(See* Hellenism; Civilisation). P.D.

GYMNASIUM. The gymnasium (derived from the word *gymnos,* meaning '' naked '', because the Greeks stripped themselves completely for sport) was specially intended, like the palaestra (q.v.), for physical exercise, but its complex of grounds and buildings was larger than the palaestra and it was generally to be found in a place planted with trees outside the city walls. Hydrotherapeutic installations were an essential feature of the gymnasium and the palaestra, which is why gymnasiums were normally planned beside a river or spring *(See* Bathing). The gymnasium at Delphi, where the athletes used to train for the Pythian games, included a circular swimming-pool, 29½ ft. across and about 6½ ft. deep, fountains with basins, a long protico, and a xystus, a sort of covered gallery with a carefully levelled ground for exercising. The three best known

Gynaecaeum. Detail of an epinetron by the Eretria Painter. About 420 B.C. Athens, National Museum.

gymnasiums at Athens were the Academy, the Lyceum and the Cynosarges, all situated a little way from the town. The Athenians used to like taking a walk to the Academy, to the west of the city beyond the suburb of Ceramicus and not far from the deme of Colonus where Sophocles was born. The Academus park was a large sacred wood, which Hipparchus, the son of Pisistratus, enclosed with a wall. Cimon, in the first half of the 5th century B.C., brought water to it, planted new trees and improved the installations of the gymnasium. The Academy was dedicated to Athena and the twelve sacred olive trees of the goddess could be seen there, but Hermes, tutelary god of gymnasiums, and Eros, the god of love, also had altars and statues dedicated to them there. Recent excavations have uncovered the ruins of the palaestra, parts of the surrounding wall and a small temple.

The Academy (q.v.) has given its name to all the " Academies " of the present day, because Plato moved there with his followers in 387 B.C. In fact, as there was no institution of advanced education, at the time of the " sophists ", in other words, of the scholars, rhetoricians and philosophers, the gymnasiums anticipated, in fact, " the cultural centres which our town-planning architects of today are designing to house in one complex everything concerned with the culture of the body and the mind. " (R. Martin). Aristotle taught at the Lyceum, and later the Cynic philosophers met each other at the Cynosarges, a gymna-

sium which seems at first to have been intended for Athenians of mixed blood, born of a citizen and a foreign woman.   R.F.

GYNAECEUM. The Greek woman, at least the woman from the middle and upper classes, lived the life of a recluse. She seldom left her house except for certain family occasions (marriages and funerals), the city religious festivals (at Athens, the festival of the Thesmophoria was actually strictly reserved for women) and for doing personal shopping (clothes and shoes), rarely on visits to friends. On all these occasions, she had to be accompanied at least by one servant. At home, she lived in a special part of the house called the *gynaikon* or the women's apartments. The gynaeceum should not be imagined with a locked door (except at night) and iron bars. It was not physical constraint, but the weight of social custom and public opinion that kept women and especially young girls separated from men and hidden away even from the sight of the men living in the house. When the dwelling comprised several storeys, the gynaeceum was usually to be found on the first floor, not far from the *thalamos,* or the room of the husband and wife, as in 4th century B.C. houses which have been discovered at Olynthus.

The women of the lower classes certainly enjoyed more freedom of movement. There was no room in their small houses for a gynaeceum. Besides, in their circles the wife often had to

Hades and Persephone enthroned in the underworld.
Votive plaque in terra-cotta from Locri.
About 470-450 B.C. Taranto Museum.
Photo Leonard von Matt.

seidon, the son of Cronus and, when power was divided among the three brothers, he was given, under the supreme authority of Zeus, the realm of the dead. He ruled from a subterranean palace, in company with his wife, Persephone, whom he had abducted from Demeter and who lived with him in the underworld for six months in the year. Hades watched over hell jealously; it was against his wishes that a few privileged mortals, like Heracles and Orpheus, tamed or beguiled the monsters such as Cerberus, who were entrusted with guarding its entrance, and penetrated alive into this world of shadows. Hades was a god from whom no one expected the slightest favour. This explains why no temple was ever dedicated to him and his image, a severe looking bearded figure, seldom appeared in art.   P.D.

contribute her share to the household income by selling goods in the market or hiring her services outside her home.   R.F.

HADES. To avoid pronouncing his dreaded name of Hades, he was often called Pluto, meaning the Wealthy One. He was, like Zeus and Po-

HAGHIA TRIADA. To the south of the broad plain of Messara in Crete, some distance from the sea, Haghia Triada was occupied by a small palace or princely villa. Its plan, consisting of two buildings at right angles to each other, simply adapted the usual Minoan layout to the features of the locality. Not far away is a necropolis with a domed tomb. Several of the most

Painted alabaster sarcophagus from Haghia Triada. About 1450-1400 B.C. Heraklion Museum.
Photo Hassia.

Palace and courtyard
at Haghia Triada.
14th century B.C.
Photo Hassia.

interesting paintings of Minoan art were found at Haghia Triada and also the famous alabaster sarcophagus, whose scenes with figures have given rise to so many different interpretations, none of which is beyond dispute.　　　　P.D.

HALICARNASSUS. Halicarnassus did not become the capital of Caria in Asia Minor until the 4th century B.C. Mausolus reigned there and there the Mausoleum, one of the Seven Wonders of the World, was built to receive the body of this prince. *(See* Mausolus).

HARMONIA. The Thebans said that Harmonia was the daughter of Ares and Aphrodite, while, according to a tradition from Samothrace, Zeus and Electra were her parents. She married Cadmus in the presence of all the gods who brought innumerable presents to the young couple. Among these was a necklace that was to be the indirect cause of the expedition of the Seven (q.v.), since Eriphyle betrayed Amphiaraus to obtain possession of it. Besides this mytholo-

gical figure, there was another Harmonia, who had no connexion, at least in the beginning, with the first and who personified the quality still denoted by her name today.　　　　P.D.

HARPIES. The Harpies were divinities, originating in the east, with the body of a bird and the head of a woman, who abducted souls. Their place in Greek mythology was unimportant. They were rather like evil spirits, whose ill-nature produced unpleasant and vexatious stituations. An example is their persecution of the wretched king, Phineus, whose food they stole or fouled whenever it was placed before him.　　　　P.D.

HEAD-DRESS. Before the Persian Wars, Athenian men paid as much attention to their head-dress as women and Thucydides has told us that they would " fasten their tufts of hair *(krobylos)* with golden pins ". The so-called Rampin Horseman in the Louvre has an elaborately curled hair style with tresses falling symmetrically behind each ear. But in later times, just before Greek youths reached the age of ephebi, they would cut

Head of an ephebe with his hair held up with a cord. Detail of a kouros. About 490 B.C. Agrigento Museum. *Photo Leonard von Matt.*

their hair and consecrate it to the gods. Only the more elegant members of the knightly class imitated the Spartans by wearing their hair long, for most Athenians in the classical period were close-cropped as we may see from the figures of the magistrates in the frieze of the Panathenaea. Athenian women remained faithful to the complicated hair styles of the korai of the Acropolis in earlier times. They also made use of the *kekryphalos*, a kind of very fetching net or scarf, which gathered the hair up from the forehead and nape and piled it on top of the head. They often wore their hair in serried ranks of curls above and behind the head. Men went barehead in the streets of the city and only wore hats in the country where they wore the *kyne*, the *pilos* or the *petasos*. The kyne (literally, dog-skin) was a leather bonnet which was mostly worn by slaves and the common people such as peasants, shepherds, craftsmen, sailors and boatmen. The pilos was more elegant; it was a high, pointed conical hat which might have a peak to protect the eyes from the sun and, although it was usually felt, it was sometimes made of leather or even metal. The *pilidion* (the name is a diminutive of pilos) was somewhat different; it was a simple felt or linen cap and in its shape and use it resembled the kyne. The most popular head-dress for travellers was the *petasos* which was a large and very wide-brimmed, low-crowned felt or straw hat with a lace so that it could be thrown back over the wearer's shoulders. It had to be tied to the head since it could be easily blown away by the wind, but it gave better protection against the sun and the rain than the pilos and kyne. Women covered their heads with a fold of their gown or mantle which they arranged as a hood. They also wore the kekryphalos (see above) which was not a hat, strictly speaking, and the *tholia*, a round, wide-brimmed hat with a peaked centre. Many Tanagra figurines have been found showing elegant women wearing a tholia.

Greek combs have been discovered such as the double comb in olive wood found in the agora of Athens, with its thirty-one fine teeth on one side, and twenty thick teeth on the other, and its spine

Feminine hair style. Detail of a statue of a kore. About 510-500 B.C. Athens, Acropolis Museum. *Photo Hassia.*

Young woman with her hair in a kekryphalos and wearing a diadem. Detail of a hydria by Meidias. About 410 B.C. Karlsruhe Landesmuseum.

decorated with ovolo and lance-head patterns. Other combs have been found made in bone, ivory, shell or bronze and some are so beautifully decorated that they are works of art in themselves. Hair was often tinted, blonde being the most popular shade. Artificial plaits and wigs were also worn.   R.F.

HECATAEUS. He was a historian and geographer, born about 540 B.C. at Miletus. His claims as a historian are questionable because, although his *Genealogies* are written in prose, they are like a mythological poem and contain the legends of Deucalion, Hellen and his sons, Heracles, the Heraclidae, and the foreign heroes, Aegyptus, Cadmus, Danaos. He does try to distinguish truth from fiction in these legendary traditions, since he begins his work: " I write about these things in so far as they appear true to me, because the Greek narratives are varied and, in my opinion, ridiculous." As a geographer, Hecataeus is the great precursor of Herodotus. His *Voyage round the Earth* comprises two books, the first called *Europe,* and the second *Asia,* but he also discusses Libya in Africa, which was then considered part of Asia. The first " universal geography ", accompanied by a map, was based on the extensive travels of the author and, like the descriptions of Herodotus, on information picked up here and there and incorporated without much critical sense. We only possess a few fragments of his work. Herodotus criticised and made fun of him, but he often borrowed from him without reference to his source. For example, the perceptive remark, " Egypt is a gift of the Nile ", was copied from Hecataeus by Herodotus, who was careful not to acknowledge his debt.
                                              R.F.

HECATE. She was an ancient goddess who was already known in 7th century Greece. She was closely connected with Artemis, but in the beginning at least her powers were more extensive. In the 5th century, she was venerated specially by women, then she became the tutelary goddess of the dead, not with the same rights as

Young boy wearing a petasos on his head. Young woman wearing a tholia on hers. Details of terra-cotta statuettes from Tanagra. Paris, Louvre. *Photo Tel.*

Priam begging Achilles to return him the body of his son Hector. Attic skyphos by the Brygos Painter. First quarter of the 5th century B.C. Vienna, Kunsthistorisches Museum.

Persephone, but as the power who presided over spells and the appearance of spirits; it was her name that magicians invoked. She was visualised as a figure holding torches in her hands, accompanied by dogs and wolves, and her powers were particularly formidable at night by the murky light of the moon with whom she was identified. She was frequently represented as a woman with three bodies, or three women standing beside each other with their backs to a column. She was often worshipped at cross-roads where her image used to be placed. P.D.

HECTOR. When the Greeks attacked Troy to win back Helen, the most courageous and intelligent of their opponents was Hector. His father, King Priam, entrusted the defence of the country to him and it was he who enjoyed the confidence of his people. He was the most likeable and human of the heroes in the Trojan camp. As such, he plays the principal role in the *Iliad* and Homer gives a sympathetic account of how, before going into battle, he lingered affectionately with his wife, Andromache, and his little son, Astyanax. His mother, Hecuba, mourned more for him, when he fell before Achilles, than for any of her own children. His biggest fight was in

fact against Achilles, after he had killed Patroclus, whom Achilles loved most dearly and was bent on revenging. He left his tent and the two heroes faced each other, but the gods had doomed Hector and Achilles triumphed. Seven times round the city, he dragged the body of his vanquished foe in the dust behind his chariot and he refused to give it to Priam for its splendid funeral, until the old king had humbly gone to him, laden with presents, to entreat the proud victor. P.D.

HECUBA. Like many other figures from Greek mythology, it is through the tragic poets, Euripides in particular, that Hecuba becomes more than a name to us, Priam's wife and the mother of numerous sons among whom Hector is the most famous. She was no more than a mother until the 5th century B.C., when tragic drama made her into the image of desolation, the embodiment of the worst misfortunes that can befall a woman, when she watched the collapse of her husband's kingdom, the death of Priam and nearly all her children. To crown her miseries, she was allotted to Ulysses as his captive, but before they could leave, she tore out the eyes of Polymestor who had killed one of her children, and was stoned by the Greeks. P.D.

HELEN. The ancients themselves did not know how to judge the woman who had represented perfect beauty on earth. Modern scholars see in her the Hellenised figure of a very ancient vegetation goddess and they may be right, but the Greeks had long forgotten her origins when they told her story. Helen was the daughter of Leda and Zeus, who to fulfill his desires changed himself into a swan. Four twins were born from this union, each pair enclosed in an egg, Castor and Pollux, Clytemnestra and Helen. The episode took place in Sparta, whose protectors the Dioscuri remained and where Helen became queen. She was hardly seven years old when she was first carried off by Theseus. She was brought back to Sparta by her brothers and soon afterwards Tyndareos, Leda's husband and the putative father of Helen, decided to arrange her marriage. The suitors were so numerous that Tyndareos, prudently planning for the future, made them swear to accept Helen's decision and come to the help of her chosen husband if some day she proved unfaithful to him. The happy man was Menelaus and the day foreseen by Tyndareos came when Paris, a young Trojan prince, landed on the shores of Sparta. He left with the young woman—and also with Menelaus's treasures—

and returned to the palace of his father, Priam, where Helen remained of her own free will for more than ten years.

As soon as he realised his misfortune, Menelaus invoked the oath sworn by all the suitors and, led by his brother, Agamemnon, the Greeks sailed to beseige Troy. From the other side of the wall, Helen watched the army that was fighting to win her back, recognised Ulysses when he slipped into the city on a secret mission, complacently accepted the admiration of the old men of Troy whose sons were dying to save her for Paris and, when Troy fell, in the midst of the massacre, coquettishly bared her breast to disarm the infuriated Menelaus, who was rushing on her with drawn sword to punish her. She returned to Sparta with her rightful husband, received Telemachus like a great lady when he was travelling over Greece in search of his father and practised every domestic virtue.

Was Helen the docile and innocent instrument of Aphrodite, who gave her to Paris as a reward for his judgment delivered in the beauty competition on Mount Ida? Or did she represent feminine infidelity, and was she the conscious cause of all the evils suffered by the Greeks and Trojans? Although the Homeric poems saw her as the tool of

Two Muses on Mount Helicon. Detail of a calyx krater by the Clio Painter. About 440 B.C. Vatican Museum. *Ph. Hirmer.*

destiny, Hesiod was already much more severe and Euripides, except for one play, condemned her outright. Philosophers and rhetoricians discussed her case and she has always been, right up to modern times, one of the most enigmatic and attractive figures ever created by the human imagination.   P.D.

HELENUS. Helenus was one of Priam's sons and the twin brother of Cassandra. Like her, he had the gift of prophecy. According to one tradition, Neoptolemus took him after the fall of Troy to Epirus, where at the end of his life he married Andromache.

HELIAEA. This was a popularly constituted juridical body in Athens, which dealt with all cases except " blood trials ", in other words, murder. *(See* Justice).

HELICON. This mountain in Boeotia is famous because it was believed to be the home of

the Muses and its name is inscribed, on a vase, beside a rock where a Muse is seated. Ascra, Hesiod's native city, was nearby and the fountain of Hippocrene, supposed to be the source of inspiration to poets, sprang from its slopes.
                                    P.D.

HELIODORUS. A Greek writer of fiction who probably lived in the 3rd century B.C. He was the author of the *Aethiopica, or the Adventures of Theagenes and Charicleia. (See* Romances).

HELIOS. Helios was not an Olympian divinity, he belonged to the race of the Titans. He was the Sun who travelled over the sky from India to the Atlantic Ocean, in a chariot drawn by four horses. Then he returned inside a large bowl to the point where he would rise again the next morning. From the 5th century B.C., artists quite often represented him as a vigorous, young man, with a beardless face and his head crowned with sunbeams, standing in his chariot and holding the reins of his impetuous team.   P.D.

Helios in his chariot. Detail of a lekythos.
6th century B.C. New York, Metropolitan Museum of Art.

HELLENISM. Divided into a multitude of states, which lay in greater or less concentration all round the Mediterranean and the Black Sea, the Greek world never enjoyed political unity, but possessed a unity of cultural ideals that constituted Hellenism, which distinguished Greeks from non-Greeks (Barbarians) and gave a spiritual coherence to brothers who were only too often enemies. Hellenism at first meant a common language for the ancients. The decipherment of a writing called Linear B (q.v.) showed that an archaic form of this language was used by the Mycenaeans at least five hundred years before Homer. In spite of dialectal differences, which literary usage lessened, everyone understood this language, while the barbarian tongues seemed like the " cheeping of birds ". The common ideal, which is implicit in everything we know about the Greeks, was more important than a common language. This Ideal was founded on the certainty that man is the measure of all things and that nothing is more beautiful than his body, more subtle than his mind or more skilful than his hands. After the gods whom they had fashioned in their own image, the Greeks thought themselves the perfect reflection of this purely human ideal and, although they sometimes paid homage to the wisdom of other peoples, they were more or less consciously penetrated with racial pride.

Ideas like these gave their religion, like their forms of government, a special stamp. Whether they came from Minoan Crete or the east, or were brought at the end of the Bronze Age by the northern invaders who settled in the south of the peninsula, their divinities became naturalised Greeks by being stripped of any characteristics that could distinguish them from human beings. They only differed from our species in their power and in the fact—there were exceptions even to this—that they were not subject to the attacks of time. Apart from this, like the ordinary mortals they resembled physically, they suffered pain, were victims of often violent passions and were plagued by anxieties, sometimes petty enough, of jealousy and precedence. Bestial and monstrous deities worshipped by other peoples were known to primitive Greece, but they were very soon expelled from the Hellenic pantheon, leaving behind only vestigial legends and a few practices of their cult, which were no longer understood by the faithful in the classical era. The Greek gods could be cruel, as we can ourselves, yet they were friendly, guided by logic and accessible to our reasoning. They ruled over free men, demanded the honours and submission that were theirs by right, but they would certainly not have accepted without contempt the fetishistic adoration with which the barbarian peoples surrounded their inhuman idols.

There was the same respect for human dignity in the political sphere. Whatever their form of government—and while preferring democracy, they also experienced dictatorship—the Greeks never considered the custodians of power as the representatives of heaven on earth; Alexander came to realise this when he demanded that they should prostrate themselves before him as before a Persian king. The gratitude of the citizens was offered especially to men like Harmodius and Aristogiton (qq.v.) who had tried to deliver their country from tyranny.

Other features could be mentioned that contributed to the idea of Hellenism, but they are all inherent in the feeling, so rare in ancient civilisations, for the excellence and beauty of human nature and the dignity of the individual. This ideal, at least as old as the Homeric poems (Thersites had the courage to face a beating rather than give up the right to criticise his chiefs), found its perfect expression in the periodic festivals at a panhellenic sanctuary like Olympia or Delphi, when Greeks, scattered all over the ancient world, gathered together. As they worshipped a god stronger and more beautiful than the finest of men, as they admired the performances of athletes who had developed the human body to its highest point, and as they listened to poets and musicians who displayed the resources of the human spirit, it was then that Greeks from all parts checked their ephemeral antagonisms and felt in their blood that they belonged to one and the same race, the race that sprang from their common ancestor, Hellen.

P.D.

HELLENISTIC. The conquests of Alexander and the expansion of the Greek world brought such changes in the way of life and thought of the Greeks that historians make 323 B.C., the year Alexander died, the beginning of a new era, which they call Hellenistic. The Mediterranean world certainly took on a new appearance from that point. The autonomy of the cities was no more than a memory; they were free to run their internal affairs as they wished, on condition that

their governments were loyal to the directives of the central authority; and they were ruled by governors, who decided in the name of the king the policy they should follow and who imposed his authority with the help of a garrison whenever it was necessary. Even the leagues that were made and unmade only existed and acted within the limits imposed by the central authority.

When we turn towards the world of ideas and their expression, the break with the past seems less than in the political sphere. Hellenistic art and literature are only the development of tendencies noticeable in the 4th century B.C. before the death of Alexander and there was nothing new about the penetration of Greek culture into Asia and Egypt or of foreign ideas into Greece. The presence of sovereigns of Hellenic origin in Alexandria, Pergamum and elsewhere only hastened a movement that had begun some time before and the prosperity of a middle class, who became important patrons of artists and writers, did not date from the establishment of the new kingdoms. Even if they had not lost their independence, the Greek cities had long before impoverished themselves too much to be able to give big commissions as they had once done in the time of Phidias and his team of assistants. Had the public bodies possessed the means to finance large enterprises, they would have clashed with the ambitions of private persons who, at

Hephaestus returning to Olympus. Detail of a hydria from Caere. About 530 B.C. Vienna, Kunsthistorisches Museum.

Hera. Inside of a white-ground Attic cup. Mid-5th century B.C. Munich, Antikensammlung.

least from the end of the 5th century B.C., thought more of their own interests than the glory of their country,

Did new tastes appear in the Hellenistic era? The inescapable conclusion to be drawn from the mass of records that have survived is that academicism was the dominant characteristic and that works like the reliefs decorating the altar at Pergamum are exceptional. In fact, the word "Hellenistic" is only useful as a chronological term when it is applied to anything other than historical events. Its value is relative even then because, although the end of the 4th century B.C. marked the beginning of this period, it is difficult to decide whether it ended with the Roman conquest or the end of paganism itself. The 3rd or even 4th century A.D. seems a preferable date to mark its termination, because in the eastern Mediterranean the Romans only substituted their rule for that of the local potentates, and only gradually at that.   P.D.

HEPHAESTUS. Like Ares, he was the son of Zeus and Hera. Although he was more

popular among the Greeks than his brother, he was in many ways a less happy person. He was lame; according to some, Zeus hurled him from the heights of Olympus because he was furious that he had taken Hera's part in a quarrel with her husband; others say that it was because he was born a weakling and his mother threw him far from her. He married the most beautiful of the goddesses, Aphrodite, but she deceived him with Ares. He was the god of fire; manual labourers were under his patronage and he himself was a blacksmith who passed his time working hard in the heat and dirt at his anvil. On the other hand, while Ares was an evil-minded god who was only happy in the midst of a battle, Hephaestus was well intentioned. As the master of fire, he taught men the crafts and, beneath his rather wretched appearance, he is one of those spirits to whom humanity has most readily expressed its gratitude.   P.D.

HERA. Her marriage to Zeus made her the most eminent of the Greek goddesses. It is quite probable that she inherited many of the functions of the Cretan goddess who ruled over all living beings and watched over vegetable life. Hera's functions were very soon whittled away and only a few rites and local names were reminders of the ancient divinity whom she had partly replaced. In Homer and in later texts and inscriptions on buildings, she was considered primarily as the patron goddess of marriage and the guardian of marital fidelity. Her own union with Zeus, however, had its stormy passages and she found it difficult to tolerate the innumerable escapades of her husband; she pursued with tenacious hatred all the women whom Zeus chose for his mistresses (Io, Leto and many others) and she vented her spite too on the children of his illicit amours; her persecution of Heracles was notable. She herself only had four children and none of them figured among the most important divinities: Ares, Hephaestus, Hebe, who was rather like a servant in Olympian society, and Ilythia, whose function was to help women in labour. One of the most important episodes in Hera's life happened in the Troad. There, Paris was asked to judge who was the most beautiful of three goddesses. Furious at her rejection, Hera unleashed her anger on the Trojans and took sides with the Greeks in the Trojan War.

P.D.

HERACLES. The huge, enervated, bloated man, propped on his club, of the Farnese Hercules is only too well known, but conveys no idea, not even a caricature, of what Heracles meant to the Greeks, the one hero whom they all, Ionians and Dorians alike, unstintingly admired. They did not all have the same conception of him, but he embodied for all of them the ideal of virile strength, courage and tenacity. For a long time he was —and for many he remains—the muscular athlete who, like the tough guy in westerns, without any apparent effort, without the flicker of an eye or the mussing of his hair, strangles the lion with its gaping muzzle, whips off the heads from the hydra's tentacles or cheerfully carries away the enormous boar, which he has captured alive. This remote and impassive athlete was often transformed into a good-natured but truculent giant, who demonstrated his vitality with a boundless and comic naïveté; he was a gross eater, a girl chaser, and attacked his enemies with the same ease, but with more passion—a Rabelaisian gusto, it has been called—than his other self did; abandoning his usual club, he brandished and twirled his enemies' bodies in space and used them to knock out the perfidious Busiris. Whether he was carried away by righteous indignation, or was master of himself, during the whole of the

The young Heracles, who was a bad pupil, beating his music master, Linus. Cup by Douris. About 490-480 B.C. Munich, Antikensammlung. *Photo Hirmer.*

Heracles strangling
the Nemean Lion,
Detail of an amphora
by Psiax 520 B.C.
Brescia Museum.
Photo Hirmer.

archaic period, he remained the incarnation of physical power, a power that hurled itself unhesitatingly, automatically, almost blindly against monsters and all the evils menacing mankind, which destiny brought his way.

Then when Greek thought became more mature, Heracles too began to think; on a metope sculptured on the temple at Olympia about 460 B.C., he appears chin on hand after his first victory, as if he were worried about the remaining tasks. His consciousness of their danger and his physical weariness gave an added merit to his challenge; each labour became for this new Heracles both a victory over himself and over his adversaries. As a consequence, the significance of the final episode in his legend underwent change. In its earliest version, the gods had considered him worthy to take a place in their assembly; then at the end of a career interwoven with athletic, military and hunting exploits, Heracles was admitted to Olympus where in addition—the finest recompense offered by a celestial jury—he received the hand of the young Hebe. From the middle of the 5th century B.C., the immortality of the hero was less a consequence of his sporting feats than of the moral courage he had shown in never refusing, whatever the cost, the battles that the salvation of mankind required of him. At one time, the gods were represented joyfully welcoming him as one of their number; now the golden apples in the Garden of the Hesperides are used as a more

subtle symbolism of immortality; the Olympian assembly disappears and it is when he receives the fruits, which he had gone so far to seek, and is seated at last in peace in the shade of the marvellous tree that Heracles triumphant becomes a peer of the gods whom death cannot touch. Once this supreme reward was no longer the prize of physical energy and matchless exploits but of a sustained effort towards moral perfection, Heracles ceased to be a purely fabulous figure and became a valuable example to simple human beings; he became a model that they should strive to imitate as well as a proof that their sufferings courageously borne would win them immortality.

After the 4th century B.C., the emphasis was laid on the sufferings and the apotheosis which was their reward. Nothing came easily to the hero, as in an earlier form of the legend. Euripides and Sophocles made him a greater figure by stressing his weakness and failures; they showed his bloodthirsty madness when, blinded by fate, he slaughtered his children, and his agonising death in the burning tunic. Theocritus described his childhood, and the tale of how love made him Omphale's slave was a favourite. Finally, during the decline of Hellenism, the day came when Glycon, the sculptor of the Farnese statue, distorted a masterpiece by Lysippus and only saw in Heracles a disillusioned old man, drained of all physical and moral strength.

These transformations of Heracles' personality

can be followed more clearly in the visual arts than in writings. Everywhere, sculptors and painters —vase painters particularly —reflected the contemporary idea of the most popular hero of all, either for edifying and religious purposes or to satisfy an inexhaustible public demand. Sometimes he appeared beardless and radiant with eternal youth, more often as a man of almost mature age, but always strong and lithe, with his face framed in a carefully combed beard and his head and body covered with the skin of the lion, his first victim. The choice of episodes and the style of presentation indicate the aspects of Heracles that were particularly appealing to different periods and it is worth noting that the earliest presentation in the 8th century, rarely depicted afterwards, was his fight with the sons of Molione, two twins who formed a single monstrous creature. By comparison, the most complete and detailed texts belong to the Roman period and only give us a stereotyped version of the legend in which poets, writers or compilers had done their best to give a coherent account of it.

Heracles' popularity attracted all sorts of narratives and episodes from different sources, which were more or less satisfactorily fitted together. Gilgamesh, the oriental god and monster-killer, can be detected behind his legend; the reason why the ancients made Boeotia the birthplace of Gilgamesh and recounted how he served an Argive prince, like him a descendant of Peloponnesian Perseus, and travelled all over the world,

was that each province had its local Heracles, whose own adventures survived and were gathered into the biography of the hero all Greece venerated.

His story is well known. Alcmene in all innocence deceived her husband, Amphitryon the king of Thebes, whose appearance Zeus assumed, and Heracles was born of this divine union. Hera, struck by a jealousy that did not lessen with time, sent two snakes when he was still a baby to kill the son whom her husband had from another, but while his half-brother, Iphicles born of Amphitryon, screamed with terror, Heracles strangled the two creatures. This episode appealed to the Hellenistic period and Theocritus described it, but it seems to have attracted as little attention before the beginning of the 5th century B.C. as the education of the hero, who was a deplorable pupil of the musician, Linus, and ended by braining him with a stool, when he could bear his lessons no longer. Until about 475, no other Heraclean theme rivalled his exploits and victories of all kinds as a subject for reliefs and vase painting, and these exploits continued to appear frequently but not exclusively.

The ancients were not agreed on the reasons why for a certain time Heracles had to obey the orders of his cousin, Eurystheus, king of Argolis, a contemptible figure who imposed twelve '' labours '' on him; he had to overcome the Nemean lion without using a sword, cut off the innumerable and renascent heads of the hydra of Lerna,

Heracles fighting with the river-god Achelous in the presence of Deianira. Detail of an Attic krater. Mid-5th century B.C. Paris Louvre.

Heracles, helmeted with the Nemean Lion skin, drawing his bow. Fragment from the east pediment of the Temple of Aphaea at Aegina. Early 5th century B.C. Munich, Glyptothek. *Photo L. von Matt.*

capture alive the boar of Erymanthus and the sacred, indefatigable hind of Mount Ceryneia, shoot down with his arrows the cloud of birds on Lake Stymphalus, clean in one day the stables of Augeas, king of Elis (he diverted the river Alpheus through the stables), master the wild bull that was ravaging Crete and the man-eating mares of Diomedes, wage war against the Amazons and win possession of the girdle of their queen, Hippolyte, fight against the triple-bodied monster, Geryon, and take away his cattle, bring back the dog, Cerberus, from Hades where he guarded the kingdom of the dead, and finally—as has already been said—he had to search to the ends of the earth, beyond the Pillars of Hercules, that is, the Straits of Gibraltar, for the golden apples guarded by the Hesperides. Some of these feats were only rarely depicted, either because they did not lend themselves to visual presentation, or more often because they were less popular with the public. Others, on the other hand, were un-wearyingly repeated, like his victory over the lion, or his return carrying the boar alive on his shoulders when, not knowing where to put it, he is about to throw it into the jar where the terrified Eurystheus has just taken refuge.

Besides the series of Twelve Labours and several episodic adventures, which always remained rather shadowy, there were others that hardly appear in written form but were evidently extremely popular from their frequent visual representation. One day, Heracles was furious because the Pythian oracle refused to give him an answer and he tried to carry off the " sacred tripod ", which Apollo had to wrench out of his hands by force. We should never have suspected the importance of this " dispute " for the hero's legend if innumerable vases, until the beginning of the 5th century, and the sculptured pediment of the Treasury, consecrated by the Siphnians at Delphi about 525, had not given it such prominence. The same applies to the story of Deianira. Sophocles' *Trachiniae* leaves little doubt about the popularity of the two episodes featured in this play, which were frequently depicted by painters: the hero's fight with the river god, Achelous, to win the hand of Deianira from him, and the murder of Nessus, the Centaur who carried the young woman over a river as a ferryman and tried to rape her. They were scenes of violence that appealed to the youthful spirit of archaic Greece and lent themselves more readily to figurative art than to psychological analysis. As soon as the emphasis began to be laid on the feelings of Heracles, literature took the lead over sculpture and painting, which had lost its popular character as soon as ceramic imagery ceased to exist. The madness of the hero slaughtering his children and his sufferings on the pyre he had built himself to put an end to his miseries are more powerfully conveyed by the writings of Euripides and Sophocles than by pictorial means that were incapable of communicating his agonies and passion. The pictures of Heracles enslaved by Omphale were only illustrations to poetical works composed in praise of Love. Side by side with this precious and tormented Heracles described by the literature intended for an intelligent and sophisticated public, there survived to the end of Hellenism the old popular figure of the hero, the Heracles « of splendid victories » whom humble folk invoked, with almost magical intentions, as their natural protector in countless situations and the bringer of good luck. P.D.

HERACLIDES PONTICUS. He was one of Plato's pupils, who took his place at the head of the Academy during Plato's last voyage to Sicily. He was upset at being refused this post at the death of Speusippus in 339 and retired to his birthplace, Heraclea, on the Pontus Euxinus. Only fragments of his various writings have survived and these show traces of a fanciful irony reminiscent of some of his master's myths. As a psychologist, he tried to defend the Platonic conception of an independent soul against the materialists of the day, by using arguments drawn from psychopathological experience. As an astronomer, he put into the mouth of Hicetas, a character in one of his dialogues, a theory of heliocentricity that was mentioned by Cicero and influenced Copernicus, as he indicated himself in the beginning of his treatise, *De revolutionibus orbium caelestium.* P.-M.S.

HERACLITUS. Heraclitus was born at Ephesus in the second half of the 6th century B.C. He belonged to a distinguished noble family and could have had an important political career if his contempt for democracy had not made him prefer solitary meditation. The Ephesians had expelled Hermodorus, his friend and one of the best of them by alleging: " We do not want anyone better than ourselves and if such exists, he must take his superiority elsewhere for the benefit of others. " Arrogance, enthusiasm, irony and pessimism mark with equal felicity his prose aphorisms, which are the surviving fragments of a work called *On Nature.* He disdained futile erudition and based his philosophical enquiries on speculative intuition. He saw war as the origin of all things. " Conflict is the father of all and king of all. He made some beings gods and others men; some slaves and others free men... Homer was wrong to hope that war would disappear from among gods and men. He did not realise that he was praying for the destruction of the universe because, if his prayer had been answered, everything would have disappeared. " This necessary conflict between opposites is also, for Heraclitus, a harmony, because the opposing forces are limited and united by each other's action, like those that keep the string of a bow taut. Similarly, in the sequence of day and night, summer and winter, life and death, an equilibrium arises through the adjustment of forces. Consequently, it is possible to conceive, beyond this existence, a unity of all things, an eternal principle and a force that is ceaselessly active. No element can represent this force better than fire. " This world, " wrote Heraclitus, " is the same for all beings; neither gods nor men have created it; it always has been, it is and it always will be a living fire, burning in the same proportion as it dies... All things are changed into fire and fire into everything, just as merchandise is exchanged for gold and gold for merchandise. " This " eternally living " fire is also the symbol of continual movement and the perpetual flow of things. Everything flows on and is in flight, nothing remains; in the same river, fresh waters always bathe you. This led Heraclitus to an ascetic morality (it is bad for man to get all he wants); to a purified religion, hostile to " pedlars of mysteries " and to those who thought they were purifying themselves " by staining themselves with blood, just like a man splashed with mud who washes his feet in mud; to an ironical vision of a universe of contrasts that is incomprehensible to the common herd (filth is more precious to pigs than limpid water, and to a donkey straw is superior to gold; sea-water is the purest and the most impure, life-giving to fish but lethal to man, etc.). Heraclitus was the first to formulate with such clarity the opposition of contraries and the law of becoming that governs those contraries, whether they are simultaneous or successive. He also anticipated, more than

Herm in the Agora of
the Italians at Delos.
2nd century B.C.
Ph. Doudot-Lamotte.

any other philosopher of classical times, the ideas
of Hegel and even Marxist dialectic, which is not
without its touch of Heraclitean irony.   P.B.

HERMAE. These were a kind of boundary
stone of extremely ancient origin. The quadrangular shaft ended in a human head, from the
middle a male sexual organ projected prominently
and, above on either side, two stumps formed
rudimentary arms. The top of the pillar curved
in to indicate a bust and the head, which surmounted it, was originally a bearded god, Zeus,
Hermes or Dionysus. These simplified images
were placed for the sake of their protective powers
in public places, particularly cross-roads, and
were the object of certain rites, rather as today in
Greece passers-by cross themselves in front of
icons enclosed in boundary-posts at the corner
of roads. It was hermae like these, right in the
middle of Athens, which some impious young
men, led perhaps by Alcibiades, amused themselves by mutilating on the eve of the expedition
to Sicily. During the 4th century B.C., particu-

larly in the gymnasiums, hermae were sculptured
in the likeness of the hero or eminent person
whose patronage would benefit the ephebi.
Several portraits of philosophers have come
down to us in this form.   P.D.

HERMES. Hermes was far from being one
of the most important gods of Olympus, but he
was one of the most picturesque figures of the
divine family. When he grew up, his functions
were minor: messenger, guide of souls to Hades
(he was called Psychopompus in this capacity),
guide of travellers, patron of traders and also
thieves; but his childhood on the other hand was
eventful. His parents were Zeus and Maia and, as
soon as he was born, he escaped from his cradle,
went as far as Thessaly and stole the cattle of
his brother, Apollo. He pulled them backwards
by their tails, so that their hoof marks pointed
in the opposite direction from the cave where
he hid them. Then he returned to his mother's
house and pretended to sleep while Apollo and
Zeus went to complain to Maia. On this expedi-

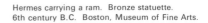
Hermes carrying a ram. Bronze statuette.
6th century B.C. Boston, Museum of Fine Arts.

HERMOGENES. He was a 3rd century B.C. architect, probably born in Priene where the urban landscape was dominated by the temple of Athena built by Pytheus. Hermogenes gave final expression to Hellenistic architecture before it was integrated into the new movement that flourished in the Roman period. This expression took a practical and theoretic form since, like his predecessors, he wrote a commentary on the buildings that he designed. The writings have disappeared, but the buildings remain: the temple and altar of Artemis at Magnesia ad Maeandrum and the temple of Dionysus at Teos, both of the Ionic order. In these two temples, he used principles of proportion that are very different from those of the classical era. The module was the width of the intercolumniation, a curious innovation that based the new system of proportions on a void, but it was also a new conception of the organisation of space and of architectural aesthetic in which structures became lighter and more airy, and greater prominence was given to planning space. While the architectural mass was set as a unified volume, the purpose of the architectural elements was to define and free the various parts of it.   R.M.

HERODOTUS. The historian and geographer, Herodotus (about 485-425 B.C.), was an Asian Greek born at Halicarnassus. His family, which was wealthy and respected, was hostile to the government of Lygdamis, a tyrant and the vassal of the king of Persia, who was the master of Halicarnassus. This is why Herodotus spent part of his youth in exile in Samos. He returned to his country with others who were banished, and drove out the tyrant. Then he began his great travels, which took him notably to Egypt and Cyrene, Syria and Babylon, Colchis, Olbia, Paeonia and Macedonia. He stayed for long periods at Athens, where he gave public readings of some parts of his works. In 443, he took part in the colonisation of Thurii, the new Sybaris, a panhellenic enterprise begun by Pericles and directed from Athens. So, after travelling all over the east, as a citizen of Thurii he was able to explore the west.

The subject of Herodotus's *Histories* is the clash of Greeks and Barbarians in the Persian Wars, but the account does not begin till Book VI,

tion, Hermes found a tortoise and, after emptying the shell, he strung it with cords made from the guts of the cattle. It was the first lyre, which Apollo took to accompany the Muses' dancing. Hermes also invented the flute and he gave other proofs as well of his ingenuity. He was represented as a lively, young god, shod with winged sandals to speed him on his way. In his hand, he held the caduceus, a sort of magic wand, wound round with two intertwining snakes, which Apollo gave him.   P.D.

HERMIONE. Hermione was not, for the Greeks, the trenchant personality whom Racine immortalised in *Andromaque*. She was the daughter of Helen and Menelaus. Her father betrothed her first to Orestes, but eventually gave her to Neoptolemus, the son of Achilles. The ancient Greeks never made her into the enamoured and fiercely jealous woman that she has become for us.   P.D.

while the whole work is divided, rather arbitrarily, into nine books each bearing the name of a Muse. As Herodotus wanted to begin by explaining the causes of the Persian Wars, of which Persian imperialism was the main one, he filled the first five books with an account of the rise of the Persian king's empire. At the same time, he took the opportunity to describe the different parts of the empire and the customs of their inhabitants, because Herodotus, like Hecataeus (q.v.) did not separate geography from history. He gave his opinion on the shape of the earth, the oceans and the vineyards of the Nile, but he was even more interested in human geography than in physical geography. Book II is entirely taken up with Egypt, its ancient buildings, its history and particularly the way of life and customs of the Egyptians. The development of the science of Egyptology since Champollion has enabled us to check the reliability of much of this and the results have generally been favourable to Herodotus. In fact, he honestly tried to find the truth. Admittedly, he lacked a critical spirit; he pours out indiscriminately all the information and tales he has been told on all sides and his informants were not always well informed themselves. Sometimes, he may cast doubt on some point or other and leave the reader to make up his own mind. In recounting events, Herodotus has all the qualities of a fluent and skilful narrator. His account is always clear and easy to follow in spite of countless digressions and he is clever at holding the reader's interest. His language is literary Ionian and still retains several characteristics of Homer's dialect. The elements of his slow, limpid sentences are co-ordinated rather than subordinated. He is credulous specially on the subject of oracles and those of Delphi in particular. Like Pindar and Aeschylus, he believes in Nemesis, that divine jealousy, which he sees as a cosmic power that engineers the fall of empires. This is the meaning of the famous stories of the tyrant Polycrates, Croesus and Xerxes.

The Greeks' love of freedom and their political ideals are clearly discussed by Herodotus, yet he can hardly be accused of partiality. This Greek from Asia Minor was better able to write about the Persians in an unbiased way than any Athenian or Spartan; Plutarch even accused him of being the " friend of the Barbarians " in his *Histories*. Actually, the strict investigations of historical research were alien to him and were not established and applied until Thucydides.

Nevertheless, this marvellous story-teller can still enchant us and, although he has not all the qualities that we expect today from the genuine historian, it is only fair to recognise that he possesses several of the indispensable ones: curiosity, a passionate enquiry into the truth, impartiality, clarity and narrative charm.   R.F.

H E R O E S . Homer refers to anyone as a " hero " who is more distinguished than the others; the bard, Demodocus, as much as Achilles, or even a group like the Danai. This is fairly close to the meaning of the word today, but it was not the most usual one among the Greeks. For them, the hero was, in the first place, the son of a mortal and a divinity, who was essentially superior to ordinary men; Theseus, Bellerophon, Perseus and others, for example, were able because of their exceptional natures to accomplish feats that were out of the ordinary. The most celebrated of them, Heracles, was admitted to Olympus after his death and, although the others were not honoured in this way, they at least seem to have enjoyed a privileged existence in the after-life. They were all venerated and offered sacrifices by the living, who hoped for their good will and favours in return. They gave their help in critical situations, just as Heracles and Theseus joined the battle of Marathon in person. Their legends originated at least as far back as the Mycenaean period and their cult remained alive as a part of popular devotion, some, like Heracles, being worshipped throughout the Greek world, others only in the region where they had been active.

The influence of a new civic consciousness and a new morality added other and more humble heroes to what may be termed this first generation. It was assumed that men to whom the state had reason to be particularly grateful, would exercise a beneficent influence over it even after their death; the founders of colonies, and men like Harmodius and Aristogiton, who had given new life to the city, were in their turn considered heroes, although they were born of mortals, and the citizens, individually or as a community, invoked their protection and paid them homage. These rites, which were called heroic to distinguish them from the worship offered to the gods, were essentially funerary with a different ritual from those demanded by the celestial powers who had never known death. They were generally performed on the *heroön*, which was regarded as the tomb of the man who was being honoured.

In the 5th and 4th century B.C. the title of hero was attributed more freely and *heroa* (plural of *heroön*) were more frequently dedicated to men of all kinds whose qualities had attracted the admiration of their fellow-citizens. During the course of the Hellenistic period and to an even greater extent in Roman times, families paid honours to their dead that had formerly been reserved exclusively to legendary figures and the sons of gods.   P.D.

HERONDAS. Herondas or Herodas probably lived in the 3rd century B.C. A papyrus, discovered in 1889, contains a dozen of his mimes (q.v.), many of which are fragmentary. They are written in the Ionian dialect, with borrowings from the Dorian and Attic dialects, and in choliambics, that is to say, "lame" iambic trimeters in which the final iambic foot is replaced by a spondee. The mimes are little plays with two or three characters, whose lively dialogues are extremely realistic studies of everyday life. The titles themselves indicate their style and tone: *The Procuress or the Bawd, The Dealer in Prostitutes, The Schoolmaster, Intimate Ladies, The Cobbler, Women to Lunch, The Spinners*, etc. These light, vivid sketches are full of amusing vignettes; people are painted in the most ordinary pursuits of their everyday lives, with their mean and vulgar preoccupations, their passions and distractions, all expressed in the racy language of the freest and most familiar conversation. Herondas does not shrink from obscenity where it would naturally appear, but he does not go out of his way to find it; he is content to introduce the crudest remarks as the context requires without either emphasis or complaisance.   R.F.

HESIOD. Hesiod was a poet of the second half of the 8th century B.C. and, after Homer, the most ancient of the Greek poets. He used the dactylic hexameter of the *Iliad* and *Odyssey*, but the subjects of his work were quite different; instead of celebrating the feats of the heroes of the Trojan War, he sang about the divine generations of the immortals in the *Theogony* and the work of peasants in his *Works and Days*. His authorship of the *Theogony* has been questioned, but the prelude, which contains his name, has a very personal flavour; in it he sings the praises of the Muses of Helicon and explains how they were responsible for his becoming a poet. Then the *Theogony* describes the beginnings of the world

with the primordial divinities of Chaos, Earth and Love from whom were born two successive generations of Olympians, first that of Cronus, then that of Zeus. The poem that Hesiod wrote at the height of his powers and that contains the sum of his human experience is the *Works and Days*. All that we know of the poet's life is to be found there too.

His father lived at Cyme in Aeolis on the shores of Asia Minor, were he ran a coastal trade. When it failed, he crossed the Aegean Sea and settled at Ascra in Boeotia, where Hesiod and his brother, Perses, were born. The father divided the patrimony between the two sons, but Perses, not content with his share, brought an action against Hesiod and the "kings" of the neighbouring town of Thespiae, in other words, the notables who dispensed justice, decided in favour of Perses. Hesiod was convinced of the justice of his cause and concluded that they had been bribed by his brother. The idle Perses lost all his money and alternately begged Hesiod to help him and threatened him with further proceedings. Hesiod dedicated his poem to Perses to teach him love of work and a respect for true justice. Hesiod also tells us that he only took ship once and then only for a brief voyage across the Straits of Euripus, which separated Boeotia and Euboea. He went to Chalcis in Euboea to attend a poetry competition, organised by the sons of Amphidamas in honour of their father who had just died. He won and dedicated the prize of a tripod to the Muses on Helicon.

The composition of *Works and Days* is disconcerting because Hesiod has little ability to link abstract ideas and his logic is shaky. It consists of a succession of maxims, allegories, myths and description, loosely strung together in which a rough, powerfully original poetry shines. After the prelude, which is an invocation to the Muses of Pieria, Hesiod elaborates the allegory of the two Eris, both goddesses of emulation, which is good, and of discord, which is bad; the myth of Pandora, the wonderfully beautiful woman, who carried a baleful jar and was sent by Zeus for the undoing of men; then the myth of the human races, which sets out in broad outline the history of mankind as a prolonged decline from the Age of Gold: the golden race of men was followed by the race of silver, of bronze, of heroes (described by Homer) and finally the race of iron to whom Hesiod is grieved that he belongs. This myth contains two real aspects of history: a memory of the age of heroes and the transition from the Age of Bronze to the Age of Iron. Hesiod is profoundly pessimistic. This pessimism can be at least partly explained by the circumstances of the poet's life, a poor peasant who had to scratch a living from the soil for himself and his family. His experience of life was bitter, he distilled it into the fable of the *Hawk and the Nightingale*, about the bird of prey that had no pity for the melodious singer, pointing to the same moral as La Fontaine's *The Wolf and the Lamb*. The two major themes of the poem, justice and work, are then developed. Hesiod becomes didactic when he describes the best way to run a farm and the work in the fields, which had to be done at the proper season. He explains in detail how to make a plough and other agricultural implements. As a warning to his reader, and first of all Perses, to prepare himself against a bad season, he gives an admirably vivid description of winter. The last part of the poem, the *Days*, consists of a sort of rustic almanac, a detailed calendar of the days of the month that are propitious or unpropitious for one occupation or another.

The Greeks considered Hesiod one of the great classical poets and placed him a little below Homer, but only a little, and children studied his work at school. R.F.

HESTIA. Hestia was the sister of Zeus and Hera, but always remained a rather obscure goddess. She personified the Home and this gave her a settled existence that left no opportunity for escapades. Her function and prestige were considerable; she was worshipped by every family and during the archaic period she figured in the processions and assemblies of divinities, which were frequently depicted by artists. R.F.

HIPPARCHUS of NICAEA. Astronomer of the 2nd century B.C. *(See* Astronomy.)

HIPPIAS of ELIS. Hippias was a sophist about contemporary with Socrates (469-399 B.C.), whom we know mainly through his caricatured portrait in two dialogues of Plato, *Hippias Major* and *Hippias Minor*. He claimed to know everything and could talk on every kind of subject: morality, astronomy, geometry, arithmetic, grammar and style, poetry and music, the genealogies of heroes and the founding of cities.

He also declared that he made his own clothes and shoes. His eloquence seems to have been empty and hollow in the extreme. R.F.

HIPPOCRATES. The most famous of the Greek physicians, Hippocrates, was born on the island of Cos about 460 B.C. and died, so it was said, a very old man in Thessaly. There is historical evidence that he was a real person, but hardly anything is known about his life. An important collection of medical treatises on miscellaneous subjects, the voluminous Hippocratic Collection, has come down to us under his name. It was edited and translated into French between 1839 and 1853 by Littré and has been carefully studied in our own day by Louis Bourgey in a thesis published in 1953. He has shown that three tendencies can be distinguished in these treatises: the first aims at developing a theoretical system related to the conceptions of nature evolved by contemporary philosophers; the second is empirical in character and probably derived from the medical school at Cnidos; the third tries to construct a rational medicine and medical code based on observation and speculation. It is in the treatises of the last group that the Hippocratic spirit can be appreciated. They include a conception of the development of diseases, their climax, recurrence and the critical point that decides the final outcome. They also show a grasp of the interdependence between the parts of an organism and a conception of the natural order with which the physician must reckon. Considerable importance is attached to rules of hygiene and a deontology based on a respect for moral values. This is why in a number of medical schools even today young doctors still swear the Hippocratic oath: " Whatever house I enter, I shall come to heal the sick... I will never give poison to anyone, even though I am asked to do so... "
P.-M.S.

HIPPODAMUS of MILETUS. Hippodamus lived in the first half of the 5th century B.C. It is difficult to decide exactly what he was; he has been variously described as a simple surveyor and the creator of an almost modern town-planning. He was put in charge of planning Piraeus and he applied to this problem of geometry the principles used in the reconstruction of Miletus, his native city, in the years immediately following its sack by the Persians in 491. P.D.

HIPPODROME. The Greek hippodrome
was the forerunner and prototype of the Roman
circus. When games on a large scale were held
by a city or panhellenic sanctuary, the sporting
events nearly all took place in the stadium (q.v.),
but this was not big enough for horse and chariot
racing, which took place in the hippodrome. In
Book XIII of the *Iliad* where Achilles held funeral
games in honour of his friend, Patroclus, the
plain of Troy was marked out as a temporary
hippodrome for the chariot racing. The competitors started from the place where the Achaeans
were gathered, swung round and returned from
the furthest point, a clearly visible and carefully
located landmark. The difficulty for the drivers
was to turn round this landmark as closely as
possible without touching it and breaking a
chariot wheel. No hippodromes have survived
from classical times, but they probably had the
same, slightly elliptical shape of the Roman
circuses, with steps or wooden stands for the
spectators generally placed near the starting
point, which was marked, as in a stadium, by a
line of cippi.

In Pindar's time, races between quadrigae
drawn by horses and mules, and horses mounted
by riders took place in the hippodrome. These
races were more highly thought of than any
others, because it was only those rich enough to
own a stable who could afford to run in them.
For the same reason, the odes in praise of such

victories were placed at the beginning of each
of Pindar's four books, the *Olympian, Pythian,
Isthmian* and *Nemean Odes.* The admirable
statue of the Delphic *Charioteer* has immortalised
one of these quadriga drivers. It was placed in
a votive chariot of bronze and was made in 478
or 474 B.C. by a Sicilian tyrant to commemorate
a victory in the Pythian hippodrome.   R.F.

HIPPOLYTUS. Racine, who based *Phèdre* on Euripides' play, has made Hippolytus a
more familiar figure to us than to the ancients. He
was the son of Theseus and an Amazon, Hippolyte, a devotee of Artemis, and lived a solitary life,
entirely occupied with hunting. The episode in
which the young man repulsed the blandishments
of Phaedra, the newly married wife of his father,
appeared in legends, but it was not till the misogynist poet, Euripides, made him the hero of one
of his plays that this mythological figure (Hippolytus may at first have been a god) acquired a
personality that popular tradition had not yet
given him. The death of Hippolytus, cursed by
Theseus and the victim of Poseidon, is wholly in
keeping with the most archaic myths in which
the gods who remained the masters of Olympus
were victorious in struggles over local deities.
                                                                          P.D.

HISTORY. Our knowledge of the different
periods of ancient Greek history varies. Some

writers concentrated their attention on one or another episode of their country's history and the writings of Herodotus, Thucydides and Xenophon enable us to follow the development of the Persian Wars and the Peloponnesian War. Other historians dealt with other episodes, but, because the quality of their work is unequal and most of it has not survived, we should know little about long and interesting periods of Greek history if our information depended on literary texts only.

For the periods when the cities were firmly established and writing widely practised, inscriptions are a useful source of information. Laws, decrees, treaties, religious prescriptions, dedications, which concerned everyone, were engraved on the walls of buildings and isolated stelae and, when these have come down to us, they are invaluable, because as records they are first hand, indisputable and preserved in writing at the very moment of their promulgation, unlike the tendentious interpretations of historians, who were biased by their personal opinions into distorting certain events. Unfortunately, although there are a large number of these inscriptions, they only constitute a small part of what originally existed and the damage suffered by most of them often makes their interpretation doubtful.

Written records are not our only source of information; archaeology is a rich mine for historians, not only for periods whose writing cannot be understood, like the greater part of the 2nd millennium B.C. in spite of the decipherment of Linear B (q.v.), but also for those whose writing is intelligible. Ruins, figurative art, particularly vase painting, and objects of all kinds, dug up from different levels of the earth, provide priceless evidence for the character of their civilisation and sometimes historical events; for example, we can deduce the exact moment when a site was destroyed from the traces of a fire on a precisely dated vase.

Of course, for later periods historians of ancient Greece seek their material in works which would not have been regarded as strictly historical. The speeches of Demosthenes and the comedies of Aristophanes dealt with current events and were written for their contemporaries, but for this very reason they give us a truer picture of Athenian society and the problems of a city on the eve of the Macedonian conquest than any historical account. Economic life would be quite unknown to us if archaeological finds had not given us an opportunity to study the international diffusion of a particular coinage, or the success of a particular workshop of bronzes or a pottery throughout the Mediterranean.

It is with such gleanings from every field that we can attempt to reconstruct the history of Greece. Whatever the gaps in our knowledge, we shall try to sketch the outlines of the life of the peoples around the Aegean Sea from its beginnings to the Roman era. Ancient Greece was never a political entity and Greek civilisation stretched all over the Mediterranean basin. (See Greece; Hellenism). It is nonetheless true that this civilisation sprang up on the land that is modern Greece. We have only recently discovered that at least some parts of this land were inhabited in the Palaeolithic Age. The remains of the Neolithic Age are numerous and widely scattered. They set some unsatisfactorily solved problems on the origins of the people, which anyway does not seem to have been homogeneous. The civilisation was comparatively well developed; the pottery was of good quality and the site of Dimini in Thessaly has produced interesting information on architecture and funeral practices. The Bronze Age, which lasted from about the middle of the 3rd millennium B.C. (it did not begin at the same time everywhere) to the end of the 2nd, is better known to us. Three parallel currents can be distinguished from the outset: Helladic on the continent, Cycladic in the Archipelago, Minoan in Crete. Each possesses its peculiar characteristics and each can be divided into three major phases, Early, Middle and Late. The Early period which lasted until about 2000 B.C. is obviously the least well known.

At the beginning of the 2nd millennium B.C., invaders from the north penetrated Greece and took possession of the land, destroying a civilisation that was not outstanding but had provided an adequate living for its people. The conquerors, who adapted themselves quite quickly to the country, were the fathers of Homer's Achaeans, the ancestors of the Ionians and, in fact, the first Greeks.

Crete was spared because it was protected by the broad stretch of sea separating it from the Peloponnesus. Its inhabitants lived in peace and enjoyed a period of great prosperity for at least five centuries. Under the probably supreme authority of a king living at Cnossos, the island expanded its fertile agriculture and built up a fleet of ships that enabled it to control exchanges with the continent and make contact with the civilisations of Egypt and the east, which were already fully developed. While the Cyclades, which had gained an important place during the 3rd millennium B.C. in the Aegean world with their trade in a hard stone called obsidian, became mere satellites of Crete, the Achaeans gradually settled down in the Peloponnesus and central Greece. After what was probably an extremely disturbed period, peace returned and the Achaeans began to enjoy a fairly high standard of life, due as much to their natural qualities as to the exchanges with Crete, which had begun at least as early as the 17th century. This standard did not equal that of the Cretans. Rebuilding splendid palaces, which had been ruined by a catastrophe in the 18th century B.C., they lived in a refinement rarely attained elsewhere in ancient Greece, and boasted a sovereign, Minos (possibly a generic name), who was admired by the Greeks and whose wisdom had brought peace and prosperity to his people. In fact, it seems that the islanders lived without any fears in unfortified towns with large buildings, where big spaces were left for storing oil and cereals, where workshops were crowded with craftsmen and manual workers and where eminent people enjoyed considerable comfort.

It was probably an attack by the Achaeans during the course of the 15th century B.C. that put an end to this happy era; whoever it was, after that the finer civilisation developed on the continent. The most important of its numerous towns was Mycenae, which may have been the capital of an empire, or simply a state whose brilliance attracted the attention of all the other cities. The royal tombs, the oldest grouped in circular enclosures, the latest placed in huge chambers shaped like beehives and actually called the beehive tombs, besides being rich, reveal an extraordinary refinement and artistic sense. The Mycenaean world differed from the Minoan in its concern with political and territorial expansion; it was not afraid of war nor distant expeditions and Mycenaean settlements are found, not only in relatively close places like Rhodes, but also as far as Cyprus and the Syrian coast, and in the other direction, as far as Sicily. The arrival of the Dorians at the end of the 2nd millennium B.C. marks a clean cut across Greek history; Mycenaean civilisation, already old and weakened, so to speak, by its expansion abroad, was ruined by the massive influx of the younger branch of its own ancestors and the invasion heralded a period

of unrest and poverty, sometimes called the Hellenic Dark Ages. During this period, which stretched from the 11th to about the 8th century B.C., memories of the past were kept alive—the Homeric poems are a return to the Mycenaean world—but a new spirit began to make itself felt. (See Dorians.)

In the political sphere, the cities that had increased in number during the former period of prosperity still existed, but oligarchic governments replaced the monarchies they had known before; the big landowners were the masters and their authority weighed heavily on the people. Hesiod lamented the sufferings of all those who were oppressed by the greed of these overlords. The miseries of war were added to the evils of social injustice; even at this point, Greece was divided into a multitude of states whose jealousies and rivalries provoked incessant conflicts. Religious associations and a common religion did nothing to diminish local animosities and, although certain festivals brought about a truce and gathered together the hostile groups at the same sanctuary, there was a feeling of insecurity everywhere. In the course of the 8th century B.C., there began a vast movement of emigration that drove thousands of Greeks out of their homeland. They went to seek their fortunes elsewhere in lands where the soil was not so poor, and founded colonies scattered from the Black Sea to the shores of Sicily and southern Italy, and sometimes further still.

This blood-letting was not sufficient to cure the cities of the evils that afflicted them; in the newly founded towns there were wars against the natives and internal dissensions, in the old states, the consequences of past injustices created problems that took long to remedy. Often legislators from outside, particularly Crete, the land of wise Minos in former times, were called upon, who tried to make their customs consistent and suppress arbitrary government. Generally, the intervention of dictators, the tyrants, was necessary to make a clean sweep, probably by brutal methods, of the differences between social classes that embittered their relationships. The struggles between different cities were no less complex than these internal conflicts. Alliances, which were formed and broken as the circumstances changed, and old quarrels that broke out afresh at every turn make the history of Greece a tissue of wars, which the ancient Greeks themselves had difficulty in distinguishing from each other. One of the most prolonged was the war waged by Sparta against Messenia, whose rich territories she wanted to appropriate.

The consequences of the Dorian invasion really lasted well into the 6th century B.C. and it was not until tyrants were governing the principal states of Greece that the characteristics of the Hellenic world begin to appear. In the second half of this century, the Greek states were scattered all over the Mediterranean. They were all independent and in all, or nearly all of them, a middle class had grown up that curtailed or reduced to nothing the part played by the old aristocracy; they were all ambitious, always eager for material wealth and often for political prestige or some kind of domination; but they were all united by their pride in Hellenism and their worship of the same gods.

Before the end of the 6th century, the tyrants disappeared everywhere except west of the Adriatic. With the exception of Sparta and a few Thessalian cities, government was now exercised by a group, in some states, the power was vested in an oligarchy or in the people as a whole, but the character of the government often changed as the result of a revolution. As a general rule, the social inequalities, which had caused so much suffering in primitive Greece, were considerably diminished. What did not change was the particularist spirit of the cities. In the opening years of the 5th century, a great danger threatened Greece; the attempt of the powerful Persian empire to dominate her. In moments of greatest danger, quite a large number of states would form a coalition against the enemy, but the entire Hellenic people never united, as in the legendary Trojan venture, under the authority of a single leader. The victories of Marathon (490), Salamis and Plataea (480-479) drove off the invading enemy, but the remaining part of the Persian Wars (q.v.) in which only a few cities were involved did not end until 449. The Greeks were already beginning to devour each other and the two cities who fought for supremacy, Athens and Sparta, dragged their allies with their uncertain loyalties after them.

The fifteen years that passed between the international truce of 446 and the beginning of a new war in 432, the Peloponnesian War, marked the apogee of Athens and one of the rare periods of peace that Greece enjoyed in all her history. Athens had grouped under her leadership the cities which, having allied themselves to her in 477 to fight against the Persians, gradually became her subjects. This was the Delian League. She exercised her authority in a cavalier fashion, but with the tributes paid to her and the genius of Pericles, she gave the whole Greek world a prestige that dazzled even the Barbarians.

In 432, the jealousy felt by the other Greek states for this great city stirred up war against her. Sparta headed the movement. For a long time the issue of the struggle was doubtful, but in 404 Sparta won, Athens lost her empire and its collapse marked a long period of uncertainty during which Sparta, Athens risen from the ruins, and Thebes fought with each other for a fragile hegemony. There was strife everywhere and the hostile groups appealed for outside help, first to the Persians from whom they only expected financial aid, then to the king of Macedonia, Philip, who intervened directly and in the end subjected the whole of Greece to his domination (338). Alexander inherited this power when he ascended the throne in 336. Outwardly, the position of the Greek cities appeared little changed; they remained autonomous, but it was a municipal autonomy. They were dependencies of a king who controlled their policy and against whom some of them tried to rebel but without success. Ultimately, it was the position of Greece as a whole that the Macedonian conquest had modified. In a few years, Alexander had won possession of all Asia Minor, Syria and Egypt.

At his death, his generals divided his empire between them and in 323, on the day the great conqueror died, a new era began, which is called Hellenistic (q.v.). It is impossible to give a detailed account of the kingdoms and dynasties that were formed, the Lagides in Egypt, the Seleucids in Asia Minor, the Antigonidae in Macedonia. What must be stressed is that the way of life and spirit of Hellenism were no longer the same; although the sovereigns were Greek, they adopted eastern ideas of monarchy straightaway; they allowed themselves to be regarded as divine persons, their rule was absolute and the collective government of the Greek cities was no more than a distant memory. Their policy was no longer the policy of cities fighting against their immediate neighbours, but policy formulated on a vast scale, affecting hundreds of thousands of subjects of whom only some possessed the meaningless title of citizen.

In 146, Rome gained possession of Greece itself,

in 133 she took over the eastern kingdom of Attalus III, King of Pergamum, and in 30 Egypt fell under her sway; everything that had been Greece, even as she was extended by Alexander's conquests, was reduced to provincial status. The difference in government was perhaps however less than that distinguishing the republican Greece of classical times from the Greece subjected to the power of Macedonia. The central government was no longer the same and the governors were foreigners, but they did not want anything beyond political domination. They did not interfere in the cultural sphere. The loss of independence had long been an accomplished fact and the Greeks had become accustomed to obeying and flattering the master and his representatives. The wealth and peace brought by the Romans were not the compensation to them for an independence that they had completely forgotten, but a benefit that no sense of shame prevented them from acknowledging publicly.   P.D.

HOMER. Homer, the earliest and greatest of the Greek poets, probably lived in the first half of the 8th century B.C. We know nothing certain about his life. Seven cities claimed the honour of being his birthplace. He may have been born in Chios and spent most of his life in Smyrna—or the other way round; they both lay between the regions of Ionia and Aeolis; the language of the *Iliad* and *Odyssey* is fundamentally Ionian, but also contains several elements of Aeolian dialect. Tradition describes Homer as blind, but if he could not see, how could he describe the earth, the sea and the sky so well ? The ancient Greeks attributed supernatural powers to blindness; the blind could see the invisible and foretell the future. Herodotus wrote about 450: " I think that Hesiod and Homer lived no more than four hundred years before me. " However, this date of 850 is rather too early for both of them, particularly Hesiod.

Most of the ancient Greeks considered Homer the author of the *Iliad* and *Odyssey*, as well as other works like the so-called *Homeric Hymns* and the *Batrachomyomachia* (Fight between the rats and frogs), which are certainly not by him. Some philologists of the Alexandrian period came to the conclusion that the text of the *Iliad* and *Odyssey* contained additions interpolated after Homer; the *Odyssey*, for example, originally ended at line 296 of Book XXIII. Other critics of the same period, who were called " separators " *(chorizontes)* went as far as rejecting Homer's authorship of the *Odyssey* altogether. The *Odyssey* seems later than the *Iliad*, but there is no reason why Homer should not have written one in his maturity and the other in his old age. In both, the style of composition is similar. Modern critics have considerably complicated the question since the memorable *Academic Conjectures, or Dissertations on the Iliad*, a book by François Hédelin, Abbé d'Abignac, written in 1666 but not published until 1715, after the author's death; and particularly since the *Prolegomena ad Homerum* by the German, F.A. Wolf, published in 1795, which, although much more tentative and less radical than the Abbé d'Abignac's work, really set off the great controversy between philologists that has hardly flagged ever since. For the romantics, who were infatuated with Ossian, the *Iliad* and *Odyssey* represented primitive poetry, the spontaneous creation of the popular genius. According to them, the two poems resulted from the combination of epic " lays " *(rhapsodiai)*, which had originally been independent and in which the soul of the Greek people expressed itself through the voice of anonymous bards. The theories of these " analysts " or " dissectors " of Homer were countless and contradictory. The conversion of some of them to the " unitarian " theory, in other words, to the generally held opinion on authorship of ancient times, caused quite a stir. The wisest thing is to go back to Aristotle. He points out convincingly in his *Poetics* that Homer's two poems differ from all the other compositions of the " epic cycle " through the unity and tautness of their action. A brief analysis of the *Iliad* and *Odyssey* will bring out this essential point.

The *Iliad* does not give an account of the whole Trojan War which, according to the legend, lasted ten years, but only a critical phase lasting less than two months. As the first line of the poem indicates, the subject is the anger of Achilles. It is true that the poet very skilfully connects by a number of scattered allusions the events that he is describing to past and future events, but he heightens the dramatic tension by concentrating the action on one major episode. The quarrel of Agamemnon and Achilles, whose captive, Briseis, is taken away from him, is followed by the intervention of his mother, Thetis, pleading his cause before Zeus, who promises to favour the Trojans until the wrong done to Achilles has been re-

Homer. Roman copy of an imaginary portrait.
2nd century B.C. Paris, Louvre.

dressed (Book I). After the lists of Achaean and Trojan troops (Book II) and the single combat between Menelaus and Paris (Book III), which are " curtain-raisers ", the first day of battle in the *Iliad* begins with Book IV and ends with Book VII. The second day is described in Book VIII, when the situation of the Achaeans, in accordance with Zeus's promise to Thetis, becomes so serious that Agamemnon sends ambassadors to Achilles in the night, but all in vain (Book IX). Book X recounts another nocturnal episode, the expedition of Ulysses and Diomedes into the Trojan camp to get information. The account of the third day of battle lasts from Book XI to Book XVIII. The peripeteia of the sending of Patroclus into battle is carefully prepared as early as Book XI, lines 596-848. The Trojans overrun the Achaean bulwark in Book XII and attack their ships in Book XIII. Lines 390-404 of Book XV are occupied with Patroclus and form the transition between Book XI and Book XVI. It is at this point that Achilles, watching Hector's setting fire to a ship, decides to send his friend, Patroclus, into the fight dressed in his own armour, but Patroclus is killed by Hector. Grief and the desire for revenge dominate Achilles' resentment and, after Hephaestus has forged new arms for him (Book XVIII), he hurls himself into the fight, looking for Hector to kill him. The fourth and last day of the battle begins with Book XX and ends in Book XXII with the death of Hector. After this Priam obtains the return of his son's corpse from Achilles (Book XXIV). The action, then, of the Iliad is a unity like that of classical tragedy and depends from beginning to end on the feelings of the protagonist, Achilles. Book I recounts the beginning of his anger and its last flickerings are described in the admirable interview with Priam in Book XXIV.

The same dramatic concentration is achieved in the *Odyssey* by a different method. At first, the events related in the *Odyssey* seem to spread over ten years, beginning with the departure from Troy to the punishment of the suitors in Ithaca: Ulysses spends a year with Circe, seven years with Calypso and further time at sea and in other landings; but the poet plunges the reader *in medias res* at the moment when he is leaving Calypso, then he leads him backwards with the account put into the mouth of the hero himself,

who is telling the Phaeacians about his previous adventures. Consequently, between the assembly of the gods in Book I and Penelope's recognition of Ulysses in Book XXIII, which ended the original Homeric poem, there is only a lapse of about forty days, less time than the *Iliad* spans. I think it shows a misunderstanding of Homer's art and his sense of composition to argue that the Journey of Telemachus, which occupies the first four books of the poem, is a post-Homeric addition. Admittedly, the journey achieves no positive results; Telemachus receives no reliable information about the fate of his father either at Pylos or Sparta and Homer is the first to point out with some humour, in Book XIII, its apparent uselessness. The poet, however, uses it to connect the return of Ulysses to the legend as a whole by taking the reader to the homes of Nestor and Menelaus, who had returned from Troy, and to describe Ithaca with Telemachus, Penelope and the suitors before the hero's arrival on the island.

In these two poems, Homer describes Achaean, or Mycenaean, civilisation four centuries before

Fight between Greeks and Trojans. Detail of the east frieze from the Treasury of the Siphnians at Delphi. About 525 B.C. Delphi Museum. *Photo Spyros Meletzis.*

his time, since he lived about 800 and Troy fell about 1180 B.C. He knew this civilisation through the traditions mostly to be found in earlier epics to which he makes several allusions in the *Iliad* (in Book IX Achilles passes the time by singing the exploits of heroes) and particularly in the *Odyssey*, when the bards, Phemius and Demodocus, sing several '' rhapsodies ''.

The Homeric language, which did not correspond exactly with any spoken idiom, but is literary and composite in character, and also the '' formula '' style of the two poems is certainly the culmination of a long development. Far from being a primitive poet, Homer is the fine flower of the Greek epic tradition. After him the crowd of Homeridae continued that tradition but without his genius *(See* Epic). Homer's superiority is striking, not only in the composition of the two poems, but also in the realism and beauty of the infinitely varied descriptions, in the striking characterisations and in the vivid images, which are more numerous in the *Iliad* than the *Odyssey*.

Homer was imitated by all the Greek poets, including lyric and dramatic writers, and by many Latin poets such as Virgil. His poems were read in their entirety at Athens during the national festival of the Panathenaea. Greek children used them as their first reading book at school. Although the *Iliad* and *Odyssey* were not '' sacred writings '' like the Bible and Koran, the Greeks accepted their authority almost without question in every sphere and referred to them as a source of information in rhetoric, strategy and even philosophy. Hellenic culture was at first defined as the knowledge and practice of the Homeric poems.   R.F.

HOSPITALITY. The Greek philosophers distinguished *philia xenike*, the friendship between guests and hosts, from the other kinds of friendship (q.v.). Those who had shared their bread and salt and slept under the same roof were united by a strong and lasting bond, which was religious in character and was transmitted from generation to generation. The piety of ancient times depended on three fundamental principles: worship of the gods, respect for parents and the care of guests. In Book VI of the *Iliad,* the Achaean, Diomedes, and the Lycian, Glaucus, challenged and talked to each other in the usual Homeric fashion before fighting. In the course of this, they realised that their paternal grandparents, Oenus and Bellerophon, had known each other and that Oenus had received Bellerophon at his house. They immediately gave up the combat, which they were on the point of beginning, and exchanged arms.

The stranger who presented himself as a suppliant was under the protection of the gods, particularly Zeus Xenios and Athena Xenia. He could not be driven away without seriously offending these powerful divinities and risking their vengeance. There existed a special ritual for supplication, which figures notably in Sophocles' *Oedipus Rex* and the *Suppliant Women* of Aeschylus and Euripides; the suppliant holding olive branches wound with fillets of wool in his hand, touched with his hand the knee and chin of the person whom he was supplicating. Euripides' *Alcestis* is a tragedy written in praise of hospitality. Admetus had just lost his wife, Alcestis, when Heracles arrived and asked to be received. Admetus hid his grief and sheltered the hero, who was given a splendid dinner, but an indiscreet servant told Heracles about the recent death of Alcestis. Heracles immediately fetched his prey back from Death and led Alcestis to Admetus, as a recompense for having been so hospitable.

Hospitality also existed in the communal and public sphere. An Athenian citizen, for example, was designated by the Spartans as their *proxenos*, or representative, of Sparta at Athens. When Spartans went to Athens, they naturally stayed with the proxenos, who was the public host of their city.   R.F.

HOURS. The feminine divinities, which we call the Hours, were really tutelary deities of the Seasons. They were nature goddesses and those who were responsible for the welfare of the state invoked their names in their most solemn oaths; because they were bound to the soil, they brought fertility and, although they hardly ever appeared in mythological tales, they probably inspired stronger and more spontaneous feelings than many Olympians who held more eminent positions.   P.D.

HOUSE. In 5th century B.C. Athens, most houses were small and unimpressive. Demosthenes said that the houses of Miltiades and Aristides were no different from those of the most humble citizens. They were built in wood, unfaced brick or a mixture of pebbles and baked earth and as a consequence the walls were so thin and fragile that robbers preferred to break their way through them rather than attempt to force the door, whence their name of "wall-piercers". The ancient Greeks did not have pane-glass windows and the openings must therefore have been rather small and like skylights. When the weather was bad they were stopped up with opaque panels. Roofs were flat. Chimneys and kitchens (when they existed, for food was often cooked in the open) were of the most rudimentary nature. The front door opened outwards and before going out it was customary to knock on it to warn the passers-by so that they could avoid being hit by the unexpected opening of the door. Most houses had one upper storey and only very rarely two. Access was usually by an outside wooden staircase. Sometimes the

House. Detail of the krater by Clitias and Ergotimus, called the François Vase. About 570 B.C. Florence, Museo Archeologico. *Photo Hirmer.*

in Athens, with several tenants all living side by side.

The 4th century B.C. houses that have survived in the best state are those found at Olynthus in Chalcidice. They are built on a nearly square groundplan with all the rooms opening not onto the street but onto an inner portico *(pastas)*, leading to a courtyard *(aule)* preceded by a vestibule *(prothyron)*. The pastas normally faced the south. On the ground floor were the reception room *(andron)* where guests were received, the ordinary dining-room *(diaiteterion)* which was also a kind of " living-room ", the kitchen, bathroom and wine-cellar; on the upper floor were the conjugal bedroom *(thalamos)* the gynaeceum and the slaves' quarters. From these already spacious houses at Olynthus were later derived the houses of the Hellenistic period, of which those at Priene and Delos are the best examples. These houses were much larger and far more decorated than those of the classical period. In order to safeguard the intimacy of the family they were without windows opening on the exterior; all the rooms opened onto a central courtyard which was usually square and furnished with a peristyle surrounding a basin; for the single row of columns of the pastas as seen at Olynthus had become a quadrangular portico. The floors were decorated with mosaics ornamented with motifs, or figures such as that of Dionysus riding a panther in the house found at Delos. The walls were covered with painted stuccos or even marble plaques. Statues were often placed in houses. The houses of the Roman period, such as those at Pompeii, are obviously a derivation from this type of dwelling created in the Greek orient.

R.F.

upper storey might be built so that it projected over the street, but the state considered balconies as an illegitimate encroachment on the public domain and took measures against them.

In the 4th century B.C., domestic architecture showed an improvement, at least in the dwellings of the richer and more leisured classes. Demosthenes was certainly exaggerating when he claimed that some politicians of his time " had built themselves dwellings that are more impressive than any public building ", but in such " residential " districts as Scambonidai at Athens, larger and more comfortable, almost luxurious houses were to be seen. But the majority of the ten thousand houses that Xenophon counted at Athens continued to resemble the humble dwellings of the preceding century. When a member of the middle classes owned a house with an upper storey, the ground floor was normally reserved for men, the women lived above *(See Gynaeceum)* as we learn from Lysias's speech *Against Eratosthenes*. Aeschines has told us that in his time blocks of flats *(synoikiai)* existed

HUNTING. Like fishing, hunting was a profession for some Greeks, a sport for others. The Spartans considered hunting to be a privileged exercise and an excellent training for war and their views were echoed by the Athenian Xenophon, a great admirer of the Spartans, in his treatise the *Cynegeticus*. In Attica hunting was also considered as a sport although game was rarer. Although a few wild beasts were still to be found in classical Greece (less numerous than in the times of Heracles and the Nemean lion), and also wolves, still to be found today in some regions, hunters mainly went after boars, deer, hares and birds such as partridges, quail, larks and thrushes. Various snares were made with nooses and springs to catch birds and small game The setting of traps was the oldest and most widespread means of hunting. For large game a deep pit was dug with sheer edges and then camouflaged with branches. A lamb was then tied to a stake at the centre, so that when a carnivorous beast heard its bleating, it approached and fell through the branches into the pit.

Hunters' weapons included the javelin, axes, clubs, daggers, sticks, bows and arrows, and slings. Birds were brought down by stones or arrows. As Xenophon's *Cynegeticus* tells us, nets were frequently used in hunting. Beaters sent hare and other small game into a net with the aid of dogs. The hunters who watched over the nets or the beaters themselves then stunned the game, or else took them alive Dogs were indispensable for this type of hunting and were so widely used that the Greek word, *kynegetes,* meant both "hunter" and "leader of dogs". Certain breeds of dog from Laconia were renowned for their speed and skill. Hunting dogs with thin snouts and sharp pointed ears were represented on painted vases. R.F.

HYMETTUS. The mountain range of Hymettus is 3,365 ft at its highest point and stretches for about 12 miles in a long, sharp line, like a wall on the eastern extremity of the plain, where Athens was built. Although Hymettus was less arid in ancient times than nowadays, aromatic plants mainly grew on its slopes even then and fed the bees whose honey is still famous. P.D.

HYPERBOREANS. The Greeks believed that in a far distant past, a mysterious people called the Hyperboreans lived in the extreme north. Apollo used to live with them before he went to Delphi and periodically paid them brief visits afterwards. Herodotus saw the tomb of the Hyperborean virgins on Delos, two girls who had brought the sacred objects of their cult from their mythical country to the sacred island and, when their mission was accomplished, died in the sanctuary. It was a Hyperborean, the soothsayer, Olen, who installed the oracle of the god at Delphi. At Delphi too, the ghosts of two Hyperborean heroes appeared miraculously and drove

away the Galatians when they invaded central Greece. The land where this mythical people lived was imagined as a kind of earthly paradise where the inhabitants lived in peace and happiness, gathering the fruits of the earth without any trouble at all. P.D.

HYPERIDES. Hyperides (390-322 B.C.) was an Athenian orator, who had been the pupil of Isocrates and Plato. He supported Demosthenes in the " patriotic " party hostile to Philip of Macedon, but he was against him in the Harpalus affair in 324 and obtained the condemnation of the great orator for venality. He died in the same year as Demosthenes after being one of the instigators of the Lamian war.

Egyptian papyri, discovered in the middle of the 19th century, have preserved quite important fragments from several of Hyperides' speeches: *For Euxenippus, For Lycophron, Against Athenogenes, Funeral Oration* Only scraps have survived of his famous pleading on behalf of his mistress, the courtesan Phryne. It is said that in the course of his peroration, Hyperides tore open Phryne's robe and revealed her breast in order to move the judges at the sight of her beauty. R.F.

HYPORCHEMA. See Lyric Poetry.

IAMBLICHUS. Iamblichus was a Neoplatonic, Neopythagorean philosopher, born about 250 A.D. at Chalcis, so it is said, where he taught after being a pupil of Porphyry. It is probable that he subsequently founded the Neoplatonic school of Syria at Apamea, which was directed after his death, about 325/6, by Sopater. In his *Lives of the Sophists,* Eunapius conveys some of the fascination exercised by his personality and teaching. The correspondence of the Emperor Julian and the extracts preserved by Stobaeus in his anthology throw light on him as a willing spiritual guide. The most extraordinary prodigies were attributed also to the "divine Iamblichus". This success at least indicates that he satisfied the appetite of his age for the marvellous, which was characteristically Hellenistic.

From his major work, *Of Pythagorean Doctrines*, there survive a *Protrepticus, On the Arithmetic of Nicomachus, On the Pythagorean Life* and a treatise called *Theological Principles of Arithmetic.* We also know the titles and possess a few fragments of works on Chaldaean mythology, the gods, the soul, etc. Besides these, scholars have confirmed the traditional attribution of the *De Mysteriis,* which is invaluable for the history of the final phase of Greek religion. Related to the development of Neoplatonism, Iamblichus seems to dissociate its logical and mystical aspects, which Plotinus for his part tried to unify, However, his concern for continuity led him to multiply the intermediaries between the Sensible, or natural world, and the Intellect. He is notable for having introduced magic and theosophy into philosophy more consciously than his master, Porphyry, had done; it is not surprising that he should have mixed them in an erotic novel of which the *Bibliotheka* of Photius has given a detailed plan. The remaining portions of his great work mentioned above show that he was anxious to put the body of Greek philosophy at the service of Neopythagorean propaganda. To further this aim, he used an extremely personal form of systematic and philological exegesis, and modern scholars have discovered a fresh interest in his work through examining it. After they had studied him as a representative of Hellenistic Neoplatonism and his influence on the Byzantine philosophers (Joannes Philoponus, Psellus, John Italus, Gemistos Pletho), they investigated his writings as a source of information for the lost works of the Pythagoreans and as a possible reflection of the young Aristotle's thought.

M.-A.V.-V.

I A M B U S . A metrical foot consisting of a short followed by a long syllable. *(See* Lyric Poetry).

I B Y C U S . Ibycus was a lyric poet of the 6th century B.C., born at Rhegium in southern Italy. He lived for a long time on Samos, then returned to Rhegium where he died. The tiny fragments of his hymns and love poems that have survived show the marked influence of Stesiochorus and Sappho. R.F.

I C A R U S . Icarus was the son of Daedalus and was imprisoned with his father by Minos, because Daedalus had helped Ariadne and Theseus to bring their adventure with the Minotaur to a successful conclusion. The two prisoners escaped into the air with wings that Daedalus had made and attached to their shoulders with wax. Ignoring the advice of his father, Icarus

flew too high and too near the heat of the sun, which melted the wax, and he fell into the sea. This legend did not win the popularity that has continued till today until a late period when it was already given a symbolic interpretation.

P.D.

I C T I N U S . Ictinus was the architect of the Parthenon, where he worked from 448 to 437 B.C. under the direction of Phidias, who supervised the whole work. Ictinus gave it an original form that provided a magnificent setting for the sculpture. We should like to know more about the early life of this great architect. He may have been born in the Peloponnesus and trained by Libon, the architect of the temple of Zeus at Olympia. His genius was sufficiently versatile to give an Attic flavour to Doric architecture in the great temple on the Acropolis. There he had to take not only various topographical and economic factors into consideration, because the Parthenon had to be built on a foundation and terrace prepared for previous projects, but also the aesthetic requirements and personal wishes of Phidias. He succeeded in creating, with the splendid material provided for him by the quarries of Pentelic marble, a work that is unique for its harmony, grace and power. The refinement and decorative quality of the Ionic order were combined with Doric severity for the first time in a temple on the Greek mainland.

Another building, less famous but very imaginative nevertheless, the Telesterion, or the Hall of the Mysteries, at Eleusis, shows that the originality of Ictinus lay in his distribution of volumes. Here again, he had to adapt the proposals of a former plan in which a huge square hall (170 ft square internally) was divided by seven rows of seven columns. Ictinus, while preserving the same proportions, increased and enlarged the spaces by eliminating more than half the columns. This he was able to do with an arrangement of the inner columns grouped on a double rectangular plan, one within the other, comprising four rows of five columns. It was modified by other architects, probably from fear of the huge spans that resulted, and the final temple had seven rows of six columns. Possibly it was this skill in distributing interior space that induced Pericles to give him the commission for the Odeum of which only the foundations remain. He may also have designed the temple of Apollo at Bassae, but it is a controversial point. R.M.

IDYLL. A short poem describing a scene from the epics or the familiar events of pastoral or middle class life in country or town. *(See Theocritus).*

ILISSUS. The Ilissus, like other rivers with romantic associations, has a sad history. This Attic stream, which flowed from Mount Hymettus, could never have had much water except after a rain storm, even at the time when Socrates walked along its banks barefoot. In our day, its dried bed had become no more than a sewer and it was covered over as a hygienic precaution.   P.D.

INNS. In ancient Greece, a number of inns, offering travellers board and lodging, existed along the main roads which were simply tracks of beaten earth. In Aristophanes' *Frogs* Dionysus asks Heracles which is the best road leading to Hades and adds: " In case it might be necessary, tell me the hosts who served you best when you went to fetch Cerberus and tell me too of the ports, the bakers' shops, the forks in the road, the fountains, the roads, the halting places, the cities, the lodgings and the hostelries without too many bugs... "   R.F.

INSCRIPTIONS. When an archaeologist excavates the site of a town or a Greek sanctuary, he is not always lucky enough to discover a fine statue or a perfectly preserved vase, but it is unusual not to find at least pottery shards, coins and fragmentary or complete inscriptions. Apart from excavations, he can often discover inscriptions on stones used again in modern buildings. The study of inscriptions is called epigraphy. *(See* the article on *Writing,* for the writing of ancient inscriptions).

The official posting of laws and decrees on tablets or wooden panels painted in white *(leukomata)* was practised by the ancient Greeks, but when they wanted to preserve a text permanently, they engraved it in lasting material, sometimes on a bronze plaque, more usually on stone *(poros),* limestone or marble.

There are innumerable texts collected in the volumes of the *Corpus inscriptionum graecarum* and each of these volumes is incomplete as soon as it appears, because new inscriptions are constantly being discovered and published (often after too long a delay). There is a great deal of variety in these texts too: dedications, epitaphs (sometimes in verse), business agreements, private transactions of buying and selling, accounts, political treaties between states, decrees of all kinds (most of these are honorific decrees), religious regulations, affranchisements, letters from rulers, etc.

Epigraphy has even preserved literary texts for us; hymns with their musical notation at Delphi, for example.

When an epigraphist discovers an inscription in the course of his travels or excavations, he should take a copy and carefully measure the stone and the letters. Besides photographing it, he should also take impressions by means of a special paper laid on the clean, inscribed surface, which is then damped and will give him a faithful mould of the text when it is dry. If the inscription is mutilated or worn away in places, he then tries to restore it with the help of all similar texts, taking care not to present his hypotheses as certainties; it is better not to make any restorations at all rather than suggest haphazard complements simply from a dislike of leaving gaps. Finally, he should publish the inscription with a translation, a commentary and, if possible, a good photograph of the stone, or at least of the impression.

Epigraphy has really revolutionised our knowledge of ancient Greece in every sphere. It has provided first hand records of the Greek language and its dialects, unlike the manuscripts of ancient authors, which are always more or less altered by copyists. The whole political, social, economic and religious history of Hellas is greatly indebted to epigraphy. Even the historian of art and literature loses by neglecting it. " Epigraphy is always bringing a fresh interest to ancient history; it is a relief to the dryness of endless discussions over texts that have been pored over for four centuries. It cuts through old controversies. It is the water of perpetual youth for our studies. It always holds the gate wide open to the realm of discovery and its delight. It is a ceaseless source of vitality for the history of antiquity in all its variety. " (Louis Robert).   R.F.

IO. Io was an Argive princess, the daughter or descendant of the river god, Inachus, and the priestess of Hera. Zeus fell in love with her and changed her into a heifer to protect her from the jealousy of his wife, but Hera was suspicious and insisted that the creature should be delivered up to her and put under the guard of Argus, the giant with a hundred eyes. Hermes succeeded in putting Argus to sleep and killing him, but Io was then pursued by a gad-fly. In her struggle to escape from this insect, which Hera had fastened to her flank, the unhappy animal fled all over Greece, swam the straits of Byzantium, which are consequently called the Bosphorus, " the cow's crossing ", wandered over Asia and finally arrived in Egypt, where she gave birth to Zeus's son, Epaphus, who was later to be the father of the Danaidae. Io then regained her human shape and was given divine honours. At her death, she became a constellation. P.D.

ION of CHIOS. Tragic poet and prose writer of the 5th century B.C.

IONIA. Ionia proper is the region on the Anatolian coast which lies round the Gulf of Smyrna, but the terms Ionian and Ionism have a wider and less precise significance. It is now thought that the Ionians constituted one of the first waves of invasion that swept over Greek territory in the beginning of the 2nd millennium B.C. and that, when they were driven out about ten centuries later, they crossed the Aegean Sea and settled in the country that bore their name.

At first, it was their dialect that distinguished the Ionians notably from the other Greeks, particularly the Dorians, who belonged to the same ethnic family and had forced them to emigrate. A more prolonged settlement on the shores of the Mediterranean among the countries of Asia Minor with their ancient civilisation, where life was easier, marked them with certain features that can be regarded as typical. They lacked the energy of the Dorians and preferred the pleasures of banqueting and long conversations to the physical effort of strenuous exercises; a certain softness went with their intellectual refinement; they were clever businessmen, loved speculating with money as well as with the things of the mind and some of the subtlest philosophers came from Ionia. A description of the Ionic order will be found in the entry on *Architecture;* the artistic and literary style of the Ionians is as easily recognisable.

Although the Ionians can be accused of indolence, their laziness vanished as soon as their interests were involved. They were some of the boldest pioneers of ancient times and the city of Miletus founded dozens of colonies and trading posts along the redoubtable shores of the Black Sea. Situated on the edge of Asia Minor, Ionia was the thoroughfare between Greece and the east. In the famous sanctuary at Ephesus,

dedicated to an Artemis who possessed some rather barbarous characteristics, the monuments and offerings showed a fusion of the two civilisations. P.D.

IONIAN ISLANDS. The Ionian Islands are the archipelago in the Ionian Sea that stretches from the mouth of the Gulf of Patras northwards along the Greek coast. The largest island is ancient Corcyra, now called Corfu, but in very early times the islands in the centre seem to have played the most important part. Archaeological discoveries in Ithaca, Cephalonia and Levkas confirm the existence, as described by the Homeric poems, of an Achaean kingdom whose chief was none other than Ulysses. Ithaca itself, the seat of the ruler, was the smallest island and, as the *Odyssey* states, " there are neither broad tracks nor meadows there. It is good for goats, but impracticable for horses ". However, Ulysses ruled the neighbouring islands that were not particularly rich either, but possessed more resources. In historic times, Corcyra alone had any importance. It was inhabited by Corinthian colonists, who founded a city there about 734 B.C., and it very quickly became a maritime power, because of its position at the narrowest point between the Adriatic and Ionian Sea, dominating the sea route between Greece and the ports of Sicily and southern Italy. It was not afraid to fight against Corinth and beat its fleet in 665. It sent contingents to found colonies along the coast of Epirus (Epidamnus and Apollonia) and had sufficient resources to build a temple to Artemis in the middle of the 6th century B.C., which was reputed to be the finest in Greece at the time. The sculptures of the pediments have been preserved. In the centre there is a horrible Gorgon from whose blood Pegasus and Chrysaor are being born and, in one of the angles, a giant can be seen fighting against the gods.

Corcyra and the other islands kept themselves out of the Persian Wars, but it was a fresh quarrel between Corinth and her colonies in 433 B.C. that sparked off the Peloponnesian War. P.D.

IPHIGENIA. When the Greeks were preparing to set sail for Troy, Agamemnon at the injunction of the soothsayer Calchas resigned himself to sacrificing his daughter, Iphigenia, to obtain favourable winds from Artemis for the fleet under his command. Clytemnestra, summoned from Argos to Aulis where the Greek fleet was

Tydeus killing the faithless Ismene, the incestuous daughter of Oedipus and Jocasta. Detail of a Corinthian amphora. About 560-550 B.C. Paris, Louvre. *Ph. Hirmer.*

concentrated, brought her daughter with her, thinking that her father wanted to marry her to Achilles. The protests of Clytemnestra against her husband's decision and the pleas of Iphigenia were in vain; however great his grief, Agamemnon would not let himself show any pity. Euripides, in a moving scene, shows the frail Iphigenia finally accepting her death as a contribution to the victory of the Greeks and the sacrifice actually takes place.

This legend covers several, complex traditions. A frequent variation was, at the moment when Calchas was going to cut the throat of Iphigenia, a hind was miraculously substituted for the young girl. Artemis herself intervened, snatched the victim from the altar and made her one of her priestesses. She was carried by the goddess to Tauris in the Crimea, where she celebrated a barbarous rite, killing on her protectress's altar the strangers who landed in the country. One day her brother, Orestes, with his friend, Pylades, disembarked on these distant shores. At the moment of sacrifice, Iphigenia recognised him. She fled with him and Pylades, carrying with her the sacred image of Artemis, which was still worshipped several centuries later in the sanctuary at Brauron in Attica. There is little doubt that this Iphigenia, humanised and romanticised by literature, was a goddess in primitive religion, very similar to the Artemis with whom she was

intimately associated and confused before eventually becoming her servant.   P.D.

IRIS. Iris was the messenger of the gods and more especially of Hera. She obeyed her faithfully, but it was she, nevertheless, who was asked to distract the attention of the goddess when Leto was going to give birth to Apollo.   P.D.

ISAEUS. Isaeus was an Athenian orator and rhetorician. Twelve of his pleadings have survived, all concerned with cases of inheritance. The most interesting is called *On the Inheritance of Philoctemon.* Isaeus possesses the same purity of language and the same stylistic elegance as Lysias, but his dialectic is more vigorous and insistent. His principal claim to glory is in having been the master of Demosthenes.   R.F.

ISMENE. Ismene was the daughter of Oedipus and Jocasta, and the sister of Antigone. In legend she at first only figured as the unhappy heroine of a banal love story; a 6th century B.C. vase painting shows her abandoned by her cowardly lover and killed by the ferocious Tydeus. Later, tragic dramatists gave her a timid personality and made her into the pathetic, frightened child of the frenzied family she was unlucky enough to be born into, incapable of doing more than lament the cruelty of fate.   P.D.

253

ISOCRATES. Isocrates (436-338 B.C.) was an Athenian orator and rhetorician, trained by Gorgias. He earned his living at first as a logographer (q.v.) then, as he could not become an orator himself because of the weakness of his voice, he opened a school of rhetoric in 393. The school was soon famous and students flocked to it from all parts of the Greek world. Among these were Isaeus, Hyperides, Lycurgus, Timotheus the son of Conon, Ephorus of Cyme and Theopompus of Chios, the latter two of whom were historians. He soon became an eminent person through the extent of his connexions and influence; he corresponded with the king of Sparta, Archidamus, with Iasus, the tyrant of Pherae in Thessaly, then with Evagoras, king of Cyprus, and with Philip of Macedon. In 338, at the age of ninety-eight, when he heard the news of the battle of Chaeronea, he is said to have starved himself to death.

Six pleadings, which he composed as a logographer, eight letters and fourteen epideictic discourses survive. These were fundamental to his work. Every teacher of rhetoric had to demonstrate samples of his art in order to attract the public in the first place and then to keep and instruct his pupils; in these set speeches, the rhetorician displayed all the resources of his art for general admiration. The most important surviving pleadings from the time before he opened his school are the *De Bigis,* which contains a sophistic eulogy of Alcibiades, and *Against Callimachus.* The main passage of the second consists of a eulogy of the peace agreements of 403, which sealed the national reconciliation of the Athenians, torn by civil war and foreign occupation. Isocrates consistently preached peace and harmony. Among the epideictic discourses, there are paradoxical eulogies in the sophistic manner: *Encomium of Helen* and *Encomium of Busiris.* Helen, as we know, was not beyond reproach and Busiris, the king of Egypt, had the reputation of being a cruel and bloody tyrant. The great works of Isocrates are the *Panegyricus, On the Antidosis* and the *Panathenaicus.*

The *Panegyricus* is so called because it is thought to have been pronounced at the solemn gathering *(panegyris)* of the Greeks at the Olympic games in 380. In it, Isocrates states his ideas on the future of the Greek cities and the whole of Hellas. He considered that Athens, his native city, had every claim to hegemony. This praise of Athens, "the Greece of Greece" is an echo of Pericles' speech in Thucydides. Isocrates

asked all the Greeks to unite under the leadership of Athens against the hereditary enemy, Persia. *On the Antidosis,* composed about 354, returns to the preoccupations of the rhetorician. He develops his theories on teaching and particularly on the way an orator should be trained. It is here that he explains what he calls his "philosophy", a kind of higher education intended for future men of action and entirely directed towards practical efficiency. The *Panathenaicus,* made public in 339 when Isocrates was ninety-seven, is like a political testament. He has no more faith, as in the days of the *Panegyricus,* that the hegemony of Athens would realise the grand design of panhellenic union against Persia. He considers several rulers in this role, notably Philip of Macedon whose son, Alexander, actually fulfilled the wishes of the rhetorician. Instead, however, of the freely consented union which Isocrates dreamed of, the Greeks were only united by force of arms after Chaeronea.

Isocrates may have been "the most influential political thinker of the 4th century" (G. Mathieu), but he was primarily a great writer of Greek prose. As he proudly claimed in *On the Antidosis,* his most finished compositions" are more like works of art informed with music and rhythm than the language heard before the magistrates". It was a cultivated prose of long, measured, rhythmical periods, with hardly a hiatus between the words and with internal assonances and rhythms. It is really musical, lyrical prose. Isocrates was undoubtedly the precursor of the balanced, harmonious eloquence of Cicero. R.F.

ITHACA. It is no exaggeration to say that Ithaca would have no existence were it not for what Homer has given it. If he had not made it the homeland of Ulysses, no one would pay any attention to this island, one of the smallest in the Ionian Sea, facing the Gulf of Patras and the Acarnanian coast. It is fifteen miles long from north to south and narrow everywhere, especially in the middle, where it is pinched into an isthmus. Rocks and mountains cover it and, as the *Odyssey* says, it possesses "neither broad tracks nor meadows", it is "impracticable for horses", just "good for goats". Although its coasts offer several safe harbours for ships, it played only an insignificant part in history.

This may be a reason for agreeing with the archaeologist, Dörpfeld, that our Ithaca, which the

Two bronze hands with gold bracelets. Taranto Museum. *Photo Leonard von Matt.*

ancients like us identified with Homer's Island. It, in very early times stole its name from the neighbouring and larger Leucas (Levkas), and that Homer thought of this latter island as Ulysses' homeland. It is a bold hypothesis, but perhaps not correct as Leucas, in very early times, was not an island. Its topography, however, does seem to correspond to that of Homer's island, whereas modern Ithaca does not. Ulysses ruled over three other islands, of which two at least, Same or Cephallenia (now Cephalonia) and Zante (now Zakinthos) were prosperous enough to assure his position among the kings of the time, which his cunning would have given a preponderant influence.   P.D.

JASON. Jason was a Thessalian hero. His eventful story goes back to ancient times when his native city, Iolcus, a poor village in historic times, was still worthy of being the seat of a king. When, after a childhood spent on the mountain slopes of Pelion under the tutelage of the centaur, Chiron, he returned to Iolcus, Jason found that his father's throne had been usurped by his uncle, Pelias. Pelias thought he was sending him to his death when he enjoined him to fetch the Golden Fleece. Under the heading, *Argonauts,* an account will be found of this expedition that took the hero across the world, spreading his name and his glory as he went. Jason brought back a stranger from Asia Minor, the sorceress Medea, whom he married in gratitude for the help she had given him in winning the marvellous ram's fleece and in ensuring the hero's escape afterwards by killing her own brother.

From that point, Medea became the dominant personality of the couple. She punished Pelias by persuading the wretched man's own daughters that they would rejuvenate him by boiling him in a cauldron. The couple then had to seek refuge with Creon, the king of Corinth. When Jason, grown tired of Medea, wanted to repudiate her and marry Creon's daughter, Creusa, Medea sent her rival a cloak that burnt the young woman to death. The culmination of her vengeance was to kill the children she had from Jason. After the expedition of the Argonauts, he obviously played a subordinate part and was overshadowed by the figure of the formidable sorceress.   P.D.

JEWELLERY. In Athens during the Persian Wars even men wore gold jewellery in their hair *(See* Head-dress) but male fashions soon became more sober and by the classical period the only male jewellery was a ring with a stone set in it which could be used for impressing seals. There were, however, exceptions, for the gilded youth of the upper classes, the long-haired "knights" of Aristophanes, used to wear metal rings around their ankles and probably other jewellery as well. A dandy like the poet Agathon would even dress and attire himself like a woman. As for the women, their toilette was never complete unless they bedecked themselves with necklaces, bracelets, earrings and metal rings around their ankles. The heavy necklaces with pendants of the Mycenaean and archaic periods were rarely worn by the time of Pericles and had become replaced by lighter necklaces from which amulets against the "evil eye" would often hang. Bracelets were worn on the arm between the elbow and shoulder when the arms were left bare, as well as on the wrist. They were usually spiral-shaped or else simple rings in gold and silver, with clasps sometimes shaped like a figurine. Bracelets were also designed like a serpent coiling on itself. At the time of Pericles, Greek women often pierced the lower ear-lobe so that they

might hang small discs in precious metals from it, sometimes decorated with rose-shapes, or else they wore necklaces shaped as animals to serve as amulets. The fashion of wearing rings around the ankle or calf was very widespread and they were believed to have a religious or magic value *(apotropaios)*. Women kept their jewels in coffers which their slaves would bring them when they wanted to bedeck themselves. This scene is frequently found on painted vases and funerary reliefs, as, for example, the splendid Hegeso stele.
R.F.

JOCASTA. The son of Jocasta, wife of Laius, king of Thebes, was Oedipus. Under the heading of this name an account will be found of how he was exposed as a new-born baby, brought up by the king of Corinth and, ignorant of who were his real parents, killed his father and married Jocasta. Their children were also involved in dark tragedies, but by that time Jocasta was already dead; she took her own life on realising the incest she had unwittingly committed. In popular legend this unhappy queen was only a shadowy character; it was the genius of Sophocles that endowed her with a tragic personality by giving dramatic expression to the sufferings which made her kill herself.
P.D.

JUSTICE. Athenian justice, the only one about which we are well informed because of the pleadings preserved in Aristotle's *Athenaion Politeia,* has two striking features: the absence of a public minister and the extraordinary number of

jurors (at least 501 in the tribunals of the Heliaea).

The city magistrates rarely took the initiative in a case themselves. In private causes *(dikai)* or public *(graphai)*, it was nearly always an ordinary citizen who set the machinery of justice in motion by his complaint, either because he had been injured personally, or because the community *(polis)* to which he belonged had suffered from the action of the man he was accusing. The denunciation of sycophants, that sore of Athenian democracy, was officially encouraged. If the accused man was found guilty, his denouncer could draw a reward amounting to half the fine imposed. It is true that the accuser had to put down a security and, if he failed to obtain a fifth

of the jury votes, he had to pay a heavy fine of a thousand drachmas.

There was, however, at Athens a police force consisting of Scythian archers, who still wore their exotic costume. Their chiefs were the " Eleven ". They could arrest a robber or criminal caught in the act and, if he confessed, execute him on the spot; otherwise they took him before a tribunal for judgment. They also brought denunciation proceedings. They were in charge of the prison and of executions; it was a servant of the Eleven who handed Socrates the cup of hemlock.

The examining magistrates were the nine archons: the chief archon for actions concerned with religion or murder; the archon *eponymos* for the private rights of citizens; the polemarch for the affairs of metics and foreigners; the six *thesmothetai* for anything that affected the material interests of the state. Citizens could not be interrogated, but torture could be applied to slaves who were called as witnesses.

Murder trials were heard by different tribunals: the Areopagus, the Palladium formed of fifty-one *ephetai*, the Delphinion, or the Prytaneis composed of the chief archon and the heads of tribes, which even passed judgment on the animals or inanimate objects that caused the death of the man.

Apart from cases of blood-shedding, the competent judicial body was the popularly constituted Heliaea. The Heliaea was an offshoot of the political assembly of citizens, or Ecclesia, in which all power resided. The Ecclesia itself could act as a court of justice; for example, in 406 B.C. it judged and condemned to death the strategi who, although they had won the naval battle of the Arginusae, were accused of causing through their negligence the death of the soldiers shipwrecked in a storm. Every citizen, when he reached the age of thirty, was eligible for the Heliaea. The total number of *heliastai* or *dikastai* was fixed at six thousand. Each year from a list of candidates drawn up by the demes (q.v.), the nine archons and their secretary drew lots for six hundred names for each of the ten tribes. They took extraordinary precautions to prevent the litigants from knowing in advance the composition of the tribunal judging then, which comprised at least 501 members, sometimes 1001, 1501 or even 2001, as if it were possible to corrupt hundreds of people! At dawn on the day on which the Heliaea was sitting, the heliastai of each tribe had to attend a meeting for drawing lots that would decide the distribution of the jurors to each tribunal, because several juries sat in judgment simultaneously. The apparatus for drawing lots *(kleroteria)*, discovered by American archaeologists in the agora, has enabled us to understand better the three chapters of Aristotle's *Athenaion Politeia* giving a detailed description of the way they worked. Then the heliastai went to the court room to which they had been assigned and sat on the wooden benches covered with rush mats. The magistrate presiding over the session sat on a platform *(bema)* at the end of the room, accompanied by the clerk, a herald and some Scythian archers to keep order. In front of him was the rostrum for pleading and a table on which the votes would be counted. The public crowded round the entrance and was separated from the judges by a barrier. The clerk read the brief drawn up by the examining magistrate. Then the president gave permission to speak in turn to the plaintiff and defendant. Each man had to speak himself without an advocate, but he was allowed to get a professional man, a logographer (q.v.), to write his speech, which he learnt by heart. Many of the legal discourses of Lysias, Demosthenes and other Attic orators were written like this at the request of a client. The pleader could also ask permission of the tribunal to have the help of a friend *(synegoros)* who was more eloquent than himself, or even to have him take his place, provided he was not a professional advocate and was not paid. All non-citizens (women, metics, slaves, freedmen) were represented in the courts by their father, husband, legal guardian, master or patron. The time allowed for the speech of each party was limited by a water-clock, a clepsydra, which worked like an hour-glass. The proceedings continued without a break and had to be completed the same day.

The heliastai remained silent from beginning to end of the session; they could not ask any questions. Then they were told to vote. In the 4th century B.C., they did this by means of two bronze discs traversed by a metal bar, one solid, the other hollow. They filed past two urns of which only the use of the first was valid. They held the discs by hiding the ends of each bar between the thumb and index finger, placed in the first urn either the disc with the hollow bar for a condemnation, or the disc with the solid bar for an acquittal, then they put the remaining disc in the second urn. When the accused was declared guilty by a majority of voices, if the penalty was not fixed by law, an " estimation of the penalty " took place; the accused was told to speak and indicate himself the punishment he considered appropriate. At this point, during his memorable trial in 399 B.C., Socrates declared that he deserved a reward instead: free food at the Prytaneum. A second vote of the heliastai decided the punishment, which could be a simple fine, partial or total confiscation of property, banishment for a period or for life, deprivation of the rights of citizenship, imprisonments or death, sometimes combined with deprivation of burial. (See Penalties, Legal for capital punishment.)

The heliastai were paid a daily allowance as compensation for the loss of their time. Obviously fools and idlers rushed to the tribunals to get the attendance counter and, while earning a living, exercised the " royal " power of a judge to decide the fate, even life, of the accused. The considerable number of heliastai developed a taste for legal proceedings and pettifoggery at Athens. Aristophanes in his *Wasps* did not spare his criticism of this kind of judicial system.

R.F.

KINGS. Although royalty was practically non-existent in Greece during the historic period, it was the normal form of government in the 2nd millennium B.C. Most of what we now know of the ancient Greek monarchy is due to the Homeric epics. Kings ruled by divine right, for they were the sons of Zeus and they transmitted the power derived from their immortal father to their eldest sons.

The functions of the kings were military, religious and civil. They assembled their soldiers, were responsible for their discipline, drew their armies up for battle and led them in the actual fighting. When they were too old to perform this role they handed over their power to their sons, as Peleus did to Achilles. There can be no doubt that they held the initiative in matters of war and peace. As sons of Zeus, the kings were also priests, and through the intermediary of soothsayers they attempted to divine the will of the gods and to appease their wrath whenever their kingdoms were struck by any calamity. It was they who performed the sacrifices. Such morally weighty responsibilities demanded great expenses and as a result, in addition to their own landed property, they were given a piece of land known as the *temenos;* the same word was later used to denote territory belonging to a god. As no tem-

ples seem to have been built in Homeric times, the public religious rites were carried out by the priest-king either in his own dwelling or in front of it. Civil power tended to take second place and the large measure of autonomy enjoyed by the family group, which was characteristic of Homeric society, and reflected Mycenae, left the king with only slight opportunities for intervention. His role was that of a supreme judge or, to be more exact, of an arbiter, since the families had the right to settle their disputes between themselves. The exercise of their religious and judicial functions brought the kings gifts and subsidies which, if Hesiod is to be believed, often vitiated their judgments. Notwithstanding, their prestige was great and even those subjects whom they welcomed and maintained as though they were their equals according to ancient custom, respected their authority, although not always without criticising them like Thersites who, as we know, did not mince his words with Agamemnon.

Such then was the Homeric and Mycenaean pattern of royalty. We do not know to what extent it was modelled after the Cretan monarchy since Minos is nothing more than a legendary name for us now.

This monarchy did not survive the troubles which broke out throughout Greece during the 8th century B.C. In circumstances now unknown to us, the nobles shared an authority which, according to the *Odyssey,* already seems to have been less solid than that described in the *Iliad.* The title of king survived in many cities but it only denoted an annual magistrature of an exclusively religious nature. True royalty as such only survived in Sparta with the peculiarity, which was not uncommon, that power was shared there by two kings who were appointed on hereditary principles, always from the same two families. Despite the fact that they were under the supervision of the ephors, the kings of Sparta remained both materially and morally endowed with powers which were at least the equal of those of the Homeric kings, and when they died their death was mourned as though they had been divine personages.

Although they were surrounded with honours, these Greek kings always remained in close contact with the people they ruled, unlike the barbarian kings, as the Greeks pointed out, especially the Great King of the Persians, who exacted blind submission from the subject peoples they ruled from a distance in their palaces.

Komos scene.
Detail of a krater
by the Pan Painter.
About 470 B.C.
Palermo Museum.
Photo Hirmer.

So different was the spirit of the two monarchical systems that all there really was in common between the Greek kings and their barbarian counterparts was their royal title. P.D.

KOMASTAI. The Greek word *komos* meant both the festival of Dionysus and the merry company celebrating it (it is the origin of our word comedy). *Komastai* were those taking part in the festival. The ceremony could have a religious character and komastai sometimes denoted legendary beings like satyrs and maenads, dancing around their god. More often, however, komastai were simply guests at a banquet who amused themselves when they left by playing, dancing, or turning somersaults with complete abandon; or they could be seen, worn out with revelling, sometimes accompanied by women, a little the worse for drink, walking the deserted streets late at night on their way home. P.D.

KOMOS. A joyous festival procession in honour of Dionysus. *(See* Komastai *and* Comedy).

KORE: KOUROS. The deliberately vague term *kouros* (pl. *kouroi*) is used by archaeologists for the type of male statuary that was most frequently made in the archaic period and similarly *kore* (pl. *korai*) is used to denote any statue of a young girl. These two types of sculpture had already been established before the end of the 7th century B.C. and were to be repeated for more than a century afterwards by sculptors who gradually developed in them the rendering of anatomy and draperies. The carving of drapery only applied to female statues, for the kouros was always represented in the nude, in the guise of an athlete so that the gods might admire the body of the being made in their image. The draperies that the korai always wore consisted either of the Dorian peplos, or the Ionian chiton and himation *(See* Clothing). In order to be consecrated in a sanctuary or set up on a tomb each statue had to render the most characteristic aspect of its sex, the male being shown as a young athlete, the female at her most demure.

Apart from this basic difference, both the korai and the kouroi were endowed with a religious dignity and were represented standing in a frontal pose, with head and body erect. One foot was usually advanced, both to ensure the stability of the statue and to give the impression that the figure could move. As in Egyptian sculpture, it was almost always the left leg that was shown

259

Kore, called the Peplos Kore. About 540-530 B.C.
Athens, Acropolis Museum. *Photo Hassia*.

Kore. About 520 B.C.
Athens, Acropolis Museum. *Photo Hassia*.

The Peplos Kore. Detail. Athens, Acropolis Museum. *Photo Hassia*.

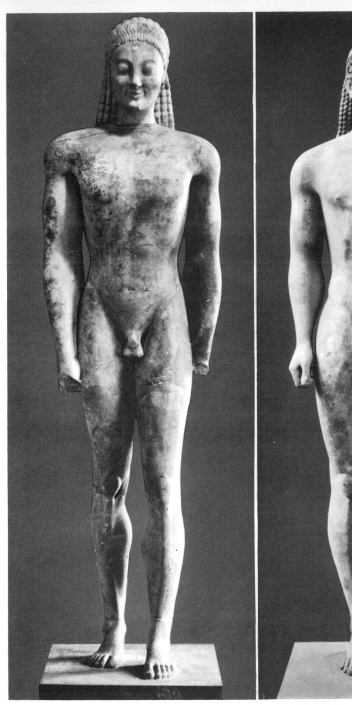

Kouros from Anavysos. About 530 B.C.
Athens, National Museum. *Photo S. Meletzis.*

Kouros from Volomandra. About 550 B.C.
Athens, National Museum. *Photo S. Meletzis.*

advancing; in the beginning, the arms were shown locked to the sides so that they would not break, but later they moved away making a somewhat timid gesture and korai were often represented holding some offering in their hands such as a flower, a fruit, or a dove. Both korai and kouroi were usually life-size and carved in marble or cast in bronze. Different materials were used for such accessories as earrings and necklaces and added later to the finished statue, which was painted in lively colours. Towards the end of the 6th century B.C., sculptors gave a livelier attitude to their figures, and no longer respected the law of frontality by which the left and the right sides of the body were composed with rigid symmetry around a central axis. In addition, expressions became less stereotyped and more individual, so that later male and female statues could no longer be classed in such strictly limited categories as kouroi and korai.   P.D.

LACONIA. This is the region that had Sparta for its capital. The Eurotas flowed through a narrow but fertile plain, hemmed in by high mountains, the most imposing of which were Taygetus to the west and Parnon to the east. There were no important cities apart from Sparta, not even Amyclae which was only well known because of its sanctuary. In the Mycenaean era, Laconia was one of the Peloponnesian provinces most profoundly influenced by Crete and some of the most interesting works of the period have been discovered at Vaphio: two daggers whose blades are inlaid with hunting scenes; and two gold cups with relief decoration, one of the capture of a wild bull and the attack of two others, the other of a wild bull led into captivity with a herd of domesticated bulls.   P.D.

LAERTES. Laertes' memory has only survived because he was the father of Ulysses. During his son's absence, he lived in retirement on his little property, far from public affairs and the difficulties that Penelope was encountering.

LAGIDES. Of all Alexander's achievements, the conquest of Egypt was probably the most momentous and lasting; the qualities of the rulers, who shaped her destinies for more than a century and a half, made the Nile valley and delta one of the poles of the new world. The diadochus (*See* Diadochi) who succeeded Alexander was called Ptolemy, the son of Lagus from whom the name of Lagides was given to the dynasty. He continued the policy begun by his master and managed the interests and susceptibilities of the Egyptians so skilfully that when in 306 B.C., following the example of Antigonus, he assumed the title of king, he set himself up as the heir of Alexander, who was himself designated by the gods as the successor of the pharaohs. He respected their timeless religious traditions, did not interfere with the priests and went no further than adding to the pantheon a deity who was to be a link between the Greeks and Egyptians, Serapis. Although his financial administration did not spare his subjects' fortunes, it was wise and well organised. He made the city of Alexandria, where he had the body of the great conqueror taken, one of the economic and intellectual capitals of the Mediterranean world. His prudence always saved him from getting involved in the intrigues and quarrels among the diadochi. He took little interest in his southern neighbours, but began the conquest of Cyrenaica, which was not finally annexed until the reign of one of his successors, Euergetes, and his attention was always attracted to Greece, particularly the islands of the Aegean, the towns along the coast of Asia Minor and Syria, which had excited the covetousness of the pharaohs from early times. In 312, he succeeded in beating off an attack by Demetrius Poliorcetes and drove back Antigonus to Pelusium in 306. His court, set up on the island of Cos, represented in his day Hellenism in all its glory. He had the wisdom to abdicate in 284 in favour of his younger son, Ptolemy II called Philadelphus, under whose rule Egypt continued to enjoy a period of brilliance. She exercised a brief hegemony in the Aegean, where the Cyclades and Samos were profoundly influenced by Ptolemy and Samothrace was controlled by one of his garrisons. Finally, in 271 he extended his power over Cilicia, Pamphylia and a large part of Syria. He married his sister, Arsinoe, in accordance with Egyptian custom. She had been his mainstay and when she died he suffered a series of reverses in Greece and Syria, which however did not affect Egypt. It was under his successor, Ptolemy III Euergetes, who reigned from 246 to 221, that danger began to threaten the dynasty. Bold and costly ventures that led the Egyptian armies as far as Bactria made inroads into the treasury and forced the government to overtax the people. Public discontent increased under the rule of Ptolemy IV

Philopater after the brilliant victory of Raphia which he won in 317 against Antiochus III; the Egyptians, conscious of their own contribution towards this success, were resentful of being treated as a subject people and having to obey officials who were entirely recruited from among the Greeks. The Hellenisation of Egypt remained superficial; there was no real exchange between the two races living side by side, and one quite clearly dominated the other. Certain cities, Alexandria, Naucratis and Ptolemais, were Greek cities built in a foreign country; the same was true of the small areas wrested from the desert, like the oasis of Fayoum. Elsewhere the Greeks simply formed the executive branch of the regime.

As a result of all this, in the 2nd century B.C. Egypt ceased to hold the eminent position she had occupied before. Her foreign possessions were gradually surrendered and trouble broke out inside the country, which Ptolemy V Epiphanes (203-182) suppressed cruelly. The wars that had ceaselessly embroiled the Ptolemaic dynasty and the Seleucids took a turn for the worse and the Romans were already beginning to take a dangerous interest in a country whose prestige and wealth still remained great. However, it was not till 34 B.C., after the inglorious reigns of a number of kings and queens, that Cleopatra, failing to seduce Octavian as she had enthralled Caesar and then Antony, committed suicide rather than figure in the triumph of the man who had just reduced Egypt to the state of a Roman province.
P.D.

LAIUS. Laius was king of Thebes and a descendant of Cadmus. When his wife, Jocasta, gave birth to a son, he ordered him to be killed immediately because an oracle had foretold that the child would murder his father and marry his mother. But it is no good trying to escape destiny. The baby was not killed, but exposed in a deserted place where he was picked up by a Corinthian shepherd. This child was Oedipus who, when he had grown up, did kill Laius during a quarrel, without knowing the ties that bound him to his victim, and afterwards married Jocasta.
P.D.

LANGUAGE. There were numerous Greek cities in the classical period and each one was an independent state, but the Greeks who lived in them felt they were brothers of the same race because of a common religion and especially because of the common language that distinguished them from all other peoples who did not speak Greek and were called "Barbarians". The decipherment of the Mycenaean tablets by Michael Ventris in 1953 *(See* Linear B) has enabled us to read pre-Homeric texts of the 14th and 13th centuries B.C. The history of the Greek tongue has a continuous development to our own day and, in spite of certain changes, modern Greek derives directly from ancient Greek. Greek is an Indo-European language like Sanskrit, Latin, the Germanic group and most of the languages spoken in Europe today; words like "mother" and "father", for example, are almost identical in all these tongues. Greek spoken at Athens, however, was not exactly the same as that spoken in Sparta or in the Greek villages of Asia Minor, Ionia or Aeolis *(See* Dialects).
R.F.

LAOCOÖN. The story of Laocoön, the priest of Apollo at Troy, has been kept alive for us by Vergil and the famous group of sculpture belonging to the Hellenistic period, now at the Vatican. When the Greeks left the wooden horse in which the best of their warriors were hidden before the walls of Troy, Laocoön did his best to dissuade the Trojans from dragging the dangerous monster inside their town. While he was arguing, two huge serpents rose out of the sea and strangled Laocoön's two sons and when he tried to rescue them he was smothered with them and died in terrible agony.
P.D.

LAPITHS. The Lapiths lived in Thessaly and legend attributed a very remote history to them. They were said to have driven the Pelasgi out of the region of Pindus and Ossa, but they are best known for their fight with the Centaurs The Centaurs were invited by Peirithous, the Lapith king, to the marriage of his daughter, Deidamia, but they disrupted the banquet by trying to carry off the young women and little boys of their hosts. In this famous battle, which has frequently been depicted in art, the Greeks considered the Lapiths were the representatives of civilisation ranged against the savage world.
P.D.

LARISSA. Larissa was founded at least as early as the Mycenaean era. In historical times it was the most important town of Thessaly and the seat of the Aleuadae dynasty. A number of famous men, Pindar, Hippocrates and Plato,

Wife of Peirithous. King of the Lapiths, carried off by a Centaur. Fragment from the west pediment of the Temple of Zeus at Olympia. About 460 B.C. Olympia Museum. *Photo Hirmer.*

stayed there, invited to the court by its half-barbarian princes who were attracted to Hellenism.
P.D.

LAURIUM. Almost at the southernmost point of Attica, on the eastern coast, seams of silver-bearing lead cropping out at Laurium were exploited in very early times, but it was not till 484 B.C. that a particularly rich deposit was discovered and became a source of wealth for Athens, which the poets described as a gift from the gods. These unexpected revenues contributed to the Athenians' victory over the Persians a few years later and in the time of Pericles helped to pay for the adornment of the Acropolis. In spite of the fortresses built in their immediate vicinity, the mines could not always be protected against enemy attack; during the Peloponnesian War, the Spartans occupied the site and enticed away the state slaves, who were quite ready to leave because their labour was so hard. As the deposits were almost exhausted early in the 2nd century B.C., at least by the methods of extraction of those times, the workings were practically abandoned. P.D.

LAWYER. When Greek citizens were summoned to court they could commission a speech in their defence from a professional speech-writer or logographer (q.v.) which they would then learn by heart. They also had the right to be assisted by some more eloquent friend, a *synegoros,* but he was not a professional lawyer, nor could he be paid *(See* Justice). R.F.

LEAGUES. In spite of an intense attachment to their independence, the Greek cities were so small that when they were faced with a strong enemy they were forced to combine with others in a union that was generally short-lived. The leagues formed in this way should not be confused either with the alliances between two or three states even though these too were often of a temporary nature, or with the amphictionies which were founded for the purely religious purpose of administering a common sanctuary. It is not surprising that these leagues did not come into existence until late, particularly during the Hellenistic period when the great kingdoms of Alexander's successors could only be resisted by forces greater than those of isolated states. The Achaean and Aetolian Leagues were sufficiently strong, from the 3rd century B.C. to the Roman conquest, to hold the balance between one side and the other in international conflicts; in fact, the Achaean League played a quite considerable part in bringing the Romans to Greece.

The first leagues known to us were rather different in character from those that sprang up later on. The Delian League offers the best example of the early type. In 477 B.C. when the Barbarians had been driven out of Greece, the Athenians, who were largely responsible for the victory, suggested that the maritime cities should help them to form a fleet powerful enough to prevent the enemy's return. The member states were given the choice of supplying ships with crews or paying a sum of money. Several states joined, but so many of them preferred to make the financial contribution that the result was an Athenian fleet equipped by money from her allies. Consequently, Athens found herself in a position to exert considerable political pressure and she was not slow to turn her allies, who were in principle her equals, into subject states. The league in fact was a means of winning hegemony for its most powerful member.

When the unfortunate outcome of the Peloponnesian War dissolved what remained of the Delian League, some members having regained their independence themselves, Sparta in her turn founded with the spoils of her enemy an organisation inspired by similar ambitions. The second league that Athens formed in 377 B.C., this time against Sparta instead of the Barbarians, was also secretly intended as an instrument for dominating others.

In the middle of the 5th century B.C. there appeared a league that was based on the fairest principles. It was formed in 448 in Boeotia to resist the menace of Athens. All the cities, however poor, were treated on an equal footing and the number of votes given to each one corresponded to the size of its population. They were grouped into eleven districts which sent sixty delegates each to the assembly; a boeotarch was appointed who, with his colleagues, exercised executive power and commanded the army; and although the assembly, a kind of Boule, was split into separate sections, decrees were only passed in a plenary session. The seat of the league was at Thebes, which did not give her a preponderant influence because of this. The league achieved a common monetary and ponderal system and had a court of justice to decide disputes; it was, in fact, organised like a city.

The Achaean and Aetolian Leagues were based on similar principles. The first was founded in the 5th century B.C. but it did not attain any importance until after the death of Alexander. It comprised the Peloponnesian cities and at one time they numbered about sixty. It was governed by two assemblies, one limited in number, the other open to all citizens, which elected the magistrates, most important of whom were the two strategi entrusted with executive powers. Aratus was a pre-eminent figure in this league from 245. His personal prestige enabled him to act more like a king than an elected magistrate and in an expedition against Antigonus Gonatas he liberated Corinth in 243, invaded Attica the following year and then beat the Aetolians. Even the king of Macedonia was forced to negotiate with him. Afterwards, he recalled the new Macedonian king, Antigonus Doson, and gave him the Peloponnesus from which he had driven out his father. Another notable personality later on of the Achaean League was Philopoemen. He succeeded in destroying the power of Sparta, which was hostile to the confederacy, and then turned against Rome, but was killed in an ambush in 182. His death deprived the league of any hope of preserving its independence against the might of Rome.

The tentative beginnings of the Aetolian League went back to quite early times, but it was not definitely organised until about 275. Its constitution was very democratic since all the citizens took part in the supreme assembly held twice a year. A council of a thousand delegates sat in the interval, but as the number of members grew appreciably (about 220, these included Acarnania, part of Phocis, western Locris, Thessaly, the Ionian Islands and finally Boeotia also), a committee limited to thirty was set up over it which made all the decisions in consultation with the two strategi, so that after a certain period this democratic league was ruled by an oligarchy. There were endless conflicts between the Achaean and Aetolian Leagues, but there is no space to give an account of them here.   P.D.

LEDA. Leda was the daughter of Nemesis who married Tyndareos, king of Sparta. Zeus was attracted to her and took the form of a swan to lie with her. Her four children were born from two eggs; Castor and Pollux in one, Helen and Clytemnestra from the other. According to some traditions, Nemesis herself was seduced by Zeus and Leda was only in charge of the eggs. Anyway, between a royal lover, a divine mother,

Warrior, traditionally known as Leonidas. Laconian. About 480 B.C. Athens, National Museum. *Photo Émile.*

whose vengeance was fearful, and children with such adventurous lives, Leda appears as a minor figure. During the Hellenistic period, with its erotic inclinations, she inspired compositions that were as academic in form as they were daring in subject.　　　　　　　　　　　　　　　P.D.

LEMNOS. The little island of Lemnos was situated almost at the mouth of the Hellespont and was reputed to be the favourite resort of Hephaestus, the god of fire, because of its volcanic character. When Zeus hurled him out of heaven, he fell on Lemnos and set up his underground forges there. It was also said that on this spot of land, far away from the usual sea routes, the Greeks abandoned their companion, Philoctetes, because of the disgusting smell from his wound. The island had little historical importance and its interest for us lies in the fact that it possessed one of the earliest remains in the Aegean of a primitive people whom the ancients called the Pelasgi: a 6th century B.C. stele bearing the roughly carved image of a man with a strange profile and an inscription in an undecipherable language whose characters seem related to Anatolian and Etruscan writing.　　　　　　　　　　　　　　　P.D.

LEONIDAS. Leonidas has become the personification of Spartan heroism. In 480 B.C., at the head of three hundred of his fellow country-men, he tried to prevent the huge Persian army from entering the narrow Pass of Thermopylae, which an invader into Greece had to go through. The Greeks were taken in the rear by an enemy contingent guided there by a traitor, Ephialtes, and Leonidas died fighting with his companions. A famous bust found in Sparta and now in the National Museum at Athens is accepted by some scholars as the portrait of this general. The face beneath the high-crested helmet contains a savage energy and there is a dynamic movement latent in the shoulders.　　　　　　　　　　P.D.

LEONIDAS of TARENTUM Lyric poet of the 3rd century B.C. Several of his epi-grams are to be found in the *Greek Anthology*.

LESBOS. Lesbos, also known as Mytilene, is the largest and most fertile island of the Aegean Sea. Like other cities who enjoyed special economic advantages, Lesbos is not given any particular importance in the history books; the Lesbians preferred their material interests and comfort to seeking an uncertain glory or some kind of supremacy in the Greek world. In spite of this, the history of Lesbos was not insignificant. Situated close to the shores of Asia Minor, it was one of the centres of the "Aeolian" people who towards the end of the Iron Age settled on the north-western fringes of Anatolia *(See* Dorians). During the 7th and 6th centuries B.C., it went through the troubles that were ended by the wise Pittacus and then fell under the domination of the Persians. After regaining its freedom with the Persian Wars, it was one of the first to join the Delian League. Although it made attempts to free itself from the sway of Athens when this became too irksome, it did not win its indepen-dence until the end of the Peloponnesian War. It then played a modest part in the complicated diplomacy of the first half of the 4th century and finally fell under the domination of Macedonia.

At one time, it had a reputation for poetry, when Alcaeus and the famous Sappho made it the centre of lyric poetry at the end of the 6th century.　　　　　　　　　　　　　　　P.D.

LETHE. Lethe symbolised oblivion; its significance was allegorical rather than mythological. The source of the river was in Hell and the dead drank its waters to lose the memories of their former lives. Similarly, the consulters of Trophonius's oracle at Lebadea in Boeotia were obliged to drink from a stream that had the same effect.   P.D.

LETO. There is no doubt that Leto, who conceived Apollo and Artemis by Zeus, was a figure of Asiatic origin. She roused the hatred of Hera against her and the goddess, using all her power to prevent the birth of the god of light, forbad every land from receiving the unhappy woman who was seeking a shelter. Only one island, which was too mean to fear anything that might happen, accepted the risk of incurring Hera's punishment. This was Ortygia, renamed Delos after the event. Apollo and Artemis guarded their mother ceaselessly and it was to revenge or protect her that they killed all Niobe's children and also Tityus who tried to rape her.   P.D.

LEUCAS. Leucas is the nearest of the Ionian Islands to the continent and it is only separated from it by a narrow channel. It is a mountainous island, which was inhabited in the Mycenaean era, and it has been argued, but without sufficient grounds, that in Homer's time it was called Ithaca. Subsequently, it had no importance in the life and history of Greece. There is a legend that the poetess, Sappho, desperate with love threw herself into the sea from one of the promontories of Leucas.   P.D.

LEUCTRA. The Spartans were beaten in a pitched battle for the first time at Leuctra. In 371 B.C. at a short distance to the south-west of Thebes, the Athenians and their Boeotian allies met the Lacedaemonian army which had come to force the Boeotians to dissolve the Confederacy that they had formed. The credit of the victory was due to the heroism of the Sacred Band (q.v.) and the tactics of Pelopidas and Epaminondas that broke the phalanx, which until then was reputed to be invincible.   P.D.

LIBANIUS. Rhetorician and literary critic (314-392 A.D.). Libanius was born at Antioch, completed his studies at Athens, then taught rhetoric at Constantinople, Nicaea, Nicomedia and Athens. When he was forty, he returned to settle permanently at Antioch. He taught St John Chrysostom and was a friend of the Emperor Julian the Apostate. Sixty-five of his speeches survive and a large number of letters.   R.F.

LIBRARY. Ancient books consisted of rolls of papyrus or parchment (See Books). We have no information on private libraries in ancient Greece although they must certainly have been very numerous. Plato's Academy doubtless possessed a library but that of Aristotle's Lyceum must have been far more important as the philosophical school was known for its encyclopaedic erudition. When Demetrius of Phalerum had been driven from Athens in 307 B.C. after ruling the city for eleven years, he was commissioned by King Ptolemy Soter of Egypt to organise what we should now call the "University" of Alexandria. Demetrius was a pupil of Theophrastus, Aristotle's friend and successor in the Lyceum. Later, Ptolemy Philadelphus bought Aristotle's personal library, and the royal library of Alexandria, which was an annexe of the Museum, finally contained almost half a million volumes. The chief librarians were nominated by the king and two of the most famous were the poet, Callimachus, who drew up the catalogue of the library, and the great scientist, Eratosthenes, the founder of historical chronology and scientific geography. The kings of Pergamum also built up a rich library and it was there that parchment was invented. Other great intellectual centres were Rhodes and Syracuse, and their public libraries rivalled those of Alexandria and Pergamum.   R.F.

LINEAR B. This is the conventional name given by Sir Arthur Evans to a system of writing which he discovered at Cnossos. The signs peculiar to this writing were engraved on clay tablets, the first of which were dug up in 1900. Since then about 5000 tablets, many reduced to broken fragments, have been discovered, most of them at Cnossos, some at Pylos from 1939 onwards, others at Mycenae from 1952. Inscriptions in Linear B have also been found on Mycenaean jars excavated at Thebes, Tiryns, Eleusis and Orchomenus, which proves the fairly widespread dissemination of this writing.

Linear B was in use at Cnossos before 1400 B.C.; paradoxically, the tablets have only been preserved for us by the fire that destroyed the palace about this date and hardened their clay. The tablets at Pylos seem to date from the 13th century B.C. and those at Mycenae from the end of the same century; evidently, Linear B was used during the Mycenaean period. It is derived from hieroglyphic writing, whose picture-signs were probably gradually replaced by signs with very simplified shapes and, like our own, was read from left to right down the page. It used eighty-seven syllabic signs of which only about sixty were in common use. Each sign represented a whole syllable with the result that there was a complete discrepancy, generally avoided in alphabetic writings, between spelling and pronun-ciation. Words of two to eight signs were sepa-rated by little vertical strokes and they were never split at the end of the line. The texts we have recovered only have a limited interest because all the tablets are in the nature of accounts rendered for merchandise, utensils, tools, etc. and we have lost hope of discovering the remains of a Mycenaean literature which, although its exis-tence is likely, could never have gone beyond the oral stage.

Linear B remained an enigma for a long time and scholars could not progress further than statistical studies on the frequency of various signs and their varying position within words. They thought that Linear B was the transcription of an unknown language and they were sure that they were confronted with a simple kind of syllabary. They did, however, also succeed in detecting the presence of declensions, the use of two genders (a discovery facilitated by picto-grams clearly indicating the receipted articles) and the relations between signs. In spite of these discoveries, all the credit for deciphering is due to a young English architect, Michael Ventris (1922-1956), who was passionately interested in the problem of the Minoan writings. After lengthy analytical investigations, Ventris hit on the idea of drawing up a table, a " grid " as he called it, in which the signs likely to share the same consonant but with different vowels were placed on the horizontal lines, and the signs sharing the same vowels, but with different consonants were placed in the vertical columns. After placing most of the signs in general use on this grid, Ventris took a group of words that were thought to denote Cretan places, and he tried to make them corres-pond with place names known from historic times. He identified by this method the names of Cnossos and Amnisus, which gave him the value

of six signs. These, in their turn, gave him the values of three vertical columns and five horizontal lines of his grid. The syllabic values isolated in this way produced elements of vocabulary bearing a certain resemblance to Greek and Ventris, although he did not at first believe in this solution, investigated the possibilities of a Greek interpre-tation. This resulted in a certain number of Greek words that all made plausible sense in their context. With the help of John Chadwick, Ven-tris continued his researches in this direction, trying to find the value of all the signs commonly used in Linear B. His theory, discussed in an article, which caused a considerable stir, " Evi-dence for Greek Dialect in the Mycenaean Ar-chives " (Journal of Hellenic Studies, 1953), was given striking confirmation shortly afterwards when it was applied to the transcription of a large tablet recently discovered at Pylos. It enabled a series of Greek words to be read on the tablet, which elucidated beyond any doubt the picto-grams inscribed on it and denoting the articles in question. Other tablets brought further confir-mation and most scholars have subscribed to Ventris's theory, that the language written in Linear B is an archaic Greek dialect which is called by the conventional name of Mycenaean.

B.N.

LITURGY. This was an Athenian institu-tion which has no equivalent in our civilisation. The state expected the wealthiest citizens to assume financial responsibility for certain public activities: organising festivals and drama competi-tions, equipping a warship and entertaining dis-tinguished guests. The archons or strategi desi-gnated officially those on whom these charges devolved and no one could refuse unless he put forward the name of another citizen whom he considered wealthier than himself. If he, in his turn, objected and alleged that he could not afford the expenses, the two parties were asked to exchange properties, which cut short the dispute about who was better able to pay them.

A liturgy was a heavy expense, so heavy that after the 4th century B.C. it had to be shared by several people. It comprised certain duties that were judged by a kind of tribunal; for example, after plays were acted the liturgists were judged on the quality of the spectacle put on at their expense. The liturgy was also an honour and the man who exercised it was regarded as a kind of magistrate. If the troupe he had financed was

Votive relief in terra-cotta from Locri. Offering brought to Persephone. About 470-450 B.C. Taranto Museum. *Photo L. von Matt.*

on the site. They are not only beautiful objects but invaluable sources of information for beliefs in the after-life. P.D

LOCRIS. Locris was one of the little provinces on the northern shores of the Gulf of Corinth. In spite of the nearness of Delphi, it was too poor to make its mark on the Greek world. It moved in the orbits of more important cities and was strongly affected by the political influence of Thebes especially. Its principal city, Amphissa, which controlled the approach to Delphi found itself on several occasions in difficulties with that town. P.D

LOGOGRAPHER. At first the word *logographos* denoted any writer of prose, particularly an historian, in contradistinction to the *poietes*, a poet. Then its meaning became more specialised and was applied to the writer of speeches composed for other people who would read or recite them before a judicial tribunal. In fact at Athens, every citizen taking part in a legal action had to speak himself; he was not allowed to employ an advocate to defend him. If he thought he was incapable of doing this himself, he commissioned a speech from a professional man, a logographer who was paid for his services, and learnt the text by heart. Many of the surviving speeches of Lysias, Isocrates, Demosthenes and others were written in these circumstances at the request of a client. Lysias's discourse, *For the Cripple,* is a typical example. R.F

LONG WALLS. When he decided to base the power of Athens on her maritime strength, Themistocles had the town and port of Piraeus prepared for this purpose. About six miles separated Athens from what was to be her access to the rest of the world by sea, six miles of plain that a hostile army could occupy without difficulty. To avoid the risk of blockade Cimon had two walls built between the two towns: one ran in a straight line, or very nearly, from Athens to Piraeus; the other, further to the south, gradually diverged from the first and ended near Phalerum. Pericles, to reduce this gap and facilitate defence, built a third wall which ran parallel to the first about 650 feet to the south of it. This fortified corridor,

judged the best, he was crowned himself—a purely honorary reward.

The main liturgies were the *choregia* and the trierarchy. The second, which was probably instituted when Themistocles built up the Athenian navy, involved the financing of a ship whose hull, rigging and crew were supplied by the state; the trierarch had to pay for the necessary repairs and upkeep of the vessel during the year that his liturgy lasted. As a compensation, he was in charge of the boat. The strategus who appointed him was not the least concerned with his competence in naval matters, only with his financial qualifications, and the real responsibility for the ship was entrusted to an experienced subordinate. The choragi undertook to recruit, support and equip at their own expense the choruses who took part in the drama competitions. According to an order decided by lot, each choragus chose a poet whose play would be performed by his troupe and, like the author and actor, the choragus received a crown when the play he had supported was judged the best. P.D.

LOCRI EPIZEPHYRII. This town was founded about 673 B.C. in Magna Graecia by colonists from Locris in Greece. The worship of the Eleusinian goddesses was widespread and several terra-cotta plaques have been discovered known as the Long Walls, secured communications between Athens and its port even in time of war. The Long Walls were destroyed by order of Lysander in 404 B.C., but Conon had them rebuilt a few years later.   P.D.

L O N G I N U S (1)   A rhetorician of the 3rd century A.D. The treatise, *On the Sublime*, was incorrectly attributed to him, as it appears to have been written in the second half of the 1st century A.D.

L O N G I N U S (2). Fiction writer of the 2nd century A.D. and author of the pastoral called *Daphnis and Chloe (See* Romances).

L O V E. Modern and sometimes ancient authors have tended to confuse Aphrodite and Eros in so far as they were divine personifications of human emotions. After all, they were mother and son, and the symbols of love. The ancient Greeks nearly always made a clear distinction between the two divinities, for they considered Aphrodite to be the goddess of physical union and carnal love, and Eros to be the god of sentiment and passion.

For the Greek philosophers who defended homosexual love, Eros was firstly the god of the *erastai* and *eromenoi*, but in theory, at least, he was the god presiding over amorous friendships which remained pure. In his *Deipnosophistae* (The Learned Banquet) Athenaeus wrote: " So far were the Greeks from believing that Eros presided over any sexual union that in the very same Academy which they had consecrated to Athena, (the virgin goddess), they set up a statue to Eros to whom they made sacrifice at the same time as Athena. "

For the Greeks then, Eros's main role was to preside over the passionate attachment of a grown man for a boy, while Aphrodite presided over the sexual relations between man and woman; but by an extension of meaning, and in second place, Eros might also be invoked in all cases of amorous passion for either a woman or a boy, and Aphrodite for any sexual relationship, be it homosexual or heterosexual. The Greeks considered beauty to be a gift from the gods and a wonderful privilege, but one which implied certain duties as it was essential to achieve both outer and inner harmony, between the soul and the body. This was the profound meaning of the words *kalos k' agathos* (beautiful and good)

which defined the human ideal of the classical period. The Homeric epics are without a single trace of " Greek love ". Paederasty (love for boys) mainly appears in Greece during the period between the 7th and 5th centuries B.C., and often was pedagogic from one aspect, since the erastai would become the mentors of their eromenoi *(See* Education). But the laws of nearly all the Greek states, and the majority of moralists formally condemned homosexual physical relations. It was rather pure friendship between an elder man and a youth that was recommended and exalted, and considered to be the source of manly virtue. Female homosexuality was rarer but certainly existed in Greece. Sappho, the female poet of Lesbos, sang with burning passion in her verses of the love she felt for her lovely pupils.

The Platonic theory of love claimed to sublimate the sentiments that Eros, the son of Aphrodite, had aroused in order to transform them into a driving force for the spirit to attain inner beauty, the knowledge of higher realities and, lastly, identification with God. The Greek romances were largely inspired by Plato's ideas and helped to diffuse them outside the circles of the philosophers, thus anticipating the " courtly " or " knightly " love of the Middle Ages.   R.F.

L U C I A N. Lucian (125-194 A.D.), a writer whose mother tongue was Syrian, was born at Samosata in Commagene by the upper reaches of the Euphrates. His family, of moderate means, decided that he should be a statue-maker, but he persuaded them to let him continue his studies in Ionia where he became an enthusiastic admirer of Greek culture. He worked as an advocate at Antioch, but soon gave up law for the profession of a wandering sophist. He lectured in Italy, notably at Rome, in Gaul, Macedonia, Greece and Asia Minor. Athens attracted him more than any other city; in 165, when he was forty, he went to live there and stayed for twenty years. Most of his masterpieces, which he read in public before circulating them, were produced in this period. In spite of his celebrity at Athens and his low opinion of the Romans, he applied for a safe and well paid administrative post in the empire because he thought he was not earning enough money. He was appointed assistant in legal affairs to the governor in Egypt and died towards the end of the reign of Commodus.

There are eighty-two pieces in Lucian's collected works, none of which are very long, but about ten of them are suspect if not definitely spurious. His favourite genre was the dialogue in the form of a short comedy like the mimes of Sophron and Herondas: *Dialogues of the Dead, Dialogues of Courtesans, Sailors' Dialogues.* The *Icaromenippos, Charon* and *Necromancy* are reminiscent of Aristophanes' fantastic situations. *Timon* was inspired by Menander's *Dyskolos.* The best writings not in dialogue form are the *Treatise on how to Write True History* (so called because, as the author declares in the preface, it contains absolutely nothing true) and the *Donkey,* if this Milesian tale packed with bawdy jokes can indeed be attributed to Lucian.

All his works are light, swift, ironical, caustic, and their biting mockery is aimed mainly at the gods and philosophers. The poets are not spared either; Lucian does not respect even those Greek writers whom he most admired, in the front rank of whom was Homer. He " was not hostile to paganism in particular but to all religion. He considered the irreligion of Epicurus to be the hallmark of Greek culture. The basic features of his conception of culture are scepticism and an educated élite in Attica. " (M. Caster). R.F.

L U X U R Y. In 594 B.C., Solon promulgated a law limiting the ostentation of women: " When they went out they were not to wear more than three garments, they were not to carry more than an obol's worth of food or drink, nor a basket more than a cubit high ". (Plutarch, *Solon,* XXI, 5). In classical Athens, the houses of some wealthy citizens were decorated with comparative luxury. Alcibiades confined the painter, Agatharchus, in his house for three months and forced him to decorate it with frescoes. Yet, the much vaunted luxury of Alcibiades' house seems modest to us; the inventory of his possessions sold in execution of the sentence, passed at the end of the trials of the Hermocopidae and Eleusinian Mysteries, mentions two cloaks, and a personal estate of which the most sumptuous furnishings were four tables in the dining rooms and twelve couches " of Milesian workmanship ". The total sum realised by the sale was only 120 drachmas. In the 4th century, Phocion's house in the Melite, a deme of Athens, was " bare and simple except for some ornamental bronze plaques " (Plutarch, *Phocion,* XVIII). Excavations at Olynthus have discovered houses of the same period, where the men's

apartment *(andron)* and the peristylar courtyard are decorated with mosaics.

Besides beds, tables, chairs and stools, furnishing also included chests and caskets for clothes and jewels. Many painted vases signed by famous artists were not used for any domestic purposes but displayed as ornaments. Vase paintings often depict *thymiateria,* tall perfume-burners in houses; the Greeks liked to perfume their houses for parties and festivals. During the classical period, simple comforts were often lacking and private bathrooms were only to be found in the richest houses, most Athenians had to wash at the basin of a fountain. Admittedly they could also go to public baths, which increased in number in the 4th century B.C. and where rooms were sometimes reserved for women.

In the Greece of the century of Pericles, precious materials, marble, gold, silver and ivory, were used mainly in temples. Phidias made two chryselephantine statues, Zeus at Olympia and Athena for the Parthenon at Athens. It was only after Alexander's conquests when Persian gold flowed into Greece that luxury could attain considerable proportions as the houses on Delos indicate with their peristyles, rich mosaics and marble statues. R.F.

L Y C E U M. Aristotle's school at Athens is often called the Lyceum because this was the name of the gymnasium, near the temple of Lycian Apollo, where the philosopher used to teach. Later on, it was also called the Peripatos, or covered walk, because it was the custom to walk up and down while carrying on a discussion, which also gave rise to the term, Peripatetic School. Its members pursued their investigations as a group into scientific and philosophical matters. In the time of Theophrastus (q.v.), who succeeded his master as head, Eudemus of Rhodes compiled a *History of Geometry* and Menon a *History of Medicine,* only fragments of which have survived. Aristoxenus of Tarentum wrote the *Elements of Harmony* and *Elements of Rhythm,* which we possess, and several works on music. We also have fragments by the historian, Dicaearchus, and Clearchus of Solis, who upheld the conception of a separate soul against several of his fellow-students and was an advocate of the active life against Theophrastus, who was in favour of the contemplative life. Theophrastus was succeeded by Strato of Lampsacus (288-269 B.C.), a physician who had much in common with

Democritus (q.v.) without going as far as his atomism; he moved towards a sort of mechanism but did not abandon the concept of qualities. The other scholarchs are less well known with the exception of Critolaus, whom the Athenians sent, with Carneades and Diogenes the Stoic, as ambassador to Rome in 156 B.C. According to Critolaus, the well-being of the soul, the well-being of the body and external well-being are all three necessary to a life lived in conformity with nature.   P.-M.S.

L Y C I A . Lycia lies at the south-western extremity of Asia Minor shut in between high mountains and the sea. In spite of its isolation, it was conquered by distant Persia, and was affected sometimes by eastern influences, sometimes by Greece, which all gave an unusual character to its art and architecture. Its funerary art was very original and in the wild beauty of its country there are still to be found isolated sarcophaguses with covers in a triangular arch just like the wooden houses that the Lycians used to live in. There is a prince's tomb belonging to the first quarter of the 5th century B.C., a curious structure consisting of a high pillar or base surmounted by a sarcophagus whose walls are decorated with scenes in relief illustrating beliefs, alien to Hellenism, of this " barbarian " people; but the influence of Greek sculpture is apparent even when the figures are those of the Harpies, carrying off souls, which have given the monument its name. The tomb of the Nereids, a century later, is much more classical. This too is a royal tomb consisting of an aedicule in the form of a temple, erected on a base of Asiatic design. The female statues placed between the columns are, like all the friezes on the base and the entablature, by Greek artists.   P.D.

L Y C O P H R O N . Lycophron was a poet of the Alexandrian period, who wrote tragedies, now lost, and a poem of nearly 1500 lines called *Alexandra* which has survived. It elaborates in obscure and amphigoric verse the imaginary prophecies of Alexandra, or Cassandra, the daughter of Priam.   R.F.

L Y C U R G U S . Lycurgus is like Daedalus in another sphere, one of the figures that the Greeks imagined to explain the existence of a number of inventions and institutions whose ori-

gins they could not bear to leave anonymous. The oldest reference to this legislator, so often mentioned by ancient and modern writers, is to be found in Herodotus and so is no earlier than the middle of the 5th century B.C. Before that, Pindar himself, although he was interested in everything relating to the Dorians, seems to be unaware of his existence and the same applies to several other writers who could at least have alluded to this illustrious figure. In Sparta itself Lycurgus was probably not unknown in the 5th century or even towards the end of the 6th century, but his reputation could not have been very great. When the Greeks began to be interested in him, they could not decide, like the Pythia herself at Delphi, whether he was a man or a god. The most contradictory tales of his origins circulated; even these were incomplete and Plutarch wondered at the outset of his biography how he was going to get to the end of it. He was of royal blood, but the kings of Sparta belonged to two different families and no one was quite sure whether Lycurgus was an Agid or a Eurypontid, whether he was king himself or the guardian and uncle of a king. According to some narratives, the Pythia at Delphi gave him the writings that he passed on to the Spartans to rule their state; according to others, he found his inspiration in Crete and only went to Delphi for ratification of the code that he brought back from his journey to the great island. Actually, the institutions attributed to him which gave Sparta its exceptional character were a series of customs and rites, almost magical acts, going back some centuries earlier. They did not know to within three centuries —from the 11th to the 8th—when Lycurgus lived and he would have done no more than formulate and codify these customs. It is arguable that the figure of Lycurgus, who may have been an actual person, did not acquire any solid reality until about the middle of the 6th century B.C. After the war against Tegea, at a time when Sparta was in danger of being torn apart by inner conflicts, an energetic ephor called Chilon tried, by returning to traditions that were being abandoned at Sparta as elsewhere, to give back strength to the state and vitality to the people. He did not claim responsibility for these reforms himself, but deliberately campaigned for this return to the past in the name of a figure that may have meant something to the Spartans, but which had probably lost all its forcefulness in the mists of distant times and forgotten generations.   P.D.

Lydia. Coin of King Croesus: a pure gold stater. Obverse: foreparts of a lion and a bull. 561-546 B.C. Basel, Antiken Museum.

LYCURGUS of ATHENS.

Lycurgus was an orator and statesman (about 390-324 B.C.) of the old Athenian nobility, who with Hyperides was Demosthenes' staunchest supporter in the struggle against Philip of Macedon. After Chaeronea (338), his fellow-citizens showed their confidence in him by making him the chief administrator in the state, a sort of Minister of Finance and Public Works. The people conferred on him the honour of burial in the Ceramicus. Only one of his speeches survives, *Against Leocrates*, an extremely severe indictment against an Athenian who had basely fled from the city on receiving the news of the defeat at Chaeronea. The speech reflects from beginning to end the rigidity and hardness of Lycurgus's character, his strong sense of duty and absolute intransigence. The style matches the thought; it is sententious, marked with intellectual effort and shows a complete contempt for gracefulness and irony, but Lycurgus strikes true, proudly and vehemently.

R.F.

LYDIA.

Although Lydia, with its capital of Sardes, had no direct access to the sea, it was one of the first of the Anatolian provinces to make contact with Greece. This was because of the policy of the Mermnadae dynasty (from about 687 to 548 B.C.) whose outstanding rulers were Gyges and Croesus; superstition as much as self-interest made them try to conciliate the gods of Olympus and we share Herodotus's astonishment at the number and sumptuousness of the offerings at the sanctuary of Delphi, specially those from Croesus. This wealth came largely from the Pactolus, a river in the region that washed down grains of gold. It seems that until 548, when she

was conquered by the Persians, Lydia was the most powerful and refined kingdom in all Asia Minor. According to some, coinage was first minted there. The idea of a tyranny may also have come to Greece from Lydia; anyway, most of the Greek tyrants established their rule over their fellow-citizens according to methods already used by Gyges.

P.D.

LYRIC POETRY.

In the history of Greek literature, lyric poetry developed after the epic and flourished in the period stretching from the middle of the 8th to the end of the 5th century B.C. The epic myth and the legendary tale still found a place in lyric poetry, but they were not essential elements as in the epic. They were often completely absent and when present they were not recounted for their own sake; the poet was content to make a passing allusion. The essence of the lyric was the poet's emotions, his own religious sentiments and those of the people on whose behalf he was singing, and the circumstances that inspired the song. The *aoidoi* and epic *rhapsodoi* (qq.v.) chanted to their own accompaniment on the lyre. Lyric poetry gave much greater importance to singing, music and dancing, consequently the epic hexameter was not sufficiently flexible for the variety of rhythms required by these melodies, and lyric metres flowered with an extraordinary diversity. The flute was added to the lyre and cithara. The Homeric tongue continued to influence lyric poets, but in spite of these borrowings, each writer expressed himself mainly in his own dialect: Aeolian at Lesbos, Dorian at Sparta, Ionian at Smyrna and Ceos. Certain traditions became established in each genre and the lyric chorus, originating in Dorian country, was always written in the Dorian dialect, even in 5th century tragedy at Athens.

The Greek lyric assumed a prodigious variety of forms. First, there is personal poetry in which the poet, writing for himself, expresses his own feelings, passions, tastes and ideas. A number of different kinds can be distinguished in it: elegiac poetry, consisting of alternate hexameters and dactylic pentameters, which was generally grave and sententious, like that of Theognis; iambic poetry that was mainly satirical and aggressive in tone, like that of Archilochus; the song or Lesbian and Ionian ode, in praise of love and pleasure, like the compositions of Sappho and Anacreon. Then there is occasional poetry composed for religious or civic ceremonies in which the poet became the mouthpiece of the community. This was the choral lyric that covered several genres: the religious *hymnos,* the solemn and noble *paian* (paean), the *prosodion* and *parthenia,* which were processional songs; the *hyporchema* with a quick beat; the dithyramb, a noisy, round chorus in honour of Dionysus; *enkomia,* or eulogies, which include the *epinikia,* songs of victory in honour of winners at the panhellenic games; and finally, the *threnoi,* or songs of mourning. The outstanding poets of lyric choruses were Alcman, Arion, Stesichorus, Simonides, Bacchylides and Pindar (qq.v.). Tragedy grew out of the dithyramb, but it still remained an independent feature at the festivals of the Great Dionysia and Thargelia during the 5th and 4th centuries.   R.F.

LYSANDER. It was in large measure due to Lysander's victory in 404 B.C. that the Peloponnesian War fought between Athens and Sparta for thirty years eventually ended. He was a curious character; a great patriot, disinterested, courageous and intelligent, yet he did not hesitate, in the interests of his country, to lie, perjure himself and stoop to bribery and, when it was a question of winning victory for Sparta, saw no shame in solliciting money from Persia which was generally considered the hereditary enemy. His guiding principle was " to sew the fox's skin to the lion's pelt ".

He was appointed nauarch, or high admiral, in 408 and used the money given to him by Cyrus, brother of the Persian king and governor general of western Asia, to raise the pay of his sailors and so lure away the Athenian crews who were attracted by the prospect of a higher salary. He was quite ready to take the offensive, but did not attack until he was sure of victory; he refused battle when he was confronted by Alcibiades, but engaged when the Athenian fleet was deprived of this brilliant leader and with these tactics, he won a great victory at Notium in 407 and another, even more decisive, at Aegospotami in 405. The second left him free to blockade Athens by sea and force it to surrender.

Not content with being victor, he virtually decided the fate of the vanquished. He refused to give his allies the satisfaction of razing the city of Pericles, but he imposed an oligarchic government on it that his intrigues had long been preparing. Intoxicated by success and the countless honours heaped on him by the cities delivered from the yoke of Athens, he made himself quite unbearable to the Greeks to whom he had promised the vintage of liberty and then, in the words of Plutarch, " only gave sour wine ". Even in Sparta itself, his insolence seemed dangerous and provoked the intervention of Pausanias II. Lysander then invaded Asia Minor and pillaged the cities of Aeolis. This roused the anger of the Persian King who demanded that Sparta should recall him. He embarked on a hazardous career and died in Phocis at the moment when the army under his command was beaten at Haliartus by a coalition of the Athenians, Corinthians, Thebans and Argives (395).
                                                                P.D.

LYSIAS. Lysias (about 440-360 B.C.) was an Attic orator, who was born at Athens, but was not an Athenian citizen. He was a metic like his father, Cephalus, a Syracusan living at Athens, and yet this metic was to be considered one of the purest of Attic writers. About thirty of his speeches survive, some of which are unfinished. Several are epideictic, like the *Olympiacus* of 388 from which only a part of the exordium remains, but most of them are pleadings composed by Lysias acting as a logographer. The outstanding discourses are *Against Eratosthenes, Against Simon* and *For the Cripple.*

Only one of Lysias's judicial speeches was written for himself and delivered by him, *Against Eratosthenes,* composed in 403. Eratosthenes, one of the Thirty Tyrants, had Polemarchus, the brother of Lysias, killed to get possession of his fortune and Lysias narrowly escaped death himself. This speech is a masterpiece of grave, measured eloquence, often tinged with irony. As a logographer, Lysias eclipsed Antiphon and even Isocrates. He excelled at making his clients speak naturally and simply, while giving them the surest arguments calculated to move and sway the judges.   R.F.

LYSIPPUS. Lysippus is an obscure personality. He was a sculptor and near contemporary of Praxiteles, but differed from him in inspiration and style. He came from Sicyon and seems to have been self-taught. Primarily a maker of bronzes, he shared the aesthetic ideal of

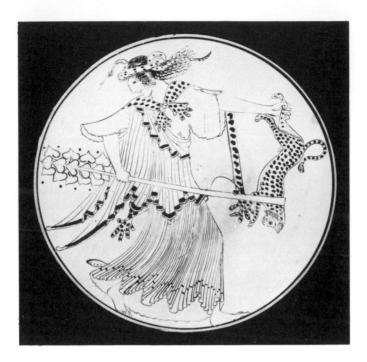

Maenad. Inside of a cup by Brygos. About 490 B.C. Munich Antikensammlung.

his Peloponnesian predecessors, an athletic ideal that the rest of Greece was abandoning. He used to say that his real master was Polycletus (q.v.) whom, of course, he had never known but whose work he had studied at first hand. Although their models of sports winners were the same, Lysippus transformed their rather ponderous strength and restful stability into a nervous suppleness, poised on the point of movement. The proportions have elongated and the face seems tense. The body is no longer facing frontwards, but always seems about to pivot on its hips; the transition from one plane to another is made imperceptibly and he obtains an almost fluid effect by the play of light reflecting from polished bronze. This in no way detracts from the vigour of the figure, its dynamism is on the contrary increased.

The masterpiece of Lysippus is the *Apoxyomenos,* known to us through bronze replicas, which probably have not retained the inner vitality of the original. It represents a nude man standing and rubbing his left arm with a strigil. Although this is not a violent movement, it possesses an extraordinary intensity. It may have been the characteristic spirit of his works that made him the

favourite sculptor of Alexander, who always carried around with him a little statue of Heracles, the *Epitrapezios,* by Lysippus. He was the only sculptor allowed to carve an image of the great conqueror. We know that he did other portraits, but it is impossible to decide exactly how much of the enormous output of the 4th century B.C. belonged to him.　　　　　　　　　　P.D.

MACEDONIA. Although the Macedonian ruling dynasty claimed descent from Heracles and therefore considered that it belonged to the Hellenic race, the Greeks continued to regard Macedonia as a barbarian country. It was difficult to reach both by land and by sea—the shoreline was far from hospitable—and the country extended from Mount Olympus and the Pindus chain of mountains, in the south and the west, to the vaguely defined frontiers of Thracia in the east, almost facing the isle of Thasos; the northern frontiers consisted of a high mountain chain through which the rivers Strymon and Axios (now called Vardar) made their way. With its greater number of mountains, its vast and marshy plains, rivers that never dried up in the summer, and its great forests, Macedonia is quite different in aspect

276

from the rest of Greece. Its inhabitants mainly lived by hunting, agriculture and stock-breeding. Macedonian civilisation was of the Danubian type until the 7th century B.C. when the foundation of numerous colonies opened the way for Hellenic influences, but there were no real towns or anything that might be called a city.

In the 7th century a royal dynasty established itself at Aigae (now Edessa) and was fairly successful in uniting the country and extending its authority over the turbulent princes who ruled over the various small tribes. In the 5th century, during the reigns of the kings Alexander I, the Philhellene, and Archelaus, the country developed closer relations with Greece. Thasos, Athens and Sparta all fought over the region of Pangaeus which was particularly rich in wood and precious metals, but the local people defended themselves fiercely. In about the middle of the 4th century, Macedonia began to play an unexpected role in Greek politics which it was eventually to dominate. In 360 B.C., King Philip II came to the throne of Macedonia and, after triumphing over the intrigues of his subjects, consolidated his authority and took advantage of the dissensions between the Greeks in order to penetrate southwards. His victory at Chaeronea in 338 made him master of the cities who had been fighting for supremacy until then, and, despite Demosthenes' efforts, Athens itself fell under Macedonian rule. Philip died in 336 and was succeeded by Alexander who transformed the hitherto anarchic and feeble nation of Macedonia into the mistress of nearly the whole of the Mediterranean world. But this hegemony was short-lived, for after Alexander died in 323 the Greek states revolted, the royal family was torn apart by internal dissensions and during the successive rules of Demetrius Poliorcetes (291), Lysimachus (285) and the Seleucids, Macedonia was simply one of many Hellenistic kingdoms until it fell prey to the Romans in 168, and was reduced to the rank of a mere province some twenty years later. P.D.

MAENADS. The Maenads were maidservants of Dionysus and followed him in procession or else accompanied him dancing. Intoxicated by mystical passion, they would run in the mountains waving the thrysus, a long stick ending with a bunch of grapes, which was one of the symbols of the cult. In their delirium, they were incapable of recognising even their own brothers and sons; and, according to the legend, it was thus that they killed Pentheus by tearing him apart in their frenzy. In imitation of these mythical figures, some Greek women in certain festivals would also enter into a trance by chewing ivy, which made them half mad, and they would then run through the forests at night, killing any small animals they might find on their way. Greek art has frequent representations of Maenads; one of the most famous was by Scopas and is now only known to us by a replica of the original.
P.D.

MAGIC. So much has been said about the rationalism of the ancient Greeks that we rather tend to forget the place that magic had in their beliefs and everyday life. Magic is even to be found at the very basis of their art since for them the image was first the exact equivalent and substitute for the being represented, in archaic times, statues were chained so that the divine protectors they embodied might be kept in the cities, and in the decoration of many of the earliest temples a special place, which might be the most visible or the most vulnerable, was reserved for figures like that of the Gorgon who were held to avert evil spirits. With the exception of Circe in the *Odyssey,* and Medea in drama, Greek literature made hardly any mention of the existence of magic and its servants until the end of the 4th century B.C. The first writer to describe it openly was Theocritus and in one of his best *Idylls* he mentions the practices of naïve souls who hoped for a miraculous fulfilment of their wishes and, more particularly, the case of a young woman who tried to make her unfaithful lover return to her. But numerous popular texts, which have survived on papyrus, show that the means used, the formulas, incantations, gestures and instruments were as varied as the desires of those who put their trust in magic. Wax or lead images were pierced with needles to bring about the death of the enemies they represented, nocturnal sacrifices were made to avenging divinities, necromancy and the use of such instruments as the *iynx,* a kind of magic top, were among the many curious measures employed by a clientele who, as time went on, came from every rank of society. There can be no doubt that magic in Greece received its main impetus from abroad, for the very name is derived from the name of the Persian priests, and the Egyptians had always been given to secret rites. From the very begin-

The sorceress, Circe, offering Ulysses a drink that would have turned him into a pig. Detail of a comic skyphos from Kabeiroi in Boetia. 4th century B.C. Oxford, Ashmolean Museum.

ning the most famous magicians, such as Medea, and the most efficacious rites came from the orient. Besides the enfeeblement of official religion, the extension of Hellenic civilisation as a result of Alexander's conquests and the fusion of peoples must all have been determining factors in the extraordinary growth of the popularity of magic in the centuries immediately preceding the Christian era. P.D.

MAGISTRACY. The magistracy was not a career for the ancient Greeks. It involved political or priestly duties as well as the administration of justice and every citizen had the chance of becoming a magistrate at some time. With the exception of certain states, where aristocratic tendencies prevailed and where the choice of magistrates was determined by class considerations, magistrates were either appointed by election or, as was more frequent, by the drawing of lots. The Athenian system of magistrature is the best known to us and we know that the importance of the various offices differed greatly; each year, the choice was made not only of the archons and strategi (qq.v.), who constituted the government properly speaking, but also of such municipal officials as the *agoranomoi,* who were responsible for the supervision of the markets. No special qualifications were required for candidature: all that was required was to be a citizen, to have never been condemned in court for any infamy, and to have honoured the patron gods of the city.

On relinquishing his office, the magistrate had to give an account of his tenure and, if his administration was suspected of being dishonest, he could be pursued by law. In several states and particularly in Sparta, special magistrates, called ephors or inspectors, were appointed with wide powers of supervision and control over the government and the administration of the laws. P.D.

MAGNA GRAECIA. The great wave of colonisation, beginning in the first quarter of the 8th century B.C., which carried the Greeks away from their homeland, fell so heavily on southern Italy and left so many emigrants there that by the end of the 6th century the term " Magna Graecia " was already being used to designate the whole region in the heel and toe of the " Boot " that stretched from the Gulf of Tarentum to the Straits of Messina. It was a thinly populated country before the arrival of the colonists, but they turned it into one of the richest lands of the western Mediterranean and at the same time a centre of Hellenic culture.

It was not, however, in these regions that the adventurous pioneers first disembarked, but at Cumae, near the present site of Naples, and then in Sicily. In 743, Chalcidians from Zancle, who had been joined by Messenians, crossed the Straits of Messina and landed at Rhegium. Afterwards, colonists, coming this time straight from Peloponnesus particularly from the little

278

province of Achaea, founded simultaneously Sybaris, on an unhealthy but very fertile plain, and Croton, in a more salubrious position that was easy to defend but had fewer economic advantages. These first arrivals encouraged others to come either to swell their own communities or to found others. In this way, an Achaean confederacy was formed with the sanctuary of Hera Lacinia, near Croton, as its spiritual centre.

The Achaeans were not the only ones to be tempted by a land that was so rich and so near Greece. Towards the end of the 8th century, the illegitimate sons of Spartan wives who had formed liaisons with *perioikoi* during the first war against Messenia, emigrated in large numbers, conquered the native population of Iapygians and founded Tarentum. From their side, the Ionians from Colophon, driven out of their country by their Lydian conquerors, settled at Siris, and about 680, the Locrians founded a city, which they called Locri. Several other towns grew up in less than a hundred years. Some of them, like Metapontum, were to have a brilliant future, while some of the smallest remained in obscurity, those, for example, that were simply used as relay stations in the hinterland on the roads leading to the western coast and Campania. Taken together, these towns occupied a continuous stretch of territory, hardly interrupted by any foreign enclaves, since the natives had been reduced with varying degrees of willingness to an almost servile condition.

The political set-up is at first sight the same as in Greece itself: a large number of states, all Greek, all autonomous, which for a very long time did not feel themselves directly threatened by a barbarian power; the Etruscans cast a hardly perceptible shadow towards the north. Briefly, nothing seemed to distinguish the situation in Magna Graecia from that in Greece itself. Its inhabitants encountered the same kind of trials and difficulties as those on the other side of the Adriatic: they fought each other bitterly and grouped themselves into short-lived confederacies against any city whose prosperity offended them; shortly after the middle of the 6th century, the wealthy Siris was forced to join the Achaean confederacy; Croton was conquered a little later by Locri, but in 511 she overcame her rival Sybaris, which was completely destroyed. These complicated intrigues, jealousies and hatreds were, on a small scale, similar to what was going on at the same period among the Greek cities. Their domestic affairs leave an analogous impression; just as in the states of Greece proper, the common people rose against the nobility and the wealthy and instituted tyrannies, which were overthrown by revolutions after a more or less brief period. We should not be misled by these similarities; although the events may well have been of the same kind, there was an atmosphere in southern Italy that gave them a great breadth and a greater violence too. In a country where the colonial settlements were scattered, where there was no lack of space, where the youth of the cities was not kept on leading-reins by a network of ancient traditions, where agriculture flourished and the richest cities, like Sybaris, carried on a profitable trade with distant ports, a freer spirit breathed everywhere, everything was easier and more spacious. It was in Magna Graecia that new experiments, born of bold initiatives, were tried out: the first known lawgiver, Zaleucus, ruled Locri; it was at Croton, then at Metapontum that the Pythagorean venture took place, and Magna Graecia was the scene of the first attempts at town-planning.

The history of this country is not independent of Greece. Although friendly and hostile contacts were naturally more frequent between cities grouped on the same territory, the states situated east of the Adriatic intervened very often in the politics of the " Italians ". Examples of this are the part that Pericles' Athens tried to play in the peninsula by founding Thurii in 443 B.C., and the friendliness shown by the Tarentines for the Spartan cause during the Peloponnesian War. Sicily particularly found herself involved in the affairs of Magna Graecia, because she was a neighbour and shared the same interests in several matters. After the Peloponnesian War, the relations between southern Italy and Greece were far from being broken off; the invitations that the Tarentines sent to Plato clearly show how close the cultural ties remained. But while Greece, before and during the conquests of Alexander, was encouraged to look eastward, the states around the Gulf of Tarentum had to defend themselves against the tribes from the Apennines, who had been aggressive and threatening. The Greek cities could not hold together a common front against an enemy whose strength and cohesion stood fast. In 392, admittedly, an Italiot confederacy was formed whoses members pledged themselves " to offer mutual help to any member when its territory was violated by the

West wing and central court of the palace at Mallia. *Photo Boudot-Lamotte.*

Lucanians ", but the barbarians found allies in Sicily and Dionysius I of Syracuse was ready to help them. However, under the leadership of Archytas of Tarentum, a little before the middle of the 4th century B.C., the victories of the league were crushing enough to ward off the danger. Shortly afterwards, when the cities were weakened by the loss of their chiefs and were again threatened, they sent an appeal for help to Greece. The only efficacious help they received came from the king of Epirus, Alexander the Molossian. When he died about 330, the danger no longer came from the Samnites, the Lucanians and Messapians, but from a far more redoubtable enemy, Rome. At first the struggle smouldered, but it soon burst into flames. Pyrrhus, also a king of Epirus, was for a long time a danger to the might of Rome. Rome, however, gained the ascendency when she took possession of Tarentum in 272. " Once Tarentum was conquered, " wrote the historian, Florus, " who would dare to raise his head ? " In fact, all the Greek towns of southern Italy then fell into the hands of the Romans.

It may seem a paradox to maintain that from the moment it was defeated, Magna Graecia played its most important part in the history of the world. Yet, it was from contact with its cities,

its art and its civilisation that Rome was introduced to Hellenism, the Hellenism whose heritage she was to hand on to the peoples of the future.

P.D.

MAGNES. Comic dramatist and a predecessor of Aristophanes. *(See* Comedy).

MAGNESIA. Magnesia was the name of two cities of Asia Minor, one situated at the foot of Mount Sipylus, north of Smyrna; the other on the banks of the Maeander, south of Ephesus. They were both of some importance in the history of Hellenised Asia. We possess the large frieze in sculptured relief which decorated in the 2nd century B.C. the temple of Artemis, the patron goddess of Magnesia ad Maeandrum.

P.D.

MALLIA. With Phaestus and Cnossos, Mallia was one of the three great Minoan palaces. It was built in the Middle Minoan I period, altered in Middle Minoan III, and abandoned shortly afterwards. It contained the customary central courtyard flanked on the west by a great portico with columns. A beautiful hypostyle chamber has been found with pillars marked with signs, which seem to have had a religious meaning, but the painting which must once have covered the walls, as in the other palaces, has no longer survived. A necropolis was also built not far from the palace.

P.D.

MANTINEA. The town of Mantinea in Arcadia was of rather late foundation, dating from 500 B.C., when five villages grouped together to form it. Its history mainly consists of its struggles against Sparta which was always trying to extend its territories towards the north. But Mantinea's fame is largely due to the battle fought there in 362 B.C. between the Spartan army and the Boeotians and their allies. Epaminondas won the victory but he was killed in the moment of triumph and his death prevented the victors from continuing their advance towards Laconia.

P.D.

MARATHON. Marathon itself is only an unimportant village some twenty miles to the north-east of Athens, facing Euboea. But the plain which separated it from the sea, where Theseus had once distinguished himself by taming a redoubtable wild bull, was the setting for one of the most decisive battles in the whole of Greek history in September 490 B.C. The Persians had landed there, guided by the dethroned tyrant Hippias, and at the very moment when they were about to divide their forces in order to attack Athens by sea and land simultaneously, the Athenian army engaged them in battle with the aid of only a single contingent sent by the city of Plataea. In a skilful manoeuvre, probably suggested by Miltiades, the Greeks concentrated their attack on the wings and were able to triumph over their numerically very superior enemy. The victory was skilfully exploited and freed Attica from the threat of invasion. It was related that to reassure his fellow-citizens, Miltiades sent a runner to Athens who made such haste that when he arrived he fell down dead from exhaustion.

The fame of the battle was great and the generation of those who had fought at Marathon, the Marathonomachoi, were mentioned as an example to posterity because of their patriotism and heroism.

P.D.

MARBLE. Despite the number and the high quality of quarries, Greece is not entirely made of marble as is often believed. Whole regions are without marble. The richest sources were in Attica, in the Cyclades, where Paros and Naxos provided marble for the Cycladic idols of the 3rd millennium B.C., and also in several parts of Anatolia. These various marbles were not all used in the same way; some, notably those from Asia Minor, were mostly used for building, while others, like that quarried from the Pentelicus near Athens, were more suitable for sculpture. Marble was by no means the only material used for relief carving and sculpture in the round. Bronze and even terra-cotta were often preferred, the first because it was more ductile and enabled the artist to suggest greater movement in his figures, the other because it was cheaper and, when it was used as a decoration for buildings, it weighed less and therefore put less strain on the supports.

Marble nevertheless was held in high esteem by architects and sculptors of building decorations. Towards the end of the archaic period it was brought at great expense from distant regions: at Delphi, for instance, the treasuries of Siphnus and Athens are built in marble from Paros; at Selinus, the figures on the metopes of a temple built in about 460 B.C. have marble heads and hands on bodies carved out of coarse limestone; at Olympia, the walls in the sanctuary of Zeus were made of conchitic limestone faced with crushed marble. Marble was often regarded as a luxury material that craftsmen had great difficulty in working, which would explain why even in Athens, in the archaic period, tufa *(poros)* was preferred both for building and for sculpture and why local stone in the Peloponnesus, as well as in southern Italy and Sicily, rivalled marble in popularity as a building material.

P.D.

MARRIAGE. In the Homeric period it was the custom in the noble classes for the father of a young girl of marriageable age to invite all the young men who seemed worthy of his daughter to take part in a sporting competition; the winner became his son-in-law. The daughter was considered part of her father's property and, if he consented to part with her, he expected compensation, whence Homer's expression that a young woman was " worth so many oxen " (before the invention of coinage, heads of cattle were the usual means of evaluation). But in Book IX of the *Iliad,* Agamemnon promised to give Achilles a considerable dowry should he agree to marry one of his daughters. When the day of the wedding came, the father of the bride would offer a large banquet and when night fell, his newly wedded daughter would be solemnly led from her father's house to her husband's home, amid the glare of torches and wedding chants.

In his *Works and Days,* Hesiod recommended thirty and sixteen as being about the best ages for a man and woman respectively to marry, and this proportion in ages was regarded as the desirable norm in the classical period. In Athens in the time of Pericles, young men married in order to have descendants and a woman to look after the household. In principle, at least, there was no question of marrying for love. Moreover, most young men never had a chance to see their future brides who were jealously enclosed in the gynaeceum (q.v.). Customs were different in Sparta where young girls took part in gymnastics and dance choruses which permitted them to appear half-naked in public.

In any case, the young woman was never consulted on the choice of a future husband, as her future was decided by her father or guardian. The suitor would usually go to her father and it was the parents who arranged the marriage for reasons of convenience or family interest; consequently marriages of convenience were the rule.

A result of the principle of endogamy, or marriage within a certain social group, was that unions between close relatives were not only authorised but even encouraged by tradition. Marriages were frequent between first cousins and marriages between an uncle and his niece were not unusual. In Athens, the only unions that were regarded as incestuous were those between parents and off-spring (as in the case of Oedipus and Jocasta) and between brothers and sisters born of the same mother, but a half-brother could still marry a sister born of the same father.

Legitimate marriage between an Athenian citizen and a citizen's daughter was characterised by *engyesis* (literally: handing over of a gage) which signified more than a mere betrothal ceremony. It was a verbal but solemn agreement entered into by two persons: the suitor and the young girl's *kyrios,* that is, her father or guardian. The two men would stand near the domestic altar where they would shake hands, the gesture having the value of an oath, and they would then exchange a few very simple ritual phrases which must have been much the same as those given in the following dialogue by Menander.

Pataecos: " I give you my daughter so that she may bring legitimate children into the world. "

Polemon: " I accept her. "

Pataecos: " I add a dowry of three talents. "

Polemon: " I also accept that with pleasure. "

It is doubtful whether the young girl whose

Wedding procession. Detail of an Attic lekythos by the Amasis Painter. About 560 B.C. New York, Metropolitan Museum of Art.

future was at stake was present at the ceremony. The dowry itself was the main sign distinguishing a legitimate marriage from concubinage.

From the moment of engyesis a marriage existed legally, and the *gamos* was normally celebrated very soon afterwards. As in the Homeric period, it essentially consisted in the solemn transfer of the young woman from one home to another. On the eve of the wedding day, sacrifices were made to the divinities who protected the unions between the two sexes—Zeus, Hera, Artemis, Apollo and Peitho (Persuasion). The fiancée first consecrated the toys of her girlhood and the familiar objects, which had surrounded her since childhood, to the gods, and then took a ritual bath after a procession had fetched water from a special fountain, the Callirhoë, which they brought in a long-necked vase called a *loutrophoros*. On the wedding day, the houses of the bride and her future husband were decorated with garlands of olive and laurel leaves. The father of the bride then offered a new sacrifice, followed by a banquet attended by his daughter, modestly veiled and wearing her best clothes with a crown on her head. The wedding feast consisted of traditional dishes, notably the sesame cakes which were a pledge of fertility. At the end of the banquet the bride received gifts and the procession then set off. In ancient times the transfer of the bride to her husband's home took on the appearance of an abduction and the old tradition was kept in Sparta. At Athens the couple was taken from one house to another on a chariot drawn by mules or oxen, the bride holding a gridiron and a sieve, parents and friends following on foot by the light of torches. Once she had arrived at her new home, the bride was given a part of the wedding cake which was made of sesame and honey, together with a quince or a date which were symbols of fertility. She was strewn with nuts and dried figs and then only unveiled herself on entering the nuptial chamber *(thalamos)*.

The day after the wedding was still a feast-day; to the accompaniment of a flute the bride's parents would solemnly bring gifts for the new household *(epaulia)* and the dowry promised by the engyesis would then be handed over. Lastly, some time later, the husband would offer a banquet accompanied by a sacrifice to the members of his phratry, who were later to receive the male children of the couple into their community and were thus officially informed of the marriage.

It is obvious that not one of these rites seemed intended to symbolise intimate union and love between the couple, for everything was aimed at the continuity of the family and the fertility of the bride, but strangely enough Greek couples rarely had many children *(See* Family). R.F.

MARSYAS. The silenus, Marsyas, was so proud of his talent on the flute that one day he boasted of being a better musician than Apollo. Apollo easily disproved him after playing a piece on his lyre and to punish the recklessness of the silenus, who had dared provoke a god, he had him flayed alive. The torture of Marsyas was represented on several sculptures of the Hellenistic period. P.D.

MASK. Before finally becoming only a childish toy, masks were first used as a ritual disguise by primitive peoples. Whether they were festival masks worn by sacred dancers, or funerary masks laid on the faces of the dead, they appear almost everywhere in the history of mankind. They were known to the peoples of the Minoan and Mycenaean civilisations; a fresco has been found at Cnossos representing a procession of personages with heads of donkeys, who were not mythological beings but simply humans in disguise. Also practised for a fairly short period was the custom of laying thin masks of gold on the faces of the dead, which reproduced their features exactly, like the 16th century B.C. masks of the princes whose tombs were found by Schliemann at Mycenae. Masks were also used in Hellenic times. In some regions they were worn by those celebrating religious ceremonies; a 6th century B.C. vase has been found at Rhodes showing a man with the head of a hare; in Sparta, at the sanctuary of Artemis Orthia, numerous votive masks have been found, all of which were human but most of them extremely caricatural, which were terra-cotta copies of the more convenient masks, probably made of light wood, worn by the faithful as they danced in honour of the goddess. When the Greek theatre was born, stereotyped masks were used by the actors to make their role more obvious, king, old man, etc.; such a device was all the more useful as all parts, even female ones, were taken by men. As a result a whole repertory of masks was built up gradually, which was later taken over by Roman comedy and tragedy. The masks accentuated the expression

Gold Mycenaean mask,
called the Mask of Agamemnon.
1580-1550. B.C.
Athens, National Museum.
Photo Spyros Meletzis.

of the personage, made his face larger and had very large mouths so that they also served as a kind of megaphone.

The appearance or magical content of all these masks was intended to give their wearers a different personality. The masks which were not worn and were made in stone or terra-cotta, representing the features of some divinity, gorgon or a protective genius, were quite different in purpose. They were either placed in a rustic shrine against a tree trunk, which had been covered with clothes to give it a human appearance, were hung from the walls of a temple, enclosed in a tomb with the dead person they were intended to help, set over a potter's hearth to dispel evil spirits or were painted on a vase to save it from breaking accidentally; they might be life-size or only an inch high, cut off at the neck or extended down with the beginning of a bust. Unlike the first mentioned masks they were not accessories of worship, but were the very image, all the more expressive as they were only faces, of the supernatural powers invoked by worshippers.   P.D.

Hare's head mask used on a ceremonial occasion. Detail of Rhodian amphora. 6th century B.C. Paris, Louvre.

MASSALIA. The city of Marseilles was originally of Greek foundation, whence its early name of Massalia. According to the legend it was in about 600 B.C. that the Phocaeans, led by Simos and Protis and accompanied by the Ephesian priestess, Aristarche landed on the site of the present city and were welcomed by the king of the country, Nann. His daughter, Gyptis, offered the betrothal cup to Protis as a sign that she had chosen him for a husband. The marriage was concluded and the Phocaeans received a small acropolis by the River Lacydon, where they installed their gods, Apollo and Artemis. But when Nann died, Massalia was attacked by his successor, Comanus. The city survived and even succeeded in founding colonies in its turn, notably at Agde (Agathe), Hyères (Olbia), Antibes (Antipolis) and Nice (Nicea).

Marseilles' importance was mainly due to its site which allowed it to direct its activities according to circumstances, either towards the south by the Mediterranean, or else towards the north along the Rhône valley. But the city never played any very great part in history and, although some of the Phocaeans, who had not sought refuge in southern Italy, settled around it after their defeat at Alalia, its influence remained somewhat limited.

P.D.

MATHEMATICS. The Greeks did not invent the science of mathematics, for its rudiments were already known to several peoples of the orient, but they did organise and construct it as a true science. After its early beginnings among the physicists of Ionia, it reached great heights in the 5th century in Pythagorean circles and reached its climax in the 3rd century B.C. in the works of Euclid, Archimedes and Apollonius of Perga, before slowly declining until the end of the ancient period. We know little about the mathematical activities of the Ionian philosophers like Thales of Miletus (about 625-585) who is traditionally and probably wrongly credited with several important discoveries in geometry (theorems such as: in a right-angled triangle, the perpendicular drawn from the right-angle to the hypotenuse cuts the triangle into two triangles similar to each other and to the original triangle). We know more about Pythagorean mathematics which were based on a metaphysical postulate: " all is number; numbers are the models of things", which was a conception that gave rise to a mys-

tique of numbers foreign to scientific thought properly speaking. The first Pythagoreans (late 6th century—early 5th century) invented number patterns formed by points (hence square numbers still in use) as a first step towards thinking of numbers geometrically. They also discussed the geometric mean: the progression of three terms such that the ratio of the first to the second is equal to that of the second to the third; i.e. $\dfrac{a}{b} = \dfrac{b}{c}$

They discovered notably irrational numbers, at least $\sqrt{2}$, which was in contrast to their marked predilection for whole numbers, and the geometric demonstration of the so-called " theorem of Pythagoras " whose content was already known in Egypt and Babylon. All these were so many decisive stages in the history of mathematics. But while the arithmo-geometry of the Pythagoreans continued throughout ancient times until Boethius, on the margins of science, mathematical research continued with the multiplication and intensive activity of study centres (late 5th and 4th centuries). Some sixty scholars, including Hippocrates of Chios, Theodorus of Cyrene and Theaetetus, the friend of Plato, all attempted to bring the theorems together in a single continuous chain and, by developing the theory of irrational numbers, they opened the way for Euclid's synthesis. Their work ended with the affirmation of the supremacy of geometry which gave its own special character to Greek science: the need for a rigorously logical demonstration combined with the construction of figures to make the truth evident to the eyes.

The thirteen books of Euclid's *Elements* were written at the end of the 4th or at the beginning of the 3rd century and were a brilliant summary of the mathematical thought of his time. Books I to IV deal with plane geometry and are fairly simple; V and VI treat of ratios and proportions and are one of the summits of mathematical thought and the foundation of algebraic geometry; VII to IX contain the theory of numbers and are the most perfect treatises of this kind to have been written until the early 19th century; X is a study of simple irrational numbers; XI and XII deal with solid geometry. The five famous postulates put at the head of Book I are proof of the mathematical rigour of a mind which did not remain content with appealing to experimental commonsense. Archimedes of Syracuse who was killed at the age of 75 in 212 B.C. was as famous an

Detail of the frieze from the Mausoleum at Halicarnassus. Fight with the Amazons. About 355-330 B.C. British Museum. *Photo Hirmer.*

engineer as he was a geometer, which explains the originality of his method, especially when he used statics (the law of the lever and the study of centres of gravity) for geometric discoveries. Among his many accomplishments were the demonstration of the quadrature of the parabola, the evaluation of the area of the sphere and the surface areas of the cone and the cylinder, research which anticipates modern integral calculus on conoids and spheroids, and a treatise on spirals which contains the first example of differential calculus, etc. Of the abundant works of Apollonius of Perga (about 300 B.C.) only the first seven out of the eight books of his main work, the *Conics,* have survived (I to IV in the Greek text, V to VII in the Arabic translation), of which the 5th book is considered to be one of the great masterpieces of Greek geometry.

After this golden age, progress went on in certain limited fields: research in spherical geometry which was necessary for astronomy, leading to the foundation of spherical trigonometry by Menelaus of Alexandria (late 1st century A.D.) and its development by Ptolemy (2nd century A.D.); development of algebraic calculus in the *Arithmetica* of Diophantus (probably 3rd century A.D.), the heir to the remote and humble Babylonian tradition; the application of mathematics to geodesy (Hero of Alexandria, 1st century A.D.), acoustics and optics (Euclid, Hero, Ptolemy). From the end of the 3rd century A.D., Greek mathematical science was only represented by commentators of whom the best known is Pappus of Alexandria (early 4th century A.D.).

J.B.

MAUSOLUS. Mausolus was one of the several small Asiatic sovereigns who managed to preserve a large measure of independence although under the suzerainty of the Persian king. He reigned over Caria, a province in the southeast of Anatolia, and made Halicarnassus into the capital city of his kingdom. He took part in Greek politics and, like many other kinglets of the time, he was very susceptible to the prestige of Hellenic civilisation. Shortly before his death in 353 B.C. he began to build his own funerary monument which was completed by his widow, Artemisia. The monument to which he gave his name became so famous that the word " mausoleum " came to be used for any tomb with architectural pretensions.

The Mausoleum both repeated and elaborated a conception that had inspired another tomb some time before: the monument of the Nereids at Xanthus. An Ionic temple, surrounded by a colonnade and surmounted by a step pyramid, was built upon a massive base measuring some 120 by 80 feet, and the whole construction reached a height of 150 feet. The base was decorated with a continuous running frieze representing the fight between Centaurs and Lapiths and Amazons. Another frieze ran around the top of the temple bearing scenes of a

chariot race. The finest sculptors of the time were commissioned for the work and included Timotheus, Scopas, Bryaxis and Leochares. Inside the building were statues of Mausolus and his family; lions, a funerary symbol, were placed between the columns; an empty chariot was placed on the summit of the pyramid. It was a strange monument in which artistic and religious themes from Asia, Egypt and Greece were combined together in a new and original manner. Although a few fragments of the decoration have survived, now in the British Museum, almost nothing has remained of the building itself, for most of the stone was used for the building of a fortress in the 12th century A.D. It is therefore very hard for us to imagine the striking impression that the building produced in its time. The peoples of the ancient world included the Mausoleum among the Seven Wonders of the World. We may ask, however, whether they did this because they found the Mausoleum as beautiful as, for example, the Parthenon, or because they were so struck by the sheer technical prowess that the monument displayed.   P.D.

MEALS. The frugality of the Greeks is famous. It is as much a consequence of the climate as of the poverty of the country. Apart from the feastings of the Homeric heroes on great occasions, and banquets which were more like drinking parties, like the one described by Plato, meals were simple and quickly eaten. There was no daily event which united the whole family round a table. Meals were taken as snacks, at the corner of a table or else in the open, as they still are by Greek peasants today.

The evening meal was the most important and it was more substantial than the hasty morning and mid-day snacks. Cakes made of wheat and barley, which country folk cooked at home and townspeople bought at the baker's shop, cloves of garlic, onions, olives, goat's cheese and purées of beans and lentils formed the staple diet. There was little meat, for it was costly and took long to prepare; game was sometimes eaten after a hunt, and an occasional chicken taken from the farmyard; a great deal of fish was eaten, for it was found in abundance off the coasts and even today it is still one of the main specialities of Greek cooking. The smell of oil must have hung heavily on the evening air, just as it does today, in summertime in the courtyards of houses where old women bend over their small stoves to fry the evening meal of red mullet. The Greeks also ate a great deal of shell-fish, squids and salted fish. Fruit was certainly appreciated as much as it is today, particularly grapes, figs and nuts. Honey was used for sweetening and for making refreshing drinks and cakes. Little wine was drunk and it was considerably watered down, but milk was often drunk and especially water, which has always been consumed in large quantities by Mediterranean peoples.

Equally simple were the meals taken by the *prytaneis (See* Prytanis) together with their guests who had been accorded this honour by a decree of the people. But even more frugal was the ordinary meal served at the mess that all citizens— even the king—were obliged to attend under Spartan law. They ate a pork stew seasoned with blood, vinegar and salt, a black broth. Apparently, you had to be very hungry and very used to it before you could appreciate it.
                               P.D.

MEASURES. Like the calendar, the system of measures differed from one city to another in ancient Greece, which made things very com-

287

plicated. Even worse, the Greeks were never sure whether they should definitively adopt the sexagesimal system of numeration, which had come from Mesopotamia, or the decimal system.

Linear measures were based on the average size of different parts of the human body: *daktylos* (finger), *kondylos* (two fingers), *palaste* (palm: four fingers), *hemipodion* (half a foot: eight fingers), *spithame* (span: twelve fingers), *pous* (foot: sixteen fingers), *pechys* (arm's length: from elbow to middle finger; a foot and a half), *orgyia* (armspan: six feet). The foot was a fundamental measure and was slightly less than the modern foot. After the orgyia came the *plethron* (a hundred feet) and the *stadion* (six hundred feet). The Greeks measured small surface areas in square feet, and large areas in square *plethra*. Measures of capacity were different for liquids and solids and varied greatly according to towns. At Athens, the *kotyle* was slightly more than half a pint; the *chous* was twelve kotylai, the *metretes,* or *amphoreus,* was 144 kotylai or about 10 gallons. For solids and notably grain, a *choinix* was about a quart, and the *medimnos* a little more than fifty quarts.

Greek weights in all countries kept constant proportions between them: a *talanton* was worth sixty *mnai,* and a mna was worth 100 *drachmai,* a drachma being worth six *oboloi* but the basic weight of the drachma was not always the same, differing notably at Athens and Aegina. The Attic talent weighed somewhat more than 5 pounds, the mna about half a pound, the drachma about 3/4 of an ounce, and the obolos about 1/8 of an ounce.   R.F.

M E D E A . Niece of Circe and, according to some authorities, the daughter of the goddess, Hecate. For the Greeks, especially from the time of Euripides onwards, Medea was the perfect example of the sorceress. Her father was Aeëtes and ruled over Colchis on the far shores of the Black Sea. Medea was in possession of all the mysteries of her native Asia and is often represented in Greek art wearing an exotic costume.

She fell in love with Jason and helped him to win the Golden Fleece, which her father had consecrated to Ares, and she then fled with him as he had promised to marry her. As Aeëtes pursued them, she killed her own brother, cut him into pieces to make her father stop to pick up the pieces, and was thus able to escape to sea with the Argonauts. She eventually married Jason—

not without difficulty for he was very reluctant to keep his word—and had children by him, the number of which varies according to different traditions. Once the Argonauts had returned to Iolcus, she took vengeance on Pelias who had hoped to send Jason to his death by making him search for the Golden Fleece. She persuaded the old king's daughters, the Peliades, that they could rejuvenate their father by boiling him in a magic liquid for which she would give them the secret formula. In order to convince them, she performed the experiment and, after throwing an old ram, cut in pieces, into the cauldron, brought out a young lamb. Naturally she did not give the same charm to the king's daughters and Pelias met his death. After this deed, Medea and Jason had to leave Iolcus and settled at Corinth. Then, when Jason decided to repudiate Medea in order to marry Creusa, the daughter of king Creon, Medea pretended to submit to his wishes, but she sent a robe and adornments which she had dipped in a magic potion, to her rival as a wedding present. As soon as the wretched Creusa put them on, she was consumed by a fire which spread to the whole palace. In order to make her vengeance still more complete, Medea killed the children she had by Jason and then fled to Athens. There she was welcomed by the king, Aegeus, by whom she had another son named Medus. She tried to kill Theseus, Aegeus's other son, but was hunted out of the country and fled into Asia with Medus, who gave his name to the Medes. According to some versions of the legend, she returned to Colchis where she finished her life after a reconciliation with her father.

Every episode in this legend has inspired artists and writers. Euripides was particularly interested by such a complex and dramatic character and her story remained a rich source of literary inspiration as time went on.   P.D.

M E D I C I N E . Two physicians appear already in as early a work as the *Iliad,* Machaon and Podalirius, who were the "sons of Asclepius", the god of medicine. When Menelaus is wounded in Book IV by an arrow in his thigh, Machaon attends to him: " He uncovered the wound where the painful weapon had struck him. He sucked the blood and smeared soothing balms over it, which his father had learnt from Chiron..." Elsewhere Homer wrote: " One physician is worth several other men. "

During the classical period, medicine was

Attending to a patient. Detail of an aryballos. Third quarter of the 5th century B.C. Paris, Louvre.

empirical and routine at least until the second half of the 5th century B.C. when Hippocrates of Cos not only built up a proper pathology with its research into causes based on rational observation, but also an admirable code of ethics; the Hippocratic oath constitutes a medical humanism that is as valid today as it was then. Yet, even after Hippocrates, there were plenty of quacks who set up as doctors because there was no qualifying examination or control over medical knowledge. Many would-be healers operated through magic formulas or interpreting dreams, a method that was practised on a grand scale in the sanctuary of Asclepius at Epidaurus (qq.v.).

There was a medical training centre at Cnidos, and possibly at Croton, the native city of the famous Democedes, who was the state physician at Aegina, then at Athens, before being appointed personal physician to the tyrant, Polycrates (q.v.) at Samos, and then to the Persian king, Darius. The most famous medical school was at Cos, where Hippocrates trained. There, the family of the Asclepiades handed down the knowledge it had acquired from father to son and were willing to share it with foreign students.

Democedes is not the only state physician known to us. A bronze tablet from Idalium in Cyprus, of about the middle of the 5th century B.C., has preserved the contract made between this town and the physician, Onasilos, and his brothers, who undertook to look after the war-wounded on payment of a lump sum. At Athens, the applicants for the post of state doctor stated their qualifications before the assembly, which chose those whom they considered the best. These were subsequently paid by the city, which put premises at their disposal for consultations, operations and the care of patients. Medicaments were also paid for by the state. The cost of this social service was covered by a special tax, the *iatrikon*.

Surgical operations remained superficial and rudimentary because the knowledge of anatomy was so scanty. As customs and religious attitudes were opposed to the dissection of human bodies, only animals were dissected. It was not till the Hellenistic period that doctors were allowed to dissect the bodies of criminals condemned to death and then medical knowledge made great progress. Herophilus of Chalcedon and Erasistratus of Iulis in Ceos, who practised vivisection, discovered the circulation of the blood twenty centuries before Harvey. During the classical period, common operations were limited to blood-letting, the injections of clysters and cupping (cupping-vessels in horn and bronze have been discovered).

A paidotribes, or gymnastic master, was often a hygienist and dietitian, who could advise athletes on the best diet to follow. He also knew how to reduce fractures, sprains and dislocations. The paedotribes, Herodicus, became a doctor in his old age.

There were also medical books for the use of the layman and he could buy drugs at the *pharmakopoles* or pharmacist, who got his own supplies from the *rhizotomos*, or harvester of roots; the culling of medicinal plants was considered an essential part of the art of healing. Doctors often supervised dispensaries where medicines were prepared under their direction. Some of these doctors were itinerant, like the sophists, and travelled from town to town offering their services. There were few specialists in Greece, except for occulists, whose principal method of caring for their clients' eyes was by using eye-washes, and dentists who knew how to fill teeth with gold.

Women could be doctors, but generally contented themselves with nursing in homes and hospitals, and specially with midwifery. Socrates was the son of a midwife. Women, particularly when their ailments were of an intimate nature, preferred to call on the services of female " healers " who practised magic rather than rational medicine.

R.F.

E m p i r i c a l M e d i c i n e . The empirical school of medicine was founded in the middle of the 3rd century B.C. by Philinus of Cos, the pupil of Herophilus. Some of its notable members were: in the 1st century B.C., Heraclides of Tarentum, who expected a " sceptical and critical " attitude in a physician, in other words, observation and judgment, and Aenesidemus of Cnossos *(See* Pyrrhon and the Sceptics); in the 2nd century A.D., Menodotus of Nicomedia and his pupil, Herodotus of Tarsus, who was the master of Sextus Empiricus *(See* Pyrrhon and the Sceptics). The empirical physicians divided diagnosis of a case *(periptosis)* into three aspects: 1) the autopsy, or observation; 2) its history, which included the Hippocratic analysis; 3) the conclusions drawn from similar cases. In the examination of the symptoms, or symptomatology, the three divisions were described as diagnostic, therapeutic, depending on the comparison of cases, and prognostic. They recommended that the greatest importance should be attached to the idiosyncrasies of the patient, that is, to his individual temperament. P.-M.S.

M E G A R A . One of the earliest cities in Greece, built on the road from Athens to Corinth.

Its origins went back to very remote times and it was supposed to have been once occupied by the Cretans. Its real importance dates from the 8th century B.C. and few other Greek states were so energetic in colonising. Its citizens founded new cities throughout the Mediterranean, in Sicily where the daughter city of Megara Hyblaea was founded in about 728 B.C., and in the Bosphorus where Byzantium was one of their creations.

Its domestic history was less remarkable. It had endured the tyranny of Theagenes, who had helped to embellish it, but it was unable to preserve its domination over Salamis which was captured by the Athenians led by Solon. Its finest period was over but it still played an important part in politics and it was largely its disputes with Athens that led to the Peloponnesian War. After Sparta's final victory, Megara only kept its prestige because of its great past. P.D.

M E G A R I A N S C H O O L . The school of Megara was founded by Euclid, the follower of Socrates (about 450-380 B.C.), who is called Euclid the Socratic to distinguish him from the geometer. His fellow-students gathered round him after the death of the master. His thought was a blend of Socratic ideas and the teaching of the Eleatic School (q.v.) which had influenced him originally. None of his writings has survived and little is known of his thought, except that he evolved a theory of reality and the unity of the Good and that he adopted a kind of logical atomism which excluded attributes and predictables. The Megarians were skilful dialecticians. They sometimes degenerated into sophistic subtleties, but their arguments often evolved profound ideas. An example of these is the argument, the so-called *kyrieuon logos*, which Diodorus Cronus developed against Aristotle's theory of possibilities; according to this argument, the possible is what is real or can become so. Other outstanding Megarians were Stilpo who stressed the imperturbability of the sage and whose students included Menedemus of Eretria, Timon the Sceptic and Zeno, the founder of Stoicism. P.-M.S.

M E G A R O N . This was the main and often the only room to be found in the most ancient dwellings discovered in the Aegean basin. In the city of Troy II that Schliemann discovered, and wrongly dated from the time of Priam when it was really built in the late 3rd millennium B.C.

archaeologists have found rectangular buildings, with a small doorway opening on one of the short sides and preceded by a modest porch, which served as a lobby. All this was the megaron. In the centre was a hearth which was used both for domestic purposes and for domestic worship. This extremely simple ground plan is also found at Mycenae and was later to be adopted by the Greeks for their temples. But once this chamber had become that of the god, the hearth, that is, the altar, was built outside the edifice and facing it, instead of remaining enclosed inside it.   P.D.

MEIDIAS. Athenian potter. His decorator, known as the " Meidias Painter ", worked in the late 5th century B.C. and was the representative of a somewhat mannered style, in which stress was laid on gracefulness, delicacy and the elegant lines of the female figures rather than on purely plastic values alone. It was known as the " flowered style "   R.M.

MELEAGER. The legend of Meleager was straightforward enough in Homer's time, but it gradually became more complicated and by the 5th and 4th centuries B.C. the story of this king's son had become almost romantic. Several days after his birth, his mother Althaea was visited by the Fates (Parcae) who told her that, when the brand that was burning in the hearth should be consumed, her son would die. Althaea thereupon extinguished the brand and carefully kept it in a coffer. When he reached manhood, Meleager gathered the greatest heroes in Greece around him to destroy the monstrous boar that was ravaging the region of Calydon. Taking part in the hunt was Atalanta, a young girl with whom Meleager fell in love. On the pretext that she had been the first to touch the boar, he gave her its head as a tribute after killing the beast himself. This distribution of spoils set off fierce quarrels among the hunters and Meleager killed his two uncles. When she was told of the death of her two brothers, not knowing who was their murderer, Althaea laid a curse on him. When she learned that it was her own son and that he was being pursued by the Erinyes because of her curse, she set fire to the brand on which her son's life depended and then hung herself.   P.D.

MELOS. The fortunate discovery in 1820—much less romantic than is sometimes supposed

—of the famous statue of Aphrodite, known as the Venus de Milo, near an oven that had been suddenly abandoned by a charcoal burner, gave the tiny isle of Melos in the Cyclades a reputation that it never had in ancient times. It had had a considerable importance in the 3rd and early 2nd millennium B.C. when it was the only source of obsidian for the Aegean world, a hard stone then greatly in demand for making weapons and tools. In Greek times properly speaking, its only historical distinction was an abortive revolt against the imperialism of Athens in 416 B.C., which was ruthlessly crushed. There is nothing to prove that the island was the source of the " Melian reliefs "—elegant terra-cotta reliefs which were placed in shrines as ex-votos or served as decorations for coffers in the first half of the 5th century B.C.   P.D.

MEMNON. Son of the Dawn (Eos) and a brother of Priam, Memnon was the king of the Ethiopians. He came with his soldiers to the help of Troy and fought against Achilles. The mothers of the two heroes were both goddesses and both implored Zeus to protect their sons. Zeus placed the fates of the two adversaries in the scales; Memnon's fate weighed the most and Eos was doomed to seek the body of her child and weep over it—a magnificent cup by Douris bears a painting of this scene—and then take it to Ethiopia, according to the legend. One tradition maintains that she succeeded in having him live among the immortals after his death.   P.D.

MENANDER. Athenian comic dramatist (342-292 B.C.). He was the " star of the new comedy " (See Comedy). He had taken lessons under Theophrastus, the author of the Characters, but he seems to have been more influenced by the thought of the Epicureans than that of the Peripatetic philosophers. He lived in his villa in Piraeus with the courtesan, Glykera, and led a quiet, studious existence, writing a hundred and eight comedies in his thirty years as a playwright. He refused to accept Ptolemy Soter's invitation to come to Alexandria. Until the end of the 19th century his works were only known by fragments handed down through indirect sources and by the Latin imitations of his comedies by Plautus and Terence. Recent papyrological discoveries have given us important fragments of several

Eos and Memnon.
Inside of a cup
by Douris. About 490 B.C.
Paris, Louvre.

plays, including the *Arbitration (Epitrepontes),* the *Woman of Samos,* the *Hero,* the *Rape of the Ringlets (Perikeiromene)* and finally in 1957, an entire play, the *Peevish Man (Dyskolos).*

The theme of his plays was nearly always that of unhappy love, either before or after marriage, but he treated this theme in a hundred different ways. What made his great reputation after his death (in his lifetime, the Athenians often preferred his rival, Philemon, in drama competitions) was not so much his skill and variety in plot construction as his refined and perspicacious observation of every nuance of human emotion and every trait of human character, which make his characters appear lifelike and true to type. They express themselves with an easy simplicity, in the racy, natural, conversational style of civilised and witty people. Menander had a wonderful facility for showing the amusing diversity of human nature and his plays contain an exquisite and refined wisdom which never becomes patronising. He is certainly less comic than Aristophanes and only rarely makes us roar with laughter, but he amuses and enchants us with the spectacle of that " human comedy " which he succeeded so well in painting with truth, delicacy, charm, and good humour. R.F.

MENECRATES. Ausonius mentions Menecrates of Rhodes as one of the seven most famous architects of antiquity and his name is found with those of other sculptors on the frieze of the great altar of Pergamum of the 3rd century B.C. He was both an architect and a sculptor and was well qualified to direct work on the Great Altar of Zeus, which stood on one of the terraces of the acropolis of Pergamum, between that of the agora and that of the temple of Athena Nikephoros. R.M.

MENELAUS. Menelaus was the son of Atreus and the brother of Agamemnon, but he is best known as the husband of Helen of Troy. Before Helen's father, Tyndareos, chose the lucky man to whom he would give the hand of the most beautiful woman in the world, he made her suitors all swear that they would unite to aid the chosen man should any misfortune befall him. Consequently, when Helen had been carried off by Paris, Menelaus was able to gather a large army, led by

Agamemnon, which captured Troy after a ten years' siege. When Troy fell, Menelaus's first impulse was to rush towards his unfaithful wife and kill her, but Helen was able to charm him with her beauty, unbaring her bosom to his sword, it is said, and appease his anger. Menelaus then took her to Sparta where she lived as a dignified queen.

Although the Greeks did not make him as ridiculous a figure as he has now become for us, they could not find any other noble qualities to attribute to him except his royal dignity and his warlike valour, but Aeschylus has movingly described his sorrow after he had been deserted and left alone in his empty palace. P.D.

MENTOR. Mentor was the friend of Ulysses, but too old to follow him on the expedition against Troy. Instead he watched over Ulysses' interests during his long absence, and acted as an adviser to young Telemachus. P.D.

MESSENIA. This was a region in the south-west of the Peloponnesus, the prosperous neighbour of Laconia from which it was separated by a high mountain. From early times it was attacked by its neighbours and it fell under their domination in the 8th century B.C., when Messenia served as the granary and manpower reserve for the warlike population of Laconia. The Messenians revolted on several occasions and were always ready to help the enemies of Sparta, but Messenia did not win independence until after the battle of Leuctra in 372 B.C. when Epaminondas built a new capital, Messene, for all those who had refused to submit to Spartan rule. The fortifications that were built around the new city were a model of military architecture in the 4th century B.C. P.D.

METICS. Most of the great Greek cities, and Athens more than any, would never have become what they did if the very restricted number of their citizens had not been supplemented by strangers who settled permanently in their city, making roots there and contributing to the life of the community by their own professions. Most of these strangers were Greeks from other states; they were so numerous that a special status had to be instituted on their behalf. They were known as metics (metoikoi), literally "those who live with". Many of these metics practised a manual

trade, established craftsmen's workshops or else went into trade, and at Athens they were placed on a nearly equal footing with the citizens. Although they could not hold office in the state or take part in the assemblies, provided they were introduced in a deme by a sponsor (prostates) and they had paid the special tax to which they were subject, they had almost the same rights as the citizens, with the exception that they could not hold land or contract a legal marriage with an Athenian woman. They were protected by the laws (their legal cases came under the jurisdiction of one of the archons, the polemarch) and they were free to practise their professions (and some who were talented orators were even able to enter politics, like Lysias or Isaeus). When they went abroad they continued to benefit from the protection of the Athenian people. They were free to practise their own religion if they were barbarians, but were still associated with the state religion and they can be seen among the bearers of offerings on the frieze of the Panathenaea. Besides these rights—privileges we might say—they had certain duties equal to those of the Athenians themselves; apart from the special tax already mentioned and another very low tax levied on those who had a business enterprise, they had the same financial responsibilities as the citizens and took part in the liturgies (q.v.). In time of war they were mobilised and served in the land army either as hoplites, or archers (only Athenians could serve in the cavalry), or in the navy, where they formed the majority of the crews.

Oligarchic regimes were never favourable to the metics although they did not go as far as Sparta, which forbade their presence in the state. But the democracies did not regard manual work as humiliating and, as they needed to develop industry and commerce, they encouraged metics to settle in their states. To encourage them further, the cities readily granted them honours and rewards. Apart from the crown they were given in special circumstances, they sometimes received the isoteleia which gave them full rights of citizenship or else exemption from certain taxes. Such gratitude was well founded for many metics contributed to the glory of Athens. Aristotle came from Stagira, the painter, Zeuxis, from Heraclea, Hippodamus, the town-planner of Piraeus, from Miletus, the sculptors, Agoracritus and Cresilas, from Paros and Crete respectively. Besides such illustrious names, countless unknown metics contributed to the prosperity of the

Athenian economy, and the Athenian people found that the metics were always ready to help them in times of greatest crisis.   P.D.

MIDAS. Midas was a legendary figure who was said to have reigned over Phrygia in very remote times.   Dionysus granted his wish that he might turn everything he touched into gold and in a very short time Midas begged the god to withdraw the gift which condemned him to die of hunger.   As a result of his magical purification in the river Pactolus the water became filled with gold nuggets.   It was Midas who had to judge the musical contest between Apollo and Marsyas (q.v.) but as he gave the palm to the silenus, the god punished him for his bad taste and sacrilege by giving him donkey's ears.   The king endeavoured to hide his disgrace by wearing a bonnet with side-pieces, known as a Phrygian cap.   It was also related that his barber was unable to keep silent about the secret he alone knew and murmured " King Midas has donkey's ears " to the soil, whereupon the reeds growing nearby all echoed his words.   P.D.

MILESIANS. Miletus was the great port of Ionia in Asia Minor, which handled the trade flowing through Lydia from inland countries as far away as Chaldaea, and she proliferated numerous colonies from the Pontus Euxinus to Sybaris. The first philosophers lived there in the 6th century B.C.: Thales (flourished between 630 and 550), Anaximander, who succeeded him in the middle of the 6th century, and Anaximenes, who died about 520.   These philosophers were not only speculative thinkers and dreamers (Thales is traditionally " the philosopher who fell down a well "), but men of action.   Thales was a military engineer who diverted the River Halys to free the way for Cyrus's army.   He could calculate from the top of a lighthouse the distance of a ship at sea and was looked upon as the father of geometry, although he probably borrowed its practical applications from the Egyptians and Babylonians. It is also likely that he owed them his knowledge of the periodicity of eclipses, which enabled him to predict the one in 584.   Anaximander, who founded the colony of Apollonia, plotted a geographical map, constructed a gnomon (a sort of sun-dial which was used for various astronomical calculations based on the length of its shadow) and a celestial sphere.   In developing their simple meteorological and cosmological theories, these early masters no longer resorted to mythology, but to images of a practical character from everyday observation.   The earth is a flat disc floating on water, according to Thales; in air, according to Anaximenes; and, according to Anaximander, a column three times as broad as it is high; around it turn wheels filled with fire escaping through holes like the stops in a flute, which correspond to the stars.   Anaximenes tried to give an idea of the celestial revolutions by comparing them to rotating millstones, or to a cap that is turned round the head it covers.   Aristotle laid great stress on Milesian conceptions of the fundamental element of things.   Thales thought it was water (probably because of the uses of the sea, the effects of the Nile waters and rain on seeds), for Anaximander it was infinity or the unlimited and, according to Anaximenes, the condensation and rarefaction of air caused cold and heat.   Among other noteworthy ideas, Thales attributed a soul to the magnet because it moves iron (hylozoism); Anaximander postulated the existence of a system of compensation through which human beings made reparation for their injustices in the course of time; Anaximenes compared the unifying action exercised by our souls, constituted of air, to the action of the surrounding, supporting air on the world.   Anaximenes had an inkling of transformism when he thought that the first forms of life, emerging from primaeval moisture, were like fishes.

Hecataeus of Miletus, the historian and geographer, who lived from about 550 to 475, was a kindred mind to these first philosophers and scientists.   His *Periegesis,* or Description of the Earth, which benefited from his extensive travels, and his *Historiai* or *Genealogia* showed the same spirit of curiosity and thirst for knowledge.   When Ionia was conquered by the Medes in 545 B.C. and Miletus destroyed in 494, most of the Ionian philosophers emigrated, some like Pythagoras and Xenophon to Magna Graecia; others like Anaxagoras of Clazomenae and Diogenes of Apollonia went later to Athens.   There are grounds for comparing the ideas of the Milesians with that of their neighbour, Heraclitus of Ephesus.
    P.-M.S.

MILETUS. When the poet, Phrynichus, performed his play called the *Taking of Miletus* before the Athenians in 493 B.C. the grief of the spectators was so noisy that the government forbade any further performances of the play.

Miletus for the Greeks had represented "the greatest glory of Ionia" until it was captured and razed to the ground by the Persians for having revolted in the preceding year. It was one of the most ancient cities the Greeks had founded on the coasts of Asia Minor when they were forced to seek safety on the other side of the Aegean during the period of the great Iron Age invasions. The native population became mixed with Cretans and Achaeans from the Peloponnesus and their descendants claimed that their ancestors were Sarpedon the Lycian, Neleus of Pylos and Miletus the Cretan, all reputed to have been the builders of the city. Miletus's future prosperity was assured by her site, for she stood between two well protected bays on a promontory where four ports were built; communications with the hinterland were easy, as Miletus was linked with Phrygia by the valley of the River Maeander, and with rich Caria by mountain passes. Their flocks of sheep found ample sustenance in this region and provided the inhabitants with a wool whose quality was highly appreciated in ancient times. In addition, agricultural resources were abundant.

These rich resources enabled the Milesians to build an important fleet and we may even talk of a Milesian thalassocracy of the 8th century B.C. as did the peoples of the time. We know for certain that Miletus was the greatest coloniser of all the Greek cities; it sent most of its settlers towards the north, mostly to the Sea of Marmara and the Black Sea, where more than ninety trading posts were set up. The city turned its attention to other areas as well and the city of Naucratis, which had been founded in the Nile delta by a consortium of Ionian states, was dominated by her. At the other end of the Mediterranean it was Miletus that kept constant commercial links with Magna Graecia, mostly through the intermediary of Sybaris. Apart from wool, it exported precious metals, furniture, especially beds, and agricultural produce. The great buildings there added to its glory and during the whole archaic period it was a nursery for artists, philosophers and scholars.

It must have suffered from internal strife as much as any other city of the times and, when the monarchy of the Neleidae had been abolished in the 8th century B.C., it was governed by an oligarchy of noblemen and the wealthy classes, followed by a tyranny. For much of the 6th century, it saw an almost uninterrupted series of civil wars, but its prestige never suffered and for the Greeks the city remained the Ionian ideal in its most perfect form. Although Ionia was conquered by Cyrus in 545 B.C., its prestige and prosperity remained unharmed and it was only when it revolted against the Persian king in 495 that the city went through its blackest period. Its fall resounded throughout the whole of the Greek world, but its citizens displayed extraordinary energy and the city soon rose from its ruins. The work of its architects had far-reaching results for Greek city-planning. As the city had been entirely destroyed, it was possible for the first time to draw up a new plan which was so bold and so revolutionary that it has been compared to some of our most recent urban achievements. The new city was divided into zones, each with its own special attributes, each sector was articulated to another and care was taken to ensure a smooth flow of traffic by building large rectilinear streets which intersected at right angles. All the credit for the rebuilding that was given to Hippodamus, a native of the town, really belongs to the architects.

The internal history of the city was less glorious for, although it had been delivered from Persian domination by the Persian Wars, it was torn by a civil strife that Athens vainly attempted to soothe in about 450. From then onwards, the history of Miletus is merely that of a city whose commerce continued to flourish and which remained prosperous despite the competition of Ephesus. It kept its wealth for centuries afterwards. This prosperity can be appreciated in the imposing, if ruined, buildings found either in the city itself or a few miles away in the ancient sanctuary of Apollo at Didyma.   P.D.

MILTIADES. Miltiades owed his fame to the important part he played in the battle of Marathon. He was the grandson of an Athenian noble who had carved himself out an estate in Thracian Chersonese in order to flee from the tyranny of Pisistratus. When the Persians invaded Attica in September 490 B.C., Miltiades was a strategus. He persuaded his fellow-citizens not to await the enemy behind the walls of their city but to go out and meet him halfway. He chose the right moment for engaging battle and his skilful tactics defeated the Persians, who were far superior in numbers. The victory gave him a popularity which he exploited in order to lead a profitless expedition against Paros. Public opinion then turned against him and he was condemned to pay a heavy fine shortly before dying from a wound received during the campaign.

P.D.

M I M E . This was a kind of comedy that consisted of short realistic sketches with two or three characters. The main representatives of this genre were Sophron in the 5th century B.C. and Herondas (or Herodas) in the 2nd (qq.v.)

R.F.

M I M N E R M U S . Lyric poet, born at Colophon in the second half of the 7th century B.C. The few surviving fragments of his work are written in the elegiac metre and sing the praises of youth, love and pleasure, and the anguish of approaching old age. *(See* Lyric Poetry).

R.F.

M I N E S . Ever since the Minoan period, the Greeks used an enormous amount of different metals. They probably imported some of them from abroad, at least in earliest times. There were, however, deposits in the Greek peninsula and the Aegean islands: there was gold in Mount Pangaeus (q.v.), at Thasos and, if Herodotus is to be believed, at Siphnus; we know the advantages the Athenians gained from the silver mines at Laurium (q.v.); the frequent occurrence of the name Chalcis in several regions is a sure indication that copper was to be found there; iron ore was mined in Laconia. The Phoenicians were supposed to have been the first to explore and exploit the mineral wealth of the earth. Nothing is more unlikely; it is unthinkable that the Greeks waited for the Phoenician thalassocracy in the 2nd millennium B.C. before looking for and discovering metals for themselves.

The mines of ancient times were very different from modern ones. Traces of galleries and shafts have been found in the ground. The deepest of these was not more than about 300 ft, which was considerable when we remember that they were dug by hand and that men had to carry up ladders the spoil and ore in baskets on their backs. The galleries were astonishingly narrow. Most of them varied in height and width between two and three feet so that the miners could only work squatting or lying down. They were so tortuous that air could not circulate and the effort required to wield picks and mattocks must have been considerable. They worked in semi-darkness by the dim light of smoky lamps hooked onto the ceiling of the tunnel.

It is hardly surprising that in the spring of 413 B.C. twenty thousand Athenian slaves revolted and took advantage of the political difficulties of the Peloponnesian War to desert the Laurium mines where they worked. Ancient writers, particularly Diodorus Siculus, tell us that the lives of miners, who were all slaves, were so wretched that special precautions were taken to force them to work and extremely severe punishments were inflicted on them. The slaves belonged, at least in Attica, to the licensees to whom the state, as proprietor of the land, had granted the exploitation of the mines. Elsewhere, the law was different and we know that the mines belonged to private persons; Pisistratus and the historian, Thucydides, owned some in Thrace. Open-cast mining was also practised and the technique was the same as in the quarries, but the greater part of Greek mineral resources was supplied by underground extraction.

P.D.

M I N O S . We do not know for certain whether Minos was the name of a specific personage or, like the Egyptian word " pharaoh ", the hereditary title of the kings of Crete. The second alternative is usually favoured by modern historians, who have given the name of " Minoan " to the civilisation that developed in the Aegean area from the 20th to the 14th century B.C. For the ancient Greeks, who made no distinction between legend and history, Minos was the son of Zeus and Europa who actually reigned over Crete, three generations before Theseus, and his power extended over the neighbouring isles. He was supposed to have had all kinds of amorous adventures. His wife Pasiphaë gave birth to Ariadne and Phaedra. His justice and wisdom were equally renowned and after his death he was appointed one of the judges of the underworld, with his brother, Rhadamanthys, and Aeachus, king of Aegina.

P.D.

M I N O T A U R . The legend of the Minotaur was one of the most popular in ancient Greece as we can see from its frequent appearance in vase paintings. The Minotaur was a monstrous being with the head of a bull and the body of a man, the son of Pasiphaë who had deceived her husband, Minos, with a bull sent by Poseidon. He

Theseus killing the Minotaur. Detail of an amphora. About 540 B.C. Berlin Museum.

lived at the end of a building known as the Labyrinth with such a complicated system of corridors that once entered, it was almost impossible to find a way out again. It was to the Minotaur that Minos sent the young men and maidens whom he exacted as a tribute from the Athenians he had vanquished. With the help of Ariadne and the thread he unwound behind him as he went, one of the chosen victims, the hero Theseus, was able to find his way in the mysterious dwelling and slay the monster.　　　　　　　P.D.

MINYANS. The Minyans were considered the oldest population of Boeotia. The name " Minyan " is also given to a fairly refined pottery, found in the region, which dated from the beginning of the 2nd millennium B.C. It was an imitation of metallic ware and did not have painted decoration, but was brushed with grey or yellow colouring, which has a very pleasing effect. It is distinguished by the precision of its forms.

P.D.

MIRRORS. The ancient Greeks used as mirrors the reflecting surface of a small disc of polished metal, which was usually made of bronze but sometimes also of gold, silver or tin. They had an average width of between 6 and 8 inches. Three sorts of mirrors were made: with handles, pedestals, or set in boxes. Handles were very varied in form and might be either cylindrical or rectangular. They sometimes consisted of a small statuette in the same metal of a female figure, shown either naked or clothed, with a ring for hanging sometimes attached under her feet. Standing mirrors had a similar figurine for a support but they were set on a kind of pedestal, which allowed the mirror to be placed upright on a

The Labyrinth. Reverse of a coin of Cnossos from Gortyna ? Heraklion Museum. *Photo Hassia.*

Mirror with stand. First half of the 5th century B.C. Paris, Louvre. *Photo Tel.*

table. The figurine and the disc might sometimes be surrounded by small representations of Eros or such fantastic animals as sphinxes and sirens. Box mirrors consisted of a base and a hinged cover and were circular or rectangular in shape. The outer cover was often richly decorated with incised figures and even reliefs. R.F.

MNESICLES. Architect of the Propylaea (q.v.) on the Acropolis of Athens built between 437 and 430 B.C. To us, he was the most sensitive of all the Greeks to the plastic qualities of architecture. When Phidias drew up his vast programme for the reconstruction of the Acropolis in the 5th century, he entrusted Mnesicles with the rebuilding of the great monumental doorway which formed the approach to Athena's domain of rock and marble. It was a difficult task; the architect had to plan and site a structure,

which had a definite practical purpose, at the extreme western end of the rocky platform, in a place which was below the great buildings inside, but dominated the exterior where the pilgrims came up the sacred way. A further difficulty was the slope of the ground from east to west.

Despite the present condition of the structure, Mnesicles' success is strikingly obvious to the modern visitor as he makes his way up around the bends of the sacred way which has been restored to its original appearance. The western façade gradually comes into view and one monumental aspect after another reveals itself until the moment when the spectator sees it in its harmonious entirety. Should he turn round after entering the first vestibule, he is overcome by a strange feeling of perfection arising from the extraordinary harmony between the design and proportions of the neighbouring buildings and the rhythmic movement of the landscape reaching to the shore of Phalerum. The great structure is also distinguished by the richness of its marble which was extracted from the quarries at Pentelicus, by the discreet polychrome effects obtained by the black stone from Eleusis for the thresholds of doorways, the technical perfection of the stereotomy, the almost symphonic harmony, so difficult to analyse, between the strong, Doric columns of the façade and the delicacy of the inner Ionic columns, soaring up towards the spacious ceiling made of marble beams, nearly twenty-three feet long, set between geometrically decorated coffering. No praise can be too great for the architect who showed such elegance in the creation of this extraordinary marble homage to Athena, the great patron goddess of Athens, which is also a homage to the goddess, Harmony, herself. R.M.

MOLOSSI. The Molossi lived in Epirus and were regarded as barbarians by the Greeks. As a matter of fact they did live outside the Hellenic world until the time when one of their princesses, Olympias, married Philip II of Macedon and became the mother of Alexander the Great. From that time the kings of the Molossi and especially a King Alexander, who was the distant cousin of the great conqueror, took part in Greek politics and Antigonus Gonatas in particular had to contend with their initiative and dynamism. P.D.

Mosaic. Lion hunt. End of the 4th century B.C. Pella. *Photo Hassia*

M O S A I C. Two or three generations ago it was thought that the art of the mosaic, which was so highly appreciated in the Roman world, had only been brought into Greece in the Hellenistic period and that its widespread diffusion was to be explained by the success enjoyed by everything from the orient at that time. But the oriental origin of mosaic has yet to be proved and recent discoveries have shown that the technique was widespread in Greece as early as the 5th century B.C. Although the number of examples is small, this may be due less to the hazard of excavations than to the modesty of the Greek household whose members were long content with only the strict necessities and who did not at first try to embellish the surroundings of their domestic life.

At Sicyon and Corinth in the Peloponnesus, at Motya in Sicily, at Athens and, most of all, at Olynthus, decorated pavements have been found showing that mosaic work was already highly appreciated before the middle of the 4th century B.C. Later, Pella and then Delos at the end of the 2nd century created remarkable examples of the art which won even greater popularity throughout Alexander's empire than in Greece itself. Apart from Syria, which seems to have produced the most famous mosaicists, Anatolia and Alexandrian Egypt were the regions where the art was most practised.

The Greek mosaics we know were nearly all intended as decorations for the floors of the most important rooms in bourgeois or princely dwellings and not as mural ornaments. Apart from several variants, the technique was the same everywhere. Elements were assembled to make a geometric, floral or figured decoration on a basis of several, superimposed, and gradually finer layers of cement. The simplest and cheapest process was to use naturally flat pebbles of different colours, but they preferred little stones that were cut into cubes (tesserae) and placed one beside the other, though because of their quadrangular form and equal dimensions, the outlines of the images tended to be rather abrupt. More refined was the technique known as *opus vermiculatum* which used cubes of different materials—stone, glass or even wood—cut irregularly according to the needs of the composition. This was a much subtler process, for the pieces were fitted together like a jigsaw puzzle and expressed the artist's intentions as precisely as a painter's brush-strokes applying touches of colour. In order to stress a line, a cloisonné effect was obtained by using lead. The variety of materials and tones gave the mosaic the subtlety of painting and mosaic pavements did in fact often reproduce the work of some famous painter. This is probably what happened with the famous *Alexander Mosaic*, which was found in a house at Pompeii, panels like that of *Ariadne and Dionysus* at Delos, the hunting scene at Pella and the *Nereids* at Olynthus, shown seated on dolphins and carrying the arms of Achilles. The outer border of these decorative panels only consisted of decorative motifs and was made on the spot but the central, figured part *(emblema)* was, as the remains at Delos prove, executed separately and then inserted, sometimes clumsily, within the outer frame. These pieces could be bought ready made from some Syrian workshop and the client would then have it set in place by local workmen.   P.D.

MUNYCHIA. This was one of the bays of the Piraeus which was used by the Athenians as a military port. It was very well sheltered and in the 4th century B.C. was surrounded by ramparts which protected the triremes kept there in reserve. A fortress was also built overlooking the whole port.   P.D.

MUSAEUS. Musaeus was, like Orpheus, a semi-mythical Thracian poet. It was said that Musaeus was the first priest of the mysteries of Eleusis, and he was credited with religious poems composed at a much later date, notably a hymn to Demeter.   R.F.

MUSES. The Muses were very ancient divinities and, although we may not agree with the ancient Greeks when they related that the first song of the Muses celebrated the recent victory of the gods over the Giants, we do know that Hesiod invoked them at the beginning of his *Works and Days* as goddesses who were well known to all and who naturally protected and inspired poets. According to the most popular tradition, they were the daughters of Mnemosyne and Zeus. For a long time they remained without any individual attributes and the nine sisters patronised every form of music and poetry equally. Their chorus was led by Apollo himself who provided the rhythm for their dances with his lyre. The Muses only developed their individual characters at a fairly late date, in the 4th century B.C. at the earliest, when an analytical spirit and a taste for allegory had become widespread. It was then that Calliope became the patron of the epic poem, Clio of history, Terpsichore of light poetry and dancing, Melpomene of tragedy, Thalia of comedy, Polyhymnia of lyric poetry, Erato of elegiac poetry, Urania, the Muse of Astronomy, and Euterpe of music. Some of these attributes, for example, history or astronomy, must obviously date from a later period when these sciences had become independent although still retaining the memory of their poetical origins.

Like the nymphs, the Muses were not represented in art for a long time except in such a vague fashion that it is impossible to identify them unless they were designated by a special inscription. Pindar mentioned their " violet curls " but this detail was to be found neither in archaic art nor in later paintings. It is in statuary of the Hellenistic period that we can often recognise the figu-

Mosaic from the House of the Dolphins at Delos. 2nd century B.C. *Ph. Jacqueline Staméroff.*

Apollo and a Muse holding a lyre. Inside of an Attic cup. Second quarter of the 5th century B.C. Boston, Museum of Fine Arts.

res of the Muses by the attributes they hold in their hands such as theatrical masks, lyres, flutes or rolled manuscripts. P.D.

MUSEUMS. Museums as we know them now, with their opening hours, uniformed attendants and works of art, classified and exhibited methodically for the instruction and delight of a large public, were unknown to the ancient Greeks. The Greek word for museum, *Mouseion*, meant a shrine with its priests, its sacrifices and its cult, which was that of the Muses (q.v.). Even when the Muses patronised intellectual activities they were never personifications as we regard them, but were always considered authentic goddesses to whom ritual honours were due. None of them protected painters and sculptors and, although it was natural that Greek " museums " should have served frequently as meeting places for philosophers, astronomers, scholars and poets, we should not be surprised that the figurative arts were only represented in the form of ex-votos as in any other shrine, and more especially in the form of real or imaginary portraits of the Sages whose spirits were supposed to inspire the learned assemblies. As in Alexandria, which was the most famous of them all, the essential part of the Greek Mouseion was the library.

Does this mean to say that the Greeks lacked those great collections of works of art which the word museum now suggests to us? There certainly were such works of art in the great sanctuaries at Delphi, Olympia, or on the Acropolis, but they were pious dedications to the gods and, from the 4th century B.C. at least, they seem to have been appreciated more for their beauty than for their religious significance. But they were still votive in purpose and their siting was determined by reasons far different from those which now determine museum lay-out, and the works exhibited were made to please the divinity rather than to be admired by human beings.

Even when the sovereigns of Pergamum and Alexandria began to gather original works or copies of the works of the most famous sculptors and painters in their palaces from the 3rd century B.C. onwards, they were not founding museums

301

Lyre player. Detail of an amphora attributed to the Berlin Painter. About 490 B.C. New York, Metropolitan Museum of Art.

M U S I C . Music held a place in the life of the Greeks that we are all too prone to forget because of the total or nearly total disappearance of all Greek musical texts. Literary works and theoretical treatises show that music was an indispensable element in the life of a Greek from earliest childhood to old age. It was an important part of religious ceremonies, for there were very few rituals that did not include chants; it was the necessary accompaniment for the oldest poems and for choruses of dancers; it was essential to the dithyramb and it filled the long intervals between the acts of comedies and tragedies; soldiers going to battle would sing, and guests at a banquet after the day's work.

The most ancient names of musicians to have come down to us are all legendary such as Orpheus, Linus and Thamyris among others. According to tradition, they were both composers of hymns and poems and the inventors of musical instruments that were still used in the classical period. There can be no doubt about the ancient origins of music in Greek civilisation; Cretan paintings of the 15th century B.C. on the sarcophagus of Haghia Triada include scenes of lyre players among those taking part in the ceremony. This is far from surprising since, in the more ancient civilisations of the east and Egypt, music was a necessity more than an art. Theoretical treatises and the few scattered indications that Greek writers have left show us fairly conclusively that Greek music was composed in various descending scales of seven notes. These scales were integrated in what were called modes, of which the most popular and probably the most ancient was known as the Dorian. It was austere and grave in mood and Plato ranked it higher in his esteem than the two others, the Phrygian and the Lydian which, for the philosopher, had the Asian faults of laxity and lasciviousness. Other modes such as the Mixolydian, the Hypodorian, the Hypophrygian and the Hypolydian were gradually added to the original modes.

Greek music seems to have remained essentially vocal, as instruments only had a secondary importance. The music was mostly choral but certain pieces were executed by soloists. Instruments were numerous but the main ones (all others were derived from them) were the lyre, for

in the modern sense. Instead, they were forming private collections for their own pleasure and they must certainly have derived some satisfaction from showing them to privileged guests whom they wished to dazzle with their riches. The general public, however, was never allowed to see these treasures.

May we say that the collection of replicas of famous sculptures in the library of Ephesus in the 2nd century A.D. was the beginning of a museum or was it rather a matter of adding appropriate decoration to an architectural setting? The works that had been reproduced were not there for their intrinsic beauty but rather because they harmonised with their surroundings.

Such collections are only found rarely in ancient Greece although they became frequent in Roman times. Moreover, it is owing to the Roman taste for collecting that so many Greek works have come down to us.   P.D.

Woman playing the double flute. Detail of a krater by the Karneia Painter. About 410 B.C. Taranto Museum. *Photo Hirmer.*

the strings, the aulos or double flute for the woodwind, and the tambourine for the percussion. Although the lyre was the noblest instrument, used by Apollo, the god of music himself, and the Muses, the double flute was capable of virtuoso effects which won those who played it a popularity equal to that enjoyed by the finest soloists of modern times.

Musical notation was alphabetic. Signs added above the letters indicated the duration of sounds and certain nuances. It seems that this notation was very complete and gave the player all the necessary indications for following the composer's intentions. The few musical texts which have come down to us were inscribed on stone in the sanctuaries of the gods in whose honour they were composed; the most famous is a Delphic paean of the 4th century B.C. Unfortunately such pieces are difficult to interpret, but there can be no doubt that the ancient Greeks raised music to the same high level of artistic beauty as the figurative arts. However, its accentuated rhythm, its modulations and some of its nuances would probably be more foreign to the ears of the modern European than a statue by Praxiteles or an archaic relief to his eyes.   P D.

MYCENAE. Mycenae was the most important city in the Mediterranean world of the 2nd millennium B.C. Although it was not the capital of an empire, it was such an influential centre that the name of " Mycenaean " has been given to the dominant civilisation which covered the area from the isles of Lipari to the shores of Syria between the 16th and the 12th centuries B.C. Mycenae was a mere village for a long period, only now known to us by its tombs which resemble all those of the Helladic world of the time. Then, in about 1900 B.C., a new Indo-European population settled on the site and Mycenaean power swiftly grew. The two groups of royal tombs, each set within a circular enclosure and dating from the mid-16th to the late 15th century, show that the princes of the time were extraordinarily wealthy; the exceptionally beautiful furnishings include jewellery, masks and pottery. No doubt this wealth did not only come from the taxes levied on the cultivators of the neighbouring plain, but

also from booty seized from bordering states and the tolls exacted from travellers on their way from Corinth to the southern Peloponnesus, who had to pass the heights on which Mycenae was situated. The palace of Mycenae looked just like a burg, at least in its final form in the 13th century. It was built on the slopes and summit of a steeply rising eminence and surrounded by walls of rough-hewn cyclopean masonry. The main doorway is surmounted by a relief representing two lions facing one another on opposite sides of a column, the symbolic image of the whole royal dwelling. Within the precinct, the remains have been found of several princely dwellings built on the ground-plan of the megaron. Outside the walls, at the same time that the ramparts and the Lion Gate were being raised, probably in the first half of the 13th century, the kings built themselves vast beehive-shaped tombs like the so-called Treasury of Atreus, now known to us as " tholos tombs ".

In modern times, we tend to consider such legendary characters as Perseus, Atreus, Thyestes, Agamemnon and Orestes as historic figures who really lived and reigned over Mycenae in the palace whose ruins we now visit. What is

Mycenae. The Lion Gate
14th century B.C.
Photo Hassia.

Mycenae. Façade
and door of the
Treasury of Atreus.
14th century B.C.
Photo Hassia.

Mycenae. The Grave Circle. 14th-13th century B.C. *Photo Boudot-Lamotte.*

certain is that the Mycenaean monarchy was rich and powerful and that, even if it did not extend its effective power, it did at least extend its political sphere of influence over a large part of the Peloponnesus, while Mycenaean civilisation spread even farther afield. In the last years of the 12th century B.C., the city was destroyed during an invasion which must have been that of the Dorians. The city never recovered; its name still figured in history but only as a secondary city that the Greeks themselves would have almost forgotten had not the poems of Homer and the tragic dramatists immortalised its past glory.   P.D.

MYCENAE (Civilisation). As Mycenae is the best known of all the cities in mainland Greece during the 2nd millennium B.C. and as it was also one of the most brilliant, its name has been given to the original civilisation that sprang up there before spreading throughout the whole of the central Mediterranean basin. As far as may be seen in those distant times whose history we do not know, Mycenae was never the capital of an empire like that of the Hittites or Egyptians. Although on certain occasions some of its chieftains were at the head of a confedera-

tion, like Agamemnon during the Trojan War, they never wielded true suzerainty over other kings. Although they might command an expedition, when their military authority was absolute, they never intervened in the government of the cities who fought under their orders and they never levied taxes on allied peoples. That love of independence, which was so characteristic of the Greeks in historic times, had already appeared. This is not so surprising, for the creators of the Mycenaean civilisation, the Achaeans as they were called, were already Greeks. What little has been deciphered of their writings, since Michael Ventris found the key in 1953 *(See* Linear B), shows that in the 15th century the language spoken in Crete and the Peloponnesus and, no doubt, elsewhere as well, was already that of Homer, if a little more archaic, and that the Hellenic pantheon was already constituted in all its essentials. Moreover, the Dorians who descended from the plains of the Danube onto the Greek peninsula at the end of the 2nd millennium B.C., are generally considered to be elder brothers of the Achaeans, who themselves had invaded along the same roads in the early centuries of the same millennium.

Mycenae. Palace of the Atridae: the megaron. 14th-13th century B.C. *Photo Boudot-Lamotte.*

When the men who founded the Mycenaean civilisation first arrived in the Peloponnesus, its inhabitants had only reached a rudimentary level of civilisation and several generations passed before a sufficiently high standard of life created the conditions for intellectual and artistic activities. In the 16th century B.C. they turned towards Crete and established relations with Egypt and the east, which brought them riches and helped them to form a civilisation. Then, in their turn, once their material power was assured, the Achaeans sent settlers to far-off regions and played an important part in the diffusion of a culture they had not themselves created, but which they had marked with the powerful stamp of their personality.

It is very difficult to determine the nature of Mycenaean religion. Numerous remains have

shown the survival of the nature goddess that the Cretans themselves had worshipped on the mountain tops or in the heart of forests, but there is no doubt that the Homeric gods were also venerated and that the main lines of Greek mythology were already laid down. It also seems certain that, during the Mycenaean period, these divinities established their patronage over certain cities and so acquired a nationalistic character. We know the art and architecture of the Mycenaeans better than their religion. Many Cretan characteristics appear in the palaces of this period but they were external features only; their spirit was different. The kings were warrior chieftains and, unlike the Minoan princes, gave precedence to security rather than comfort. Cnossos is the residence of a rich proprietor who was never haunted by the fear of invasion, but the Mycenaean palaces, perched high up on the hill-tops, often resemble fortresses. The interior lay-out of their palaces was less homogeneous and less subtly articulated than in Crete and certain technical innovations were introduced by the invaders, such as sloping instead of terraced roofs, since snow and rain were frequent in the Balkans from where the Achaeans originally came. Like the Cretans, the Achaeans were painters, but in this art, as in ceramics, they showed a kind of stiffness radically different in spirit from the highly imaginative spontaneity of the Minoans. Forms and themes are similar but there is no risk of confusion between the works that have survived. Long before the arrival of the Dorians a taste for geometrical patterns, not without a certain dryness, had appeared in Mycenaean art. Like the Cretans, the Mycenaeans were fond of personal ornament and were accomplished goldsmiths, but among the objects

that have come down to us it is weapons such as swords and daggers that predominate. A warrior people, they were attached to everything connected with a martial life; in life they shut themselves up in their citadels: in death, they were buried with all their warlike equipment. We might be tempted to conclude that Mycenaean society was more hierarchical and paramilitary in organisation than that of Crete, but we have very little evidence and we cannot be sure of this. Yet, when we look at the strong walls of the palace, the majestic aspect of the Lion Gate and the imposing grandeur of the Treasury of Atreus, and when we consider all the gold that the sovereigns had accumulated in their tombs, we cannot help feeling that these greedy and jealous chieftains were far removed in spirit from the Cretan princes whose palaces were so often open, whose vast courtyards were so ready to welcome the whole population of the city as it came streaming in to applaud the exploits of acrobats and bull-fighters.   P.D.

MYRMIDONS. People of southern Thessaly whose name has come down to us through the Homeric poems. Achilles seems to have been their king.

MYRON. The *Discobolus* is such an accomplished masterpiece that it is easy to understand why the fame of its creator, the sculptor Myron, should have endured throughout the centuries more than that of Pythagoras or any other contemporary sculptor of the same school. Surviving replicas of this famous work enable us to reconstitute the bronze original which was lost at the end of the classical period. The statue was that of a young athlete, his body tensed, leaning forward, the legs unequally bent, the right arm stretched out almost in a straight line from the shoulder, as though pulled out by the discus he is about to throw, the left arm bent back towards the knees, the head turned back. The abrupt torsion of the hips, the instability of the pose (too fleeting for the eye to observe from nature and, in fact, the cinematograph has proved that it does not exist in reality) and the intensity of movement would all give an effect of fatigue were it not that the harmonious composition of lines forms a kind of arabesque, as though the figure were inscribed in a medallion; in fact, it reminds one of the images painted by archaic decorators inside a cup and enclosed in its own whirlwind of movement.

The *Discobolus* was not Myron's only work, for

Bronze dagger inlaid with gold and silver from the royal tombs at Mycenae. 16th century B.C. Athens, National Museum. *Photo Spyros Meletzis.*

The Discobolus. Roman copy of a work by Myron. Original about 450-440 B.C. Vatican Museum. *Photo Anderson-Viollet.*

the group consecrated on the Acropolis, which showed Marsyas with the flute that Athena had disdainfully let fall, has been reconstructed. Another work in the same spirit as the *Discobolus* is the *Ladas,* an admirable statue of a runner panting, standing on the tips of his toes, and the bronze *Cow,* consecrated in Athens, of which we have no dependable replica. It was not Myron who created the fashion for intense movement and unstable balance in statues; everywhere in the same period, between 475 and 450 B.C., other sculptors, who were not of Attic origin like himself, but from Ionia like Pythagoras of Samos, from Aegina like the artist of the east pediment of the temple of Aphaea, or from Crete like Cresilas in his youth, all aimed at an effect of intensity and tried to give the ephemeral impression of instantaneity. Myron was not a pioneer but, by profiting from the experiments of his predecessors and contemporaries, he succeeded in producing the perfect expression of the " realistic " style of sculp-

ture that the pure classicists, Phidias and Polycletus, later condemned in the style of their own works.   P.D.

MYSIA. Mysia was a region in the northwest of Asia Minor. It never had any importance politically as an independent state. Its very isolation and obscurity attracted the attention of Lysimachus (q.v.) when, in 283 B.C., he was looking for a sure hiding place for his treasures. The place he chose was Pergamum (q.v.), the only part of the province to win lasting fame.

P.D.

MYSTERIES. The name mysteries was given to all the ceremonies and religious rites in which only initiates *(mystai)* took part. Although the mysteries of Eleusis, consecrated to Demeter, became the most famous, this was only because they were among the most popular. Many other mysteries about which we now know very little had been instituted in honour of the same goddess in certain demes of Attica, and in honour of other divinities elsewhere, such as the Cabiri at Samothrace and near Thebes.

The mysteries were officially recognised by the cities who protected and encouraged their celebration, but they were not a state religion in any way. They were under the direction of priestly families whose ancestors had received their instructions from the lips of the divinity itself, initiations were held individually and, though the law punished any act that the priests might hold to be sacrilegious, there was nothing to oblige citizens to take part in the cult. We might say that the state offered its services to a religion that remained private in principle, even when the number of its faithful had increased out of all proportion. That they were private may well have been because originally, in a remote past going back to the Mycenaean period, they had been the religions of a single family or a very restricted group, which did not admit participants from outside into the ceremonies of the mysteries unless they had first undergone a series of formalities. The word " formalities " may seem strange to us and yet, judging by the mysteries of Eleusis, which we know better than any others, it is the perfect word to describe at least the first stage of the initiation.

All that was asked of the candidates was to purify themselves carefully and then take part in a secret ceremony in which sacred objects were no doubt revealed to them and finally recite certain sacred formulas. Admission to the higher degrees involved far more difficult tests.

We may well ask what the initiates hoped to gain by admittance to these mysteries. It seems that the mystery cults, which had originally been those of agrarian divinities, very soon took on a profounder significance. The powers that presided over fertility ensured rebirth and a new existence for plants after their seasonal disappearance; and the cycle of vegetation, with its alternation of death and life, repeated itself every year. By analogy, at Eleusis any way, it was thought that the divinities who had been honoured would protect human beings after their death.

What does seem certain is that the initiates, who might come from every class of society, even the humblest, had the impression that they were in direct, personal contact with the divinity. As a result they practised the cult with a fervour which was lacking when they paid homage to other divinities. Moreover, moral ideas tended to appear among the initiates, which gave the mystery religions a spiritual value that distinguished them from the official religions.   P.D.

MYTHOLOGY. We do not know if the female figure shown so frequently in Cretan art, either sitting under a tree or perched up on a mountain top, brandishing serpents or flanked by wild beasts, represents a single divinity, endowed with several different attributes, or else a number of goddesses who resemble one another like sisters of the same family. This means that at present we still do not know whether a Minoan mythology existed or not. For while religion is, in the words of Littré, " the whole of all the doctrines and practices which constitute the relationship between mankind and divine power ", mythology is " the story of divine personages " (and semi-divine personages we may add) and " of polytheism ", polytheism implying that each of these personages is distinguished from the others, not only by his attributes, but also by his individual character and life story.

No sooner do we enter the Hellenic world through the poems of Homer, than we are struck by the multiplicity and diversity of superhuman beings and by the precision with which the individuality of each is stressed. Such precision is only understandable if a pantheon, familiar to both the poet and his public, had long been established. We do know that such a pantheon had grown up well before the end of the 2nd millennium B.C., from studying the Linear B texts (q.v.), which mention the names of some of the gods of classical Greece like Apollo or Dionysus, who may have been gods brought with them by the invading Achaeans and therefore quite different in origin from the Cretan goddess. The divine society that Homer described may well have been modelled on the human society of Greece during the golden age of the Mycenaean civilisation. There is an absolute sovereign, Agamemnon or Zeus, whose vassals tremble when he frowns; younger brothers such as Menelaus or Poseidon, high and mighty lords who nonetheless respect the orders of their master; and then all the vassals of lesser importance, but still chieftains of well defined domains, whom the king gathers around him, either to celebrate or to give advice, before he takes his irrevocable decisions. If the sovereign's authority was less than Homer would have us suppose and if the social structure was in fact less solid, we need not be surprised that the poet should have idealised reality to a certain extent. If the image he gives us of the world of the gods corresponds to beliefs current in his time, how incomplete this image must be! Behind the majestic Olympian assembly, whose composition and character he established more or less definitely for the future, there is no trace of that barbaric swarm of divinities which others, including Hesiod, were later to try to reduce to some semblance of order. The fact is the gods were not eternal and those who ruled the world in the *Iliad* and the *Odyssey* were themselves the descendants and successors of divine generations. Some of their members had survived and kept an eminent position, such as Gaea and Hecate, while others were dethroned, relegated to memories of the past, or even buried, like the Titans, in the depths of the earth by order of their victors.

Hesiod's *Theogony* relates how out of the original emptiness, or Chaos, Gaea, the Earth, was born, and gave birth to all the rest beginning with the Sky (Uranus) which was " capable of covering her completely ". Out of their union were born horrible monsters, but also goddesses who were still honoured in the classical period, and twelve Titans of whom the lastborn, Cronus, emasculated his father with the aid of his mother and became master of the world. Although Uranus had been a fearful tyrant, his son Cronus was no better. In order not to be dispossessed by his sons, he ate all the children whom his sister, Rhea, bore him except the lastborn, Zeus. He was saved by his mother's ruse, when she made the unsuspecting Cronus swallow a stone swaddled with rags as a substitute. When he reached manhood, Zeus forced Cronus to disgorge his brothers and sisters, Hestia, Demeter, Hera, Poseidon and Hades, by giving him a magic potion. Then together they waged war on Cronus and the other Titans, defeated and chained them up for all eternity in the darkness. In turn they had children, some of whom became divine such as Apollo, Artemis, Hermes, Aphrodite, Athena, Dionysus, Ares, Hephaestus, while others, who were born of unions with mortals, took their place in the confused cohort of the heroes.

This then, was how an empire was formed by a dynasty who took up residence on the cloudy heights of Mount Olympus after having quelled the revolt of the Giants, not without difficulty, and reigned over the world until the end of the pagan era. Under Zeus's supreme rule each of the divinities we have mentioned was given either a well determined domain (Poseidon received the sea and Hades the kingdom of the dead) or a well defined function (Hera as protector of fiancées and wives, Demeter as patron of agriculture). But this neat account is not an accurate picture of the way successive beliefs actually evolved; the Greeks did not venerate Cronus before they worshipped his son. This outline of divine prehistory was elaborated in a century in which Asian influences, impregnated with traditions, were making themselves felt. It was an attempt to explain the order that Zeus and his kin had brought ready made with them when, in the long distant past, they had taken possession of a Greece ruled only by divinities of the Cretan type. This scholarly explanation had little impact either on official religion or popular beliefs; we should not know of such a cosmic system if it were not that we still have Hesiod's *Theogony* which is the oldest known, if not the only attempt, at a synthesis of this kind and if mythographers had not transmitted information culled from works that the ancient peoples themselves do not seem to have consulted much. Even in its beginnings the Greek pantheon lacked the beautiful and simple clarity that we are tempted to ascribe to it. The divinities, who had been hierarchically classified and given well defined attributes as early as the time of Homer, may first have been the gods of different geographical regions. They would have begun their career by reigning over various cities whose inhabitants looked to them for protection of their lives and all their activities, over their harvests, herds, health, and enterprises, both warlike and peaceful. This universality of function would have resulted in all the divinities resembling each other. When the Greek world became conscious of its spiritual unity and when leagues, such as that formed against Troy, were formed, it became necessary to find each of these local gods an individual place in a world which was becoming united, and it was then that family links were established between them, that their ranks, orders of precedence and functions were determined. Politics also intervened in modifying their relationships to one another; Hera may have owed her eminent rank on Mount Olympus to her patronage of Argolis, which was the fief of Agamemnon in the time of Mycenaean greatness, and when Athens had annexed its neighbour Eleusis, Athena was somewhat eclipsed in her role as agricultural goddess by her rival, Demeter.

Even more than the gods, the heroes were attached to a single city and although some, like Heracles, were renowned throughout Greece, others were little known beyond the boundaries of their small states. Their personalities often remained rather ill defined, but others were involved in adventures whose equivalents may be found in the folklores of many countries. Long before they became the protagonists of classical tragedy, they had made their impact on popular imagination and their legends were illustrated in vase paintings. The ancient Greeks also believed that these personages had really existed in a distant past and the citizens of the states that they protected were proud of their exploits. We now know that many of these heroes were none other than oriental figures whom the Greeks had adopted, forgetting that they had first heard of them through the stories that sailors had brought back with them.   P.D.

NAUCRATIS. It was difficult for the Greeks to found colonies in well organised countries governed by an administration of long standing like Egypt. Commercial relations existed between the Nile valley and the principal Greek

Sailing ships. Disembarkation ladders and steering oars attached to the sterns. Detail of a cup by Nikosthenes. About 525-520 B.C. Paris, Louvre. *Photo Hirmer*.

ports, especially those in Asia Minor, and Herodotus tells us that Amasis conceded the town of Naucratis to the Greek merchants who traded in his country. We do not know exactly when it was founded, but it probably dates back to the last quarter of the 7th century B.C. and seems to have been founded by the Milesians. It quickly became a gathering point for all the Greeks in Egypt who had not been enrolled as mercenaries in the armies of the pharaohs. Sanctuaries to the Greek gods were built there and it appears that by the middle of the 5th century, the town enjoyed extraterritorial privileges. We do not quite know the nature of its political regime; it was probably a sort of municipal autonomy. The population was very mixed; nine port prefects each represented a different city, and all these cities were situated on the seabord of Anatolia.

It survived for a long time, even into the Ptolemaic era, in spite of the crushing rivalry of Alexandria, which was almost its neighbour. The most prosperous era of its history was in the 6th century, when all the trade between the Greek world and Egypt passed through Naucratis. Its main export was cereals and in return it imported timber and slaves, captured by cities like Thasus in Thrace and Macedonia, and, more important still, silver which fetched higher prices in Egypt than in Greece. There is hardly any need to point out that cultural contacts accompanied commercial exchanges and Naucratis was

for a long time the port of communication between the two civilisations.   P.D.

NAUSICAA. The figures of young girls rarely graced the literature of early times. Nausicaa was one of them. She appears in the *Odyssey* as the daughter of Alcinous, king of the Phaeacians, welcoming Ulysses, when his last shipwreck threw him, naked and covered with foam, onto the shores of the island of Pteria, which is generally identified with Corfu. While her companions, who were playing ball with her on the beach, fled in terror, Nausicaa looked after the unfortunate man, clothed him and took him as a guest to her father's palace.   P.D.

NAVIGATION. The Greeks are reputed a nation of sailors, but they are wary sailors who, to be like Ulysses, never really trusted the sea. Hesiod said in the *Works and Days* that he had only taken ship once in his life and that was to cross the Euripus which separated the island of Euboea from the continent. He advised Perses to be careful of the dangers of sea travel. During the classical era, the Athenian thalassocracy cleared the seas of pirates and sailors had only bad weather to fear.

The Greeks used anchors, but did not know about the rudder attached to the stern-post which swings on an axis; they guided their ships with a long oar placed on the poop. This may have been one of the reasons limiting shipping tonnage, but there were others: boats were pulled onto dry land during the bad weather season and even at night when the sea was rough during the navigation months. The lack of good sea charts, compasses and powerful beacons restricted sailing to the daytime and good weather, without losing sight of land. Boats hugged the coast as closely as possible and sailed from island to island so that they could find shelter at sundown. Corcyra (Corfu) and Tarentum were generally ports of call on the voyage from Piraeus to Sicily. Boats were hauled onto land with false keels. To avoid sailing round the Peloponnesus and encountering the frequent storms off Cape Malea, ships sailed through the Saronic Gulf and Gulf of Corinth, and were dragged on wooden logs the length of the *diolkos*, or slipway, whose track runs beside the present Canal of Corinth, and in some parts coincides with it. *(See* Shipping). R.F.

NAXOS. Naxos is not only the largest, but also the most fertile and pleasantest of the Cyclades. We know little of its history during the 3rd and 2nd millennium B.C. Cycladic idols found on the island prove that it was inhabited and civilised in very early times. According to the legend, Theseus abandoned Ariadne there on his return from Crete and Dionysus came to console her.

In the first centuries of Hellenism, Naxos certainly exercised a real hegemony over her neighbours. The most important archaic buildings and sculpture on Delos were offerings from Naxos; it is enough to mention the row of lions on an esplanade facing the Sacred Lake, and the colossus, about 36 ft high, which fell later on and knocked down the magnificent bronze palm tree dedicated by the Athenian, Nicias. In the 6th century, Naxos was ruled by the tyrant, Lygdamis, who concluded a friendly alliance with Pisistratus of Athens. The alliance survived a change of regime and, after being devastated by the Persians during the Persian Wars, Naxos was one of the first to join the Delian League. It was not long before it revolted, but unsuccessfully. Later, after the victory of Sparta in 404, the course of its history became independent of Athens. It suffered the same vicissitudes as the other Cyclades during the Hellenistic period. P.D.

NEMEA. Since the legendary times when Heracles, on the orders of Eurystheus, killed the only lion that figures in Greek myths, Nemea was one of the great sanctuaries of Greece. Every four years, the games were held there that were celebrated in Pindar's *Nemean Odes*. The only surviving ruin of the sanctuary is a temple, built and decorated by Scopas. P.D.

NEMESIS. Nemesis does not figure very largely in Greek mythology. She was the daughter of Night and it was said that Zeus loved her. According to one tradition, she laid the egg from which Helen, Clytemnestra and the Dioscuri were hatched. The egg was found by a shepherd who took it to Leda. In spite of the scantiness of these legends, Nemesis was considered one of the most powerful of the divinities and the Greeks showed her the greatest respect. Her function was to see that the measure was observed in all things, that everyone stayed in the place allotted to him by Destiny, and to protect the gods from encroachments by mortals. She punished pride in all its forms and did not permit any enterprise to go forward that would change the natural order: when the Persian king decided to pierce the isthmus of Mount Athos, to allow a passage for his ships, she stirred up a storm that wrecked his fleet; when Polycrates (q.v.) tried to defy fate and pay for the excessive happiness he enjoyed by throwing his favourite ring into the sea, she refused the sacrifice that he intended to impose on

Stater from Naxos. Reverse: Silenus holding a cup of wine. About 460 B.C. Sicily, Private collection. *Photo L. von Matt.*

Nereid. Sculpture from the Nereid Monument at Xanthus in Lycia. About 410 or 380 B.C. British Museum.

the gods and returned the tyrant's ring in the stomach of a fish brought to his table by a fisherman. The greatest fault a man could commit in the eyes of the Greeks was to indulge in excess; "Nothing too much" was one of the precepts enjoined at Delphi, and Nemesis was entrusted with seeing that the injunction was observed. Although the eminent persons of the world had particular cause for fearing her, she sometimes punished humbler people whose thoughts had become too ambitious. Even in our day, Greek peasants do not like to be complimented on the beauty of their children; the old fear of the goddess still survives among them.

Nemesis was worshipped as a goddess in several regions of Greece. The Athenians notably dedicated a sanctuary to her about 430 B.C. at Rhamnus, which seems to have been very popular. Agoracritus, Phidias's friend, made the statue of the goddess. P.D.

NEOPLATONISM. *See* Plotinus.

NEOPTOLEMUS. Neoptolemus, also called Pyrrhus, was the son of Achilles and took part in the Trojan War after the death of his father. He distinguished himself by his courage and also by his savagery. When Troy fell, he killed Priam although he had taken refuge at an altar, smashed the skull of little Astyanax, Hector's son, and sacrificed Polyxena, the king's daughter, on the tomb of Achilles. He was given Andromache as part of his booty, but he also married Hermione, the daughter of Menelaus. On his return to Greece, he settled in Epirus. As his marriage was barren, he went to consult the oracle at Delphi. There Orestes, at the instigation of Hermione whom he loved, killed Neoptolemus during a quarrel that he had begun himself. According to other traditions, Orestes had nothing to do with his death, which was brought about by the Delphians and the hatred of Apollo. P.D.

NEREIDS. *See* Nereus.

NEREUS. Nereus, "the old man of the sea", is a benevolent god who figures largely in sailors' lore. In the divine genealogies he appears as the son of the Sea (Pontus) and Gaea, the Earth. Thus he was older than Poseidon, but the relations between the two deities were rather distant; they leave the impression that as the two gods possessed similar attributes, the younger relegated Nereus to the sphere of popular piety and arrogated an official position for himself from which the elder had been ousted. Nereus and Doris, the daughter of Oceanus, had fifty daughters, the Nereids, who were very beautiful and had nothing else to do than to spin, sing and dance on the waves. The two outstanding members of the bevy were Amphitrite, who married Poseidon, and Thetis, who married a simple mortal, Peleus, and became the mother of Achilles. P.D.

NESSUS. The Centaur, Nessus, used to carry travellers on his back over the river Evenus. One day, having taken Deianira over in this way, he tried to rape her. The husband of the young woman, Heracles, came to the rescue in time and killed him. Before he died, Nessus took his revenge by giving Deianira a little of his blood,

Winged Nike adjusting her sandal. Bas-relief from the parapet of the Temple of Athena Nike. About 410-407 B.C. Athens, Acropolis Museum. *Photo H. Müller-Brunke.*

N I C I A S (1). An Athenian politician of the second half of the 5th century B.C. and one of the leaders of the conservative party, he had little liking for Pericles and was uncompromisingly hostile to the demagogues who succeeded him. Nothing in his life or actions indicated a trenchant personality; his moderation and respect for the gods appealed to the Athenians. He was elected strategus several times, commanded the troups on several expeditions of the Peloponnesian War and negotiated a truce with Sparta in 421. He was a man of the middle way. He died in 413.

P.D.

N I C I A S (2). An Athenian painter active in the second half of the 4th century B.C. He worked for clients living in different regions, notably in Ephesus. The subjects of his works seem to have been mythological, but we only know them by their titles. His masterpiece, called *Nemea,* depicted an allegorical character. According to tradition, he painted marble statues carved by Praxiteles *(See* Polychrome Sculpture). P.D.

N I K E . Nike is one of those divinities who show how naturally the Greeks personified abstractions even as early as the 8th century B.C. Hesiod in his *Theogony* makes Nike the daughter of the Titan, Pallas, and Styx. Nike represented no more than Victory and only a desire for logic created this piece of genealogy which the ancient Greeks ignored after Hesiod. Nike was primarily considered as a secondary aspect of more important divinities. On the Acropolis, the Athenians worshipped an Athena Nike, and an Athena Ergane, or the Worker, was venerated in a nearby sanctuary. The Athena Nike was surrounded by other Nikes, sacrificing in her honour, who could have been taken for emanations of the goddess they were worshipping. The Nike figures were represented as young women with long wings who could fly over the heavens carrying a crown for the victor. This crown was not a reward for warlike exploits only, but also for success in musical, literary and sporting competitions and Nike could be seen placing it like a pledge on the heads of those who had a glorious career before them; for example, on the pediment of the Parthenon, Nike is depicted crowning Athena as

telling her that it was a philtre which would bring back Heracles to her if he were unfaithful. The blood was really a violent poison. When Deianira smeared it on a tunic and sent it to her husband, who had proved faithless, the tunic clung to the hero's body and burnt him so cruelly that it killed himself. P.D.

N E S T O R . Nestor was the embodiment of wisdom and experience among the Greek chiefs of the Trojan War. He was older than the others and on several occasions he spoke with the authority of a man conscious of a life full of brilliant action. He was accompanied by his son, Antilochus, one of Achilles' closest friends and one of the bravest of the Greek warriors. The figure of Nestor acquired a greater interest for us when his palace was discovered at Pylos in Messenia. There, too, in recent years, several tablets written in Linear B (q.v.), the Mycenaean script deciphered by Michael Ventris, have come to light. P.D.

she issues from Zeus's head. Her personality tended to acquire a more romantic aspect in the Hellenistic epoch, which is admirably embodied in the famous Louvre statue found at Samothrace.

P.D.

NONNUS. An early epic poet who wrote the *Dionysiaca. (See* Epic).

NYMPHS. The nymphs were female nature divinities. They had no great literary importance, but their worship played a large part in the lives of humble people. The powers of the nymphs were limited, but each one was the essence and tutelary deity of a natural object and in a particular place. Whether the nymph was associated with a fountain, a shrub, a rock or a field, she knew the peasants intimately like neighbouring friends and they, in their turn, addressed her more easily than the remote Olympians; they left simple offerings

Nymph abducted by a silenus. Obverse of a silver stater from Thasos. About 420 B.C. Basel, Antiken Museum.

before the habitations of their protectresses and there was no need to go through the intermediary of a priest for this; the epigrams of the *Greek Anthology* are sophisticated versions of the vows actually made by peasants with a less literary talent to these divinities. There were also sanctuaries dedicated to nymphs in the towns; one of them lies on the southern slope of the Acropolis at Athens. These seem to have taken young girls and newly wedded wives specially under their protection. Nymphs are hardly identifiable on reliefs and vase paintings unless they are indicated as such in an inscription; in fact, they appear as draped women who are not characterised by any particular attributes. P.D.

OATH. Oaths were important in the life of the Greeks. They were guaranteed by the gods in whose name they were sworn and it was the gods themselves who were offended if they were broken. In a society founded on religion like that of Greece, there could be no better way of sealing an agreement and they were used in both private and political life. The god who was most usually invoked was Zeus; his name was then followed by an epithet which meant " protector of the oath ". But varying according to place, the circumstance and the period, various other divinities or even local heroes were invoked for oaths. As it was considered unseemly for women to swear by a male god, it was usually the goddess Hera that served as guarantor. Even the immortals themselves engaged themselves by oaths and in Homer's poems Zeus swore by the Earth, the Heavens and the Styx. Because he was all-seeing, Helios, the Sun was also very much favoured for oaths.

The oath was a religious act and to assume its full solemnity it had to be sworn with the eyes raised heavenwards, the hands clasped in front of the body, standing in a sanctuary before an altar. If the swearer touched the altar or the statue of the god, the oath became all the more strongly binding. It was accompanied by a sacrifice. In Athens there was a special stone on which all who wanted to swear an oath could stand. Every oath ended with an imprecatory formula that invoked divine wrath against anyone who did not keep his word and a punishment that would strike even future generations.

Oaths were taken in public life as well as in private affairs. Solon's fellow-citizens swore to remain faithful to his institutions by an oath and

young Athenians only acquired their civic rights after having sworn to defend the homeland and obey the laws. The same practice was frequent in many other cities. Magistrates took oaths before taking up their duties, whether they were political or judiciary, and the two contracting parties to a treaty engaged themselves in the same manner. The words of the oath and the name of the person who had taken it were often engraved on a stele, which was then placed in a sacred spot. P.D.

OCEANUS. Oceanus was the son of Uranus and Gaea, so he belonged to the most ancient of the divine generations and was older than Poseidon himself who inherited most of his attributes. He was the river that encircled the earth and was the source of all the other rivers, but it was Poseidon whom sailors venerated, not Oceanus. His daughters, the Oceanids, were only some among his numerous progeny. Hesiod said there were about forty Oceanids, but other writers mention a larger number. P.D.

OEDIPUS. Oedipus is the central character in Boeotian myths. An oracle told his father, Laius, that if he had a son, this son would kill him, marry Laius's widow and take possession of his kingdom. As soon as he was born, Oedipus was condemned to death, but the man who was entrusted with the deed dared not kill the defenceless child and left him exposed on the mountain. There was every likelihood that he would be eaten by wild animals, but a shepherd in the service of Polybus, king of Corinth, who was passing by, picked up the baby, took him home and brought him up as his own child. Oedipus's courage and intelligence were so outstanding in the midst of the little peasants that when he came into the presence of Polybus as a sequel to a slight affair (he had struck the son of a nobleman), he was adopted by the king who was childless. He forgot his origins himself and believed that he was the real son of Polybus. When he grew up, he consulted the oracle at Delphi and was horrified to be told that he would kill his father and marry his mother. In an attempt to escape his destiny, he decided not to return to Corinth and left in the direction of Thebes. He had a dispute on the way with the retainers of an old man's retinue, which he encountered, and killed the unknown old man and his men. The old man was Laius, but he did not learn this until much later. When he arrived at Thebes, the citizens were striken by a double disaster: the king had just been assassinated while on a journey, and a monstrous animal, the sphinx, devoured some of the young people of the country every day. The queen, Jocasta, had proclaimed that she would give her hand and her kingdom to any man who would deliver the city from this scourge. Oedipus presented himself before the sphinx, which did not kill its victims immediately but asked them a riddle first and slaughtered them when they could not guess the answer. Oedipus was the first to answer the monster's question: which being walks on four feet in the morning, two at noon and three in the evening? Oedipus realised that it was a man, who crawls on all fours in babyhood, then walks normally until the day when old age forces him to lean on a stick. When the sphinx saw its riddle solved, it threw itself in pure chagrin into a chasm and was killed on a rock. As the husband of Jocasta, ruler of a rich country that he governed wisely, the father of two sons, Eteocles and Polynices, and two daughters, Ismene and Antigone, Oedipus was respected by everyone and remained happy until Thebes was ravaged by plague. The oracle at Delphi was consulted on how the epidemic could be stopped and answered that Laius's murderer should be driven out, because this unpunished crime was a stain on the whole country. Oedipus

led the enquiry for the murderer himself and, in *Oedipus Rex*, Sophocles shows how the truth came out little by little and Oedipus, who still believed himself to be the son of Polybus, learnt how he had unwittingly committed the double crime of murder and incest. Jocasta hanged herself, while Oedipus tore out his own eyes so that he might no longer see the light of day, and left for exile, a wretched man, cursed by his subjects and accompanied only by Antigone, his daughter, who remained faithful to him until his death. According to Athenian tradition, he died at Colonus, near Athens, after meeting at last in Theseus, king of Attica, a man who could understand his greatness and the tragedy of his destiny. Another of Sophocles' plays, *Oedipus Coloneus*, shows the two heroes conversing in the sacred grove where Oedipus later disappeared, leaving Theseus the secret of the place where his remains would rest and protect the city that had received him in his misfortune.

The dark fate of Oedipus did not end there. The curse laid on him fell on his descendants also. His two sons fought each other for possession of the kingdom and killed each other in battle, and Antigone, in spite of the official prohibition, gave the honours of the dead to Polynices and was, in her turn, executed by Creon's order. Creon, Jocasta's brother, had acted like a traitor from the

Oedipus and the Sphinx.
Inside of an Attic cup. About
430 B.C. Vatican Museum.
Photo Anderson-Viollet.

expulsion of Oedipus to the death of his nephews because he coveted the succession. P.D.

OIL. *See* Olive Trees.

OLIVE TREES. Olive trees and vines were the main agricultural products of Attica. During the Peloponnesian War, the enemy army cut down all the olive trees, which was a disaster, because it takes ten years for a tree to begin giving fruit and much longer before it is fully productive. Olive gathering sometimes appears in vase painting. It was done by hand and with long, flexible canes. A mortar was used for the pressing, with a spout, or a hole in the bottom where the marc ran out. Another method in use was an oil-mill consisting of two stones, one fixed, the other movable, which was turned by slaves. R.F.

OLYMPIA. Olympia, lying about 14 miles from the sea in Elis, a remote, peaceful little province, was one of the most sacred places of the Greek world. It was cut off from the centre and east of the Peloponnesus by high mountains; communications were easiest with Messenia, Laconia and the district of Patras. Neither the legendary fame of a glorious Mycenaean past, nor the appearance of the site in a gently undulating countryside offer any explanation for the future development of the sanctuary. It was situated on the ruins and in the environs of a humble village and for a long time, during the period following the arrival of the Dorians, it was no more than a sacred grove. A female divinity was originally venerated there but Zeus, the lord of Olympus, joined her and became the principal deity. He was the successor of his father, Cronus, who had once been worshipped on the neighbouring hill of Kronion. Zeus remained in the plain. His devotees were the neighbouring peasants who, from the 9th to the 8th centuries B.C., dedicated rudimentary figurines to him made of bronze and terracotta, representing cattle, horses and birds, and who burnt their sacrifices on an open-air altar. The first sacred edifice was not dedicated to him but to his divine wife. The remains of this Heraeum were discovered beneath the 6th century Heraeum whose columns are still standing today. The presence of Zeus himself was so strong in the grove of Altis, at the foot of Kronion, that at this period they felt there was no need to build him a temple.

It was in his honour that the peasants of the district celebrated games from the very beginning and held athletic competitions. We do not know

Olive harvesting. Detail of an amphora. Third quarter of the 6th century B.C. British Museum.

Olympia. Temple of
Hera. 6th century B.C.
*Photo Louis-Frédéric
Rapho.*

how the reputation of these games (q.v.) became so widespread nor why athletes from further away wanted to compete. By 776 B.C., the year of the first Olympiad, the ceremonies were already international in character. Probably the influence of Argos was at first a decisive factor in the success of the festival. Later on, the Spartans occupied a dominant place in the competitions and, while remaining panhellenic, the great games always attracted a majority of Dorians. The quadriennial celebration of the games, the international truce accompanying them, the prestige of the victories won there, all explain how the modest sanctuary in Elis became, in the course of the 7th century, and remained one of the centres of Greek civilisation. The buildings around the sanctuary were insignificant in normal times, but for a brief period, once every four years, the representatives of the entire Greek world were to be found united there in veneration of Zeus and glorification of Hellenic athleticism. After 776, Greek chronology everywhere was calculated according to the festival, each Olympiad consisting of four years *(See* Chronology).

It must have seemed strange at a time when the least important divinity possessed his habitation that the lord of the place should remain unhoused; so about 470 B.C. it was decided that a temple should be erected to him, a magnificent Doric building, rather elongated in form, designed by a local architect, Libon. It was constructed of ordinary stone, covered with a thin coat of stucco, with pediments and metopes carved in Parian marble. The building was completed in about fifteen years, but the chryselephantine statue, focal point of the worship, was not made until about 430 by Phidias. The decoration of the tympanum illustrated, on the eastern part, Zeus helping the hero, Pelops, when he took possession of the Peloponnesus and, on the west, the glory of Apollo, Zeus's son, whose pacificatory intervention gave victory to the Lapiths when they were unjustly attacked by the Centaurs. The twelve labours of Heracles, a Peloponnesian hero, were depicted on the frieze. Consequently, although the themes had a local character, their interest was not narrowly provincial but appealed to all Greeks.

319

Olympia. Portico of the palaestra. 3rd century B.C. *Photo Hassia.*

At the beginning of the 6th century, the treasuries (q.v.), built in a row on a terrace that was an extension of the temple of Hera, had all been erected on sites consecrated by the Dorians. The most recent of these treasuries dates from the 5th century. Scattered in the layers of the sanctuary innumerable ex-votos have been found, most of them made of bronze, which were offered up in the treasuries by humble devotees. Others, which were more important and were dedicated by the victors themselves or the cities they came from, have unfortunately been lost.

There were also two very ancient enclosures situated right in the heart of the sanctuary. One was dedicated to Pelops, the first prince of the Peloponnesus, the other to Hippodamia, his wife, whose hand he won when he was the victor in the first chariot race run at Olympia. There is no space to describe all the buildings gradually erected in the sanctuary. They were not all religious in character: the assembly halls, the senate and the

Runner. Bronze statuette. Early 5th century B.C. Olympia Museum. *Photo Deutsches Archäologisches Institut, Athens.*

Olympia. Temple of Zeus. 470-456 B.C. *Photo Louis-Frédéric Rapho.*

prytaneum were used by the administrators of the sacred places and their worship; Phidias's workshop, which the Byzantines later adapted as a church, was built for the great master to make the statue of the god; the Macedonian princes, then the Romans, erected numerous buildings there, which are not all of equal interest. The most important place in Olympia for the ancient Greeks was certainly the stadium which was laid out to the east of the sanctuary. It has been systematically excavated and one can still see the starting lines in stone prepared for the runners.

It is natural to compare Olympia and Delphi because the two sanctuaries were the most revered places of the Hellenic world. They were not rivals. While Delphi, because of its oracle, was involved in all the events of history and, in spite of the prudence of its priests, found itself taking up a position between cities or parties in the same state, Olympia kept itself above the fray. The competitions taking place there stirred up passions that sprang more from athletic pride than politics. The only reward coveted by the competitors and the states, which sent them as their champions, was the slender olive branch circling their brows, a moral reward dissociated from all material interest. The ancient Greeks might very well try to circumvent Apollo whose replies would give or withdraw possession of a territory; from Zeus of Olympia they asked nothing but his approval for those physical and moral qualities that together were designated by the word *arete*. P.D.

OLYMPUS. Olympus is part of a vast and complex mountain range stretching northwards into Thessaly, southwards into Macedonia and to the Gulf of Salonika in the east. Its principal peak, Olympus, is 9570 ft and there are eight others higher than 8450 ft. It is almost inaccessible (it was first climbed in 1913 and thoroughly explored for the first time in 1921) as it is cut up with precipices and valleys and flanked by hills. In ancient times, it lay at the farthest point of Greece proper, far from any large towns, a mysterious, cloud capped peak that was considered the abode of the gods. The legendary giants in a vain effort to reach the gods in their domain had to pile

321

Ossa (6490 ft) on Pelion (5300 ft), both being fairly near. Apart from its mythological significance, Olympus had little importance in Greek life. Other mountains too, Olympus in Bithynia for example, bore the same name.   P.D.

OLYNTHUS. Thirty years ago, the name of Olynthus, made famous by the speeches of Demosthenes, was primarily associated for us with Athens' struggle against Philip of Macedon. Now this little town of Chalcidice, near the Macedonian frontier, interests us mainly as the best example of Greek town-planning in the 5th century B.C. It was rebuilt after the destruction of the Persian Wars, and its expansion about 440 led to the building of a new district at the foot of the acropolis, which has been excavated by the Americans. The plan consists of big avenues, sixteen to nineteen feet wide, running from north to south, which follow the geographical characteristics of the site. These are cut at right angles by narrower streets which form rectangular areas of uniform size, measuring about 116 ft from north to south, and about 283 ft from east to

west. Two rows of five houses were built on each of these areas. In spite of a few minor variations owing to the irregularities of the site, this lay-out excluded all picturesque or impressive effects; it fulfilled the practical aims made fashionable by Hippodamus of Miletus, which are common enough in our day but were rather rare at that time in Greece.

Another reason for the archaeological interest of this town arises from its destruction by the Spartans in 379 B.C. As a consequence of this, we can consider that any works of art or objects found on the site belong to a date previous to this; even if the site was occupied again afterwards, it is very doubtful that it enjoyed any real prosperity. It is one of the chronological landmarks, unfortunately only too rare, that we possess for the study of styles.   P.D.

ORACLES. The entry under *Divination* discusses inductive divination which depends on the observation of phenomena and the interpretation of signs. The present article will be concerned with the second kind, *mantike*, a

Lapith woman struggling with a Centaur. Fragment from the west pediment of the Temple of Zeus at Olympia. About 460 B.C. Olympia Museum. *Photo Walter Hege.*

Mount Olympus.
Photo Boissonnas.

sort of delirium or ecstasy *(mania* in Greek, *furor* in Latin), which Plato considered far superior to the first. It was practised by prophets like Bakis, and particularly sibyls and pythias whom the god was supposed to inspire directly without the intermediary of any sign. It was also experienced by " dreamers " who were given revelations in their sleep.

The sibyls were legendary figures who probably first appeared during the great religious movement of the 8th century B.C. whose mystical character encouraged a belief in intuitive divination, which was generally inspired by Apollo. The Dionysiac mysteries sprang from the same movement and at Delphi, for example, Dionysus was associated with Apollo. The sibyls of Cumae, Delphi and Erythrae were famous; during the Roman era there were as many as twelve of them. The Trojan sibyl, Cassandra, was a sort of prototype of all the others. Apollo, who loved her, gave her the gift of prophecy and she told the Trojans of the misfortunes that threatened them. After the city had been taken, Agamemnon led her captive to Mycenae. In his *Agamemnon,* Aeschylus depicts the prophetic delirium that seizes Cassandra like a physical pain and takes the form of several crises separated by calm periods.

Zeus delivered his oracles at the sanctuary of Dodona. About the 7th century B.C., divination began to be practised in the sanctuaries of Apollo, the son of Zeus, who was kindly disposed towards men and informed them of the will of his father. The sceptical Lucian enumerated the principal oracles of Apollo: Delphi, the most famous of all, then Colophon, Xanthus, Claros and Branchidae.

At Claros the oracles were delivered by a prophet, not a prophetess. The adyton, or place of mysteries forbidden to the profane, which was used for divination, has recently been excavated by Louis Robert in a remarkable state of preservation. The sanctuary of Branchidae, or Didyma, was also in Asia Minor, on the territory of the great city of Miletus. There a prophetess delivered the oracles of Apollo and German excavations have brought to light the lay-out of the adyton as at Claros. Delphi (q.v.) for a long time overshadowed all the other oracular sanctuaries of Apollo and it is most unfortunate that its adyton was completely destroyed.

When Apollo took over Delphi, the former sibyl of Delphi whose " rock " was kept in the sanctuary of Gaea, the Earth, became a pythia, that is, a Delphian subordinated to the priests of the place and the " prophets " of the sanctuary, a sort of temple official who, on certain days, served as an intermediary, or medium, between Apollo and men. She delivered oracles by drawing lots at any time except unpropitious days *(See* Divination), but the "inspired" consultation of the adyton only took place in principle once a month, on the 7th, apart from three winter months; however, extraordinary consultations were permitted.

The consulters, either private persons or delegates from a city, first had to pay a tax *(pelanos)* and offer a sacrifice, usually a goat. Before it was killed, the priests sprinkled it with cold water. If it remained still under the shower, this was a bad sign, but if it shuddered and trembled, this indicated that the god was present and the priests "led the Pythia into the temple". The consulters who had been granted the *promanteia* (the right of consulting the oracle first) by the city of Delphi went in first, followed by the rest. Inside, lots were drawn among the two groups, distinguished in this way, to decide who should consult the oracle first. The priests and the consulters crossed the temple and went down to the subterranean place, or manteion, divided, as at Claros and Miletus, into two rooms; they stayed in the first while the Pythia went alone into the adyton proper, where she sat on the cover of a high tripod. As she was separated by a door or a simple curtain from the first room, the consulters could not see her at the moment when she was prophesying, but they could hear her. Besides the tripod in the adyton, there was also the sacred stone called the *omphalos (See* Delphi), the gold statue of Apollo and the tomb of Dionysus.

The ancient Greeks spoke of a telluric exhalation, the *pneuma,* which was supposed to rise from the earth underneath the tripod and cause the delirium, or "enthusiasm", of the Pythia. She also chewed laurel leaves, the tree sacred to Apollo, some varieties of which are poisonous. But her "ecstasy" was probably simply induced by auto-suggestion, in other words, by a process of religious psychology which is not necessarily hysteria. The replies of the Pythia were often inarticulate and obscure. They had to be interpreted and given form by the "prophets", who generally put them into hexameters like those of Homer. A large number of these oracles, authentic or false, have come down to us either through Greek writers, particularly Herodotus and Plutarch, or through inscriptions.

Apollonian divination at Delphi and elsewhere belonged to the day and to light (Apollo was also the sun god of the Greeks), but there was also an inspired divination, nocturnal in character, based mainly on the interpretation of dreams *(oneiromanteia).*

At Epidaurus in Argolis, Asclepius, the god of medicine and son of Apollo, had a sanctuary that did a thriving business especially in the 4th century B.C., where the suppliants were sick people. After accomplishing the preliminary rites, they used to lie beneath a huge, two storied portico, which was used as a dormitory and was called the *enkoimeterion* (place of sleeping), or the *abaton* (holy and secret place). There, lying on animal skins, they received from Asclepius during their sleep either a miraculous, instantaneous cure, or a dream prescribing the treatment appropriate for their maladies. Stelae found at Epidaurus have preserved for us an extraordinary record of innumerable cures of this kind. The same process of incubation was followed at Oropus near the frontier between Attica and Boeotia, at the Amphiareion, the sanctuary of the prophet-king Amphiaraus, hero of the Theban legend. At Lebadia in Boeotia, the land of innumerable oracles, there was the sanctuary of the hero, Trophonius, a deep fissure in the mountain-side. The consulter who was brave enough to face the terrors of the passage underground was led to the far end of the fissure where he received the revelations of Trophonius in visions and through voices. He was afterwards conducted back by the same path, bewildered and battered by the ordeal.

Nekromanteia, the evocation of the spirits of the dead to question them, was known to the Greeks. The prophecies given by Tiresias to Ulysses in Book XI of the *Odyssey,* and the summoning of the ghost of King Darius in Aeschylus's *Persians* are proofs of this.

Throughout the ages, dreams have been regarded as an important source of divination, although Homer already realised that dreams were ambiguous and that it was difficult to distinguish between deceitful and false dreams (those that come to us through the ivory gate) and true dreams (those that pass through the gate of horn). Moreover, dreams could include all the prodigies and portents observable in waking hours. Consequently, a good interpreter of dreams had to master the whole science of divination, and *oneirokritike* finally comprised a body of extremely numerous and complex doctrines, which may be the origins of the *Keys to Dreams* still read today.

R.F.

ORCHOMENUS. Orchomenus was with Thebes the oldest and most important city of

Boeotia. She was the most brilliant centre of Minoan civilisation on Greek territory towards the end of the 3rd millennium B.C. Her prosperity survived invasion; she existed in the Mycenaean period and Homer celebrated her glory and wealth. During the archaic era, she joined the Boeotian Confederacy and during the Persian Wars supported the Persians. When at the end of the Peloponnesian War Thebes adopted a democratic constitution, Orchomenus which, up to that point, had maintained good relations with Thebes, broke away from her and the Spartans found an ally in Orchomenus in 395 and 394 B.C. After their victory at Leuctra, the Thebans were quite prepared to destroy her, but they did not carry this out until later when Epaminondas was no longer there to intercede for Orchomenus. Another town, situated in Arcadia, bore the same name.　　P.D.

ORDERS. The term, orders, is applied to the different kinds of proportions and decorations of the column and the entablature it supports. Their importance to an architecture like that of the Greeks, where the column is significant of the style, can hardly be exaggerated; the style of a building is mainly determined by the orders. Although by the end of the 6th century B.C. the Doric and Ionic orders, which came into existence about the same time, were to be found all over the Greek world, they were at first limited to their own geographical areas. The Doric order dominated the Greek peninsula, Crete, southern Italy and Sicily; the Ionic originated along the Asia Minor coasts of the Aegean Sea from where it spread to the large neighbouring islands and the Cyclades. Although their different characters can perhaps be explained in the beginning by the nature of the materials at the disposal of the first builders, they also corresponded with the clearly defined, almost opposing temperaments of the people who used them; severity and logic were characteristic of the Dorians in contrast to the easy-going charm, the fancy and inventive imagination of the Ionians.

Doric capital from the Temple of Hephaestus at Athens. About 430 B.C. *Ph. Deutsches Archäologisches Institut, Athens.*

Ionic capital from the Temple of Artemis at Sardis. 4th century B.C. *Photo Hirmer.*

Corinthian capital from the Tholos at Epidaurus. 4th century B.C. Epidaurus Museum. *Photo Hassia.*

Doric frieze. The cornice runs along the upper edge, beneath are the metopes decorated with bas-reliefs separated by the triglyphs. The guttae beneath the triglyphs prevent water from falling onto the unprotected architrave underneath. Frieze from Temple C at Selinus. About 470 B.C. Palermo Museum. *Photo L. von Matt.*

The Doric order emphasised the structural lines of the building. The column sprang directly from the stylobate or floor. The geometric lines of the capital with the square abacus and echinus, make no attempt to conceal the fact that it is constructed to support the architrave and reduce its bearing. The architrave, bare of all decoration, looks like a beam serving as a rest for the extremities of other transversal beams that form the base of the roof framework. Only the ends of these beams can be seen. Grooved by three vertical flutes, they form the triglyphs and the interval between them, generally filled with a slab, constitutes the metope. The alternation of triglyphs and metopes, which forms the frieze, is one of the most distinctive features of the Doric order. The frieze is surmounted by the cornice, which supports the double slope of the roof framework, and architrave, frieze and cornice together comprise the entablature. The emphasis on the functional character of all the constructional elements gives a reassuring impression of solidity while satisfying the Greek taste for geometry.

The Ionic order, on the contrary, enveloped in all kinds of embellishments the very real and carefully calculated strength of its architecture. The attention is focused particularly on the column. It is more slender than in the Doric order, and is enlarged and reinforced at its extremities.

The shaft rests on a base that distributes the weight over the foundation through a number of superimposed discs, each larger than the next, set on a square dado. The middle is often encircled by rings called astragals. The top is crowned by a capital that lacks the sturdy appearance of the Doric, but in the words of Choisy it resembles " a double band of flexible matter that is quickened until the tension rolls the extremities in on themselves; it is rather like a spring that transmits the weight of the architrave to the shaft ". The architrave consists of two or three slightly projecting fascias joined to the frieze by a moulding. The frieze is not divided by triglyphs, but forms an unbroken strip circling the entire building which can be left plain but is nearly always decorated with paintings or reliefs. It is noteworthy that buildings of the Ionic order are richly decorated with ornamental motifs, such as ovolos, anthemia, astragals and arabesques, over the base of walls and door-frames. This decoration sought after an effect of elegance and stylishness that was sometimes not far from ostentation.

The Corinthian order was very popular from the end of the 5th century B.C. and, as this indicates, was added at a late date to the two canonical orders. Callimachus, a carver contemporary with Phidias, is said to have invented it. It was really only a development of the Ionic column with its capital surrounded with sprays of acanthus leaves. P.D.

ORESTES. Orestes was still a child when his mother, Clytemnestra, killed his father, Agamemnon, with the help of her lover, Aegisthus. He fled to his uncle, Strophius, whose son, Pylades, became his inseparable friend. There, a grown man, he planned revenge, returned secretly to Mycenae and killed Clytemnestra and Aegisthus. This parricide automatically aroused the vengeance of the gods and the Erinyes pursued the wretched man who found no rest until the Areopagus (q.v.), an Athenian tribunal, summoned by Athena, acquitted him after a brilliant pleading by Apollo. A ritual purification at Delphi finally cleansed him of the stain of spilling blood. There was also a story, the subject of Euripides' *Iphigenia in Tauris,* that Orestes, accompanied by Pylades, landed at Tauris, the present Crimea, where the king used to sacrifice all strangers. But the priestess entrusted with killing the victims was Iphigenia, Orestes' own sister, whom Artemis had rescued from the knife of Calchas when he was about to sacrifice her at Aulis, substituting a hind for the young girl. Iphigenia, Pylades and Orestes fled from Tauris, carrying with them the statue of the goddess, and

it was this statue that was said to be the one worshipped in the sanctuary at Brauron (q.v.) in Attica. P.D.

ORPHEUS. The essential elements in the legend of Orpheus are quite simple. He was a Thracian prince, son of a muse, Calliope or Polymnia, who was so gifted with poetic genius that even the most savage creatures, the fiercest beasts and even the trees were spell-bound by the charm of his creations. The earliest literature invoked his name and he is already mentioned in the Homeric hymns as the first poet. Jason took him on board his ship, the Argo, so that the rowers could keep time to the rhythm of his cithara and he would encourage his companions in their ordeals. On his return to Thrace, he fell in love with the nymph, Eurydice, and was inconsolable when she died from a snake bite. He went down to the underworld, charmed the guardians of that terrible place and was granted the return of Eurydice to the living on one condition, that while he was leading her back to the frontier between the dead and the living, he should not look back at her. His impatience was too great to obey the order and the young woman, before reaching the earth, was taken back by the messenger of the shades, Hermes Psychopompus, who gave her back to Hades.

Death of Orpheus.
Detail of an Attic
stamnos by Hermonax.
470 B.C. Paris,
Louvre.

Tradition varies on the way Orpheus' life ended. It was said that he was killed by Thracian women, and his head and lyre, thrown into the river Hebrus, were carried by the current to the island of Lesbos. Orpheus was not only a poet: he was also regarded as the founder of a mystery religion which had a lasting popularity throughout the Greek world. P.D.

ORPHISM. Orphism was a religious movement that is difficult to define with any precision. Some historians talk about "Orphic mysteries" and "Orphic conventicles"; these would have been secret societies similar to the Dionysiac *thiasoi* from which they were derived as the result of a reform attributed to Orpheus. In fact, Orpheus, the Thracian singer, was a "prophet" of the Dionysiac religion. Other historians assert that in ancient times the term, Orphic, was only applied to isolated individuals, like sorcerers or diviners, or to books. A whole literature, which has almost entirely disappeared, was considered the work of Orpheus. What remains does not go back earlier than the 6th century B.C. It contains all the elements of a mythology, preceded by a theogony, or divine genealogy. The distinctive elements of this Orphic theogony was the primordial Egg from which the entire universe had been hatched; the importance of the goddess, Night, who brought forth the heavens and earth; and the myth of Zagreus. There are numerous variants of this myth but the main outlines were as follows. The young god, Zagreus, who was promised the sovereignty of the universe, was borne from the sacred union of Zeus and his daughter, Persephone. The Titans, the enemies of the child, seized and killed him and then ate him. It is the story of the death of Orpheus, with the Titans substituted for the maenads. But Zagreus was a god. Zeus recovered his heart, which had escaped the voracity of the Titans, and resuscitated him from this organ and later handed him the government of the world.

Since in some versions of the legend, Zagreus comes to life again in the person of Dionysus, it has been suggested that its aim was to explain the fusion of the Cretan god, Zagreus, with the Thracian god, Dionysus. But the myth is primarily concerned with the rite of omophagia, the manducation of raw flesh that the *mystai* (initiates) of Dionysus indulged in and the Titans practised before them on the body of the same god.

Men are descendants of the Titans. Conse-quently, they have a soul in which the tendencies towards happiness and unhappiness are mixed, because the Titanic nature was in itself inferior, but the Titans absorbed a divine element, the flesh of Zagreus. This divided soul was enclosed in the body like a prison, or a tomb (*Soma,* body = *sema,* sign) and it seemed to carry the burden of an ancient misdeed that had to be painfully expiated. This misdeed may have been the crime of the Titans but this is not at all clear.

It is useless for man to try to deliver himself from his corporal prison by suicide, because the impure soul is subjected to the relentless law of cyclic existences. As soon as it leaves one body it is condemned to incarnation in another and this cycle of rebirth is eternal for the uninitiated. To those who knew the revelation of Orpheus, a road to salvation lay open. The Orphic led a life of abstinence and renunciation, in obedience to the strict rules decreed by the ancient prophet. He was forbidden to eat animal flesh, because the belief in the transmigration of souls implied a respect for all life, so he was a vegetarian. Besides, the liberation of the soul would be compromised by anything that strengthened the corporal element, source of all impurity. For the same reason, it was forbidden to bury the dead in woollen garments because wool comes from an animal.

The Orphic life not only entailed mortifications, but also incantations, lustrations and purifications of all kinds. When the soul, after several earthly existences alternating with infernal punishments, was finally purified and freed from earthly bonds, it took its way towards the divine abode where it enjoyed an eternal happiness. The road there was beset with snares and perils. Consequently the initiated was scrupulously instructed on the itinerary he must follow, which Orpheus had followed before him, as well as on the passwords he had to utter.

Fragments of this kind of guide to the after-life have been preserved for us in the inscriptions on gold plaques discovered in tombs in Crete and southern Italy. They consisted of a kind of amulet hung round the neck of the dead man to help his memory. It is not absolutely certain that these texts are Orphic, but this is the most likely explanation. It has been argued recently that the dead wearing these amulets were Eleusinian initiates. Here is a translation of some of these tablets.

"You will find a fountain, with a white cypress growing beside it, to the left of the dwellings in Hades. Be careful not to go near that fountain.

You will find another, pouring out water from the Lake of Memory. Some guards stand before it and you should say to them: I am the son of Earth and the starry Heavens; consequently, I belong to a heavenly race. I am dry and dying of thirst; give me quickly some of the water flowing from the Lake of Memory. ' They will let you drink from the divine fountain and immediately afterwards, you will reign with the other heroes. "

Another tablet is inscribed with the words that the initiated should address to the infernal gods.

" I come from a community of pure souls, oh, pure sovereign of the underworld, Eucles, Eubulus, and you other immortal gods! I am proud to belong to your blessed race, but destiny has struck me down... I leapt out of the cycle of crushing punishment and grief and sprang with swift foot towards the longed-for crown. I took refuge in the bosom of the Lady, queen of this underworld. " The goddess replies: " Oh, fortunate spirit! You have become a god from the man you were. " The initiate replies in his turn with the mysterious formula: " Young goat, I have fallen into milk. "   R.F.

OSTRACISM. This was a procedure peculiar to Athens without any equivalent elsewhere. It was instituted by Cleisthenes in 507 B.C. to prevent the return of tyrants, who had been driven out three years previously, and was applied about ten times up to 417 when it fell into disuse. It was a preventive measure against anyone who had made himself too prominent in the public eye and seemed a possible aspirant to dictatorship, even though, according to the famous story, it might be used against so just a person as Aristides.

Every year the people were officially consulted and decided whether there were any reason for applying it. If any citizen thought that the ambitions of a man constituted a potential menace to the institutions, he wrote his name on an *ostrakon*. If the same name was indicated by six thousand voters, the person had to leave Attica for ten years. At the end of this period, as it was not a penalty involving the loss of civil rights, he could then return to his country, where he would find his possessions untouched and could enjoy his rights as a citizen again. No member of his family was ever molested during his absence.

Nike of Olympia by Paeonius. About 420 B.C. Olympia Museum. *Photo Deutsches Archäologisches Institut, Athens.*

Paestum. Temple of Hera II, called the Temple of Poseidon. Behind it is the Temple of Hera I, called the Basilica.
Photo L. von Matt.

The excavations of the agora at Athens have brought to light some of the voting shards, some of which bear distinguished names such as Themistocles and Aristides. The ostrakon was not, as was formerly thought, an oyster shell, which would anyway have been difficult to write on, but a fragment of a broken vase. Instead of being thrown away, it was used for the voting, the name of the undesirable person being written on it with a brush. P.D.

PAEAN. A kind of lyric poem with a solemn and dignified rhythm. *(See* Lyric Poetry).

PAEONIUS of EPHESUS. Paeonius was an architect of the 4th century B.C. who was associated with Democrates in the reconstruction of the new temple of Artemis at Ephesus after the fire of 356. He then supervised the lay-out of the site of the colossal temple of Apollo at Didyma, assisted by Daphnis of Miletus. He belonged to the line of Ionian architects, beginning with Rhoecus. Their work was characterised by proportions which appeared immense to the other

Greeks who did not imitate them much. R.M.

PAEONIUS of MENDE. Paeonius of Mende, the sculptor of the *Nike of Olympia,* who lived in the 5th century B.C., elaborated and gave new life to a traditional subject of sculpture, the winged figure in movement, through his pictorial and decorative treatment of wind-blown drapery that clung to the body and revealed the form beneath. The *Nike of Olympia* was depicted alighting in a final flutter of wings on the pedestal of a commemorative monument dedicated in Altis by the Messenians. The weight of the body falls on the bare, left leg, while the right leg is thrown back and clearly visible under the folds of drapery, which was originally held at one corner by the right hand, accentuating the clinging effect of the light, wind-tossed material. The peplos is fastened on the shoulder but it has all the lightness of Ionian drapery. Its folds and puckers are so disposed that they emphasize the movement carried from the fluttering wings through the body, stressing the suppleness and elasticity of the Nike's descent on to the earth. According to the dedicatory inscription, Paeonius also won the prize for the acroteria on the temple of Zeus. R.M.

PAESTUM. The ruins of Paestum, on the Gulf of Salerno, were fairly easy to reach even before the age of tourism, and, as long ago as the 18th century, they attracted artists and classicists who could admire in them the first known example of a Greek architectural lay-out. Paestum, however, had only been Greek for a relatively brief period. It was probably founded about 650 B.C. on a site that was already inhabited in the Palaeolithic Age, and a hundred years later was sufficiently prosperous to build a beautiful Doric temple, called by the old name of the Basilica. At the very end of the 5th century, the population was swollen by all the defeated Sybarites driven out from their own home. This began a brilliant period that ended about 400 when the highland Lucanians siezed the town. The conquerors seem to have subjected it to a thorough process of dehellenisation and, known until then as Poseidana, it was given the name that the Romans turned into Paestum. For six years, from 332 to 326, the Greeks under the leadership of Alexander of Molossia, a nephew of the Macedonian king, tried to gain the upper hand, but the Lucanians retained their dominant position and even went so far as to forbid the use of the Greek language. In 273, a Roman colony was settled on the site, which gave the city back its prosperity and individuality.

The surrounding wall is about three miles long, the most ancient parts having been built in the 6th century B.C. The site has by no means been thoroughly explored and so far two groups of sanctuaries are to be seen separated by an agora, which later became the forum. To the south, lie two large temples, still wrongly named the Basilica and the temple of Neptune, the latter really being dedicated to Hera; and to the north, the so-called temple of Ceres, which actually belonged to Athena. These huge edifices, built between the middle of the 6th century and about the middle of the 5th, present anomalies beside the purely Greek features of their plan and decoration, which are hardly surprising in this distant province.

About 7½ miles from Paestum on the banks of the river Sele, there lies an archaic sanctuary of Hera, where two temples were also built. They are lavishly decorated with sculptures in a rather provincial but vital style. The variety of themes depicted on the metopes are a particularly interesting feature.   P.D.

PAINTING Hardly anything survives of an art that the Greeks prized at least as much as sculpture. Their painting had a long history going back in Crete to the end of the 3rd millennium B.C. Even in the Early Minoan age, their fondness for colour is apparent in the choice of the stone, green, black and grey steatite, breccia, alabaster and other marbles, which were scooped out into the shape of vases; and the potters of the flambé, or flame-mottled decoration of the Vasiliki style, gave tones to the clay ranging from black to brown and from red to orange. Besides this, the inner walls of houses were painted in tiered bands of flat colours applied to the wet plaster and, for the first time, figurative motifs appeared. It was in the 17th century B.C., when the palaces destroyed by some catastrophe were being rebuilt, that Cretan painting reached its peak. Large and small state rooms and domestic quarters were made gay with brightly coloured frescoes wherever there was space available. Nearly five hundred, almost life-size figures, divided into two

Two young girls performing a religious dance. Metope from the Temple of Hera at the mouth of the River Sele. About 510-500 B.C. Paestum Museum. *Ph. L. von Matt.*

Minoan painting.
Detail of a
sarcophagus from
Haghia Triada. About
1450-1400 B.C.
Heraklion Museum.
Photo Hassia.

registers, stretched out in a procession along one of the corridors of Cnossos, but on another, rather cramped space there is a whole crowd milling together to watch some spectacle in a style of miniature fresco that was very popular. This term describes the size, but not the spirit of these works, because nothing could be less meticulous or larger in conception than these paintings; sometimes there is a complete absence of detail in the mass of figures and the artist has just given sketchy outlines in bright colours to a few silhouettes against a uniformly dark background. Very often, however, the figures have an individual character like the famous *Parisienne*. The painting is small and suggests the midinettes that Toulouse-Lautrec and some of the impressionists were painting at the time that Cnossos was being excavated. As a matter of fact, the whole of Cretan painting has much in common with impressionism; it shares the same indifference to photographic exactitude, the same desire to suggest rather than to explain. The human face is reduced to its essentials: a sharp profile, large expressive eyes, a generous mouth and untidy hair tossed about by the frenzy of dancing. Movement, arrested in mid-action, was what these artists loved to paint whether their subject was

acrobats, bulls in full career, fishes undulating in a marine ballet or the gentler motions of a cat watching its prey or elegant young women fluttering round in a society gathering. Nothing is static, nothing is stiff. Gaiety of colour matches this intoxication of movement; it has no connexion with reality but is used to accentuate the liveliness of the picture. The painter knew that neither birds nor monkeys were blue, but the blue is so pretty and is such a striking contrast with the background red that its unreality is quite unimportant. This Cretan mural painting, whose vitality is so attractive, seems thoroughly original to us, but though this may be true of its effects and inspiration, its technique was not original but derived from Egyptian art on which it was first based. As in Egypt, a brownish ochre was used for the flesh tints of men in contrast to the whiteness of women. As in Egypt too, the painter often worked on a surface in slight relief; the famous *Prince with Lilies* of which only some fragments are authentic, was executed by this method which is found in several examples in the mastabas of the Nile valley. But, as so often in the history of Greek art, when the Egyptians were the forerunners, the Hellenes almost immediately gave an original stamp to their borrowings.

Minoan painting. Fragment of a fresco from Cnossos: the "Parisienne". About 1500 B.C. Heraklion Museum. *Photo Giraudon.*

The work of the Cretans who decorated vases is as admirable as the fresco paintings. They have the same spontaneity and the same skill, but they chose different subjects; they did not for this purely decorative work attempt the human figure or narrative and dramatic scenes and they only used flora and fauna as motifs arranged tastefully over a vessel whose decoration had to conform to its shape: graceful plants in delicate colours undulate lightly, small sea animals, nautiluses and murexes, and the supple tentacles of octopuses are scattered, crowded or wound over the length of tall amphorae and the rounded bowls of heavy kraters. Although the magnificent spontaneity of the Kamares style (17th century B.C.) tended to stiffen in the Palace style, yet all this painting on walls and vases fascinates us with its joy, its love of life and sensitiveness, which seem essentially Cretan qualities. Painting was a much more flexible medium for these particular characteristics than sculpture; it was the natural expression of the Cretan temperament and it may never again have flowered so brilliantly among the Greeks of later times.

As soon as Mycenaean civilisation spread over Greece, painting became less important, perhaps because its architecture did not offer frescoists the same space and light, perhaps too because spontaneity was no longer appreciated at this period as it had been in the past. The techniques and subjects remained the same, but the processions of chariots and bear hunts which decorated the palace of Tiryns are the insensitive imitations of careful followers who no longer understood and no longer felt a living interest in a subject that they copied without conviction. The same is true of the vase decorations; the octopuses that clutch the bellies of stirrup-vases have lost their savage vitality. There was a prevailing tendency towards stylisation which anticipated the geometric austerity of the following centuries.

We hesitate to include in a history of painting the considerable output of what is called the Geometric Period, not because during the whole of this era, which stretches from the 10th to the 8th century B.C., the only graphic art we know appears on clay vases and engraved metal buckles

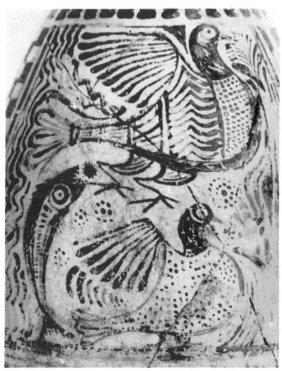

Minoan painting. Detail of a vase from Phaestus. 14th century B.C. Heraklion Museum. *Photo Hassia.*

Attic painting of the geometric period. Detail of a krater from the Dipylon Cemetery. Mid-8th century B.C.
Athens, National Museum. *Photo Hirmer.*

—until the end of the 4th century B.C. our knowledge of painting is always indirect—but because
the taste for abstraction has never been taken so
far and because, in the absence of any figurative
painting, we feel rather uneasy when we apply
the same word to these skilful networks of lines in
the form of crosses, swastikas, meanders and
losanges as we use for the work of Rembrandt
and Delacroix. But we must accept the idea that
until the end of classicism the Greeks included
under painting what is really only coloured
designing. True enough, about 800 B.C., this
designing emerged from abstraction and human
figures and animals were traced in the midst of
purely linear motifs, but it was not till the time of
the Parthenon in the second half of the 5th century B.C. that they began to be concerned with
the qualities which characterise painting to us:
tone, shadow and perspective.

Nothing is stranger than the first attempts at
figuration of the 8th century Greeks. A single
scene, the burial of the dead, was represented to
begin with; the actors in the scene, the dead man
himself, the mourners, the horses drawing the
funerary chariot, were treated as stylised puppets,
like a row of geometric figures: a triangle for the
torso, a circle for the head, a trapezium for the

arms lifted and bent over the hair which is being
pulled out as a sign of grief. Gradually the bodies
acquired substance and even opacity, which was
increased by the technique then in use of
presenting them as silhouettes, or chinese shadows, in black against the beige background of
baked clay. The inner details only appeared little
by little, beginning with a black dot for the eye
placed in the middle of the circle representing
the face.

Contact with eastern civilisations revealed to
the Greeks a painting that they soon imitated.
Until then, Athens had been the innovator, but
afterwards it was the ports of call in the Levant,
Crete, Rhodes and Corinth, that offered new ideas
to artists. Decorative motifs and subjects were
copied from those commonly used in Cyprus,
Syria and sometimes Egypt: birds, fish, wild
animals and monsters. Although the silhouette
style was not abandoned, salient features were
drawn, touches of red and white, sometimes an
ivory slip over the background of the vase, gave
the whole decoration a variegated brilliance, like
the oriental carpets imported into Greece at that
time which must have inspired the vase painters
on more than one occasion. This Orientalising
Style, as it is called, dominated the 7th century

B.C. It was the century that saw the first temples built round the first statues and just as bas-relief appeared to decorate those temples, so paintings were done for the same purpose. The painted metopes of the temples at Thermum and Calydon date from about 650. They are plaques of clay, baked in a kiln like vases and decorated by the same processes as an amphora or a krater, except that there are more colours in them, green and yellow as well as black, red and white; but they were still flat colours and it is quite easy to imagine the same workshop producing vases and plaques of this kind. Apart from the process of fabrication, these painted metopes are identical with sculptured metopes, so we can reconstitute from the surviving bas-reliefs the appearance and subjects of painted decorations in the sacred buildings of the period.

After the 7th century, Greek art tried to rid itself of oriental influences and, having learnt new techniques abroad, artists fashioned a style that would express their own ideals. The Corinthians had already made a rather isolated attempt to paint pictures in which the human interest was predominant and a small vase of about 650 may well give us a better idea of a large mural painting than the cramped designs on the Thermum metopes; the oinochoe, or small wine jug, known as the Chigi Jug, with its line of warriors advancing in time to the sound of music, who might just as well be the subject of a mural. The Homeric poems were a source of inspiration for painters and on Attic vases of about the same period Ulysses is depicted blinding the Cyclops and hiding himself before escaping from the cave under the belly of a ram.

How far the subjects dear to vase painters can give us an idea of single frescoes and panels is an unavoidable question that must dominate anyone's enquiry into early painting. Until at least the end of the 6th century, most vase decorations had a mythological, epic or religious association which would be quite in keeping with the demands of priests who wanted to embellish the houses of their gods with works of art. There are some Laconian vases of the 6th century where the painted area has obviously cut in two a figure from a picture that continued to the left and right on the model from which the potter had only copied a fragment.

There is no space here to list the different schools which, throughout the Greek world from Ionia to Sicily, must have included some great painters if the quality of their products is any guide. Their very names have nearly all been lost and it was not till the last years of the archaic period that there lived a certain Cimon of Cleonae whose name and reputation survived to the time

Painting in the Rhodian orientalising style. Detail of the Levi oinochoe. Middle of 7th century B.C. Paris, Louvre.

Painted metope from the Temple of Apollo at Thermum. Late 7th century B.C. Athens, National Museum. *Photo Hirmer.*

within the contours bare apart from the brush lines; hence the name of the style. This line drawing made psychological expression possible which was indispensable for the dramatic interest of a scene and which the rudimentary character of the old methods could not render. In less than two generations enormous progress was made in depicting anatomical details, movement, even the feelings of the characters. Encouraged perhaps by the brilliant results offered them by the new technique, innumerable artists, all Athenians by birth or adoption, decorated hundreds of vases of all shapes but with a marked preference for cups. There were no colour effects, apart from the contrasting red and black, but the draughtsmanship and composition are admirable. Many of the artists are anonymous, but others, proud of their talent, signed their works; so we know of a Brygos (q.v.; he may have been only a potter who entrusted the decoration of his products to others), a Douris (q.v.) and a Makron. It would be unjust to deny these draughtsmen an originality that sprang from the joy they took in their work, but it seems, nevertheless, that they were following in paths already pointed out to them by painters who did not work for commercial purposes.

The most famous of these painters lived later, about 470 B.C. He was called Polygnotus (q.v.). His influence was felt in his lifetime by artisans who, like him, ranged their figures at different levels in an attempt to render an impression of space and, like him, struggled to express with a rictus or a movement of the eyes the violent passions felt by their characters. This was only a first step; Polygnotus and his rival, Micon, were soon outstripped by Zeuxis and Parrhasius (qq.v.), whose works have been lost but who seem to have been the first Greeks to conceive painting in the same terms as we do ourselves. According to descriptions in early writers, Zeuxis set some of his scenes in a landscape where he tried to give an impression of depth by foreshortening and the use of shadows. Although the palette of these artists was still extremely restricted (Polygnotus only used four colours), their use of tone indicates a less exclusively linear vision of reality. This kind of progress meant that the vase decorators with the limited means at their disposal were incapable of reaching the level of the great artists; however

of Pliny. Yet it was probably in competition with these now forgotten artists that the Athenian potters about 530 B.C. found a technique which gave greater clarity to their designs. Until then, the practice of painting figures in silhouette and covering them entirely with black, still persisted from the Geometric Period. About the beginning of the 7th century the details within the figure were marked by incising them with a burin, which cut through the coating of black varnish and scratched the clay, tracing a clear outline for the muscles and the folds of garments. Touches of white on the flesh of women and the hair of old men or on some bit of clothing, and accents of blue-red helped to distinguish one figure from another in the opaque masses and brightened the rather too sombre appearance of the whole. This technique is known as the Black-Figure Style. Pictorially it lacked clarity and was replaced about 530 by the Red-Figure Style. The contours of the figures, all the details within this outline and the accessories of the scene rendered before by incisions, were now drawn by a fine brush, just as in a modern drawing. The background was coated with black varnish leaving the red clay

Black-figure painting. Detail of a plate painted by Psiax. Komast dancing accompanied by a girl flute player.
About 520-510 B.C. Basel, Antiken Museum.

Red-figure painting.
Detail of a stamnos.
Mid-4th century B.C.
Paris, Cabinet des
Médailles.

much they livened their figures with bright red, white and gold, and with other colours like blue in the following century, they remained far inferior to the painters of sanctuaries. Because of this cleavage between craft work and fine art, vase painting is not a guide to what the great painting of the 4th century B.C. was.

This is a pity because it was just this century that seems to have been the great age of Greek painting. The leading personality was Apelles (q.v.), the friend of Alexander the Great, whom we only know from literary sources, but the reputation of fellow-artists like Protogenes and Aëtion rivalled his. Mosaics, some almost contemporary,

and the mural decoration of Roman villas at Herculaneum and Pompeii must have been inspired by the best known works of painters at that time or during the Hellenistic period, but it is difficult to decide how closely these late works have reproduced Greek models. Technique certainly improved rapidly because, by the 3rd century B.C., compositions were given atmospheric depth; the planes, although quite distinct from each other, recede gradually into the back-

Palace at Phaestus.
State room looking
onto the central court.
15th century B.C.
Photo Hassia.

ground and a romantic, picturesque nature pro-
vides a setting for the figures in paintings that
have an affinity with our own 18th century art.
These changes were very likely due to influences
from Egypt and Asia Minor. The rational severity
of Greek linear art may well have been softened
and eventually transformed by a current of
romanticism.

The last authentic examples of Greek painting
we possess are no later than the beginning of the
Christian era. This does not mean to say that it
was not produced after this date and there must
have been paintings executed in Greece that
would have shown how Byzantine painting had
developed from Greek art; it is most unfortunate
that they have not survived.   P.D.

PALACES. As the sovereign's residence or
the seat of an assembly, the palace had no place
in a democratic regime where no private person,
even though he wielded real power, dared to rise
ostensibly above his fellow-citizens and where the
magistrates drew their authority from the will of
the people and not from the sumptuousness of the
setting in which they held their sessions. This is
why in the Aegean basin, all the existing palaces

belong to a period either before the establishment
of the Hellenic political ideal or are contemporary
with the Hellenistic monarchies. Moreover, the
latter are only to be found in regions that the
Greeks once considered barbarian.

In the second millennium B.C., palaces were
built in great numbers, at first in Crete, then in the
Achaean world, especially the Peloponnesus.
There are marked differences between the two.

The palaces of Minoan Crete are the oldest; the
most important and best preserved of these are at
Cnossos, Phaestus and Mallia. They were first
erected in the 20th century B.C., but did not
acquire their final appearance until two or three
hundred years later after reconstruction and often
extensive alterations. They were planned to fulfil
a greater variety of functions than our modern
palaces: residences of the king, his family and his
entourage, as well as political and religious
centres. They were real villages, built round a
rectangular courtyard that was the geometric
focus of a multiplicity of activities; royal apartments, state rooms, little sanctuaries, archive
depositories, workshops where the court artisans
worked, storehouses where the provisions needed
by the community were kept, all had their place in

this complex that was divided into clearly defined quarters. Between the different sections, which fitted into each other in such a complicated way that the plan of these places gave rise to the legend of the Labyrinth, there were long corridors and small courtyards providing access to the rooms. There were no vast perspectives and no attempt to impress subjects who did not have an oriental veneration for their kings, but a great desire for comfort and convenience which have no parallel until times near our own. One of the most striking features of these palaces is the carefree attitude of their builders who did not show the slightest concern for military defence; they sited them on easily accessible places and did not surround them with the thick walls that provide such a marked contrast with Achaean palaces.

These, whose finest examples are to be found at Mycenae, Tiryns and Pylos, are like feudal castles of the Middle Ages, built on abrupt heights, with gates designed to discourage attack as much by their impressive appearance as by their narrowness. There was no complex centred on a courtyard. Isolated buildings, scattered on different levels over the eminence chosen by the lord, housing either the prince and his family, or the

retinue of his officials and servants, were enclosed within walls beyond which they never spread. The most important of these buildings was the megaron (q.v.). Clearly, they differed radically from the Cretan palaces. Nevertheless, these Achaean palaces, built during the 15th century B.C., were influenced by Minoan civilisation, an influence which is recognisable in the details, the fondness for luxury and the profusion of painted decoration on the walls.

The Mycenaean palaces did not survive the Dorian invasions and several centuries elapsed before royal residences were again built. But these seemed modest beside the palaces we have just described, especially compared to those of the oriental world, to that of the Persian king, or even those of his vassals, the satraps of Asia Minor. The best known is at Palatitsa. It is hardly more spacious or luxurious than a private house. There is a portico in front of a façade, which is about 260 ft long, and the entrance is a triple passage formed by two rows of Ionic columns. In the centre of the building, a spacious, peristylar courtyard is surrounded by small rooms on two sides and, on the east, by two large rooms: one is square and could have been used as a dining-hall as it is next door to the kitchens, the other circular, containing the remains of a throne, which suggests that it was reserved for official receptions. Very likely the palaces of great capital cities, like that of the Ptolemys, were resplendent and quite different. Unfortunately, nothing remains of them. P.D.

PALAESTRA. This word is derived from *pale,* wrestling, one of the five exercises of the pentathlon *(See* Education), but jumping, boxing, pancratium and several other sports were also practised there. If the palaestra was too small for races, they were run in the stadium or gymnasium (qq.v.). Palaestrae could be either public or private. Those reserved for training children seem to have been mainly private and were named after the proprietor or founder. Adults generally exercised in public palaestrae. Like gymnasiums, they were provided with hydrotherapeutic installations *(See* Bathing) because the Greeks washed them-

selves before and after every spell of physical exercise. The *paidotribes,* or gymnastic teacher in his red cloak supervised the children's palaestra It was really an open-air sports ground, square in shape and surrounded with a wall. On one or two sides were covered-in rooms used as cloakrooms, rest rooms furnished with benches *(hedrai)* and so known as *exedrai,* baths, shops selling oil and sand, because the pupils rubbed oil over themselves before exercising and rolled in sand afterwards. The palaestra, like the gymnasium, was decorated with statues or busts of the god, Hermes, patron of athletes. R.F

PAN. Pan was a minor rustic divinity worshipped particularly by Arcadian shepherds but also familiar to peasants throughout Greece. He was said to be the son of Hermes and a nymph The Greeks imagined him as a small, bearded creature, the upper part of his body human except for his horns, the lower part a goat. Solitary places attracted him and he loved playing a seven piped flute, called pan pipes after him. He was extremely lascivious, spied on women and young people but was too humble to have amorous adventures except with nymphs and peasants; a sculpture from Delos depicts Aphrodite striking him with her sandal when he dared to try to seduce her P.D

PANAETIUS. Panaetius was born at Lindus, Rhodes, about 180 B.C. and was a pupil of the Stoic, Antipater. He spent fifteen years at Rome with Scipio Aemilianus, whom he accompanied on his Mediterranean voyages, and then returned to Athens to help his master, whom he succeeded in 129. He died himself between 110 and 100. His theories on the virtues and the personality were adopted and discussed by Cicero in his treatise, *De Officiis.* The beauty of the universe and the way nature is transformed by the hand of man occupy a prominent place in Panaetius's philosophy, which reflected the conceptions of a man of integrity and a man of the world. P.-M.S.

PANATHENAEA. Like human beings, the immortals had their anniversaries and every year in August the Athenians celebrated the Athenaea, the anniversary of their protectress,

Pan and Aphrodite. Marble sculpture from Delos. 2nd century B.C. Athens, National Museum.

Procession of the Panathenaea. The Ergastinai. Fragment of the frieze from the Parthenon. About 447-436 B.C. Louvre. Photo Tel.

Athena. Every four years, the festival was specially magnificent and was called the Panathenaea. The institution probably did not go back to the legendary Erichthonius, as they claimed, or even to Theseus, but it is likely that, when Pisistratus celebrated it with pomp for the first time in 566 B.C. to enhance the prestige of the state, he was only developing, on the model of Olympia and Delphi, a festival that had already existed for a long time.

The Panathenaea lasted for four days. The essential event was offering the presents of the people to the goddess and, when the Delian League had been founded, those of the allies. The festival began one evening with dancing, singing and torch races, which continued into the night. At dawn the next day, the people, or at least their representatives, gathered together at the Ceramicus and from there the great procession set off which has been idealised for us in the Ionic frieze of the Parthenon. It made its way across the lower town and the agora, stopping from time to time at a kind of temporary altar. At its head was a waggon in the form of a ship and, spread over the mast and yard like a sail, was the peplos, the ritual present for the goddess, which the noblest women of the city, called the *ergastinai*, had been weaving for nine months. This garment, embroidered with the battle between the gods and giants, would be draped on the antique statue of the goddess in the temple of

Athena Polias, not in the Parthenon. Behind the waggonship walked the ergastinai, the Kanephoroi, aristocratic young women carrying baskets of sacred objects, and the leading personalities of the city. They were followed by the sacrificers with their animals, bulls and rams, whose meat would be shared between the goddess, the officiating priests and the tribes. A little farther away came the representatives of the metics with their wives who were honoured by being entrusted with bowls full of honey and hydriai whose contents would be offered to the goddess. The procession ended with mounted units of the army, a brilliant cavalcade which Phidias gave a somewhat disproportionate place in his frieze. At the foot of the Acropolis, the slope was too steep for the waggonship to climb; at this point it was abandoned and the peplos was carried folded on the arm. When they all arrived at the Acropolis, the procession stopped and sacrificed to Athena Hygieia, protectress of health. Finally, it proceeded to the old temple (when this was destroyed, the *xoanon*, the primitive wooden statue, was kept in the eastern part of the Erechtheum) where the offerings were given to the goddess and the animals were killed, some of which had been supplied by the allies.

Although this ceremony was the central point of the Panathenaea, it was not the only part. The festival also included music competitions and games. The victors received a small quantity of the oil harvested from the olive trees sacred to the goddess, which was placed in a special kind of amphora called Panathenaic amphorae.   P.D.

PANDORA. Pandora, according to Hesiod, was the first woman, fashioned and given life by Hephaestus and Athena. Zeus sent her to Epimetheus, brother of Prometheus, who married her. Unfortunately, Pandora opened a firmly sealed box which it was forbidden to touch. The jar contained all the evils, which escaped and spread all over the earth. Terrified at what she had done, Pandora shut the box in which only Hope remained.   P.D.

PANGAEUS (Mount). The mass of Pangaeus, rising to 6418 ft, is situated on the borders of Macedonia and Thrace, and did not geographically form part of the Hellenic world, but it was important in the life of the Greeks and their history. From the 6th century B.C., the fame of its riches, the forests growing on its slopes and the gold mines concealed in its depths haunted their imagination. The Thasians were the first to fight with the local tribes for control of the mysterious mountain whose imposing mass

they could see from their country. The Persians, in their turn, were attracted to it. Then, when they had been driven out about 475 B.C., the Athenians and Spartans tried to gain possession of it and in the course of their savage struggles the local inhabitants joined in.

Mount Pangaeus was not only a source of almost inexhaustible material wealth; it was also one of the favourite retreats of Dionysus where the maenads felt themselves carried away by the most rapturous of mystical transports.   From far away, devotees of the god would turn nostalgic thoughts towards these peaks " where the spirit blew ".   In ancient times for restless, religious minds such as these, Pangaeus represented what Athos, its neighbour, was later to become for many Christians, the holiest of mountains.

P.D.

PARCAE. The Parcae, whom the Greeks called the Moirai, personified Fate. Each human being had his personal Moira, but there also existed, as far as we can clarify ideas that always remained vague and changeable, the Moirai who determined the fate of the world in general and who imposed their will on the gods of Olympus themselves.   P.D.

PARIS. Paris was one of the numerous sons of Priam, the old king of Troy. He was not one of the most distinguished of them except perhaps for his beauty. He was asked, nevertheless, by the three goddesses, Hera, Athena and Aphrodite, to decide which of them was the most beautiful. Paris chose Aphrodite and she promised as a reward that he should be loved by the woman who was considered the most lovely of mortals. Paris set off in search of her and at Sparta he met Helen. She followed him and so began the Trojan War. During the ten years it was fought out beneath the walls of Troy, Paris was far from being the bravest of the leaders and the Trojans even reproached him for cowardice. In spite of this, he was the one to vanquish Achilles by shooting an arrow from a distance into his heel, the only vulnerable part of his body. He was not present at the fall of Troy because he had been mortally wounded by Philoctetes.   P.D.

Panathenaic amphora: running race. 4th century B.C. British Museum. *Photo Boudot-Lamotte.*

The Parthenon designed by Ictinus and Callicrates. 447-436 B.C.

PARNASSUS. The peak of Parnassus, 8062 ft, dominates from afar the Gulf of Corinth, but it is not the highest mountain in Greece; it is only one of the most imposing and the sacred character of Delphi, nestling in a part of its rugged relief, adds to its grandeur. The Muses, under the patronage of Apollo, lived on its slopes as well as on the neighbouring Mount Helicon. Also on its slopes, near the Corycian Cave, the Bacchantes, the followers of Dionysus, gave themselves up to their wild orgies when they were possessed by the spirit of the god.

P.D.

PAROS. This beautiful name evokes all the purity of Greece; the finest marble ever used by sculptors was hewn from the island quarries which can still be seen today. Paros was also a centre of trade and art; Thasos was colonised from Paros; the poet, Archilochus, was born there; and the most splendid ceramics of the archaic period were produced by the workshops

of Paros. All this activity and distinction seemed to die out at the end of the 7th century B.C. Paros then became one of the unremarkable Cyclades which were overshadowed by the glory of Delos and the power of Athens.

P.D.

PARRHASIUS. We only have at best a second hand knowledge of the painter, Parrhasius. He came from Ephesus and was active in the last third of the 5th century B.C. Several stories have come down from the ancient Greeks of his inordinate pride and the luxury of his life. His contemporaries considered him the most typical representative of his art and Socrates chose him as interlocutor when he wanted to discuss painting. One of his most famous works was the *Demos*, the People of Athens, whom he represented, if Pliny the Elder is to be believed, as " changeable, quick to anger, unjust, inconstant and at the same time easily swayed, merciful, glorious, arrogant, humble, courageous and cowardly; briefly, everything at once ". We may

345

Horsemen on the north frieze from the Parthenon. 447-436 B.C. British Museum. *Photo Hirmer*.

conclude from this obviously imaginative description that Parrhasius tried to capture the expressions of his figures. He is credited with a *Theseus* who " seemed fed with roses "; the phrase suggests the taste of the period for a rather affected grace. The titles of other paintings indicate that in spite of this tendency towards drawing-room elegance, he did not shrink from heroic subjects: *Contest for the arms of Achilles, Ulysses feigning Madness, Philoctetes Wounded, The Torture of Prometheus*. He probably made them an opportunity for expressing the pain and passion felt by his characters.   P.D.

PARTHENIA. Processional song. *(See* Lyric Poetry).

PARTHENON. In 447 B.C. when Athens was engaged against other Greek towns in a war that threatened her very existence, Pericles decided to take up again on behalf of his party an old project that had once been proposed, the erection on the Acropolis of a temple to the national goddess, Athena. Pericles conceived this temple not only as a replacement for more ancient edifices dedicated to the goddess on the

sacred plateau, but also as a political manifestation that would symbolise the strength of the democratic ideal; Athena, who would be housed in it, would not be a remote Olympian, she would be both the patroness and first citizen of the regenerated city that the popular party was in process of creating. The conclusion of peace in 446 and the authority of Pericles pressed forward the work which was begun in 447, completed in 438, except for the sculptures which were finished in 432. Pericles gave the general directives, but it was his right hand man in everything concerned with the fine arts, Phidias, who was put in charge of the enterprise. He chose Ictinus and Callicrates for his architects. The instructions he gave them were to provide a shelter suitable for the size and character of the goddess's statue which he was going to make himself. It was chryselephantine, that is, made of gold and ivory, and measured forty feet including the base. The Parthenos, or Virgin, was a standing figure, clothed in a peplos, on which the aegis lay, and wearing a helmet elaborately decorated with symbolic figures, a sphinx flanked by two winged horses. She was armed, but her lance was propped against her left arm while her left hand held the shield up on the

Metope from the
Parthenon. Fight
between a Lapith and
a Centaur. 447-436
B.C. British Museum.
Photo Hirmer.

347

Fragment from the east pediment of the Parthenon. Aphrodite and Dione (?). 447-436 B.C. British Museum. *Photo Braur*

Fragment from the east pediment of the Parthenon. Head of a horse from the Chariot of Selene. 447-436 B.C. British Museum. *Photo Hirmer.*

Fragment from the east pediment of the Parthenon. Dionysus. 447-436 B.C. British Museum. *Photo Boudot-Lamotte.*

ground; like the people she personified, after the peace of 446, she had nothing to fear from her enemies either within or without, and the Victory, which she offered in her right hand to her worshippers, crowned the successes they had gained through the democratic party in armed conflicts as well as in economic and political rivalries. Such was the image, with an entirely novel conception, for which and around which the Parthenon was built. This was a larger temple (q.v.) than usual so that the statue should not be cramped in the naos, which measured the traditional hundred Attic feet in length, like that of the Hecatompedon, the old temple replaced by the Parthenon. As in the Hecatompedon, too, and in accordance with a custom peculiar to the local cult of Athena, the opisthodomos opened into a second room, independent of the naos and without any communication with it; this was what was strictly termed, we do not know why, the *parthenon,* or the room of the Virgin. The treasure of the goddess and the state was deposited in it.

The sekos, or sacred precinct, laid out in this way, was surrounded by a peristyle of eight columns on the short sides (and not six as in most temples) and seventeen on the long sides. The whole building, in Pentelic marble, measured 228 ft from north to south, and 101 ft from east to west. The order was Doric, but with important modifications: the four columns supporting in the centre the ceiling of the second room, the parthenon, were Ionic; besides the regular frieze of the entablature outside, there was another, Ionic in style, which ran unbroken round the sekos under the ceiling of the peristyle, in a place that Doric architecture had never decorated. This frieze, which could only be seen with difficulty from below, must have assumed a special importance in the eyes of Pericles and Phidias because of its subject. It represented, transferred into a world where men and gods were on familiar terms, the procession of the Panathenaea (q.v.) which gathered together the whole people every four years to carry the peplos, woven by the noblest young women of the city, to the ancient statue of Athena. On the principal façade on the east, the gods were depicted around Athena to whom the priests were offering the garment. The procession was deployed in two parallel files the length of the two long sides on the north and south. The preparations for the procession were

349

represented on the western façade. Leading it were the *ergastinai* who had woven the peplos, then the bearers of offerings with the sacrificial beasts, and last but not least the cavalry of the city. There is no doubt whatever that the purpose of the frieze was to illustrate what was almost an alliance between the people of Athens and the immortals, who received them as familiars, almost as equals in their assembly.

The metopes of the Doric frieze were less original, but the choice of the four subjects developed on different sides of the building was deliberate. On the two façades the theme of victory, already glorified in the chryselephantine statue, was repeated: the victory of the Athenians over the Amazons on the western façade and the victory of the gods over the giants on the eastern were subjects that Phidias had already depicted on the shield of the colossal Athena; the name of the national hero, Theseus, was associated with the first and the daughter of Zeus had been in the vanguard of the second battle. The long south side illustrated, beside a brief incident to the glory of the old king, Erechtheus, the fight between the Centaurs and the Lapiths. Along the northern, perhaps to discourage wars by showing their inanity, Phidias carved the end of the Trojan War, the sack of the town, the triumph of Helen and the departure of the victors to a fate as sombre as that of the vanquished.

The subjects of the pediments, where a pre-eminent position was still reserved for the gods, were concerned with the legendary past of Athena. On the east, there appeared the miraculous birth of Athena; to have issued straight from the head of Zeus gave greater prestige and power to the protectress of the city. On the west, there was the dispute between Poseidon and the goddess for possession of Attica; the Athenians, chosen as arbiters, passed judgment in favour of the goddess; it was fitting that this memorable occasion should have been celebrated in one of the most prominent places of the building where the alliance between the citizens and their patron goddess had once more been sealed.

This decorative ensemble, which was so clearly conceived in the same spirit as the chryselephantine statue of Athena, must surely have been by the same hand. Phidias probably called on the help of several sculptors, especially for the Doric frieze, but it is very likely that he drew the cartoons, supervised and put the finishing touch to their execution. His work remained intact for several centuries, evoking an admiration which has echoed down to our day. Then in the 5th century A.D., Phidias's statue was taken to Constantinople and, under Justinian, the temple became a church before being converted to a mosque in 1460. These transformations were accompanied by important architectural changes. In 1687, a bombardment directed by the Venetian, Morosini. destroyed the building, where a supply of gunpowder had been stored, almost completely. It was from this pile of ruin that Lord Elgin took away in 1816 several pieces of sculpture which have remained since in the British Museum. Patient and scholarly restoration from the beginning of this century has reconstructed at least the outlines of the Parthenon.   P.D.

PATROCLUS. The friendship of Achilles and Patroclus has remained legendary. The two men were brought up together in Thessaly at the court of Peleus and were never parted. Patroclus played a brilliant second to his friend; he shared all his exploits and even replaced him and dressed in his armour when Achilles refused to join the battle against the Trojans. He was killed by Hector in a fight described by Homer. Achilles re-entered the conflict to revenge him, killed Hector and dragged his corpse round Troy during the splendid funeral that he celebrated for his friend.   P.D.

PAUSANIAS(1). Pausanias was a name borne by two famous Spartan kings. One led the Greeks when they defeated the Persians at Plataea in 479 B.C., but during the complicated intriguing of the following years, he probably concluded a secret pact with Xerxes. The ephors feared a coup d'état on his part and summoned him to give an explanation. Pausanias took refuge in the temple of Athena Chalkioikos where he died of starvation, because it would have been a sacrilege to have dragged him out of it.

The other Pausanias was reigning at the time when Lysander had just crushed the power of Athens and was behaving mercilessly towards the conquered. Pausanias intervened and re-established peace in the city rent by internal conflict.   P.D.

PAUSANIAS (2). Pausanias was a traveller of the 2nd century A.D., who wrote a

The wounded Patroclus tended by Achilles. Inside of a cup by the potter Sosias. About 500 B.C. Berlin Museum.

Periegesis, or description of Greece, in ten volumes, covering Attica, the various regions of the Peloponnesus, Boeotia and Phocis including, Delphi. This work, although it is devoid of literary merit, is one of the most useful of its kind as a source of information for ancient Greece, its religious customs, topography and buildings. His reliability has often been questioned but his critics have often, too, been forced to admit that they were wrong to doubt his evidence. P.D.

PEGASUS. When Perseus killed the Medusa, a winged horse, Pegasus, was born from its blood. He served Zeus, but one day, through the wish of Poseidon according to some, of Athena according to others, he arrived at the fountain of Peirene at Corinth just when Bellerophon was setting off for Lycia. Pegasus became the hero's faithful servant and it was through his help that he killed the Chimaera. Winged horses frequently appear in Greek and oriental art. They are often dragging the chariot of Apollo and his sister, Artemis. The very fact that the principal episode of his legend takes place in Lycia indicates the eastern character of this Pegasus, although it sets his birth in the west. Very often in sculpture and still more in vase painting, a Pegasus is represented alone without Bellerophon. Probably until at least the end of the 6th century B.C., Pegasus was

Pegasus. Reverse of a coin from Corinth. Paris, Cabinet des Médailles.

Peleus struggling with Thetis. Melian terra-cotta. 5th century B.C. British Museum.

attributed with magic qualities that were a protection against evil and it was only much later that he came to symbolise poetic inspiration because of his flights into space. P.D.

PELASGIANS. Early writings often mention the Pelasgians, Leleges and the Carians who were said to have occupied in very remote times the lands that later became Greek. It is impossible to know whether this idea had any basis in historical reality. The three peoples were localised in fairly clearly defined regions: the Pelasgians were described as natives of Thessaly and were supposed to have founded Argos and Larissa; the Carians, who had withdrawn to the south-west of Asia Minor in historical times, and the Leleges were scattered over most of Greece proper. But already by the 4th century B.C. the historian, Ephorus, and certainly many of his contemporaries seemed to consider these names as vague terms designating the different peoples whom the Greeks had encountered, absorbed or driven away during their own migrations. False etymology attributed to the Pelasgians a wall called the Pelargikon, or Pelasgikon, which enclosed a place in front of the Acropolis where storks used to nest. P.D.

PELEUS. The legendary life of Peleus is full of dramatic episodes, but his marriage with the

Nereid, Thetis, is the only one that will concern us here. As she was a goddess, she did not welcome the idea of marrying a mortal, but Zeus had commanded this because an oracle had foretold that her son would be more powerful than his father. It could have been dangerous for the Olympians if she had married a god, because her offspring would then have been in a position to make himself master of Olympus.

Thetis, who like all marine deities could assume several different shapes, changed herself into fire, water, wind, a tree, a bird, a tiger, a lion, a snake and a cuttle-fish in an attempt to escape from Peleus. But Peleus had been warned by the Centaur, Chiron, that he must persist. In the end, Thetis regained her human form and the wedding took place in the presence of all the gods who all brought gifts. This scene was frequently depicted by vase painters, notably on the François Vase of about 570 B.C. Achilles was the son born from this union. P.D.

PELIAS. Pelias was Jason's uncle who sent him to bring back the Golden Fleece to prevent him from ascending the throne of Iolcus, where Pelias was regent. When his hopes were disappointed and Jason returned victorious from the expedition, he had to surrender the throne to him. As he was growing old, Jason's wife, Medea, persuaded his daughters that they could rejuvenate him by witchcraft; all they needed to do was to boil him in a cauldron. This they did with fatal consequences for the old man.   P.D.

PELOPIDAS. The name of Pelopidas is inseparable from that of his friend Epaminondas (q.v.). Thebes owed her freedom from the domination of Sparta to both of them in 379 B.C. and in 371 they won the brilliant victory of Leuctra over the Spartan army which until then had been considered invincible.

PELOPONNESUS. A geological subsidence almost completely cut off the end of the Greek mainland from the rest of the continent, leaving it attached by the Isthmus of Corinth, which is about four miles across. This peninsula was called the Peloponnesus, that is, the island of Pelops, who was supposed to be one of its first rulers. No particular characteristic distinguished it from the rest of Greece, nor did it constitute a political unity on its own. As elsewhere in the Hellenic world, there were several cities, all living their own lives and maintaining as far as possible their independence.

The brilliant Mycenaean civilisation, which soon spread beyond the Gulf of Corinth, developed in the Peloponnesus because of its comparative proximity to Crete. The peoples, driven out by the invaders from the north at the beginning of the Iron Age, took refuge in its highland plateaux and mountains, particularly in Arcadia, where access was difficult. But it was also around these plateaux that the invaders themselves settled and it was at Sparta, Olympia and Argos that the Dorian way of life was most firmly entrenched. Thus the Peloponnesus is primarily a geographical term and the history of the peninsula forms part of the history of Greece as a whole.   P.D.

PELOPS. Pelops was the eponymous ruler of the Peloponnesus, but he originally came from Asia Minor. His father, Tantalus, used him to test the perspicacity of the gods. When he was a child, he killed him, cut him into pieces and offered the morsels to the gods in a stew to see if they would detect the ingredients. Except for Demeter, who was distracted by the recent loss of her daughter, Persephone, they were not deceived and punished Tantalus with the torture associated with his name. They resurrected the little Pelops and gave him an ivory shoulder to replace the one that Demeter had absent-mindedly

eaten. When Pelops grew up he attracted the affection and unfailing protection of Poseidon. He asked for the hand of Hippodamia, princess of Elis, whose father, Oenomaus, had declared that he would only give her to the man who could beat him in a chariot race. This was a trick he had devised after an oracle had predicted that he would be killed by his son-in-law. As his team of horses were divine and were given him by Ares, he thought he was sure of winning, and his competitors were killed immediately after their defeat. Twelve claimants had already been vanquished and killed when Pelops presented himself. Horses from Poseidon and the treachery of Myrtilus, the king's charioteer who by loosening the axles of his wheels caused his death, ensured victory for Pelops, who married Hippodamia and became king of the Peloponnesus. To commemorate this victory, he instituted, so it was said the Olympic games. According to Pindar, their origins did in fact go back to the funeral games celebrated near the tomb of Pelops at Olympia. Thyestes and Atreus, founder of the tragic family of the Atridae, were two of his numerous children.   P.D.

PENALTIES (LEGAL). Besides pecuniary penalties (fines, total or partial confiscation of goods) the Athenian tribunals could also inflict exile temporarily *(phyge)* or for life *(aeiphygia)*, deprivation of the rights of citizenship *(atimia)*, imprisonment and the death penalty. Socrates drank hemlock, but death by poisoning was a mitigation of capital punishment, a sort of permissive suicide. The place of execution was outside the town, near the northern Long Wall between Athens and Piraeus. For a long time it was thought that the death penalty called the *apotympanismos,* at Athens, was the " plank torture ", which consisted in fixing a carcan to the neck of the condemned man, fastening his four limbs to a large plank with crampons and leaving him exposed in the sun until he died. This sort of crucifixion certainly existed in Athens but it seems to have been reserved for pirates. It seems more likely that the apotympanismos was decapitation or flogging to death. Flagellation on the wheel, branding and the carcan were inflicted on slaves. Sacrilegious persons and traitors were condemned to precipitation into the gulf of the Barathrum and stoning.   R.F.

PENELOPE. Penelope was the wife of Ulysses and became the symbol of conjugal fidelity for succeeding ages. Although some ancient traditions refer to the adulterous affairs of this worthy matron, she has remained for us the woman whom Homer described, defending the family home for twenty years—ten while Ulysses was fighting at Troy and ten which he spent on his return journey to Ithaca—protecting her husband's domain against the ambitions of rivals, bringing up her son, Telemachus, and rejecting offers of marriage from the young nobles of the country. Her ruse for avoiding an outright refusal of their proposals is well known; she put off her reply until the day when the tapistry she had begun should be completed and every night she undid the work of the daytime. One of the most moving scenes of the *Odyssey* is where she meets her husband again whom she did not at first recognise, asking him questions which Ulysses alone could have answered. Once the wooers had been killed, she finally handed over to her husband the heavy responsibilities which she had so courageously assumed.   P.D.

PENEUS. More than any Greek writer, Virgil has created for us the poetic associations evoked by. the name of Peneus, the little river flowing from the Pindus mountains that waters the green Vale of Tempe. It does not dry up in summer and its banks are green with large trees and fields which must seem idyllic to anyone coming from the aridity of the Northern Sporades.
                              P.D.

PENTELICUS. The plain of Athens is closed towards the north-east by the huge, majestic chain of Pentelicus like a wall. The quarries there were worked for centuries to extract the marble used in so many Greek buildings.

PENTHESILEA. Penthesilea was queen of the Amazons. She led her companions to the help of Priam during the siege of Troy, where she fought with Achilles and was pierced by his sword. According to one legend, just at the moment when the young woman sank fatally wounded, the two warriors fell hopelessly in love with each other and a splendid Attic cup, made a little after 450 B.C., shows the long passionate look they exchanged.   P.D.

PERFUME. The Greeks used perfumes a great deal. They were originally made in Syria

from where their production spread notably to Rhodes and Corinth. At Athens in the myropolion, the " perfume market ", which occupied a whole section of the agora, these perfumes were sold in specially shaped vases: alabastra, aryballoi and pyxides. Perfumes were an important part of the toilet of men as well as women. It was the custom to anoint the body with perfumed oils after a bath. Guests were perfumed at banquets; Callias, the host of Xenophon's *Symposium,* suggests to his guests that he should send for the perfumes, but Socrates objected and said that perfumes were only fit for women. Praxagoras in Aristophanes' *Ecclesiazusae* and Myrrhina in his *Lysistrata* perfumed themselves specially before making love. *Thymiateria,* the tall perfume-burners so frequently depicted on 4th century B.C. Attic vases, were not only to be found in gynaeceums and banqueting-halls, but were also used in religious ceremonies. Perfume was sprinkled on statues of the gods and funerary stelae instead of incense. Corpses were covered with perfume, sometimes even embalmed, and the flasks containing the scented oils were placed in the tombs.   R.F.

PERGAMUM. About 50 miles to the north of Smyrna, Pergamum is perched on an abrupt rock that rises nearly 1000 ft above the plain and nearby valley of the Caicus. Until the break-up of Alexander's empire, it was nothing but a nesting place for eagles, fought over by kinglets who wanted to gain possession of the province of Mysia. Then its impregnable position made Lysimachus (q.v.) choose it as the depository of his treasure of nine thousand talents, which he entrusted to his officer, Philetaerus. It was a misplaced confidence, because he betrayed his master, first offering his services to Seleucus and then, in 281 B.C., proclaiming his independence. The nine thousand talents helped him to build a strong monarchy and Pergamum became the capital of one of the most important kingdoms of the Hellenistic world.

It never achieved the splendour of Alexandria. The construction of the town was gradual; the final phase of its development during the reign of Eumenes II (197-159 B.C.), when some of its finest buildings were erected, came a long time after its foundation. Imposing ruins still give some idea of what it looked like then. From the beginning, its architects realised that they had to be guided by the nature of the site and that the terraces on the rocky slopes would offer their

Fragment of the frieze from the Altar of Zeus and Athena at Pergamum. The gigantomachy. 197-159 B.C. Berlin Museum.

successors excellent positions for future buildings. The town actually grew from the top of the hill downwards. In the time of Philetaerus, it was confined to the summit, where the palace was built, and the upper terraces with the temple of Athena. Successive walls were erected to surround an increasing number of buildings, military edifices such as arsenals and barracks, new temples and especially porticoes, which stretched over the terraces that grew broader as the slope grew gentler. The theatre, one of the most imposing perhaps ever built in ancient times, was constructed in a rocky recess, from where there is an incomparable view over the plain. Huge level areas break the slope of the acropolis, linked by winding streets or stairways.

Pergamum was not only a triumph of town-planning; the example of Alexandria encouraged the Attalids to make their capital an intellectual centre. They provided it with a library and a museum and invited artists to it. Some of them reproduced classical masterpieces with fashion-able modernisations, others were more venturous and broke new ground, like the sculptors who carved romantic, over life-size figures of the Gigantomachy on the sides of the great altar, dedicated by Eumenes II to Zeus, the remains of which are now in Berlin.　　　　　　　　P.D.

PERICLES. In 472 B.C., a young man called Pericles was chosen as choragus to produce Aeschylus's drama, the *Persians*. So began, under the sign of greatness, the career of the man whose name was to become the symbol of Athens' glory. He came of a noble family; for generations the Alcmaeonidae had been in the forefront of state affairs and two of them had recently attracted so much attention to themselves that a decree of ostracism (q.v.) had exiled them for ten years. Either from conviction or expediency, Pericles immediately sided with the popular party. He became the follower of the democrat, Ephialtes, whom he succeeded as party leader in 462. In the struggle against Cimon and the oligarchs, he had a series of measures passed that made every citizen, without distinction of class or wealth, eligible for the highest offices in the government including the archonship; the granting of the *misthophora*, a daily allowance, enabled the poorest to exercise their rights of citizenship, and sit in the assemblies and tribunals without suffer-ing any financial loss.

Anxious that his country should occupy a domi-nant position, Pericles at first used his influence towards an Athenian victory, in a series of wars, waged at some cost, against the Persians, Corinth, Aegina, Thebes and Sparta. The peace of

Bust of Pericles. Roman copy of an original by Cresilas. About 440 B.C. Berlin Museum.

he had repudiated his wife. She bore him a son whom he succeeded in legitimising, in spite of a law forbidding the union of citizens and metics which he himself had advocated. Aspasia was intelligent and cultivated; she was the first woman in Greece to hold a sort of literary salon where artists, philosophers and noble women used to meet each other. A novelty like this did not fail to cause scandal; not content with malicious gossip, a certain Hermippus, a comic writer, brought an action against her. The main charges were serious: procuring and impiety. To defend his mistress and get an acquittal, Pericles, who had nearly reached the end of his career, had to plead in person for the mercy of the tribunal.

He had already been challenged a little before, probably in 433, in the same indirect manner, when his enemies had accused his friend, Phidias, of malversation and forced him into exile. Pericles had entrusted him with his most cherished project: to rebuild the Acropolis as a symbol of the greatness of Athens and its democracy. For fifteen years he had followed, step by step, the progress of an enterprise whose success would be the glory of his country and of the party he led and which gave much later the name of the Age of Pericles to all this second half of the 5th century. He had not only spared nothing towards its realisation, he had smoothed away every difficulty and found the necessary money, but there is no doubt that he had recognised in Phidias the man who understood his design better than anyone. To attack Phidias was to attack Pericles himself. Nevertheless, even after the great artist had left, he did not abandon what he considered the crown of his achievements; the work on the Acropolis was not interrupted and the actions brought against his entourage did not lessen his activity.

It was his initiative that made Athens throw herself into the Peloponnesian War to establish her supremacy and undermine the power of Sparta. It is idle to speculate, as has sometimes been done, whether its development would have been different and the outcome not so catastrophic if Pericles had not died of plague in 429, a short time after war had broken out.   P.D.

Callias, signed in 449 with the king, then in 446 a thirty year truce concluded with Sparta, assured a peace for Greece that she had not enjoyed for a long time. The credit for the victory, which was dearly bought and had nothing triumphal about it, was not entirely due to Pericles; his old enemy, Cimon, had also deserved well of his country. Pericles' tenacity, intelligence and political skill won such prestige for him that, from 443 to his death in 429, he was elected strategus every year and, although he shared this office with nine colleagues who changed periodically, his personality was so dominant that he practically ruled supreme over the affairs of the state. In 443, Thucydides, the leader of the oligarchic party, was driven out by ostracism, and military expeditions ruthlessly conducted from 441 to 439 forced the cities of Samos and Byzantium to remain in the Athenian alliance when they were trying to regain their freedom. Before such success, criticism, which was often sharp, and ridicule heaped on him from satirical writers, Aristophanes specially, who nicknamed him the Olympian, had little effect.

Pericles, however, had his weak points. His enemies attacked him through his mistress, Aspasia. She was a Milesian and for love of her

PERSEPHONE. Persephone, or Kore, was the daughter of Demeter. She was carried off by Hades to the underworld while she was playing

with her companions. The desolate Demeter looked for her child everywhere and was threatening to interrupt the fruition of the earth when the king of Eleusis, Celeus, or his son, Triptolemus, told her the name of her abductor. During her stay with Hades, Persephone had eaten six pomegranate seeds, which gave her husband a magic power over her, so that she had to spend a part of the year with him and could only rejoin her mother for the remaining months. While she is with her mother, everything grows abundantly on the earth; her time in the underworld corresponds with the winter months when the earth is barren. Persephone was thus the counterpart of Demeter as a goddess of vegetation. She was also queen of the dead and her position seems to have been more important than that of her husband.

P.D.

PERSEUS. Vase painting and sculpture more than literary texts show that Perseus was one of the most popular of the Greek heroes from as early as the 7th century B.C. at least. He was born in Argos and his mother was Danaë, the daughter of Acrisius, who shut her up alone in a bronze tower because an oracle had foretold that her son would kill Acrisius. Zeus visited the unhappy prisoner as a shower of gold and

Acrisius's precautions were thwarted. Perseus was born without his grandfather's knowledge and when he was told about it, he shut the mother and child into a wooden chest and threw it into the sea. The chest did not sink but drifted with the waves to the little island of Seriphus. The two castaways were rescued by a fisherman called Dictys, who brought up the child. The king of the country, Polydectes, wanted to get rid of Perseus because he protected Danaë against his advances, and ordered him to fetch the head of Medusa. Medusa was the only one of the three Gorgons who was not immortal. With the help of Hermes, who gave him a pair of winged sandals, to speed him on his way, and Athena, whose magic helmet made its wearer invisible, Perseus succeeded in decapitating Medusa in her sleep. He put the head of his victim in a sack, also given him by his divine protectors, so that he should not on any account look at it, because even in death, the head could petrify anyone who saw it. He flew rapidly away to Seriphus, where he revenged himself and put his mother out of danger by simply taking the head of Medusa out of the sack and turning Polydectes and his companions into stone statues.

On the journey, back, Perseus crossed Ethiopia and met a beautiful princess, Andromeda, whom Poseidon had tied to a rock under the guard of a

357

Palace at Phaestus.
Theatre dating from
the time of the first
palace. 18th century
B.C. *Photo Hassia.*

monster. He did this to punish the effrontery of
her mother, Cassiopeia, who had boasted that she
was more beautiful than all the Nereids. Perseus
delivered the young woman who was given to
him in marriage. He had incidentally taken the
precaution to eliminate the other claimants by
showing them the Gorgon's head. Later on, Perseus wanted to return to his own country, Argos,
but he dared not, he had, in fact, fulfilled the
oracle's former prediction by killing his grandfather, whom he had never actually seen. The
accident occurred when he was throwing the
discus at some funeral games at Larissa, where he
was unaware of Acrisius's presence. So he exchanged the kingdom of Argos, where he was
the legal heir, with Tiryns and Mycenae, which
belonged to his cousin, Megapenthes.   P.D.

PHAEDRA. Phaedra is one of the Greek
heroines who appear as characters in modern
drama. She was the daughter of the legendary
Minos and Pasiphaë, and married Theseus who
already had a son, Hippolytus, from his first
marriage with the Amazon, Antiope. In Euripides'
Hippolytus, the source of Racine's *Phèdre,* when
Theseus was away, Phaedra fell in love with the
young man, who rejected her advances, and the
wretched woman, tormented with desire and
remorse, killed herself after falsely accusing
Hippolytus of seducing her. As early as the 4th
century B.C., artists had been inspired by the
unhappy figure of Phaedra. It has been recently
suggested that Phaedra was originally a goddess
who gradually lost her divinity and became an
unfortunate queen.   P.D

PHAESTUS. It was in the south of Crete, at
Phaestus, that the first palace of a prince was built.
The remains of this building and its successor
have been discovered beneath the ruins of two
large palaces that rivalled those of Cnossos from
the 19th to the 15th century B.C. Both these
palaces, the second of which is the finer and more
complete, were planned and built according to
the usual architectural principles of Crete at that
time. There are the large, rectangular court and
the various rooms stretching along two sides of it:
the state rooms and living quarters, the places of
worship, the offices and food stores. The features
of special interest in the present state of the palace
are the propylaeum, which anticipates those of
historical times in Greece, and a splendid staircase, to the west, leading to the first floor. Like

the other palaces, those at Phaestus were decorated with paintings. P.D.

PHALERUM. Before the port of Piraeus was constructed in the 5th century B.C., the Athenians used the neighbouring harbour of Phalerum as their outlet to the sea. Excavations have uncovered evidence of occupation from the 7th to the 6th century B.C., notably some interesting vases of the final phase of the Geometric Style. Its situation, ill protected from enemy attack as well as sea winds, made Phalerum unsuitable for the sea traffic on which the Athenians depended so much and eventually led to its abandonment. P.D.

PHERECRATES. Athenian writer of comedies in the late 5th century B.C. *(See* Comedy).

PHIDIAS. On the shield of the copy we possess of Phidias's Athena Parthenos there is a spirited figure of a Greek; a gaunt body, broad back, rather large head, a forehead made more prominent by baldness, the face framed by a rounded beard. According to Plutarch, this is the self-portrait of Phidias. If we are indeed lucky enough to possess it, it is unique of its kind. The tradition is unauthenticated, but not improbable, and it would be all the pleasanter to be able to accept it as we know hardly anything about Phidias himself. He was an Athenian, the son of a certain Charmides. He was probably born about 500 B.C. and began as a painter but very soon made a reputation for himself as a sculptor. About 470, he did a statue of Athena Areia, their patron goddess, for the Plataeans; it was 26 ft high with a body in gilt wood, a head and extremities of Pentelic marble. At Delphi, he executed a group in memory of Miltiades. He must also have worked at Eleusis and the Tiber Apollo and Demeter of Cherchel are considered to be replicas of his work. His favourite materials were bronze, gold and ivory, and his two most admired statues, the Athena Parthenos and the Zeus of Olympia, were chryselephantine.

Soon after 450, Pericles commissioned him to supervise the great works he planned to embellish Athens and it is likely that he did not limit himself to decorating the Parthenon, but designed down

to its last detail the imposing plan for the reconstructed Acropolis. He made three statues himself of the goddess for the sanctuary: one in gold and ivory, the Athena Parthenos, a colossal standing figure, towering right in the centre of the temple; and two others of bronze which stood in the open

Statue of Athena from Varvakeion. Roman copy of the Athena Parthenos executed by Phidias in 438 B.C. Athens, National Museum. *Photo Spyros Meletzis.*

air: the Athena Promachos, also a gigantic sculpture that seemed to watch over the city, and the Athena Lemnia, which was smaller and less formidable.

These statues disappeared centuries ago, but the remains of the pediments and two friezes from the Parthenon allow us to share the admiration of the Greeks for the man whom they considered the greatest of sculptors. Simplicity in the grandeur of a conception seems to us his outstanding quality; confident of himself and his genius, he did not have to strain himself to impress the world with the image he had formed of it. His innate nobility never stiffens into solemnity; he created like nature herself, with a richness that must sometimes have come near to exuberance.

He gathered a large group of assistants round himself whom we know mainly by the funerary stelae of anonymous sculptors. We can only speculate on the work of his most distinguished followers, Agoracritus, Alcamenes, Callimachus (qq.v.), which has survived in copies of uncertain identity. Their talent was considerable but they were never able to free themselves completely from the dominating influence of their master which marked their style inescapably. P.D.

PHIGALEIA. *See* Bassae.

PHILEMON. Playwright of the New Comedy. *(See* Comedy).

PHILIP II. The most convincing proof of the legitimacy of Alexander the Great, who was said to be the son of his mother's adultery, was the genius of his father, Philip II of Macedonia; the task he accomplished was so formidable that he was perhaps even more distinguished than the son whose name eclipsed his own.

He came to power at the age of twenty-three as the regent of his nephew whom he later completely evicted from the throne. The country had just suffered a serious defeat and was disintegrating, but in a few months (359-358 B.C.), by a combination of ruse and violence, he succeeded in reuniting Macedonia and welding her into a strong state. He reorganised the army, which employed mercenaries although it was national, and created the famous phalanx to which Alexander owed some of his military success.

He had to open an access to the outer world for a country which had been isolated by its geography and the primitive character of its people. The conquests of ports giving it an outlet to the sea brought him into conflict with the Greeks, specially the Athenians, whose economic interests had attracted them into the region of Mount

Pangaeus (q.v.) and east of the Gulf of Salonica. Three years spent as the hostage of Epaminondas and Pelopidas (qq.v.) had taught him how to handle his neighbours; there was no reaction from Athens when he took possession of Amphipolis in 357 and Potidaea in 356. Then he pushed his conquests eastwards and occupied Crenides, which the Thasians had founded a short time before, and renamed it Philippi after himself.

After this, he turned his attentions to Greece itself. An intervention in the internal affairs of Thessaly took him to Thermopylae in 353, which gave him an opening into Hellenic politics, but he did not take advantage of this immediately; instead of trying to penetrate further south, he turned northward, took possession of Olynthus in 348 and destroyed it. This victory, following on a number of incidents, alarmed the Athenians, and Demosthenes, who had on several occasions already expatiated on the Macedonian danger, tried to rouse his fellow-citizens to take a vigorous course of action, against the advice of his rival, Aeschines. Philip, however, continued with his slow but sure erosion to consolidate his positions; an Athenian embassy in 346, which included the two great orators just mentioned, failed to make him restore the territories he had conquered. After a few years, during which there were several incidents between Athens and Macedonia and a veiled hostility without war actually being declared, the final phase of the drama began in 340. In the course of an operation against Byzantium, Philip seized 180 Athenian ships, which were cruising near the Bosporus. This was war. Athens succeeded in grouping a fair number of cities into a league against her adversary, but Philip, chosen by the amphictionies (q.v.) as leader of a campaign against the sacrilegious city of Amphissa, took advantage of this to advance far into Greece. He overcame Elatea in 339 and in 338 crushed the Athenians and their allies at Chaeronea.

This victory made him master of Greece. Although he destroyed Thebes, he was lenient towards the other states, left them a nominal autonomy and only insisted that they should group themselves into a confederacy whose policy he decided but in which he did not take a direct part; the fact remains that he ruled over the whole of Greece through his intermediaries. He was getting ready to launch this confederacy against the Persians, the hereditary enemies of Greece, when he was assassinated in 336. It was his son, Alexander, who completed the work that had been begun so brilliantly to the glory of Macedonia.

P.D.

PHILIP V. Macedonia enjoyed one of its most brilliant periods under the reign of Philip V. He succeeded Antigonus Doson in 220 B.C., when he was seventeen years old, and spent a large part of his life waging war against the Aetolian League on the one hand and against the Romans on the other. He concluded an alliance with Hannibal in 216 and left him to attack their common enemy in Italy itself, while he harried the Romans in Illyria where they had gained a foothold. He pursued his activities intelligently and efficaciously, at one time and another, in Illyria, the Peloponnesus and central Greece where he supported Aratus and the Achaean League with varying success. In 206 and 205, he was in a position to negotiate on more honourable terms with his different enemies. He then tried to dominate the Aegean; he occupied Samos in 201, besieged Chios and finally attacked Attalus, advancing through Anatolia as far as Pergamum and into the heart of Caria.

In 200, the Romans began a major offensive against Greece and in 197 they beat Philip's troops at Cynoscephalae in Thessaly. Macedonia had to stop her interventions in Greece and paid a heavy

Philoctetes wounded and abandoned on the Isle of Lemnos. Beside him are the bow and arrows bequeathed him by Heracles. Detail of an Attic lekythos. About 430-420 B.C. New York, Metropolitan Museum of Art.

indemnity to the conquerors including the loss of her fleet. However, in her struggle against the ambitions of Antiochus III, Rome modified her policy and sought a reconciliation with Philip. He took advantage of the circumstances to renew his incursions into Greece and try to enlarge his kingdom. The Romans rejected him and he died a disillusioned man.   P.D.

PHILIPPUS of OPUS. Philippus was a philosopher and astronomer, the pupil of Plato whose last work, the *Laws,* he edited when his master left it unfinished at his death. It is likely that he wrote the *Epinomis,* a short treatise intended to complete the *Laws* which is always included with it in modern editions and which some scholars attribute to Plato himself.   P.-M.S.

PHILISTION. Philistion was a native of Locri in Magna Graecia and became physician to the tyrant, Dionysius of Syracuse. He was a follower of Empedocles (q.v.) and took over the theory of the four elements from him. He stressed the importance of good breathing for health and developed a theory of the vital breath, or Pneuma, which had a considerable influence later on. His

Treatise on the Heart is included in the Hippocratic collection and Plato seems to have been influenced by some of its descriptions in the *Timaeus.* There is a remarkable discussion in it of how the sigmoid valves function but the intelligence and the remaining principles of the soul were situated in the left ventricle according to Philistion.   P.-M.S.

PHILOCRATES. Philocrates cuts a rather poor figure beside Demosthenes and Aeschines whom he accompanied as ambassador in 346 B.C. to Philip II of Macedonia (q.v.) to negotiate an end to hostilities. His name, however, was given to the treaty, which was then concluded, because he had it ratified by the Athenians. The treaty was an inglorious compromise that sacrificed the Phocians, whom Athens had promised to defend, and left undecided most of the thorny questions between the two states.   P.D.

PHILOCTETES. Philoctetes was the companion of Heracles in his last moments. The hero asked him to light the pyre on which he wanted to die, making him swear that he would never reveal the place where he was going to take

362

Bronze bust of a philosopher found in the sea near ...ticythera. Hellenistic period. Athens, National Museum.
Photo Spyros Meletzis.

...is life, and bequeathed him his bow and arrows. ...hiloctetes broke the promise he had made and ...his was why, according to one version of the ...egend, he was bitten by a snake when he arrived ...vith the other chiefs on the shores of Troy. The ...vound smelt so disgusting that his companions ...bandoned him on a desert island, where he ...tayed for ten years. Then the Greeks learnt ...hrough an oracle that they would never take ...'riam's city without his help because they had to ...e armed with the arrows of Heracles to conquer ...:. Ulysses was sent with Diomedes to find the ...vretched man and, by means that vary according ...o different traditions, they succeeded in bringing ...'hiloctetes back to the Greek camp, where ...Machaon, the son of Asclepius, cured the snake ...ite.   P.D.

PHILON of ALEXANDRIA. Philon ...vas a member of the Jewish community in ...Alexandria and its leader. The first husband of ...Queen Berenice was one of his nephews. In ...$9 A.D. he went as an envoy to Rome to beg ...Caligula to exempt his community from the obliga- ...ion to worship the emperor. Caligula refused but ...he Emperor Claudius gave him satisfaction in 41. ...'hilon's account of this mission has come down ...o us. We do not know the exact date of his death ...nd various dates for his birth have been suggested ...etween 40 and 13 B.C. Although he was deeply ...ttached to Judaism, Philon had a thorough ...ppreciation of Greek culture and a sound ...hilosophical training. His work is an invaluable ...ource of information both for Stoic doctrine and ...or the rites of the Therapeutae, a Jewish sect in ...Egypt connected with the Essenes. In his works ...e explains the Bible by allegorical methods and ...describes the stages of the spiritual life and the ...iscesis of the soul, turning from evil and ascend- ...ng to God until it attains ecstasy. Philon's theo- ...ogy included several divine powers, the principal ...of which was the Word, or Logos. This Greek ...ranslation of the Hebrew *dabar* (word) denoted ...in important conception in the Stoic system, the ...nnate reason that animates the world. The Logos, ...he Idea of Ideas *(See* Plato) was for Philon the ...rinciple and instrument of creation that marks its ...reatures with its image.   P.-M.S.

PHILOSOPHY. The ancient Greeks drew up a list of Seven Sages, who were men of experience and famous for certain maxims they had enunciated. Later, a distinction was made between these sages *(sophoi)* and, on the one hand, the sophists, who were specialists of argu- mentation, and on the other, those who simply considered themselves " friends of wisdom " *(philosophoi)*. This was the origin of the word " philosophy ", which soon came to designate any more or less systematic conception of the world and man. The first Greek philosophers were Milesians who were trying to find an explanation for the substance of things. The monism of Parmenides of Elea stood in contrast to Heracli- tus's doctrine of flux. The problem of the relations of the One and the Many, propounded so strikingly by Heraclitus, was offered different solutions by Democritus, who developed an atomistic conception, and by Anaxagoras and Empedocles. Into this current of thought, Empe- docles introduced ideas on the destiny of the soul that derived from Pythagoras. Socrates' preoccu- pations were different from philosophical systems of nature elaborated on these lines. Conscious of his own ignorance and that of others, he firmly laid the basis of moral philosophy and prescribed the knowledge of the self. His ideas had very varied developments. First, there was the work of Plato who reacted against the amoralism of the sophists with a moral system depending on the absolute supremacy of the Good, which shines through the world of Ideas. The legislator who has attained this notion of the Good by dialectic ought to impose it on the City. Although Aristotle reacted against Platonic inspiration, he remained strongly influenced by Platonism, and elaborated a system in which the world is dependent on God, conceived as thought thinking itself. He rejected the separate Ideas, which Plato himself had criticised, but explained reality as the expression of forms on matter. Another development of Socrates' thought took place in the small schools where the masters had been strongly influenced by him. They were the source of the great philosophical systems that were developed in the Hellenistic period when the conquests of Alexander had burst the bounds of the city state; Pyrrho's scepticism and the ideas of Epicurus drew on Socrates, as well as his Cyrenaican followers and Democritus. Zeno of Citium, followed by Cleanthes and Chrysippus, reacted against Epicureanism; they worked out the Stoic system in which Socratic thought reappeared with a Platonic element, coloured by the traditions of the Megarian school and a purified Cynicism, and completed by physics inspired by Heraclitus. As a contrast to these new dogmatisms, there grew up the relativism of the so-called Third or New Academy at Athens, directed by Arcesilaus and Carneades. Stoicism itself evolved; the radical intellectualism of Chrysippus was followed by the dualistic conceptions of Panaetius and his follower, Posidonius, the author of a new and impressive synthesis of the knowledge of his time (Middle Stoa period). The influence of Platonism reappeared again in these. The Academy, in its turn, drew nearer to the Stoa and Cicero, who admired Philon of Larissa, head of the Academy, and had also attended classes by Posidonius, often comes very near to Stoicism. The Stoicism of imperial Rome, represented by Seneca, Epictetus and Marcus Aurelius, was chiefly concerned with the consciousness and self-examination of the individual. Philon of Alexandria had already anticipated Neoplatonism and its full development came with Plotinus, who had steeped himself in Plato's thought. Plotinus leads his reader to the supreme level of the One and describes the descent through various interme-

diaries to the Many. His main followers were Porphyry, Iamblichus, Proclus and Damatius. The last of these found a refuge with his associates at the Persian court of King Chosroes I when the Emperor Justinian closed the School of Athens in 529 A.D. P.-M.S

PHILOXENUS. A lyric poet born at Cythera (435-380 B.C.). Philoxenus was invited to Sicily by Dionysius I but was soon thrown into the Latomiae quarries at Syracuse from where he succeeded in escaping. He died at Ephesus. He revenged himself on Dionysius by making crude allusions to the tyrant in his most celebrated dithyramb (See Lyric Poetry), the Cyclops, in which he took up the story in Book IX of the Odyssey and introduced a topical element into it through the episode of the love of Polyphemus for the sea nymph, Galatea, who rejected the monster.
R.F

PHOCAEA. This little town on the Anatolian coast to the north of Smyrna had a rather brief existence because it was among those taken by Cyrus in 545 B.C. when its inhabitants abandoned the town in a body. But for a period covering less than a hundred years, its colonising activity was so intense that it is not an exaggeration to speak of a Phocaean thalassocracy during the early 6th century. They went as far as Spain to the coast of Cadiz, but their ventures were mainly directed to the mouth of the Rhone valley and what is now the French Riviera. They not only founded Massalia, the present Marseilles, but also Theline (Arles) and probably several other towns of Languedoc, the Barcelona region and perhaps also Monaco. About 560, they settled on the east coast of Corsica, at Alalia (Aleria), which was extremely useful to them when the Persians drove them out of their home town and they found a refuge here. Their activities continued and alarmed the Etruscans and Carthaginians, who attacked and vanquished the Phocaeans at Alalia in 535. They then took refuge at Rhegium from where some of them left to found a colony at Elea.
P.D

PHOCION. Phocion was one of the staunchest supporters of the peace party at Athens during the troubled period when Macedonia was gradually conquering Greece. At a time when Demosthenes was trying to rouse his fellow citizens against Philip, Phocion was preaching an entente with him. After the battle of Chaeronea in 338 B.C., he was entrusted, with Aeschines and Demades, to negotiate with the victor. When the death of Alexander the Great was announced and his compatriots revolted against the Macedonian domination, he preached moderation and intervened with Antipater (q.v.) when the inevitable repression came. It was not surprising then, that the democrats, returned from exile with the help of Polyperchon, should condemn him to death as a collaborator.   P.D.

PHOCIS. The glory and misfortune of Phocis was the presence of the sanctuary of Delphi in this humble mountain province.   Incidents that elsewhere would not have been of great moment were liable there to degenerate into sacred wars with several cities joining in to ensure their influence over the sacred place where Apollo delivered his oracles. Philip II of Macedonia (q.v.) made the Third Sacred War (355-345 B.C.) a pretext for invading Greece for the first time and, in spite of the courage of Philomelus and Onomarchus, the Phocian army was crushed by the Macedonians.   P.D.

PHRATRY. The phratry in primitive tribes was a group of families and the religious character of the institution gave it an official status right into the classical period. Citizens presented their new-born children to the phratry and this was the equivalent of enrolment at a registry office.   As soon as democratic regimes were set up at Athens and the other states, the phratry lost the political and social importance it had possessed while aristocratic families occupied a leading place.
                                    P.D.

PHRYGIA.   Hellenic influence never succeeded in changing the profoundly Anatolian character of the people in this province situated in the north-west of Asia Minor. To the Greeks it represented strange and barbaric Asia, and the term "phrygian" was applied as readily to a musical mode that shocked the traditionalists, or a clinging garment, or the bonnet worn by the barbarians. It was from Phrygia, too, according to the Athenians, that those oriental divinities came who were such formidable rivals to the Olympians in the days of Aristophanes and Euripides. The Phrygian art we know bears the mark of its Anatolian predecessors even when it was produced by Hellenised artists.   P.D.

PHRYNE. Phryne is not the only courtesan of ancient Greece whose name is known to us, but she is one of the best known, as much for her liaison with the sculptor, Praxiteles, as for the story told in connexion with her. When she was standing trial before her judges on a charge of impiety, her defender, Hyperides, tore her chiton from her, exclaiming, " Can such beauty be guilty? "—and won her case.

We know little about her life. Her real name was Mnesarete.   She was a native of Thespiae in Boeotia and probably settled in Athens in 372 B.C. when her country was conquered and pillaged. In one of its sanctuaries she dedicated a statue of Eros, which Praxiteles had given her, and also her own portrait. If, as is rather doubtful, she was the model for the *Aphrodite of Cnidos* and it was really the replica of her portrait that was found at Arles, her beauty was dignified, serene, and well rounded, the kind that Mediterranean people, who are not particularly susceptible to the charms of a slender figure, would find extremely seductive.   P.D.

PHRYNICUS.   A tragic playwright and predecessor of Aeschylus. *(See* Tragedy).

PHYLACOPI.   Phylacopi on the island of Melos is one of the oldest inhabited sites in the Cyclades. The town was first founded at the end of the 3rd millennium B.C., but had to be reconstructed, first, in the early part of the 2nd millennium, then again in the second half. It owed its prosperity to the trade in a soft stone called obsidian which at that time was used for making sharp-edged tools, lance-points and arrows. The whole of the Aegean basin came to Phylacopi for the precious material. It is not surprising that in the ruins of the second town, frescoes were found, bearing the traces of Cretan influence, which are an eloquent testimony to its inhabitants' wealth.
                                    P.D.

PHYLE. The word *phyle*, which can be translated as " tribe ", was used by the Greeks to denote very different organisations at different periods.

It was first used for ethnic groupings whose origins were lost in the mists of time. These groups flourished until the end of the archaic period and united all those who took part in the same form of worship, although they might not claim to be the descendants of a common ancestor. When they invaded the Greek peninsula, the people known as the Ionians were already divided into four tribes and the Dorians, who came later, were divided into three. This tripartite and quadripartite division survived the dispersion of these peoples throughout the Mediterranean world and was found even in the colonial settlements of the 7th century B.C. As the conquerors could not integrate the conquered native peoples into their tribes, which were formed around ancestral cults at the time of their invasion, they grouped them in additional tribes to which they tended to give inferior status; Sicyon is a characteristic example of this.

These new creations, which were political in inspiration and not religious, were a first step towards the transformation of the concept of the phyle, which was completed in Attica during the final years of the 6th century B.C.

It was Cleisthenes (q.v.) who divided his fellow-citizens into ten phylai unrelated to former divisions, in his attempt to give his country a democratic constitution and to break down the traditional framework of society. Each phyle was placed under the protection of a hero, designated by the Pythia, whose statue stood in the agora of Athens, and all acts concerning the phyle were affixed to the pedestal of this statue. The phylai were both territorial and administrative. Each contained citizens from three districts, the first being in the city and its suburbs, the second on the Attic coast *(Paralia),* the third in the plain and the mountains of the interior *(Mesogaea* and *Diacria),* and, as each phyle also grouped people of different origins and interests, the old local traditions were eliminated.

The phyle that had been made in this way of three different sections then became an administrative and political cell in the new state. It had a relative autonomy, with its own religious organisation established in the sanctuary of its patron deity, its own resources and budget, and its own deliberative assemblies. The city's institutions were based on the decimal pattern of the phylai. As there were ten phylai, the year was divided into ten prytanies, in each of which a phyle took turns in wielding the executive power through the intermediary of the fifty delegates it sent to the Council of Five Hundred, the Boule. Similarly, there were ten regiments of hoplites, ten squadrons of horsemen, ten strategi, treasurers, and other magistrates. From that time, all the phyle had in common with the ethnic and religious group of early times was its name.　　P.D.

PINDAR. Pindar (518-438 B.C.) was a lyric poet born in Boeotia, near Thebes. His talent was precocious; he was just twenty years old when he composed his tenth *Pythian Ode.* He travelled a great deal, not only to the great games, whose victors he celebrated, at Olympia, Delphi, the Isthmus of Corinth and Nemea, but also to Sicily, to the court of the Syracusan tyrant, Hieron, to the court of Theron, the tyrant of Agrigentum, and perhaps also to Cyrene to King Arcesilas. He visited Aegina and Athens several times.

Pindar excelled in all kinds of lyric poetry. Fragments have survived of *Hymns, Paeans, Dithyrambs, Parthenia, Hyporchemata, Enkomia,* etc. *(See* Lyric Poetry). The only complete poems we possess—and the music has been lost even of these—are his *Epinikia,* or *Triumphal Odes,* collected in four books, each one corresponding to a panhellenic games gathering: the *Olympian, Pythian, Nemean* and *Isthmian Odes.*

Pindar refers to the victory itself in a few dry, concise phrases, without any descriptive details. What interested this aristocratic poet, who believed in the transmission of the hereditary virtues of a race, was the immortalising of the victor's family and native land, not forgetting the gods from whom all success comes, nor the festival that offered the athlete an opportunity to distinguish himself. In the middle of the ode, he nearly always places a divine or heroic myth, swiftly evoked, rather than narrated, with two or three features of the legend, which he assumes is familiar; and projects a brilliant light on these chosen aspects of the story. He generally ends with some religious and moral reflexions on the human condition (man is only an ephemeral being, the dream of a shadow), solemn advice to princes and nobles and, finally, allusions to his own genius, which are like the signature of the poet. Like his contemporary, Aeschylus, Pindar was an orthodox religious thinker. His conception of the dignity and omniscience of the gods was too exalted for him to accept all the tales about the gods indiscriminately; in the first *Olympian Ode,* for example, he does not hesitate to modify the fable of Tantalus and Pelops to make it more in keeping with his religious notions. He was more afraid of misrepresenting the gods than anything else, because it was really " blaspheming ".

Pindar's odes are formed in triads, each comprising a strophe, an antistrophe and an epode. They give an impression of disorder because the poet did not trouble about regular composition;

he passed rapidly, without any transition, from one subject to another, borne along by his inspiration and the association of ideas. His poetry is grand, brilliant and powerful, but it cannot be fully appreciated without the music; only the "librettos" of these operas" have survived in which poetry, singing and dancing were closely associated.   P.D.

PIRACY. Piracy in the Mediterranean in ancient times was a real institution, as it continued to be in the modern world until comparatively recently. We have no information about it in the Bronze Age, but Plutarch mentions a tradition that Minos had already taken measures to suppress it. Although there is no actual proof, it is likely that it flourished without any difficulty when coastal defences were not organised and there were not many ships on the sea. Besides, in the Homeric period, a sailor would be normally asked when he embarked, " Are you a pirate ? " Was a distinction made between trade and piracy ? Probably, the two activities were closely connected according to circumstances, and a sea-trader would pay for or steal the merchandise and slaves he wanted, depending on the reception he found on the coast. Some peoples had a reputation for piracy; besides the Phoenicians and Cilicians, the neighbouring Cretans and Tyrrhenians, that is, the Etruscans, were mentioned for their propensity to it; but the Samians and several other peoples were certainly not averse from intercepting boats that came their way or raiding the villages when they had put into port. As soon as a maritime power established itself, its first aim was to ensure the safety of the seas, but the struggle always had to begin again. Even at the peak of Athenian power in the 5th century B.C., acts of piracy were common and, during the troubles of the Hellenistic period, populations abandoned several places on the coast and founded villages in the interior to escape attacks from the sea.   P.D.

PIRAEUS. The victories of Mycale (479 B.C.) and Salamis (480 B.C.) made the Athenians realise their maritime potentialities. Encouraged by Themistocles, they decided to build a large fleet and the poorly protected harbour of Phalerum (q.v.) was abandoned. They chose the nearby site of Piraeus to make a port. On either side of the peninsula of Acte, there were three bights of different sizes offering three ports that would meet all their requirements; Munychia, Zea and a much larger basin called Cantharus. They had their special uses from the beginning; the arsenals were constructed at Zea, warehouses and commercial buildings were built along the Cantharus. The agglomeration was fortified and soon afterwards the communication with Athens, about six miles away, was protected by the Long Walls (q.v.).

The town itself grew up in two phases, the first in the time of Themistocles, the second under the government of Pericles, about thirty years later. The famous architect, Hippodamus of Miletus (q.v.) planned the main divisions of its lay-out, and their boundary stones, found in their original places, have preserved the principal demarcations: " Limit of the port and the street.—Limit of the public anchorage.—Public area from this street to the port. " It was only in the second phase, that the sites of the agora and the various districts were decided.

As soon as it was founded, Piraeus became of considerable importance to the life of Athens; it was the only outlet to the sea, so it had to be protected from all enemy incursions and its blockade would have paralysed the whole country with famine. It developed very rapidly and, as was natural, a large number of metics settled there and maintained Athens' flourishing trade with the outside world. Bankers, and money-changers, ship outfitters, businessmen of all kinds and dockers gave this port the vital and colourful appearance that Alexandria would have later on, or Naples in the days of sailing vessels and perhaps Marseilles in our own times. Many exotic cults, especially the Egyptian deities, found a refuge in this cosmopolitan centre, before penetrating to the heart of Athens.   P.D.

PISISTRATUS: PISISTRATIDS. Pisistratus seems typical to us of those tyrants whose political attitudes anticipated the " enlightened despots " of 18th century Europe. His dictatorship over Athens lasted from 561 to 528 B.C. with two breaks covering fourteen years when he was sent into exile. His sons succeeded him at his death. Hipparchus, one of them, seduced the sister of Harmodius and was assassinated in 514 by Harmodius and Aristogiton (qq.v.), the Tyrannicides, who became heroes of freedom. Hippias, the other son, was driven out in 510 by the democratic revolution of Cleisthenes (q.v.).

Pisistratus was of noble birth and distinguished himself by repulsing the attack of the Megarians.

Head of the Rampin Horseman. Attic. Mid-6th century B.C. Paris, Louvre. *Photo Chevojon.*

head of Athena and the emblem of the owl, brought the country an unprecedented prosperity. Public works gave employment to the labouring classes while it made life easier for all citizens. An attempt at town-planning was made with the straightening of some streets, and the construction of drains and fountains.

The sanctuaries were restored with the dual purpose of increasing the prestige of Athens and showing a proper piety to the gods: the Acropolis was given a monumental entrance which must have influenced Mnesicles (q.v.) when he built the Propylaea; the Hecatompedon, the temple of Athena, was enlarged and embellished with a marble pediment; off the plateau, Pisistratus laid the first stones of a gigantic temple, the Olympieum, which was not finished until the reign of the Emperor Hadrian; and the sanctuary, as yet a modest one, was built for a god whose worship was spreading, Dionysus. Partly from inclination and partly to discourage from politics an aristocracy, which was hostile to tyranny, Pisistratus and his sons surrounded themselves with a brilliant court whose tastes were reflected in the preciousness of works of art like the *Rampin Horseman* in sculpture and the Little Master cups in ceramics. Numerous offerings dedicated to the gods, especially marble statues of korai and kouroi (qq.v.) are as much an indication of the wealth of the patrons as the skill of their artists. Literature was not neglected: Pisistratus had an edition of the Homeric poems prepared that would establish a standard version from an unreliable tradition; he invited Anacreon and other poets to his court. It was under the tyranny that Athens, in nearly every sphere, found the orientation that was to remain hers and the era of Pisistratus could with some justification be counted among the " great ages ". P.D.

He took advantage of his popularity by inducing the city to grant him a body-guard on the pretext that his security was threatened. The guards seized the seat of government, the Acropolis, for him and established his power over Athens. He was driven out after a few years, but returned in triumph led, so it was said, by Athena herself, in actual fact by a beautiful woman who was made to look like the goddess. His reign was brilliant and his administration sound. He assured the peasants the possession of their patches of ground, developed the cultivation of the vine and did everything to prevent a drift from the countryside and the consequent increase of the urban proletariat to a dangerous degree. In the towns, crafts were encouraged; the potteries increased in number and Black-Figure vases excelled in the fierce competition of the international market with their Rhodian and Corinthian rivals. Commercial exchanges benefited from the peace that followed the generally peaceful relations of Pisistratus with the other tyrants. Wise financial administration, the introduction of a twenty per cent tax and the minting of coins, bearing the

PLATAEA. Plataea was only a small town in Boeotia and she owed her fame to the great battle fought between the Greeks and Persians in 479 B.C. The Greeks won and their victory, following the one at Salamis, was decisive; it was after Plataea that Mardonius, the Persian general, ordered his troops to evacuate Greece. The Plataeans, who behaved heroically on this occasion and had already faithfully supported the Athenians in other battles, were jealously detested by the neighbouring Thebans. In 431, the Thebans attacked the town and this aggression, which was unsuccessful, was one of the causes of the Peloponnesian War. It was a fatal war for the little city, because in 427, after a long siege, it was taken by the Thebans without receiving any help from its Athenian allies. The town was razed and the inhabitants massacred.   P.D.

PLATO. Plato was born at Athens about 428/427 B.C. into an aristocratic family connected with Codrus and Solon. His first master was Cratylus, a Heraclitean philosopher who stressed the rapid flux of sensible things, he then joined the circle around Socrates. In the normal course of his career, he would have entered political life, but he was equally disillusioned by the injustices under the government of the Thirty Tyrants with which his uncle, Charmides, was associated, as under the democratic reaction that put Socrates to death. So in 399/398, he travelled widely in Egypt, Cyrenaica, Sicily and southern Italy. On his return, he bought the park called the Academus and set up there an establishment for philosophical, scientific and political investigation called the Academy (q.v.). He returned twice to Sicily in 367 and 361 in the hopes of setting up an ideal government at Syracuse with the help of the tyrant Dionysius I and his uncle, Dion, whom Plato had converted to his idea of the philosopher-king, but his visits ended badly each time. He died at Athens in 348/347 without completing his last work, the *Laws*.

Plato's work consists of philosophical dialogue, each of which opens with a specific question and suggests a broad view of the problem that is very often left to the reader to decide for himself. Scholars have succeeded over the last hundred years in establishing a chronological classification of the dialogues, which can be divided into three periods.

I. Early period.

The dialogues considered as youthful works often end in apparent failure and are known as the aporetic dialogues, from the word *aporia*, dead-end, difficulty; the reader can find a reason for this in the hints scattered through a dialogue. Generally speaking, it can be said that Plato was trying to reach, behind the flow of appearances, the absolute realities that would enable him to escape from relativism and attain a stable knowledge. Socrates' teaching had shown him such realities

in the sphere of morality: the virtues; but they also existed in the world of mathematical essences (the Pythagorean, Archytas of Tarentum, and later on the geometrician, Eudoxus of Cnidos, helped him to understand this world) and as aesthetic values in the sphere of the Beautiful. He called these realities " Forms " or " Ideas "; they are both notions and structural types. Together they rise like a pyramid towards the culminating Idea, that of the Good, which alone can give an understanding of the universe and its justification (*Republic*, Book VI) and towards which the dialectical method leads us. Knowledge of these essences is directly associated with the reminiscence or memory of knowledge that is acquired before birth *(Meno)*. The soul, in fact, pre-exists the body and survives it; this was a harmonising factor essentially bound up with the idea of life, because by its very nature it excluded death *(Phaedo)* and is described later in the *Phaedrus* as a self-moved principle (*Phaedrus*, sec. 245). Several myths or parables illustrate the destiny of the soul. After death it is judged (*Gorgias;* end of the *Republic*, Book X, myth of Er). A thousand years after this judgment, it chooses a different destiny. The myth of the *Phaedrus* describes the gods driving in chariots round the vault of heaven, probably that of the stars, beyond which stretches the world of Ideas that they contemplate. Below the gods and the vault of heaven, drive the chariots of the souls and the most privileged among them can glance at the supercelestial world; it is just this view that reminiscence will bring back to them later on. It will also make them recognise the Idea of Beauty, which they have formerly contemplated, when they see earthly beauties. Although Plato had insisted on the unity of the soul in the *Phaedo*, he gives a tripartite image of it in the *Phaedrus:* the charioteer (reason) and two horses (the noble passions and the base).

This doctrine provided the foundation for a personal morality according to which it is better to suffer injustice, which damages the soul, than to commit it; and a political morality that explains both the nature of the evils afflicting cities and the remedy proposed by Plato. They result from the loss of natural simplicity and from the fact that only imperfect societies exist, each necessarily derived from the other: timocracy or a false aristocracy, selfish oligarchy, anarchic democracy and finally tyranny. The remedy lies in the selection, scientific and philosophical education of the governors, who will be entrusted with establishing a political community in which the conflicts of family interests would be avoided by fusing the families into the city.

II. Middle period.

In a series of great metaphysical dialogues, Plato brings together the strongest objections that can be marshalled against his theory of Ideas *(Parmenides,* 1st part) and thoroughly examines the bases of knowledge. In the *Theaetetus,* he first of all criticizes knowledge, derived from sense-perception, and the relativism of Protagoras, and finally shows that opinion, however sound, is not a reliable foundation. In the *Sophist* he attacks the Eleatic tradition, arguing that besides Being, the existence must be recognised of what he calls " the other " whose presence allows movement and thought. In the last part of the *Parmenides,* he examines more deeply the difficulties created by conceptions of the One and the Others. To explain the genesis of Being, the *Philebus* introduces the Pythagorean notion of the limited acting on the infinite which results in a mixture whose cause should be investigated. Beside the ascending dialectic, an increasing importance is given in the *Philebus* to a descending dialectic, or apprehension by the method of division; since the Good cannot be apprehended in its essence, it is attained under the three aspects of beauty, proportion and truth; and morality is replaced by certain pure, intellectual pleasures. Finally, the *Statesman* contrasts the flexibility of true politics with the rigidity of law.

III. Late period.

In the marvellous work called the *Timaeus,* Plato elaborates a whole cosmology and biology whose influence lasted for centuries. He returns to political problems in the unfinished *Critias.* The huge work of the *Laws,* which occupied the last years of his life, is like an encyclopaedia of politics and their metaphysical foundations. He cast it in the form of a constitutional system for an imaginary city, which offered a less rigorous solution than the ideal city outlined in the *Republic* and was also more feasible. In the last book of Aristotle's *Metaphysics,* there are references to the " unwritten teachings of Plato "; his theories on ideal numbers would have held an important place in them.

Plato's thought has exercised a considerable influence over the development of philosophy through the ages. His philosophical profundities are expressed in a delightful style and he never fails to introduce his moral, political and scientific preoccupations gracefully. The myths give a sensitive and poetic form to important ideas for those who would be discouraged if they were couched in abstract terms, but at the same time they create problems for those who are capable of thinking in abstractions. They are fundamental problems, like those formulated at the end of the *Parmenides,* and philosophers are still trying to find a solution to them. They never cease to stimulate the mind to a profounder contemplation. P.-M.S.

PLEIADES. The seven stars in the constellation of the Pleiades were originally seven sisters, the daughters of Atlas. This metamorphosis was brought about by Zeus to screen the young women from the love of Orion, a Boeotian hunter, who had pursued them for five years. P.D.

PLOTINUS. Neoplatonist philosopher born about 205 A.D. Nothing is known of Ammonius Saccas, who taught Plotinus at Alexandria from 233 to 242 and attracted him to philosophy. He took part in the ill-fated expedition organised by the Emperor Gordian against Persia, which he had joined in the hope of meeting the eastern sages. After this he settled in Antioch, then Rome where he taught until his death in 270. His follower Porphyry (q.v.) collected the fifty-four treatises, left by his master, into six *Enneads* or groups of nine treatises. These treatises generally begin by the statement of a technical problem, from a commentary by Plato or Aristotle. The problem, taken as a starting-point, is gradually related to the whole system of Platonic doctrine as elaborated by Plotinus. In this way, the system is developed little by little from different points of view.

Plotinus leads his reader up from the sensible world to the intelligible world which penetrates it and whose brilliance can be seen in physical beauties. In order to conceive it, he invites his reader to disregard matter and space. This intelligible world, which Plotinus calls *Nous* or Divine Intellect, holds within itself the radiant assembly of the Ideas, but it is necessary to rise above this harmonious multitude to the supreme principle, which Plotinus, like Plato, calls the One and which is ineffable; it is the First Principle or first hypostasis. It is possible to approach this principle through the intellect (by analogy or by

Scythian archer acting as a policeman. Decoration on a plate by Epictetus. About 525-520 B.C. British Museum.

negation, for example), but it cannot really be attained except in ecstasy. From it emanates Nous, the second hypostasis, and from Nous itself a third hypostasis, Soul, proceeds, which in its turn projects the natural world. Plotinus sometimes seems drawn towards a monist conception where even matter is the product of a rational evolution, but he generally only sees it as a negative reality and there more often appears in his work a dualism that implies the fall of the Soul, attracted like Narcissus to its own reflection. Consequently, it descends into bodies and is differentiated without in any way being fragmented. The choice lies with each of us to decide the level where we wish to come to rest. Emanation, or procession, and conversion, are the two themes that dominate Plotinus's thought. Their alternation has inspired many of the great philosophies through the centuries.   P.-M.S.

PLUTARCH. The philosopher and historian, Plutarch (46-126 A.D.), was born at Chaeronea in Boeotia and belonged to an old, middle class family. He finished his studies at Athens, when he was about twenty; they included rhetoric and especially philosophy and the sciences. He also went to Alexandria in Egypt, and several times to Italy, particularly Rome, where he taught philosophy and made several friends. When he was about forty, he returned to Chaeronea to settle, but he still made several short visits in Greece, mainly to Delphi where he accepted the duties of Apollo's priest. In spite of his sacerdotal functions, the municipal offices he assumed at Chaeronea, the responsibilities of looking after his children (he had at least four sons and a daughter) and his estates, he led the peaceful life of a sage and scholar.

Plutarch wrote a great deal and, although a large number of his works are lost, the surviving part is about as voluminous as Plato's. It falls into two parts: the *Lives* and the *Moralia* which could be called more accurately *Miscellaneous Works;* several treatises collected under this title are concerned with general philosophy, the sciences, historical studies and theology, as much as with morality. Often entertaining and curious, it is also a mixture of unusual insights, a great deal of information on Greek religion and civilisation, and

some rubbish. The most elaborate literary works are dialogues, notably the *Amatorius, De sera numinis vindicata,* and the *Pythian Dialogues.*

Plutarch's reputation rests on the *Lives* in which he sets the life of an illustrious Greek and Roman side by side in each volume and ends by making a comparison between them. It is the approach of a historian, but the preoccupations of the psychologist and moralist also enter the work, because he was more concerned with painting characters than describing battles. His talent as a narrator is consummate; he can describe with extraordinary economy a person, or bring a whole scene before the eyes of his reader. Plutarch has told us about the childhood, way of life, ideas and feelings of great men where other historians have only described their exploits and public attitudes. Everyone knows or thinks he knows, what is a " Plutarchean hero ". The influence of the Lives has been considerable on all European literature, from Amyot's translation in the 16th century up to the end of the 18th century. Plutarch is not a great writer; his style is sometimes heavy and diffuse; but his work is an epitome of the whole of Hellenic antiquity and is immensely interesting on this account.   R.F.

POLICE. The Athenian police, the only one we know a little about, had a two-fold function like our own; they had to keep order and see that

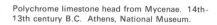

the city laws were observed and also arrest criminals.

In certain instances, the first task was entrusted to citizens recruited from the ten tribes; the five hundred guards of the arsenals and the fifty protecting the Acropolis, for example; but in the city itself, it was entrusted to Scythian archers. They were public slaves, about a thousand in number, who camped on the Areopagus hill and should not be confused with the Scythians engaged in the army as auxiliaries. They retained their native costume which was so different from that of the Greeks: pointed cap, short tunic and tightly fitting trousers. They were responsible for policing the streets and were at the disposal of presidents of the assembly and the tribunals for keeping order.

There was no criminal police in the strict sense of the term; Athens had no Quai des Orfèvres or Scotland Yard. The Eleven, magistrates who were also called "supervisors of ill-doers", were in fact charged with arresting criminals and thieves, but only if they were taken *flagrante delicto,* or if a citizen delivered them into the hands of the magistrate. Action against an unknown person did not exist. The machinery of justice (q.v.) did not initiate criminal proceedings itself, but was set in motion by the complaint of a private citizen or magistrate. The preliminary investigation was carried out by one of the nine archons (q.v.; which one depended on the nature of the crime) and he certainly did not hold one of those criminal investigations that enthrall our own age. Informing *(See* Sycophants) was the main source of supply for the prison population; the police only had to pick up the offender.   P.D.

POLYBIUS. Historian (210-128 B.C.), born at Megalopolis in Arcadia. As the son of the Achaean strategus, Lycortas, who was the friend of Philopoemen, Polybius was introduced to politics at an early age. In 183, he was given the honour of carrying the ashes of Philopoemen back to his country. After the victory of Aemilius Paullus at Pydna in 168 over Perseus, the king of Macedonia, Polybius was inscribed on the list of a thousand hostages deported to Italy. He stayed sixteen years in Italy and was filled with admiration at the sight of Roman discipline and Roman virtues in the golden age of the Republic. He became friendly with the sons of Aemilius Paullus, Fabius, Publius and Laelius. Publius, better known as Scipio Aemilianus, persuaded Cato to free the Achaean hostages in 150. Polybius returned to Greece, but Rome had become a second country to him; he returned to it several times, accompanied Scipio on his campaigns and was with him at the taking of Carthage in 146. He died about 128 after falling from his horse.

Several of Polybius's works have been lost: *Life of Philopoemen, Treatise on Tactics, History of the Numantine War.* His main work, the *Universal History,* has not survived intact. Its forty books recount the conquest of the world by Rome from the beginning of the Second Punic War (221) to the taking of Corinth (146).

Polybius's history was pragmatic, in other words, concerned with the narrative of events, and epideictic, that is, containing a discussion of the sequence of causes and effects. His early training in public affairs gave depth to his analysis of the motives of statesmen, national characteristics and institutions; his studies on the constitutions of Sparta, Rome and Carthage are models of exact information and penetrating comment. Polybius's historical method is like Thucydides'. Compared with Livy, who used his work extensively, it is the " Graeculus " who has a positive, realistic spirit, while the Roman is very much preoccupied with his style and expression. As a writer, Polybius was extremely clear, but his style is dull and heavy. His cast of mind was much more scientific than literary. Like all early historians, he was also a geographer; his extensive travels and his gifts of observation enabled him to give improved and more precise information about the earth than his predecessors. His work is more valuable for its substance than its form. His lucid and profound comments on his own times show that he was one of the most trenchant minds of antiquity.   R.F.

POLYCHROME SCULPTURE. The practice of colouring statues and reliefs is common to all primitive peoples. The Greeks practised polychromy not only in archaic times, but also in the classical and Hellenistic periods. The Cretans had already, perhaps under Egyptian influence, accentuated some of their frescoes with a slight relief, so that it is difficult to decide whether the *Prince with Lilies* at Cnossos should be described as a painted relief or a fresco in relief. The Greeks picked out their statues and carved friezes with bright colours, which not only gave them an added vitality but also hid the poor quality of the stone, which they first used, under a coat of paint. In the beginning their colours were extremely vivid, intense blue and bright red. During the classical period, when the sculptor's material of fine marble no longer needed to be hidden, they did not give up polychromy but the colours were more varied and less aggressive. Painting statues required skill and Praxiteles called on the services of one the greatest artists of the day, Nicias (q.v.). Other sculptural materials besides stone were painted; the remains of pale blue, pink and gold can still be detected on numerous terra-cotta figurines and a patina was brushed onto bronze whose effect is difficult to imagine.
                                                    P.D.

POLYCLETUS. Few Greek sculptors produced so little and there are few whose influence was so lasting and so profound. Many portrait sculptures of the Roman period are only more or less skilful adaptations or replicas of one of the rare statues that Polycletus cast in bronze.

He cannot, however, be credited with creating a new type. A Sicyonian by birth, he was trained in the school of the Argive master, Ageladas, became a citizen of Argos and remained faithful to the Peloponnesian tradition: his most famous works, the *Doryphoros*, about 445 B.C., and the *Diadumenos*, about fifteen years later, are recognisably the descendants of a long line of kouroi (q.v.). He was not content to give vitality to the eternal type of the kouros, as Calamis had already done at Athens, by breaking its immobility and stiffness, but had rethought, remodelled and made it the ideal of the male body perfected by athletics.

The Diadumenos. Roman copy of a bronze by Polycletus. About 400 B.C. Athens, National Museum.
Photo Spyros Meletzis.

Brought up on the Pythagorean theory of numbers, he had thought deeply on the question and his statues were the plastic illustrations of the *Canon,* the treatise he had written on the proportions of the human body. The initial module was, it seems, the breadth of the finger, but the Canon was something quite other than " a multiplication table that is both complicated and over-simple " (J. Charbonneaux); constant contact with nature modified the artificiality that might have resulted from a too strict dependence on geometry. Observation, too, corrected the errors of calculation and the Diadumenos is like a " recast and improved edition " of the Doryphoros.

The aim that Polycletus set himself inevitably made his statues look more or less alike; the monotony that the ancient Greeks accused him of can be explained by his desire to make all his figures perfect models whose exemplary qualities would be immediately obvious. He did everything so that the athlete could compare his own body with the sculptured image and correct his own imperfections accordingly; the head was bent slightly on one side to accentuate the line of the neck, the arms were held away from the body to free the chest completely, the legs gave an impression of both suppleness and strength.

Polycletus did not only represent the athlete in the prime of life; the gracious figure of an ephebe, the *Kyniskos,* was much admired and, when the priests of Ephesus held a competition for the figure of an *Amazon,* they preferred the work of Polycletus to that of Cresilas and Phidias. But as far as we can judge from replicas, these works were based on the same principles and embodied the same human ideal, which was that of Hellenism itself. P.D.

POLYCRATES. The most popular story about Polycrates is the instructive anecdote told by Herodotus, in which he tried in vain to cheat destiny by voluntarily sacrificing a precious ring to pay the lowest price for an excessive happiness that would certainly incur the wrath of Nemesis, the goddess of measure. This colourful character deserves better than just to be the hero of an edifying tale, invented at that. His father was a ship supplier and he himself was the head of industrial enterprises. About 533 B.C., he seized power by force in his native Samos at a period when the large island was flourishing. For some time the Samians had been making vases and textiles which the island sailors used to sell to the most distant ports of the Mediterranean, but the government was still in the hands of a landed aristocracy attached to privileges that its functions no longer justified, and traditionally linked with Miletus, the rival commercial city. Polycrates, with military aid from Lygdamis, the tyrant of Naxos, completely reduced the power of this nobility and did everything to enable Samos to hold the leading place on the international markets. Agriculture was encouraged, specially stock-farming; new breeds of sheep were imported, which must have been an asset to the textile industry. One of his most notable achievements was to organise a large emporium where the products of the whole Mediterranean world were exchanged. The reconstruction of the port encouraged sea-traffic and nothing was neglected to attract strangers; Polycrates even made Samos a pleasure resort where sailors liked to put into port. Improvements were made in the town and it was in the reign of Polycrates that Eupalinus built the aqueduct which made him famous. In its immediate environs, the sanctuary of Hera also benefited from Polycrates' attentions and the new temple he built rivalled the one at Ephesus in size and beauty.

Polycrates himself led a splendid existence. Surrounded by artists, scientists and poets (Anacreon was attached to his court), he lived a gay and luxurious life and, in consequence, earned a reputation that made him a suitable choice for the hero of the ring story. He realised that this prosperity could not be maintained if his country did not possess a military force. So he fortified the capital, engaged mercenaries and his fleet became the most powerful in the Aegean. At the same time, he negotiated alliances with Amasis, the king of Egypt, and Arcesilas, king of Cyrene. Through a combination of privateering and conquest, Samos exercised a hegemony over the Cyclades that also extended over the Anatolian coast as far as the region of Miletus. It roused the fear and jealousy of the other Greeks and the Lacedaemonians even besieged the town in 524 B.C. but without success. Ambition drove Polycrates to engage in a complicated policy to the east which was to prove fatal to him. Lured by the promise of a huge subsidy, he fell into an ambush set by the satrap of Magnesia and was crucified in 522. P.D.

POLYGNOTUS. None of Polygnotus's work has survived so we have to take the word of the early Greeks that he was one of the greatest painters at the beginning of the classical period between 475 and 440 B.C. We have a certain amount of information about him. He was born at Thasos, where his father, Aglaophon, had already been a painter. He painted two large compositions, the *Last night of Troy* and *Ulysses summoning the Dead* for the Cnidian Lesche, a large assembly hall at Delphi. He spent most of his life at Athens, where he was made an honorary citizen of the town because he had painted the Stoa Poikile without payment. He also executed a *Fight between Greeks and Amazons* and a *Battle of Marathon* for the Theseum. He occupied a high position in the city and it was said that Elpinike, the sister of the strategus, Cimon, was his mistress; but he returned before his death to his own country where his name appears on a list of magistrates.

Aristotle praised the moral tone of his works and Pliny informs us that he was the first to give expression to faces and render the transparency of clothes. He tried to suggest space by placing his figures on different planes, while his predecessors had lined them up, one in front of the other. After 460, the innovations credited to him were introduced into vase painting which indicates their immediate success with the public.

P.D.

POLYNICES. Polynices was the brother of Eteocles and became his rival in the struggle for power at Thebes, after Oedipus had left. *(See* Seven against Thebes).

POLYPHEMUS. Like his brothers, the other Cyclopes, Polyphemus only had one eye and lived like them on the produce of his herds, isolated from civilisation. Like them, too, he was a savage and, in the island where he lived, he used to capture strangers and eat them with relish. When Ulysses, driven by a storm, landed on his estates, Polyphemus shut him up with his companions in the cave where he lived and each evening ate two of the unfortunate Greeks. As the first move in his plan of escape, Ulysses first offered him wine, a new drink to the Cyclops which he liked but which sent him to sleep. The shipwrecked sailors took advantage of his stupor to sharpen a stake, which they thrust into the only eye of the monster, then escaped in the morning by holding on to the bellies of the Cyclops' rams when he let them out of the cave as usual. His gigantic fingers groped over the backs of the sheep in vain; Ulysses, with his surviving companions, gained his freedom and took to the sea.

The refined culture of the Hellenistic period turned Polyphemus into the bashful lover of the nymph, Galatea.

P.D.

POLYXENA. Polyxena is one of the most touching figures of the Trojan story. She was one of the numerous daughters of Priam and Hecuba. Before the ruin of her country, she was involved in an episode that was often illustrated by artists. One day when she was accompanying her young brother, Troilus, to fetch water from a fountain outside the city walls, the two children were attacked by Achilles, who was lying in wait to kill

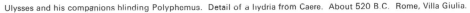
Ulysses and his companions blinding Polyphemus. Detail of a hydria from Caere. About 520 B.C. Rome, Villa Giulia.

Achilles, Polyxena and Troilus at the fountain. Detail of a Laconian dinos. 6th century B.C. Paris, Louvre.

them. The little Troilus lost his life and Polyxena only saved hers by running away. Her escape only delayed her eventual fate, because when Troy was taken, she was sacrificed, some say by Neoptolemus, others by all the Greek chiefs, on the tomb of the savage Achilles who, even in death, still demanded victims. P.D.

PONTUS EUXINUS. The sea which the Greeks called the Pontus Euxinus, or the " Hospitable Sea ", is the Black Sea. It was an antiphrastic designation inspired by the hope of placating by this flattery a sea that is still feared by sailors today. The voyage through the winds sweeping from the steppes must have been hard for the colonists who, as early as the 8th century B.C., came mainly from Miletus and founded numerous settlements on the north coast in the Crimea and Bessarabia, many of which grew into flourishing cities. They were the intermediaries, in fact, that carried on the profitable exchanges between mainland Greece, whose only wealth was her industry, and the vast territories of southern Russia, where there was an unlimited wheat supply and timber, and where the Scythian princes were eager to sell slaves in exchange for artists to adorn the precious gold objects that have been found in their tombs. P.D.

PORPHYRY. Porphyry was born at Tyre in 234 A.D. and went about 254 to study in Athens. He learnt grammar, mathematics and specially philosophy with Longinus. It may have been on the advice of Longinus himself that he

went to Rome in 263 in his thirtieth year to study the philosophy of Plotinus (q.v.). Plotinus's teaching was a constant appeal to a spiritual life culminating in ecstasy. In this atmosphere of psychic tension, Porphyry was probably exhausted by excessive asceticism and mystical concentration. In 268, he suffered from neurosis and contemplated suicide. One of his biographers, Eunapius, said: " He resented the fact that he had a body and was a man. " Plotinus realised this spiritual crisis and advised him to travel, so he left for Sicily and stayed at Lilybaeum. Plotinus died in 270. Porphyry then probably returned to Rome and succeeded his master. About this time, he married Marcella, the widow of a philosopher. In 301, he wrote the *Life of Plotinus* and issued the complete edition of his master's works, arranged in artificial groups under the title of *Enneads*. He died shortly afterwards, probably between 301 and 310.

His commentaries on Plato and Aristotle have nearly all been lost, but there have survived either whole, or in fragments: a vegetarian treatise, *De Abstinentia;* a little manual of pagan piety, *Ad Marcellam,* in the form of a letter to his wife; a short but important treatise on logic, generally called the *Isagogus*. His major work, *Adversus Christianos*, is the most weighty refutation of Christianity that Hellenism produced. Porphyry takes up his main position on history and literary criticism; for him " the evangelists were the inventors, not the historians, of the things they relate about Jesus ", so he set out to stress all the contradictions and discrepancies to be found

The Athenian Stoa at
Delphi. 478 B.C.
Photo Hassia.

in the Old and New Testament. His criticism also extended to the dogmas, sacraments and life of the Church. Porphyry was one of the masters of the west and had a decisive influence on the development of medieval thought.   P.H.

PORTICO. Porticoes were an important feature of ancient Greece. These long open galleries, one wall of which was replaced by a row of columns, were airy and shady, and they provided shelter from wind, rain and sudden storms. They were a meeting place for friends, where the latest news circulated, where one could relax in the hottest part of the day and where sellers set out their wares. They were, in fact, one of the most indispensable of the public buildings; they were built at sanctuaries as resting places for pilgrims, near theatres to shelter the spectators if the performance was interrupted by a storm, and round the agora in cities. In their simplest form they were just canopies, but when they were dedicated at Delphi or Olympia by a city; or, like the one at Delos, the munificent gift of a king anxious to win popularity, porticoes were given majestic proportions. The finest, like the portico given to the Athenians by Attalus II, king of Pergamum from 159 to 138 B.C., comprised a storey and their width required a second row of columns

along the axis of the building to support the roof.
          P.D.

PORTS. As the resources of the Greeks, who were a sea-faring people, depended almost entirely on sea-borne trade, they were forced at an early period to prepare harbours along the shores they used. For quite a long time their ships were so small that they found it quite satisfactory to haul them onto the shore when they landed for the evening, but this primitive practice was obviously inadequate after a while. Many towns were built along well-sheltered bays, which provided a safe anchorage, but security and convenience required artificial constructions as well and, in fact, the remains of several harbour installations have been discovered. Breakwaters were built between the two arms of a bight to protect them against high seas and enemy attack. The natural rock was used as far as possible in the construction of the breakwaters, which were planned on the same principles as buildings on firm land. These walls of hewn stone were given solid foundations and, like those at Thasos and elsewhere, were often real fortifications. If necessary, the sea-bed was excavated to give ships an adequate draught. Ideally, the passage between the two breakwaters was so arranged that pilots did not have to

Poseidon wearing a chlamys and brandishing his trident. Silver stater of Poseidonia. About 540 B.C. Naples, Museo Nazionale. *Photo Leonard von Matt.*

struggle against winds and currents. Sometimes to prevent sanding up, narrower openings were left in the mole so that the waves could wash away the gradual accumulation of sand.

The Greeks generally built different ports for their naval boats and the commercial shipping. They thought nothing of making more than one; Piraeus had three, Syracuse had two, one of which was immense. The largest and most convenient were at Alexandria, where the island of Pharos was joined to the town by a sea-wall on either side of which were two ports.

The quays were planned skilfully and thoughtfully. Warehouses and repositories naturally found a place on them, but there were also cultural and civic buildings which gave a liveliness to the shipping world, probably similar to the bustle of the great Mediterranean ports of our own day.

P.D.

POSEIDON. Poseidon was the brother of Zeus and probably, as in the Mycenaean royal families, occupied a rather inferior position. The realm of the waters fell to his share; he ruled over the seas and the ocean, but it seemed that he also held sway over the rivers, springs and lakes.

Subsidiary divinities, like Nereus, were under his orders and his wife, Amphitrite, shared the undersea empire with him. Armed with the trident which was his attribute, he stirred up the waves into violent movement that " shook the earth ". The more or less transitory liaisons that he had with goddesses and mortals generally produced monstrous beings like the Cyclops, Polyphemus, Pegasus, the brigand Sciron whom Theseus killed, or Orion, the accursed hunter. Poseidon was honoured particularly by sailors, who often dreaded him and everyone knows how relentlessly he persecuted Ulysses on his return journey to Ithaca. He was a majestic looking god; artists gave him very much the same appearance as Zeus and, when his trident is missing, it is hard to distinguish him from his brother. P.D.

POSIDONIUS. Posidonius (135-51 B.C.) was born at Apamea on the Orontes. He studied at Athens and was taught by Panaetius, then he settled in Rhodes, where he opened a famous school, which was visited by Pompey and Cicero. When he became prytanis of the city, he was sent to Rome as ambassador in 86. His extensive travels in the west took him to Gaul and Spain, as far as the Atlantic. Only a few fragments of his encyclopaedic work have survived. Seneca discussed his theory of the origins of civilisation which attributed all the major inventions to the sages. As a historian, he continued the work of Polybius. His geographical works were often quoted by Strabo. He evolved a theory that explained tides by the influence of the sun and the moon, in conformity with the Stoic conception of universal sympathy. Posidonius was also a mathematician and astronomer and constructed a planetarium. In psychology, he discussed the radical intellectualism of Chrysippus and worked out a theory of the passions which we know about through Galen. This synthesis of knowledge was crowned by a mythology, the substance of which is still discussed by scholars. Several of them have thought that a mystic eschatology can be deduced from his work. He seems to have subordinated fate to Zeus through nature as an intermediary, instead of making them identical as the early Stoics had done. P.-M.S.

PRAXITELES. Praxiteles was one of the most admired and imitated artists of ancient times. He was an Athenian, the son of a good sculptor, Cephisodotus, whom we know through replicas of an allegorical group, *Peace bringing Abundance,* executed in 375 B.C. We know hardly anything of Praxiteles' personal life. His activity stretched over the second quarter of the 4th century B.C., probably ending about 330 or 320. He seems to have enjoyed a certain position in Athenian society; he was rich and admired. His liaison with the courtesan, Phryne, who was probably his model, is the only striking episode in his life that has been handed down from antiquity.

He owed his lasting success to the fact that he gave expression to the contemporary taste for grace and elegance. His age was tired of the rational austerity of past times and his work embodied the reaction towards sensuousness. He did not produce statues of athletes, or majestic and severe divinities, but he never grew tired of sculpting the features of young, handsome gods, modelled from the more graceful bodies of young women and ephebi: Apollo, a slightly ambiguous Apollo perhaps, with his long hair and rather broad hips *(Apollo Sauroctonos),* sometimes

Torso of the Aphrodite of Cnidos. Roman copy of an original by Praxiteles. Mid-4th century B.C. Paris, Louvre. *Photo Sougez.*

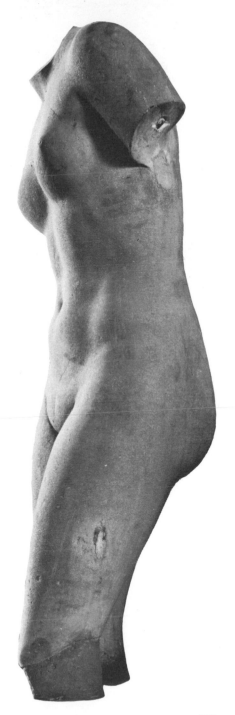

Aphrodite of Arles. Roman copy of an original by
Praxiteles. About 350-330 B.C. Paris, Louvre. *Ph. Sougez.*

Hermes holding the infant Dionysus. About 350-330 B.C.
Olympia Museum. *Photo H. Müller-Brunke.*

Artemis *(Diana of Gabii),* Hermes *(Hermes of
Olympia),* and particularly Eros, the god of Love,
and his mother Aphrodite. One of his works
caused a scandal. This was the Aphrodite erected
at Cnidos; no veil covered her beauty; the humanity
of the goddess, represented as a beautiful model,
and her complete nudity were something quite
new at the time. The Greeks were certainly not
prudish and there had always been lascivious
scenes depicted in their art, but because they were
used to seeing courtesans undressed, they were
all the more shocked to see a similar freedom
associated with a goddess. In spite of this, the
Aphrodite of Cnidos was afterwards the most

imitated and reproduced statue of the Hellenic and Roman worlds. Praxiteles represented Aphrodite in other attitudes; the *Aphrodite of Arles* in the Louvre, half draped with a garment slipping over her hips, is a copy of one of his finest creations.

Praxiteles embodied the same ideal of feminine beauty in all these statues; there was nothing delicate in their strong, well rounded forms. Delicacy of proportion was reserved for the slender neck, supporting the small, sharply defined head, which was adorned with the complicated convolutions of a hair-style ending in a thick knot on the nape of the neck. It was a sensual image possessing little sensitiveness; the features of the face, tight mouth and hard eyes suggested some of the malice that inspired Mérimée's short story, *La Vénus d'Ille.*   P.D.

P R I A M . In Greek art and literature, Priam appears as a majestic figure who played a rather unobtrusive part in Troy, which he reigned, compared to Hector, the most valiant of his fifty sons. He was the husband of Hecuba and a benevolent, pious patriarch who accepted in his family the presence of Helen, the cause of so much misfortune. He watched the youngest of his sons, Troilus, fall under the blows of Achilles, went to the savage hero to plead in person for the corpse of Hector and, on the fatal night when Troy fell, was killed himself by Neoptolemus beside the altar where he had taken refuge.
                                                          P.D.

P R I E N E . Priene, the neighbouring town to Miletus on the coast of Asia Minor, had very little historical importance; its real interest today is in the way its inhabitants adapted the plan of their new town to an extremely hilly site when they were forced to leave the old site which was covered with sand from the River Maeander. There was a difference in level of nearly a thousand feet between the highest and lowest points of the new Priene. They preferred to make a fair number of streets into stairways rather than abandon the regular square network characteristic of town-planning in the preceding century. The result was that movement in vehicles was practically impossible.

From the middle of geometrically divided areas of houses, there rose public buildings. some of which, like the Bouleuterion, or the Senate House are among the best preserved, the finest and most interesting architecture of this period. The site, perched on a precipitous hill, is superb and it is a curious experience today to walk through the almost intact streets of the dead city.   P.D.

P R I E S T . A priest among the Greeks was not, as in religions familiar to us, a man called by a personal vocation to divine service. He was an ordinary individual, a citizen like any other, who was designated sometimes by heredity, more often by election or even drawing of lots to fulfil in the name of the community the rites and ceremonies required by a god. During the period of monarchical regimes, the sovereign naturally served as the intermediary between his people and the immortals, just as within the family the functions of officiant normally devolved on the father. When monarchies disappeared, the attributes of the sovereign were divided between different persons. Although the notion of priestly functions, invested in the king subsisted in an archon-king, or Basileus, at Athens who bore the main responsibility for religious affairs, priests, like magistrates, were appointed, not for their suitability, but by the hazards of voting or drawing lots and, like them, they were temporary because most of their powers were limited to a year. No one was barred from the priesthood, unless he had committed a serious offence against the city that would have deprived him of all civic rights and severed him from the community. Some cults, particularly the mysteries (q.v.), would very likely have had permanent officiants, recruited from a few privileged families, who normally succeeded from father to son, but this was exceptional. Apart from his conduct of ceremonies, nothing distinguished the priest from the mass of citizens. When he was officiating, he carried a crown on his head or some other attribute; the rest of the time, he mixed with the crowds and was dressed like them. No special qualifications were required of him either. As religion was completely formal, there were no theological problems, no points of conscience to clear up, no moral advice to preach and no sermons. Everything was comprised in the fulfilment of certains customs and the practice, which did not have to be consistent, of a purely outward rectitude.

The business of the priest was to serve the divinity. He was responsible for the preservation of the statue, the upkeep of the temple, its orderliness and cleaning the sanctuary. He had a whole staff under his authority who did the menial jobs; for example, Euripides shows the young Ion sweeping out the house of the god. He administered the property of the god under a commission, the equivalent of the modern parish council. This property was of all kinds; it not only covered the offerings of the faithful, but might also include land, sometimes built on, slaves, etc. Finally, the priest presided over the ceremonies which were not, as in some religions today, weekly or daily, but were performed on fixed dates or at the request of an individual. The sacrifices were the most important part of these. Professionals generally killed the victims; the priests, whose presence was not always necessary, merely pronounced the formulas and accomplished the movements prescribed by the ritual. There was no need for a long apprenticeship for this either; the priest had not only watched the ceremony performed since his childhood, his assistants and perhaps manuals were there to guide him.

In certain places, the priesthood was neither so simple nor so flexible as this; age limits were imposed in some (we know that some cults were ministered by children) and celibacy was obligatory, especially for women, in others. None of this necessarily applies to the priesthood of the non-official, Asiatic and Egyptian religions, which were being introduced into the Greek world as early as the 5th century B.C.; their priests were governed by rules decreed by the barbarian religions that foreigners had imported into Greece itself.

P.D.

PROCLUS. Proclus was one of the last Neoplatonists of the School of Athens. He was probably born in 412 A.D. at Byzantium of Lycian parents. When he was very young they took him to Xanthus in Lycia, where he studied at first. He continued at Alexandria and, when he was about twenty, landed at Piraeus to complete his philosophical training at Athens. He became a follower of Plutarch and Syrianus, then succeeded these two masters. Except for a brief visit to Asia Minor, he stayed in Athens and devoted himself to teaching and writing. He died in 485 and was buried with Syrianus near Mount Lycabettus. Marinus, his successor, wrote a biography, divided according to the Neoplatonic hierarchy of virtues, which is full of remarkable events.

A considerable amount of Proclus's work survives. Among his most important productions are two epitomes, one fairly short, the *Elements of Theology*, the other much fuller, the *Platonic*

Theology; the commentaries on Plato's *Parmenides, Timaeus, Republic, Alcibiades* and *Cratylus;* the commentary on the first book of Euclid's *Elements;* and three short treatises on Evil, Fate and Providence.

Before forming an idea of Proclus's thought it must be remembered that he was mainly concerned, like Plotinus, with interpreting and keeping alive the teaching of Plato, but in the face of new problems he had to develop and refashion Platonism. He tried to find a place for everything valid in the work of philosophers (Aristotle and the Stoics, for example) since Plato. Besides this, he endeavoured to incorporate the religious ideas introduced from the east and reinvigorate the mythological traditions of antiquity which were threatened by the rising tide of Christianity. Consequently, the work of Proclus is perhaps the richest synthesis we possess of Greek Neoplatonism.

J.T.

PRODICUS. Prodicus was a sophist of the 5th century B.C., born at Iulis in the island of Ceos. He went to Athens several times on embassies. Aristophanes paid tribute to his " knowledge and wisdom ". Prodicus was the author of the famous apologue of Heracles standing at the fork of two roads, one the way to Vice, the other to Virtue. Socrates thought his moral philosophy was sound and sent pupils to him. Where rhetoric and style were concerned, he analysed the distinction between words of similar meaning to the point of pedantry, as we can see in Plato's *Protagoras*. No doubt his struggles towards precision of vocabulary were praiseworthy and useful.

R.F.

PROMETHEUS. Prometheus was the son of a Titan, Iapetus; Atlas and Epimetheus were his brothers and Zeus his cousin. His relations with his cousin, the Lord of the Universe, were so bad that Prometheus has been made into the symbol of humanity's revolt against the gods. In fact, the ancient Greeks did not see such a profound significance in this figure, who was rather the embodiment of ingeniousness and guile for them, though admittedly these were in the service of mortals. Zeus was twice tricked by Prometheus. One day during a sacrifice, Prometheus asked him to choose the part of the victim he preferred and the remainder should be given to men. Zeus chose what seemed to be the best morsel but it turned out to be cleverly disguised fat and bones. Another time, Prometheus stole a spark of fire, either from the chariot of the sun or from the forge of Hephaestus, because Zeus had deprived men of it to revenge himself for the deception of the sacrificial meat. The punishment was terrible. He chained Prometheus to a rock in the Caucasus and sent an eagle to eat away his liver which always grew again. The torment would have continued for all eternity if Heracles had not killed the eagle with an arrow. According to some traditions, it was Prometheus and not Hephaestus who fashioned the first men from clay.

P.D.

PROPERTY. The only form of property known to the early ages of Greece was landed property, that of the earth, the fruits it bears and the cattle that graze on it. The Homeric poems reflect the memory of a time when that property did not belong to an individual but to a family and was consequently inalienable, since it had to be transmitted intact to following generations. After this, the principle of joint possession ceased to be sacrosanct. Paris left his father to build his own house, others marked out a field for themselves in waste land and, when the collective responsibility of the family was involved, even communal property was sometimes cut up.

In this way, the conception of personal property evolved but not without difficulties. Hesiod describes the lamentable plight of small landowners who, as a result of a bad harvest or some other misfortune, borrowed money by mortgaging their ground and, crushed by the weight of a debt that increased ceaselessly with the exorbitant interest rates of the times, they not only had to surrender it to the rich men who had advanced them the profits on their crops, but often had to repay the loan they had contracted with their liberty. This state of things had a good deal to do with the pressure on thousands of colonists to leave their homeland. It had much, too, to do with the establishment in several cities of tyrannies that tried to win the support of humble people by relieving their poverty.

It was not a tyrant, however, but the sage, Solon, who passed a law at Athens, forbidding imprisonment for debt and, although its precise application remains obscure, it succeeded in freeing mortgaged land, though probably it did not go so far as to abolish debts entirely. Not content with this reform, which seems to have settled the social question, he tried to hasten the break-up of overlarge estates into small holdings in order to give an opportunity of possessing land to a greater number of citizens; he decreed that the principle of joint possession was not obligatory and gave the right of inheritance, not only to the eldest son but also to the younger ones and to daughters; if the dead man had no legitimate son, his illegiti-

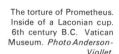
The torture of Prometheus. Inside of a Laconian cup. 6th century B.C. Vatican Museum. *Photo Anderson-Viollet.*

West front of the Propylaea on the Acropolis at Athens, built by Mnesicles. 437-432 B.C. *Photo Hassia.*

mate sons could claim his goods or the testator could even bequeath his lands to someone outside the family.

This instituted the era of small and average size properties guaranteed by the law. Each year when he entered on his office, the archon proclaimed by herald that " what each possesses he shall continue to possess as absolute master ", and the oath sworn by members of the Heliaea contained the following: " I will not consent either to an abolition of private debts or to a division of lands and houses belonging to the citizens ". The phrase " to the citizens " was clearly specified because only they had the right to possess land. Metics were excluded, but other forms of ownership were open to them, notably in industry and business.

As in everything, conditions in Sparta differed radically from those at Athens. There the whole belt around the city was state property. The head of each family was given a lot and another lot was added to this in Messenia. It was this lot, worked by helots, which provided the livelihood of the family. However, his possessions were not limited to this small holding; if he was rich enough, the Spartan could acquire, outside the city zone in conquered territory, his own land which he could do what he liked with and leave to his children. P.D.

PROPYLAEUM. In Greek this denotes any monumental entrance, but it suggests to us before anything else, just as it did to the Greeks, the edifice erected by Mnesicles (q.v.) between 437 and 432 B.C. on the Acropolis at Athens. These Propylaea (they are always in the plural because their importance led to the designing of a complex and multiple building) replaced a more humble building, dating from the time of Pisistratus, whose modest appearance was no longer suitable for the grand architectural ensemble that Pericles planned. They dominated the top of a steep slope which pilgrims climbed along a winding path. At the end of it were two wings that projected from the portico like arms welcoming the crowds. This portico, in the Doric order, was the approach to a hall, open to the exterior on the west side but enclosed on the other three sides, whose ceiling was supported by slender Ionic columns. Here visitors could rest a while after their stiff climb. The far wall on the east separated the profane world from the sacred precinct. It was pierced by five doors; the largest one in the centre communicated with a ramp provided for the sacrificial victims, while the other four were used by people. A second Doric portico, opening onto the sanctuary, formed the counterpart on the east to the one on the west. Mnesicles had planned widely splayed wings projecting from this building but, probably from lack of funds, the design was only partially realised; the room, called the Pinakotheke, used for exhibiting the work of great painters, was part of it. Even incomplete as they remained, the Propylaea of the Acropolis were much admired by the ancient Greeks who imitated them at Lindus on the island of Rhodes, and Epaminondas would have liked to have transported them to the citadel of Thebes. They not only admired them for their dignity and simplicity, but also for the skill of the architect who had adapted his design to the irregularities of a sloping site. He was admired, too, for the way he had combined the whiteness of Pentelic marble with the black Eleusinian limestone of the plinths. P.D.

PROTAGORAS. Philosopher and rhetorician (485-411 B.C.), born at Abdera in Thrace. Protagoras was one of the most famous sophists of his time. He went several times to Athens where he met Pericles. He made his pupils pay as much as a hundred minas, or ten thousand drachmas, for a course of lessons. At the beginning of the *Protagoras,* Plato conveys some of the intense excitement caused by the arrival of the celebrated teacher among the young Athenians. He was condemned for impiety at Athens about 416. He was drowned in a shipwreck.

The agnosticism of Protagoras had points in common with the scepticism of Gorgias. His most famous saying is: " Man is the measure of all things. " In language and the art of speaking, Protagoras was primarily a grammarian and a logician. His followers learnt how to use words precisely and build up apparently irrefutable arguments. R.F.

PROTEUS. Proteus was a servant of Poseidon and a sea-god who looked after the herds of seals. He possessed the gift of prophecy and, like other legendary water beings, he could metamorphose himself into fire and water as well as into an animal. Menelaus, however, succeeded in mastering him and extracting answers to his questions. P.D.

PROXENOS. Ambassadors (q.v.) were only appointed for the temporary duration of their mission; permanent international relations were maintained by the *proxenoi.* Strictly speaking, they were only " hosts " *(xenoi)* and *proxenia* was a particular example of ancient Greek hospitality. Their function corresponded more closely to that of the modern consul than to that of our ambassadors, but they did not belong to the nation whose interests they were protecting; Callias, the proxenos of Sparta at Athens was an Athenian on whom Lacedaemonia had conferred this honour, which was also a financial responsibility.

It was an honour because when Callias went to Sparta, he enjoyed a special status. We possess thousands of decrees of proxenia that enumerate the privileges of the proxenos. The most usual for him and his descendants were exemption from taxes, inviolability of the person, the right to a place of honour *(proedria)* at all the festivals organised by the state, and the ability to acquire land and a house. At Athens the proxenoi were entertained at the Prytaneum.

It was a financial responsibility because the proxenos had to bear heavy expenses. He had to provide financial assistance and protection for citizens from the city he represented and sometimes even board them in his own home. He also had to stand surety for them and help them in all the commercial transactions in which they were involved. Obviously his obligations were even greater to the ambassadors of the city he represented; he not only had to present them to the Senate and Assembly, he also had to provide board and lodging for them.

During the Hellenistic and Roman periods, when the cities had lost their independence, the office of proxenos became purely honorary, but it was nonetheless sought after. R.F.

PRYTANEUM. In primitive Greece, the fire that burnt night and day in the house of the chief, or prytanis (q.v.), was not only the family fire; it symbolised the continuity of the state. This was why, even after the fall of the monarchies, the place where the communal fire burnt was called the prytaneum and those who looked after it, the prytaneis.

Although it was a sacred place in the city, the prytaneum was not a temple. Sacrifices were offered there, but no other form of worship was celebrated; it remained a secular edifice, which explains its simplicity and the variety of its plan. This was designed large enough to accommodate the associated functions exercised by the prytaneis. If more space was required, they did not hesitate, as the example of Athens proves, to construct other buildings, independent of the place where the fire burned and sometimes quite far from it, which were used for the administrative and political activities of the prytaneis. The long accepted idea that prytaneums were always built on a circular plan has been contradicted by the facts.   P.D.

PRYTANIS. The original meaning of *prytanis*, like archon, was someone who commanded and Zeus was still described by Aeschylus as a prytanis. Like the archon (q.v.), as the states evolved, it was not long before the prytanis became a highly placed magistrate with particular functions.

We know most about the functions and status of the prytanis at Athens, specially from the beginning of the 5th century B.C. For the entire period of 35 to 39 days that constituted a *prytaneia,* the fifty senators, from one of the ten tribes instituted by Cleisthenes (q.v.), represented the whole people. These were the prytaneis. Every day one of them, chosen by lot and eligible once only, held for twenty-four hours the symbols of authority, the state seals and the keys of the public Treasury. They assumed as a body the administrative, political and religious responsibilities of the state and, although these remained distinct from the executive powers, they made them one of the highest authorities in the state. They looked after the perpetually lighted hearth of the goddess, Hestia, which was probably their original function; foreign ambassadors were presented to them; it was their duty to fix and announce the dates of assemblies, settle the agenda and preside over them. They took their meals in common at the expense of the state; the representatives of foreign powers and citizens chosen for their exceptional distinction were invited to dine with them. The man who had been singled out by lot as their leader spent the night in the place where he and his colleagues had held their sessions. The place, whose site has been discovered in the agora quite near the Bouleuterion, the Senate House, looked like a large house at first. After the sack of Athens by the Persians in 480 B.C., it was rebuilt quite modestly on a circular plan. It was called the Skias, or more commonly, the Tholos. It was distinct from the Prytaneum, properly so called, which was somewhere at the foot of the Acropolis, but we do not know the exact site.   P.D.

PSYCHE. Psyche, whose name in Greek means " soul ", only acquired a literary personality in later times. She was a young girl who was visited every evening in a wonderful place by a lover who refused to reveal his identity or to let her see him. One time, she disobeyed his order, leaned over him in his sleep and recognised Eros himself. But a drop of oil fell on him from her lamp and woke up the god, who disappeared forever. Psyche set off in search of him and became the prisoner of Aphrodite, who was jealous of the young girl's happiness, but she bore courageously the misfortunes that befell her. Eros helped her secretly and the two lovers were eventually happily united.   P.D.

PTOLEMY (1). Ptolemy was the name borne by the sovereigns of the Lagides (q.v.) dynasty who reigned over Egypt after the death of Alexander.

PTOLEMY (2). Claudius Ptolemaeus, commonly known as Ptolemy, was the last and most famous of the great astronomers of antiquity. Nothing is known of his life except that he worked at Alexandria from 127 to 151 A.D. Besides his famous *Guide to Geography* and two treatises on *Optics* and on music, the *Harmonica,* we possess four of his astronomical works; the most important is the *Mathematike Syntaxis,* generally known as the *Almagest,* from the name given it by Arab scholars, which is a complete survey of the geocentric system; the *Planetary Hypothesis* is a corrected summary of his theory of the planets; the *Phases of the Fixed Stars* is a calendar of the rising and setting of the stars, established for five different latitudes; and the *Catalogue of the Stars,* which is fuller than Hipparchus's and arranged according to original calculations of co-ordinates. He also compiled the *Tetrabiblos,* a compendium of Hellenistic astrology, which combined some discoveries of scientific astronomy with the fossilised methods of Babylonian origin currently used in astrology. Ptolemy has often been accused of borrowing all the material of his work from his predecessors without acknowledgment, but careful investigations have brought to light his personal contribution, which is considerable. His principal achievement is to have completed the detailed theory of the planets begun by Hipparchus, which was based on eccentric circles and epicycles *(See* Astronomy). Hipparchus had done the work on the sun and moon; Ptolemy fundamentally reshaped the theory on the moon and elaborated that on the five little planets He introduced into their six systems, comprising the eccentric and epicycle, a third circle called the equant whose centre did not coincide with that of the eccentric. The circular movement of the epicycle on the eccentric was constant in relation to the centre of the equant but not in relation to the centre of the eccentric. By doing this, he had shaken the principle of uniformly circular movement, while actually trying to keep it as a basis, and behaved like a true scholar, at least by modifying it according to observed phenomena. It is this strict respect for observed phenomena that led him to discover the evection and nutation of the moon and to calculate its parallax.   J.B.

PURIFICATION. Every act of worship required that the participants should be in a state of purity. It was a physical and corporal purity obtained by aspergation or immersion, not by confession or an examination of conscience, and Greek piety attached considerable importance to it. At the entrance to sacred places, sanctuaries and even agoras, bowls were placed filled with water, which had been drawn as prescribed from special springs, and everyone going into these places, like a Catholic entering a church today, had to wet his fingers, at least as a symbol. Before praying, the worshipper purified himself similarly with water, just as the victim was sprinkled before sacrifice, or anyone entering a death-chamber.

Although water could wash away the superficial defilements that life necessarily left, there was one impurity it could not cleanse, that of blood-shedding. Except in war, even involuntary murder made the murderer a danger to anyone approaching him, not in the sense in which we speak of a "public enemy", but because its pollution was a miasma that was infectious; like a plague victim, he contaminated everything he touched until a solemn purification had made him a normal human being again. This purification from blood-shedding had to be performed with blood, which was sprinkled from a sacrificial victim, just as Apollo, the chief deity of purification, had cleansed Orestes by splashing him with the blood of a young pig.   P.D.

PYLOS. A short time ago we only knew of the splendour of Pylos, the capital of Triphylia, from literary sources, specially Homer. Excavations on the west coast of the Peloponnesus have recently dug up the remains of a Mycenaean palace proving that tradition had not misled us. Its architecture was similar to that of other sites of the same period. The most important find was a large number of inscribed tablets which the deciphering of Linear B (q.v.) has enabled us to study. They have already begun to give us precious information on this period only known until now through archaeological remains.   P.D.

PYRRHON and the SCEPTICS. Pyrrhon of Elis, the Sceptic model, was the contemporary of Theophrastus (4th century B.C.). Like Socrates, he wrote nothing down. His pupil, Timon of Phlius, in his praise of him, placed him higher than any other philosopher. Pyrrhon seems to have absorbed on the one hand the Socratic tradition transmitted by the philosophers of Elis (school of Phaedon) and the Megarics (Bryson); and, on the other, the ideas of Democritus (q.v.) tinged with Cyrenaic thought *(See* Aristippus) through Anaxarchus of Abdera, whom he joined to follow Alexander's expedition to the east. There he witnessed the spiritual strength of the fakirs or gymnosophists. It was probably this third influence that induced Pyrrhon to interpret for the Greeks " the Hindu ideal of renunciation both in meditation and practice " (L. Robin). His contemporaries were struck by his imperturbable impassivity *(ataraxia),* his gentleness and quietude. He counselled silence *(aphasia)* and indifference, " no more this than that ", while still conforming to the way of life led by his fellow-citizens.

In the 3rd and 2nd centuries B.C., the New Academy of Arcesilaus and Carneades, in its struggle against Stoic dogmatism, gave a Sceptic interpretation to Platonism as well as to " Socratic ignorance ", which ended in a relativist attitude. This school, however, should be distinguished from the Sceptic school proper. In the 1st century B.C., Aenesidemus of Cnossos, who lived at Alexandria *(See* Medicine, Empiric) wrote some *Pyrrhonian Discourses* and classified the main types of argument that demonstrate the relativity of understanding and the consequent impossibility of dogmatic assertion. These were the ten *tropoi,* or modes, for the suspension of judgment *(epoche):* variations of perception due to distance, age, state of health, frequency, etc.; variations in moral judgments and criticisms of causal reasoning. The list of tropoi was subsequently condensed and reduced to five, then two: the criticism of evidence and the criticism of demonstration.

At the end of the 2nd and beginning of the 3rd centuries A.D. the physician, Sextus Empiricus, gave a very full account of Sceptic thought: the *Outlines of Pyrrhonism* and another work which is a criticism of the principal philosophical and scientific systems of antiquity. While the first Sceptics were mainly preoccupied with moral questions and although Sextus, too, recommended the moderation and quietude that derives from the suspension of judgment, he was primarily concerned with methodology. He pointed out the absence of any valid criterion of truth, and demonstrated the inadequacy of the syllogism, where the major premiss is only true if the conclusion is verified, and of causal reasoning. True to the spirit of empirical medicine (q.v.), he contented himself with observing the existence of concomitances and consecutions, which anticipated the positive approach that was eventually adopted by science.   P.-M.S.

PYRRHUS. The life of Pyrrhus, king of Epirus from 307 to 272 B.C., is the life of an extraordinary adventurer, which would provide all the ingredients for a spectacular film: distant expeditions, courage and generosity, brilliant actions including a set battle-piece in which a charge of elephants threw panic into the ranks of the Roman army. Opposite him would play his adviser, the diplomat Cineas, with the artificially conventional features of an old man with a long beard, who utters the maxims of Plutarch and counsels of moderation that we should expect

from the wisdom of antiquity. Nothing of this would be fundamentally false.

Episodes abound, in fact, in the career of this warrior who could not bear inaction and was always ready for the most daring enterprises. When he was two years old, his father was overthrown by a revolt and Pyrrhus was carried secretly over a river in full spate to the king of Illyria, Glaucias, who took pity on the small child and refused to hand him over to the rebels. At the age of twelve, he was able to ascend his father's throne, but was driven from it in 302. He then went to Asia Minor to his brother-in-law, Demetrius Poliorcetes, and fought beside him at the battle of Ipsus (301) in which the former generals of Alexander were ranged against each other. In spite of his youth (he was thirteen years old then), he distinguished himself by his courage. Demetrius lost and entrusted Pyrrhus with the government of Achaea and Argolis, then sent him as a hostage to Alexandria where he stayed for two years. Although the young man was accustomed to the rough life of Epirus and Illyria, he was able to adapt himself to the refined atmosphere of the court; Ptolemy II appreciated his gifts and Berenice gave him the hand of Antigone, the daughter of her first marriage. He was given the means to win back his throne and at the age of twenty-two firmly established himself in his own kingdom of Epirus. As soon as he felt strong enough to intervene in international politics, he contracted further marriages with barbarian princesses, broke with Demetrius, penetrated into Macedonia, proclaimed himself king of this country (288) and invaded Thessaly, but was driven back to his own territory in 285. Various annexations enlarged Epirus, towards the north and south, and in 281 he responded to the appeal of the Tarentines who were looking for an ally against Rome. He embarked on a series of expeditions, overcame the Romans at Heraclea by using the elephants, negotiated with the vanquished army, then sped to the help of Sicily, threatened by Carthage, and proclaimed himself king. A defeat in front of the town of Lilybaeum forced him to retreat into Magna Graecia where he pillaged the sanctuary of Persephone at Locris. He was compelled to abandon Italy in 275. On his return to Epirus, he began to pursue his old ambitions again, became king of Macedonia a second time, penetrated deep into Greece, crossed the Peloponnesus, but failed to take Sparta. He then turned towards Argos and it was during street fighting there in

272 that he lost his life, killed by a tile thrown by an old woman from the roof of her house.

It was a strange fate which has inspired the most contradictory judgments from his day to our own. He has been compared to Alexander. His life was certainly no less romantic than the great conqueror's and perhaps it was only a perverse fate that turned an exceptional character and a warrior full of energy and courage into a mere adventurer.   P.D.

PYTHAGORAS. Pythagoras was born at Samos in 570 B.C. and went to southern Italy as many Ionians were doing at that time. There he founded a religious association which took over power in Croton about 530. This confraternity believed in the doctrine of the reincarnation of the soul into the bodies of men or animals and even certain plants. Pythagoras was reputed to have the gift of memory which enabled him to recall his former lives. The sect practised a severe discipline which included soorccy, respect for the authority of the master, ritual purifications, memory exercises, examinations of conscience, and various taboos especially concerning food. Pythagoras taught a cosmology similar to those of the Milesians (q.v.). It differed from theirs by the essential place it gave to numbers, which were represented by points juxtaposed to form square, triangular and rectangular figures. "Things are numbers", he said. He discovered the relations of simple numbers (2/1, 3/2, 4/3), which determine the principal intervals of the musical scale (fourths, fifths, octaves), and thought that the distances separating the heavenly bodies observed the same proportions; this was the origin of the idea of a harmony in the spheres and the importance attached to music. But the discovery of the theorem that bears his name showed that it was impossible to generalise these concepts and that irrational numbers exist arising, for example, from considering the ratio between the side of a square and the length of its diagonal.

After the death of Pythagoras, his followers divided into the conservative group of *akousmatikoi*, who devoted themselves to arithmology, and the mathematicians whose point of view was largely scientific. Archytas of Tarentum, mathematician, engineer and politician, who had a great influence over Plato, belonged to this second group, and also the physician, Alcmaeon of Croton (q.v.). Empedocles (q.v.) adopted the Pythagorean theories of the soul and its reincarna-

tions or metempsychosis. Some Pythagoreans fled to Phlius after a revolt that drove them from power. At the beginning of the Empire, a Neopythagorean school was formed which had a considerable influence under Nigidius Figulus. An underground basilica with stucco decorations illustrating symbolically the life of the soul, belonging to this sect, was discovered at Rome in 1920.   P.-M.S.

PYTHAGORAS of RHEGIUM. Although the sculptor, Pythagoras, was born in Samos in the last quarter of the 6th century B.C., he is more often than not described as of western origin. This mixed strain in him and his style are a reflection of the exchanges taking place in the early 5th century between Ionian art with its refined forms, embroidered draperies, mannered features and hair, and Dorian art which was characterised by the statues of muscular athletes with their firmly constructed and powerful volumes. Written sources contain a long list of these victorious athletes in the great panhellenic competitions, whom Pythagoras immortalised in his bronzes and Pindar in his odes.   R.M.

PYTHIA. The Pythia was a woman in the sanctuary at Delphi, who prophesied in the name of Apollo while she sat on the tripod. In early times she had to be a virgin. Diodorus Siculus relates how one Pythia was abducted by a young man and after that a Delphian of a "canonical" age, over fifty, was chosen. From the moment the Pythia had been appointed by the priests of Apollo, she was considered the "wife of the god" and had to live a solitary and chaste life. At the time of the Delphic oracle's greatest prosperity, there were as many as three Pythias working there together: two "ordinary" Pythias, who took it in turn to mount the tripod, and a "deputy" Pythia *(ephedros)* who was ready to replace either of her failing colleagues. In Plutarch's time, during the Roman period, a single Pythia was quite sufficient to reply to the questions of the dwindled number of consulters.

A Pythia with white hair is represented on an amphora in the Museo Nazionale, Naples, which illustrates the opening of Aeschylus's *Eumenides* where the Pythia plays a part.

Plutarch, who was a priest of Pythian Apollo, describes the tragic death of a Pythia in his dialogue, *On the Disappearance of Oracles.*

R.F.

Victory of Samothrace.
About 190 B.C. Paris,
Louvre. *Photo Vigneau.*

PYTHICRITUS. Pythicritus was born at Rhodes and is probably the sculptor of the winged *Victory of Samothrace*, the magnificent Nike caught alighting on the prow of her ship. The body is thrown forward and supported by the right leg while the left remains free. The unity and dynamism of the movement are emphasised by the sweep of the wings, both outstretched but at different heights, and by the skilful treatment of the drapery, lifted by the currents of air, gathered in multiple folds, or clinging to the body and revealing through its transparency the breasts and outlines of the legs and stomach. This subtle interplay of contrasts in the drapery, flying free in

one place, whipped by the wind against the body elsewhere, accentuates the movement emanating from the body. It is particularly powerful in the parts left virtually naked by the clinging drapery and further intensified by the oblique line of the garment skilfully folded between the legs. R.M.

PYTHIUS. According to Pliny and Vitruvius, this Ionian architect was the designer of the temple of Athena Polias at Priene and the Mausoleum at Halicarnassus, Caria, which is counted among the Seven Wonders of the World. He is typical of that point in the middle of the 4th century B.C. when Greek architecture achieved a graceful,

390

airy equilibrium between the masses, at times rather heavy, of the classical period and the dry, effete gracility of the Hellenistic era. In the technical treatise where he discusses his own work, Pythius defends the Ionic order, which was more flexible and better suited to his temperament than the severe Doric. He set out extremely exacting requirements for the training of the architect whose knowledge of the arts as well as the sciences should make him one of the most cultivated men of his time. His scientific, almost mathematical conception of architecture is reflected in the temple he built on a prominent terrace in the centre of the new town of Priene (q.v.) about 340.

A few years before, about 350, Pythius and the Parian, Satyrus, were commissioned to build a mausoleum for the Carian prince, Mausolus, by his wife, Artemisia. The sculptured ornament was done by four masters of the time, Scopas, Timotheus, Bryaxis and Leochares. All these artists, some of whom were both architects and sculptors, were applying Greek plastic forms to an architectural conception that was more oriental than Hellenic. This type of monument enjoyed considerable popularity; it spread into Syria and, in the Roman period, was to be found even in the western parts of the empire, indicating that the work of Pythius had a profound and widespread influence.
R.M.

Q U I N T U S o f S M Y R N A . Epic poet of the late period. *(See* Epic).

RELIGION. Greek religion was neither revelation nor dogma: it was born out of a constant and profound sense of the divine and an innate certainty in every man of the existence of powers beyond mankind that surpassed human possibilities and were capable of arousing human admiration and wonder by their very grandeur, their miraculous nature and such natural phenomena as earthquakes and the sudden emerging of a spring. They were also capable of feats which it seemed impossible for any human to accomplish without some kind of external aid. But for people like the Greeks, who were never at ease with abstract ideas and who could find nothing in nature to surpass man in intelligence and willpower, these invisible forces, whose actions they admired or simply endured, could only be deployed by beings resembling mankind except for their immortality and the wide range of their powers. Such a conviction was spontaneous among the ancient Greeks. The anthropomorphism of the gods was not a poetic creation, even though art and literature made great use of it as we know. Contrary to the opinion that used to be widespread in the modern world, centuries of scientific thought were needed before what had first been held to be a divine manifestation became accepted as a physical phenomenon. The French poet, Boileau, reversed the real process when he wrote: " Echo is no longer a sound resounding in the air but a nymph in tears lamenting Narcissus. "

The Greek peasant, standing in front of a curiously shaped rock, whom I heard exclaim, " It's not natural. God must have made it, " had, on the other hand, slipped back effortlessly to the attitude of antiquity.

We know too little about the Minoan civilisation to be certain whether the female figure represented on so many buildings and especially on intaglios, either standing on a mountain top or under a tree, or else surrounded by animals, is a single goddess in every case or one of several, who all resembled one another and exercised joint dominion over the world. Anyway, we must take it for granted that the figures personified the reproductive powers of nature and that their bared bosoms were symbols of the fertility of the soil and the human race. The god, often shown accompanying them, usually seems to have held a minor position as prince consort.

The character of these images underwent no change in the Mycenaean period but the deciphering of the Linear B (q. v.) script not only revealed the names of some of these divinities, such as Hera and Dionysus, but also proved that, at this time at least, they had begun to acquire separate identities. It must certainly have been at this time that the feudal pantheon ruled by a male god and probably formed on the model of Mycenaean society was created. According to the Homeric poems it already had a long past and was well organised. Not all the divinities were indigenous to Greece for some—Zeus, the great lord, seems to have been one of them—had been brought to Greece by the Indo-European invaders who had destroyed the power of Minos, while others may have been brought back by the Mycenaeans after their wanderings in the orient. Some of the female divinities appear to have been the direct heirs of the great Cretan goddess, like her bestowing fertility on every living thing, although under new auspices and under different names according to the regions that had adopted them. It is questionable whether these gods, whom Homer endowed with such brilliant life and who never ceased to be venerated by the Greeks from that time, were able to satisfy the spiritual needs of their worshippers and that deep rooted feeling which, as we have discovered, lay at the basis of Hellenic religion. They all represented a certain power, and it was to conciliate this power that they were always worshipped But, with his brothers Hades and Poseidon one of whom ruled over the dead and the other over the seas, the great Zeus, gatherer of the clouds and all-powerful master of the world, was the only deity with well defined attributes, precisely as if he were the sovereign of a determined realm. The others, with the exception of Iris and Hebe who were nothing more than servants, were without any special function in early times; they were the personal gods of a leader and consequently of his people rather than the incarnations of any physical or moral quality that later mythographers were to ascribe to them. Apollo was the protector of the Trojans and he used his bow and arrows mainly to strike down their foes; Aphrodite was certainly the fairest of all the goddesses but the main use she made of her power over the hearts of mortals was in favour of Helen; Athena put her valour and wisdom at the disposition of the Greeks, Ulysses in particular. No doubt, when these gods revealed themselves to their worshippers, they inspired them with a feeling of awe which allowed the latter to see through their disguise, but they only showed themselves to the lords of the earth like Ulysses, Achilles, and Nausicaa, a prince's daughter, and it was for such alone that they consented to leave the palace on the summit of Olympus among the clouds, where they resided like the monarchs of Mycenae. The common people never saw the gods and only knew them through the intermediary of their kings. There can be little doubt that the common people shared the general fervour of their leaders and that they felt the need for direct protection no less than the nobles. On several occasions, especially in the *Odyssey*, Homer casually mentions the sanctuaries of the nymphs. They were divinities of a humbler order, living in villages, watching over a field, a spring or a wood. Modest descendants of the Cretan Great Mother, they assured the prosperity of orchards, the health of the peasants and their herds. During the whole of antiquity, it was mainly to the nymphs and their male counterparts,

such as Pan, that the common people addressed their prayers. Although written texts are lacking, archaeological finds have shown scenes of peasants, who did not dare approach the Olympians, making their requests to these minor deities, offering them the first fruits of their harvests together with vases and images whose value lay more in the sincerity of the giver than the intrinsic worth of the objects themselves. The dedicatory verses in the *Greek Anthology* are more refined and elegant transcriptions of the naïve but sincere dedications that could be read by the thousands throughout the rustic shrines. It is not surprising that these divinities resembled each other from one village or province to another, or shared the same very widespread attributes, since the preoccupations of their worshippers were the same everywhere. Each divinity, however, had its own well defined geographical domain and each township had its own patron deity or deities, although their number was never very great since the populations were so small.

The great gods also had their special spheres of influence although they may not have been so strictly localised. In the first place, they were the protectors of a sovereign who provided their nourishment, who maintained them and saw to their protection, and who sought to please them by organising festivals, dances and competitions in their honour. Once the monarchies had fallen, the gods became the patrons of the new communities who took the place of the kings. The cities then annexed and monopolised these divinities whose function it was to watch over them. Although the gods were apparently identical, local cults gave them a particular character and the fact that her name was linked with a certain locality prevented Hera of Samos from being confused with her namesake from Argos. There were some gods whose authority extended beyond the limits of a single city; this happened when several neighbouring states combined together, for economic or political reasons, to maintain a shrine in common. Some of these associations, or amphictionies (q. v.) as they were called, disintegrated before they could expand, but others drew pilgrims from the whole of the Greek world, either because the deity delivered oracles or for some other reason came to have a great reputation that gave it a panhellenic character.

The disappearance of the monarchies brought the faithful closer to their gods by giving them a part of the responsibilities that had formerly been assumed by the kings. Each citizen was obliged to take part in the worship and to abstain from committing any deed that might harm the community by rousing the wrath of its divine protectors against it. But at the same time, the feeling that he was lost among a crowd deprived each citizen of the hope of coming into direct contact with the divinity or of meeting an immortal one day, as Ulysses met Athena, or some peasant encountered Pan or the village nymphs, with mingled feelings of religious terror and pride, on the mountain side amid his grazing goats. This did not prevent the individual from begging favours from the Olympians; the young bride would invoke Hera, and the shopkeeper would call upon Hermes for aid but such requests, accompanied by offerings and sacrifices, were like striking a bargain. There was nothing in it that could satisfy mystical aspirations. The priests themselves, more often than not, were only officials performing rites whose former significance had sunk into oblivion.

Morality itself received little inspiration from the behaviour of the gods for, although Zeus was always careful to render justice as befitted a good ruler, neither he nor the members of the family, whose head he was, could be taken as examples of virtue. Adultery, falsehood, theft, and acts of cruelty were all frequent occurrences in the world of the Olympians.

Very soon, the spirit of logic and the sincere piety of certain Greeks, like Hesiod, made them attempt to bring some order into this pantheon which had been so vaguely defined for so long. They tried to determine relationships and origins, to justify the supremacy of the gods by their victories over the forces of evil and to exalt the sovereign majesty of Zeus. Later, when Greek thought had matured and when it no longer regarded power and victory as the only valid justification for the empire of the Olympians, there were many Greeks like Aeschylus and Pindar who drew a veil over the misdeeds of the gods, and preferred to praise the profundity of the gods' designs, their wise administration, and the protection they granted to all who honoured them with a sincere piety. Others, who were somewhat tired of official religious ceremonies, which they only accomplished out of a sense of civic duty, turned towards the few divinities capable of inspiring love in their followers with a fervour that sometimes reached great heights of passion. Among these divinities

were Dionysus, who inspired ecstasy in his faithful as they communed with him, and Demeter, giver of bread, who promised her followers a happiness that would endure after death. This was the origin of the mysteries (q. v.). The traditional figures of the past were soon joined by others in the 5th century B.C. and after. These newcomers mostly came from the east like Bendis, Sabazius and others, whose exoticism and emotional appeal attracted a public in which women occupied an increasingly important place.

It is tempting to attribute the development of hero-worship to the same insufficiency of official religion. In principle, hero-worship is connected with funerary beliefs. For a long time, the privilege of being admitted to the company of the gods after death had been reserved for only a few exceptional mortals such as Heracles or the legendary founders of cities. In the 4th century B.C., perhaps in imitation of oriental practices, the Greeks began to consider divine all those whose merit had won them the right to grateful recognition by their fellow-mortals. As time went on, they became less exacting and by the beginning of the Christian era all the dead were considered as heroes.

To follow the slow but sure evolution of the Greeks towards monotheism and Christianity lies beyond the scope of this article. Obviously, since earliest times the gods of Greece were not only the human, too human figures depicted by Homer. We should not let his epic vision blind us to the sincerity of a religious feeling in the Greeks that sometimes reached the heights of mysticism.
P.D.

RHADAMANTHYS. Rhadamanthys belongs to the Cretan tradition which considered him to be the son of Zeus and Europa, like his brothers Minos and Sarpedon. In the eyes of the Greeks he represented wisdom and justice. He was said to have given its laws to Crete and he was made one of the judges in the underworld. But neither Rhadamanthys nor the other judges were empowered to weigh the good and the evil deeds committed by the dead during their lifetime, it was only in recognition of the functions they had discharged so perfectly on earth that they remained paragons of judges in the nether world.
P.D.

RHAPSODES. A rhapsode was a declaimer of epic poems. A rhapsody is a section of an

sition, elocution and oratorical gestures. The exordium had to include the *captatio benevolentiae*. Next came an account of the facts, followed by the argumentation and the reply to the adversary's anticipated arguments *(prokatalepsis)*. The thesis was developed by the process of amplification *(auxesis)* and the speech was brought to an end by a vigorous recapitulation. Many teachers paid particular attention to the harmony of each phrase through rhymes *(homoioteleuta)*, the perfect balance of different propositions *(parisa)* and the use of numerous " figures of speech ", which were carefully classified.

In a democracy like that of Athens, in which the assembly and the tribunals were so important, eloquence had a very special place; before the state could be governed, the people had to be won over with the art of words.

This is why rhetoric, although it began in Sicily, was so highly developed at Athens. The schools of Antiphon, Isaeus and Isocrates (qq.v.) were among the most famous. In the Hellenistic and Roman periods, the teaching of the art of oratory remained the basis of the " all-round " education *(enkyklios paideia)*. R.F.

RHODES. The island of Rhodes did not owe its great prosperity only to its natural wealth but also to its geographical position, which made it an almost compulsory port of call between Egypt and the Phoenician ports on one hand, and the towns of the Aegean on the other. Mycenaean civilisation flourished at Rhodes before the arrival of the Dorians who settled on the island. The three most ancient towns in Rhodes, Ialysus, Camirus and Lindus, formed with the island of Cos, and Cnidus and Halicarnassus on the mainland, the confederation which was known as the Dorian hexapolis. During the 7th and 6th centuries B.C., colonisation and trade in far-off countries gave the island a very important place in the Hellenic world and products from Rhodes were exported as far as the western Mediterranean.

The art of this period is particularly interesting. We know little of the sculpture but ceramic art is represented by vases which must have been fashioned after models in metal. They were decorated in the oriental manner with bands of animal

epic that could be recited on its own. In his *Ion* Plato has given us a delightful account of the rhapsody. *(See* Epic; Homer).

RHETORIC. Themistocles' and Pericles' eloquence owed nothing to rhetoric; when they were beginning their careers, it was not yet being taught in Athens. Rhetoric originated in Sicily in the first half of the 5th century B.C. The founder of the science was Corax and he had a pupil, Tisias, who became the master of Gorgias (q. v.).

The teaching of the rhetors was based on the principle that in every debate there are two contradictory theses, one strong and the other weak. By laying stress on verisimilitude, rhetoric was supposed to assure the triumph of the weaker thesis. Rhetors had provided themselves with a whole battery of commonplaces *(topoi)* and taught their pupils the art of invention, compo-

Temple at Lindos
in Rhodes. *Photo
Boudot-Lamotte.*

motifs whose composition and colours were
reminiscent of tapestry work.

After domination by the Persian king, and then
association with the Athenians in 478 B.C., the
citizens of the three great states of the island
joined in founding a new city in 408, giving it the
name of the island itself, Rhodes. It was sited
in the extreme north of the island, facing the coast
of Anatolia. In a short time, this new city eclipsed
all the others in importance. At first it remained
faithful to the alliance with Athens, whose democratic regime it had adopted; then in 356 B.C.,
it fell under the influence of Mausolus, king of
Caria. It fought without success against Alexander and then joined the Ptolemys because the
main part of its trade was with Egypt. In 305, it
was victorious in its resistance to the attacks of
Demetrius Poliorcetes (q.v.). The Hellenistic
period was a time of greatest prosperity for
Rhodes and its international trade brought it
considerable wealth. Although its influence was
not as great as that of Alexandria, in the Helle-

The Levi oinochoe. Rhodian. Mid-7th century B.C.
Paris, Louvre.

nistic period it was still a centre of the arts and produced such works as the famous *Colossus*, now unfortunately lost, and the *Victory of Samothrace*, and Rhodian sculptors also seem to have taken a large part in the execution of the friezes on the Altar of Zeus at Pergamum. In the very different style of traditional academicism, they also achieved a certain distinction.   P.D.

RHOECUS. Rhoecus was an architect, born in the late 7th century B.C. on the island of Samos which the tyrant, Polycrates (q.v.) made famous for its buildings and cities. He contributed to the building of Hera's sanctuary at the beginning of the 6th century before Polycrates' tyranny. He was a bronze-worker as well as an architect and found an inventive mind in Theodorus, his associate. Theodorus was an engineer, bronze-founder, toreutic-worker, engraver and, according to tradition, made successful innovations in the technique of bronze-casting. They travelled together in Egypt and returned deeply impressed by its monumental architecture, which influenced their conception of the first great temple of Hera. Their concern with the surroundings and the lay-out as a whole was also something new at the time, and they landscaped the countryside before starting to build; the vague horizons above the low and marshy delta of the River Imbrasus, where the temple of Hera was sited, were bounded to the north by a portico and to the south by a peristyle building, which formed the frame-work for the great Ionic temple. The great hypostyle chambers of Egyptian temples probably inspired this forest of columns, at least 102 in number, which gave the name of " labyrinth " to the temple whose proportions were different from any hitherto known in Greek architecture. The construction of this enormous mass required a special technique for the foundations, which Theodorus's engineering had perfected. He also invented the towers and machines necessary for the cutting and emplacement of the columns and elements of the entablature. Besides the monumental character of the design, the complexity and richness of its various elements all contributed to make the temple the luxurious expression of a rich civilisation that had been strongly influenced by foreign styles.   R.M.

ROMANCES. There is no exact word in Greek for " novel ", but the kind of fictional narrative found in the myth is as old as Hellas itself and it cannot be said that the Greeks ever lacked creative imagination. But the romance was never a mere tale, for it purported to relate the lives and deeds of several characters revolving round a hero and heroine, who were in love with each other. The tribulations, which the lovers had to suffer and which separated them, were countless and included storms and shipwrecks, attacks by brigands and pirates, but the most terrible of all were those provoked by their own exceptional but pernicious beauty that aroused the most fearful jealousies and rivalries around them.

The oldest of these Greek romances, the *Adventures of Chareas and Callirhoë*, probably dates from the 1st century B.C. It was the work of a Greek from Asia Minor, Chariton of Aphrodisias (a town in Caria). The setting is the Greek world at the end of the 5th century, where the action moves from Syracuse to Miletus, from there to Babylon, Phoenicia and Cyprus, before coming back again to Syracuse. Chariton often quotes from the *Iliad* and the *Odyssey*—poems which themselves are epic romances.

Xenophon of Ephesus, the author of the *Ephesiaca*, may have lived in the 2nd century A.D. His work also dealt with the heroic fidelity of a man and wife, Habrocomes and Anthia. The tone of the romance is always edifying and religious and at times almost mystical.

The only one of these romances to have remained famous to this day is also the shortest and the most erotic: *Daphnis and Chloe*, a " pastoral " rather than a romance properly speaking. It was written by Longus who, like Xenophon of Ephesus, seems to have lived in the 2nd century A.D. In this story of two children, abandoned by their parents who left them with valuable tokens *(gnorismata)* that would enable them to recognise each other, we find a theme which frequently recurs in the tragedies of Euripides and the New Comedy.

The *Aethiopica*, or *Theagenes and Charicleia*, was the work of Heliodorus who lived in the 3rd century A.D. The story is about two fiancés who only marry at the end of the book after narrowly escaping death on a hundred occasions. In the work, Theagenes appears as a " knight in waiting " and the humble slave of " his lady ".

About the same time, Achilles Tatius, a native of Alexandria, wrote the *Adventures of Leucippe and Clitophon*. The narrator is Clitophon himself; he falls in love with Leucippe but his love is not immediately returned and it is only after a long siege that he is able to win the heart of his lady love.

These romances were highly fashionable in the 16th and 17th centuries. We know that when Racine was fifteen years old he devoured Heliodorus's *Aethiopica* and said he knew it by heart. The story is full of the most conventional and unlikely incidents, but, nonetheless, these works are still very appealing and give us a highly coloured, lively, and very convincing picture of life in the ancient world.   R.F.

S A C R I F I C E . The sacrifice was the essential act of worship and for its origins we must turn to the belief, which was innate among the Greeks, that the anthropomorphic divinity had the same needs as the ordinary mortal. Not only did it need a roof over its head, the temple, and clothing—the offering of a peplos to Athena (*See* Panathenaea) is a typical example—it also needed food and drink. In the first instance, a sacrifice was the offering of food and drink to the deity. Drink was offered in the form of a libation: milk, wine, blood or any other liquid prescribed by the rites required for the circumstances, was poured on an altar, which represented a dining-table, or on the ground if the deity belonged to the underworld. Food offerings might consist of cakes, fruits or meat. If it was meat, the animal that the deity preferred was brought before the altar and immolated by the priests, who alone were competent in such a matter, and the pieces of flesh reserved for the divinity were then burnt. It was usually customary to divide the victim into three portions, one for the god (generally not the best part), one for the officiating priest, and one for the donor, who might be either a single person or a community. Sacrifices of this nature were offered on countless occasions either by a people as a whole, a single social group or a private person, on feast days, after a harvest (when the first fruits were offered), as thanksgiving for the success of some enterprise or favour received, or before some undertaking when the higher powers were besought to ensure its success. A sacrifice was made each time the divinity was invoked, whether it was to seal an oath, to wash away some defilement, or to avert a calamity. In the last instance, it seems that the victim was charged with the evil miasmas to be dispelled and consequently, instead of being eaten, the meat

Sacrificing a pig.
Inside of an Attic cup.
Last quarter of the
6th century B.C.
Paris, Louvre.

Moscophoros: a man carrying a young calf for sacrifice. Attic. Mid-6th century B.C. Athens, Acropolis Museum. *Photo Alinari.*

it was governed by strict rules. A minutely detailed ritual, probably derived from the very primitive superstitions and taboos of early man, regulated the nature of the offerings and the ceremonial. It was a great sacrilege to offer an ox to a divinity if it preferred a goat in certain circumstances; it was a great mistake to sing a paean if silence was the rule for the ceremony; and, although the god worshipped might be the same, he would require different rituals according to the shrine in which he was being worshipped. Above all, it was imperative not to perform the ritual in the same way when invoking a celestial power and a power of the infernal regions.

The function of the priests was precisely to see that these rules were observed. Generally, they did not themselves give the mortal blow to the victim; this devolved either on the donor, or on skilled subordinates who knew how to prepare the victim, how to deck it with fillets, symbolising its consecration to the divinity, how to cut off a few of its hairs according to the religious laws, and how to cut its throat and quarter it. It was the priest's function to indicate the required gesture and words; he was in charge of the musical accompaniment, chose the right moment and the formula for the prayer or oath without which the sacrifice was useless or even harmful to the donor.

There is no space here to mention all the various sacrifices, nor even to give some detailed examples. What must be stressed is the exceptional importance that the sacrifice had for the ancient Greeks whose piety went hand in hand with superstitious traditionalism. The frequent appearance of such ceremonies in Greek vase painting reveals both their variety and the place they held in the private and public life of Greek society. We have no space, either, to go into the controversial matter of human sacrifices, although we know that such a barbarous practice was not entirely unknown to the Greeks; the immolation of Polyxena was not an isolated instance. The problem here is to discover what motive lay behind such practices and whether the sacrificers were seeking anything beyond the sanctification of a very human desire for vengeance, by making sure that the gods were involved.

P.D.

of the animal was burned entirely. Such a sacrifice was known as a holocaust.

Far more unusual was the sacrifice, almost in the modern sense of the word, when some precious and greatly esteemed object was thrown away in order to give proof of modesty before the gods and to avoid arousing their jealousy by a display of excessive happiness quite incompatible with the human condition. The most famous example of this kind is that of Polycrates (q.v.), throwing a precious ring into the sea so that other goods he prized even more might not be taken from him. But the gods refused to be deceived by such a minute offering and Destiny was not to be bought by the tyrant at such a paltry price.

As the sacrifice was the supreme act of piety,

SACRILEGE. The Greeks used the general term " impiety " to cover a series of acts prejudicial to religion which they unanimously disapproved and could condemn with legal sanction. To annex a piece of land which was the property of a divinity, to destroy the olive trees of Athena, to profane a sanctuary even by the mere fact of entering it in a state of impurity, bully supplicants, divulge mysteries, practise sorcery, leave the dead unburied and introduce new cults, without the authorisation of the people, were all offences against the divine laws that no one could commit without laying themselves open to public obloquy.

Such a condemnation only followed when the acts risked upsetting the social structure or compromising the interests of the state or the party in power. When in the early 6th century B.C., the clergy of Delphi accused the inhabitants of Crisa of having extorted money from the pilgrims on their way to the sanctuary, this act of sacrilege gave the Thessalians an excellent excuse for destroying a city that had offended them on the pretext that they were accomplishing a pious duty.

From the time of Solon, the laws of Athens punished certain acts of impiety by fines, banishment or death but it sometimes happened that the state would step aside in cases of minor importance so that the priests involved in the affair could punish the accused with the gentler sanctions at their disposal; during periods of stability, particularly during the first years of Pericles' government, these laws remained almost a dead letter. When the opposition raised its head again, it found accusations of impiety a useful weapon which it used with varying degrees of success against Pericles' friends, against philosophers who debauched young people and introduced ideas contrary to accepted theological beliefs and against Aspasia, who was not only reproached with procuring but with having introduced new divinities into the state.

During the difficult times of the Peloponnesian War and the crisis that followed the downfall of Athens, trials for impiety multiplied. They were all the more dangerous for the accused as the nation was in peril and scapegoats had to be found. The most sensational of these trials was that held in 415 B.C. which ended in the condemnation of Alcibiades and his misguided young accomplices, who had parodied the mysteries (q.v.) and mutilated the sacred boundary stones, sculpted with the image of Hermes, that lined the streets of Athens; such a sacrilege was likely to provoke the gods into wreaking their vengeance on the people as a whole. Socrates' trial in 399 B.C. was also for impiety but he might not have been condemned if the Athenians, who had been aroused against the sophists in general by Aristophanes and a few others, had not held the whole intellectual class responsible for the country's misfortunes and if some of Socrates' followers had not been among the most dangerous of the oligarchs. The real reason for the condemnation of the great philosopher, like the majority of those brought to court for impiety, was not so much for being irreligious as for having committed an offence against the integrity of the state, to use a modern formula.   P.D.

SALAMIS. For a long time the arid little island of Salamis, lying in the middle of the bay of Eleusis, meant nothing more to the Athenians than a forward bastion, which had to be held to prevent the Megarians or anyone else using it as a base for incursions against their territory. It was only in 612 B.C. through Solon's initiative that they finally annexed the rock from which they could expect little material benefit, but after the Persian Wars the name of Salamis was proudly cited as a symbol of victory. It was in the narrow straits between the island and the coast of Attica that the small fleet of the Greek confederates, led it seems by Themistocles, practically wiped out Xerxes' fleet before his very eyes on September 29th, 480 B.C., depriving him of naval support for his ground troops.

The outline of the battle is fairly well known from descriptions left by Herodotus and Aeschylus, although they only tally approximately. We are told that the Persian navy was hampered by its very numbers and that, as the ships were unable to deploy themselves in a line, they fell an easy prey to the Greeks. " Their hulls overturned, the sea was hidden under a mass of wreckage and bleeding corpses; the shores and reefs were littered with the dead and what was left of the barbarian vessels rowed away in disordered flight. " Such is the description given by Aeschylus in his tragedy the *Persians*. He goes on to say: " The Greeks struck and dashed their brains out with broken oars and fragments of wreckage as though the Persians were tunny or fish emptied out of a net. A great cry broken by sobs reigned

over the open sea until the dark hue of night brought an end to all. " P.D.

SAMOS. Samos, facing Cape Mycale, is the largest of the Aegean islands. Very different in appearance from the Cyclades, it resembles the landscape of Asia Minor from which it is separated by narrow straits less than a mile and a half wide. The island is crossed by high mountains running from east to west, bordering plains of which one, in the south, was the site of one of the most important of Hera's sanctuaries by the edge of the sea. Samos was first settled in the 3rd millennium B.C., then becoming Ionian, and the fertility of its soil and the initiative of its inhabitants gave it a prosperity which reached its peak under the reign of the tyrant, Polycrates (q.v.), who came to power in about 532 B.C. It was at this time that the port was modernised, the architect, Eupalinus, built an underground aquaduct nearly 1140 ft long, improvements were made in the capital, and the raising of a magnificent temple in the sanctuary of Hera made Samos a centre of attraction for pilgrims, traders and mariners from not only Ionia but the whole of the eastern and central Mediterranean. Polycrates established relations with Egypt and Samos pursued a policy of colonial expansion, which it had begun in the 7th century, by sending settlers as far as the coasts of Spain and even beyond Gibraltar. The death of Polycrates and the conquest of the island by the Persians brought an end to its political importance if not to its prosperity, but when the Persians left Greece, Samos was one of the first to join the Delian League. In 439 B.C., it was subdued by Athens after rebelling against the city and it was given a democratic regime. At the end of the Peloponnesian War, it became a satellite of Sparta and did not fall under Athenian influence again until 366. It regained its autonomy in 322 after the fall of Athens but only to pass under the virtual control of the Ptolemys and, after that, it lost all its former importance.

In its most brilliant period during the archaic era, it was more than one of the indispensable pawns on the chessboard of Greek politics and one of the first markets of the Greek world; it was also a centre of the arts. A bronze-working process was invented by the Samians, Rhoecus

Statue of the goddess, Hera, dedicated by Cheramyes. Samos. Mid-6th century B.C. Paris, Louvre. *Photo Braun.*

(q.v.) and Theodorus, and a whole school of sculpture then developed whose vivacity and spontaneity distinguished it from the heavy Milesian style of its Ionian rivals. P.D.

SAMOTHRACE. The island of Samothrace with its inhospitable shores, facing the Gulf of Saros, rises like a giant pyramid from the sea. It had first been inhabited by a people known to the Greeks as the Pelasgi, and was probably also settled by the Tyrseni, who came from Anatolia and had established themselves in the neighbouring island of Lemnos. The Samians sent colonists to the island, probably in the early 7th century B.C., but Samothrace continued to remain outside the Greek world, isolated by its storms and sea mists. However, a sanctuary of the Cabiri, gods with a mystery (q.v.) cult who protected navigators, gave Samothrace a fame far surpassing that of richer cities, especially in the Hellenistic period. Temples were built and offerings consecrated, the most famous and the most beautiful of which was the *Victory of Samothrace* that recent studies have shown to date from the 2nd century B.C. P.D.

SANCTUARIES. Like many other words we use to translate Greek terms, the word " sanctuary " is only a very approximate equivalent for what the ancient Greeks understood by the word *hieron*. The fact is, of course, that the religious attitudes of the Greeks were quite different from ours; for them, the sanctuary was primarily the place where a divinity, resembling a human being and with the same needs, had his actual residence; its function as a place of worship was subordinate to this. No matter what the differences between Greek sanctuaries, whether they were in humble villages or at Delphi and Olympia, they were above all places where the god had chosen to live. Although some natural phenomenon such as a grotto or a spring may sometimes explain why it was in one precise spot and not in another that the deity had chosen to take up his residence, the reasons for his choice at the majority of sanctuaries remain unknown to us, as they did even to the ancient Greeks themselves. The arrival of the divinity was usually lost in the mists of time and most sanctuaries had already been inhabited—sometimes by different titularies—long before the historical period, like Delos, to mention only one example.

The land belonging to the god *(temenos)* was, like that of human beings, limited by boundary stones or a wall *(peribolos)* and, as everything within these limits was divine property, it was sacred. No profane building could be raised there, but an altar was practically indispensable on which the faithful could place and often burn food offerings to win the god's favour. The god was generally materialised in the form of a statue which was not only his image, but an integral part of himself and identified with him, according to primitive superstition. This was why his devotees were not content to offer it food only, but cleaned it, covered it with clothes and sometimes even chained it so that it should remain among the people who counted on its protection. Although the statue might remain in the open, as in some rustic sanctuaries, it was thought that the god would be better pleased if he were sheltered under a roof, in a house reserved for his sole use to which the public would not have access, in a word, a temple (q.v.). The various offerings consecrated to the god by the pious faithful would be placed either in the temple itself or elsewhere within the sacred domain. In the countryside and in earliest times, such offerings were laid out on tables, fastened to the ground by pegs or else hung from the branches of a tree, according to their nature. The best furnished sanctuaries had special chambers in which the offerings were placed, like the Chalkotheke on the Acropolis at Athens, which contained offerings in bronze. Although water was nearly always required for the ceremonies, it was not always possible to set up fountains within the sacred enclosures and they were sometimes situated outside the peribolos. There was often a sacred wood growing within the enclosure and the temple of Zeus at Olympia was built on a site that had previously been planted with trees. The richest sanctuaries contained adjacent buildings where the faithful could rest *(exedrai*, or rooms with benches, and porticoes), and the priests live and keep the accessories of their ritual.

Most sanctuaries were those of a local divinity, who protected the village or the state on whose land he had chosen to dwell. But there were also panhellenic sanctuaries that drew worshippers from all over the Greek world, like those at Olympia, Delphi, Dodona and Delos, among others. Although the significance and structure of these sanctuaries were the same as the others, the offerings were both richer and more numerous and, in addition to the various buildings we have just mentioned, small buildings known as treasuries (q.v.) were built by the different cities to hold the gifts offered to the sanctuary by their people. Like the public buildings, porticoes and other structures set up by munificent rulers in the Hellenistic period, these treasuries were sited in the best possible position in the space available. They were set up where they could be best seen, as near to the temple as possible or else where they could triumphantly out-face the consecrated structure of some other rival state. These panhellenic sanctuaries were not only the geometric centres of Hellenic civilisation and spiritual capitals, where the inhabitants of the most distant colonies could come to worship at the very source of their culture, they were also the meeting ground for all the hatreds and rivalries that set one city against another.

Let us try to picture the scene that was normally repeated once every four years, when the usual coming and going of isolated worshippers gave way to the massive arrival of pilgrims in official delegations, representing the states where they were citizens, for the great festivals or *panegyreis*. As they made their way towards the sanctuary, they were accompanied by a crowd of private pilgrims attracted by piety, greed or simple curiosity. They passed between a number of buildings, all erected at different periods and in different styles, and as they crowded into every corner of the sacred enclosure, they would compare the richness of the offerings being made and show their admiration for the consecrations that most struck their imaginations. At Delphi for example, two buildings faced one another, one built to the glory of the Athenians, the other to the glory of the Spartans and each visitor could give expression to his sympathies for one or the other of the states represented. As the pilgrim walked along the Sacred Way leading from the entrance of the enclosure to the temple, he could appreciate the glory of the different states who, by the gift of a statue, the erection of a treasury or an inscription engraved in a well chosen spot, tried to impress the passer-by with their superiority in these reminders to all the Greeks, and to the god himself, of the victories they had won. These rivalries became even more open when the champions of the different cities competed against one another in the games held in the stadium attached to the sanctuary. Through their splendour and the ideal of Hellenic universality they represented,

the games contributed quite as much to the reputation of the sanctuaries where they were held as the religious ceremonies themselves. No doubt it was the oracle that drew the greatest crowds to Delphi, but it was above all to see the races and the sporting championships that pilgrims went to Olympia.   P.D.

SAPPHO. Poetess from Lesbos who lived in the late 7th and early 6th century B.C. She was born on the island of Lesbos at Eresus, or Mytilene, into a noble family. Sappho (or Psappho to give her real name in the Aeolian dialect) married and had a daughter called Cleis. She knew Alcaeus (q.v.), was banished from her country where civil strife was raging and went to Syracuse in Sicily, but her exile was short and she returned to live to a ripe old age. Her love for the handsome Phaon and her suicide by leaping from the promontory of Leucas, when she was rejected, are pure legend.

Sappho directed a kind of boarding school for aristocratic young girls, placed under the patronage of the Muses, the Graces and Aphrodite. She wrote verses burning with passion to some of her pupils. The ancient Greeks called Sappho the " tenth Muse " and sometimes compared her work with Homer's. What little we know of her work confirms their opinion. She was able to express the physical effects of amorous passion with power and simplicity. The expression of her personal feelings was associated with nature and the universe as a whole, for they seemed inseparable from the emotions and anguish she felt. Her verses are full of constant references to water, fire, the rivers, the sun and the stars, linked to the stirrings or the joy of her own heart by a process of subtle, secret harmonies which give her poetry a strangely modern accent.
                                                                           R.F.

SARCOPHAGUS. The custom of placing the bodies of the dead in a decorated sarcophagus did not originate in Greece. The same practice is found in Minoan Crete where sarcophaguses in terra-cotta or soft stone have been discovered in several necropolises where the Cretans may have been simply copying the Egyptian custom. Most famous of these sarcophaguses is that of Haghia Triada, with its sides painted with scenes of a religious character whose exact significance has given rise to a great deal of controversy.

During the archaic period, decorated sarcophaguses were only used in the Smyrna region and the somewhat restricted term of " Clazomenian sarcophaguses " has been given to a series of thick, earthern coffins in which the corpse was left exposed to the view of the family before burial. The coffin itself was undecorated but it was surrounded by a border with representations of mythological, heroic or animal scenes in a technique similar to that of vase paintings. It was in Asia again that sarcophaguses were used later and several have been found in the necropolis at Sidon, containing the remains of local princes who had come under strong Hellenic influence. From about 450 to the end of the 4th century B.C., four of these sarcophaguses have enabled scholars to follow the different stages in the evolution of the bas-relief. The most ancient is very Ionian in spirit and depicts a satrap hunting and feasting; another, more exotic in form (known as the Lycian Sarcophagus), was clearly inspired by the art of the Parthenon, but the most famous is also the most recent and is called the Alexander Sarcophagus because the Macedonian king is shown taking part in the battle scenes carved on the sides.

Apart from the Anatolian sarcophaguses of the late Hellenistic period, Athenian artists made great marble sarcophaguses for export under the Roman empire. They were decorated with mythological scenes which had both mystical and symbolic significance for their Roman buyers.

P.D.

SARDES. The city of Sardes lay far from the sea, perched on the Anatolian plateau, and both its position and its people's race placed it outside the Hellenic world. But its prestige was so great among the Greeks that it has to have an entry in this book. It was the capital of Lydia and was destroyed by the Cimmerians in about 635 B.C. It was then ruled over by the powerful dynasty of the Mermnadae whose last representative was none other than the famous Croesus. Like his predecessors, and to an even greater extent, Croesus was immensely rich and favourably disposed to the Greeks. Herodotus has given us an impressive list of the presents he sent to Delphi and other sanctuaries. The same historian has related the interview, which is probably imaginary, between the over-confident sovereign and Solon. When Sardes was taken by the Persians and Croesus was led to the pyre in 546, he realised the truth of what the wise Athenian, Solon, had told him: " Call no man happy till he dies, he is at best but fortunate. " At the last moment Cyrus spared Croesus' life and made him his counsellor. Even under Persian domination, Sardes continued to welcome the Greeks and it was there that the exiled Alcibiades found refuge. Excavated objects, notably stamped terra-cotta plaques, show the great influence of Greek art on this barbarian country. P.D.

SARONIC GULF. The Saronic Gulf extends from the northern shores of Argolis as far as Cape Sunium, to the Isthmus of Corinth

Sarcophagus from Gournia. Minoan. 13th century B.C. Heraklion Museum. *Photo Hassia.*

and along the coasts of Megara and southern Attica. A few fairly large islands lie scattered throughout the gulf, of which the most famous is Aegina.

SATYRS. The satyrs, often confused with Sileni, were nature daemons who formed part of Dionysus's train. They were peaceable creatures but possessed by a love for wine and lechery. They were usually represented as human beings, but with a goat's or a horse's tail at the base of their spine, and pointed ears. They often had two horns protruding from their forehead. Until the middle of the 5th century B.C., they were represented in vase paintings with bestial features— flat-nosed, thick-lipped, with flowing hair and beards—but later, although their features remained irregular, their expressions became more pensive and sometimes even melancholy. They were often shown playing the flute or the syrinx or dancing friskily. Sometimes, especially in the Hellenistic period, like Pan, only the top half of their bodies was human and their legs were a goat's. Because the actors were disguised as satyrs, the name of satyr play was given to the fourth type of play that Greek playwrights used to present in competitions.   P.D.

SCEPTICISM. *See* Pyrrhon and the Sceptics.

SCHOOLS. Ancient Greece did not have any state schools that were founded and maintained by the city. Although parents were encouraged to send their children to schools, these were all private and charged fees. As a result, even when the education of all citizens was theoretically compulsory, many were only imperfectly educated when pupils and parents lacked the means to pay their teachers. Teachers were generally hard-up mediocrities whose services were obtained after rather sordid haggling. Schoolmasters were assisted by readers who not only taught the pupils but sometimes, like the father of the orator, Aeschines, " prepared the ink, washed the stools, and swept the class-room. " The children sat on low stools and wrote on their knees around a teacher who sat on a chair or even in an armchair. From the walls hung the equipment used by the *grammatistes* and the *kitharistes* such as lyres, and baskets full of scrolls which were used for reading and exercises. The children practised writing by forming letters on wax

tablets with a sharpened point, or else by drawing them with a brush on potsherds, or on papyrus with a pen. They used cruciform rulers to draw straight lines on which they wrote sentences with all the words joined together. Memory-training was important and the pupils often read and recited in chorus. The master also taught arithmetic and perhaps even a few rudiments of geometry, and it was at schools that music was learned.

There do not seem to have been any real school-holidays as we know them, but feast days were so numerous in Greece that there was little risk of overwork for the children. Moreover, there was no proper curriculum, nor any examinations or competitions to complete the studies. The state certainly exercised some kind of supervision over the schools, but only in the field of morals and never intervened in teaching matters which were left to the discretion of the teacher.

We do not know when the first schools were started in Greece although, from a passage in Aristophanes, we may conclude that they existed before the Persian Wars. Some authorities have also been tempted to relate their development to the social movements of the 6th century B.C. which gave new importance to the classes of traders and craftsmen. On the other hand, although there was never any kind of university, properly speaking, in the Hellenic world, it is highly probable that in the 3rd century B.C. some teachers made their establishment into more than a primary school and that the children of the bourgeoisie were already preparing in them to follow higher courses of instruction given by private tutors, rhetors or philosophers, or else the heads of such semi-religious, semi-professional institutions as the School of Cos which produced so many eminent physicians.   P.D.

SCOPAS. Of all the sculptors that came from Paros, the island of marble, Scopas is the most famous. He was active in about the middle of the 4th century B.C. and was one of the first Greek artists to hire his services to whoever could afford them. Early in his career he became the architect of two Peloponnesian temples: one at Nemea, the other at Tegea. He may also have done the sculptures decorating the second of these temples; one of the pediments represents the Calydonian hunt and the few fragments that have been found confirm the ancient Greeks' description of Scopas's style, with their massive

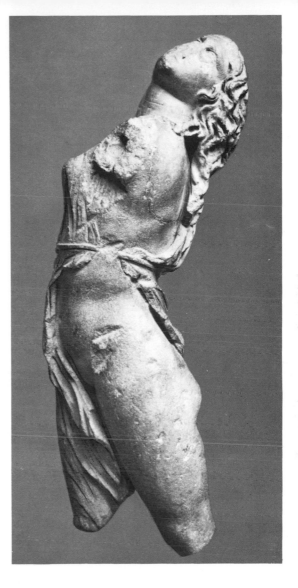

Roman copy of a work by Scopas. Dancing maenad. About 350 B.C. Dresden Museum.

hoods, sunken eyes under thick brows, their passionate expression, and the rather romantic disorder of the hair.

Scopas is thought to be one of the artists commissioned by the priests of Ephesus to decorate the temple of Artemis. He is also said to have helped with the decoration of the Mausoleum at Halicarnassus and some of the slabs of the frieze which remain, depicting the fight between Amazons and Greeks, have been attributed to him. One of these Amazons closely resembles a statuette in the museum at Dresden which we are justified in considering a replica of Scopas's famous *Maenad*, with her tunic opened wide, her hair flowing, her head thrown back, staring eyes, and brandishing the kid she had torn apart alive in her ecstasy. This was the first image in Greece of a hysterical mysticism and it suggests that Scopas had been strongly influenced by the irrational cults of Asia.

Scopas also worked at Samothrace where he executed the allegorical image of Desire *(Pothos)*. The statues that are supposed to be a replica of this work show us quite a different aspect of his talent; they are rather languid and completely lacking in the energy and violence that Scopas had been the first to introduce into sculpture.

P.D.

SCULPTURE. No matter what may have been said in the past, neither the richness of her natural resources in marble, nor the pure lines of her landscape and the clear light of her skies in any way predestined Greece to become the birthplace of sculpture. Of all the arts practised by the peoples of the Mediterranean it was sculpture that came last when painting, architecture and even literature already had a brilliant history. Admittedly, Cycladic artists had created curious marble idols as early as the 3rd millennium B.C. These figurines were carved in thin slabs, were almost always small in scale, sometimes tiny, the form of the body was schematised to an extreme degree, with the head thrown back at the end of an unnaturally long neck, the arms were folded over the chest and the legs stretched out straight. Some statuettes consisted only of a torso and a neck and looked rather like a violin; this is because they were images of a goddess of fertility and, for magical reasons, only the sex and the breasts were significant, and these were always strongly marked. It may be that these now dead faces in which only the ears and the nose were carved in relief once had painted mouths and eyes. Other more animated, more complete, and larger types of figurines, like the flute player in the National Museum in Athens, were exceptional. Such experiments were never taken any further and it seems that no sculpture was produced in the 2nd millennium. In Crete, sculpture was restricted to terra-cotta or bronze figurines, and more rarely,

405

there appeared ivory or pottery statuettes. Apart from votive animals, these figures represented goddesses or perhaps priestesses, who wore ritually low-cut bodices and bell-shaped skirts, and brandished serpents in their hands; or else male worshippers wearing loin-cloths and shown shielding their eyes before the radiance of the divinity. Large scale sculpture was not unknown in Mycenaean civilisation but little was produced. A famous head from Argolis, the Lord of Asine, is all that remains of a life-size statue. The other famous example of Mycenaean sculpture is, of course, the bas-relief of the lions facing each other on the Lion Gate at Mycenae, on either side of a column symbolising the palace, but these fierce beasts seem to have been directly imported from Asia, where monsters and wild beasts guarded the entry to royal dwellings in the same manner. Grandiose as is this work, it has no equivalent in Mycenaean civilisation.

After three or four centuries during which there are no signs of its existence, sculpture reappeared in the course of the 8th century B.C. in the form of votive figurines, such as sacrificial animals and worshippers, all treated in the geometric style that is seen at its most perfect in vase painting of the time. Such works may only be clumsy copies of Asiatic models; the first large scale statues, carved from about 650 B.C., were certainly made after oriental or Egyptian models. They were images of gods or cult statues (the first temples were built to house them) or images of mortals which were either consecrated in sanctuaries or set up over tombs. Until the 5th century, they were always uniform in type, shown erect, immobile, the head held straight, the left leg usually pushed forward, the arms hanging straight down alongside the body or else bent in front of the body to hold a distinguishing attribute. The male figures, *kouroi* (q.v.), were shown completely nude like athletes whereas the female figures, *korai* (q.v.), were shown wearing their finest apparel. They were all represented in solemn attitudes, they were all young and all seemed to be trying to appear as beautiful as possible; but never, not even in the image of a donor, did the sculptor make any attempt to produce a portrait or to recreate an individual likeness. It was the attribute alone that identified the god represented, and it was only

Large statuette of a woman. Cycladic art. Amorgos. 3rd millennium B.C. Athens, National Museum. *Photo Spyros Meletzis.*

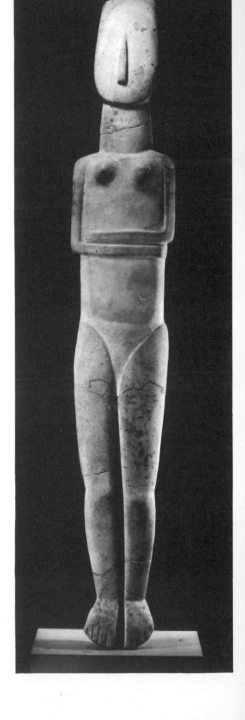

the inscription on the base or the body of the statue that gave the name of the donor or the deceased person represented. Apart from this type of statue, examples of which may be counted in hundreds, there were few others: seated figures of kouroi draped in long robes (such a type was quite frequent on the coastline of Asia Minor); figures shown in action or carrying an offering like the *Moschophoros* of Athens carrying a calf on his shoulders, or horsemen winning a race. These last were the most lively and prove that the stiff attitude of the kouroi and korai was not so much due to any clumsiness on the part of the sculptor as to the desire of the donor to show himself frozen in a rigid religious posture of attention. Some of these archaic statues were made of soft limestone *(poros)*, others of marble, but many others were of bronze although only a few rare examples have survived to this day. They were painted in lively colours. But stone was the main material for carvings in bas-relief and poros, conchiferous limestone or marble was used according to the region. Stone very quickly took the place of terra-cotta, which had been used only as long as buildings were too fragile for the tops of their walls to bear the weight of a stone frieze or pediment. It was in fact at the tops of walls that relief sculpture first appeared, for these were the places where it could best be seen on sacred buildings. Its purpose was magical at first and then decorative, but in a short time it became didactic; the figure of the Gorgon, whose mass dominates the façade of the temple of Artemis at Corfu, repelled evil from the sacred building, the Calydonian Hunt carved on the treasury of Sicyon at Delphi illustrated a beautiful story, but the scene of the defeat of the Giants on the pediment of the Hecatompedon of Athens was intended to show the faithful the triumph and grandeur of the gods. They were coloured with lively red and blue tints, with some pieces made of bronze, and no matter how high these edifying scenes might be set they could not fail to attract the attention of pilgrims. The contrast between the Ionic and the Doric styles in sculpture was never so marked as it was during the archaic period, between the late 7th and the early 5th centuries B.C. The Doric style first appeared in the rather harsh form of " daedalism. " Statues char-

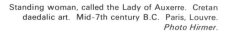

Standing woman, called the Lady of Auxerre. Cretan daedalic art. Mid-7th century B.C. Paris, Louvre.
Photo Hirmer.

Unfinished kouros.
Naxos. 6th century
B.C. Athens, National
Museum. *Photo
Boudot-Lamotte.*

acteristic of this, seemed to have been hacked out of the stone and must have fairly closely resembled the primitive wooden statues or *xoana*, some of which still existed in the 2nd century A.D.; the *Venus of Auxerre* in the Louvre, almost certainly of Cretan provenance, is a good example. The head was set on an angular body and the thin, triangular face was framed by a thick wig. The features were accentuated excessively, with long pointed noses, slipper chins, a thin slit for the mouth and intense eyes, in an attempt to give expression to the face. Then, in about 600 B.C., the triumph of the athletic ideal made sculptors concentrate on the body itself, on its vigour, somewhat heavy in Argolis and more nervous in Corinth, on the structure of the torso, the play of muscles and the suppleness or the weight of limbs. The face itself remained expressionless. When the artist wanted to enliven it—after all, it was the image of a man, a thinking being—he contented himself with drawing the ends of the lips upwards in a stereotyped smile, which was not always free from foolishness. The total effect remained somewhat strained, tense, and dominated by an unrelenting discipline. It was because of this sense of discipline that the Doric relief harmonised with its setting of metopes and pediments. This strictly measured, inconvenient space inevitably led to a grave, severe, clear style; we can see in the treasury of Sicyon at Delphi, that what the

Unfinished metope
from the Temple of
Hera at the mouth of
the River Sele.
Heracles struggling
with Antaeus. About
540 B.C. Paestum
Museum. *Photo
Leonard von Matt.*

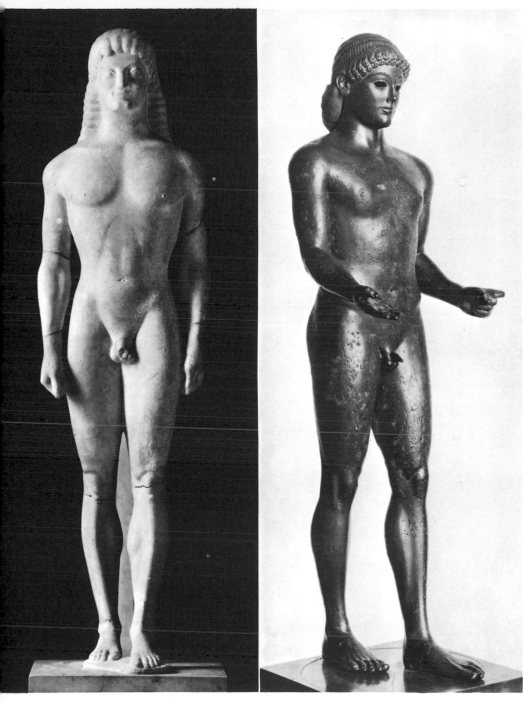

Kouros from Tenea. About 550 B.C. Munich,
Glyptothek. *Photo Hirmer.*

Apollo of Piombino. Dorian art. First quarter of the
5th century B.C. Paris, Louvre. *Photo Sougez.*

Head of a kouros, called the Rayet-Jakobsen Head. About 520-510 B.C. Copenhagen, Glyptotek Ny Carlsberg.

Head of a kore. About 520-510 B.C. Athens, Acropolis Museum. *Photo Hassia*.

work lost in charm it gained in power. In contrast, Ionian sculpture appears less austere, not so much in its subjects, as in its spirit. The kouroi are more fragile in form and the aim of the winsomely adorned korai is to please; they seem to smile more spontaneously and their more relaxed attitude suggests the luxurious softness of Asia. The continuous band of the frieze is like a wordy and undisciplined story enlivened by every kind of picturesque detail, as in the Delphic treasury of Siphnus. Attic sculpture displayed a happy combination of the two tendencies, for it lightened the austerity of the Dorian style with a grace free from either solemnity or affectation; the long series of korai found on the Acropolis, and what remains of the Gigantomachy, carved on the pediment of the Hecatompedon, already pointed the way to future developments. As a matter of fact, from the beginning of the 5th century B.C., the period of technical apprenticeship had come to an end and the differences between the various schools were diminishing. Although the sculpted decoration of the Sicilian temples might still be called Dorian in spirit, the pediments of the temple of Aegina, carved between 490 and 475, and even those of Olympia, of about 460, show a certain eclecticism in their tendencies and the Attic influence appears in their sense of drama and their intense life. It was at about this time that sculptors first emerged as well defined personalities whose names were the admiration of the peoples of antiquity. Generally we only know their works by replicas of the Roman period, and we can hardly ever be certain of the attribution of the statues that have survived. Although Myron's *Discobolus* or Polycletus's *Diadumenos* have been easily identified, many other admirable creations have remained anonymous like the *Charioteer* of Delphi or the *Ludovisi Throne*. Our knowledge of Phidias would be vague indeed if he had not made a personal contribution to the decoration of the Parthenon. Our lack of knowledge is all the greater as the majority of statues were of bronze and it was only by chance that some of them were saved from being melted down when metal became scarce. The artists mentioned, as well as

The Charioteer, dedicated by Polyzalus of Gela to Apollo at Delphi. About 475-460 B.C. Delphi Museum. *Ph. Hirmer.*

Opposite page
Head of the Charioteer of Delphi.

Votive stele to Athena.
Attic relief. About
470-450 B.C. Athens,
Acropolis Museum.
Photo Hirmer.

Three-sided relief, called the Ludovisi Throne. Girl playing a double-flute. Young woman burning incense. The birth of Aphrodite (?). About 460 B.C. Rome, Terme Museum. *Photo Alinari.*

Head of Athena. Detail of the metope "Heracles and the Stymphalian birds" from the Temple of Zeus at Olympia. About 460 B.C. Paris, Louvre. *Photo Dontenville.*

many others who were less illustrious, were all dominated by a classic ideal which, without betraying reality by a withered and anaemic imitation, gave a purified image of all that it represented, freed from all baseness, all feebleness and all accidental contingencies. Phidias's divinities and Polycletus's athletes are all for various reasons paragons of the human race; an astonishing observation mingled with idealisation led to the creation of types who, by their stable beauty, are even truer than the flesh and blood examples which served as their models. This was a living sculpture that was only interested in the human being—mortal or god was virtually the same to the sculptor—and neither nature nor animals, with the exception of those like the dog or the horse who are so intimately associated with our life, were represented, and even the Centaurs themselves lost much of their primitive savagery. The output of sculpture was considerable in the forty years from about 450 to about 410 which is known as the Age of Pericles. The great centre was Athens where the Parthenon was decorated under Phidias's direction and where the Acropolis was peopled with statues, several of which were colossi. Workshops that were once very independent came under Attic influence; even the pure Argive art of Polycletus felt it. Although it encouraged the creation of so many buildings and sculptures, the relative tranquillity reigning in Athens until 432 rather softened the Athenians and led to a reaction against the severity of Phidias's ideals. The catastrophes of the Peloponnesian War and the fall of Athens in 404 not only ruined Greece's prosperity and made any ambitious enterprise unrealisable, but completed the disruption of traditional attitudes. After this new experience of suffering, the Greeks were more easily moved by all that deserved pity such as the weakness of old age and infancy, the fragile grace of womanhood and the torment of the passions. At the same time their faith in the power of reason was eroded by contact with Asia where many artists now went to seek their fortunes.

It was these tendencies that Cephisodotus, Praxiteles and Scopas, the greatest sculptors of the 4th century B.C., expressed in one form or another. Their tormented faces of accursed heroes, the mystical frenzy of a maenad possessed

The athlete Agias. Copy of a work by Lysippus. About 325-300 B.C. Delphi Museum. *Photo Boudot-Lamotte.*

Head of the
Ephebe of
Marathon.
Photo S. Meletzis.

Opposite page
The Ephebe of Marathon.
Bronze. About 340-300
B.C. Athens, National
Museum. *Photo Hirmer.*

by her god, and the sensual charms of seductive
adolescents or thinly draped goddesses are far
removed from the austere ideals of preceding
generations of sculptors. Although Lysippus, the
friend of Alexander, certainly intended to exalt
athletic force in his statues, his figures had none
of the reassuring poise of past sculptures. Instead,
they possess the elusive fluidity of a suppleness
that seemed to be shaken by a nervous shudder
even when they are immobile. Anxiety dominated
sculpture. In this age of dislocation, artists set
out to perpetuate the memories of those in the
present or the past who seemed to represent more
or less stable values by their qualities and the services they had rendered. Although portrait art
was practically unknown until late in the 5th century B.C., real or imaginary portraits of philosophers and politicians, who had won the reco-

gnition of a generation searching for moral stability, were made in ever increasing numbers. The
servility of the public, the vanity of sovereigns,
governors and important personages made portrait sculpture one of the most widely practised
genres in the Hellenistic period. Its fullest development was in Asia. From the 4th century B.C.,
Asia Minor became the favourite home of sculptors. There, they could be sure of earning a living
through commissions, better than in impoverished Greece. Although Athenian artists
carved a great number of funerary stelae representing the deceased with his family, the art of
the bas-relief reached far greater heights in about
350 on the temple of Ephesus or friezes of the
Mausoleum of Halicarnassus.

After Alexander's conquests, Greece, and
Athens in particular, remained the centres of the

academic style but the new centre of creative art was at Alexandria, Antioch, Tralles and Pergamum. The new tendencies found a brilliant expression there: a taste for nature, sometimes appearing in '' pictorial reliefs, '' at others in the creation of open-air sculpture and garden statuary like the *Farnese Bull;* a sense of caricature that produced the grotesque figures made in Alexandria and southern Italy; and a love for the tragic taken to extremes as in the famous frieze of the *Gigantomachy* on the base of the altar of Zeus at Pergamum.

Neither this sometimes breathless romanticism nor the cruel realism of the Alexandrian school found a very wide public. Most sculptors re-mained faithful to the traditions of a past of their own choosing which might be classical or even more remote. Praxiteles' success inspired a number of imitations which were often admirable (one being the *Venus de Milo*, dating from about 100 B.C.) but the taste of art lovers also encouraged the formation of an archaising school which tried to recapture the naïvety of the 6th century. Above all, fortunately for us, hundreds of copies were made of ancient works that were soon to disappear. The manufacture of these replicas continued up to the time of the Antonines and it is mainly from them that we know so much of what may well be the most glorious sculpture the world has ever seen.　　　　　　　　　　P.D.

Crouching Aphrodite. Roman copy of an original by Doidalsas. First half of the 3rd century B.C. Paris, Louvre. *Photo Tel.*

Aphrodite, called the
Venus of Cyrene.
Roman copy of a
Greek original of the
1st century B.C.
Rome, Terme Museum.
Photo L. von Matt.

421

Nyx. Fragment of the frieze from the Altar of Zeus and Athena at Pergamum. 197-159 B.C. Berlin Museum. *Photo Hirmer*.

Portrait of a man found at
Delos. Bronze. Early 1st
century B.C. Athens,
National Museum.

SCYRUS. Scyrus is not quite half way between Euboea and Lesbos but its isolated position
placed it outside the main sea-routes and it was
always considered as a lost island without any
links with the great centres of civilisation. Its
reputation was only due to legendary traditions.
It was in Scyrus that Achilles was hidden by his
parents among the daughters of King Lycomedes
in the hope that he would escape the destiny that
awaited him before the walls of Troy. It was also
in Scyrus that Lycomedes hurled Theseus from a
rock when Theseus had voluntarily exiled himself
on the island after giving Athens its first constitution. In 470 B.C. the Athenian, Cimon, discovered the body of the hero which he brought back
to his country with great pomp. It should be made
clear that the Athenian general did not go to
Scyrus merely to fulfil this pious mission but to
take possession of the island, expel its inhabitants
and install colonists who, at a time when sea
power was developing, could from their remote
look-out watch the comings and goings of
warships.   P.D.

SCYTALE. The scytale was a stick of a
determined breadth which the Spartans used to
ensure the secrecy of certain public messages they
sent, such as orders from ephors to generals away
leading an expedition. A leather ribbon on which
the message was written was rolled around the
stick and it could only be read if it was rewound
again on another stick of the same size. As a
result the word " scytale " finally came to denote
the message that had been sent in this fashion.

SCYTHIA. The semi-nomadic Scythians
lived on the steppes of southern Russia and the
centre of their empire lay between the rivers
Dnieper and Don. They were warriors and hunters
and wore a costume very different from that of
the Greeks, consisting of tight trousers, a kind
of vest and a pointed cap. Their favourite weapon

423

Unfinished Doric
temple at Segesta.
5th century B.C.
Ph. Leonard von Matt.

was the bow. Their tribes were ruled by kings.
They soon established relations, which were often
friendly, with the Greek colonists and, although
they had an original art of their own they readily
adopted Greek styles. Their nomadic life explains
their lack of architecture and sculpture, but they
liked to decorate their weapons of war, notably
their quivers, and they wore fine, rich apparel.
The bowmen who served as policemen in Athens
were all recruited from Scythia.   P.D.

S E A L S . Stones engraved for use as seals were
to be found throughout the east in Crete and then
later in Greece.   In the classical period, all
important documents and even letters were sealed
with a little wax or clay on which the imprint of
the seal was stamped.   The state also used seals
to authenticate official deeds and in Athens it was
the *epistates* (president) of the *prytaneis* who had
the safekeeping of the seal of the city (*See* Prytanis). The public seal was reddened by fire and
was also used to brand the slaves of the state.
In order to avoid the possibility of a seal's being
duplicated, Solon prohibited sellers of seals to
keep an impression once it had been sold.   The
seal was also used as a signature.   R.F.

S E G E S T A . Capital of the Elymi. Segesta
was situated in the mountains of western Sicily
and was constantly at war with Selinus (q.v.)
and is only mentioned here because of the admiration its inhabitants showed for Greek civilisation.
Its influence can be seen in their coins, which
included splendid tetradrachms with representations of a hunter and his dog; a little 3rd century theatre and especially the great Doric temple
begun in the 5th century B.C. and never completed. Its majestic ruins can still be seen today
towering up in the grandiose landscape.   P.D.

S E L E U C I D S . *See* Seleucus I.

S E L E U C U S   I . Seleucus I had the largest
domain of all the Diadochi (q.v.). In addition to
the kingdoms of Babylonia, Media and Persia
which he had won in 321 B.C. for the part he had
played in the murder of Perdiccas, the regent
of the central power, he also took over Syria and,
when Lysimachus died in 281, he annexed Asia
Minor as well. His troops proclaimed him king
of Macedonia but he never lived to enjoy the
title for he was assassinated in 280. Even when
he had given up the exercise of his authority over
the easternmost provinces acquired by Alexander

such as Parthia, Armenia and the Indian frontier region shortly before 300, the extent and diversity of the empire he had built himself made effective rule difficult. It was in vain that he and his successors founded one Greek settlement after another throughout the empire, for these scattered townships were never able to ensure the unity of peoples who had only felt Hellenic influence at its most superficial. Seleucus very soon concentrated on Syria, whose shores gave onto the high seas and whose well sheltered ports lay at the end of the caravan and merchant routes from Mesopotamia and even further afield. He set up his capital at Antioch, which he founded himself. From there he was able to keep an eye on the movements of the Lagides (q.v.), who had renewed the claims of the ancient pharaohs to Syria; these were now all the more dangerous as no treaty had settled any frontier between the two kingdoms.

The kingdom was also threatened by other dangers. In 270 the Galatians made their way into Asia Minor and, although Antiochus I defeated them before the town of Sardes, he had to let them settle in the valley of the Halys in a country which then became known as Galatia. Next there was the question of relations with Pergamum. After its governor, Philetaerus (q.v.), had betrayed and robbed his master Lysimachus (q.v.), he first elected to serve Seleucus, then in 262 demanded his independence so that his successors always had to reckon with the policies of the Seleucids.

The main struggle over the future of the kingdom was played out in Syria and, from the advent of Antiochus I to the throne in 280 until the treaty of Apamea in 188, no less than five wars were fought between the Lagides and the Seleucids for possession of this strip of land, which was so vital for a dynasty whose prosperity depended on the maintenance of the link between Mesopotamia and the Mediterranean. There is no need to trace the monotonous course of these wars which often took place far from the country disputed (during the third war between 246 and 241 the fighting took place at Sardes), nor is there any need to describe the reigns of the mediocre succession of rulers between the death of Seleucus I and the advent of Antiochus III in 223.

Antiochus III was the only one of these rulers to deserve to be called "the Great." Having first rid himself of those high placed officials who had proved to be incapable or dishonest, he restored the empire that his predecessors had gradually allowed to disintegrate. Although he was unable to recover possession of Parthia, which had become an independent kingdom in 249, or Bactria, he signed treaties of friendship with both states and reduced Asia Minor to submission again after its governors had shown an excessive independence of action. He invaded the kingdom of Pergamum and, in order to wipe out the stain of the defeat he had suffered at the hands of Ptolemy IV at Raphia in 217, he reconquered the part of Syria that the Lagides had seized.

The kingdom of Seleucus had almost been brought together again when Antiochus was faced by the power of Rome. After he had been defeated in the decisive battle of Magnesia ad Sipylum to the north of Smyrna, Antiochus signed a treaty at Apamea in 188 which wiped out all his former achievements. Syria continued to exist

Metope from Temple E at Selinus. Artemis and Actaeon. About 460 B.C. Palermo Museum. *Ph. Leonard von Matt.*

Selinus. Temple C: view from the north-west. About 550-530 B.C. *Ph. Leonard von Matt.*

as a nation and even triumphed in a victorious campaign against Egypt in 170, but was forced through lack of money to attack the Jews and it steadily declined as a power until Pompey finally reduced it to the rank of yet another Roman province in 64 B.C.   P.D.

SELINUS. No Greek site ever left such imposing ruins as those still to be seen in Sicily on the deserted site now called Selinunte. The town had been founded in about 650 B.C. at the south-western extremity of the island by colonists from Megara Hyblaea, which was a settlement on the eastern coast, itself peopled by Dorians who had arrived a century earlier. The Selinians settled over a wide area on a great open space around an acropolis which they reserved for sanctuaries. Their trade with the Greeks and the Carthaginians soon made them prosperous and they built other sumptuous temples to the east and the west on neighbouring plateaux. As good merchants, they cared more for material benefits than politics and their town had little importance in Sicilian history. But they were often at war with the Elymi of Segesta (q.v.) and it was in the course of one of these conflicts that the Carthaginians, who had allied themselves with the other side, took and destroyed Selinus in 409. A new and smaller city was built in 407

which vegetated until the middle of the 3rd century when the Carthaginians destroyed it once more, this time for good. The site was never inhabited again and it was an earthquake in the Middle Ages which gave the surviving buildings their present ruined aspect.

Except for that of Demeter Malophorus to the west, the temples have remained anonymous and are now designated by letters of the alphabet. They date approximately from 550 to 450 and one, temple G, was never completed. They were all built in the Doric order and most of them, in the Sicilian manner, have a chamber situated behind the cella and communicating with it, known as the adyton. Remnants of sculpted decoration from nearly all the temples can be seen in the museum at Palermo. Notable pieces are the metope showing Perseus slaying the Gorgon, and Apollo in a chariot seen in a frontal view, from temple C, belonging to the late 6th century B.C.; the metopes of Heracles and Antiope, Artemis and Actaeon, and Zeus drawing his wife towards him, from temple E, dated about 470.   P.D.

SEMELE. Semele was the daughter of Cadmus and Harmonia and the mistress of Zeus by whom she gave birth to Dionysus. Before the child's birth, she implored Zeus to show himself to her in all his splendour. As the god had promised to grant Semele's every wish, he was unable to refuse and Semele died burned by the divine fire she had herself provoked. Zeus then took the child from her womb and hid it in his thigh until it was time for it to be born.   P.D.

SEVEN AGAINST THEBES (EXPEDITION).

Boeotian legends inspired artists and poets for centuries. One of the most famous of them all, which notably inspired Aeschylus's great tragedy, was that of the Seven against Thebes. The story is as follows. Oedipus had two sons. After he had become aware of the crimes he had involuntarily committed and put out his own eyes, he was tended by Antigone but insulted and ill-treated by his two sons, Eteocles and Polynices, whom he then cursed. Once Oedipus had left Thebes, they decided that they would share the royal power alternately. But when it was time for him to hand over the throne, Eteocles refused to make way for Polynices. Polynices then sought refuge at the court of the king of Argos, Adrastus, and married his daughter. Adrastus promised to return his kingdom to him and led an expedition with seven chiefs including a famous soothsayer called Amphiaraus. The seven chiefs were unable to capture Thebes and during the decisive battle the two enemy brothers clashed in single combat with such fury that they both perished. Their uncle, Creon, then took power in Thebes and organised sumptuous funeral rites in honour of Eteocles but forbade anyone to bury Polynices who had been guilty of taking up arms against his homeland. It was then that Antigone obeyed the " unwritten laws " by disobeying Creon and burying her unfortunate brother with her own hands without fear of the pain of death she knew awaited her.

Ten years later the sons of the Seven, known as the Epigoni, reopened the war against Thebes to avenge the defeat and this time they were successful and captured the city.   P.D.

SHIPPING.

Greek merchant ships were called " round " or " hollow " in contrast to the shallower and narrower ships of war. They depended almost exclusively on sail and were much slower than the triremes. The largest of the merchant ships weighed scarcely four hundred tons (for reasons for this limitation of tonnage See Navigation). In the 5th century B.C., the formerly wealthy ports of Corinth and Aegina were eclipsed in importance by Piraeus, which had been modernised by Themistocles and which was the centre of an intense commercial and military activity. Later Piraeus lost its primacy to the ports of Delos, then Alexandria and Rhodes (See Commerce).

The navy was also created by Themistocles and consisted of triremes, ships with three rows of oars, which replaced the old pentekontoroi; these were manoeuvred by fifty oarsmen who all sat in a single rank and they were therefore described as monereis (vessels with a single bank of oars). The trireme was some fifty yards in length and somewhat less than seven yards in width, a long rapid vessel which could carry about two hundred men. The main body of the boat was in deal, except for the keel which was made of oak

Ship. Detail of a Proto-Corinthian krater. First half of the 8th century B.C. Toronto, Royal Ontario Museum.

Athenian trireme. Bas-relief. Athens, Acropolis Museum.

so that it might better withstand haulage ashore which was a frequent practice in ancient Greece. The prow was decorated with a pair of great eyes, which had an apotropaic value, and was tapered to a stem carrying the pointed ram which could pierce the hull of an enemy vessel. The poop was raised and curved in a volute, or like a swan's neck, forming the *aphlaston;* this with the ram, constituted the trophy should the ship be captured. The trireme had only one mast with a main-yard and a square sail; when the sail was not in use the mast was lowered towards the poop and lay horizontally on supports. Sail was only used when no enemy was in sight, and for extra speed sail might be used together with oars, but in combat all manoeuvres were made with oars only. Two large oars, placed on the outside of each side of the poop, served for steering. The oarsmen of the three ranks, placed one above the other, were known as *thranitai, zygitai* and *thalamitai,* the last sitting in the lowest part of the vessel, in the hold with the sides pierced by portholes. The Athenian trireme had 170 oarsmen: 62 thranitai, 54 zygitai and 54 thalamitai. Naturally, the oars were of unequal length, those of the thranitai were more than ten feet long, and those of the thalamitai some five feet. In addition to the 170 oarsmen, the crew consisted of about ten topmen who handled the sails and rigging as well as the bailers; ten naval soldiers *(epibatai),* equipped like hoplites and posted in the bows, whose duty it was to repel the enemy in case the ship was boarded and to leap onto the enemy's decks, and lastly the officers. They were: the

trierarch, or captain, and his staff, which consisted of the pilot, the quarter-master *(keleustes)* who transmitted orders to the oarsmen and gave them the beat with the help of a flute-player *(trieraules),* the officer of the prow who stood on the forecastle *(proreus),* the steward's mate, and a few other officers who supervised the oarsmen.

R.F.

SIBYL. The legendary prophetesses called sibyls are far more famous than the male prophets who were known as " Bakides ". The most ancient sibyl of all seems to have been the Trojan Cassandra, the beloved of Apollo. She had received the gift of prophecy but, as she refused to give herself to the god, he decided that her prophecies would be considered false by all who heard them. The " Sibyl's rock " at Delphi in the sanctuary of the Earth, the first prophetess, was associated with Herophile who was said to have given oracles there before the first pythias (q.v.) and even before Apollo's arrival at Delphi. Other famous sibyls were those of Erythrae (of whom the philosopher Heraclitus of Ephesus spoke with reverence) and Cumae. As many as twelve sibyls could be counted in the Roman period *(See* Oracles; Divination).

SICILY. " A vast land, rich in marvels that astonish and attract other nations, abundant in its goods, strong in the multitude of its people "; this was how the Latin poet, Lucretius, described Sicily in his time. And although " the triangular island surrounded by its eddies and

Casemates, called the Cave of the Cumaean Sybil.
Photo Leonard von Matt.

indenting the Ionian sea with its wide bays " had been a Roman possession for a long time, it remained a Greek island in the poet's eyes. Greek indeed it is in many of its aspects and its landscapes with their dark blue skies, the hard, pure lines of its jagged mountains and its broken, rugged coastline.

Its population had once been Greek and largely consisted of colonists who had begun arriving in the 8th century B.C. from Euboea, Corinth, Megara and Rhodes. Its civilisation, which influenced even the native tribes in the hinterland and the Punic trading posts on the west coast, was also Greek and the magnificent ruins, which may still be seen by the modern tourist, are equally Greek.

Sicily held an exceptional place in the Hellenic world. Although it could have been a meeting ground for the cultures of the east, north Africa and the west by its situation, it was not. One of the island's most recent historians has even declared that Sicily had only been " one of the culs-de-sac of Greek civilisation " which is explained by the fact that what the colonists were looking for and found there in the first place were large areas of cultivatable land and rich corn harvests. But the most perfect creations of Greek civilisation were to accumulate in this isolated pocket, especially in the 5th century B.C. and the reason, this time, was the exceptional wealth of the island. It was because the cities were so prosperous that they were able to build such outstandingly large and lavish buildings, and invite the artists, poets, scholars and philosophers who were unable to earn a living in their own countries.

Sicily had already been visited by the Achaeans and perhaps even the Cretans of the Minoan period, but we know nothing of the island's history before it was settled by the Greeks. First came the Euboeans who established a footing on the east coast and seem to have founded Naxos in 757 B.C. Then colonies increased in number and some even developed enough to send out settlers in their turn. Although the exact dates are controversial, Sicilian settlements occurred in the following order: Megara Hyblaea, in the mid-8th century B.C., named after the settlers' homeland; Leontini, peopled by Chalcidians from Naxos; and, most important, the city of Syra-

cuse, which was to have such a brilliant history, founded in 733. After a pause the southern coast was settled in its turn. In 688 the Rhodians founded Gela; Megara Hyblaea founded a subsidiary city at Selinus in about 650 at about the same time that Zancle was sending colonists to Himera. In 580 the city of Agrigentum was founded by colonists from Gela. Other towns, too numerous to mention here, were also founded and at the same time local townships began to be hellenised. As the Greeks had not yet had to face the hostility of the Carthaginians, whose trading posts in the west of the island did not impede their activities, we may say that by the late 7th century B.C. Sicily was truly a Greek island.

But the system of government differed in many respects from that in force on the other side of the Adriatic. The colonists, who had come to exploit the natural resources of the island, had shared out the land (we do not know on what principle it was apportioned among the settlers) and the natural play of economic laws soon gave rise to a landowning class which remained dominant for a long time. It took much less interest in industry and commerce than agriculture, and its

429

Sicily. Temple F at
Agrigentum, called
the Temple of
Concord. About
450-440 B.C. *Photo
Leonard von Matt.*

main aim was to increase its estates. As a result, conflicts ceaselessly broke out between the cities, who all wanted to enlarge their domains, and the military leaders, all chosen from among the land-owning nobility, became powerful enough to establish a tyranny. Consequently, this tyranny was not an institution basing itself on the people in order to fight against the great nobles as in other Greek countries; nor did it develop industries to provide work for a large number of workers; it was simply a creation of the upper classes, intended to defend their interests.

There is no space to give a detailed account of the constant struggles within the cities themselves or against each other, nor of the repressions of the natives' attempts to throw off the yoke of the colonists. What should be noted, however, was that the very prosperity of Sicilian states and their desire for expansion brought them into conflict with the Carthaginians in the west of the island. Matters came to a head in 480 B.C. when the Carthaginians synchronised their action with that of the Persian king in the Aegean in order to wage an offensive against the Greeks.

Gelon, tyrant of Syracuse, defeated the bar-

barians at Himera in a memorable battle that, according to tradition (probably false), was fought on the same day as the battle of Salamis. Even though this victory saved Sicily from an external threat it did not bring peace to the island nor diminish Syracuse's desire for domination. In the course of the 5th century B.C., the city came under a number of different regimes. It was more powerful than ever after its victory against the expedition sent by the Athenians in 413 and the government of Dionysius I seems to have given it control of the whole island. But the tyrant's hopes were frustrated and Sicily underwent a new period of internecine strife which was only brought to an end by Timoleon, a general from the Peloponnesus. Between 344 and 340, he brought peace again to a land that had been ravaged by so many wars and revolutions and in 339 the Greeks made peace at last with the Carthaginians. But the conflict broke out again after a short time and in 306 Agathocles, a gifted adventurer, needed all his talents to establish his authority over almost all of Sicily.

At the end of the First Punic War, Sicily came under Roman domination, but it was by its intermediary that much of Hellenic civilisation was absorbed by its still primitive conquerors.   P.D.

SICYON. Sicyon was not one of the most important cities in ancient Greece. It was situated on the northern coast of the Peloponnesus, some twelve miles from Corinth. Its most brilliant period was under the tyranny of the Orthagoridae, a family whose founder, Orthagoras, seized power in about 670 B.C. after his military victories. The most striking member of this dynasty was his grand-nephew, Cleisthenes, who reigned from 601 to 570. He was responsible for democratic reforms which changed the face of the state and it was owing to him that the three Dorian tribes which had hitherto been dominant were humiliated and dispossessed in favour of a fourth which grouped together all those who had been defeated during the return of the Heraclidae. The result was that an unprecedented racialist sentiment, unknown in any other Greek city, was born in Sicyon. Cleisthenes distinguished himself from other tyrants in the rest of Greece by his military talent. He answered the appeal of the Amphictionic League of Delphi for help and in 590 took part in the war against Crisa. He also took arms against Argos, the champion of the Dorians, and his hatred for the city was so great that he forbade the recital of the Homeric poems that celebrated its former glory. Cleisthenes gave his daughter in marriage to the Athenian, Megacles, and the wedding was the occasion for a festival that was still remembered in the time of Herodotus, for love of magnificence was part of his nature and the arts flourished during his reign. In later centuries, her sculptors, bronze-workers and schools of painting gave Sicyon a place that was more than honourable in the history of Greek civilisation. One of its greatest artists was none other than Lysippus (q.v.), the sculptor so much admired by Alexander. On the other hand, as it lacked both commerce and industry, the city was politically undistinguished. It only emerged from seclusion in 254 when Aratus brought it into the Achaean League which it led for the next thirty years. For a while, it was chosen by the Romans to be a companion city for Corinth, but this proved too much for such a modest city and it soon fell into decline. In 25 A.D. it was completely devastated by an earthquake.   P.D.

SILENI. Modern scholars have made a careful distinction between sileni and satyrs. In fact, it seems that the ancient Greeks themselves made no difference, but thought of them both as companions of Dionysus, beings of human appearance, some with goats' tails, others with a horse's tail, all with pointed ears and flattened noses. The sileni should not be confused with Silenus, in the singular. He was an old man, just

Sicily. Tetradrachm from Catane signed by Heracleidas. Apollo. About 415-400 B.C. Sicily, Private collection. *Photo Leonard von Matt.*

like his fellow-sileni, but outstanding among them for his wisdom, which he probably inherited from the union of his mother, a nymph, with Hermes or Pan. P.D.

SIMONIDES. Lyric poet who lived from about 550 to 460 B.C. He was born at Iulis, a tiny town on the little Ionian island of Ceos. He lived at Athens at the court of Hipparchus, son of Pisistratus, then at the courts of the princes of Crannon, Pharsalus and Larissa. He was already seventy years old at the time of the Persian Wars when he went to Sicily to the court of Hieron, the tyrant of Syracuse.

He was a court poet who demanded very high prices for the set pieces he was commissioned to write. He had practised every kind of lyrical genre, notably epigrams, dithyrambs, paeans,

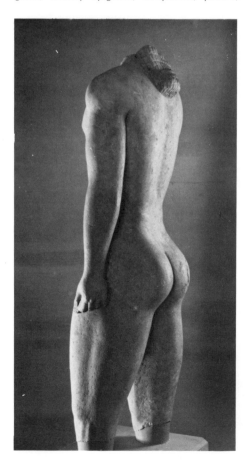

hyporchemes, epinikia and threnodies *(See Lyric Poetry)* but only about a hundred lines remain of his work.

In his poems Simonides expressed a likeable, cheerful wisdom with a great deal of wit and charm. He also wrote effective poems based on myths like the one describing how Danaë was abandoned in a chest with her young son, Perseus, on the high seas. His soft and haunting poetry and his subdued feeling are forerunners of the style of Pindar and Aeschylus rather than Euripides. He was the uncle of Bacchylides (q.v.). R.F.

SIRENS. For us the word " siren " suggests the image of a fish-woman, swimming in the storm-tossed waves. This was a comparatively late conception which originated during the last centuries of the pagan period and was popularised during the Middles Ages. The Greek sirens were birds with human heads, of either sex (in the archaic period they were often bearded), the prototype of which had come from Egypt and the east. They were musicians and essentially funerary " Muses of the other world "; they called the living to their death (the episode in the *Odyssey* in which Ulysses resists their enchantment is well known) and accompanied the souls of the dead into the remote kingdom where they were to dwell, consoling and cheering them with their songs. Sirens were often represented on the pediments of funerary stelae over the image of the deceased. P.D.

SISYPHUS. Sisyphus was the son of Aeolus and belongs to Corinthian legend which made him an ancestor of Bellerophon. His ingenuity was unrivalled and many inventions were attributed to him. His talent may well have been excessive and it would seem that the punishment he suffered showed how greatly the gods were disturbed by a man whose intelligence threatened to change the order of things. He was sent to Hades where he was condemned to push a boulder up a very steep slope, but always in vain for it continually fell down again. For the Greeks he remained the symbol of cunning. P.D.

SLAVERY. Every rich Athenian owned at least fifty slaves, to say nothing of the Greek

Torso of a kouros from Megara Hyblaea. First half of the 6th century B.C. Syracuse, Museo Archeologico.

Ulysses tied to the mast of the ship to escape the enchantment of the Sirens. Detail of a stamnos. About 480 B.C. British Museum.

statesman, Nicias, who owned more than a thousand, while the average bourgeois could count at least ten in his household. There were also many slaves belonging to the state and others belonging to the gods so that in 5th and 4th century B.C. Athens at any rate, the majority of the population was composed of slaves; the proportion may even have been as high as two thirds. The proportion was probably the same in other Greek cities, although even higher in Sparta where the number of citizens was constantly decreasing. It therefore seems all the more surprising that this huge population of slaves should have accepted its condition so meekly and that slave revolts—those of the helots being a different matter—should have been so rare. One of the main reasons was that men do not revolt against what they hold to be the laws of nature and that to the minds of the ancient Greeks, at least until the Hellenistic period when a few voices began to be raised in protest, slavery was an institution accepted by all. It was as old as the world itself and was solidly established among all the other peoples known to the Greeks. Just as horses and dogs were regarded as the natural servants of man, it was admitted without discussion, as an obvious fact, that men were not only born to serve other men, but also to belong to them body and

soul—if they had a soul at all. " Some individuals ", wrote Aristotle, " are as inferior to others as the body is to the soul or the beast is to man. The use of their physical powers is the only benefit to be gained from these individuals; they are destined for slavery by nature itself since there is nothing better for them than to obey. " Such a point of view was so common and seemed so much a part of the order of things that it was even accepted by those who were its victims.

The facts, however, contradicted Aristotle's theory, for the greatest inequalities existed between slaves and some were of outstanding capabilities. It could not have been otherwise. War and piracy were the great sources of supply for slaves; all who were not put to the sword when a city was captured, and all who had been taken alive by corsairs were sold into slavery. Plato owed his new-found liberty to the generosity of a Cyrenaean who had bought him at the market of Aegina. Some slaves were doctors, others were teachers and archivists and in the 4th century B.C. some, like Pasion and Phormion who were later enfranchised, became the trusted colleagues of great bankers and men with whom even the state had to reckon. In about the same period, the running of the main administrative services of the city was assured by public slaves. It is true that such slaves were the exception, for the majority were only humble servants who had been captured in the barbarian regions of Thracia or Asia Minor, or else born into slavery and raised by their masters who wished to assure themselves of a constant supply of manpower.

The condition of the slaves varied greatly according to the character of the master and their occupation. Many worked in the countryside where they helped their master to cultivate his parcel of land, labouring beside him, often on an almost equal footing; others remained in the house as servants and cannot have led a particularly hard life; still others were hired out by their masters because of their special capabilities and to be the possessor of a slave who was a good cook and who could be hired out on demand, was to have a steady source of extra revenue. Other slaves led a nearly independent existence such as those who were entrusted by their masters with the running of a shop or a manufacture. Even more varied were the occupations of the state slaves who might serve as humble roadsweepers or ushers in a court of law, as a director of archives or a public executioner, not to mention the Athenian police force which was composed of slaves from Scythia. The only slaves whose existence was really to be pitied were those who were used in mills to turn the millstone or particularly those who spent their lives toiling in the suffocating shafts of mines.

In theory, slaves owed total obedience to their masters. They were objects that the owner could dispose of as he pleased, selling them apparently without the least concern for any family ties that might be thereby broken, setting them to any employment he pleased, punishing them, imprisoning them, putting them in a carcan and branding them. The law helped the owner to recapture runaway slaves and international agreements even allowed him to cross frontiers in search of the fugitive. If the master was implicated in a criminal case, he was even entitled to demand that his slaves be put to the torture to make them confess what they knew. The slave had no legal rights and any money he might earn belonged to his master, who might, if he so wished, leave him a part, out of kind-heartedness or self-interest. But in certain cities, especially at Athens, the law did protect the slave against injuries inflicted by a third party.

A consequence of the naturally humane character of the Greeks was that most slaves could bear their lot almost cheerfully. They were often treated like servants of modern times, sometimes with that friendly familiarity which may still be seen in Greece between the mistress of a household and her maids, and they would be regarded as members of the household—all the more as they were not likely to leave it suddenly. Although the unions they might contract between themselves were not recognised by law, they were recognised *de facto* by their masters who would raise the resulting offspring who naturally belonged to them. Slaves took part in private and sometimes even public religious ceremonies. In times of emergency they were incorporated into the city and they might be mobilised in the army or, as was more often the case, the navy, where they served as oarsmen. It was possible for slaves to become free men, either by buying their freedom with the savings they were often allowed to keep by their master, or else by being enfranchised directly by the master during the latter's lifetime, or else by his testament. The newly freed slave did not thereby become a citizen and in Athens he was placed on an equal footing with the resident foreigner.   P.D.

SMYRNA. An Amazon was said to have given her name to the city of Smyrna in remote times. In ancient times, Smyrna was merely one of many cities that lay along the west coast of Asia Minor and was overshadowed by such cities as Ephesus and Miletus. The archaic settlement at the end of the gulf has recently been discovered. It is some three or four miles distant from the present site which dates from the Hellenistic period. It was then and during the ensuing Roman period that Smyrna developed to its greatest extent.   P.D.

SOCRATES. Socrates was born in Athens in 470 B.C. His father, Sophroniscus, was a sculptor and his mother, Phaenarete, a midwife. He died at Athens in 399 by drinking hemlock, after the people's tribunal had decided by a vote of 280 for and 220 against that he had been guilty of not believing in the gods of the state, of having introduced new divinities and corrupting the youth of the city. Although all the philosophical schools that followed him in Greece claimed him as their founder, he wrote nothing and his disciples all interpreted his teachings in their own manner. In 423 Aristophanes caricatured him in his play the *Clouds*, showing him as a sophist and a naturalist but also a meditative man absorbed in his spiritual exercises. His portrait in Xenophon's *Memorabilia* is rather flat but Plato portrayed him with extreme vividness in his Dialogues, although probably not without crediting him with a number of his own ideas.

Socrates declared that the only thing he knew was that he knew nothing (the feigned ignorance known as Socratic irony), but as the Delphic oracle had declared that no wiser man than Socrates was to be found, he carried out a survey among his fellow-citizens. While feigning ignorance, he skilfully questioned them on the knowledge they claimed to possess and on their pretended virtues. He saw that men were ignorant of what they believed themselves to know and he made them contradict themselves but, at the same time, his questions led them along the road to discovery (Socratic *maieutike* or awakening of minds). His questions generally dealt with moral problems and often aimed at the definition of the virtues and their relationship with knowledge, which led his interlocutor to a thorough examination of the moral subject. " No one is ever voluntarily evil " is one of the few positive affirmations credited to Socrates. He declared that he could detect a sign that forbade him to commit certain deeds (the daemon of Socrates) and this must certainly have been one of the reasons for the accusation brought against him, the other probably being his popularity with the aristocratic youth of the time who flocked around him to hear his words (Alcibiades, Critias, Plato, etc.). But the circle of his listeners included many other disciples like Antisthenes who became the head of the school of the Cynics, Eucleides who founded the school of Megara, and Aristippus of Cyrene, among others. P.-M.S.

S O L O N . " I come to herald Salamis the beautiful, bringing a poem filled with songs as proclamation. I should like to change my homeland and belong to Pholegandros or Sikinos [obscure isles] rather than to Athens, for soon it will be said among men: Here was one of those Athenians who abandoned Salamis. Let us go then to Salamis to fight for that pleasant island and reject such an intolerable shame. ". These are a few lines from the poem which brought an aristocrat by the name of Solon into the limelight in Athens in about 612 B.C. It is highly doubtful whether Solon did in fact lead the troops who recaptured the island from the Megarians, just as it is prob-

ably an imaginary scene that describes the poet wearing travelling costume, covered with dust, making his exhortation in the street, standing on the boundary stone from which public announcements were made.

Although he did not give up his poetry, Solon set himself the task of resolving the grave political and social problems of his homeland. He was named archon in 594 when he was nearly fifty years old and restored civil peace by proclaiming an amnesty. He introduced a reform known as the *seisachtheia;* the details are not known to us but we do know that, although it did not abolish debts, it did at least free the lands and the bodies of the debtors from distraint. " How many men, sold or forced into exile by debt, have I brought back to Athens! " Solon exclaims in one of his poems. Besides these social reforms and measures to develop the activities of the citizens (fathers who neglected to provide their sons with a trade were punished), he made a number of political reforms which became wrongly known as the constitution of Solon. They were half measures but they did modify the Athenian regime. The four property-owning classes were completely changed, magistrates were designated according to a new procedure and the assemblies were transformed. These were all measures that finally broke the hold that the family groups *(gene)* had over the individual. After accomplishing what he considered to be his mission, Solon retired and travelled abroad. He returned to Athens only to see his fellow citizens fall back into civil strife and Pisistratus usurp the supreme power for personal ends a year before he died (561). P.D.

S O P H I S T . There was nothing pejorative in the meaning of the word " sophist " at first; on the contrary, it denoted any man who was skilled in a certain art but particularly a teacher of philosophy or rhetoric. The sophists made their first appearance in the mid-5th century B.C. Before that time, Greek youths only received an elementary education from the *grammatistes* who taught them reading, writing and arithmetic, and the *paidotribes*, or master of gymnastics, and the musician who taught them to sing and play the lyre and the flute. The sophists were the first teachers of higher education and were always on tour. In each town where they stopped they gave lectures to display their knowledge and talent, which attracted new students who followed them and accompanied them on their travels. These lessons were very expensive and, according to Plato, the sophist, Protagoras, earned more than ten times as much as a sculptor like Phidias. The sophists brought a new approach into Greek thought; most of them were sceptics and their incisive criticisms spared neither the social order nor religion and several were prosecuted for impiety. *(See* Gorgias; Hippias of Elis; Prodicus; Protagoras).   R.F.

SOPHOCLES. Tragic dramatist (496-406 B.C.). He was born in the village of Colonus near Athens and was the son of a rich arms manufacturer. He was well educated and at the age of sixteen he was chosen as a lute player to lead the chorus of young people who celebrated the victory of Salamis by a paean. Twice appointed strategus, he never shirked his civic duties; he also held office in 443/442 as one of the *Hellenotamiai*, and, in 413 after the Sicilian disaster, *proboulos*. He was a more productive writer than Aeschylus and was said to have written 123 plays. He won the first prize in dramatic competitions more often than his rival and was never classed third, that is, last. He won his first triumph at the age of twenty-eight in 468.

Plutarch tells us that Sophocles himself said that he had written in three different, successive styles. He first imitated Aeschylus's " magnificence ", then he adopted an " incisive " and " very studied " manner, which was probably rather precious, before succeeding in giving each of his characters the most natural and most suitable tone. But we only have examples of Sophocles' third manner; his seven surviving tragedies belong to a " Selection " that had been made in Roman times according to pedagogic criteria, and they all date from the second part of his career. They are as follows, in the most probable order of their composition: the *Trachiniae*, *Antigone* (performed in 441), *Ajax*, *Oedipus Rex*, *Electra*, *Philoctetes*, and *Oedipus Coloneus*. The last play, in which Sophocles sang the praises of the deme where he was born, was written when the poet was nearly ninety years old and was only performed after his death, in 401. The *Trachiniae* is inspired by the legend of Heracles: Heracles' jealous wife, Deianira, sends him the shirt dipped in the blood of the Centaur, Nessus, and he dies in terrible agony. *Oedipus Rex*, *Oedipus Coloneus* and *Antigone* belong to the Theban cycle. In the first, as a result of the plague that ravages Thebes,

Oedipus learns the horrible truth in the course of his investigations: an unknown man he killed was none other than his father, Laius, and Jocasta, his widow, whom he had married afterwards, was his own mother. *Oedipus Coloneus* dramatises the death or rather the mysterious disappearance of Oedipus, who had acquired a kind of religious majesty as a consequence of all his misfortunes. *Antigone* is the drama of the conflict between established order as represented by Creon, and moral conscience, incarnated by Oedipus's daughter, who violates the king's decree by strewing earth over the body of her brother, Polynices, who had died an enemy of Thebes. The other three plays are inspired by the Trojan epic cycle: Ulysses and Neoptolemus go to Lemnos to seek out the sick Philoctetes who has kept the weapons of his friend Heracles, without which Troy cannot be captured. Impelled by his natural sincerity and pity, Achilles' young son frustrates Ulysses' design, but Heracles, the *deus ex machina*, makes Philoctetes decide to take ship for Troy. In *Ajax*, the hero of the title is passed over in favour of Ulysses by the Achaeans, who give him Achilles' arms. Ajax goes mad and commits suicide despite the touching efforts of his companion, the tender Tecmessa. The theme of *Electra* is the murder of Clytemnestra by Orestes. It had already been treated by Aeschylus in the *Choephoroe*, but Sophocles' art gave it new life.

Sophocles developed the study of character in drama considerably. Although he was certainly a believer, his theatre shows the gods and destiny allowing greater liberty of action to mortals; their influence remains in the background while the human will is the main-spring of the action. Unlike Aeschylus's characters, Sophocles' human beings are no longer mere playthings in the hands of the gods. All his protagonists are moved by a lucid, firm and unshakeable will which determines the action of the play. This contains few events; their main function is to vary situations and so give the characters the opportunity to express the reactions of their sensitive natures and the struggles of their souls. The catastrophes which afflict them are due more to themselves than to the gods. The pathos of Sophocles' drama is heightened by the fact that his heroes are nearly always struck down just when they are most confident of escaping their menacing destinies; this gives an added poignancy to Oedipus in *Oedipus Rex*, Clytemnestra in *Electra*, and

Creon in *Antigone*. This sudden, complete change in their fortunes and this immediate collapse, which they have themselves brought on, are the final failure of all their hopes and all their efforts. The drama of Sophocles creates a lesser feeling of terror than that of Aeschylus but the pity is more intense.

Sophocles' style is naturally adapted to the discussions and passionate dialectic of the characters who confront one another. His lyric poetry is less rich and more concentrated than that of Aeschylus; it is also calmer and more relaxed, Apollonian rather than Dionysiac. Like Phidias's sculptures, his drama is in the grave and noble classic mould; in other words, it has the maturity of an art that has reached its plenitude.   R.F.

SOPHRON. Mime writer of the 5th century B.C. *(See* Mime).

SPARTA. Sparta's destiny was a strange one. Although the city was always considered to be one of the most important in Greece, even by its enemies, it was in reality only a large country town spread over an area of several miles and it was so poor in public buildings that, as Thucydides said, " If one day all that remained of it were its sanctuaries and the foundations of its public buildings, posterity would find it hard to believe that its power ever matched its reputation. " Its institutions were held up to the world as examples by the wisest of the philosophers but, although no one was aware of the fact at the time, they were survivals of such primitive customs and rites that ethnologists have found them again, in almost identical form, among the most backward peoples of Polynesia and Africa. Lastly, although this state had made it a principle to proscribe the activities of craftsmen and merchants, all the most tangible remains of ancient Sparta are its small manufactured objects, which it exported far abroad, such as terra-cotta vases and bronze statuettes, whose high quality made archaic Sparta the rival of the most renowned art centres of the time.

The site of Sparta does not seem to have been inhabited before the 9th century B.C. but the immediate neighbourhood has yielded up important vestiges of Creto-Mycenaean civilisation. Amyclae, only a few miles to the south, was then a capital and nearby the tholos tombs of Vaphio have given us precious daggers with encrusted blades and two golden goblets, one decorated with the scene of the capture of wild bulls, the

Golden cup from Vaphio near Sparta. Minoan art. 16th century B.C. Athens, National Museum.
Photo Roger-Viollet.

437

other with their taming. When the Dorians crossed the Peloponnesus, and came to this southern province, they founded Sparta by the banks of the Eurotas, one of the few rivers in Greece that never dries up during the year. The site of Sparta was a vast valley, limited to the east by the Parnon chain of mountains, to the west by the snow-capped peaks of the Taygetus. Its prosperity was assured by its olive groves, orchards, its fertile fields and the vines growing on the mountain slopes. Laconia, as the province was named, was not naturally enclosed in isolation; it communicated with the outer world through its port at Gythium, and with the rest of Greece by passes linking it to Arcadia and, even though the way was harder, to Messenia in the north-west. Sparta's inward withdrawal into itself was no more due to geographical conditions than to the kind of austere life that its laws imposed on its citizens. It even began to assert itself as a state by a policy of expansion, conquering rich Messenia and making thrusts to the north and east towards Argolis and Arcadia with whom it was to have so many conflicts in the course of history.

It would be rash to offer the conquest of Laconia and neighbouring regions as an explanation for the strict hierarchical system which distinguished between true Spartans (known among themselves as *homoioi*, citizens with equal rights to hold offices of state) and the *perioikoi* and helots. Although the name of Lacedaemonian was given to the whole population of Laconia, it covers three quite distinct population groups: citizens with full rights who were the true masters of the state; the perioikoi who were grouped on the borders of the country, administered themselves and owned land although they were subject to the Spartans to whom they paid taxes and for whom they had to fight in case of war; finally, the helots, who were serfs attached to the soil, with no legal rights whatsoever. Although this class division was as old as Sparta itself, it does not seem to have been based on any ethnic differences between conquerors and conquered.

From the beginning, too, certain very old customs were adopted in Sparta which could also be found in other parts of Greece and especially in Crete. Far from abandoning them as time went on, the Spartans established them all the more firmly, probably about the mid-6th century B.C., by attributing their institution to the legendary Lycurgus. Sparta was the only really Greek city which remained faithful to the principle of royalty. Its two kings were hereditary and came from two families, who were never joined by blood, and shared a power that must have been very similar to that of the Homeric kings. They were both military and religious leaders and they enjoyed considerable prestige. As in the society to which Agamemnon belonged, warriors assembled to hold council with them, and twenty-eight of them were chosen by popular acclamation to join with their rulers in forming the *gerousia* which was probably an assembly of " privileged men " rather than a meeting of elders. This assembly reigned supreme until the 8th century B.C. when the kings had to submit to the supervision of ephors (q.v.), magistrates whose exact function, origin and designation are still far from clear. The other Spartans then formed a popular assembly with greatly reduced powers.

The way of life of the Spartans (whose number varied and gradually diminished; in their most flourishing period they must have numbered some nine thousand) astonished all the other peoples of antiquity. All work was forbidden them. Their subsistence was provided by a plot of land tilled for them by helots and perioikoi, and the homoioi would bring the produce of their land to a common table, which was a kind of mess where attendance was compulsory. These warriors lived an essentially communal life and family ties counted for little with warriors for whom marriage meant nothing more than brief clandestine visits to their wives before returning to sleep for the rest of the night in their dormitories. As soon as he was born, a child belonged to the community. It was not his father but the representatives of the state who had to decide whether he was to be exposed until he died or else merited survival so that he might serve the state. As soon as a boy was seven years old, he was snatched from his mother's care and enrolled in a troop of boys of his own age, where his way of life changed periodically as he grew older. Before reaching puberty, the boys began to associate with men, to follow their example, and to develop relationships which would guide them later in life. Then, as amongst certain Pacific tribes today, to become a man the boy was obliged to live apart, far from the others, sleeping on the ground, living by petty pilfering and even winning virile dignity by shedding the blood of helots who had the misfortune to be outdoors after nightfall, a mysterious and savage custom which stupefied

Plain of Sparta and Mount Taÿgetus. *Photo H. Müller-Brunke.*

the other Greeks and was known as the *krypteia*. After this retreat, the young Spartan took his place in the city and thereafter belonged to a group of warriors with whom he ate and whose existence he shared. The Spartan was obliged to marry but, as has been said, he did not leave his group once he had done so. Consequently, the woman enjoyed great freedom, for, far from living in seclusion as was the custom in the rest of Greece, she lived outdoors, practised violent exercises to make her even stronger and administered a household with which the husband was forbidden to concern himself. She was an object of scandal to other Greeks with her scanty tunic that hardly covered her thighs. " Even if she wanted to, a young girl could not be virtuous in Sparta, leaving the house, as she did, thighs naked and tunic flapping, to take part in the sports of the stadium and palaestra with young men, " said Euripides, although Spartan boys and girls lived apart in an atmosphere that almost amounted to hostility. Other customs that astonished the Greeks were the Spartans' indifference to adultery

and the possibility, according to Plutarch " for a virtuous man, who admired the merits and fertility of another's wife, to know her with the agreement of her husband and plant his seed in such fine soil, and thus have excellent children born out of an irreproachable union. " For the Spartans, the only thing that counted was the vigour of the breed.

The mistake of the ancient Greeks lay in thinking that such customs—so different from their own—had been instituted by a human will, by the legendary Lycurgus, in order to safeguard a state avid for power; for such customs date from the very beginnings of human society and are derived from the oldest and least planned superstitions. It is nonetheless true that by their very existence such customs had very important consequences for the development of Sparta. It was not in vain that young men passed their childhood subjected to the harshest of disciplines or that men were made to live side by side in an army. The education of young people neglected intelligence but gave great importance

439

Young Spartan girl running. Bronze statuette. 6th century B.C. British Museum.

to communal exercises and movements done to the rhythm of music so that the Spartan choruses were the most famous of all, and the phalanx, a Spartan creation, was as much a corps de ballet as it was an instrument of war. Strikingly enough, when the Spartans were painfully struggling against the Messenians in the 7th century, they invited the foreign poet Tyrtaeus to guide them and strengthen their courage. '' It is fine to die, falling in the front rank, as a man of courage, fighting for his country, '' sang Tyrtaeus, and '' let each set his feet firmly on the ground, bite his lips... and brandish his strong spear with his right hand as he waves the fearful plume on his helmet. ''

The Spartans made the most sparing use of their army but for centuries it triumphed on every battlefield and enormous scandal was created in 425 B.C. when it was learned that Spartan hoplites had surrendered on the island of Sphacteria instead of dying where they stood. Many Greeks and even barbarians made use of Spartan military valour when necessary, and the prestige of Athens itself appeared more fragile than Sparta's which had come to symbolise all the energy of the Dorian world despite its roughness. The greatness of Sparta, in fact, depended on

the renown of what were considered to be its virtues. Until the mid-6th century this greatness was a reality, for besides its military campaigns, the prosperity of the commerce and industry, which were managed by the perioikoi, gave a solid basis to Spartan power. When the ephor, Chilon, encouraged Sparta to shut itself in its own past and, practise what was known as *xenelasia*, forbidding its citizens to go abroad and putting obstacles in the way of foreigners' visits, and persisted in only using iron bars for currency, which were so heavy that a cart was needed to carry them when any important amount was involved, at a time when silver and bronze coinage had become current in the rest of Greece, Sparta began to be no more than a magnificent façade. It was still to have valiant generals like Leonidas, the hero of Thermopylae, Brasidas, who captured Amphipolis in 423, and Agesilas in the early 4th century; it was still to perform many brilliant exploits and even to have clever politicians like Lysander, who triumphed over Athens in 404, but it slowly died of internal exhaustion, the diminishing number of its citizens, and the disproportion between the number of plots of land and the men who obtained revenues from them. Sparta also died because of the unease felt by its citizens when they were confronted by a civilisation that evolved while their own stood still. After Athens had fallen in 404, more than one Spartan felt attracted by the easy life of the people he had conquered and rebelled against his own regime; officers were found pillaging the public treasuries and the high morality of the city of Lycurgus became nothing more than a past memory. After trying to extend its sway over the rest of Greece in the 1st half of the 4th century B.C., Sparta was swept away like other cities in the storm of the Macedonian conquest. Unlike Athens, it had no monuments to show Roman tourists; already, as Chateaubriand was to do much later, they came to the banks of the River Eurotas to seek the legendary memories of a splendid past. P.D.

SPHINX. Minoan civilisation and then the Greeks borrowed the myth of the sphinx from Egypt and the orient, but the Greeks were too realistic and logical a people to attach any great importance to such a legendary monster with a lion's body, a woman's bust and head, and long wings. In Crete, the sphinx, like the griffon, was the companion of the divinities who reigned over nature and protected even the dead. At the time the Dorians came, it had almost been forgotten, but it was adopted by the Greeks during the period of colonisation when there was a vogue for the exotic from abroad. The sphinx then joined other animals, both real and fantastic, in vase paintings at Rhodes, Corinth and even other cities which were less directly in contact with Asia. The sphinx might have completely vanished from the Greek repertory of legendary beings, together with the taste for exoticism, in the early 6th century B.C., if it had not acquired a certain funerary significance and if it had not come to be linked with one of Greece's most popular legends, that of Oedipus. Consequently, it was often represented facing the Theban hero. It recurs more frequently in the high classical period where it figured among the decoration of funerary monuments. When religions and themes from Egypt

Sphinx. Proto-Attic incense-burner in terra-cotta. 7th century B.C. Athens, Kerameikos Museum. *Photo Deutsches Archäologisches Institut, Athens.*

Stadium at Delphi.
Photo
H. Müller-Brunke.

and the orient penetrated into Greece in the 4th
century B.C., the sphinx won a new popularity.
                                                   P.D.

SPORADES. In contrast to the Cyclades,
which all lie close to one another, the isles of the
Sporades are more widely scattered throughout
the Aegean. The name is mostly used to designate the islands facing Euboea and Thessaly
such as Skiathos, Skopelos, Skyros (Scyrus)
and a few others of lesser importance. Because
of their distance from the mainland and the aridity
of their soil they are among the poorest regions
of Greece.   P.D.

STADIUM. Like the gymnasium and the
theatre, the stadium was one of the most characteristic buildings in Greek civilisation. It was
rectangular in shape, with one end rounded and
ending in tiers of seats, which also lined the two
long sides. Quite often, as at Delphi, one of the
long sides of the stadium was set against the
slope of a mountain so that the far side had to

be built over a supporting base. The length of
stadiums varied from place to place but they were
generally about 600 feet long. The word, *stadion*,
was also used to denote the same length.

The main, but not the only sport that took place
in the stadium was the running competition. The
starting line was marked by a row of cippi or
truncated columns, not far from the round tiers
of seats on one of the narrower sides of the stadium. At the far end of the track, a single cippus
(terma) marked the point where runners who
were racing twice around the stadium had to turn
to come back to the starting line. The single,
double and quadruple stadium runs were speed
contests but long distance races might be as long
as twenty-four stadiums or about two and a half
miles. Races were also run in armour when the
contestants wore the heavy armour of the hoplite,
and relay races were held between two teams,
when the runners held lighted torches, a type of
race called the *lampadedromia*. The stadium was
also used for the four other exercises of the pentathlon, jumping, wrestling, discus and javelin

throwing, as well as for boxing and the pancratium. Only horse and chariot races were held in the hippodrome (q.v.), which was much larger.

When the panhellenic games were held at Delphi, Olympia, the Isthmus and Nemea, the stadiums near these sanctuaries, like those built near towns, could also be used for meetings and musical performances in the open air.   R.F.

STATUES. Although statuary does not seem to have been very important in the 2nd millennium B.C. *(See* Sculpture), it occupied an eminent position in Hellenic civilisation from the 7th century onwards. The importance of the statue was less on account of its artistic worth than for the religious significance that the Greeks attributed to it even at fairly late periods. They believed that the statue incarnated the being it represented, whether mortal or divine. There were four different types of statue.

The cult statue was lodged in a temple specially built for it and represented the master of the sanctuary. The worshippers would address the statue, standing in front of it, and offer it sacrifices on the altar.

The votive statue represented a believer who wished to give it as a sign of his piety, either because he had some favour to ask or because he wanted to give thanks for some favour such as victory in the games. The votive statue was set up in the sanctuary and the donor would try to place it as close as possible to the statue of the god so that the latter would constantly have the image of his worshipper before his eyes and be disposed to think kindly of him.

The funerary statue was set on tombs. It only seems to have stood on male tombs for such statues only represented males.

Decorative sculpture formed part of buildings and was often in the round as, for example, when it was on the top of a building. This also had a religious significance and it was only in the Hellenistic period that statues sometimes tended to be profane, but there is still some doubt on this point for some images that have been considered to be purely secular were in fact inspired by legends and cults now lost to us.   P.D.

STELE. For the Greeks, the word " stele " also meant a column and a pillar, but for archaeo-

Grave stele, called the Giustiniani Stele. Young woman holding a pyxis. Early 5th century B.C. Berlin Museum.

443

Grave stele of Hegeso.
Late 5th century B.C.
Athens, National
Museum..
Photo S. Meletzis.

logists it only means a thin slab of stone fixed to the ground firmly and set up on a tomb, in a sanctuary or some public place, to commemorate some deceased person, a pious ceremony or some act related to the life of the city.

The funerary stele was first only a roughly hewn slab of stone to mark the site of a grave. As art developed, it became decorated with engraving, painting or relief sculpture, bearing some image relating to the life of the deceased. In the Myce-

naean period, stelae usually bore illustrations of hunting or warlike scenes. But all figurative decoration vanished from stelae from the end of the Bronze Age to the beginning of the 6th century B.C. The image of the deceased was then placed in the ground, as though the dead man was emerging from the tomb to receive the homage of the living. Such images were stylised; their aim was not to give any exact likeness but simply to indicate the type of person who had

died and his place in society, showing whether he had been a farmer, athlete or soldier, for example. When ideas on the after-life had changed in the course of the 5th century B.C., the deceased was no longer represented as though he were still in his grave; he was shown surrounded by his family, ready to leave for the Blessed Isles, which are the destination of all who leave us, and the style repeated that of the white-ground lekythoi. As these monuments were made in advance and were bought ready made from the marble-cutters, an inscription was made at the last moment to give the name of the dead person lying under the stele.

The votive stele was intended to remind the immortals constantly of some act of piety. The ceremony itself of the offering to be commemorated, the libation or sacrifice, was represented. Mortals were shown standing respectfully before a god who could be recognised by his greater size. The image was accompanied by an inscription, usually brief, which often only mentioned the name of the deceased. Stelae commemorating public acts belonged to the same category, for nothing could be done or decided upon in the state without the approval of the gods. The formula " to good Fortune, " which is found in most inscriptions, is in reality a pious invocation. Naturally, the text was given the most prominent place on the stele; it might be the transcription of a decree, the list of the clauses of a treaty, or the articles of a code of laws. If there was any figurative decoration, it consisted of symbolic ornaments such as wreaths for a citizen that had been honoured by his community, or else images of one or several divinities whose presence sanctioned the decision transcribed on the stele.

P.D.

STESICHORUS. Lyric poet (640-550 B.C.). Stesichorus is a pseudonym and means " master of the chorus ". The poet's real name was Teisias and he was probably born in Sicily at Himera. His best known poems were hymns which were sung by a motionless chorus to the accompaniment of a lyre, in honour of the heroes whose adventures Stesichorus celebrated in a new and original manner. Only a very few fragments of his hymns have survived, together with a number of titles such as *Geryoneis, Cerberus,*

Scylla, the *Boar Hunters* (of Erymanthus), the *Iliupersis* (taking of Troy), the *Returns*, the *Oresteia* and *Helen*. The last was followed by a palinode, since it seems that Helen had been displeased with the poet and had struck him with blindness, from which he only recovered after he had composed a second poem in which he contradicted the assertions in the first, at least, so Plato tells us in the *Phaedrus*. R.F.

STOICISM. The Stoic school was founded in opposition to that of Epicurus in 300 B.C. by Zeno of Citium (Cyprus). Zeno lived from 332 to 262, came to Athens in 312, studied in succession under the Cynic philosophers, Crates and Stilpon *(See* Cynicism), and Xenocrates and Polemon, the scholarchs of the Academy, and Diodorus Cronus of Iasos. He then taught in the Stoa Poikile, the frescoed hall, which gave the school its name. He recommended men to lead coherent lives in conformity with nature which is animated by a rational and igneous breath of life, the *logos*. The universe emanates from this *logos* and is periodically reabsorbed by it at the

445

end of the Great Year in a purifying fire (universal conflagration). The Great Year was a long cycle—estimated by the Stoic, Diogenes the Babylonian, at 365 times 10,800 years—at the end of which the stars and constellations would return to the positions they were in at the beginning. The logos was also to be seen in the fatal chain of causes (destiny) whose necessity is recognised by the wise man. Because he knows the logos, which is present within himself, a man can lead a rational life. He can refuse to follow the evidence of his senses or give in to his passionate impulses. The wise man is master of himself and only accomplishes perfectly virtuous deeds. As for indifferent deeds, he must prefer those that conform to nature and can be justified by reason.

Zeno was succeeded by Cleanthes of Assos who was scholarch from 262 to 232, and author of a *Hymn to Zeus* in which he declared his submission to destiny, the divine order of the world. He was followed in turn by Chrysippus of Soli, who directed the school from 232 to 204. He reorganised and completed its doctrine, which he defended against Arcesilaus's objections; the lines of his contribution lay in developing the logic and, in particular, the theory of hypothetical syllogisms, dealing with the problem of the relation between destiny and liberty, and elaborating an intellectualist theory of the passions. From 204 to 129 the school was successively directed by Zeno of Tarsus, Diogenes the Babylonian, and Antipater of Tarsus. Early Stoicism was then succeeded by Middle Stoicism whose most famous masters were Panaetius and Posidonius (qq.v.). Panaetius was born at Lindus, on the island of Rhodes, in about 185 and stayed for a long time at Rome with Scipio before directing the school from 129 until his death in about 109. He was the author of famous works which inspired Cicero and Plutarch: *On Providence*, *On the Nature of the Gods*, *On the Tranquillity of the Soul*. For Chrysippus's intellectualist monism he substituted a dualist theory of man in which irrational impulses are opposed by natural tendencies. He also elaborated a theory of the virtues and a theory of persons (the name then given to masks) which marks a date in the history of the idea of personality. His pupil, Posidonius of Apamea (q.v.), lived from 135 to 50. He founded a famous school at Rhodes where he performed official duties and Cicero was among his students. He made a long trip to the west of Europe as far as the Atlantic coast of Spain. He also constructed a vast synthesis of the knowledge of his time. Strabo has described his theory of the tides; the influence of the sun and moon was an indispensable part of it and it illustrated the Stoic idea of universal sympathy. Cicero has also mentioned an astronomical device, a planetarium, which he built. Seneca has discussed his theory of the origins of civilisation and techniques and how he attributed their invention to sages. Although sufficiently solid proof is lacking, he has also been credited with a vitalistic dynamism and a mystical eschatology.

Stoicism had a great influence in Rome under the empire, notably inspiring the works of Seneca and Epictetus (q.v.) and the emperor, Marcus Aurelius, who wrote his journal in Greek. We still find Stoic philosophers at the end of the 3rd century A.D. at the time of Plotinus (q.v.) for the doctrine had endured for nearly six centuries, and even today, its influence survives.   P.-M.S.

STRABO. Historian and geographer, born at Amaseia in Pontus about 60 B.C. As a historian, Strabo followed Polybius (q.v.) by giving an account of universal history from 146 to the foundation of the Roman Empire. As a geographer, he left a complete picture of the ancient world at the beginning of the empire in his surviving work, the *Geography*.   R.F.

STRATEGUS. In Athens, command of the army belonged to one of the archons (q.v.), the polemarch, until the early 5th century B.C. Like his colleagues, the polemarch was chosen by lot from a fairly restricted category of citizens who were quite accustomed to bearing arms so that in a time when courage was the first thing that counted in a victory, such a means of selection would not create any grave problems. When Cleisthenes' (q.v.) reforms created the ten new tribes to give a frame-work to the state, each tribe formed a military unit which still remained under the supreme, but soon purely nominal, authority of the polemarch but which had its own command formed of officers elected by the people; the first of these officers were called the strategus. This reform happened to coincide with the enlargement of the archonship, which was still drawn by lots as before, but from among a much larger number of candidates than in the past. Even if allowances must be made for corruption and inevitable intrigues, the archons were largely incompetent and strategi necessarily became more important than officials drawn by lot from a list of five hundred names, all the more as Athens was in the throes of a crisis and the business of war had become more complicated than in the past.

Each strategus belonged to a tribe and, in principle, they formed a college and took turns in commanding the army, every tenth day. Experience very soon made them give up such a senseless system and at the start of each expedition a decree named the magistrate who was to lead it and assume full responsibility. To ensure the unity of military operations, his authority extended over the navy and his opinion naturally carried the greatest weight during negotiations with allies or enemies so that the polemarch soon lost all effective power. The great worth of some strategi also helped to deprive the other archons of their essential attributes. The strategi had an enormous advantage over the archons for, by a derogation which was quite unique in Athenian administration, they were elected for a year but their term of office could be extended indefinitely so that it was possible for them to launch long-term enterprises without being doomed from the beginning to leave them unfinished. This was the explanation of Pericles' uninterrupted tenure of office from 443 to 429.

This vaguely defined power was very great for a time. Not only did the strategus command the army, attend to details of mobilisation, conduct the campaign, ensure discipline, administer the war budget and often levy tribute from allies, he was also called upon to act as a diplomat and, on several occasions, to represent his country abroad. The reports that he sent to the senate and the assembly contained advice that was often thinly disguised orders and when he appeared before the popular assembly, which he had the right to summon for an extraordinary session, he was the first to put forward his proposals. He also had the right to participate in the most secret councils.

Admittedly, such extensive powers in a country that was radically hostile to tyranny were limited by rules which were the same for all Athenian magistrates. The *dokimasia* (q.v.) was severer for them, since it seems that they had to be the father of at least one legitimate child and to own property in Attica. They had to keep the people constantly informed of their activities and to justify themselves when replying to the harsh criticisms that were often made against them.

If they made an ill advised manoeuvre, they risked such grave charges as illegal behaviour and, if they were ordered to investigate affairs concerning national defence, these cases were judged not by them but by the regular tribunals. Lastly, on relinquishing office, they had to render accounts that were closely scrutinised and they were personally responsible for the funds that had been entrusted to them. However, this rendering of accounts was only compulsory when they had finally relinquished office, and it did not take place if they were immediately re-elected. The efficacy of these democratic guarantees is proved by the fact that not one of the strategi ever tried to become a tyrant.

In few other magistrates' offices did the personality of the man elected count for so much; Pericles' supremacy led to an unlimited expansion of functions that were not restricted by any rules. After his death, the office of strategus became less important because none of his successors was able to assume it as brilliantly as he had done. The strategi then renounced all political influence and confined themselves to the performance of the military duties which were their only real function. In the second half of the 5th century B.C., five were given particular and clearly defined responsibilities in the army: one was the strategus of the hoplites and became the most important of the strategi; another was in charge of national defence; a third was directed to keep watch on the coasts, actually, two strategi shared this duty; a fifth had to distribute military liturgies (q.v.); while the five remaining strategi were given well defined missions according to circumstances. When Athens lost its independence, the office was still an important one but the activity of the strategus was necessarily restricted since the city had become no more than a municipal body. Athens was not the only city to have strategi; the post was to be found in several other Greek states. The functions of the strategi were always important but they varied in considerable detail according to period and place.   P.D.

STYMPHALUS. Stymphalus is in the north of Arcadia. Its fame rests chiefly on the exploit of Heracles, which he accomplished there, when on the orders of Eurystheus he delivered the region from the monstrous birds that haunted the nearby lake. There was also a town of Stymphalus, even mentioned by Homer, whose ruins have now been found. It was situated on the borders of Argolis, and usually chose to associate with this state.   P.D.

SUNIUM. Cape Sunium lies at the extreme end of the pointed Attic promontory and both the distant landscapes of Argolis and the isles of the Cyclades may be seen from it. It was the site of a sanctuary of Poseidon and the ruins of its Doric temple still dominate the surroundings. It was built in the second half of the 5th century B.C. and was originally surrounded by porticoes, and was approached through propylaea.   P.D.

SUPPLIANTS. Anyone who had committed a serious offence that might incur the displeasure of the gods against his community, either family or city, found himself automatically excluded from society. Until a ritual purification had washed the defilement (q.v.) from him, he depended on the pity of his fellows for his means of survival. He became a suppliant. Excluded from sanctuaries, he held a branch in his hand and begged help which piety enjoined them to give him; but, in certain cases, this was dangerous as the suppliant's defilement could contaminate those who came near him, until the day when a religious purification regularised the offender's position. Suppliants, however, were not necessarily criminals; they might simply be unfortunate men driven from their homes by some reverse. Their very misfortunes sanctified them and it was impious to reject them. The type of the suppliant was sufficiently well known for Aristophanes to use it in a parody of Euripides and his heroes who were always so miserable.   P.D.

SYBARIS. Sybaris was founded on the western shore of the gulf of Tarentum by colonists from Achaea in the 8th century B.C. The extraordinary fertility of the soil soon gave the city a legendary prosperity. Equally legendary was the softness of its inhabitants, who were accused by their enemies of spending their lives in idleness and luxury, refusing to make any effort and hardly able to bear even the activity of their slaves who toiled around them. Such a charge is obviously false; so much gold would not have poured into the town if its population had not been industrious. In 510 B.C. Sybaris was attacked by the Crotonians, led by the famous Milo, who was attracted by the prospect of so much booty. The city was completely destroyed and the inhabitants were forced to flee for shelter to neighbouring cities.   P.D.

Heracles killing the Stymphalian birds. Detail of an Attic amphora. Late 6th century B.C. British Museum.

448

Temple of Poseidon
at Cape Sunium.
About 440 B.C.
Photo Hassia.

SYCOPHANT. The sycophant was a man who was an informer by trade in order to win the reward given to any accuser whose denunciation was proved to be founded by the tribunal. The origin of the word which really means " he who shows figs " is obscure *(See* Justice).

R.F.

SYNOECISMUS. In the eyes of the Athenians, nothing contributed more to Theseus's glory than the fact that he had brought all the inhabitants of Attica, who had been living until then in dispersed scattered hamlets, into a vast community of which Athens became the centre. This operation had been given the name of synoecismus, meaning regrouping. It was not a transfer of populations; everyone remained in his home; it was a political unification and the creation of a city-state in which people, who had formerly been living in small anarchic clans, were united by a common cult, around a common centre and lead-

er. Theseus's personality is so legendary that it is not certain he achieved such an important feat, but the reality of the synoecismus is beyond doubt (it is worth remembering that the name of Athens is a plural), and we know that it occurred one or two centuries before the end of the 1st millennium B.C. Other cities in historical periods were also founded by the same process, when several, unimportant villages decided to unite in order to make a common front against the difficulties facing them.

P.D.

SYRACUSE. " Syracuse, immense city, temple of Ares, that ardent warrior, divine nurse of men and iron-barbed horses " was Pindar's description of the city. It was one of the first to be founded in Sicily and in its time occupied a dominant position on the three-pointed isle. Its beginnings were modest: in about 633 B.C., Corinthians led by Archias settled on the islet of Ortygia and then spilled over onto the mainland

449

along the vast bay facing them, and fortified the plateau of Achradina. The foundation of the city was marked by bitter quarrels, for the rich landed proprietors, the *gamoroi*, ruthlessly dominated the common people composed of craftsmen and sailors. Less than a century after its creation, Syracuse was populated enough to be able to found colonies in its turn, at Acrae, Casmenae, and later at Camarina.

Meanwhile, wars raged between the cities, and in 485 the city was captured by Gelon, the tyrant of the rival city of Gela. He made his new conquest into the capital of a vast domain and brought there the population of other cities, including his own, so that for the whole of the 5th century B.C. Syracuse enjoyed an incomparable prosperity. It covered itself in glory in 480 when Gelon crushed the Carthaginians before Himera, when he went to the aid of his son-in-law, Theron of Agrigentum. In 478, Gelon was succeeded by his brother, Hieron, and the new reign was marked by a series of successes that Pindar later celebrated; in 476 probably, after expelling the inhabitants of Catana and Naxos, Hieron founded the new city of Aetna over which his son Dinomenes was to rule; in 474, he sent his fleet to help the Greeks of Cumae and defeated the Etruscans before this city; lastly, in 472, the only prince able to compete with him, Theron of Agrigentum, died and he won a brilliant victory over the tyrant's successor, Thrasydaeus. He triumphed in the Olympic games on several occasions, and received artists and poets at his court, notably Aeschylus, who had his *Persians* performed at the court and wrote his play *Aetnae* in praise of his host.

When a democratic government was established in 466, Syracuse dominated a good part of Sicily, its commerce was prospering, its admirable coinage was sought after and its wealth had excited the cupidity of the Athenians, who showed great optimism in hoping to capture the city during the Peloponnesian War (414). But the expedition was badly prepared and, badly led; it began under gloomy auspices and ended in a disaster that even further increased Syracuse's reputation. Countless Athenians perished in the famous quarries of the Latomiae. where their captors had confined them, or else only escaped death to be sold into slavery.

In 405 a new danger threatened the city. In order to repel an attack of the Carthaginians, the

Syracuse. The Latomiae: quarries where the Athenian prisoners were shut up and a great number died.
Ph. Leonard von Matt.

450

Syracusans appealed to a new tyrant, Dionysius I, who reigned until 367. He began by enclosing the city and the plateau dominating it, behind powerful walls, 18 miles long, whose key point was the fortress of Euryalus, a masterpiece of military architecture. Syracuse was then able to withstand the assault of the Punic troops under Himilco's command (396), and twenty years later the war ended, at least for a time. Meanwhile Dionysius had founded the towns of Ancona and Adria on the Adriatic coast of Italy and acted as the champion of western Hellenism when he took an active part in the negotiations between mainland Greece and the king of the Persians. But the Carthaginian peril was always present and, having re-established a democratic regime, Syracuse called upon Agathocles for help in 316. He carried the war into Africa in order to save both his country and his own power (310). In 265 the government was headed by Hieron II, whose policy of alliance with the Romans gave his fellow-citizens nearly fifty years of tranquillity.

It was after the rupture of this alliance that Syracuse suffered the catastrophe from which it never recovered; after a siege led by Marcellus, in the course of which Archimedes was killed, the city was captured in 212 and most of its accumulated treasures were carried off to Rome.

Little trace now remains of the city's glorious history stretching over more than four hundred years. The visitor has only to see the two bays on either side of the city, barely cut by the canal separating Ortygia from the mainland, to understand why these two marvellous ports—one narrow and lacking some of the natural facilities of the other, larger and better protected harbour—should have contributed so much to the wealth of the city into which all the riches of the vast granary that was Sicily came pouring. The imposing mass of the Euryalus and the proud fortifications surrounding Syracuse can still be admired. In its final form, given to it by Hieron II, the theatre is one of the finest to survive from the Hellenic world, but so little remains of the sanctuaries and temples that modern guide books hardly give them a mention. The oldest is that of Apollo, whose proportions were lengthened by its double row of columns along the façade. Following a common practice in Sicily, the opisthodomos was replaced in the same position by an adyton, a closed chamber which only communicated with the cella. The order is Doric, the columns monolithic, and their low height and the flat capitals pressing down on them must have given a rather squat appearance to the whole structure. Nevertheless, the mason was proud enough of his work to leave his signature on the columns. The Olympieion is some ten years earlier in date and was built in about the middle of the 6th century B.C., but it is almost entirely destroyed. The temple of Athena was built at the time of the victory of Himera and is more skilfully designed. Its plan is very simple and conforms strictly to the canons, but certain refinements that the architects of Greece only adopted rather later may be seen in the construction; the two last intercolumniations on either side are progressively reduced to correct the optical illusion that would make them appear larger if they were mathematically equal to the others.

The buildings that once must have graced the city have all disappeared together with the hundreds of individual works of art that the Romans carried away. Perhaps the only consolation that remained for the Syracusans was that the " ferocious victors, " as Horace called them, were to develop a taste for things of beauty.

P.D.

TANAGRA. Tanagra was an obscure village in Boeotia which only owes its present reputation to the craftsmen who made the little terra-cotta figurines that have been found by thousands in the tombs of the region. These craftsmen handed down the art from father to son during the whole of the Hellenic period. When they were first found, the success of these " dolls " was so great that the name Tanagra was indiscriminately used for all antique terra-cotta figurines regardless of their provenance *(See* Figurines). P.D.

TANTALUS. The legend of the endless torture of Tantalus goes back to the 6th century B.C. According to one version, Tantalus was condemned in the underworld to be constantly in fear of a huge boulder threatening to crush him; according to another, he was always frustrated in his efforts to drink water, which ran away when he lifted it to his mouth, and to eat fruits just out of

Decadrachm of Syracuse designed by Cimon. Late 5th century B.C.
Ph. Leonard von Matt.

Silver coin of Tarentum. Phalanthus, the founder of the city, riding on a dolphin. 470-460 B.C. Naples, Museo Nazionale. *Photo L. von Matt.*

his reach. The reasons for his punishment remained obscure and it was uncertain whether he was being made to suffer because he had betrayed the secrets of the gods, stolen nectar and ambrosia from a divine banquet to which he had been invited, or for having served up to his guests the body of his son Pelops (q.v.) whom he had killed and who was resurrected by the gods.   P.D.

TARENTUM. Tarentum was one of the most brilliant of the many cities of Magna Graecia. It had been founded in the last years of the 8th century B.C. by illegitimate Spartans who were said to have been banished as the result of an unsuccessful conspiracy. The legendary Phalanthus, who was probably a marine divinity, and the hero, Taras, were said to have presided over the city's foundation. The settlers first had to fight against the native tribe of Iapygians before being able to settle on the site, which had been assigned to them by the oracle of Delphi. It was an excellent site, as it was in the best sheltered part of the gulf to which the new city gave its name. The city was Dorian in its origins, its dialect, forms of worship and organisation. It became

Young girl acrobat. Terra-cotta from Tarentum. Hellenistic period. Taranto Museum. *Photo Leonard von Matt.*

prosperous through developing its agriculture, industry and commerce, and maintained profitable relations with Miletus, the richest of the Greek cities in Asia Minor.

Tarentum had to fight against its barbarian neighbours such as the Messapians, Lucanians and Samnites, and celebrated its victories with ex-votos at Delphi. It also took part in the internecine wars between the Greek cities, both in Magna Graecia and on the other side of the Adriatic; its Laconian origin is not by itself enough to explain its hostility to Athens at the time of the foundation of Thurii (443) and during the Peloponnesian War. In the 4th century B.C. the city began to assume a leading position. The threat of the native peoples had then become much more serious than in the past. Under the leadership of Archytas, who was strategus for seven years running, probably from 367 to 361, Tarentum headed an Italiot confederation with its centre at Heraclea, a town founded in about 433. The city managed to crush Apulia and Lucania and its prestige was never as great as it was at this time. But this success was short-lived. Once the confederation had broken up, Tarentum appealed to the king of Epirus, Alexander of Molossia, for aid in fighting against the barbarians. From then onwards, the history of the city was that of wars, both successful and unsuccessful, against the natives, and a complicated series of manoeuvres in which the Greek cities of southern Italy and Sicily sometimes fought with her and sometimes against her. The situation worsened when Tarentum was faced by the power of Rome. Despite Pyrrhus's aid and such brilliant victories as that of Heraclea in 280, the city fell in 272, leaving the conqueror, in the words of a Latin historian, " all its marvels, its gold, its purple, its statues and its pictures ".

The history of Tarentum was not only bound up with politics and warfare. From its beginnings, it had been an art centre and its production had been considerable. All we need mention here is its coinage and the thousands of terra-cotta figurines that its modellers had made. As such a rich city would have attracted foreign artists, it must have been what we should now call an " art city ".

After its defeat, it did not lose its autonomy immediately and its total collapse only came with

The River Eurotas and Mount Taÿgetus. *Ph. Boudot-Lamotte.*

Head of a woman, called Hygeia, found at Tegea, Arcadia. About 350 B.C. Athens, National Museum. *Ph. S. Meletzis.*

the Punic Wars. It then became merely one of the many Greek cities that Greece's own fall had plunged into irremediable decadence. P.D.

TARTARUS. The underworld (q.v.) where the dead resided was a subterranean domain, but even deeper underground lay Tartarus, the place where the gods emprisoned the enemies they had vanquished, such as the Cyclopes who had revolted against Uranus and were delivered by Zeus when he took possession of the world, the Titans who had been vanquished by the Olympians, and all the greatest sinners who had committed sacrilege by encroaching on divine privileges. P.D.

TAXES. It was an accepted principle in Greek cities that citizens who could be called upon at any moment to defend their country were exempt from all payments because of this obligation. At Athens, no direct taxation was imposed on them except for a few taxes that were levied on contractors of public works. Direct taxes did exist, however, but they only affected foreigners domiciled in the country, the metics *(metoikoi)*. Even these were quite mild: twelve drachmas a year for a man, six for a woman, a residents' tax, in fact.

There were exceptional circumstances in which financial demands were made on the citizens. When war was declared, for example, the assembly of the people decided the gross sum required of which one sixth had to be paid by the metics and the rest by the citizens. This contribution of about two or three per cent was payable by everyone possessing property valued at one thousand drachmas or more. We do not know when this levy, the *eisphora*, was first made; probably at the outbreak of the Peloponnesian War. It was levied on several occasions and the method of collection was reorganised in 378 and 362 B.C., when the tax-payers were divided into groups, the *symmoriai*. The aggregate wealth of each was approximately equal, so the sum contributed by each was the same. The tax-payers within each group paid a sum proportionate to their income. Naturally, disputes were frequent on the value of an individual's property and the amount he ought to pay. Besides, this the state imposed *leitourgiai*, or liturgies (q.v.), on the richest citizens to meet

some of its expenses. These were such a heavy burden that they caused frequent court appeals and proposals for exchanging properties.

Needless to say, only very small states could work a system like this, whose simplicity and economy are startling compared to the complex organisation of modern finances. P.D.

TAYGETUS. This was a high mountain chain bounding the plain of Sparta to the west. Its highest peak was about 7903 ft high. It was there that the young Spartans went to exercise and acquire the endurance that made them the best soldiers in Greece.

TEGEA. Tegea was the only important town in the rural province of Arcadia. Its history mainly consists of its quarrels with Sparta, to whose authority it had to submit on several occasions. Scopas decorated and may even have built its temple, consecrated to the local goddess Athena Alea, and a few humble vestiges still remain of his work.

An enigmatic marble head, supposed by some

Temple of Hephaestus, called the Theseum, at Athens. About 449-444 B.C. *Photo Chéruzel.*

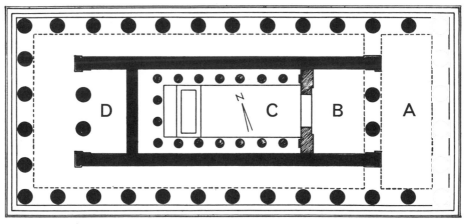

Plan of the Temple of Hephaestus at Athens. A. Portico. B. Pronaos. C. Naos. D. Opisthodomos.
B, C and D constitute the sekos.

authorities to be that of Hygieia, one of the most beautiful examples of 4th century B.C. art, has been found on the site.   P.D.

TELEMACHUS. Telemachus was Ulysses' only son. When his father left for the Trojan War, he was only a child, whose education was super- vised by Mentor. As the *Odyssey* tells us, when Telemachus reached manhood he defended the kingdom of Ithaca against rival claimants and sailed to Pylos and Sparta to ask survivors of the great expedition for news of his father. He returned to Ithaca just in time to help Ulysses reconquer his throne and massacre the claimants.   P.D.

TEMPLE. For the Greeks the temple was not like a church, a mosque or a synagogue where the faithful would gather for an act of worship, but the dwelling of the divinity himself. Except in the relatively rare sanctuaries where the god rendered oracles and received those who wished to consult it, the only mortals permitted to enter its sacred domain were the priests and sacristans responsible for its maintenance. There was no need for the temple to be large, for the statue with which the god was identified, was the only thing placed in it. Although the god might wish to have some of the offerings of his pious worshippers near him, only the most precious and fragile were ordinarily placed in the temple; the others were put else where in the sanctuary. The statue of the god had to be placed so that he could see and smell the food and drink that were burned or poured on his altar. Except in very archaic times, the altar was set in the open for convenience and hygienic reasons, but the temple door opened onto it so that, when they made a sacrifice, the worshippers could see the holy image before them.

As the ordinary house was taken as a pattern for the dwelling of the god, the original form of the temple resembled it closely; in the earliest periods, it was no more luxurious (the temple of Apollo at Delphi was only a hut made of branches at first); for a long time, it was built of wood and brick and always designed according to the same plan, generally oblong but sometimes with an apse, in certain regions of mainland Greece. At the end of the 8th century B.C., votive models in terracotta show the main characteristics of the temple that was later to develop into a more complex structure. It was a simple chamber in which the god resided (the *naos* or *domos,* or *cella* as it was called in Latin) preceded by a narrow vestibule (the *pronaos*) protected by a porch. A pointed roof was set over a window where the pediment was later to be built. The vestibule evolved into the portico at the same time that the *opisthodomos* was set at the back of the building, as much from a desire for symmetry as to provide a new place for offerings. The opisthodomos resembled the pronaos in every respect except that the " room at the back " (the meaning of the term) did not communicate with the naos. The complete structure, consisting of the essential naos and its two annexes, constituted the *sekos*. Some temples, especially those in Sicily, but also others of which the Parthenon is the most famous, had a second chamber placed between the naos and the opisthodomos, which was often a secret place or *adyton*. The structure was usually raised on a three-tiered platform known as the *krepis*, which protected the base of the building against water seeping in when the walls were of brick. The wish to give the divine dwelling a more beautiful appearance led architects to surround the whole of the sekos with a colonnade. The temple is then said to be peripteral (dipteral if there was a double row of pillars); it is called prostyle, or amphiprostyle, if the portico only runs along one or two façades; the building is also termed hexastyle, octostyle or dodecastyle according to whether there are six, eight or twelve columns on the façade. The order (q.v.), chosen by the architect, determined the architectural style of the temple more than any of these peculiarities. P.D.

TEN THOUSAND. The poverty of the soil often obliged Greeks to serve as mercenaries for a foreign power, as in 401 B.C. when a Lacedaemonian by the name of Clearchus enrolled some ten thousand fellow-Greeks to help Cyrus II to dethrone his brother, Artaxerxes, the king of Persia. After marching over much of Asia and fighting Artaxerxes' armies at Cunaxa near Babylon, the mercenaries lost their chiefs who were treacherously assassinated by the Persians. They turned back in an attempt to find their way back home across the mountains of Armenia and along the Black Sea. This extraordinarily long and arduous journey has been described by Xenophon, who took the leadership of the army after the deaths of the generals. His famous account, the *Anabasis*, does not only record the courage and endurance of the Greeks, but by revealing the weaknesses of organisation in the Persian empire, helps us to understand why Alexander was able to overthrow it with such ease three generations later. P.D.

TERPANDER. Lesbian poet of the 7th century B.C. Like all the lyric poets, Terpander was a musician and a famous *kitharistes*. He came to mainland Greece, notably to Sparta and Delphi, where he made some important innovations in music. So little now remains of his verse that he is hardly more than a name to us. R.F.

THASOS. The little island of Thasos lies on the edge of the Aegean, some three or four miles from the Thracian coast, and differs from most of the other Aegean islands in its pleasant climate, its abundance of running water and the luxuriance of its vegetation. In the early 7th century B.C., a few colonists from Paros settled there to seek their fortune in a less poverty-stricken country than their own. Their first impression of Thasos was unfortunate and the poet Archilochus, who was a member of the expedition, was horrified by the savage aspect of the island with its great trees, and rugged mountains, running in an uninterrupted chain from south to north, which he compared to a donkey's spine. Although the Parians seem to have settled on the island without any great difficulty, they soon had to face the hostility of the Thracians, a rough warrior race before whom the poet did not hesitate to throw away his shield so that he could run away more quickly.

We know almost nothing of the history of Thasos until the end of the 6th century, but it is clear that the colonists soon overcame their fears and that they established good relations with their neighbours. We also know that they were able to tame and cultivate the island, for Thasos had become one of the richest cities in Greece by the time of the Persian Wars. It sold wine from its well kept vines as far abroad as Egypt and Syria, as well as wood from the colonies it founded and slaves that it procured from Thrace. Gold was also extracted from mines, which were exhausted fairly quickly but which left traces that Herodotus was still able to see about 450 B.C.

This prosperity enabled the inhabitants to collect works of art whose richness and beauty may be seen from the French archaeological excavations. Unfortunately the excavated buildings are in a poor state, but we can still recognise the sanctuaries of Apollo and the patron divinities of the island, Heracles and Dionysus. The statues set up as early as the 6th century B.C. were sometimes of colossal size and often beautiful, but their originality is questionable since they reflect Athenian and eastern influences, according to the fashion of the moment. We can assume that the islanders were clever traders, a people used to comfort, who loved luxury, and whose patriotism was based on self-interest. Thasos meekly endured the Persian invasion, and in 477 agreed to follow the politics of Athens, until it felt that its commercial interests were in danger and it revolted (464-462). The revolt was a failure; it ended in the total subjection of the island, which was only delivered from Athenian domination in 404 when Sparta emerged victorious from the Peloponnesian War. Mean-

while, internal troubles had broken out, which left Thasos in such a poverty-stricken state that more than twenty years elapsed before it recovered its former prosperity if not its prestige.

Although little was done to improve the city and no notable works of art were created during the latter half of the 5th century B.C., the 4th century was a period of comparative brilliance. Sanctuaries and public building were reconstructed and once again trade flourished even with remote countries. But it was only after 166, when the island was annexed by the Romans, that life became really agreeable and even luxurious again for the inhabitants. The agora was renovated, lined with marble porticoes and filled with portrait statues of the leading citizens and officials, and the emperors to whom the island owed many various benefits. But art was no more original than it had been in the archaic period. The restless seeking after new themes and techniques, common to all young peoples, which gives early art its savour and a charming naïvety; was no longer to be found. The works we know are often talented in their execution but their academic coldness often leaves us unmoved. It was not until the last centuries of the ancient world that its artistic activity became interesting again, perhaps because it was then that the island recovered the splendour of its archaic period.   P.D.

T H E A T R E . The most typical and the best preserved of all Greek theatres is at Epidaurus. It consists of some fifty tiers of seats, arranged in a semicircle on a hill-slope, flanked at either end by a supporting wall, with a circular stage three-quarters surrounded by the lower row of tiers, as though held in a pincer-grip; the stage area, the orchestra, is 67 ft in diameter and its centre is marked by a round altar; facing the hemicycle is a long building, sufficiently low not to obstruct the view of the majestic and peaceful countryside from the tiers. It was built by Polyclitus the Younger in the second half of the 4th century B.C., but he was not the inventor of the design which combines three elements, without any material link between them, into a perfect unity. The nature of the ceremonies celebrated in honour of Dionysus had imposed these elements on his immediate predecessors and on the first troupes, of which Thespis *(See* Tragedy) had been one of the leaders about 530 B.C., and which had been content with movable stages; Polyclitus, admittedly with an incomparable sense of propor-

Theatre at Epidaurus. About 350 B.C. *Photo Hirmer.*

tion, had only harmonised them. The Greek theatre had begun as a simple chorus singing praises to their god around an altar *(thymele)* when all that was needed was a circular, flattened area (the *orchestra*), around which sat the spectators, on the ground or, if the site permitted, the slopes of a hill.

When the day came that a protagonist broke away from the chorus in order to conduct a dialogue with it on a theme that was no longer exclusively Dionysiac, the Greek theatre may be said to have been born. In the first half of the 5th century B.C., Aeschylus and Sophocles made first one and then two other actors accompany this protagonist. To concentrate attention on them, they were placed in isolation on a narrow and slightly raised platform, at a tangent to the central track, from which they could still easily communicate with the chorus, which remained in the orchestra. This platform was adjacent to an erection (the *skene*). Movable, painted panels *(pinakes)* were placed on its walls by way of scenery and the roof was used by divinities

appearing in the play. Inside the hut, where props were kept as in the wings of a modern theatre, the actors, each of whom might play several parts, could change before coming out onto the platform.

As this new arrangement meant that the spectators could only sit round three-quarters of the circle instead of surrounding it entirely as they had done in the past, they sat together on an elevation, and it became the rule to install theatres at the foot of a hill whose slope was reserved for the public. At first, wooden tiers of seats were built but they were uncomfortable and sometimes collapsed disastrously, so in the late 5th century B.C. they were gradually replaced by permanent and better arranged stone tiers. Access to this semi-circular bowl (the *koilon,* or *cavea* as it was called in Latin) was both from the top where openings had been made in the walls, and from below where a passage *(parodos)* was pierced between the ends of the stage and the wall supporting the tiers. Although the stage was empty when the performance began and the chorus entered on the track, it was filled with

Proedria seats in the theatre of Dionysus at Athens. End of the Hellenistic period. *Photo H. Müller-Brunke.*

was raised so that it was much higher than the orchestra and had no communication with it. At the same time, the wall at the back no longer marked the end of the wings only; it became an architectural feature, almost as high as the koilon, and was hollowed with decorative niches for statues.

The structure of the Roman theatre owes much to that of the Greek theatre of the Hellenistic period, but the Romans made quite extensive changes to the design; for example, the tiers of seats were supported by masonry rather than the slope of a hill, and the seats were arranged in a semicircle instead of round three-quarters of a circle.   P.D.

THEBES. Thebes was one of the most important towns in Boeotia but in the historical period it never enjoyed the brilliance it had known in the 2nd millennium B.C. According to legend, it was founded by the Phoenician, Cadmus, who gave his name to the citadel, the Cadmea. Oedipus was king of Thebes and it was against his city that the Seven Chiefs of Argos took arms. Although Thebes was a rival of Orchomenus, it succeeded in dominating the League that Boeotia formed and played the leading role during the brief period in the 4th century B.C. when Boeotia established its hegemony over the rest of Greece. It was destroyed by Alexander in 336 and never recovered. It was an agricultural centre; it could never be said to have been a " great city ", and never built any monument worthy of admiration.   P.D.

spectators both before and after the spectacle, as they gained or left their seats on the tiers. Stairs and gangways divided the koilon and enabled spectators to move more easily. The first row of seats, the *proedria,* was reserved for important people and was on a level with the orchestra without being in any way separated from it. In both conception and achievement the Greek theatre was perfectly adapted to its functions and, with admirable subtlety, it changed with the character of the plays to be performed in it. Although the chorus had first been the only object of the performance, its importance diminished with time. In Aeschylus's tragedies, its importance was more or less equal to that of the actors, but Euripides greatly reduced its role and, in the comic or tragic plays of the 4th century B.C. and the Hellenistic period, it was almost completely eclipsed by a plot in which the protagonists were all individuals. The structure of the theatre was then adapted to this development; as the actors no longer held a continuous dialogue with the chorus, the stage, rather as in the modern theatre,

THEMIS. Themis, now familiar as a conventional figure holding a sword and a pair of scales to symbolise justice, was once a savage goddess who belonged to the race of Titans. She was the daughter of Gaea and Uranus, and the sister of Cronus, and belonged to the monstrous generation which preceded the Olympians as rulers of the world. Themis had been the wife of Zeus long before Hera and among the children she bore him were the three Fates, Clotho, Lachesis and Atropos, whom the Greeks called the Moirai and who wove the threads of human destiny. She established oracles; an Attic cup of the second half of the 5th century B.C. shows her sitting on the Delphic tripod she occupied long before Apollo. According to legend, it was also Themis who had determined rites, instituted laws, and been the first to distinguish between what was permitted and what offended the divine order.

She was a redoubtable figure, almost the only survivor of the powers born when the world had been created, and even gave advice to Zeus. She was the incarnation of supernatural law and became the personification of Justice; as such, she was more or less identified with Nemesis and pursued crime and excess. Consequently, the figure, which the allegory-loving Hellenistic period had conceived as law-giver to the Olympians, has evolved into the personification that inspires the just sentences of judges today.

P.D.

THEMISTOCLES. Few other men played such a decisive role in the life of Athens as Themistocles, for he made this hitherto somewhat inward-turned city into the greatest naval power in the Hellenic world. He was born of a modest family but he won his first honours at an early age; he was chosen archon at the age of thirty in 493 B.C., and strategus in 490.

According to Thucydides, he was able " to distinguish in advance and in the middle of events between what was advantageous and what was harmful ". Even before the Persian Wars, he had started to transform Piraeus, which seemed to him to be a better port for the fleet he dreamed of creating than the open roads of Phalerum. After Marathon and despite the opposition of the hoplites, who were proud of having won a decisive victory on land, he persuaded his fellow-citizens to build ships and to set aside for this purpose the products of the silver mines that had been discovered in Laurium in 483. During the second Persian War, it was Themistocles' eloquence and cunning that persuaded the Peloponnesians not to withdraw behind the Isthmus of Corinth but to engage the Persian fleet in the straits of Salamis, a decision that resulted in the great victory of 480 which freed Greece from the Persian threat. As soon as the enemy was repelled, Themistocles fortified Athens and Piraeus despite the protests of the Spartans who were very unwilling to see their rivals strengthen themselves. He reorganised the command of the navy and had new triremes built. It was owing to his efforts that three years after Salamis the Athenian fleet was strong enough for the peoples of the islands to offer spontaneously the command of their own fleets to the Athenian strategi. This was the

formation of the Delian League in 477 which made Athens the head of a virtual empire. Themistocles had to struggle ceaselessly, especially against his own countrymen, to achieve all this. They did not re-elect him strategus after Salamis and preferred to appoint Aristides, called the Just, and a valiant soldier, Cimon, to this post. They reproached him with being more hostile to Sparta than the Persians and in 472 he was ostracised. There followed an extremely complicated series of intrigues led by Themistocles against Sparta. He was hunted and condemned by default in Athens and first took refuge at the court of his personal enemy, Admetus, king of the Molossians, imploring his hospitality, then at the court of the Persian king to whom he may have offered his services, and who covered him with honours. He died of an illness at Magnesia ad Maeandrum in 464, without seeing his homeland again.

P.D.

THEOCRITUS. Poet of the Alexandrian period, born at Syracuse in about 300 B.C. After vainly asking for the help and protection of Hieron II, the tyrant of Syracuse, Theocritus turned to Ptolemy Philadelphus who granted his request. He stayed on the Island of Cos and then settled at Alexandria, where he became a court poet like Callimachus. He was a composer of idylls. The word *eidyllion* was a diminutive (from *eidos*) which meant " brief picture ", or " little poem "; it denoted only the form and not the content of this type of poetry which could be very varied; it might be an epic fragment, a scene from family life in the town or the country, either pastoral or middle class. Like all the Alexandrian poets, Theocritus gave a preponderant place in his poetry to the description of love which is why the word " idyll " has its present romantic connotations.

The rather conventional, pastoral vein, which notably influenced Virgil and Longus, appeared in many of Theocritus's idylls: *Thyrsis,* the *Shepherds,* the *Goatherd and the Shepherd,* the *Bucolic Singers,* the *Harvesters* and the *Thalysia.* The *Cyclops,* where Polyphemus is shown in love with the nymph, Galatea, owes much less to Homer than to Philoxenus of Cythera. *Hylas* is an account of Heracles' love for the beautiful young man of that name who was taken away from him by naiads from a spring. The *Sorceresses* describes the fierce passion of a young girl who resorts to incantations and philtres to bring back her unfaithful lover. The *Childhood of Heracles* is a genre-like interpretation of mythology: Amphitryon and Alcmene are shown as ordinary, peaceful middle class parents whose sleep is interrupted by an unforeseen incident. The *Women of Syracuse* is a real mime (q.v.) about two young women of Syracuse, who settle at Alexandria and go to the festival of Adonis together. Few other ancient works are as lively and pleasing as this idyll with its racy, uninhibited dialogue, its carefree spirit and its popular expressions.

Theocritus succeeded better than any other poet of his time in avoiding the reefs of erudition. He touches us by his profound and vibrant sensibility, his love of nature and his dramatic gifts. The variety of his talent, the beauty of his descriptions of town and countryside, his wit and the virtuosity he displays in his handling of language and dialect all make him a great poet.   R.F.

THEOGNIS. Elegiac poet of the 6th century B.C., born at Megara. The collection of elegies, which has survived under his name, contains nearly 1400 lines but among them we can recognise passages by Solon, Mimnermus and Tyrtaeus and it is difficult to decide Theognis' share in them with any certainty. In his poetry, he addresses the young Cyrnus and offers him his experience of life and of mankind. His didacticism is pedantic and glacial. He was an aristocrat and a fanatical doctrinaire whose racialism condemned any misalliance with the people whom he hated and despised. The elegies were famous because they contained many well coined maxims but there is very little real poetry in them.   R.F.

THEOPHRASTUS. Theophrastus was born at Eresus on the island of Lesbos in 372 B.C. He was the pupil of Aristotle at the Peripatetic school and succeeded him at the head of the school, which he directed for more than thirty years from 322 until his death in 288. His considerable and varied work embraced every field of knowledge, like his master's, which he completed and corrected on several important points, notably the conception of the universal first cause, which is studied in an important fragment of the *Metaphysics,* and the theory of the intellect. He completed the theory of the syllogism by the study of hypothetical and disjunctive syllogisms. His *Opinions on Physicists* have been the basis for ancient histories of philosophy. His works which have survived are the *Characters,* which

La Bruyère translated and imitated, and two remarkable botanical works: the *Aetiology of Plants* and the *Enquiry into Plants*. Only fragments of his other works have survived.
                                                                    P.-M.S.

THERA. Thera, now known as Santorin, is not only one of the most picturesque islands in the Aegean and a particularly remarkable field of study for the vulcanologist, it is also of great archaeological interest, as the people who settled there in the 3rd millennium B.C. have left traces of their activities. In the historical period, the Dorians colonised Thera in the early 1st millennium and influenced its artistic production, especially ceramics. Lastly, it should be noted that Cyrene on the north African coast was founded by colonists from Thera.   P.D.

THERAMENES. Theramenes was one of the Athenians who were hostile to the democratic regime in Athens at the time it had reached its acme under Pericles. When the expedition against Syracuse during the Peloponnesian War failed, he was among those who established a new, oligarchic constitution in 411 B.C. It reserved the exercise of political rights to only five thousand citizens of whom four hundred wielded uncontrolled power. The regime did not last but Theramenes remained faithful to his hatred of democracy by collaborating with Sparta and negotiating the capitulation of his country in 404. After Athens' defeat, he was one of the Thirty Tyrants who instituted a real reign of terror for several months. But as he was one of the more moderate members of the tyranny, Theramenes himself was suspected by the more violent of his colleagues, who were strongly backed up by the Spartans, and was put to death.   P.D.

THERMOPYLAE. The four miles of narrow road between the Malian Gulf and the high mountains lay on the main invasion route from the north and were always a strategic point of the highest importance. The pass of Thermopylae was one of the keys to Greece. It was there that the Spartan general, Leonidas, waited at the head of a small force for Xerxes' countless troops, in July 480. Even if some of the Persian soldiers had not been led along a goat-track by a traitor and taken the Greeks by surprise from the rear, it was unlikely that Leonidas with his three hundred compatriots and seven hundred Thespian

Theseus landing at Delos. Detail of an Attic krater, called the François Vase. About 570 B.C. Florence, Museo Archeologico. *Photo Hirmer.*

soldiers could ever have held the enemy at bay, no matter how determined they were not to give way. They all died fighting, covered with a glory that ensured them undying fame. As Herodotus said, "they fought with the sword, with their hands, and with their teeth" to the last soldier. Later, they were commemorated by the famous couplet: "Go, stranger, and tell Lacedaemonia that we lie here in obedience to her laws."

P.D.

THESEUS. Unlike Heracles, Theseus was not worshipped throughout the Hellenic world. Although he happened to be born at Troezen, Theseus was a true Athenian, the son of one of its kings and the founder of the state, and by a campaign of political propaganda the Athenians succeeded in making him almost the equal in reputation and deeds of the son of Zeus and Alcmene. So that his origins should be as impressive as Heracles', they altered tradition by making him the son of a god as well, declaring that his father was Poseidon, who reigned beside Athena on the Acropolis. However, according to the best known and certainly the oldest version of the legend, his father was Aegeus whom Pittheus, king of Troezen, married, in spite of his marked indifference, to his daughter Aethra in order to accomplish an oracle. Aegeus lost no time with the young woman but, when he left her, he showed her the cache where he had hidden his sandals and his sword under a heavy rock. When the child she bore reached adolescence,

he proved his strength by lifting the heavy boulder and, equipped with the objects hidden there, went to Athens where he won his father's recognition.

Theseus's trip to Athens was the occasion for his first exploits. The countryside was infested by brigands, who felt certain of their impunity because Heracles was in Lydia, near Omphale, at the time. Theseus showed that he was quite the equal of this hero by killing Periphetes whose club he kept; Sinis, who used to attach his victims to a pine tree which he bent to the ground and then released so that the unfortunate wretch would be catapulted through the air; Sciron whom he threw from a cliff into the sea; Cercyon, and Procrustes, a sadistic madman who made all his prisoners fit the exact length of a bed on which he laid them, either by stretching them or by cutting off their feet. Besides all this, he rid the region of Crommyon, a ferocious sow who had killed several people.

His arrival at Athens dashed the hopes of his cousins, the fifty Pallantides who, until then did not know of his existence and hoped to share Aegeus's heritage one day. In order to defend himself against their ambushes Theseus killed them all. He then placated the Athenians by capturing a monstrous bull, which had been ravaging the plain of Marathon, just as Heracles had done in Crete.

But Theseus's greatest adventure was the slaying of the Minotaur in Cnossos. This monster was half-human, half-bull and every nine years made the Athenians pay him a tribute of seven youths and seven maidens which he devoured alive. As the son of a king, Theseus insisted on joining the band of victims and it was said that he proved he was the true son of Poseidon by throwing a ring in the sea during the crossing and then retrieving it. On his arrival, he seduced Ariadne, the daughter of King Minos. She gave him a thread, which he unwound as he made his way into the Labyrinth and used to find his way out of the palace, apparently with no exit, after he had killed the Minotaur. With the young people whose lives he had saved, he left the island accompanied by Ariadne but he abandoned her on the nearby isle of Naxos, where Dionysus found her and fell in love with her. By the beginning of the 6th century B.C., the Athenians would tell how, on his way back, he stopped at Delos where he consecrated a statue that Ariadne had given him, and how, with his companions, he danced a dance before the " altar of the horns " that was later to become the ritual " dance of the crane " (geranos) whose movements recalled the windings of the Labyrinth. The Athenians used the story to prove how ancient were the links between them and the island which was vital to anyone who wanted to gain control of the Cyclades. On his return, Theseus became king. Aegeus had committed suicide from pure grief when he saw the boat returning from Crete with the black sail to signify mourning. This had been hoisted on their departure and Theseus had forgotten to replace it with a white sail as a sign of the expedition's success.

From this point in his life, most of the stories about Theseus take on a political significance, like that about Delos, although they remain legendary. In the classical period he was credited with an intense political activity, which both anticipated and justified that of the Athenian statesmen of the 5th and 4th centuries B.C. Through the process of synoecismus (q.v.) he grouped all the formerly autonomous hamlets around Athens into a single state. In order to stabilise this new unity, he gave a new lustre to the Panathenaea (q.v.) and created a political organisation which Athenians liked to consider as the forerunner of the future democracy. He was also credited with the very temporary annexation of Megara and with halting an attack by the Amazons at the very foot of the Acropolis. It was his own fault that the war with the valiant Amazons had broken out. One of the many women he had fallen in love with (Ariadne, Helen when a girl, Phaedra and many others) was Antiope, an Amazon whom he had treacherously kidnapped. Her companions made the expedition to free her and in 480 their defeat was regarded as a centuries old anticipation of the Athenian victory over the Persians.

Even stranger was the story of Theseus's descent into the underworld. His friend, Pirithous, king of the Lapiths, wanted to win Persephone and Theseus went with him down to the domain of the dead. He was kept prisoner there until the day when Heracles (note the constant desire of the Athenians to associate the two heroes in order to exalt Theseus!) came to deliver him and set him back again on the throne of Athens. When he returned from the underworld, Theseus found his kingdom in such a state of disorder that he took refuge at the court of King Lycomedes at Scyrus who, probably nervous about the merits and reputation of his guest, threw him from the top of a cliff.

Theseus continued to protect the Athenians even after his death. He was seen fighting at the battle of Marathon in the shape of a hero of prodigious stature and some years later Cimon found his tomb on Scyrus and brought his bones back to Athens, where they were buried in a tomb fit for a king who was considered to have been the father of his country.   P.D.

THESPIS. The earliest of the tragic dramatists. (See Tragedy).

THESSALY. Thessaly was the northernmost province in ancient Greece and several of its features distinguished it from the rest of Hellas. It was crossed by the River Peneus, surrounded by wooded mountains, and was richer and more fertile than the rest of Greece; it was also highly suitable for livestock breeding, not only sheep and goats but also oxen and horses. Although it did not lack outlets on the sea, it was mainly an agricultural province and its trade was never very prosperous. It had been the centre of a fairly developed civilisation in the Neolithic period and was settled at about the end of the 3rd millennium B.C. by the Minyans, who were long remembered by the Greeks, as they made very fine ceramics, characterised by its grey or yellow colour. In the Homeric period, Thessaly was said to have been the homeland of Achilles but his was the only great name to figure in the history of the region. The Thessalian way of life encouraged the establishment of a land-owning aristocracy and never allowed a true democracy to take root there as it had elsewhere. The country was divided between principalities, who united in the 6th century B.C. into a confederation whose power more than once disturbed neighbouring peoples, particularly the Phocians. The time of its greatest strength was in the first half of the 4th century, when it was led by the tyrants of Pherae, Jason and Alexander. It was reorganised in 364 by Thebes, then by Philip of Macedon and finally by the Romans in 197. The main town was Larissa, which does not seem to have been much more important than the other towns which were all humble agricultural centres. The most famous was Pharsalus; it was there that Caesar triumphed over Pompey's army in 48 B.C.   P.D.

THETIS. Thetis was one of the fifty daughters of Nereus. She had been raised by Hera to whom she always remained very attached. According to one legend, it was out of consideration for Hera that Thetis refused Zeus's amorous advances but other versions claim that both Zeus and Poseidon, who both desired her, renounced her after an oracle had told them that any son she bore would surpass his father in power. Consequently, although she was a goddess, she was forced to marry a mortal. She only did so after considerable resistance and when Peleus came to marry her, she tried to escape from him by taking on a great variety of shapes, especially that of a lion; for she had the gift of being able to change at will. The episode was often represented by artists and ended with Peleus's triumph.

The wedding was celebrated on Mount Pelion in the presence of all the gods, which was another subject frequently treated by vase painters. The couple had several children whom Thetis tried to make immortal by throwing them all into the flames but the only result was that they died. Peleus snatched away their seventh-born, Achilles, just as she was beginning another of her insane attempts. Annoyed at only being able to give birth to human beings, Thetis then left Peleus and came back to live with her sisters, the Nereids. From the depths of the sea, she kept watch over Achilles and hid him among Lycomedes' daughters on Scyrus to prevent him from leaving on the Trojan expedition which she knew would

prove fatal for him. She provided his weapons and, when they were taken by Hector from the corpse of Patroclus, she had others forged by Hephaestus which were then brought to the young hero by a troop of Nereids mounted on dolphins.   P.D.

THIEVES. Aristophanes' comedies give the impression that clothes' thieves were particularly numerous in the classical period; they mostly used to operate in the palaestrae and gymnasiums where athletes undressed for their exercises. House burglars also existed in ancient Greece but, as houses were built of unfaced brick and the walls were rather thin, they preferred to break a hole through the walls rather than force the doors, which would be shut by a solid cross bar and bolt; hence their name of " wall-piercers ".
    R.F.

THOLOS. The word *tholos* or its equivalent *skias*, which we translate as " rotunda ", originally meant the umbrella-shaped roof of primitive huts, with a tuft of leaves crowning it at the summit.

Thetis. Detail of the neck of an amphora by Oltos. About 530-520 B.C. Paris, Louvre.

Tholos at Marmaria, Delphi. 4th century B.C. *Photo Ullstein.*

A certain number of tholoi are known to us by texts or else by ruins as at Delphi, where a partial reconstruction now allows us to admire its slim elegance; at Epidaurus, a masterpiece by the architect, Polyclitus, in the 4th century B.C.; in the agora of Athens where the *prytaneis (See* Prytanis) assembled to eat in common; at Sparta, where it was used as a concert hall; besides many others, mentioned by Pausanias, in particular, in his *Description of Greece.*

What all these tholoi had in common was their circular form and the strange cone-shaped roof from which they derived their name, but they differed considerably in the care lavished on their construction. Those at Delphi and Epidaurus were surrounded by a circle of columns which was not to be found everywhere; the finest were of marble, others, like that at Athens, were built of brick. Inside, there was only space for a more or less roomy chamber with wooden supports propping up the roof beams, as at Athens; but the floor of the tholos at Epidaurus covers three narrow concentric corridors which archaeologists have not yet succeeded in explaining. It should be added that certain buildings bear carvings of miniature representations of tholoi which were offered as ex-votos to the deceased or the divinities.

It would seem that, despite differences of detail,

the tholos was far from being a mere architectural fantasy, but was linked to certain funerary beliefs and to chthonian cults. According to the most recent and likely interpretation, the tholos at Epidaurus was the tomb of Asclepius, the master of the sanctuary and the hero whom Zeus had struck with a thunderbolt before admitting him to the company of the gods. Not every tholos was a tomb but it seems at least that they were all originally associated with some form of hero-worship.　　　　　　　　　　　　　　　P.D.

THRACE. Even when it was conquered by Philip II and became a possession of the Macedonian rulers, and later of the Romans, Thrace was never regarded as part of Greece. The Greeks never ventured in this wild and mountainous country which extended as far as the Danube in the north, and as far as the Black Sea in the east. The primitive peasants and hunters living there spoke a language quite different from Greek, worshipped gods of which only a few were gradually to make their way into the Greek pantheon, were divided into warlike tribes and obeyed kings. But the country was rich in minerals, wood, vines and cereals; it also supplied slaves and mercenaries, and through the intermediary of colonists who had settled along the shores of the

Aegean, the Marmara or the Black Sea, the Greek world developed trading links with Thrace as early as the 7th century B.C. The local rulers were jealous of their independence and attempts by the Athenians and Spartans to seize hold of the mines of Mount Pangaeus were sharply repulsed. Even Philip and Alexander of Macedon did not impose their authority on this turbulent people without difficulty.   P.D.

THRASYBULUS. Although he was not a leading figure in Greek history, Thrasybulus did play a decisive part in Athenian life on at least one occasion. During the Peloponnesian War, he skilfully led several operations against Sparta. He supported Alcibiades and, when the Thirty Tyrants had destroyed the democratic regime, he fled to Thebes with several of his compatriots and headed a liberation movement. In December 404, he led a little group of banished Athenians, overwhelmed a frontier post at Phyle and then, joined by numerous partisans, seized hold of Piraeus. The Thirty counter-attacked but they were beaten and their defeat brought down the Tyranny (January 403).

Thrasybulus then contributed to the restoration of democracy. After first advising his fellow-citizens to adopt a prudent attitude towards the Spartan conquerors, he urged them to take revenge in 395 and proposed an alliance with Thebes. When fighting broke out again with Sparta, he commanded the Athenian contingent at the battle of Nemea in 394. He was defeated and had to retire from politics for a while, but he regained his prestige when, in 389, his fleet of forty ships forced the northern states of Thasos, Samothrace and Byzantium to acknowledge the hegemony of Athens. This was a short-lived triumph for in 388, when he fell in a surprise attack, he was about to be summoned back to Athens to justify the pillaging for which he was responsible.   P.D.

THRENODY. Poem expressing the sadness of mourning. *(See* Lyric Poetry).

THUCYDIDES. Athenian historian (about 462-395 B.C.). He was the son of Oloros and related to the family of Miltiades and Cimon. From his father he inherited gold mines in the region of Strymon in Thrace. As he was rich, he could attend the lessons of the sophists and then devote himself to lengthy studies with a view to writing a work on the Peloponnesian War. He was acquainted with Anaxagoras, Antiphon, Gorgias and Prodicus (qq.v.). In 430 he caught plague, and in 424, after being elected strategus, he arrived too late to prevent the town of Amphipolis from falling into the hands of the Spartan general, Brasidas. He was judged, sentenced and banished and had to spend the next twenty years in exile until the end of the war, but this exile proved beneficial for his work, because it gave him a great deal of leisure and the opportunity to gather information from both sides.

His book is unfinished. It stops with the events of the year 411, and this last and eighth book does not seem to have been revised and corrected by him. The history was continued after this point by Xenophon in his *Hellenica Oxyrhynchia*.

Thucydides was born only about twenty years after Herodotus but his conception of history was quite different. In his preface, he gives a picture of ancient Greece in which his strict, objective method can already be seen at work. He tries to extract the " kernel " of truth that the Homeric poems may contain. Then he discusses the principles governing his investigations, which are very similar to those of modern historians. He did, however, attribute numerous speeches to statesmen and strategi, which could not have been exactly reported, but he was honest enough to warn the reader of this. For him, these speeches were a convenient means of showing the reader, not only the motives and characters of the speakers, but also the chain of events, at least as it appeared to him; for, with his lucid and penetrating mind, he had long reflected on the course of events, their causes and effects, and on the psychology of both crowds and leaders. He was really trying to lay down a philosophy of history; his grounds for presenting his work as " an acquisition for always " and as a lesson that would be of value for all time were that he believed in reason and thought that, as the same causes produce the same effects, his work would hold useful lessons for future generals and politicians. He firmly established the date of the war he described by the synchronisms listed in Book II, which clearly fix the outbreak of hostilities. The successive years of the war are counted from this one, then he carefully distinguishes, within each year, the different stages of the narrative.

Thucydides was the first of the ancient historians to give economic and social facts their true importance. On several occasions, he gives precise indications of the material and financial resources of the main belligerents. But in his eyes, human intelligence was far more decisive than any economic factor, especially if it was combined with energy and boldness. He had a gift for psychological analysis and observed the particular traits in the characters of Pericles, Cleon, Nicias and Alcibiades, and also those of the Athenian and Spartan characters in general, which were quite different. As he had been a strategus, he was experienced in political and military matters and knew what he was writing about far better than any historian shut up in his study. He had such a respect for science and such a love for truth that impartiality seemed the most natural thing in the world to him. He was never deceived by appearances. In his account, his first concern is for precision and clarity, but when some event seems exceptionally important to him, he lingers over the scene and draws on all the sources of rhetoric to describe it.

Thucydides wrote in the archaic Attic dialect, which was still close to Ionian, and was firm rather than supple. His style, especially in speeches and set pieces, was consciously abstract, concise, difficult and even obscure, full of antitheses, dissymmetries, abrupt breaks of syntax, litotes, and all the figures of speech that were taught by the rhetors. It was a style designed for effect, which may sometimes jar, but which reveals the writer's constant effort to express the finest and subtlest nuances, to outline an idea with the greatest precision and give each thought its full weight. Thucydides' history is both a work of art and a work of science. No other period of ancient history is so brilliantly lighted as these twenty years of the Peloponnesian War, as they are recounted in the pages of Thucydides. As a historian he outclasses even his successors.

R.F.

THURII. In 446 B.C., Pericles, who wanted to ensure Athens' position in the richest regions of Magna Graecia, advised several different cities to unite in founding a colony on the gulf of Tarentum, but his appeal was ignored and only the Athenians set off for the new site which was given the name of Thurii. The town prospered, but its main interest for us lies in the fact that it served as an intermediary between Athens and southern Italy. People from every walk of life took part in the expedition and, once they had settled down in this distant country, they continued to practise the trades of their homeland. Pottery workshops were set up that remained faithful to Attic traditions. Their vases were the same as those being made in Athens. These potters formed a school and it would be true to say that the Italiot style, which was strongly inspired by Greece, originated at Thurii.

P.D.

THYESTES. The Greeks made legendary beings out of figures who may have really existed at the time of the establishment of Mycenaean power, and the adventures they spun round them suggest a climate of violence which is not at all unlikely at a time when the Achaean feudal system was in its beginnings. Thyestes was the son of Pelops and Hippodamia. He was deprived of power by his elder brother, Atreus, the ancestor of the illustrious family of the Atridae. An implacable hate sprang up between the two brothers. Thyestes had three sons whom Atreus massacred. He then invited Thyestes to a banquet on the pretext of a reconciliation and served the unhappy father the flesh of his own children. Thyestes had to take flight without being able to avenge this crime, but another of his sons, who had escaped the butchery, murdered Atreus.

P.D.

TIRESIAS. When he was still young, the Theban, Tiresias, had seen Athena naked, while she was taking her bath in a river. Although this act of sacrilege was involuntary, Tiresias was struck by blindness, but his blindness did not prevent him from foreseeing the future and he became the best known of all the prophets of legend. It was to consult him after his death that Ulysses evoked the shades of the underworld.

P.D.

TIRYNS. Tiryns is one of the great names of the Achaean world. It was said to have been founded by Proetus, brother of Acrisius, king of Argos, and built by Cyclopes from Lycia. Among its rulers were Perseus and then Eurystheus for whom Heracles performed his labours. The site, a mound three hundred yards long on the edge of the Gulf of Argolis, was inhabited from the 3rd millennium B.C. The circular and very modest residence of a chief then stood on its summit and the town may already have overflowed on to the nearby plain. A larger palace, whose ground-plan we do not know, was built there in the 16th century B.C. and the acropolis was surrounded by a ram-

Tiryns. Mycenaean casemates. 13th century B.C. *Photo Müller-Drunke.*

Tiryns. The ramparts: view from the west. *Photo Hassia.*

part. During the 14th and 13th centuries, this rampart was enlarged and rebuilt, and in its final state, it consisted of a triple enceinte built in terraces from the top of the mound down to the plain. The palace, whose ruins have remained, also dates from this period which was the most brilliant in the city's history.

The French writer, Edmond About, has described Tiryns as " a little heap of large stones ", but it is the witticism of a disrespectful and hurried tourist; one has only to leave the nearby road and climb up the steep slope of the acropolis to see the imposing ruins of one of the best preserved of Mycenaean fortresses. A ramp, more than 15 ft wide, which could have been used by chariots, leads to the first doorway opening into a corridor between two walls; this leads to the fortified entrance of the upper terrace which was probably similar to the Lion Gate at Mycenae. The terrace, which was reached by this way, preceded a monumental propylaeum through which the palace itself was approached, with its grand courtyard, its megaron, altar, bath-room and adjacent chambers. All that now remains of these rooms are the foundations. On the other hand, there have survived, in a very impressive state of preservation, the systems of casemates, covered galleries and subterranean stairways which were dug in the rock under the entrance terrace and were extremely important to the military life of the fortress. But nothing can equal the imposing impression given by the ramparts. They are between 24 and 57 ft thick, built of enormous blocks, some of which were simply set one on top of the other, while some were carefully cut by the masons and jointed before they faced the wall. The ramparts were skilfully made to follow the contours of the terrain with bastions, salients and ravelins, whose defensive qualities are the admiration of military specialists even today.

P.D.

TISIAS. Sicilian rhetor, the pupil of Corax. *(See* Rhetoric).

TITANS. The Titans, who must not be confused with the Giants who belong to a much later generation in divine genealogy, were the six male children that Gaea bore to Uranus. The most important was Cronus who became the father of Zeus. Oceanus was also a Titan and he helped Zeus when he wanted to seize power.

P.D.

TOILET. *See* Bathing, Clothing, Cosmetics, Fan, Footwear, Head-dress, Jewellery, Mirrors, Perfume, Umbrella.

TORTURE. Torture was inflicted on slaves who had to give evidence in court *(See* Justice).

TOWN-PLANNING. In Greece as elsewhere, town-planning only began long after the foundation of most towns. The sites of towns were originally chosen because they could easily be defended, because the land was rich, or because they were near a sanctuary, or for some similar reason, and they developed haphazardly, without any preconceived plan. Necessary changes were made with varying degrees of success according to circumstances; tyrants, like Pisistratus and Polycrates, courted popular favour by having fountains built in their cities that lacked water.

When the Greeks began to take an interest in town-planning it was far too late to change the appearance of towns with a long history except in some details, which was why a visitor to Athens in the 3rd century B.C. wrote: " The town is very dry and badly laid out because of its great age... a stranger suddenly coming upon it might wonder whether this really was the famous town of the Athenians ".

Circumstances were rather different in towns founded by the colonists which started from nothing. As Roland Martin has shown in his authoritative study of Greek town-planning, what little we can still see of the original lay-out of Greek towns, before later alterations and rebuilding, seems to show that private and public buildings were not built according to any kind of overall plan; although streets tended to intersect at right angles more frequently in colonies than in the metropolis, this was only to facilitate land distribution among the settlers, for the plots of land that were drawn by lot among the newcomers were usually rectangular in shape.

The first city to be built according to a rationalised plan was Miletus, twenty years after it had been destroyed by the Persians in 494 B.C. Articulated residential quarters, which made the best use of the contours of the land, were built on each side of a central sector that was reserved for administrative, religious and commercial buildings. The town was divided into squares by numerous, rectilinear streets, wide enough to allow traffic to flow easily (the two main thoroughfares were 25 ft wide). It was not the streets, however, that determined the lay-out but the blocks they enclosed. Each quarter had its own character depending on its particular conditions. Functional town-planning, in fact, was being created; one of the most striking innovations was the introduction of separate zones, each with its own characteristics.

Not even the name of the designer of the new city of Miletus is known to us, but one of his successors did win great fame, Hippodamus of Miletus (q.v.) who was asked by Themistocles to rebuild the Piraeus. His work, however, seems to have been limited to defining the different sectors of the city and directing the laying-out of the boundaries. Politico-philosophical theories played their part in the project as well as purely practical considerations and we know from Aristotle that Hippodamus was " the inventor of the division of states according to the orders of citizens ".

Other considerations were soon taken into account and, mainly through Hippocrates' influence, city-planners later paid attention to such factors as the direction of the winds, exposure to sunlight and, in a word, to all conditions necessary to health. The districts of Olynthus (q.v.), built about 440-430 B.C., are a good example of the way in which the theories that had been elaborated in preceding years were adapted to local conditions.

In Greece itself and Asia Minor, several cities were planned with the same ideas; but it was not until Alexandria was founded in 331 B.C. that the aim of town-planning developed from the purely functional to creating surroundings that would also be impressive. We do not know what Dinocrates of Rhodes' plan was like, but it is safe to assume that it was based on this principle. Spaciousness was its distinguishing characteristic as it was of all Alexander's foundations. The main streets were 50 to 65 ft wide, if not more, and the architect had carefully calculated the effect produced by the magnificence and variety of the splendid buildings and parks set along the avenues of the city. For the first time, the impression on foreign visitors was taken into account as well as the comfort of the inhabitants.

The masterpiece of this type of impressive town-planning was probably Pergamum (q.v.). When Lysimachus placed Alexander's treasures there in the early 3rd century B.C., the town was a mere eagle's nest, but under the dynasty of the Attalids it became one of the most beautiful cities in the Hellenistic world. The neighbouring plain was dominated by an acropolis over 1,000 ft high. On its steep slopes, architects who were all inspired by the same principles from generation to generation, succeeded in building temples, porticoes, a gymnasium, markets, an arsenal and houses, which harmonised as a whole with the landscape and were individually adapted to the rugged terrain in the most practical and logical manner. Town-planning up to this point provided a basis for the alterations and improvements made by the Romans in every town to which they attached a particular importance and it was the Romans who were to give a new appearance to such ancient cities as Athens.

P.D.

T O W N S . The Greeks had fairly dense centres of population at every period in their history, but it was only in the Hellenistic era that large towns, in the modern sense of the word, grew up. On the whole, most Greek towns remained villages, divided by vegetable gardens, courtyards, probably waste ground and even fields. Areas where food could be grown by their owners were considered an amenity even inside the ramparts. Few traces of habitation have been found on level ground suitable for small scale farming, so the earliest villages must have been built on steep slopes and rocks. Naturally, the appearance of towns varied according to place and period. In the 5th century B.C., towns like Miletus or Piraeus, for example, were planned as a whole with some ideas of hygiene and convenience (See Town-planning). But even these towns and, to a greater extent, those that had been founded earlier were characterised by the narrowness of their streets and the confused huddles of houses within each built-up area. The excavated quarter near the theatre at Delos is often quoted as a typical example. It is built on very broken ground and narrow alleys, sometimes intersected by stairways, wind between the blind walls of houses that only receive daylight from an inner courtyard; the steps, leading to the upper storeys, encroach on the over-narrow streets which have a gutter down the middle to carry away waste water. It was only at a late date that the agora took on its dignified character. There was no street lighting and on moonless nights it was advisable to walk with a torch. It is quite possible that the popular quarters were much the same even in the great towns of the Hellenistic period although the centre at least was planned much more spaciously, with wide avenues leading to esplanades, which not only eased the flow of everyday traffic but were ideal for processions and the celebrations of great festivals. Streets always intersected at right angles and pavements may then have made their first appearance for the benefit of pedestrians.

A town is not an empty setting and both in the earliest towns and in those built on the most advanced principles of town-planning in the later periods the dominant characteristic must have been the presence of their noisy, lively, talkative Mediterranean crowds; like so many Greek towns today, they were made as much by their people as by their buildings.   P.D.

TOYS AND AMUSEMENTS. Aristotle mentions the *platage*, a rattle or castanet, as one of the toys of small children, which was invented by the philosopher and statesman, Archytas of Tarentum. Older children played with balls and dice made of knuckle-bones *(astragaloi)*. They were also given small chariots to pull, miniature painted vases, horses on wheels and all sorts of model clay animals: pigs, hens, doves, etc. Little girls were generally given dolls, some of which were jointed like marionettes *(neurospasta)*. The children probably liked best of all the toys they made themselves. In Aristo-

phanes' *The Clouds*, the good-natured Strepsiades, talking about his son, said, " He was still a mite, no higher than that, when he used to model clay houses at home, carve boats in wood, build little chariots of leather and make wonderful frogs from the rind of pomegranates. " Children used to amuse themselves with live animals too: dogs, ducks, quails, mice, weasels and grasshoppers. They played hopscotch and used hoops and tops; swung on seesaws, leap-frogged and carried each other piggie-back in a game called *ephedrismos*. They used nuts for marbles and they competed in throwing stones and bits of broken pottery as near as possible to a line drawn on the ground. The toy we call a yo-yo was known to the Greeks and perhaps the young model of the *Ephebe of Anticythera* may have indulged in it. Children and ephebi practised balancing exercises like trying to stand as long as possible on a full leather-bottle, which had been previously oiled. There were innumerable variations of ball or balloon games. The ball was sometimes hit with sticks curved at the end rather like our modern hockey *(keratizontes)*.

Young and old enjoyed the spectacles of fighting animals, cats against dogs, and cockfights, which were often cruel and bloody. Gamecocks were often very expensive. They were given garlic and onions to make them fiercer and bronze spurs were attached to their own spurs. The Athenian magistrates organised cock-fights in the

Game of ephedrismos.
Detail of an oinochoe
by the Shuvalov
Painter.
About 430-420 B.C.
Berlin Museum.
Photo Hirmer.

Game of hockey. Attic bas-relief. About 510 B.C. Athens, National Museum. *Photo Émile.*

theatre every year and bets were laid on them. Games of chance were innumerable, ranging from the game of " heads and tails " played with bronze coins, subdivisions of the obol, knuckle-bones and beans, to a variety of games with dice *(kuboi)*. Specimens of these dice in baked clay have been found. The best throw, or " Aphrodite's cast ", was three sixes (they generally played with three dice); the worst was three ones, or the " dog's cast ". *Petteia* was a kind of backgammon or draughts; Homer's heroes used to play " with counters ". The Greeks also amused themselves with something like our game of goose, which consisted in moving pieces or stones over an area marked out like a dice. *Kottabos* was a favourite game at banquets. A drinker aimed the wine left at the bottom of his cup at a particular object and uttered the name of the person whom he loved as he threw. If the wine landed on its target, he took it as a good omen that his love would be successful. They liked complicating the game by filling a vase, chosen for the target, with water and floating little clay saucers on it. The players tried to sink these tiny vessels and the kottabos prize went to the man who succeeded in causing the largest number of miniature shipwrecks. Another version of the game was to balance a little plate on top of a long, vertical, metal rod and try to dislodge it by throwing the remains of a wine-cup on it.   R.F.

Children's games. Detail of an Anthesteria oinochoe. Second half of the 5th century B.C. Paris, Louvre.

TRAGEDY. The origins and even the name of tragedy (" song of the goat ") are obscure. It may originally have been the chorus that sang and danced during the sacrifice of a he-goat to Dionysus, the god of the theatre. It has also been suggested that the satyrs of the Dionysiac procession were represented by members of the chorus disguised as goats. Whatever the explanation it was the round chorus of the dithyramb *(See* Lyric Poetry) that gave birth to tragedy.

The dithyramb was sung and danced by the chorus around the altar of Dionysus, called the *thymele*. In theatres of the classical period, this

473

altar remained in the centre of the circular *orchestra* where the chorus sang and danced *(See* Theatre). Certain dithyrambs, like Bacchylides' Poem XVIII called *Theseus*, already contained a dialogue between the chorus and a person who was not merely a reciter; the role in this poem was taken by Aegeus, the father of Theseus. According to tradition, it was the Athenian, Thespis, a native of the deme of Icaria, near Marathon, who was the first to produce a truly dramatic action.

The Greeks have always had an instinct for mime. The most ancient religious ceremonies always included real " tableaux vivants " in which various episodes from divine or heroic mythology were represented, like the Crane Dance at Delos in memory of the turns and twists of Theseus in the Cretan Labyrinth, and the Septerion at Delphi, which represented the fight between Apollo and the serpent, Python, and the purification of the god at Tempe. In one sense, tragedy could also be said to derive from the " epic drama ", for in Homer the recital is often interrupted by the speeches and dialogues of the characters. Arion's (q.v.) dithyramb owes much to the epic poem.

According to Horace's *Ars Poetica*, Thespis went with his tragedies from village to village on a wagon throughout Attica before having them performed in Athens. He was the actor—there was only one at the time—and also combined the functions of producer, impresario, author and ballet master. He was active in about 560 B.C. at the beginning of Pisistratus's tyranny, but the institution of competitions of tragedies at the city Dionysia *(See* Festivals) only dates from about 530. In Thespis's time or a little later, it became the custom to illustrate three successive episodes from the same legend. Each of these episodes constituted a tragedy and altogether they made up a linked trilogy. Next came a fourth play which was specially related to the Dionysus legend, as the chorus was formed by satyrs, the companions of Bacchus. This play became the satyric drama which transformed all tragic trilogies into a tetralogy. Linked trilogies were soon abandoned during the 5th century, and the satyric drama was often replaced by a special type of tragedy, like Euripides' *Alcestis*, which was without a chorus of satyrs. The only trilogy that has survived intact is Aeschylus's *Oresteia* and the only satyric drama that has come down to us in a complete state is Euripides' *Cyclops*.

Phrynichus, an Athenian like Thespis, also only used a single actor who was able to act several different characters in succession. There was hardly any action in his plays but the Athenians long remembered the sweetness and harmony of the songs he gave his chorus. The themes of most of his plays were taken from legend but he broke new ground in having the *Taking of Miletus* performed in Athens some time after 494 B.C., which moved the audience deeply. After the battle of Salamis, he wrote another topical play, the *Phoenissae*, which in a way anticipated Aeschylus's *Persians*.

Aeschylus gave new lustre to tragic performances. He added a second actor, the *deuteragonistes*, who was subordinate to the *protagonistes*, and when the young Sophocles had brought the number of actors up to three, Aeschylus followed his example by making use of the *tritagonistes* in his turn. Greek tragedy never used more than three actors, each playing several different roles in succession, but the playwright might also use silent performers. Sophocles definitely gave up the linked trilogy and, although he lessened the relative importance of the lyric pieces sung by the chorus, he increased the number of chorists from twelve to fifteen. Lastly, Euripides was the first to use the prologue for a convenient but artificial exposition of the theme, when a god or one of the characters in the play would announce the theme of the play to the audience and give a résumé of the events preceding the action to be represented.   R.F.

TRALLES. Tralles, the modern Aidin, is a town in Caria which only became important in the Hellenistic and Roman periods. It was first mentioned by Xenophon. It was then called Seleuceia on the Maeander and in 133 B.C. it became part of the Roman Empire. It was an agricultural centre and conducted most of its trade with Miletus, sending it the produce of the very rich plain which surrounded it. In the Hellenistic period, a school of art grew up which followed closely the ideals of the classical period.
                          P.D.

TRAVEL. Spartans could not go abroad without a special permit from the ephors, but other Greeks often travelled outside their country, especially for trade and to see the panhellenic games which were periodically held at great sanctuaries such as those of Delphi and Olympia. Others, like Solon, Hecataeus of Miletus and

Fragment of the north frieze from the Treasury of the Siphnians at Delphi. Gigantomachy. About 525 B.C. Delphi Museum. *Photo Hirmer.*

Herodotus, travelled to instruct themselves and were a kind of early tourist, but they were exceptions; it was only under the Roman Empire that there was much travel to see " the wonders of the world ".

There were no good roads in ancient Greece and certainly nothing that could be compared with the Roman roads. Roads were simply beaten earth tracks, which stopped at river fords, and they were rarely wide enough for two chariots to pass one another from opposite directions without difficulty (according to legend, this was why Oedipus killed his father, Laius). Inns (q.v.) existed, however.

No part of Greece is more than sixty miles from the sea; consequently, most travel was by sea, at least in fine weather. The real centre of Hellas was the Aegean with its numerous isles that served as ports of call between Europe and Asia *(See* Navigation). R.F.

TREASURIES. In panhellenic sanctuaries, the Greek states asserted their particularism by placing all the private or public offerings of their citizens in the same building, which was quite separate from that of the other communities. These edifices, the treasuries, were built on a simplified plan of the temples, with a vestibule and a closed chamber, corresponding to the naos and the pronaos, a pediment and a carved frieze. They were not places of worship, but they belonged to the god as they were built in the sacred enclosure, and they had to be beautiful in appearance to prove to both the divinity and the public how great was the richness and piety of their builders. According to the amount of land that was available, each city tried to find the best site for its treasury, either inside the sanctuary so that it might be easily seen from along the sacred way, or else close to the temple. The treasuries were usually built to commemorate some fortunate event. At Delphi the treasury of the Siphnians was built in about 525 B.C., one of the most richly decorated of its kind ever built; and that of the Athenians, financed with a tenth of the booty taken from the Persians, was built to thank Apollo for having saved the city by giving it victory at the battle of Marathon in 490.

P.D.

TREES (SACRED). The Greeks do not seem to have practised tree worship, although a sacred tree cult had existed in Minoan Crete, where numerous seals have been found representing a female figure, goddess or priestess, sitting under trees of uncertain species. It may however be assumed that the trees in these images are not so much objects of veneration as symbols of the creative power of nature. This may be a survival of oriental religions. In any case, we know that Leto, whose Asiatic origin is certain, leant against a palm tree to give birth to Apollo and that the palm tree always remained sacred at Delos. In the forests of Epirus, the rustling of the oak trees of Dodona in the wind was held to reveal the will of Zeus. On the whole, the tree played a very modest part in the religion of the ancient Greeks.   P.D.

TRIBE. *See* Phyle.

TRIPTOLEMUS. Although there are several versions of the legend, it seems that Triptolemus was the son of Celeus, the king of Eleusis. When Demeter came to the town in search of her daughter, she was all the more grateful for the hospitality she was given there as she had not been welcomed everywhere she went. When she had found Kore again, she expressed her gratitude by giving Triptolemus the mission

of teaching mankind how to use corn and a famous relief from Eleusis shows the two goddesses giving the sacred ear of corn to the young man.

They also gave him a chariot drawn by winged dragons to help him in his task.   P.D.

TROJAN WAR. Although the history of the Aegean peoples must have been dramatic enough during the 2nd millennium B.C., the Trojan War was the only episode to leave profound traces in the memory of the Greeks and the only event to appear as a homogeneous and logically constructed incident. Its reality was never doubted by the ancient Greeks and today, although we no longer blindly believe what Homer and the tragic dramatists tell us, the successive discoveries of the last hundred years have made us realise that the scepticism of some 19th century scholars was unjustified, that the Trojan War was not a poetic invention and that it did, in fact, largely correspond to actual historical events. What is still widely disputed is the date of these events, whether they took place in the early 12th century B.C. according to the most widely accepted tradition (Eratosthenes gave 1183 as the date of the capture of the city), or earlier in the 14th century. What is certain is that the site of Troy has been found and that the city that occupied the seventh stratigraphical layer was destroyed by fire at the same time that the Mycenaean civilisation dominated Greece. Archaeological investigations have also shown that the remains of the main towns of this civilisation correspond to what Homer called the most important cities of the time. Moreover, the picture that the *Iliad* gives us of the Greek people and its army has been largely confirmed by modern archaeologists. Although we should not give the episode all the importance attributed to it by the ancient Greeks, and although we should not regard the Homeric poems as a historical work and believe implicitly in all the legends surrounding the heroes, we must recognise that the Homeric tradition contains a good deal of truth. Just how much of it is historical fact may never be known.

It all started when Hermes was ordered to take the three goddesses, Hera, Athena, and Aphrodite, before Paris after they had been quarrelling

Triptolemus in his winged chariot holding wheat-ears. Detail of a lekythos attributed to the Berlin Painter. About 490-480 B.C. Syracuse Museum. *Ph. Leonard von Matt.*

Farewell of Hector and Andromache. Detail of a Chalcidian krater. About 530-525 B.C. Würzburg, Martin von Wagner Museum. *Photo Hirmer.*

over an apple that Eris, Discord, had thrown in their midst saying that it belonged to the fairest of the three. Paris, the son of Priam, the king of Troy, chose Aphrodite after she had promised him that in return she would give him the love of Helen, the wife of Menelaus, the king of Sparta. Helen was so beautiful that before giving her to Menelaus in marriage, her father, Tyndareos, made all her other noble suitors promise to come to the aid of the fortunate bridegroom should anyone try to take his wife from him. As the final choice of a husband had not yet been made, each suitor took the oath, secretly thinking that if they were chosen they would then benefit from the support of their former rivals. After giving his judgment, Paris sailed for Sparta, accompanied by Aeneas. to claim the reward for his arbitration. He was well received by Menelaus who had to leave for Crete after entreating his wife to look after their Trojan guests. Encouraged by Aphrodite, Helen allowed herself to be seduced and Paris carried her away, with Menelaus's treasure, too, according to some traditions. The two lovers fled to Troy where Paris took his place again among his fifty brothers in Priam's palace. On returning to Sparta, Menelaus found his home empty, reminded the other suitors of their promise

and so gathered the principal Greek chieftains together. There is no need, at this point, to underline the legendary character of this episode even if it was accepted as truth by the ancient Greeks, for it is only in fairy tales and romances of chivalry that princes combine to return a beautiful but faithless wife to her lawful husband.

There is less need to be sceptical about the expedition itself, no matter what the cause that provoked it, such as economic necessity or the desire for conquest. Command of the operations was given to Agamemnon, the king with the largest domains and most powerful army, who ruled over Argolis from his palaces at Argos and Mycenae and who may also have held sway over other provinces in the Peloponnesus. Although we need not accept all the horrible details given by the ancient Greeks, we have no reason for disbelieving that Agamemnon's father, Atreus, had ruthlessly seized the throne from his brother, Thyestes, whom he brutally murdered, and that the family had more than one crime on its conscience. Agamemnon himself had married Clytemnestra, the sister of Helen, whose brother-in-law he was twice over since Menelaus was his step-brother. The main chiefs placed under his command were Nestor, king of Pylos, Ulysses, king of Ithaca, Achilles from Thessaly, Ajax, the son of Oïleus, who commanded the Locrians, and another Ajax, the son of Telamon, the hero of Salamis, the Cretan Idomeneus and still others too numerous to mention. Each one brought his vassals and his soldiers and also his ships, which were needed for the transport of such a huge army. The place of assembly was at Aulis, on the Attic coast, facing Euboea. Despite the signs that the augur, Calchas, judged favourable for the success of the campaign, lack of a wind prevented the departure. Calchas then said that to raise the wind it was necessary for the head of the expedition to sacrifice his own daughter, Iphigenia, to the goddess, Artemis, who reigned over the site. Agamemnon bowed to this necessity and on his orders Clytemnestra herself led Iphigenia to Aulis, thinking that her daughter was going to marry Achilles. Clytemnestra's fury and despair when she learned the real reason for the journey, Agamemnon's hesitations as he was torn between his duties as a leader and his duties as a father, the anguish of Iphigenia who agreed to die to serve the Greek cause after a moment of revolt, all inspired some of the most beautiful passages in Greek drama. Modern scholars now think that, with the primitive religions of the time, it was not unlikely that a military expedition should begin by a human sacrifice. What we do not know is whether a human sacrifice really was made or whether Iphigenia's place had been taken by a hind, according to an ancient tradition, and whether Iphigenia herself might not have been a goddess who had become confused with Artemis.

Once the goddess had been placated, the army was able to embark. As they sailed towards Troy, they stopped to abandon one of their chiefs, Philoctetes, on the isle of Lemnos, which was deserted at that time for he had accidently injured himself and the smell coming from his wound became unbearable to his companions. The Greeks then laid siege to Troy but the city was the most powerful on the Anatolian coast and only fell after ten years. It was defended by huge ramparts, whose remains can be seen today, and its warriors were no less courageous than the Greeks, especially Hector whom Homer made into one of the most human characters in the *Iliad*. No memories remain of the first nine years of the siege; the quarrel between Achilles and Agamemnon, which Homer immortalised, took place in the tenth year. Agamemnon had captured Chryseis, the daughter of a priest of Apollo, in an ambush, but as he refused to return her to her father in exchange for a ransom, the god

Ajax carrying the body of Achilles. Detail of the handle of the François Vase. About 570 B.C. Florence, Museo Archeologico. *Photo Hirmer.*

Fall of Troy. Detail of a cup by Brygos. About 490 B.C. Paris, Louvre.

struck the Greek army with a plague and Agamemnon had to give way before the pressure of his soldiers and return the girl to bring an end to the epidemic. He then tried to make Achilles pay the price of his concession by making the hero give him the most beautiful of his captives, Briseis. Although Achilles refused at first, he ended by obeying the supreme commander, but he retired from the fight, shut himself up in his tent and let the Greeks go on fighting without him. As he alone was able to stand up to Hector, the Greeks suffered one reverse after another. His friend, Patroclus, then obtained his consent to borrow his weapons and armour. When he appeared on the battle-field, the Trojans took him for Achilles and were filled with terror, but Hector came forward to meet him and slew him in single combat. Patroclus's death left Achilles inconsolable and to avenge him he put on a new suit of armour that Hephaestus had specially forged for him, went out of his tent, killed Hector and dragged his body around the walls of Troy. He did not survive his friend for long and by an irony of fate the invincible hero was killed by the least valorous of his enemies; Paris shot an arrow into his heel, the only vulnerable part of his body, and brought his career to an end.

The Greeks finally took Troy by ruse and not by force. They pretended to give up their enterprise and embarked again, but left an enormous wooden horse in which the best of their chiefs were hidden before the town. Despite Laocoön's warnings, the Trojans were so overjoyed at seeing the siege come to an end that they dragged the wooden horse inside their walls. While they feasted that night, the Greeks crept out of their hiding place, opened the city gates to their companions who had sailed back, and massacred the Trojans. Aeneas, whom Priam esteemed most highly after Hector, only saved his life by flight. The king himself sought refuge on the altar of the gods, but he was pitilessly slain by Achilles' son, Neoptolemus, while Hector's widow, Andromache, vainly tried to protect her son, Astyanax; they too were massacred. Every man was slaughtered, all the women were led away as slaves; the most famous was Cassandra, the prophetess and daughter of the king, who had to follow Agamemnon to Argos where she shared his sinister fate. Victory did not bring the trials of the Greeks to an end, for Menelaus alone, or almost alone, came peacefully back to Sparta with Helen, a wiser Helen whom he had forgiven and who, the *Odyssey* tells us, behaved nobly as a queen. All the other Greeks were struck by misfortune: Ulysses had to wander for ten years before returning to Ithaca, Ajax of Salamis committed suicide because he was refused the share he claimed of the booty, his namesake was struck by a thunderbolt by Poseidon for having defied the gods. The most lamentable fate of all was that of Agamemnon, whose wife, Clytemnestra, had taken Aegisthus as a lover during his absence; the adulterous couple murdered him in his bath and the disaster that had struck him and the crimes committed by his family all had their repercussions on his children, on Electra, his daughter, and Orestes, his son, who slew Aegisthus and Clytemnestra to avenge him and then became insane.

No other event struck the imagination of the Greeks as much as this partly legendary war. It did not only inspire the *Iliad;* all the tragic dramatists used it as a subject, it haunted the Greek imagination, was constantly referred to by writers, inspired sculptors from the beginnings of Hellenic art to the Roman period, and vase painters never tired of representing its heroes and their adventures.

If it had not inspired the poet whose works were taught to every Greek at school, the memory of this war would not have endured for so long, for there must have been other wars of the same period which were quite as bitter but which have left no trace. It took on a symbolic meaning for the ancient Greeks; in their eyes it represented the triumph of Hellenism over the barbarians (in the ancient sense of the word) and the victory of their civilisation over those of Asia. In the struggles between east and west, it remained the typical example of the victory of light and human dignity over darkness. P.D.

TROY. The town of Troy, also called Ilium, was situated in Asia Minor near the sea, by the straits of the Dardanelles, at a point where its inhabitants could keep watch on the sea-traffic between the Aegean and the Sea of Marmara, and also where traders, afraid of the difficult crossing of the straits, could unload their merchandise to take it on board again, after the dangerous crossing, and use land routes for a certain distance. This was the explanation of Troy's prosperity during the late 3rd millennium and several periods in the 2nd millennium B.C.

In 1870, the German, Schliemann, filled with enthusiasm after reading Homer, decided to devote his fortune and his time to the exploration of the site. The excavations have continued ever since and have shown that several successive cities were built on the same site, a rocky spur dominating a plain through which the River Simoïs peacefully winds its way. The richest of these towns and the second in chronological order, dates from the 22nd century B.C. Already surrounded by powerful fortifications, it contained art treasures of rather rough workmanship but great material value, no doubt the product of the tribute that was levied on the traders whose passage was supervised by the kings. The appearance of the royal dwellings hardly corresponded with such opulence; standing behind the enormous walls surrounding the plateau, they were isolated buildings which generally consisted of a single room preceded by a vestibule. It was not until Homer's Troy that we find a city comparable with the one described in the epic. This city is the seventh in stratigraphical order; the others are less interesting. What was the date of this Homeric Troy? According to ancient tradition, it was destroyed by Agamemnon's Achaeans in 1183, but some authorities today believe that the famous war took place about the beginning of the 14th century B.C. Afterwards, the site was only occupied by towns of very minor importance until the Roman period, when the city, then called Ilium Novum occupied a certain position in the provincial life of the region. P.D.

TYRANNICIDES. In 514 B.C., two Athenians, Harmodius and Aristogiton, assassinated Hipparchus, one of Pisistratus's two tyrant sons. Although their deed had been inspired by personal motives, they were hailed as heroic liberators of their country and, as soon as democracy was established in 510, the greatest Athenian sculptor, Antenor, made a bronze statue of them. As the statues were later carried away by the Persians, another group, which we know by replicas, was made in 477 by Critius and Nesiotes and placed in the agora. The tyrant's killers (this is the meaning of the word tyrannicides) remained symbols of patriotism and love of freedom in the eyes of the Athenians. P.D.

TYRANNY. No form of government known to the Greeks was judged more severely than tyranny. This was the name they gave to the exercise of power by a man whom force had placed at the head of the state. A regime without any legal or religious justification could only be a scandal which rhetors and philosophers were not slow to condemn. But the frequency of tyrannies proved that they answered a real need and during the 7th and 6th centuries B.C. most Greek cities experienced a tyranny of varying duration; the average was one or two generations. The exceptions, among the most important cities, were Argos and Sparta, Aegina and Thebes. The institution spread everywhere, from the Anatolian coast to Sicily and Magna Graecia, where it lasted much longer than elsewhere. Sicyon had the Orthagoridae as tyrants; Corinth, Cypselus and his descendants; Athens, Pisistratus and his sons; Samos, Polycrates—the list is too long to continue. It seems that the model and technique of the coup d'état had come from Lydia. An energetic man, whose birth or military successes had already given him a certain reputation, would gather together a group of thugs who, by ruse or force, would capture the leaders of the state and disarm the citizens. He would then have himself elected to some important office which put the reins of the state in his hands, unless he preferred to govern through an intermediary; he took care not to call himself a tyrant. Seizure of power by these usurpers was encouraged by the poverty of the people; in every city, they were already bringing pressure to bear on the greedy nobles who had shared out the spoils of the kings. In his *Works and Days*, Hesiod has described the injustices and abuses that were committed: court verdicts were bought and tenants were crippled by debts so that they had to sign away their freedom. Even the wisest legislators like Solon were unable to redress the situation by regular means. Everywhere, the tyrants found support from the crowd of the disinherited. They ensured a means of subsistence for everyone by brutal methods and—we do not know how—solved the question of debtors and creditors. They gave the countryfolk security of tenure and bettered the living conditions of the city-dwellers by multiplying public works of general utility, especially by building aqueducts and fountains. Their great enemies were the nobles whom they had dispossessed and who disapproved of what they called demagogy. Either by force or, more skilfully (as Louis XIV of France was to do), by distracting them with a whirlwind of festivities, the tyrants succeeded in overcoming this opposition. One happy result of such a policy was an unprecedented flourishing of art and literature. Tyrants competed for poets and musicians; Anacreon, for example, was called from distant Samos to Athens. Pisistratus went farther than any other tyrant in his taste for brilliance but not even in this domain did his behaviour differ from that of other tyrants. They all acted according to the same principles, supporting each other, willingly contracting family alliances by marriages, mutually rendering services in a kind of Holy Alliance. They did not seek war, for they knew that their power was largely dependent on their prestige and that a defeat would be fatal for them. No tyranny ever lasted for very long and the dynastic ambitions of the usurpers were frustrated probably because the very prosperity they gave their cities sharpened their citizens' desire for liberty.   P.D.

TYRTAEUS. Tyrtaeus was a 7th century B.C. poet and a native of Aphidnae, but whether this was the Attic or the Laconian village of the same name we do not know. Whichever it was, he lived at Sparta. His most famous works were his marching songs, a kind of paean that soldiers sang when they were attacking the enemy, and especially his elegies *(See* Lyric Poetry). Tyrtaeus was primarily a " supplier of uplift ", warlike uplift that would have been specially appreciated in a military town like Sparta.   R.F.

ULYSSES. Ulysses is one of the most engaging and representative figures of Hellenic mythology. Although he took a leading part in the Trojan War and greatly contributed to the final victory of the Greeks by his advice, he gave the most convincing proof of his qualities during his long voyage, described by Homer in the *Odyssey*, which eventually took him back to his kingdom of Ithaca where his wife Penelope, his father Laertes, and his son Telemachus were waiting for him. Ulysses' outstanding characteristic was his great humanity. His companions were not only his subjects but his friends, and they did not only obey him because he was a king like Agamemnon but, above all, because they recognised him as a man of exceptional genius, capable of overcoming every difficulty. Ulysses was obviously convinced that there was no circumstance in which intelligence and ingenuity could not win through. Whether he was faced by the sorceress, Circe, or the giant, Cyclops, or cast up by the storm on the shores of the Phaeacians, he always knew how to behave. He had great courage and never flinched before any danger, but he had less faith in his strength and courage than in his cunning and wits. He was

Ulysses landing after shipwreck on the Isle of Pteria. Detail of an Attic amphora. Third quarter of the 5th century B.C. Munich, Antikensammlung.

cunning was required, such as obtaining the help of Philoctetes whom the Greeks had wantonly abandoned on the isle of Lemnos or spying in the enemy's territory. After Nestor, whose experience made his counsels invaluable, Ulysses' advice was the most highly esteemed in the chiefs' assembly.

After the capture of Troy, Ulysses did not return home for ten years. He had aroused the hatred of Poseidon and suffered a fearful shipwreck. His voyages took him where no Greek had ever set foot before.

He conjured the shade of the soothsayer, Tiresias, when he wanted to see into the future, and saw the dead clustering around the ram he had to sacrifice for this magical ritual. After ten years of wandering, and years spent on Ogygia where Calypso, who had fallen in love with him, retained him, he was finally taken back home by Alcinous, king of the Phaeacians, who left him on the shores of Ithaca one night, while he was asleep. His wife had waited for him for twenty years, refusing to despair and rejecting the many suitors who hoped to become rulers of the island by marrying her. Disguised as a beggar, recognised only by his old dog, his swineherd, Eumaeus, and his nurse, Euryclea, Ulysses found Penelope again and, with the aid of Telemachus, slew the suitors who had installed themselves in his palace and were plundering his lands. The rest of his life was uneventful and he modestly ended a career during which he had shown those qualities of intelligence, perseverance, courage, submissiveness to the gods and confidence in them, which made him one of the most admirable, certainly the most beloved representative of their race in the eyes of his fellow-countrymen.

P.D.

not haughty like Ajax and remained the ideal of the moderate man for the Greeks, and it was because he was so typically Greek that the goddess, Athena, always protected him, tried to save him from dangers and appeared under one form or another to guide him in the midst of his difficulties.

The story of Ulysses is familiar. Faithful to the oath that the kings had taken, to help Menelaus recover his wife Helen, he regretfully left his little island, the fields he had tilled himself, his faithful servants, his wife and his small son who was later to go in search of him. Even before the campaign started, Ulysses distinguished himself in a difficult situation, when he found Achilles who had been hidden by his parents among King Lycomedes' daughters on the isle of Scyrus. During the war he performed missions in which

UMBRELLA. In a hot, sunny country like Greece, this accessory of a woman's dress must have been useful. The Greek umbrella was very much like the modern one; a circular piece of tissue was stretched over several spokes converging on a ring that slipped easily along a rod held in the hand. The umbrella was generally held over the woman by a slave who walked behind her and protected the whiteness of her complexion.

R.F.

UNDERWORLD. We know hardly anything of the ancient Greeks' ideas on death and the fate awaiting mortals in the next world and it may well be that their ideas on the subject were no more clear than ours. The absence of dogma gave rise to all kinds of beliefs which varied considerably according to different periods, regions and social classes. Documents of the times are singularly unenlightening, since it is inconceivable that the man in the street, Pindar and Plato, all preoccupied by this subject, should have shared identical conceptions. What texts do tell us is the opinion of the most eminent minds which had rid themselves of popular superstitions, and for the latter, evidence is offered by archaeological excavations, the appearance of tombs and the nature of the offerings laid in them, all of which we are prone to interpret inaccurately.

It may be assumed that during the centuries previous to the historical period, the deceased was considered to retain certain vestiges of existence as long as he had not been reduced to a skeleton. His arms, his everyday possessions and some foods were laid in the the tomb beside him, but if the tomb was opened again so that another body might be placed in it, the gifts were unhesitatingly taken back again and the bones of the deceased were thrown in a corner without the least sign of respect being shown for them. Neither in Crete nor in the Mycenaean world have we found any reliable evidence of a funorary cult: even the famous sarcophagus found at Haghia Triada, which dates from the late Minoan period (15th century B.C.) has not furnished any proof of such a cult, for the ceremonies represented on its sides are not necessarily in honour of the deceased and their meaning remains unknown to us. Equally indecisive is the Grave Circle at Mycenae.

Of the two beliefs that nothing survived of the deceased, or, on the contrary, that his soul survived in a world far remote from that of the living, the second seems to have been the more common in Homer's time. In one of the most famous books of the *Odyssey* we are told how Ulysses conjured up the dead by means of a hole he had dug in the ground and near which he had sacrificed victims whose blood attracted the shades of those he had known in life. In this epoch, it was believed that after death men lived a kind of half existence under the earth their bodies, which were customarily burned from approximately the 11th cen-

Elpenor, Ulysses and Hermes in the underworld. Detail from an Attic pelike by the Elpenor Painter. About 440 B.C. Boston, Museum of Fine Arts.

Charon. Detail of a white-ground lekythos. About 440 B.C. Karlsruhe, Landesmuseum.

tury B.C. onwards, were deprived of their fleshly covering and were no more than wraiths which only assumed a fleeting semblance of vitality after absorbing the blood of the victims. It also seems that all the dead were gathered in a shadowy domain, the underworld, ruled by Hades and his wife, Persephone. The description has come down to us of Achilles striding through the fields of asphodels in this sombre kingdom. In this other world, everyone continued to lead the existence which had been his in life. Except for a few impious souls whose crimes against the gods had been particularly serious, no distinction was made there between the good and the bad, and no reward or punishment was handed out in accordance with each soul's behaviour during his lifetime. According to the legend, Minos was certainly a judge but only because this had been his function on earth, and it would seem that his jurisdiction did not extend to acts committed before death. Was the image that Homer gave of death shared by his contemporaries? Shortly after the writing of the *Odyssey*, Hesiod alluded to those far-off isles where the gods carry the souls of those they had loved. These isles were situated beyond the Ocean and offered a happy

sojourn of an ill determined nature to those who had been led there by the Breezes. It seems that in later times the two conceptions existed side by side in the minds of the Greeks, and increasingly clear traces of the second are found from the 5th century B.C. onwards in the writings of Pindar and other writers and on certain funerary monuments like the one called the Tomb of the Nereids in which a Lycian prince was laid to rest in the early 4th century B.C. But the underworld hell was not forgotten, for it was there that Aristophanes led Heracles and Dionysus, that Euripides sent Heracles in search of Alcestis and that Orpheus ventured in order to bring Eurydice back to earth.

Since Homer's time this hell had taken on a topographical reality. Although it was not known in what part of the world lay the way that led to hell, it was said that access to it lay on the other side of a river, the Styx, which had to be crossed on a boat rowed by the hideous Charon, a scene often found on late 5th century B.C. funerary lekythoi. Permission to embark on Charon's boat was only granted to those to whom the living had accorded the ritual honours, those who had been buried or cremated according to due form, and those whose tomb contained the modest obolus that the sinister boatman exacted as a toll. All other souls were distressed spirits who no longer belonged to any world and who did not know where to go. The Styx ran round the kingdom in the centre of which stood the palace where Hades and Persephone dwelt and the door was constantly guarded by a monstrous being, Cerberus, a dog with three heads covered with serpents for hair. Living beings who had succeeded in passing through the doors of this palace without first dying were rare indeed and only a few mortals protected by the gods and by their initiation into certain mysteries had succeeded in this enterprise. Others, like Pirithous and Theseus who had come, it is true, with the culpable design of carrying away Persephone, were severely punished, like Theseus who was never able to rise from the seat on which the infernal sovereigns had invited him to sit. Virgil in his *Aeneid* and the mythographers have given us a picture of hell with a precision which, it may be seen, in no way corresponded with the ideas of their predecessors. But there can be no doubt that between the time when the *Odyssey* was composed and the 5th century B.C., the logical Greek spirit had already given the sombre kingdom of the nether world a substantiality that was more reassuring for mortals than the nebulous chaos that Ulysses had succeeded in conjuring out of nothingness for a few instants. The place where the dead regained contact with the world of the living had even been established and archaeologists have discovered a sanctuary in Epirus, which was believed to have been built by one of the entrances into the underworld.

P.D.

U R A N U S . Uranus was the Sky. The legends about him belong more to theogony and philosophical conceptions concerning the world than to mythology proper. His function varied according to the system. Generally he was made the husband of Gaea, the Earth, who gave birth to several children. The last born of these, Cronus, put an end to this proliferation by castrating his father with a sickle. P.D.

W A R S . The first event that literature tells us about Greek history is a war, the War of Troy, and Homer only recounts a very brief episode from it. Following this, our grandparents' history books unfold a long tissue of battles and an imposing list of generals. Less importance is attached today to these tedious struggles, full of brilliant feats of arms, but whose monotonous strategy is of more than doubtful interest for children. It must be remembered that the image of war is traced almost without a break over the background to a civilisation that now holds all our attention; from one end to the other of its history, Hellenism lived through war, peace was never more than a brief interlude and everyone knew that it was short-lived. There were local wars between the innumerable cities, which were jealous of each other and always ready to fight over a few acres of land; wars waged by coalitions, when the increasing strength of one state threatened to destroy the delicate balance of international power; and there were civil wars.

Only the most famous of these almost uninterrupted conflicts will be mentioned here: two wars of doubtful chronology, one probably at the end of the 8th century B.C., the other a hundred years later, that ended with Sparta conquering the rich Messenia, in spite of the heroic resistance of Aristomenes; the Lelantine War in which

Chalcis and Eretria, in Euboea, struggled against each other for several generations during the 7th century B.C.; and the Sacred Wars, which broke out three times, at the beginning of the 6th century B.C., in 448, and from 356 to 346 under the pretext of protecting the sanctuary at Delphi, an excuse that served the Thessalians, the Athenians and their Phocian allies in turn, then finally Philip of Macedon. There were two conflicts, which, until the conquests of Alexander, were far more extensive than any of the others, the Persian Wars and the Peloponnesian War.

The Persian Wars provide an almost unique example in their history of the Greeks forming a coalition to ward off a danger from abroad. The king of the Persians, Darius I, had ruthlessly crushed a revolt of Greeks in Asia Minor in 494 B.C. and he decided to attack Hellenism at its centre, on the other side of the Aegean, to avoid a recurrence of such rebellions. In 490, the Persian fleet sailed towards Athens, which was guilty of having encouraged the revolt. The Persians disembarked on the plain of Marathon and the only help Athens could find was in a few troops sent as reinforcements by the little town of Plataea. Miltiades, who commanded the army, advanced his men in front of the enemy and, contrary to all hopes, won a victory. The success was all the more impressive because the Greeks were far outnumbered and, if Miltiades had not made skilful use of the terrain, the Greek cause would have been lost. Darius gave up the venture, but his son, Xerxes, decided to try again. He laid his plans with the greatest care, enormous armies were concentrated in Asia Minor and he even went so far as to cut a canal through Athos, which was almost an island, to ensure an easier passage for his fleet. The danger was so great that the Greeks decided to act together. An inscription, engraved on the bronze serpent supporting the tripod offered to Apollo after the victory, gives us a list of the confederates; thirty-one cities pledged themselves at a congress assembled at Corinth to fight together against the common enemy. Sparta and Athens headed the league. Although the Spartan, Leonidas, died heroically when the Persians tried to penetrate through the Pass of Thermopylae, the real credit for the Greek success was due to Athens; it was Themistocles who lured the Persian fleet into the narrow roadstead of Salamis where it was annihilated by the combined navy of the Greeks. The following year, 479, a land battle at Plataea finally drove the

Persian army out of Greece, while the allied fleet won a fresh victory at Mycale, off Samos. The war continued for a long time and did not end till 449, but the worst was over in 479 and the prestige of such brilliant victories, largely owing to the initiative of Athens, gave her through the Delian League a virtual hegemony over most of the Greek cities.

It was, in fact, the jealousies and odium roused by this hegemony that caused the Peloponnesian War. This was purely a Greek war, a fight to the death between the two leading cities, Athens and Sparta, each one dragging other states in its wake, some of which changed from one camp to the other. An Athenian decree of 432 against the inhabitants of Megara sparked off hostilities. In the beginning, Athens, who held the trump cards in the struggle, was weakened by an epidemic of plague, which lasted for several years and killed the man whose presence at the helm was more than ever necessary, Pericles. The leaders who succeeded him were not of his calibre: the demagogue Cleon, the timid Nicias, then Alcibiades, whose brilliant qualities were not sufficient compensation for his ambition and unscrupulousness. The outstanding personalities on the Spartan side were Brasidas, a skilful and courageous general, and particularly Lysander. For a long time the war was limited to partial campaigns, sorties into enemy territory and expeditions against neutral cities, like Melos from whom Athens was demanding help. In 421, the opponents, discouraged by the slender result obtained, concluded a peace associated with the name of Nicias. This peace was broken in 414. At the time, Athens had already involved itself in the most famous episode of the whole war. Encouraged by Alcibiades, it had sent a fleet against Syracuse to support its ally, Segesta. Ill prepared, badly conducted and hampered by the fact that its initiator, Alcibiades, had fled into exile to escape an accusation of sacrilege, the expedition ended in disaster in 413. The absence of these large forces away from Athens gave the Spartans far more opportunity for action in Greece itself and, after a series of half-successes and reverses, an oligarchic revolution broke out at Athens in 411. This revolution provoked various reactions among its allies and enabled several of them to break away from the Delian League. At this point, one of the most distinguished personalities Sparta had ever produced, Lysander, appeared on the scene. He owed his success as much to his diplomatic sense, which won over the help of all those who, whether in Athens itself or among its subject states, were tired of its political regime and longed for a change, as to the military talents that won him victory at Aegospotami in 405. Partly as a consequence of this dissidence, he laid seige to Athens in 404 and it had to surrender.

Herodotus has related the history of the Persian Wars and tried to explain their origins. Thucydides is the historian of the Peloponnesian War. The two wars do not owe their renown entirely to the qualities of these two great writers; they were in fact the most important, the most characteristic and the most significant of all the conflicts that the Greeks had to endure before the struggle against Philip of Macedon and the conquests of Alexander.   P.D.

WINE. Wine for the Greeks was the drink of kings, the divine " gift of Dionysus ". Wine and oil were Attica's main exports. The grapes were crushed in vats under the feet of the harvesters. Fermentation in vats was neither prolonged nor systematic so that it was difficult to keep wine for any length of time unless salt water or other ingredients (each wine-growing region had its own particular recipe) were added. Unlike the modern Greeks, the ancient wine-makers did not add resin to their wine. Their ingredients were sometimes aromatic such as thyme, mint cinnamon or honey, and some sort of spirits were also made. The wines of Thasos, Chios, Lesbos, Rhodes and other " vintages " were particularly renowned. At Thasos, the export and import of wines was strictly controlled by law and frauds were prosecuted.

Wine for local consumption was poured in goat or pig-skin bottles. Wine for export was kept in large terra-cotta jars *(pithoi)*, the equivalent of our modern casks, and then poured in clay amphorae which were lined inside with pitch. The handles of the amphorae were stamped with the names of the merchant and certain local magistrates whose seal was a guarantee rather like the French " Appellation contrôlée ".

The Greeks rarely drank wine in the pure state. Before each meal, wine would be mixed with a greater or lesser quantity of water in a large vase known as a krater. In Book IX of the *Iliad*, when Achilles receives the envoys from Agamemnon, he orders Patroclus: " Take a larger krater, make a stronger mixture and give a cup to all. " Servants

Woman ladling wine mixed with water out of a stamnos. Detail of a stamnos. Second quarter of the 5th century B.C. Oxford, Ashmolean Museum.

would take wine from the krater with ladles, or *oinochoai*, and then fill the cups which were also made of clay. Wine was also used for libations in honour of the gods and for the " erotic " game known as *kottabos (See* Toys and Amusements).

R.F.

WOMEN. During the Minoan and Mycenaean ages, women seem to have enjoyed equality or near equality with men, in the Homeric poems, Helen, Andromache, Hecuba, Penelope, Nausicaa and her mother, Arete, behave and speak with great freedom and the men do not treat them in any way as inferiors. After the Dorian invasions, which marked the beginning of the Iron Age about the 11th century B.C., things were very different. Hesiod is already a misogynist. The position of women is best known to us during the classical period.

Sparta has to be considered quite separately; on this point as on so many others, it is a special case. There, young girls, like the boys, exercised in public, running races, wrestling, throwing the discus and javelin. They appeared almost naked in processions. In his *Life of Lycurgus*, Plutarch tells us: " The Lacedaemonian women were too forward and behaved with a thoroughly masculine boldness towards their husbands. Their authority was unquestioned in the home and they gave their opinions freely on the most important matters in public affairs ". As a matter of fact, as they did not hold office either in the assembly (the *Apella*), or in the senate (the *Gerousia*), and had no political rights, it was only by influencing their husbands that Spartan women could express their opinions on state affairs.

At Athens and most of the cities, the picture is very different. The state only took cognisance of the citizens that constituted it; it ignored women, just as it ignored foreigners, metics, slaves and children. The Athenian woman was not free to decide her own life. Her lord and master, her *kyrios*, had every right over her person. In very early times, he could kill or sell her with impunity. A law of Solon forbad anyone to sell his daughter or sister unless she was proved to have had intercourse with a man before marriage. The kyrios of a young girl was her father, or failing him, her

half-brother, or after him, the nearest relation on the paternal side of the family. The kyrios of a married woman was her husband, but if he died, she came under the authority of her father again and he could remarry her as he wished. A father not only had the power to arrange his daughter's marriage during his lifetime, but could also decide it in his will and his heirs enjoyed the same power after him. However, we know that the first husband, if he knew that he was at the point of death, sometimes designated the man who was to replace him. An Athenian woman could not go to law herself, but was represented by her kyrios. Nevertheless, it can be said that, although she enjoyed no civil rights herself, she possessed a " potential citizenship ", which she transmitted to her sons. This held good particularly after a law of Pericles, passed in 450 B.C., decreed that to be an Athenian citizen a man had to be the son, not only of a citizen, but also of the daughter of a citizen. The case was a little analogous to that concerning the family possessions and patrimony, which a woman could not administer herself but of which she was often considered the trustee, particularly in the case of an *epikleros* girl, that is,

487

an orphan whose father died without leaving any male heir. To ensure the transmission of the patrimony and the continuity of the ancestor cult, the father's nearest relative was obliged by law to marry the epikleros and, if he was already married, he could free himself and get his wife married to someone else. Thus, the Greek woman was, in the eyes of the law, a perpetual minor; her legal position was hardly superior to that of a slave. Social custom allowed the married woman a certain freedom of action; within narrow enough limits it is true, that is, within the home.

A young girl led a much more monotonous and confined existence at Athens than in Sparta. She remained shut up in the women's apartments, the gynaeceum (q.v.), shielded from the sight of men, even those living in the house; she was not enclosed by iron bars or locked doors, except probably at night, but by the binding power of social custom. While the young Athenian boy, when he reached the age of seven, went to the school of the *grammatistes*, soon after to that of the *kitharistes*, then to the *paidotribes* (master of the gymnasium), his sister received no further education than what her mother and nurse could give her, who were probably illiterate themselves. Euripides, who invariably modelled the heroines of his tragedies on the Athenian women of his day, shows Iphigenia in Tauris incapable of

writing a letter herself. Divorce (q.v.) was easily granted when the man wanted it, but almost impossible when the woman alone asked for it.

Xenophon's *Oeconomicus* reveals both the strict subordination of the woman and her relative independence when, once she was married, she ran the house where she was the *despoina*, the mistress. She took part in the domestic religious observances and was the *consors sacrorum* of her husband. In fact, religion conferred a dignity on women that the civil laws denied her. There took place even at Athens, the festival of Demeter, the Thesmophoria, which was kept by the matrons, and from which men were absolutely excluded. Middle class women hardly ever left home except for family celebrations, city festivals and when they had personal shopping to do and they were always accompanied by a servant. It was quite a different matter for the women of the lower classes, who had to earn their living and their humble dwellings would hardly have been large enough to allow for the isolation of the gynaeceum.

During the time of the sophists, those radical thinkers who challenged everything, protests were heard against the inferior condition of women, as well as slaves. Socrates and several of his followers proclaimed the natural equality of the two sexes. Finally, the Peloponnesian War,

Women spinning wool. Detail from an Attic lekythos by the Amasis Painter. About 540-530 B.C. New York Metropolitan Museum of Art.

which lasted for thirty years, hastened the evolution of social habits; as the men were constantly on guard duty on the ramparts or campaigning, their wives had to take their place and assume greater responsibilities.

During the Hellenistic period, girls had their own schools and women occupied a much more important place in society. This can be seen clearly in the papyri on which marriage contracts, like the one quoted in the article on *Contracts*, have been preserved for us to this day.   R.F.

WRITING. Archaic Greek of the Mycenaean period, before Homer's time, was written in a syllabic notation composed of 87 different signs, which was deciphered in 1953 by the Englishman, Michael Ventris *(See* Linear B).

Another syllabic system survived in parts of the Greek world until the classical period, as in Cyprus for example, but this was an anachronism, for by about the 8th century B.C. most Greeks had adopted and adapted the " Cadmean letters ", the Phoenician alphabet which was much simpler than syllabic writing since it had only some 25 signs. The Greek *alpha* is derived from the Phoenician *aleph*, the Greek *beta* from *beth* and so on. Greek alphabets differed markedly from one another according to regions and dialects (q.v.); for example, the Chalcidian alphabet was not quite like the Ionian alphabet which was used at Athens. As the language was ceaselessly evolving, some sounds vanished, like that which was represented by the letter *digamma* (the Latin F); this was already on its way out in Ionian in Homer's time, but the same letter survived much longer in other dialects, as well as in the notation of numbers in which it stood for 6.

The Greeks did not possess any special signs for numbers and usually represented them by means of the letters of the alphabet. The first nine letters stood for numbers 1 to 9, the next nine for multiples of ten (*iota* stood for 10, *kappa* 20, etc.) and the last nine for hundreds (*rho* was 100, *sigma* 200, etc.). To make this total of 27 letters, not only had the *digamma* (6) been kept, but also the *koppa* (90) and the *sampi* (900). After 1,000, letters were given a kind of *iota* written underneath to the left (*alpha* in this way became 1,000, *beta* 2,000, etc.), but for high numbers the word *myrioi* or *myriades*, which meant 10,000, was generally used. Inscriptions have been found with another numerical system which was similar to that of the Romans; a vertical stroke was one

unit, so that 1111 would mean 4, and then the initials of words were used for five *(pi)*, ten *(delta)*, hundred *(epsilon)* and thousand *(chi)* for the notation of these numbers.

In the classical period only capital letters were used and there were no signs for punctuation or intervals between words and phrases. The habit of writing from left to right was only slowly adopted and many, very ancient inscriptions are written alternately from left to right, and then right to left, the system being called *boustrophedon*, that is, after the manner in which a team of oxen make furrows when pulling a plough. It was only much later that cursive writing, with characters rather like our miniscules, appeared. The habit was then adopted of separating words, punctuating sentences, and marking the breathing (rough or smooth) and the accents.   R.F.

XANTHUS. There would be no need to mention the small Lycian town of Xanthus in the south-west of Asia Minor were it not that it provided an excellent example of how Greece influenced the barbarian princes of that area. Recent excavations have shown that Athenian potters sent highly valuable vases to that far-off region from the mid-6th century B.C. Xanthus has also been long known for its two monuments, called the Harpy Tomb (about 480 B.C.) and the Nereid Monument (about 380 B.C.; according to some, about 410). Both were decorated by Greek artists who bent their talent to the representation of local scenes.   P.D.

XENOPHANES. According to Plato, Xenophanes was the founder of the Eleatic school (q.v.). He was born at Colophon in about 570 B.C. and left Ionia when it was conquered by the Persians (545). Sixty-seven years later he was still writing. He went as an *aoidos* (q.v.) from town to town reciting his poems of which some lines still survive. They are remarkable for the degree of their philosophical inspiration. In his poetry he criticised dogmatism, polytheism and anthropomorphism and proclaimed the existence of a single god who had no resemblance to mankind. He also seems to have followed in Anaximander's footsteps by making palaeontological observations on certain fossils and he elaborated a theory of progress.   P.-M.S.

XENOPHON. Athenian writer (426-355 B.C.). Although his father, Gryllus, was not a nobleman he must certainly have belonged to that class of well-to-do proprietors, knights or *hippeis* that Aristophanes described as the natural enemies of demagogues. Xenophon's passion for horse-riding and hunting as well as his conservative opinions presumably came from his childhood and family milieu. He was a disciple of Socrates before he took ship for Asia where, in 401, he took part in the expedition of the Ten Thousand (q.v.) which he later recounted in his *Anabasis*. In 396, he went to Asia again with his friend, Agesilaus, king of Sparta, and when the latter was recalled to Greece, Xenophon fought with the Spartans against his compatriots at the battle of Coronea in 394. He was then banished and sent into exile by the Athenians, although they may already have ostracised him in 399. He was deprived of all his possessions but he was given a large country estate at Scillus, in Elis near Olympia, by his Spartan friends. Here he lived for more than twenty years with his wife Philesia, who bore him two sons, Gryllus and Diodorus, and led the life of a rich and cultured landowner, riding over his lands to supervise his farm-workers, hunting, receiving friends and writing his books. About 367, the sentence of exile was rescinded and shortly afterwards he returned to Attica. In 362 his son, Gryllus, who had been serving in the Athenian cavalry, was killed in a skirmish before the battle of Mantinea.

Xenophon was both a man of action and a man of letters. As a writer, his numerous works were of such a range and variety that he can best be described as an essayist. Some of his works were inspired by his lifelong veneration for Socrates: the *Apology*, the *Memorabilia* (the memories of Socrates) and the *Symposium*. Others were historical: the *Anabasis*, *Agesilaus*, and the *Hellenica* (the Greek history which continued Thucydides' work up to the battle of Mantinea, from 411 to 362). Like the *Memorabilia*, the *Anabasis* belongs to the genre of memoirs, because Xenophon relates in it the story of a military expedition, which he accompanied, and his own part in it. Other works were both technical and didactic, describing the best training for a horseman, hunter, head of a family and a statesman: *Hipparchicus* (cavalry officer), *On Horsemanship*, *Cynegeticus*, *Oeconomicus* and *Cyropaedia*, but the last work, describing the education of Cyrus and the way the great conqueror organised his empire, was also a historical novel—the first of its kind. Other writings were of a political nature: the

Polity of the Lacedaemonians, *Hieron* or *The Tyranny*, and the *Polity of the Athenians*.

Nearly all his works, especially the *Memorabilia*, *Symposium*, *Anabasis*, and *Oeconomicus*, are highly readable. When he writes on Socrates, he is admittedly less profound than Plato, but Plato attributed many of his own personal ideas to the master; Xenophon was a simpler and perhaps a more reliable witness, when he described Socrates conversing freely and pleasantly with his friends without a hint of pedantry. As a historian, Xenophon is certainly very inferior to Thucydides, but his narrative is clear, easy and witty and has great qualities of its own. Apart from certain aristocratic lapses, his language is natural and graceful. His style is that of the " plain blunt man ", who makes no claim to be a writer but writes as he speaks, with ease, distinction and wit. Talented essayist as he was, Xenophon treated too many subjects to excel in every one of them. He was the originator of two new literary genres: the biography *(Agesilaus)* and the novel *(Cyropaedia)*. The ancient Greeks gave him the nickname of the " Attic bee ". Although Xenophon ranks somewhat beneath the greatest writers, he earned himself an important and lasting place in Greek literary history. P.-M.S.

ZEUS. Zeus was worshipped as the master of gods and men throughout the whole of the Greek world. Even when a city had a special veneration for some other divinity, Zeus still took first place. It was probably in the Mycenaean period that he came to the fore and relegated to second place the goddess whom the Cretans had first adored. From that time, armed with the lightning with which he exterminated his enemies, he sat on his throne among the clouds on the summit of Mount Olympus, as a patriarchal ruler surrounded by other divinities, most of whom were his own children. Although he shared some of his powers among them, he controlled them all and his will was always supreme. He was the son of Cronus and only a ruse on the part of his mother, Rhea, saved him from being devoured at birth by his father. He was secretly raised by the Curetes and the nymphs in a grotto in Crete, before he dethroned his father and established his power over the world, although not until he had crushed the revolt of the Giants against his new dynasty. The universality of his cult explains the multitude of legends associated with him; there is hardly a region in Greece that had not once been the

Zeus hurling a thunder-bolt.
Bronze statuette. About 450 B.C.
Athens, National Museum.
Photo Spyros Meletzis.

scene of one of his exploits which peopled the Greece of the heroic age with his descendants. From Homer's time at least, his legitimate spouse was Hera, but his previous wives were Metis, Themis, Dione and Mnemosyne. Greek artists represented Zeus as a mature, but not an old man, of majestic aspect, wearing a great beard and looking as though he were about to knit his brows in a moment of temper, when the whole of Olympia would tremble. He generally carried a sceptre, unless he was wielding a thunderbolt, and he was often shown accompanied by his favourite bird, an eagle. The most famous statue of Zeus was the colossal gold and ivory figure that Phidias made for the temple of Olympia.   P.D.

ZEUXIS. Zeuxis was a painter, born early in the 4th century B.C. at Heraclea in Sicily. He was a contemporary of Apollodorus, the " painter of shadows ", whose technical innovations he skilfully used in his own work. The period saw a revival in painting which had been eclipsed for a time by sculpture, made supreme among the arts by Phidias. Polygnotus mastered space in his works: Zeuxis showed his mastery in the treatment of light. The titles of some of his most famous works, *Helen at her Toilet, Eros crowned with Roses, Child with Grapes, Heracles in the Cradle, The Centaur's Family*, suggest the early 4th century taste for sentimental themes, the light and graceful treatment of women and children against a new background where country landscapes replaced the traditional column representing a portico or a city palace. The Centaur's family was shown tenderly gazing at the baby Centaur as it frolicked in the grass. According to those who saw his works, Zeuxis' treatment of light effects, his contrasting tones, carefully studied play of shadows on draperies, and the accentuated contours of his figures stressed the grace and femininity of his figures rather than their force and plastic volume.   R.M.

491

Imp. Les Petits-Fils de Léonard DANEL, LOOS (Nord).

Adria

ETRURIA

Massalia

Emporiae

Hemeroscopium

Cumae

Paestum

Sybaris

MAGNA

Croton

GRAECIA

Segesta

Locri
Epizephyrii

SICILY

Naxos

Selinus

Carthage

Agrigentum

Syracuse

Epidamnus

Tarentum